FUNDAMENTALS OF MARKETING

McGRAW-HILL SERIES IN MARKETING

ALLEN, SPOHN, and WILSON: Selling Dynamics
BAIER: Direct Marketing
BOWERSOX, COOPER, LAMBERT, and TAYLOR:
    Management in Marketing Channels
BRITT, BOYD, DAVIS, and LARRECHE: Marketing
    Management and Administrative Action
BUELL: Marketing Management: A Strategic Planning
    Approach
COREY, LOVELOCK, and WARD: Problems in
    Marketing
DeLOZIER: The Marketing Communications Process
DOBLER, LEE, and BURT: Purchasing and Materials
    Management: Text and Cases
ENGEL: Advertising: The Process and Practice
GUILTINAN and PAUL: Marketing Management:
    Strategies and Programs
GUILTINAN and PAUL: Readings in Marketing
    Strategies and Programs
JOHNSON, KURTZ, and SCHEUING: Sales
    Management: Concepts, Practices, and Cases
KINNEAR and TAYLOR: Marketing Research: An
    Applied Approach
LOUDON and DELLA BITTA: Consumer Behavior:
    Concepts and Applications
LOVELOCK and WEINBERG: Marketing Challenges:
    Cases and Exercises
MONROE: Pricing: Making Profitable Decisions
MYERS: Marketing
REDINBAUGH: Retailing Management: A Planning
    Approach
RUSSELL, BEACH, and BUSKIRK: Selling: Principles
    and Practices
SHAPIRO: Sales Program Management: Formulation
    and Implementation
STANTON and FUTRELL: Fundamentals of Marketing
STROH: Managing the Sales Function
WRIGHT, WINTER, and ZEIGLER: Advertising

WILLIAM J. STANTON
University of Colorado

CHARLES FUTRELL
Texas A&M University

**McGRAW-HILL
BOOK COMPANY**

New York • St. Louis
San Francisco • Auckland
Bogotá • Hamburg
London • Madrid
Mexico • Milan
Montreal • New Delhi
Panama • Paris
São Paulo • Singapore
Sydney • Tokyo • Toronto

FUNDAMENTALS OF MARKETING

**EIGHTH
EDITION**

FUNDAMENTALS OF MARKETING

2 3 4 5 6 7 8 9 0 K G P K G P 8 9 4 3 2 1 0 9 8 7

ISBN 0-07-060943-8

This book was set in Times Roman by Waldman Graphics, Inc.
The editors were Sam Costanzo, Elisa Adams, and Linda A. Mittiga;
the production supervisor was Joe Campanella;
the designer was Jo Jones.
The photo editor was Caroline Anderson.
The drawings were done by Danmark and Michaels.
Cover photograph by R. Tesa, Int'l Stock Photo.
Arcata Graphics/Kingsport was printer and binder.

See Photo Credits on pages 655–656.
Copyrights included on this page by reference.

Library of Congress Cataloging-in-Publication Data

Stanton, William J.
    Fundamentals of marketing.

    (McGraw-Hill series in marketing)
    Includes bibliographical references and indexes.
    1. Marketing 1. Futrell, Charles.   II. Title.
III. Series.
HF5415.S745   1987   658.8   86-18492
ISBN 0-07-060943-8

TO

KELLY AND LITTLE JOE

BOB AND JUANITA

William J. Stanton and
Charles Futrell

ABOUT THE AUTHORS

William J. Stanton is a Professor of Marketing at the University of Colorado, in Boulder. He received his Ph.D. from Northwestern University. For over 30 years, Professor Stanton has worked extensively with both undergraduate and graduate students at Colorado, developing teaching-learning materials as well as curricular programs.

As an extension of his teaching interests through the years, Professor Stanton has worked in business and taught in several management development programs for marketing executives, some of which were in Europe, Mexico, and Canada. He has also served as a consultant for several business organizations and engaged in research projects for the federal government.

Fundamentals of Marketing has been translated into Spanish, Portuguese, Italian, and Indonesian languages, and separate editions have been adapted (with coauthors) for students in Canada, Australia, and Italy. Professor Stanton has lectured at universities in Europe, Asia, Mexico, and New Zealand. He is also the coauthor of the most widely used textbook in sales management courses, and he has written journal articles, monographs, and other books.

In a survey of marketing educators, Professor Stanton was voted one of the leaders in marketing thought, and he is listed in *Who's Who in America* and *Who's Who in the World*. In his "spare" time he thoroughly enjoys jogging, skiing, gardening, and traveling.

Charles Futrell is Professor of Marketing at Texas A&M University. He brings a rich and varied background of professional experience as he joins Professor Stanton as coauthor for the first time in this edition.

Before beginning his academic career Professor Futrell worked in sales and marketing capacities for eight years with the Colgate-Palmolive Company, Upjohn Company, and Ayerst Laboratories. An excellent classroom teacher, he has written or cowritten five successful texts for the college and professional audience, and his work in sales and marketing management has appeared in numerous national and international journals. Professor Futrell also serves as a frequent reviewer for several academic journals including the *Journal of Marketing* and the *Journal of Marketing Research*. In his fifteen years as a university instructor and teacher for various executive development programs and the Bank Marketing Association, he has developed numerous innovative instructional materials including computer simulations, computerized classroom materials, and video exercises.

Professor Futrell enjoys coaching Little League baseball, photography, and fishing.

CONTENTS IN BRIEF

Preface xvii

PART ONE MODERN MARKETING AND ITS ENVIRONMENT 1

Chapter 1 The Field of Marketing 2
Chapter 2 The Marketing Environment 20
Chapter 3 Strategic Marketing Planning 38
Chapter 4 Marketing Information Systems and Marketing Research 60
Cases for Part 1 81

PART TWO TARGET MARKETS 89

Chapter 5 Market Demographics and Buying Power 90
Chapter 6 Social-Group and Psychological Influences on Buyer Behavior 110
Chapter 7 The Industrial Market 134
Chapter 8 Market Segmentation and Forecasting Market Demand 156
Cases for Part 2 180

PART THREE THE PRODUCT 187

Chapter 9 Product Planning and Development 188
Chapter 10 Product-Mix Strategies 214
Chapter 11 Brands, Packaging, and Other Product Features 230
Cases for Part 3 251

PART FOUR THE PRICE 257

Chapter 12 Price Determination 258
Chapter 13 Pricing Strategies and Policies 284
Cases for Part 4 303

vii

PART FIVE

DISTRIBUTION 311

Chapter 14 Retailing: Markets and Institutions 312
Chapter 15 Wholesaling: Markets and Institutions 344
Chapter 16 Channels of Distribution: Conflict, Cooperation, and Management 362
Chapter 17 Management of Physical Distribution 386
Cases for Part 5 406

PART SIX

PROMOTION 415

Chapter 18 The Promotional Program 416
Chapter 19 Management of Personal Selling 438
Chapter 20 Management of Advertising, Sales Promotion, and Publicity 460
Cases for Part 6 486

PART SEVEN

MARKETING IN SPECIAL FIELDS 493

Chapter 21 Marketing of Services 494
Chapter 22 Marketing in Nonbusiness Organizations 512
Chapter 23 International Marketing 532
Cases for Part 7 558

PART EIGHT

IMPLEMENTING AND EVALUATING THE MARKETING EFFORT 567

Chapter 24 Marketing Implementation and Performance Evaluation 568
Chapter 25 Marketing: Societal Appraisal and Prospect 590
Case for Part 8 614

Appendix A: Marketing Arithmetic 617
Appendix B: Careers in Marketing 630
Glossary 642
Photo Credits 655
Indexes 657

CONTENTS

Preface   xvii

PART ONE

MODERN MARKETING AND ITS ENVIRONMENT   1

1. THE FIELD OF MARKETING   2

Nature and Scope of Marketing   4
Present-Day Importance of Marketing   6
The Marketing Concept   10
Marketing Management and Its Evolution   12
Broadening the Marketing Concept   15
Structural Plan of This Book   16
Summary   17

2. THE MARKETING ENVIRONMENT   20

External Macroenvironment   22
External Microenvironment   31
An Organization's Internal Environment   33
Summary   34

3. STRATEGIC MARKETING PLANNING   38

Managing a Marketing System   40
Nature and Scope of Planning   44
Strategic Company Planning   46
Strategic Marketing Planning   53
Summary   57

4. MARKETING INFORMATION SYSTEMS AND MARKETING RESEARCH   60

What Is a Marketing Information System?   61
Need for a Marketing Information System   62
Benefits and Uses of an MkIS   64

ix

Relationship between Marketing Information Systems and Marketing Research — 64

Scope of Marketing Research Activities — 65

Procedure in Marketing Research — 65

Who Does Marketing Research? — 77

Status of Marketing Research — 78

Summary — 79

Cases for Part 1 — 81

1. Sierra National Bank—*Applying the Marketing Concept* — 81

2. Bookworms, Inc.—*Planning a Marketing Research Project* — 83

3. The Harrisonburg-Rockingham Chamber of Commerce—*Designing a Marketing Research Project* — 85

PART TWO

TARGET MARKETS — 89

5. **MARKET DEMOGRAPHICS AND BUYING POWER** — 90

Market Opportunity Analysis — 92

Population: Its Distribution and Composition — 93

Consumer Income and Its Distribution — 102

Consumer Expenditure Patterns — 105

Summary — 107

6. **SOCIAL-GROUP AND PSYCHOLOGICAL INFLUENCES ON BUYER BEHAVIOR** — 110

Importance and Difficulty of Understanding Consumer Behavior — 111

Cultural Influences — 115

Social-Group Influences — 117

Psychological Determinants of Buyer Behavior — 123

Decision-Making Process in Buying — 129

Summary — 131

7. **THE INDUSTRIAL MARKET** — 134

Nature and Importance of the Industrial Market — 136

Characteristics of Industrial Market Demand — 141

Determinants of Industrial Market Demand — 143

Summary — 153

8. **MARKET SEGMENTATION AND FORECASTING MARKET DEMAND** — 156

Guidelines in Market Selection — 158

Nature of Market Segmentation — 158

Bases for Market Segmentation 161

Target-Market Strategies 169

Forecasting Market Demand 172

Summary 177

Cases for Part 2 180

4. Hubbard Manufacturing Company—*Analysis of a Market* 180

5. Mercury Airlines—*Handling an Important Customer* 182

6. Draper Furniture—*Consumer Buying Behavior* 185

PART THREE

THE PRODUCT 187

9. PRODUCT PLANNING AND DEVELOPMENT 188

The Meaning of *Product* 189

Classification of Products 192

Importance of Product Innovation 198

Development of New Products 200

New-Product Adoption and Diffusion Processes 205

Organizing for Product Innovation 207

Why New Products Fail or Succeed 209

Summary 210

10. PRODUCT-MIX STRATEGIES 214

Product Mix and Product Line 215

Major Product-Mix Strategies 215

Concept of the Product Life Cycle 220

Planned Obsolescence and Fashion 224

Summary 228

11. BRANDS, PACKAGING, AND OTHER PRODUCT FEATURES 230

Influences of Product Features on Business Functions 231

Brands 232

Packaging 240

Labeling 242

Other Image-Building Features 244

Summary 248

Cases for Part 3 251

7. First National Bank of Woodbury—*Adding a New Product* 251

8. Peter Rabbit Toy Shoppe—*Adding a New Line of Products* 252

9. Dependable Drugs—*Brand Strategy* 254

PART FOUR

THE PRICE 257

12. PRICE DETERMINATION 258

  Meaning of Price 259
  Price Importance in the Economy 261
  Pricing Objectives 262
  Factors Influencing Price Determination 264
  Basic Methods of Setting Prices 268
  Cost-Plus Pricing 268
  Break-Even Analysis 274
  Prices Based on a Balance between Supply and Demand 277
  Prices Set in Relation to Market Alone 279
  Summary 282

13. PRICING STRATEGIES AND POLICIES 284

  Discounts and Allowances 286
  Geographic Pricing Strategies 290
  Skimming and Penetration Pricing 292
  One-Price and Flexible-Price Strategies 293
  Unit Pricing 294
  Price Lining 294
  Resale Price Maintenance 295
  Leader Pricing and Unfair-Practices Acts 296
  Psychological Pricing—Odd Pricing 297
  Price versus Nonprice Competition 298
  Summary 300

  Cases for Part 4 303

  10. Colwell Manufacturing Company—*Pricing a New Product* 303
  11. Green Valley Landscaping Company—*Pricing a Service in a New Company* 305
  12. Winkleman Manufacturing Company—*Pricing Strategy for a Proposed New Product* 306

PART FIVE

DISTRIBUTION 311

14. RETAILING: MARKETS AND INSTITUTIONS 312

  Middlemen and Channels of Distribution 314
  Nature of Retail Market 316
  Retailers Classified by Sales Volume 321
  Retailers Classified by Product Line 325

Retailers Classified by Form of Ownership — 326
Retailers Classified by Method of Operation — 331
The Future in Retailing — 339
Summary — 341

15. WHOLESALING: MARKETS AND INSTITUTIONS — **344**

Nature and Importance of Wholesaling — 346
Merchant Wholesalers — 353
Agent Wholesaling Middlemen — 355
Future of the Wholesaler — 359
Summary — 359

16. CHANNELS OF DISTRIBUTION: CONFLICT, COOPERATION, AND MANAGEMENT — **362**

Conflict and Cooperation in Distribution Channels — 364
Selecting Channels of Distribution — 371
Determining Intensity of Distribution — 377
Selecting and Working with Individual Middlemen — 380
Legal Considerations in Channel Management — 381
Summary — 383

17. MANAGEMENT OF PHYSICAL DISTRIBUTION — **386**

Importance of Physical Distribution Management — 388
Total-System Concept of Physical Distribution — 389
The Strategic Use of Physical Distribution — 392
Physical Distribution Management — 395
The Future in Physical Distribution — 403
Summary — 403

Cases for Part 5 — 406

13. Rexford Company—*Selecting a Distribution Channel to Minimize Conflict* — 406
14. Diebold Equipment Company—*Changing the Channels of Distribution* — 408
15. Pesco Fastener Corporation—*Evaluating a Distribution System* — 410
16. Shapely Sack Company, Inc.—*Physical Distribution Strategy* — 412

PROMOTION — 415

18. THE PROMOTIONAL PROGRAM — **416**

Meaning and Importance of Promotion — 418

PART SIX

The Communication Process 421
Determination of Promotional Mix 422
Determination of Total Promotional Appropriation 429
The Campaign Concept: An Exercise in Strategic Planning 431
Regulation of Promotional Activities 432
Summary 435

19. **MANAGEMENT OF PERSONAL SELLING** **438**

Nature and Importance of Personal Selling 440
The Strategic Personal Selling Process 445
Strategic Sales-Force Management 448
Operating a Sales Force 448
Evaluating a Sales Person's Performance 454
Summary 457

20. **MANAGEMENT OF ADVERTISING, SALES PROMOTION,**
AND PUBLICITY **460**

Nature of Advertising 462
Objectives of Advertising 467
Developing an Advertising Campaign 468
Evaluating the Advertising Effort 472
Organizing for Advertising 474
Nature of Sales Promotion 475
Importance of Sales Promotion 476
Strategic Management of Sales Promotion 477
Publicity and Public Relations 481
Summary 483

Cases for Part 6 486

17. Eagle Steel Supply Company—*Promotional Program in*
an Expanding Market 486
18. Concord Portrait Studios—*Promotional Program to Enter*
a New Market 488
19. The Klothes Kloset—*Promotional Program for a Small Retailer* 490

PART SEVEN

MARKETING IN SPECIAL FIELDS 493

21. **MARKETING OF SERVICES** **494**

Nature and Importance of Services 496
The Marketing Concept and Service Marketing 500
A Strategic Program for the Marketing of Services 502

Future Outlook in Service Marketing 508

Summary 509

22. MARKETING IN NONBUSINESS ORGANIZATIONS **512**

Nature and Scope of Nonbusiness Marketing 513

Nonbusiness Attitude toward Marketing 517

Developing a Strategic Program for Nonbusiness Marketing 518

Implementation of Marketing 527

Summary 529

23. INTERNATIONAL MARKETING **532**

Domestic Marketing and International Marketing 533

Importance of International Marketing 534

Structures for Operating in Foreign Markets 537

A Strategic Program for International Marketing 539

International Trade Balances 552

Summary 556

Cases for Part 7 558

20. DataCorp of Virginia, Inc.—*Marketing Strategy in a Service Organization* 558

21. Hoover Furniture Rental Company—*Competitive Strategy in a Service Firm* 560

22. Valley College—*A Single-Sex Institution with Enrollment Problems* 562

23. Cooper Supply Company—*Distribution Channel to Reach a Foreign Market* 564

PART EIGHT

IMPLEMENTING AND EVALUATING THE MARKETING EFFORT 567

24. MARKETING IMPLEMENTATION AND PERFORMANCE EVALUATION **568**

Implementation and Planning Interrelationships 570

Marketing Implementation 570

Evaluating Marketing Performance 576

Analysis of Sales Volume 579

Marketing Cost Analysis 581

Summary 588

25. MARKETING: SOCIETAL APPRAISAL AND PROSPECT **590**

Basis for Evaluating Our Marketing System 591

Criticisms of Marketing 592

Consumerism: A Criticism of Our Marketing System   597
Responses to These Criticisms   599
A Societal Orientation in Marketing   604
Broadening the Marketing Concept   609
Summary   611
Case for Part 8   614
24. Peerless Chocolate Company—*Designing a Strategic
    Marketing Mix*   614

APPENDIX A: MARKETING ARITHMETIC   **617**

The Operating Statement   617
Markups   621
Analytical Ratios   624

APPENDIX B: CAREERS IN MARKETING   **630**

Choosing a Career   630
What Are the Jobs?   632
Where Are the Jobs?   636
How to Get a Job   639
Conclusion—A Personal Note   641

GLOSSARY   **642**

PHOTO CREDITS   **655**

INDEXES   **657**

Name Index   657
Subject Index   660

THE BOOK—UPDATED FOR THE 1990s

Our first goal in revising this text for the 1990s was to reflect the major social and economic forces presenting serious challenges to business and particularly to marketing today. Thus many changes have been made in this edition to introduce recent developments and new concepts and thereby prepare students for marketing in the text decade.

As we move through the late 1980s and prepare for the 1990s, our socioeconomic setting is quite different from what it was when this book was first published. Both the economic growth rate and the birth rate have slowed in industrial nations. Values are changing as all of us become concerned about our social and physical environment and quality of life. The role of women continues to change significantly, and computers are dramatically altering many aspects of our lives. Foreign competition seriously affects many industries. Our text reflects all these influences.

THE MAJOR CHANGES IN THIS EDITION

Of the many changes reflecting our focus for the 1990s, the most immediately noticeable is the change in the physical appearance of the book. The new design which features full-color photographs and drawings is a dramatic improvement over the preceding edition and provides immense pedagogical benefits—the book is a delight to read and to teach from.

We also have made many significant changes in the content of the book. At the beginning of each chapter, there is a real-world vignette accompanied by related photographs. A new chapter (3) is now devoted to strategic marketing planning, thus reflecting the interest in this topic in marketing courses. Throughout the text we continue to develop this topic at a level and depth of coverage that we feel is appropriate for a beginning course in marketing. A new chapter (2) now is devoted to the marketing environment. We have also written a separate chapter (8) on market segmentation and demand forecasting.

The previous two chapters on sociological and psychological aspects of consumer buying behavior now are condensed and combined into one chapter. We also have condensed our treatment of pricing into two chapters, instead of three as in previous editions. This was done by covering price determination in a single chapter. The treatment of sales promotion and publicity in Chapter 20 has been expanded. The

THE BOOK—ITS BASIC STRUCTURE

discussions of types of consumer and industrial products have been moved to the introductory chapter (9) on product planning. Chapter 24 now includes coverage of the implementation stage in the management process (as well as the previous coverage of the evaluation stage).

Twelve of the 24 cases are new and several other chapters have been substantially rewritten. All material, including countless new examples, has been updated throughout the book. Except for some classic references, virtually all referenced sources are from the 1980s, including 1986. We have also prepared a much expanded and improved package of teaching and learning supplements (see below for full descriptions of each item).

Those familiar with the earlier editions will find that we retained the features that made the book an outstanding teaching and learning resource. The writing style continues to make the material clear and interesting to read. The organization is appropriate; material flows logically with a section-heading structure that makes for easier reading and outlining. We provide many excellent end-of-chapter discussion questions. Most of these are thought-provoking and involve the *application* of text material, rather than being answerable "straight out of the book." The 24 short cases each focus on a topic covered in the text, and they provide students an opportunity for problem analysis and decision making.

We also have retained and updated such teaching-learning features as chapter objectives, chapter summaries, and a glossary. The key terms and concepts are highlighted in bold type throughout the text and are summarized in a list at the end of each chapter.

The basic theme, approach, and organization have been retained from previous editions. The central theme is that marketing is a total system of business action rather than a fragmented assortment of functions and institutions. While some attention is directed to the role of marketing in our socioeconomic system, the book is written largely from the viewpoint of marketing executives *in an individual firm.* This firm may be a manufacturer or a middleman, a business or a nonbusiness (nonprofit) organization, and it may be marketing products or services.

The marketing concept is a philosophy that stresses the need for a marketing orientation compatible with society's long-run interests. This philosophy is evident in the framework of the strategic marketing planning process. A company sets its marketing objectives, taking into consideration the environmental forces that influence its marketing effort. Management next selects target markets. The company then has four strategic elements—its product, price structure, distribution system, and promotional activities—with which to build a marketing program to reach its markets and achieve its objectives. In all stages of the marketing process, management should use marketing research as a tool for problem solving and decision making.

This framework for the strategic marketing planning process is reflected generally in the organization of the book's content. The text is divided into eight parts. Part 1 serves as an introduction and includes chapters on the marketing environment, strategic marketing planning, and marketing information systems. Part 2 is devoted to the analysis and selection of target markets—either consumer or industrial markets.

Parts 3 through 6 deal with the development of a marketing program, and each of these parts covers one of the above-mentioned components of the strategic marketing mix. In Part 3 various topics related to the product are discussed. The company's price structure is the subject of Part 4, and Part 5 covers the distribution system, including the management of physical distribution. Part 6 is devoted to the total promotional program, including advertising, personal selling, and sales promotion.

Part 7 is devoted to marketing fundamentals as they are applied to three special fields—the marketing of services, marketing in nonbusiness organizations, and international marketing. Part 8 deals with the implementation and evaluation of the total marketing effort *in an individual firm*. Part 8 also includes an appraisal of the role of marketing *in our society*, including the subjects of consumer criticisms and the social responsibility of an organization. At the end of the book there are two appendices, one on marketing arithmetic, and the other a discussion of careers in marketing and how to get a job.

TEACHING AND LEARNING SUPPLEMENTS

The textbook is only the central element in a complete package of teaching and learning resources that have been considerably revised and expanded for this edition. This package includes:

- *Instructor's manual* with outlines for each chapter plus several hundred articles that have been outlined to provide examples not found in the text, and commentaries on the cases, end-of-chapter questions, and exercises from the *Study Guide*.
- *Study Guide* with chapter outlines, test questions, real-world readings for each chapter, and exercises that involve the students in practical marketing experiences.
- *Test bank* that includes an extensive assortment of multiple-choice and true-false questions for each chapter. This test bank also is available in computerized form for mainframe and microcomputers.
- *Color transparencies* that include all the figures from the book. We also provide lecture-outline transparencies for each chapter.
- *Cases for computer use.* Eight of the cases in the text are set up for use with Lotus IBM personal-computer software. They are indicated in the text by this symbol: ⚿.
- *Simulation exercise* for use on an IBM PC. This is a simple, one-product simulation calling for nine decisions primarily in marketing.

ACKNOWLEDGMENTS

Many people—our students, present and past colleagues, business executives, publishers, and other professors—have contributed greatly to this book over the years. In this edition several of the cases were written by other people, and in each instance the authorship is identified. The revised and expanded *Study Guide* once again was prepared by Thomas J. Adams of Sacramento City College. The excellent test bank was prepared by Charles L. Martin of Wichita State University. For their fine efforts in adapting some of our cases for use on personal computers we especially want to thank W. Austin Spivey, Raydel Tullous Spivey, and Jerre B. Richardson, all at the University of Texas at San Antonio.

Many of the changes that we made in this edition were inspired by the in-depth review provided by the following professors:

George Avellano	Central State University, Oklahoma
Newell Chiesl	Indiana State University
Barbara Coe	North Texas State University
Helen Darus	Jefferson Community College, Kentucky
Les Dlabay	Lake Forest College, Illinois
David Georgoff	Florida Atlantic University
Melinda German	University of Kentucky
Joseph P. Guiltinan	La Salle University
Kathleen Krentler	San Diego State University
Ron Lennon	Towson State University, Maryland
Ken Mangun	Roosevelt University, Chicago
Peter Sanchez	Villanova University
Dick Skinner	Kent State University
David T. Wilson	Pennsylvania State University

Many thoughtful comments, suggestions, and criticisms also were generated in a focus-group discussion held at a Southwest Marketing Association meeting. The participants in that discussion were:

Gary Clark	Northern Illinois University
Barbara Coe	North Texas State University
Jane Cromartie	University of New Orleans, Lake Front
Charles Heltin	Eastern Kentucky University
Jim Lumpkin	Baylor University
Ron Moser	Middle Tennessee University

Finally, we would like to recognize, with grateful appreciation, the creative efforts of the people at McGraw-Hill who did so much to make this book an excellent teaching and learning resource.

William J. Stanton

Charles Futrell

MODERN MARKETING AND ITS ENVIRONMENT

An introduction to marketing, the marketing environment, strategic planning, marketing research, and the role of marketing in business today

The first part of this book is an introduction to the field of marketing. In Chapter 1 we explain what marketing is, how it has developed, and how it is continuing to develop. We look at the role of marketing both in our overall socioeconomic system and in the individual organization. This individual organization may be a business firm or a nonprofit organization; it may be marketing products, services, ideas, people, or places; and it may be marketing them domestically or internationally.

In Chapter 2 we discuss the environmental forces which shape an organization's marketing program. Then in Chapter 3 we discuss the management process in marketing and introduce the concept of strategic marketing planning. Chapter 4 explains the role of marketing information systems and describes the procedure in a marketing research investigation. Marketing information systems and marketing research are major tools used in strategic planning, problem solving, and decision making.

In Search of
EXCELLENCE

Lessons from America's
Best-Run Companies

Thomas J. Peters and
Robert H. Waterman, Jr.

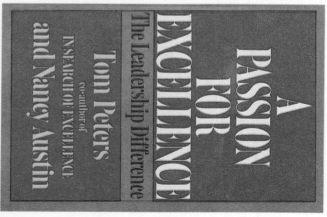

A
PASSION
FOR
EXCELLENCE

The Leadership Difference

Tom Peters

co-author of
IN SEARCH OF EXCELLENCE

and Nancy Austin

C H A P T E R

1

THE FIELD OF MARKETING

CHAPTER GOALS

This chapter is an answer to the question "What is marketing?"—and the answer may surprise you. After studying this chapter, you should understand:

- The meaning of marketing—its broad definition and business-system definition.

- The present-day importance of marketing, both in the total economy and in the individual firm.

- The marketing concept.

- The difference between selling and marketing.

- The four-stage evolution of marketing management.

- The broadened view of the marketing concept.

n Tom Peters' and Bob Waterman's book *In Search of Excellence* and in Peters' follow-up book, *A Passion for Excellence* co-authored with Nancy Austin, the authors identified about 50 business organizations that had a history of successful performance. Included in this group were such well-known companies as the following:

IBM
McDonald's
3 M
Frito-Lay (PepsiCo)
Johnson & Johnson
Marriott
Procter & Gamble

Delta Airlines
Hewlett-Packard
Boeing Aircraft
Maytag
Wal-Mart Stores
Walt Disney Productions
Standard Oil (Indiana)

Two traits that every one of these companies possessed were outstanding leadership and "turned-on" people. The workers' performance was the result of management's listening to workers and displaying a respect for the dignity and creativity of workers.

Two additional traits—"two edges of excellence"—found in each of these organizations were (1) a drive to provide superior service and quality to customers and (2) a drive to innovate—to develop new products and services. In other words, *every one of these companies was marketing-oriented*. In dealings with their customers, these firms gave top priority to finding out what the customers wanted and then creatively developing products and services to satisfy those wants.[1]

Now as we approach the end of the 1980s, it is increasingly clear that marketing is the name of the game in both business and nonbusiness organizations. Moreover, as we prepare for the 1990s and look forward to the next century, marketing will continue to be where the action is. Gone is the spirit prevailing in the 1970s when shortages and the energy crisis focused attention on financial and legal management. An "analysis paralysis" hit many organizations as they looked inward to cut costs, quantify everything, and take forever to make a decision.

Today companies want a president with marketing experience—someone who understands such concepts as target markets, product life cycles, and market segmentation. These companies are seeking a renewal of the risk-taking, dynamic, entrepreneurial spirit that companies need if they are going to grow and be successful.[2]

[1]Thomas J. Peters and Robert H. Waterman, Jr., *In Search of Excellence: Lessons from America's Best-Run Companies*, Harper & Row, New York, 1982; and Thomas J. Peters and Nancy Austin, *A Passion for Excellence: The Leadership Difference*, Random House, New York, 1985. Some of the companies cited in the first book have run into problems in the marketplace since that book was written. However, this situation in no way negates the basic points made in those books and highlighted in this section.

[2]"Marketing: The New Priority," *Business Week*, Nov. 21, 1983, p. 96.

NATURE AND SCOPE OF MARKETING

One day early last summer two boys placed written notices in their neighborhood announcing a lawn-care service that they had just started. They also went door to door to spread the word in person about their new venture. Whether these young entrepreneurs realized it or not, they were engaging in marketing. At the other end of the size scale, General Electric also engages in marketing when it realizes that the railroads need more powerful, yet energy-efficient engines. G.E. then develops, sells, and delivers to the railroads a new model of engine to fill that need.

In a business firm, marketing generates the revenues that are managed by the financial people and used by the production people in creating products and services. The challenge of marketing is to generate those revenues by satisfying customers' wants at a profit and in a socially responsible manner.

Broad Dimensions of Marketing

But marketing is not limited to business. Whenever you try to persuade somebody to do something—donate to the Salvation Army, fasten a seat belt, lower a stereo's noise during study hours in the dorm, vote for your candidate, accept a date with you (or maybe even marry you)—you are engaging in a marketing activity. So-called non-business organizations—they really are in business but don't think of themselves as business people—also engage in marketing. Their "product" may be a vacation place they want you to visit, a social cause or an idea they want you to support, a person they are thrusting into the spotlight, or a cultural institution they want you to attend. Whatever the product is, the organization is engaging in marketing.

As you may gather, marketing is a very broad-based activity, and consequently, it calls for a broad definition. **Now the essence of marketing is a transaction—an exchange—intended to satisfy human needs and wants. That is, marketing occurs any time one social unit (person or organization) strives to exchange something of value with another social unit. Our broad definition then is as follows:**

Marketing consists of all activities designed to generate and facilitate any exchange intended to satisfy human needs or wants.

In this book the terms *needs* and *wants* are used interchangeably. In a limited physiological sense, we might say that we "need" only food, clothing, and shelter. Beyond these requirements we get into the area of "wants." More realistically in our society today, however, many people would say that they "need" a telephone or they "need" some form of mechanized transportation.

CONCEPT OF EXCHANGE

Now let's examine the concept of **exchange** as this term relates to marketing. Exchange is one of three ways in which a person can satisfy a want. Suppose you want some clothes. You can sew them, knit them, or otherwise produce the clothes yourself. You can steal them or use some form of coercion to get the clothes. Or you can offer something of value (money, service, other products) to another person who will voluntarily exchange the clothes for what you offer. It is only the third type of transfer that we call an exchange in the sense that marketing is taking place.

Within the context of our definition of marketing, for an exchange to occur the following conditions must exist:

1. Two or more social units (people or organizations) must be involved. If you are totally self-sufficient in some area, there is no exchange and hence no marketing.
2. The parties must be involved voluntarily, and each must have wants to be satisfied.
3. Each party must have something of value to contribute in the exchange, and each party must believe it will benefit from the exchange.
4. The parties must be able to communicate with each other. Assume that you want a new sweater and a clothing store has sweaters for sale. But if you and the store are not aware of each other—you are not communicating—then there will be no exchange.

Within this broad definition of marketing, then, (1) the marketers, (2) what they are marketing, and (3) their potential markets all assume broad dimensions. The category of **marketers** might include, in addition to business firms, such diverse social units as (a) a political party trying to market its candidate to the public; (b) the director of an art museum providing new exhibits to generate greater attendance and financial support; (c) a labor union marketing its ideas to members and to the company management; and (d) professors trying to make their courses interesting for students.

In addition to the range of items normally considered as products and services, **what is being marketed** might include (a) *ideas*, such as reducing air pollution or contributing to the United Way; (b) *people*, such as a new football coach or a political candidate; and (c) *places*, such as industrial plant sites or a place to go for a vacation.

In a broad sense, **markets** include more than the direct consumers of products, services, and ideas. Thus a state university's market includes the legislators who provide funds, the citizens living near the university who may be affected by university activities, and the alumni. A business firm's market may include government regulatory agencies, environmentalists, and local tax assessors.

The category of "what is being marketed" can include some interesting things.

Business Dimensions of Marketing

Our broad (or macro) definition tells us something about the role of marketing in our socioeconomic system. But this is a book about the business of marketing in an individual organization within that system. These organizations may be business firms in the conventional sense of the word *business*. Or they may be what is called a nonbusiness or a nonprofit organization—a hospital, university, United Way, church, police department, or museum, for example. Both groups—business and nonbusiness—face essentially the same basic marketing problems.

Now many executives in those organizations, as well as many household consumers, think they already know a good bit about the business of marketing. After all, churches run newspaper ads and museums sell copies of famous paintings. And people at home watch television commercials that persuade them to buy. These people purchase products on a self-service basis in supermarkets. Some have friends who "can get it for them wholesale." But in each of these examples, we are talking about only one part of the totality of marketing activities. Consequently, we need a micro, business definition of marketing to guide executives in business or nonbusiness organizations in the management of their marketing effort.

A nonbusiness "business" also engages in marketing.

BUSINESS DEFINITION OF MARKETING

Our micro definition of marketing—applicable in a business or nonbusiness organization—is as follows:

Marketing is a total system of business activities designed to plan, price, promote, and distribute want-satisfying products, services, and ideas to target markets in order to achieve organizational objectives.[3]

Marketing is:
a system: of business activities
designed to: plan, price, promote, and distribute
something of value: want-satisfying products, services, and ideas
for the benefit of: the target market—present and potential household consumers or industrial users
to achieve: the organization's objectives.

This definition has some significant implications:

- It is a managerial, systems definition.
- The entire system of business activities must be customer-oriented. Customers' wants must be recognized and satisfied effectively.
- The marketing program starts with the germ of a product idea and does not end until the customer's wants are completely satisfied, which may be some time after the sale is made.
- The definition implies that to be successful, marketing must maximize profitable sales over the *long run*. Thus, customers must be satisfied in order for a company to get the repeat business that ordinarily is so vital to success.

PRESENT-DAY IMPORTANCE OF MARKETING

Today most nations—regardless of their degree of economic development or their political philosophy—are recognizing the importance of marketing. Economic growth in developing nations depends greatly upon those nations' ability to develop effective distribution systems to handle their raw materials and their industrial output. Even countries with some major state-owned industries (Great Britain, Sweden, Italy) are looking to modern marketing practices as a way to improve their economic health.

---

[3]This definition is essentially the same as the one used in all previous editions of this book. We modified our original definition slightly to conform generally with a revised American Marketing Association definition. The AMA definition is as follows: "Marketing is the process of planning and executing the conception, pricing, promotion, and distribution of ideas, goods, and services to create exchanges that satisfy individual and organizational objectives." See "AMA Board Approves New Marketing Definition," *Marketing News*, Mar. 1, 1985, p. 1.

And communist countries are using advertising, pricing, and other marketing activities to improve their domestic distribution systems and to compete more effectively in international trade.

Importance in the American Socioeconomic System

But it is in the United States that marketing has developed to the greatest extent. Aggressive marketing practices have been largely responsible for the high material standard of living in the United States. Today, through mass, low-cost marketing, we enjoy products that once were considered luxuries and that still are so classified in many countries.

In the United States, modern marketing came of age after World War I, when the words *surplus* and *overproduction* became an important part of the economics vocabulary. Since about 1920, except during World War II and the immediate postwar period, a strong *buyers' market* has existed in the United States. That is, the available supply of products and services has far surpassed effective demand. There has been relatively little difficulty in producing most goods. The real problem has been in marketing them. During recession periods, business people soon realize that it is a slowdown in marketing that forces cutbacks in production. It becomes evident that "nothing happens until somebody sells something."

The importance of marketing in the business world might be more easily understood in quantitative terms. *Between one-fourth and one-third of the civilian labor force is engaged in marketing activities.* Furthermore, over the past century, jobs in marketing have increased at a much more rapid rate than jobs in production. The great increase in the number of marketing workers is a reflection of marketing's expanded role in the economy and the increased demand for marketing services.

Another measure of the importance of marketing is its cost. On the average, about *50 cents of each dollar we spend at the retail level goes to cover marketing costs.* These costs should not be confused with marketing *profits*, however. Nor should it be assumed that products and services would cost less if there were no marketing activities.

AN ECONOMY OF ABUNDANCE

The type of economy we have in the United States largely explains why marketing is so much an American phenomenon. Unlike other economies, ours is an economy of abundance. This means that as a nation, we produce and consume far beyond our subsistence needs. Although marketing exists in every type of *modern* economy, it is especially important for successful business performance in a highly competitive economy of abundance.

American marketing activity has the task of encouraging the consumption of the vast output of American industry. Although modern marketing has been successful, its success has not been greeted with joy in all quarters. Many social and economic resources are scarce and are becoming more so. A number of respected students of social and economic systems have raised serious questions concerning the influence that marketing has on the allocation of these resources. The question they raise is whether too much marketing is leading to a misallocation of resources. Is marketing accepting its responsibility to guide our use of economic resources toward socially desirable goals? We may be so successful in marketing automobiles and fashionable clothing that we overlook more basic values, such as education, slum clearance, and the elimination of pollution. In other words, are we marketing the wrong things?

CREATION OF UTILITIES

The range of utilities created by marketing is another indication of its importance in our socioeconomic system. **Utility** may be defined as the attribute in an item that makes it capable of satisfying human wants. Marketing creates four types of utility—time, place, possession, and image utility—and plays a supporting role in creating form utility.

Form utility is what we ordinarily refer to in business as production—the physical or chemical changes that make a product more valuable. When lumber is made into furniture, form utility is created. This is production, not marketing. However, marketing research may aid in the decision making regarding product design, color, quantities produced, or some other aspect of production.

Place utility is created when a product is made readily accessible to potential customers. **Time utility** is created when a product is available to customers when they want it. **Possession utility** is created when a customer buys the product—that is, the ownership title is transferred to the buyer.

Furniture produced in Grand Rapids, Michigan, in April is of little value to a woman in Los Angeles who wants to buy the furniture for a Christmas present. However, by performing marketing activities—in this case, transporting the furniture to Los Angeles and locating it in a store near where that woman lives—we have added value to the furniture. That is, marketing has created *place utility*. Then by storing the furniture—another marketing activity—from April until December, marketing has created *time utility*. Finally, *possession utility* is created when the woman buys—acquires ownership title to—the furniture.

Image utility is a more subjective, difficult-to-measure concept. It involves the emotional or psychological value that a person attaches to a product or brand because of the reputation or social standing of that product or brand. Marketing, especially

advertising and other forms of promotion, often contributes much to the creation of image utility.

Image utility ordinarily is associated with prestige or high-status products such as designer clothes, expensive foreign automobiles, or certain residential neighborhoods. However, the image-utility value of a given product may vary considerably depending upon different consumers' perceptions. What is a high-image-value product for your parents may mean nothing to you. A certain hairstyle or makeup that is beautiful to one group may be considered ugly by another group. As it is so aptly expressed in an old Irish saying: "It's all a matter of taste, said the lady as she kissed her cow."

Importance in the Individual Firm

Marketing considerations should be the most critical factor guiding all short-range and long-range planning in any organization, for two reasons. First, the core of marketing is customer want-satisfaction, and that is the basic social and economic justification for the existence of virtually all organizations. Second, marketing is the revenue-generating activity in any organization—nothing happens until somebody sells something.

Too often, unfortunately, American business has been oriented toward production. Products are designed by engineers, manufactured by production people, priced by accountants, and then given to sales managers to sell. That procedure generally won't work in today's environment of intense competition and constant change. Just *building* a good product will not result in a company's success, nor will it have much bearing on consumer welfare. The product must be *marketed* to consumers before its full value can be realized.

Today a company must first determine what the customers want and then build a product and marketing program to satisfy those wants, hopefully at a profit. Many organizational departments in a company are essential to its growth, *but marketing is still the sole revenue-producing activity.* This fact sometimes is overlooked by the production managers who use these revenues and by the financial executives who manage them.

Importance to You

Okay, so marketing is important in our economy and in an individual organization. But why should you personally study marketing? What's in it for you? Our answer to these questions consists of three points. First, the study of marketing should be fun and exciting to you because you are participating in marketing in so many of your daily activities. You buy various articles in different stores. You watch television with its advertising commercials, and you read magazines and newspaper ads. As a college student, you are part of your school's market and you might complain about the price (tuition) of the service (education) that you are receiving. Truly, marketing occupies a large part of your daily life. If you doubt this, just imagine for a moment where you would be if there were no marketing institutions—no retail stores, no advertising to give you information, etc.

A second reason for your studying marketing is to make you a better-informed consumer. When you buy a product, you'll understand something of the company's pricing or branding strategy. You'll understand the role of promotion and the role of middlemen (retailers and wholesalers) in distribution.

THE MARKETING CONCEPT

The third reason for studying marketing ties in with your career aspirations. If you are a marketing major, you can learn about the many career opportunities in the field. We especially suggest that you read Appendix B (Careers in Marketing) at the back of this book. Those of you who plan a career in accounting, finance, or some other business field can learn how marketing affects managerial decision making in your field. Finally, some of you may seek a career in a nonbusiness field. You may work in the field of music, psychology, health care, government, education, social work, etc. It is highly likely that organizations in any of those fields will be involved in marketing.

<table>
<tr><td>PROFILE OF A CEO</td></tr>
</table>

— a composite of the chief executive officer (CEO) of a large U.S. corporation.
— and please note the "route to the top" section in the career path below.

The position:

Title: Chairman and chief executive officer.
Compensation: $473,500 salary and bonus plus several benefits.
Workload: 60 or more hours in an average week.
Drawbacks: Insufficient time for family and outside interests.

Career path:

→ **Route to the top: Sales/marketing.**
Number of employers: 2.4.
Years with present company: 23 years.
Number of locations with present company: No more than 2.

The person:

Age: 56.6 years.
Marital status: In first marriage.
Religion: Protestant.
Education: Advanced degree.
Ranking of priorities: Family first, then work, country, and community.

Source: Adapted from a survey of CEOs of Fortune 500 companies by Heidrick & Struggles, an executive search firm, as reported in USA Today, Aug. 16, 1985, p. 1B.

As business people have come to recognize that marketing is vitally important to the success of a firm, an entirely new way of business thinking—a new philosophy—has evolved. It is called the *marketing concept*, and it is based on three fundamental beliefs (see Fig. 1-1):

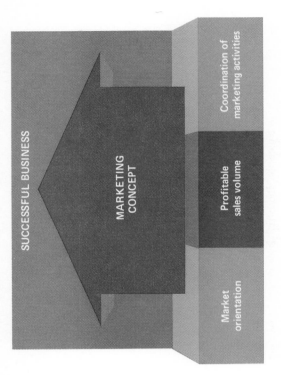

FIGURE 1-1
The marketing concept is built on three foundation stones.

(Figure content: SUCCESSFUL BUSINESS / MARKETING CONCEPT / Market orientation / Profitable sales volume / Coordination of marketing activities)

- All company planning and operations should be *customer-oriented.*
- The goal of the firm should be *profitable sales volume* and not just volume for the sake of volume alone.
- All marketing activities in a firm should be *organizationally coordinated.*

In its fullest sense, the **marketing concept** is a philosophy of business that states that the customers' want-satisfaction is the economic and social justification for a firm's existence. Consequently, all company activities should be devoted to determining customers' wants and then satisfying those wants, while still making a profit over the long run.

Difference between Marketing and Selling

Unfortunately, even today many people, including some business executives, still do not understand the difference between selling and marketing. In fact, many people think the terms are synonymous. Instead, these concepts actually have *opposite* meanings.

Under the *selling* concept, a company makes a product and then uses various selling methods to persuade customers to buy the product. In effect, the company is bending consumer demand to fit the company's supply. Just the opposite occurs under the *marketing* concept. The company finds out what the customer wants and then tries to develop a product that will satisfy that want and still yield a profit. Now the company is bending its supply to the will of consumer demand.

We can summarize the contrasts between selling and marketing as follows:

Selling

1. Emphasis is on the product.
2. Company first makes the product and then figures out how to sell it.

Marketing

1. Emphasis is on customers' wants.
2. Company first determines customers' wants and then figures out how to make and deliver a product to satisfy those wants.

(*continued*)

Banks also are marketing, instead of selling.

MARKETING MANAGEMENT AND ITS EVOLUTION ■

3. Management is sales-volume-oriented.
4. Planning is short-run-oriented, in terms of today's products and markets.
5. Stresses needs of seller.

3. Management is profit-oriented.
4. Planning is long-run-oriented, in terms of new products, tomorrow's markets, and future growth.
5. Stresses wants of buyers.

For a business enterprise to realize the full benefits of the marketing concept, that philosophy must be translated into action. This means that (1) the marketing activities in the firm must be fully coordinated and well managed, and (2) the chief marketing executive must be accorded an important role in company planning. As these two moves occur, marketing management begins to develop. **Marketing management** is the marketing concept in action.

Since the Industrial Revolution, marketing management in American business has evolved through three stages of development, and a fourth one is emerging. However, many companies are still in the earlier stages. And as yet only a few firms exhibit the managerial philosophies and practices characteristic of the most advanced developmental period.

Production-Orientation Stage

In this first stage, a company typically is production-oriented. Executives in production and engineering shape its planning. The function of the sales department is simply to sell the company's output, at a price set by production and financial executives. This is the "build a better mousetrap" stage. The underlying assumption is that marketing effort is not needed to get people to buy a product that is well made and reasonably priced.

During this period, manufacturers have sales departments—marketing is not yet recognized—headed by sales managers whose main job is to operate a sales force. This form of organization predominated in the United States until about the start of the Great Depression in the 1930s.

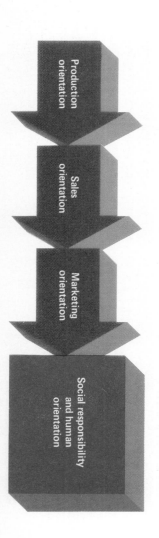

Production orientation

Sales orientation

Marketing orientation

Social responsibility and human orientation

Sales-Orientation Stage

The Depression made it clear that the main problem in the economy no longer was to make or grow enough products, but rather to *sell* the output. Just *producing* a better mousetrap brought no assurance of market success. The product had to be sold, and this called for substantial promotional effort. Thus, the United States entered a period when selling and sales executives were given new respect and responsibilities by company management.

Unfortunately, it was also during this period that selling acquired much of its bad reputation. This was the age of the "hard sell"—pictured in terms of the unscrupulous used-car sales person or the door-to-door encyclopedia sales people. What is more unfortunate is that even today many organizations still believe that they must operate with a hard-sell philosophy to prosper. And as long as there are companies operating with a hard-sell philosophy, there will be continued (and justified, in the authors' opinion) criticisms of selling and marketing. In the United States the sales era generally extended from the 1930s well into the 1950s, although no specific dates sharply define any of the four stages.

Marketing-Orientation Stage

In the third stage, companies embrace the concept of coordinated marketing management, directed toward the twin goals of customer orientation and *profitable* sales volume. Attention is focused on marketing, rather than on selling, and the top executive in this area is called a marketing manager or a vice president of marketing. In this stage, several activities that traditionally were the province of other executives become the responsibility of the marketing manager. For instance, inventory control, warehousing, and aspects of product planning are often turned over to the marketing

Customers like convenience banking.

manager. These managers should be brought in at the *beginning*, rather than at the end, of a production cycle. Marketing should influence all short-term and long-range company planning.

The key to implementing the marketing concept successfully is a favorable attitude on the part of top management. As an executive at the Chase Manhattan Bank once stated: "Marketing begins with top management. Only top management can provide the climate, the discipline, and the leadership required for a successful marketing program." The president of Burroughs Corporation caught the spirit of firms that have fully embraced the marketing concept when he said, "Any company is nothing but a marketing organization." The president of Pepsi-Cola said, "Our business is the business of marketing."

We are *not* saying that marketing executives should hold the top positions in a company. The marketing concept *does not* imply that the president of a firm must come up through the marketing department. We say only that the president must be marketing-oriented.

Most American firms are now in this third stage in the evolution of marketing management. The marketing concept has generally been adopted by both large and medium-sized companies. How well many companies have actually implemented the marketing concept, however, is still questionable. Many companies are using the appropriate titles and other external trappings, but they are paying little more than lip service to the concept. In the apparel industry, for example, some observers believe that a combination of foreign competition plus the lack of a marketing orientation will force many manufacturers out of business by 1990.[4] The AT&T case illustrates what an enormous job it is for a giant, heavily manufacturing-oriented corporation to become marketing-oriented. This large organization was forced to divest itself of the regional Bell Telephone companies and also to give up its monopoly position in long-distance telephone service. Top marketing executives were hired from other companies and AT&T entered new fields—even competing with IBM. In this situation you would think that a marketing orientation would be a natural and obvious corporate strategy to employ. Yet for the first few years following the divestiture, the corporation was still essentially a manufacturing-oriented organization and the manufacturing executives still were in control.[5]

Social Responsibility and Human-Orientation Stage

Social and economic conditions in the 1970s and 1980s have led to the fourth stage in the evolution of marketing management—a stage characterized by its societal orientation. It is increasingly obvious that marketing executives must act in a socially responsible manner if they wish to succeed, or even survive. External pressures—consumer discontent, a concern for environmental problems, and political-legal forces—are influencing the marketing programs of countless firms.

[4] *Marketing News*, Jan. 18, 1985, p. 1. For a report on some other traditionally non-marketing-oriented industries (textiles, transportation, consumer durables, and retailing) and their struggles to become more marketing-oriented, see Edward G. Michaels, "Marketing Muscle," *Business Horizons*, May–June 1982, pp. 63–74.

[5] Monica Langley, "AT&T Marketing Men Find Their Star Fails to Ascend as Expected," *The Wall Street Journal*, Feb. 13, 1984, p. 1.

Many people are realizing that there are finite limits to our natural resources. We have already experienced shortages of several resources. Consequently, this fourth period might be viewed as a "survival" stage. Marketers must be supply-oriented—whether we mean the supply of raw materials, of energy resources, of clean air and water, or of just the "good life" in general.

Perhaps this fourth stage may also be viewed more broadly as a human-orientation period—a time in which there is a concern for the management of human resources. We sense a change in emphasis from materialism to humanism in our society. One mark of an affluent society is a shift from consumption of products to services, and a shift in cultural emphasis from things to people. In this fourth stage, marketing management must be concerned with creating and delivering a better quality of *life*, rather than only a material standard of *living*.[6]

BROADENING THE MARKETING CONCEPT

The wave of consumer protests starting in the late 1960s—the rise of *consumerism*—was an indication to some people that the marketing concept was a failure. Others went so far as to suggest that the marketing concept is an operational philosophy that *conflicts* with a firm's social responsibility.

From one point of view, these charges are true. A firm may totally satisfy its customers (in line with the marketing concept), while at the same time be adversely affecting society. To illustrate, a steel company in Ohio might be satisfying its customers in Texas with the right product, reasonably priced. Yet at the same time this company is polluting the air and water in Ohio.

The marketing concept and a company's social responsibility can be quite compatible. They need not conflict. The key to compatibility lies in extending the *breadth* and *time* dimensions in the definition of the marketing concept.

Regarding *breadth*—let us assume that a company's market includes not only the buyers of the firm's products, but also other people directly affected by the firm's operations. Then, under this broader definition of customers, the marketing concept and the social responsibility of the firm can indeed be compatible. In our example, the Ohio steel mill has several "customer" groups to satisfy. Among these are (1) the Texas customers of the steel shipments; (2) the consumers of the air that contains impurities given off by the mill; (3) the recreational users of the local river affected by waste matter from the mill; and (4) the community affected by employee traffic driving to and from work.

This broadening of the marketing concept is consistent with our previously discussed, broad definition of marketing. There we recognized that a given marketer may have several different target markets.

Regarding the extended *time* dimension—we must view consumer satisfaction and profitable business as goals to be achieved *over the long run*. If a company prospers in the long run, it must be doing a reasonably good job of satisfying its customers' current social and economic demands.

[6]See Leslie M. Dawson, "Marketing for Human Needs in a Humane Future," *Business Horizons*, June 1980, pp. 72–82.

This firm is not satisfying some of its customer groups.

Thus, the marketing concept and a company's social responsibility are compatible, if management strives *over the long run* to (1) satisfy the wants of product-buying customers, (2) satisfy the societal wants affected by the firm's activities, and (3) meet the company's profit goals.

STRUCTURAL PLAN OF THIS BOOK

The overall plan of this book is to use the managerial-micro approach to study the strategic management of the marketing activities in an individual organization. The book is divided into 8 parts consisting of 25 chapters in total.

Part 1 provides us with the background and framework within which we can build our marketing program. The first chapter has covered the nature, importance, and evolution of marketing. In Chapter 2 we see that a company's marketing activity is shaped largely by external, uncontrollable environmental forces, as well as by the environment within the firm. Chapter 3 explains the marketing management process and the fundamentals of strategic planning in a marketing organization. Chapter 4 covers a marketing information system and marketing research—the main tools used by marketing executives to aid in their decision making.

Part 2—Chapters 5 through 8—deals with the identification and analysis of a company's target markets. In Chapters 5, 6, and 7 we examine the demographic, sociological, and psychological influences on buying behavior in consumer and industrial markets. We discuss the topics of market segmentation and forecasting market demand in Chapter 8.

Parts 3 through 6—Chapters 9 through 20—are devoted to designing and developing a strategic marketing mix. A marketing mix is a combination of the four elements that constitute the core of a marketing program. The four are an organization's product assortment (Part 3), price structure (Part 4), distribution system (Part 5), and promotional activities (Part 6).

In Part 7 we discuss the strategic management of a marketing program in three special fields—the marketing of services (Chapter 21), marketing in nonbusiness, nonprofit organizations (Chapter 22), and international marketing (Chapter 23).

Part 8 deals with the implementation of strategic planning and an evaluation of the performance of the organization's marketing program. In Chapter 24 we use a micro approach to evaluate the performance of the marketing effort in an individual firm. In Chapter 25 we use a macro approach as we evaluate the role of marketing in our socioeconomic system.

For additional help and information we have provided two appendices at the back of the book. One covers the fundamentals of marketing arithmetic, and the other discusses careers in marketing and how to get a job in marketing.

SUMMARY

In a broad sense, marketing is any exchange activity intended to satisfy human wants. In this context we need to look broadly at (1) who should be classed as marketers, (2) what is being marketed, and (3) who are the target markets. In a business sense, marketing is a system of business action designed to plan, price, promote, and distribute want-satisfying products, services, and ideas to markets in order to achieve organizational objectives.

Marketing is practiced today in all modern nations, regardless of their political philosophies. But marketing has developed to the greatest extent in the United States because this country has an economy of abundance. One of every three or four people is employed in marketing, and about half of what consumers spend goes to cover the costs of marketing. Marketing creates time, place, possession, and image utility, and it contributes a bit to the creation of form utility.

The philosophy of the marketing concept holds that a company should (1) be customer-oriented, (2) strive for profitable sales volume, and (3) coordinate all its marketing activities. Marketing management is the vehicle that business uses to activate the marketing concept. Our socioeconomic structure—and marketing management is part of it—has evolved:

- from an agrarian economy in a rural setting,
- through a production-oriented, subsistence-level economy in an urban society,
- and then through a sales-oriented economy,
- into today's customer-oriented economy, featuring a society of abundance with discretionary purchasing power.

Looking to the future, our attention is shifting to societal relationships:

- to the quality of our life and environment.
- to the conservation and allocation of our scarce resources.
- to a concern for people.

These point up the need to broaden the marketing concept to include satisfaction of *all* a company's markets, while generating profits *over the long run.*

KEY TERMS AND CONCEPTS

The numbers refer to the pages on which the terms and concepts are defined. In addition, see the glossary at the back of the book.

Marketing (broad definition) 4
Concept of exchange 4
Marketing (micro, business definition) 6
Economy of abundance 7
Utility: 8
  Form utility 8
  Place utility 8
  Time utility 8
  Possession utility 8
  Image utility 8

Marketing concept 10
Marketing management: 12
  Production-orientation stage 12
  Sales-orientation stage 13
  Marketing-orientation stage 13
  Social-responsibility stage 14
Broadening the marketing concept 15

QUESTIONS AND PROBLEMS

1. Explain the concept of an exchange, including the conditions that must exist for an exchange to occur.

2. In the following marketing exchanges, what is the "something of value" that each party contributes in the exchange?
   a. Your school ←——→ You as a student.
   b. Fire department ←——→ People in your hometown.
   c. Flour miller ←——→ Bakery.
   d. United Way ←——→ Contributors.
   e. Hilton Hotel ←——→ Publisher's sales meeting.

3. In line with the broader, societal concept of marketing, describe some of the ways in which nonbusiness organizations to which you belong are engaged in marketing activities.

4. For each of the following organizations, describe (1) what is being marketed and (2) who is the target market.
   a. San Francisco Forty-Niners professional football team.
   b. Airline Pilots Association labor union.
   c. Professor teaching a first-year chemistry course.
   d. Fire department in your city.

5. Give some examples of creating:
   a. Time utility.   c. Image utility.
   b. Place utility.   d. Form utility (marketing's contribution).

6. One writer has stated that any business has only two functions—marketing and innovation. How would you explain this statement to a student majoring in engineering, accounting, finance, or personnel management?

7. One way of explaining the importance of marketing in our economy is to consider how we would live if there were no marketing facilities. Describe some of the ways in which your daily activities would be affected under such circumstances.

8. Explain the three elements that constitute the marketing concept.

9. Explain the difference between marketing and selling.

10. Name some companies that you believe are still in the production or sales stage in the evolution of marketing management. Explain why you chose each of them.

11. "The marketing concept does not imply that marketing executives will run the firm. The concept requires only that whoever is in top management be marketing-oriented." Give examples of how a production manager, company treasurer, or personnel manager can be marketing-oriented.

CHAPTER

2

THE MARKETING ENVIRONMENT

CHAPTER GOALS

A variety of environmental forces impinge on an organization's marketing system. Some of these are external to the firm and thus are largely uncontrollable by the organization. Other forces within the firm generally are controllable by management. After studying this chapter, you should understand:

- How the following macroenvironmental factors can influence a company's marketing system:

  a. Demography.   d. Social and cultural forces.

  b. Economic   e. Political and conditions.   legal forces.

  c. Competition.   f. Technology.

- How the external microenvironmental factors of the market, suppliers, and marketing intermediaries all can influence an organization's marketing program.

- How the nonmarketing resources within a company can influence that firm's marketing system.

- The need to coordinate the marketing activities within an organization.

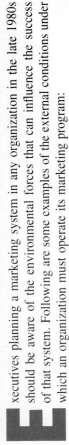

xecutives planning a marketing system in any organization in the late 1980s should be aware of the environmental forces that can influence the success of that system. Following are some examples of the external conditions under which an organization must operate its marketing program:

- Our population is growing old, and the average age will continue to rise.
- Regional shifts in population are increasing the economic and political power of the South and West.
- Computers are dramatically changing many aspects of our lives.
- Foreign competition is seriously affecting many of our industries.
- The role of women in society, employment, and politics is continuing to change significantly.
- Minority groups—both native-born and immigrants—are putting their imprint on politics, eduation, business, athletics, and other aspects of American life. And their numbers are growing at a faster rate than is the population as a whole.
- The two so-called superpowers—United States and Russia—face challenges and a declining position in many parts of the world—a situation that for America was unthinkable only three decades ago.
- Public confidence in, and respect for, government has declined sharply over the past two decades. Yet, despite the public's frustrations with government, polls show that people generally do not want to dismantle government services or change the basic institutions.
- The number of people earning a college degree increased signficantly over the past 20 years. Yet, with few exceptions, the biggest employment growth during the next 10 years will be in occupations that do not require a college degree.
- Medical "miracles" are curtailing illnesses ranging from childhood diseases to killer diseases such as cancer and heart ailments. At the same time, many Americans simply cannot afford adequate medical care. The runaway medical costs in the United States are a major economic problem.[1]

---

[1]Adapted from "10 Forces Reshaping America," *U.S. News & World Report*, Mar. 19, 1984, p. 40.

The above conditions are part of the external environment of marketing, and as such, they present a set of strong challenges to marketing executives. A company's marketing system must operate within the framework of forces that constitute the system's environment. These forces are either external or internal to the firm. The *internal forces* are inherent in the organization and are controlled by management. The *external forces*, which generally *cannot* be controlled by the firm, may be divided into two groups. The first is a set of broad (*macro*) influences such as culture, laws, and economic conditions. The second group we shall call (for lack of a better term) the firm's *microenvironment*. This group includes producer-suppliers, marketing intermediaries, and customers.

EXTERNAL MACROENVIRONMENT

■

The following six interrelated macroenvironmental forces have considerable effect on any organization's marketing system. Yet they are largely *not* controllable by management. See Fig. 2-1.

- Demography.
- Economic conditions.
- Competition.

- Social and cultural forces.
- Political and legal forces.
- Technology.

Note that we just said that these forces are *largely*, but not *totally*, uncontrollable by management in a firm. That is, a company may be able to manage its external environment to some extent. For example, through company and industry lobbying and contributions to a political action committee (PAC), a company may have some influence on the political-legal forces in its environment. Or new-product research and development that is on the technological frontier can influence a firm's competitive position. In fact, it may be *our* company's technology that is the external environmental force of technology that is affecting *other* organizations.[2]

―――――――――

[2] For several examples of environmental management strategies that companies can use to influence the uncontrollable environmental forces discussed in this section, see Carl P. Zeithaml and Valarie A. Zeithaml, "Environmental Management: Revisiting a Marketing Perspective," *Journal of Marketing*, Spring 1984, pp. 46–53.

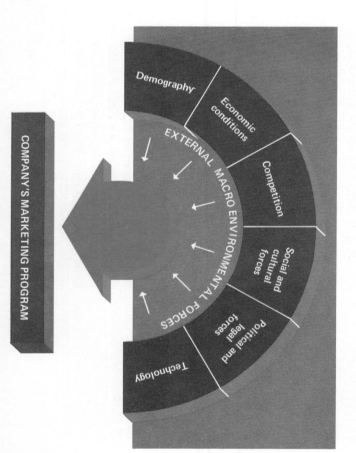

FIGURE 2-1
Major forces in a company's macroenvironment.

If there is one similarity among the above six environmental factors, it is that they are subject to change—and at an increasing rate. We noted some of these changes and new environmental conditions in our chapter-opening vignette. Others will be discussed in the remainder of this section.

Demography

We may define **demography** as the statistical study of human population and its distribution. It is especially important to marketing executives, because people constitute markets. Demography will be discussed in greater detail in Chapter 5. So at this point we shall mention just a couple of examples of how demographic factors influence marketing systems.

In the mid-1980s, for the first time in our history, the number of people 65 and over surpassed the number of teenagers—and this gap will widen considerably by 1990. The marketing implications in this trend are substantial. Johnson & Johnson, for example, introduced Affinity, a shampoo "for hair over 40." Cosmetic firms are featuring in their ads such actresses as Catherine Deneuve and Linda Evans, who are over 40, and Joan Collins and Sophia Loren, who are over 50. This is quite a contrast to the youth-driven promotions of a decade ago. Many movies deal with subjects of interest to older people. Even restaurants—International King's Table chain, for example—are catering to the tastes and incomes of people over 60.

Another significant demographic development is the rapidly growing marketing comprised of single people. In 1940 fewer than 3 percent of all adults lived alone. Today, nearly 12 percent of the adults (21 million in 1985) live alone. More than 60 percent of these singles are female, and over half of these single women are widows. One aspect of the singles' psychology is especially significant for marketers—these people don't necessarily look on their single status as something only temporary.

The marketing implications in this demographic force are almost limitless. The frozen-food industry caters to this market with high-quality foods and a great variety of menu offerings. Corning Glass Works (Pyrex) introduced a line of Little Dishes—small food containers for microwave-oven use. Auto manufacturers are catering to the female singles market. Dealers will even change the angle of the gas pedal to accommodate high heels. Home builders are designing homes, condominium units, and other housing ventures especially for the singles market.[3]

They say you're not as
innocent as you seem.

They say you have a past.

They say you cry too easily
and laugh too much.

They're right, you do.

So do I.

Now wear my perfume.
And let them talk.

SOPHIA

Some firms now aim at older-age markets.

Economic Conditions

People alone do not make a market. They must have money to spend and be willing to spend it. Consequently, the **economic environment** is a significant force that affects the marketing system of just about any organization. A marketing system is affected especially by such economic considerations as the current stage of the business cycle, inflation, and interest rates.

STAGE OF THE BUSINESS CYCLE

Marketing executives should know what stage of the business cycle the economy currently is in, because this cycle has such an impact on a company's marketing system. The traditional business cycle goes through four stages—prosperity, recession,

---

[3]Cindy Skrzycki, "Digging for Dollars in the Singles Market," *U.S. News & World Report*, Feb. 10, 1986, pp. 46–47.

depression, and recovery. However, various economic strategies have been adopted by the federal government that have averted the depression stage in the United States for over 50 years. Consequently, today we think in terms of a three-stage cycle—prosperity, recession, recovery—then returning full cycle to prosperity.

Essentially, a company usually operates its marketing system quite differently during each stage. Prosperity is characterized typically as a period of economic growth. During this stage, organizations tend to expand their marketing programs as they add new products and enter new markets. A recession, on the other hand, typically is a period of retrenchment for consumers and businesses. People can become discouraged, scared, and angry. Naturally these feelings affect their buying behavior which, in turn, has major implications for the marketing programs in countless firms.

Recovery finds the economy moving from recession to prosperity: the marketers' challenge is determining how quickly prosperity will return and to what level. As the unemployment rate declines and disposable income increases, companies expand their marketing efforts to improve sales and profits.

INFLATION

Inflation is a rise in price levels. When prices rise at a faster rate than personal incomes, there is a decline in consumer buying power. Many countries today are plagued with extremely high rates of inflation. During the late 1970s and early 1980s the United States experienced what for us was a high inflation rate of 10 to 14 percent. While inflation has declined in recent years, there still is a fear that higher rates may return. Consequently, this spectre continues to influence government policies, consumer psychology, and business marketing programs.

Inflation presents some real challenges in the management of a marketing program—especially in the area of pricing and cost control. Consumers are adversely affected as their buying power declines. At the same time, they may overspend today for fear that prices will be higher tomorrow.

INTEREST RATES

Interest rates are another external economic factor influencing marketing programs. When interest rates are high, for example, consumers tend to hold back on long-term purchases such as housing. Consumer purchases also are affected by whether they think interest rates will increase or decline. Marketers sometimes offer below-market interest rates (a form of price cut) as a promotional device to increase business. Auto manufacturers used this tactic extensively in the mid-1980s, for example.

Competition

A company's competitive environment obviously is a major influence shaping its marketing system. Any executives worth their salt should be constantly gathering intelligence and otherwise monitoring all aspects of competitors' marketing activities—that is, their products, pricing, distribution systems, and promotional programs. Also, a significant related environmental force shaping the destiny of many American firms today is the factor of *foreign competition*. Two aspects of competition that we shall consider briefly here are the types of competition and the competitive market structure in which companies may be operating.

TYPES OF COMPETITION

A firm generally faces competition from three different sources. The first is the competition from marketers of directly similar products. Thus, in personal computers Tandy competes with Apple, IBM, Compaq, and other brands. Fischer skis compete with Dynastar, Atomic, K-2, Olin, Rossignol, and several other brands. The second type of competition is from substitute products. In this situation a manufacturer of vinyl stereo record albums must compete with laser discs, tape cassettes, and even substitute products in the home-entertainment field. In the third type of competition we recognize that every company is competing for the customer's limited buying power. So the competition faced by a producer of tennis rackets might be a new pair of slacks, a garden tool, or a car repair bill.

COMPETITIVE MARKET STRUCTURES

Four basic types of competitive market structures exist in the American economy today. The four are pure competition, monopolistic competition, oligopoly, and monopoly. Figure 2-2 is a summary of the characteristics of each category. A company's marketing program is influenced considerably by the particular type of competitive structure in which the company operates.

Pure competition is a market situation in which there are many small buyers and sellers, each with complete market information. No single buyer or seller controls market demand, market supply, or price. The product is homogeneous—i.e., each seller markets the same product. It is easy to enter or leave this type of market. Pure competition is rarely, if ever, attained in the real world. Rather, it is a theoretical concept—an ideal. Something close to pure competition often is found in the marketing of agricultural products such as cereal grains or fresh fruits and vegetables.

In a market situation of **monopolistic competition** there are many buyers and sellers, but they lack complete market information. Each seller is attempting to gain a differential advantage over its competitors. This advantage may be differences

Sometimes competition can be direct.

FIGURE 2-2
Characteristics of competitive market structures.

CHARACTERISTIC	STRUCTURE			
	Pure competition	Monopolistic competition	Oligopoly	Monopoly
Number of competitors	Very many	Many	Few	One
Size of competitors	Small	Varies	Large	There are none
Nature of product	Homogeneous	Differentiated	Homogeneous or differentiated	Unique—no close substitutes
Seller's control over price	None	Some—depends on degree of differentiation	Some—but be careful	Complete (within regulations)
Entry into industry	Very easy	Easy	Difficult	Very difficult

Social and Cultural Forces

in the product, its brand or packaging, the distribution system, promotional appeals, or customer services. The idea is to get the buyer to perceive an attractive difference in what this seller is offering and therefore select this particular seller's product. Because of these perceived differences, the sellers have more control over their product and price, even though the sellers are marketing essentially similar products. Monopolistic competition is the most prevalent competitive structure in the United States today. It exists in the marketing of countless products and services.

An **oligopoly** is a market structure wherein only a few large sellers, marketing essentially similar products, account for all or almost all of an industry's sales. In the United States, examples of oligopolistic industries include cola drinks, autos, breakfast cereals, auto tires, steel, aluminum, cigarettes, and beer. Usually the strong competition and/or large initial investment will make it very difficult for a new firm to enter an oligopoly.

When planning its marketing strategies, each seller must consider the possible reactions of the few competitors. For example, all sellers tend to charge the same price. If one firm raises its price, its sales drop off considerably. If a firm cuts its price, all competitors will follow and the new market price simply settles at a lower level. Consequently, the last thing an oligopoly wants is a price war.

A **monopoly** is a market structure in which only one firm is marketing a particular product or service, and there are no close substitutes. This situation is typical, for example, in the gas and electric utilities market in any given metropolitan area. Because of their unique market positions, public-utility monopolies are heavily regulated by governmental agencies. Sometimes patent protections (17 years maximum) can provide a company with something close to a monopoly position when the product is a significant improvement over existing products. This situation existed for several years in the case of Polaroid cameras, Xerox copiers, and various pharmaceutical drugs.

The impact of the sociocultural environment on marketing systems is reflected in several sections of this book. Most of two chapters—6 and 25—is devoted to the topic. To add to the complexity of the task facing marketing executives, cultural patterns—life-styles, social values, beliefs—are changing much faster than they used to. At this point we shall note just a few of these changes that have significant marketing implications.

EMPHASIS ON QUALITY OF LIFE

Our emphasis today is increasingly on the *quality* of life rather than the *quantity* of goods. The theme is, "Not more—but better." We seek value, durability, and safety in the products we buy. Looking ahead, we will worry more about inflation, crime, and interest rates, and less about keeping up with the neighbors in autos, dress, and homes. Our growing concern for the environment and our discontent with pollution and resource waste are leading to significant changes in our life-styles. And when our life-styles change, of course marketing is affected.

ROLE OF WOMEN

One of the most dramatic occurrences in our society in recent years has been the changing role of women. What is especially significant is the breaking away from the

Marketers know that the role of women is changing.

traditional and sometimes discriminatory patterns that have stereotyped the male-female roles in families, jobs, recreation, product use, and many other areas. Today, women's growing political power, economic power, and new job opportunities have considerably changed their perspectives and those of men as well.

ATTITUDES TOWARD PHYSICAL FITNESS AND EATING

In recent years an increased interest in health and physical fitness seems generally to have cut across most demographic and economic segments of our society. Participation in physical fitness activities from aerobics to yoga (we could not think of an activity beginning with a Z) is on the increase. Stores supplying activity products and service organizations catering to this trend have multiplied. Public facilities (bicycle paths, hiking trails, jogging paths, and playgrounds) have been improved.

Paralleling the physical fitness phenomenon, we are experiencing significant changes in the eating patterns in the United States. Our sensitivity level is being raised with respect to the relationship between our diet and major killing diseases such as heart attacks and cancer. Consequently, there is a growing interest in weight-control eating, foods low in salt, additives, and cholesterol, and foods high in vitamins, minerals, and fiber content. Health foods truly have moved into supermarkets.

IMPULSE BUYING

In recent years there has been a significant increase in impulse buying—that is, purchases made without much advance planning. A shopper may go to the grocery store with a mental note to buy meat and bread. In the store, he may also select some fresh

We want convenient shopping hours.

peaches because they look appealing or are priced attractively. Another shopper, seeing some cleansing tissues on the shelf, may be reminded that she is running low and so may buy two boxes. These are impulse purchases.

A key point to understand is that some impulse buying is done on a very rational basis. Self-service, open-display selling has brought about a marketing situation wherein planning may be postponed until the buyer reaches the retail outlet. Because of the trend toward impulse buying, greater emphasis must be placed on promotional programs to get people into a store. Displays must be more appealing because the manufacturer's package must serve as a silent sales person.

DESIRE FOR CONVENIENCE

As an outgrowth of the increase in discretionary purchasing power and the importance of time, there has been a substantial increase in the consumer's desire for convenience. We want products ready and easy to use, and convenient credit plans to pay for them. We want these products packaged in a variety of sizes, quantities, and forms. We want stores located close by, and open at virtually all hours.

Every major phase of a company's marketing program is affected by this craving for convenience. Product planning is influenced by the need for customer convenience in packaging, quantity, and selection. Pricing policies must be established in conformity with the demand for credit and with the costs of providing the various kinds of convenience. Distribution policies must provide for convenient locations and store hours.

Political and Legal Forces

To an increasing extent, every company's conduct is influenced by the political-legal processes in society. Legislation at all levels exercises more influence on the *marketing* activities of an organization than on any other phase of its operations. The political-legal influences on marketing can be grouped into five categories. In each, the influence stems both from legislation and from policies established by the maze of government regulatory agencies. The categories are:

1. *General monetary and fiscal policies.* Marketing systems obviously are affected by the level of government spending, the money supply, and tax legislation.

2. *Broad social legislation and accompanying policies set by regulatory agencies.* Civil rights laws and programs to reduce unemployment fall in this category. Also included is legislation controlling the environment—antipollution laws, for example, and regulations set by the Environmental Protection Agency.

3. *Governmental relationships with individual industries.* Here we find subsidies in agriculture, shipbuilding, passenger rail transportation, and other industries. Tariffs and import quotas also affect specific industries. In the 1980s, government *deregulation* has had a significant effect on financial institutions and on the airline, rail, and trucking industries.

4. *Legislation specifically related to marketing.* Marketing executives do not have to be lawyers. But they should know something about these laws, especially the major ones—why they were passed, what are their main provisions, and what are the current ground rules set by the courts and regulatory agencies for administering these laws.

The laws tend to fall into two groups. One group is designed primarily to

TABLE 2-1   SUMMARY OF SELECTED MAJOR LEGISLATION AFFECTING MARKETING

Designed primarily to regulate competition:

1. *Sherman Antitrust Act* (1890). Prohibits monopolies and combinations in restraint of trade.

2. *Federal Trade Commission (FTC) Act* (1914). Prohibits unfair competition.

3. *Clayton Antitrust Act* (1914). Regulates price discrimination, exclusive dealing, tying contracts, and interlocking corporate directorships.

4. *State Unfair Trade Practices Acts* (1930s). Prohibit "loss-leader" pricing (selling below cost). Laws still in effect in about half the states.

5. *Robinson-Patman Act* (1936). Amends the Clayton Act by strengthening the prohibition of price discrimination. Regulates price discounts and allowances.

6. *Wheeler-Lea Act* (1938). Amends the FTC Act; broadens and strengthens regulation of unfair or deceptive competition.

7. *Lanham Trademark Act* (1946). Regulates brands and trademarks.

8. *Celler-Kefauver Antimerger Act* (1950). Amends the Clayton Act; prevents corporate mergers where the effect may be to substantially lessen competition.

9. *Consumer Goods Pricing Act* (1975). Repeals federal laws supporting State fair-trade laws. Does away with state laws allowing manufacturers to set retail prices.

10. *Various deregulation laws pertaining to specific industries:*
    a. Natural Gas Policy Act (1978).
    b. Airline Deregulation Act (1978).
    c. Motor Carrier Act (1980).
    d. Staggers Rail Act (1980).
    e. Depository Institutions Act (1981).

Designed primarily to protect consumers:

1. *Pure Food and Drug Act* (1906). Regulates labeling of food and drugs and prohibits manufacture or marketing of adulterated food or drugs. Amended in 1938 by Food, Drug, and Cosmetics Act.

2. *Meat Inspection Act* (1906). Regulates meat-packing houses and provides for federal inspection of meats.

3. *Various textile labeling laws that require the manufacturer to indicate what the product is made of:*
    a. Wool Products Labeling Act (1939).
    b. Fur Products Labeling Act (1951).
    c. Flammable Fabrics Act (1953).
    d. Textile Fiber Products Identification Act.

4. *Automobile Information Disclosure Act* (1958). Requires manufacturers to post suggested retail prices on new passenger vehicles.

5. *Kefauver-Harris Drug Amendments* (1962). Requires (a) that drugs be labeled with their generic names, (b) that new drugs be pretested, and (c) that new drugs get approval of Food and Drug Administration before being marketed.

6. *National Traffic and Motor Vehicle Safety Act* (1966). Provides for safety standards for tires and autos.

7. *Fair Packaging and Labeling Act* (1966). The "truth in packaging" law that regulates packaging and labeling.

8. *Cigarette Labeling and Advertising Acts* (1966, 1969). Require manufacturers to label cigarettes as being hazardous to health and prohibits TV advertising of cigarettes.

9. *Consumer Credit Protection Act* (1968). The "truth in lending" law that requires full disclosure of interest rates and other financing charges on loans and credit purchases.

10. *Fair Credit Reporting Act* (1970). Regulating the reporting and the use of credit information.

11. *Consumer Product Safety Act* (1972). Establishes the Consumer Product Safety Commission with broad powers to regulate the marketing of products ruled unsafe by the commission.

12. *Consumer Product Warranty Act* (1975). Increases consumers' rights and sellers' responsibilities under product warranties.

13. *FTC Improvement Act* (1980). Limits the power of the Federal Trade Commission to set and enforce industry trade regulations. In effect, reverses the trend toward more FTC protection of consumers.

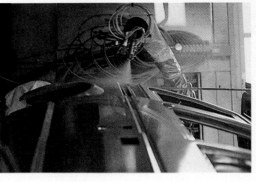

Robots are changing marketing patterns.

regulate and maintain competition, and the other is primarily intended to protect the consumer. Table 2-1 is a summary of the main laws in each group. We shall not continue our discussion of marketing legislation at this point. Instead, we shall cover the relevant legislation in the appropriate places throughout this book.

5. *The provision of information and the purchase of products.* This fifth area of government influence in marketing is quite different from the other four. Instead of telling marketing executives what they must do or cannot do—instead of the legislation and regulations—the government is clearly helping them. The federal government is the largest source of secondary marketing information in the country. And the government is the largest single buyer of products and services in the nation.

TECHNOLOGY

Technology has a tremendous impact on our lives—our life-styles, our consumption patterns, and our economic well-being. Just think of the effect of major technological developments like the airplane, plastics, television, computers, antibiotics, and birth control pills. Except perhaps for the airplane, all these technologies reached the large-scale marketing stage only in your lifetime or your parents' lifetime. Think how your life in the future might be affected by cures for the common cold, development of energy sources to replace fossil fuels, low-cost methods for making ocean water drinkable, or even commercial travel to the moon.

Major technological breakthroughs carry a threefold market impact. They can:

• Start entirely new industries, as computers, robots, and lasers have done.
• Radically alter, or virtually destroy, existing industries. Television crippled the radio and movie industries; wash-and-wear fabrics hurt commercial laundries and dry cleaners.
• Stimulate other markets and industries not related to the new technology. New home appliances and frozen food gave homemakers additional free time to engage in other activities.

Technology is a mixed blessing in other ways, also. A new technology may improve our lives in one area, while creating environmental and social problems in other areas. The automobile makes life great in some ways, but it also creates traffic jams and air pollution. Television provides built-in baby-sitters, but it also has an adverse effect on family discussions and on children's reading habits. It is a bit ironic that technology is strongly criticized for creating problems (air pollution, for example), but at the same time we look to technology to solve these problems.

Monitor the Environment

We have finished our discussion of the major external environmental forces that shape an organization's marketing system. When you stop to think about it, you may realize what a monumental task a marketing executive has in adjusting to these external influences. Obviously, the more executives know about their environment, the better the job they can do in planning and operating their company's marketing systems. One key to learning about the environment is to monitor it in a systematic, ongoing fashion. In each of the six environmental categories, marketing executives should be alert to trends, new developments, and other changes that may present marketing opportunities or problems for their particular firm.

Management should assign this monitoring responsibility specifically to certain people or departments in the organization. Most of the information probably will be derived from a systematic review of existing sources of information such as periodicals, news releases, and government publications. Personal discussions with particular information sources typically are valuable. In some situations, a company may regularly conduct its own marketing field research to determine some aspect of consumer behavior or competitor activity.

EXTERNAL MICROENVIRONMENT ■

Three environmental forces are a part of a company's marketing system, but are external to the company. These are the firm's market, producer-suppliers, and marketing intermediaries. While generally classed as noncontrollable forces, these external elements can be influenced to a greater degree than the macro forces. A marketing organization, for example, may be able to exert some pressure on its suppliers or middlemen. And, through its advertising effort, a firm should have some influence on its present and potential market. (See Fig. 2-3.)

The Market

As both an external force and a key part of every marketing system, the market is really what marketing and this book are all about—how to reach the market and serve it profitably and in a socially responsible manner. The market is (or should be) the focal point of all marketing decisions in an organization. This tremendously important factor is the subject of Part 2 (Chapters 5 to 8), and it crops up frequently throughout the text.

WHAT IS A MARKET?

The word *market* is used in a number of ways. There is a stock *market* and an automobile *market*, a retail *market* for furniture and a wholesale *market* for furniture. One person may be going to the *market*; another may plan to *market* a product. *What, then, is a market?* Clearly, there are many usages of the term in economic theory, in business in general, and in marketing in particular. A *market* may be defined as a place where buyers and sellers meet, products or services are offered for sale, and transfers of ownership occur. A *market* may also be defined as the demand made by a certain group of potential buyers for a product or service. For example, there is a farm *market* for petroleum products. The terms *market* and *demand* are often used interchangeably, and they may also be used jointly as *market demand*.

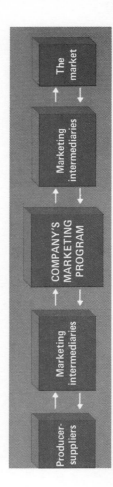

FIGURE 2-3
External microenvironment of a company's marketing program.

These definitions of a market may not be sufficiently precise to be useful to us here. Consequently, in this book a **market** is defined as people or organizations with wants (needs) to satisfy, money to spend, and the willingness to spend it. Thus, in the market demand for any given product or service, there are three factors to consider—people or organizations with wants (needs), their purchasing power, and their buying behavior.

We shall employ the dictionary definition of *needs*: A need is the lack of anything that is required, desired, or useful. As noted in Chapter 1, we do not limit needs to the narrow physiological requirements of food, clothing, and shelter essential for survival. In effect, in our discussion, the words *needs* and *wants* are used synonymously and interchangeably.

Markets are people—with wants, money, and a spending mood.

> A **market** is people or organizations with
> → Needs (or wants) to satisfy
> → Money to spend
> → Willingness to spend it

Suppliers

You can't sell a product if you can't first make it or buy it. So it is probably rather obvious that **producer-suppliers** of products and services are critical to the success of any marketing organization. In our economy a buyer's market exists for most products. That is, there is no problem in making or buying a product; the problem is usually how to sell it.

Marketing executives often do not concern themselves enough with the supply side of the exchange transaction. However, the importance of suppliers in a company's marketing system comes into focus sharply when shortages occur. But shortages only highlight the importance of cooperative relationships with suppliers. Suppliers' prices and services are a significant influence on any company's marketing system. At the same time, these prices and services can very often be influenced by careful planning on the part of the buying organization.

Marketing Intermediaries

Marketing intermediaries are independent business organizations that directly aid in the flow of products and services between a marketing organization and its markets. These intermediaries include two types of institutions: (1) resellers—the wholesalers and retailers—or the people we call "middlemen" and (2) various "facilitating" organizations that provide transportation, warehousing, financing, and other supportive sellers needed to complete exchanges between buyers and sellers.

These intermediaries operate between a company and its markets and between a company and its suppliers. Thus they complete what we call "channels of distribution" or "trade channels."

In some situations it may be more efficient for a company to operate on a "do-it-yourself" basis without using marketing intermediaries. That is, a firm can deal *directly* with its suppliers or sell *directly* to its customers and do its own shipping, financing, and so on. But marketing intermediaries do perform a variety of services. They are specialists in their respective fields. Typically, they justify their economic existence by doing a better job at a lower cost than the marketing organization can do by itself.

The environmental forces that influence a company's marketing program are not limited to external factors. An organization's marketing system is also shaped to some extent by two sets of *internal* forces that are largely controllable by management. One set of these internal factors are the organization's resources in *nonmarketing* areas. The other set of internal influences is the environment and resources *within the marketing department.*

AN ORGANIZATION'S INTERNAL ENVIRONMENT

Internal Nonmarketing Resources

A company's marketing system is influenced by the firm's production, financial, and personnel capabilities. If management is considering adding a new product, for example, it must determine whether existing *production facilities* and *expertise* can be used. If the new product requires a new plant or machinery, *financial capability* enters the picture. Other nonmarketing forces are the *company's location*, its *research and*

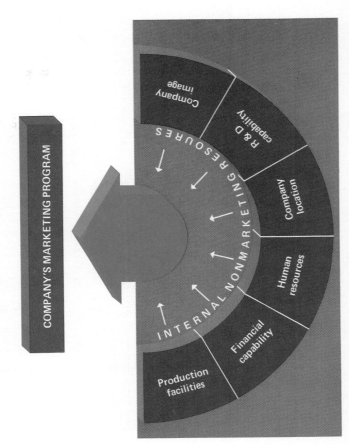

FIGURE 2-4
A company's marketing environment.

development (R&D) *strength* as evidenced by the patents it holds, and the overall *image* the firm projects to its public. Plant location often determines the geographic limits of a company's market, particularly if high transportation costs or perishable products are involved. The R&D factor may determine whether a company will lead or follow in the industry's technology and marketing. See Fig. 2-4.

Another environmental consideration here is the necessity of coordinating the marketing and nonmarketing activities in a company. Sometimes this can be difficult because of conflicts in activity goals and executive personalities. Production people, for example, like to see long production runs of standardized items. Marketing and sales executives want a variety of models, sizes, and colors to satisfy different market segments. Financial executives typically want tighter credit and expense limits than the marketing people feel is necessary to be competitive.

Internal Marketing Environment

The notion of encouraging cooperation and minimizing conflicts should not be limited only to relationships involving marketing with the other departments in a company. Far from it. The environment *within* the marketing department certainly can have a considerable influence on a company's marketing system. Consequently, we cannot have sales executives fighting with advertising management any more than we can have sales-force executives fighting with production or financial executives.

Nevertheless, occasions may arise when the existing marketing environment will shape or change the marketing planning. To illustrate, management may be considering whether to add a certain new product. The decision is made against it because the firm's distribution system cannot handle the proposed product. Or a firm may want to enter a new market, but the existing sales force cannot handle this additional assignment. And the company is not prepared at this time to develop a new sales force for the new market.

Environmental Conclusion

To wrap up this chapter, we have designed Fig. 2-5—a combination of three previous figures—showing the environmental forces as they combine to shape an organization's marketing program. With an understanding of the environment within which they operate, marketing executives now can engage in the strategic planning which hopefully will lead to a successful marketing program. This strategic marketing planning—as part of the total management process in marketing—is the topic of the next chapter.

SUMMARY ■

A company operates its marketing system within a framework of ever-changing forces that constitute the system's environment. Some of the forces are broad, external variables that generally cannot be controlled by the executives in a firm. Demographic conditions are one of these macro influences. Another is economic conditions such as the business cycle, inflation, interest rates, and unemployment. Management must be aware of the various types of competition and the competitive structure within which a given firm operates. Social and cultural forces, including cultural changes, are another factor to contend with. Political and legal forces, along with technology,

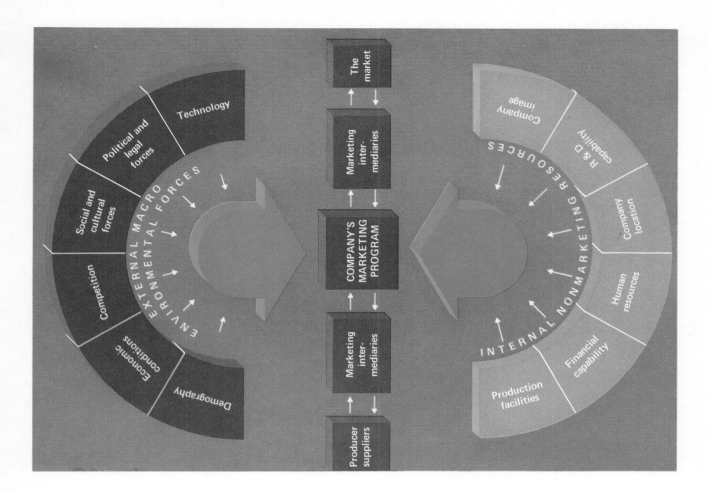

round out our group of external macroenvironmental influences. Management should establish a system for monitoring these external forces.

Another set of environmental factors—producer-suppliers, marketing intermedi-

FIGURE 2-5
A company's marketing environment.

aries, and the market itself—is also external to the firm. But these elements clearly are a part of the firm's marketing system, and they also can be controlled to some extent by the firm. At the same time, a set of nonmarketing resources *within* the firm (production, facilities, personnel, finances, and so on) influences its marketing system. These variables generally are controllable by management, as are the environmental elements within the marketing department.

KEY TERMS AND CONCEPTS ■

Demography 23

Economic conditions: 23
   Business cycle 23
   Inflation 24
   Interest rates 24

Types of competition 25

Competitive market structures: 25
   Pure competition 25
   Monopolistic competition 25
   Oligopoly 26
   Monopoly 26

Social and cultural forces 26

Cultural changes 26

Political and legal forces 28

Technology 30

Environmental monitoring 30

The market 31

Producer-suppliers 32

Marketing intermediaries 32

Nonmarketing resources in a firm 33

QUESTIONS AND PROBLEMS ■

1. It is predicted that college enrollments will decline during the next several years. What marketing measures should your school take to adjust to this forecast?

2. For each of the following companies, give some examples of how its marketing program is likely to differ during periods of prosperity as contrasted with periods of recession.
   a. Campbell soups.
   b. Building materials.
   c. Videocassette recorders.

3. If interest rates are high, how is the situation likely to affect the market for the following products?
   a. Timex or Swatch watches.
   b. Schwinn bicycles.
   c. Adidas athletic shoes.
   d. Sony television.

4. Compare the economic characteristics of the competitive market structures of oligopoly and monopolistic competition.

5. Give some examples of how the changing role of women has been reflected in American marketing.

6. What are some of the marketing implications of the increasing public interest in health and physical fitness?

7. What should be the role of marketing in treating the following major social problems?

   a. Air pollution.
   b. The depletion of irreplaceable resources.
   c. The retailing situation in ghetto markets.
8. Give some examples of the effects of marketing legislation in your own buying, recreation, and other everyday activities. Do you believe these laws are effective? If not, what changes would you recommend?
9. Using examples other than those in this chapter, explain how a firm's marketing system can be influenced by the environmental factor of technology.
10. Explain how each of the following resources within a company might influence that company's marketing program.
   a. Plant location.   c. Financial resources.
   b. Company image.   d. Personnel capability.
11. Specify some internal environmental forces affecting the marketing program of:
   a. Pizza Hut.   c. A local disco night club.
   b. Your school.   d. Clairol (hair-care products).

STRATEGIC MARKETING PLANNING

CHAPTER GOALS

The marketing system must be managed—and its activities must be planned—for effective operation within its environment. After studying this chapter, you should understand:

- The management process as it applies to marketing.
- The meanings of some basic management terms.
- The nature, scope, and importance of planning in marketing.
- Some fundamentals of strategic company planning and strategic marketing planning.
- The concept of the marketing mix.

For almost 99 years the Coca-Cola Company followed essentially the same simple, yet very effective, strategy. The company sold one product—Coca-Cola syrup—to its bottlers and to other industrial users such as soda fountains, restaurants, and bars. It sold to the consumer market one product—Coca-Cola in the familiar 6½-ounce, distinctively shaped, green glass bottle. The company's marketing progam was a huge success. Coke's market share dominated the soft-drink industry. The product achieved something akin to a national symbolism and mystique.

Then in the 1970s some of the environmental forces that we talked about in Chapter 2 began to seriously affect Coke's market position. Competition finally began to impact on Coca-Cola. Life-styles changed as we became more health and physical-fitness conscious. These trends had a negative impact on products with sugar and caffeine. Our tastes also changed in that we preferred more variety in soft drinks.

These environmental influences brought about some significant changes in Coca-Cola's strategic marketing planning. The company's packaging strategy was changed and Coke appeared in 12-ounce cans, 2-liter plastic bottles, and other containers. To implement a strategy of market segmentation and to meet competition, the company broadened its line of cola drinks to include a Diet Coke, caffeine-free Diet Coke, Tab, caffeine-free regular Coke, and Cherry Coke.

Then in April 1985 Coca-Cola announced the biggest change of all. Near its 99th birthday, Coca-Cola changed its formula and introduced a new, sweeter drink called New Coke and discontinued producing the traditional Coke. This change came after 4½ years of planning and $4 million of marketing research.

But something had gone wrong in the research and strategic planning. Soon after an apparently successful introduction of New Coke, Coca-Cola began to experience real static from the marketplace. Lovers of the traditional Coke were outraged. They stockpiled the old Coke while supplies lasted. They telephoned and wrote letters to the company. They formed protest groups. The net result was that 3 months later (July 1985) the company brought back the traditional coke—calling it Coca-Cola Classic. The Classic Coke was marketed side by side with the New Coke on store shelves.

Whatever the future outcome may be for Coca-Cola, that company provided us with a classic example of how environmental forces can shape a company's strategic marketing program. In the preceding chapter we saw that a company's marketing system is strongly influenced by external environmental forces and also by the firm's internal environment. Now in this chapter we shall consider how a company manages its marketing activities within its environment. Specifically, we shall discuss the management process as it applies to a marketing program, and one major part of this management process—namely, strategic planning. Our coverage will be brief and at a level that seems reasonable for your first course in marketing.

MANAGING A MARKETING SYSTEM ■

Within its environment, a company must plan, implement, and evaluate its marketing system. That is, the organization must *manage* its marketing effort—and must do this effectively.

The "marketing" part of the term *marketing management* was defined in Chapter 1, but what about the "management" part? The terms *management* and *administration* are used synonymously here. They may be defined as the process of planning, implementing, and evaluating the efforts of a group of people toward a common goal. Through management, the combined group output surpasses the sum of the individual outputs.

The Management Process

The management process, as applied to marketing, consists basically of (1) planning a marketing program, (2) implementing it, and (3) evaluating its performance. The **planning** stage includes setting the goals and selecting the strategies and tactics to reach these goals. The **implementing** stage includes forming and staffing the marketing organization and directing the actual operation of the organization according to the plan. The **performance-evaluation** stage is a good example of the interrelated, continuing nature of the management process. That is, evaluation is both a look back and a look ahead—a link between past performance and future planning and operations. Management looks back to analyze performance in light of organizational goals. The findings from this evaluation of past performance then are used to look ahead in setting the goals and plans for future periods. (See Fig. 3-1.)

Throughout the past 20 years a tremendous amount of attention in business has been devoted to the planning phase of the management process. Several planning models were developed and most of the large companies used one or more of these models. The popular term for this activity—virtually a buzzword in business—is strategic planning. In the next major section of this chapter, we shall briefly discuss strategic planning—especially strategic marketing planning. Business also typically devotes much time and effort to the performance-evaluation activities in the management process.

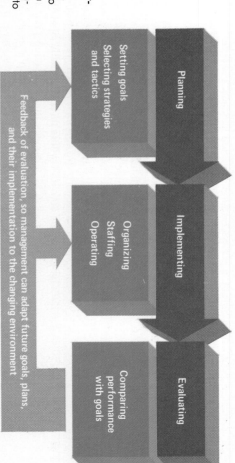

FIGURE 3-1
The management process in marketing systems.
Plans are implemented, and performance results are evaluated to provide information used to plan for the future. The process is continuous and allows for adapting to changes in the environment.

Planning
Setting goals
Selecting strategies
and tactics

Implementing
Organizing
Staffing
Operating

Evaluating
Comparing
performance
with goals

Feedback of evaluation, so management can adapt future goals, plans, and their implementation to the changing environment

In their preoccupation with strategic planning and performance evaluation, however, business executives typically have given relatively little attention to the implementation stage of the management process. In the authors' opinion this is a very unfortunate state of affairs. After all, if you don't carry through with your plans and put them into practice—that is, implement them—then your plan really is of no value at all. You may have the best plan for an upcoming ball game, but if you can't execute that plan—make it work in the game—then that plan is not worth very much to you.

An encouraging prospect at this point, however, is the fact that in recent years many companies have become disenchanted with the lopsided emphasis on strategic planning. Executives are becoming increasingly vocal in their demand for more effective *implementation* of their company's plans.

In Parts 2 through 6 of this book we shall be discussing the planning and development of a marketing program in an organization. Periodically throughout those chapters we shall be dealing with the implementation of marketing plans. Then, near the end of the book, we devote an entire chapter (Chapter 24) to the implementation and evaluation stages of the marketing management process.

Some Basic Management Terminology

Several basic terms continually appear in discussions of the management of a marketing system. These terms sometimes are used carelessly, and they may mean different things to different people. Consequently, at this point let's look at the way these terms will be used in this book.

OBJECTIVES AND GOALS

We shall treat these two terms—objectives and goals—as synonymous to be used interchangeably in all our discussions. An **objective** (or **goal**) is something that is to be attained. Effective planning must begin with a series of objectives that are to be reached by carrying out the plans. The objectives are, in essence, the reasons for the plans. Furthermore, the objectives should be stated in writing, to minimize (1) the possibility of misunderstanding and (2) the risk that managerial decisions and activities will not be in accord with these goals.

To be effective, the goals also should be stated as specifically as possible:

Too vague, too general	More specific
1. Increase our market share.	1. Next year, increase our market share to 25 percent from its present 20 percent level.
2. Improve our profit position.	2. Generate a return on investment of 15 percent next year.

STRATEGIES

A **strategy** is a broad, basic plan of action by which an organization intends to reach its goal. The word *strategy* (from the Greek word *strategia*) originally was related to the science or art of military generalship. A strategy is a grand plan for winning a battle as a step toward achieving the objective of winning the war.

In marketing, the relationship between goals and strategies may be illustrated as follows:

Goals

1. Reduce marketing costs next year by 15 percent below this year's level.

2. Increase sales next year by 10 percent over this year's figure.

Possible strategies

1a. Reduce warehouse inventories and eliminate slow-moving products.
1b. Reduce number of sales calls on small accounts.

2a. Intensify marketing efforts in domestic markets.
2b. Expand into foreign markets.

Two companies might have the same goal, but use different strategies to reach that goal. For example, two firms might each aim to increase their market share by 20 percent over the next 3 years. To reach this goal, one firm's strategy might be to intensify its efforts in the domestic markets. The other company might select the strategy of expanding into foreign markets.

Conversely, two companies might have different goals but select the same strategy to reach them. As an illustration, suppose one company's goal is to increase its sales volume next year by 20 percent over this year's sales. The other company wants to earn a 20 percent return on investment next year. Both companies might decide that their best strategy is to introduce a major new product next year.

TACTICS

A **tactic** is an operational means by which a strategy is to be implemented or activated. A tactic typically is a more specific, detailed course of action than is a strategy. Also, tactics generally cover shorter time periods—are more closely oriented to short-term goals—than are strategies.

Let's look at some examples:

Strategies

1. Direct our promotion to males, age 25–40.

2. Increase sales-force motivation.

Tactics

1a. Advertise in magazines read by this market segment.
1b. Advertise on television programs watched by these people.

2a. Conduct more sales contests.
2b. Increase incentive features in pay plans.
2c. Use more personal supervision of sales people.

To be effective, the tactics selected must parallel or support the strategy. It would be a mistake, for example, to adopt a strategy of increasing our sales to the women's market—and then advertise in men's magazines or use advertising messages that appeal to men.

POLICY

A **policy** is a course of action adopted by management to routinely guide future decision making in a given situation. Policies typically are used on all levels in an organization—from the presidential suite down to new workers. It may be company *policy*, for example, to have a union leader on the board of directors. Sales managers may follow the *policy* of hiring only college graduates for sales jobs. In the office, our *policy* may be that the last person leaving must turn off the lights and lock the door.

A policy typically is an "automatic decision-making mechanism" for some situation. That is, once a course of action is decided upon in a given situation, then that decision becomes the *policy* that we follow every time the same situation arises. For example, to reach the goal of a certain sales volume in our company, suppose we decided on a strategy of offering quantity discounts in pricing. The relevant tactic we selected was a certain detailed discount schedule. Now, once those decisions have been made, we can follow the pricing *policy* of routinely granting a quantity discount according to our predetermined schedule.

CONTROL

Many writers and business executives refer to the management process as consisting of planning, implementation, and *control*. In this book we use the term *performance evaluation* to represent the third activity in the management process. To speak of *control* as only one part of the management process seems to your authors to be a misleading and unduly restricted use of the term.

Control is not an isolated managerial function—it permeates virtually all other managerial activities. For example, management *controls* its company operations by virtue of the goals and strategies it selects. The type of organizational structure used in the marketing department determines the degree of *control* over marketing operations. Management *controls* its sales force by means of the compensation plan, the territorial structure, and so on.

Levels of Goals and Strategies

When discussing objectives, strategies, and tactics, is it important to identify the organizational level that we are talking about. Otherwise, we run the risk of creating confusion and misunderstanding, for a very simple reason: What is an *objective* for an executive on one organizational level may be a *strategy* for management on a higher level.

As an illustration, suppose one executive says, "Our goal is to enter a seven-state Western market next year and generate a sales volume of at least $1 million." A second executive says, "No—entering that new market is only a strategy. Our goal is to increase our market share to 15 percent next year." A third executive says that the second is wrong. "Increasing our market share is our strategy," is this person's argument. "Our goal is to earn a 20 percent return on investment."

Actually, all three executives are correct. They simply are speaking from the perspectives of different organizational levels in their firm. These relationships may be summarized as follows:

- *Company goal:* To earn a 20 percent return on investment next year.
- *Company strategy (and marketing goal):* To increase our share of the market to 15 percent next year.
- *Marketing strategy (and sales-force goal):* To enter a seven-state Western market next year and generate a minimum sales volume of $1 million.

And so on down to an individual sales representative. This person's goal may

Tactic: Run this ad in a men's magazine unless you want her to buy it for him.

Life's an adventure. Live it!

L'HOMME Roger&Gallet
PARIS

be to exceed quota by 15 percent, and the proposed strategy may be to average three more sales calls per day.

In any case, for a particular *level of objective*, a *strategy* is a plan of action designed to reach that objective. *Tactics* then are the operational details that implement this plan.

We now are ready to talk about developing a marketing program in an organization. To do an effective job in developing such a program, however, management first should prepare a strategic plan for the total organizational effort. Then this total-company planning should be followed by strategic planning in the organization's various functional divisions, including marketing. The success of a company's marketing effort depends largely upon management's ability to strategically plan a marketing program within the environmental framework discussed earlier in this chapter and then to carry out that plan.

But before we discuss strategic company planning, let's first understand the concept of planning in general.

NATURE AND SCOPE OF PLANNING

■

What Is Planning?

There's an old saying to the effect that if you don't know where you are going, then any road will take you there. That is, you need a plan. If you don't have a plan, you cannot get anything done—because you don't know what needs to be done or how to do it. In simple English, **planning** is studying the past to decide in the present what to do in the future. Or deciding what we are going to do later, when and how we are going to do it, and who will do it.

In business management one type of planning that we find very useful is the more formal concept called strategic planning. **Strategic planning** may be defined as the managerial process of matching an organization's resources with its marketing opportunities over the long run. Note (1) that strategic planning is a total-company concept and (2) that it involves a long-run orientation.

The concept of planning is not new. However, market and economic condition in recent years have led to a better understanding of the need for formal planning. Truly, any success that management has in increasing the profitability of marketing operations depends in large part upon the nature of its marketing planning. Formal planning is one of the most effective management tools available for reducing risks.

Scope of Planning Activities

Planning may cover long or short periods of time. **Long-range planning** (for 3, 5, 10, or even 25 years) usually involves top management and special planning staffs. It deals with broad, company-wide issues such as plant, market, or product expansion. **Short-term planning** typically covers a period of 1 year or less and is the responsibility of lower- and middle-echelon executives. It involves such issues as planning next year's advertising campaign, making merchandise-buying plans in a store, or setting sales quotas for a sales force.

The planning activities in an organization may be conducted on three or four different levels, depending upon the size of the organization and the diversity of its products or services. These planning levels are as follows:

1. **Strategic company planning.** At this level, management defines the organization's mission, sets the organization's long-range goals, and decides on broad strategies formulated to achieve the goals. These long-range, company-wide goals and strategies then become the framework within which departmental planning is done. This total-company planning takes into consideration an organization's financial requirements, production capabilities, labor needs, research and development effort, and marketing capabilities.

2. **Strategic business unit planning.** In large, diversified organizations, a modification of strategic company-wide planning has emerged in recent years. For more effective planning and operation, the total organization is divided into separate divisions called *strategic business units* (SBUs). Each SBU is, in effect, a separate "business," and each SBU conducts its own strategic "business-wide" planning.

3. **Strategic marketing planning.** At this level, management is engaged in setting goals and strategies for the marketing effort in the organization. In smaller or nondiversified organizations, the SBU planning and marketing planning may be combined into one strategic planning activity. Or, in small, single-business organizations, the top three levels of planning (company, SBU, marketing) may be combined into one planning activity.

Strategic marketing planning includes (1) the selection of target markets and (2) the development of the four major ingredients in a company's marketing program—the product, the distribution system, the pricing structure, and the promotional activities. In Parts 3 to 6 of this book, these four ingredients will be considered individually.

4. **Annual marketing planning.** The annual marketing plan is one part, covering one time segment, of the ongoing strategic marketing planning process. It is a master plan covering a year's marketing operations for a given product line, major product, brand, or market. Thus, this plan serves as a tactical operational guide to the executives in each phase of the marketing effort for the given product or market.

STRATEGIC COMPANY PLANNING ■

Strategic company planning is the managerial process of matching an organization's resources with its marketing opportunities over the long run. This process consists of (1) defining the organization's mission, (2) setting organizational objectives, (3) evaluating the strategic business units (this is called *business portfolio analysis*), and (4) selecting appropriate strategies so as to achieve the organizational objectives. (See Fig. 3-2.) The strategic planning forces will be influenced considerably by the external

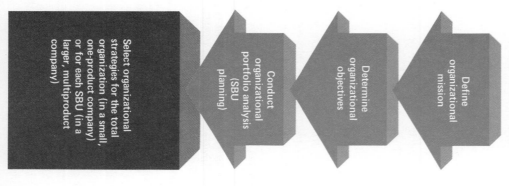

Define organizational mission

Determine organizational objectives

Conduct organizational portfolio analysis (SBU planning)

Select organizational strategies for the total organization (in a small, one-product company) or for each SBU (in a larger, multiproduct company)

FIGURE 3-2
The strategic planning process for the total organization.

macroenvironmental forces that we discussed earlier in Chapter 2. It probably is obvious that management's planning also will be influenced by the organization's internal resources such as its financial condition, production facilities, research and development capabilities, etc.

Define Organizational Mission

The first step in the strategic planning process, as applied to the organization as a whole, is to clearly define the company's mission. For some firms, this step requires only the review and approval of a previously published mission statement. But, for most firms, this step in formal planning really has never been clearly articulated.

Defining an organization's mission means answering the question, "What business are we in?" And further, management may also ask, "What business *should* we be in?" Unless the organization's basic purpose is clear to all executives, any efforts at strategic planning are likely to be ineffective.

Kodak's mission is to market memories.

An organization's purpose, or mission, should be stated in writing and well publicized. A properly prepared statement of company mission can be an effective public relations tool. The statement should not be too broad or vague—nor should it be too narrow or specific. To say that our mission is "to benefit American consumers" is too broad and vague. To say that our business is "to make tennis balls" is too narrow. Neither statement provides sufficient guidance to management.

Traditionally, companies have stated their mission in production-oriented terms: "We make telephones (or furnaces, or skis)." Or management might say, "We are in the railroad business (or in furniture manufacturing, or in the motion-picture business)."

Today, in line with the marketing concept, organizations are urged to be marketing-oriented in their mission statements. Executives should be thinking in terms of the benefits they are marketing and the wants they are satisfying. (See Table 3-1.) Thus, instead of saying, "We make telephones," a phone company should define its mission as the marketing of communication services. Instead of "making furnaces," the Lennox Company's mission should be stated as the marketing of home climate control. Not only are these marketing-oriented mission statements more attractive to the public, but they also serve to broaden a company's market and extend the company's life. If your mission is to make furnaces, you will be out of the business when furnaces are replaced by heat pumps or solar heating units. But if your mission is to market climate control, then you can discontinue furnace production, switch to alternative energy sources, and continue competing with the new generation of heating and air-conditioning companies.

TABLE 3-1 WHAT BUSINESS ARE YOU IN?

	Production-oriented answer	Marketing-oriented answer
AT&T	We operate a long-distance phone company.	We market a communications system.
Exxon	We produce oil and gasoline products.	We market energy.
Penn Central	We run a railroad.	We provide a transportation and materials-handling system.
Levi Strauss	We make Levi's blue jeans.	In wearing apparel we offer comfort, fashion, & durability.
Xerox	We make copy machines.	We market automated office systems.
Eastman Kodak	We make cameras and film.	We market beautiful memories.
Revlon Cosmetics—the president said:	"In the factory we make cosmetics."	"In the drugstore, we sell hope."

Determine Organizational Objectives

The next step in the strategic planning process is for management to decide upon a set of objectives that will guide the organization in accomplishing its mission. These objectives can also serve as guides for managerial planning at lower levels in an organization. And they provide standards for evaluating an organization's performance.

In effect, the definition of what business we are in and a statement of our goals are critically important to the marketing effort in our organization. The mission statement tells us something about the markets to be served, and the objectives give us some direction in determining how we will implement the marketing concept. Together, the statements of mission and objectives should help us to be marketing-oriented rather than production- or sales-oriented.

At any level of strategic planning, the objectives should be clearly stated *in writing*. Such statements should avoid meaningless platitudes. Objectives should be action-stimulators, because objectives are achieved by actions that carry out plans.

The organization's objectives should be realistic and mutually consistent. To be effective, each objective should be stated in *specific* terms, and, wherever possible, the objectives should be *quantitatively measurable*. Some examples of objectives that illustrate these criteria are as follows:

Too general: To increase the company's profitability.

Not measurable: To improve the company's public image.

More specific: To increase the company's return on investment to 18 percent within 2 years.

Measurable: To receive favorable recognition awards next year from at least three consumer or environmental groups.

Conduct Organizational Portfolio Analysis: Strategic Business Unit (SBU) Planning

Many organizations are so diversified that total-company planning cannot serve as an effective guide for the executives who manage the component divisions of the organizations. Certainly in the Philip Morris Company, for example, the mission, objectives, and strategies in the tobacco division are quite different from those in the Miller brewing division. Most large and medium-sized companies—and even many small firms—are multiproduct, and even multibusiness, organizations.

Consequently, for more effective planning and operation, the total organization should be divided into major product or market divisions. These divisions are called *strategic business units* (SBUs)—a term coined some years ago by a major consulting firm in its work with the General Electric Company. Each SBU may be a major division in an organization, a group of related products, or even a single major product, or brand.

To be identified as an SBU, a unit should possess these characteristics:

- It is a separately identifiable business.
- It has its own distinct mission.
- It has its own competitors.
- It has its own executives and profit responsibility.
- It may have its own strategic plan.

To illustrate, some possible SBU divisions are as follows:

General Electric: Electrical motors, major appliances, jet engines, medical equipment, lighting equipment, electronic supplies, etc.

A university: Different schools (engineering, business, education, law, etc.) *or* different teaching methods (on-campus courses, television courses, correspondence courses).

Sears, Roebuck: Retail-store divisions, insurance company (Allstate), real estate brokerage business (Coldwell-Banker), securities brokerage business (Dean Witter), and credit-card division (Discover card).

Sears' retail stores: Auto supplies, furniture, large appliances, plumbing and heating equipment, home furnishings, women's apparel, men's apparel, sporting goods, hardware, etc.

The trick here is to set up the proper number of SBUs in an organization. If there are too many, then the management can get bogged down in the planning, operating, and reporting details. If there are too few SBUs, each unit covers too broad an area to be useful for managerial planning and control. A survey of the 1,000 largest industrial firms in the United States reported that the typical company had about 30 SBUs.[1]

The total organization may then be viewed as a "portfolio" of these businesses. And *a key step in strategic planning* is an evaluation of the individual businesses in the organization's portfolio. This evaluation is called a **business (or product) portfolio analysis.** Or we can use the broader term **organizational portfolio** analysis, to imply the use of this planning concept in nonbusiness, nonprofit organizations.

A portfolio analysis is made to identify the present status of each SBU and to determine its future role in the company. This evaluation also provides guidance to management in designing the strategies and tactics for an SBU. Management typically has limited resources to use in supporting its SBUs. Consequently, management needs to know how to allocate these limited resources. Which SBUs should be stimulated to grow, which ones maintained in their present market position, and which ones eliminated? A business portfolio analysis is designed to aid management in this decision making.

Select Organizational Strategies

By this point in its strategic planning, presumably the organization has determined where it wants to go. The next step in strategic planning is to design the ways to get there. These are the organizational strategies—the broad, basic plans of action by which an organization intends to achieve its goals and fulfill its mission. We are speaking about selecting strategies (1) for the total organization in a small, one-product company or (2) for each SBU in a larger, multiproduct or multibusiness organization.

Several models have been developed that management can use as a guide in its selection of appropriate organizational strategies. To illustrate the possible strategic

[1]Philippe Haspeslagh, "Portfolio Planning: Uses and Limits," *Harvard Business Review,* January–February 1982, p. 65.

use of these models, at this point we shall describe very briefly three of them. Any further discussion of these and other planning models really is outside the scope of this book.

PORTER'S GENERIC-STRATEGIES MODEL

Professor Michael Porter of the Harvard Business School has developed a model in which he identifies the following three generic strategies to achieve success in a competitive market:[2]

- *Overall cost leadership:* Produce a standardized product at a low price and then underprice everybody else.
- *Differentiation:* Market at a higher-than-average price something that customers will perceive as being unique in quality, design, brand, or some other feature.
- *Focus:* Concentrate on a small specialty market (particular consumer group, geographic market) or a segment of the product line.

Porter's model is shown in Fig. 3-3. Companies in the upper left-hand end of the curve are profitable even with a small market share, because their products and/or markets are specialized and command above-average prices. Firms at the upper right-hand end of the curve also are successful. This is because either they differentiate their products or else they have a large market share because of low prices and low costs. It is the firms in the middle (low) part of the curve that are in trouble. They have low profits and a modest market share because they have nothing going for them.

[2]This discussion is adapted from Walter Kiechel, III, ''Three (Or Four, or More) Ways to Win,'' *Fortune,* Oct. 19, 1981, p. 181; and by same author, ''The Decline of the Experience Curve,'' *Fortune,* Oct. 5, 1981, p. 146. See also Michael E. Porter, *Competitive Strategy: Techniques for Analyzing Industries and Competitors,* The Free Press, New York, 1980.

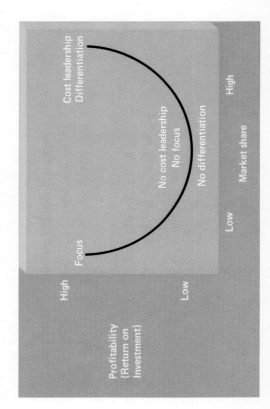

FIGURE 3-3
Porter's generic-strategies model.

FIGURE 3-4
Boston consulting group's strategic
planning matrix.

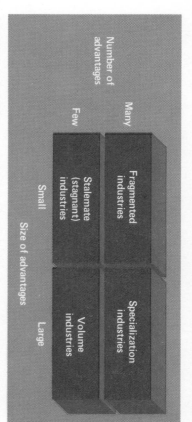

BOSTON CONSULTING GROUP MATRIX

The Boston Consulting Group (BCG), a well-known management consulting firm, has developed a new strategic planning matrix.[3] This new matrix replaces an earlier, widely used one that had developed some shortcomings in the competitive environment of the late 1970s. See Fig. 3-4.

On the vertical axis is plotted the number of ways the company can obtain a marketing advantage, from few to many. On the horizontal axis we plot the size of the advantage, ranging from small to large. The resulting model may be divided into four cells, each identifying a different strategic industrial situation, as follows:

• *Stalemate (stagnant) industries:* Very few advantages, and they are small—steel or uncoated paper, for example.

• *Volume industries:* Very few advantages, but they are big—such as the cost advantage in a large aluminum plant.

• *Fragmented industries:* Many competitive advantages, but each one is limited in size—as in the restaurant industry.

• *Specialization industries:* Many competitive advantages, and they are large—Japanese automobile manufacturers or television manufacturers, for example.

PRODUCT/MARKET EXPANSION STRATEGIES

Most statements of mission and objectives reflect an organization's intention to grow—to increase its revenues and profit. In such cases, an organization may take either of two routes in its strategy design. It can continue to do what it is now doing with its products and markets—only do it better. Or the organization can venture into new products and/or new markets. These two routes, when applied to markets and products, result in the following four strategic alternatives.[4] See Fig. 3-5.

• *Market penetration:* A company tries to sell more of its present products to its

[3]This discussion is based on Kiechel, "Three . . . Ways to Win," pp. 184, 188.
[4]H. Igor Anshoff, "Strategies for Diversification," *Harvard Business Review,* September–October 1957, pp. 113–124.

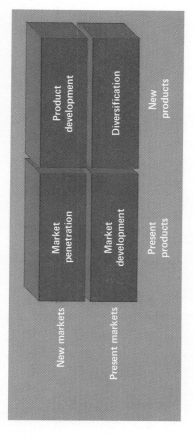

FIGURE 3-5
Organizational strategies for product/market expansion.

present markets. Supporting tactics might include an increase in expenditure for advertising or personal selling.

- *Market development:* A company continues to sell its present products, but to a new market. Thus, a manufacturer of power tools now selling to industrial users might decide to sell its small portable tools to household consumers.
- *Product development:* This strategy calls for a company to develop new products to sell to its existing markets. A stereo records company recently introduced laser discs to its present customers.
- *Diversification:* A company develops new products to sell to new markets. Sears, Roebuck, for example, has diversified into real estate, securities, and a credit-card program.

STRATEGIC MARKETING PLANNING

After completing the strategic planning for the total organization and for each SBU, then management can do the planning for each major functional division, such as marketing or production. The planning for marketing (or for any functional division, for that matter) should be guided by the total organizational or the SBU mission and objectives.

The Planning Process

The **strategic marketing planning process** consists of these steps: (1) conduct a situation analysis; (2) determine marketing objectives; (3) select target markets and measure the market demand; (4) design a strategic marketing mix; (5) prepare an annual marketing plan. See Fig. 3-6.

A *situation analysis* is a review of the company's existing marketing program. By analyzing where the program has been and where it is now, management can determine where the program should go in the future. A situation analysis normally includes an analysis of the external environmental forces and the nonmarketing resources that surround the organization's marketing program. A situation analysis also includes a detailed review of the company's present marketing mix—its product and its pricing situation, its distribution system (including suppliers and middlemen), and its promotional program.

FIGURE 3-6
The strategic marketing planning process.

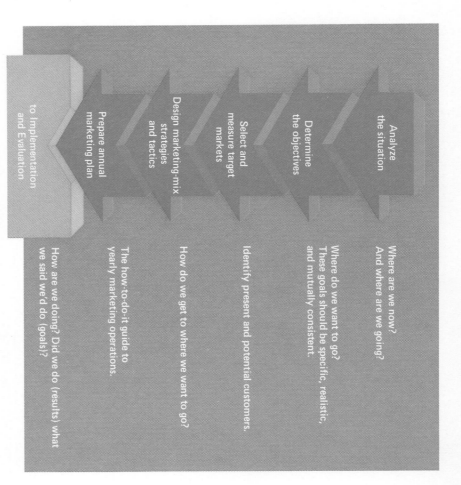

The next step in the marketing planning process is to *determine the marketing objectives*. As with organizational objectives, the marketing goals should be realistic, specific, measurable, and mutually consistent. And they should be clearly stated in writing.

The goals at the marketing level are closely related to the company-wide goals and strategies. In fact, a company strategy often translates into a marketing goal. For example, to reach an organizational objective of a 20 percent return on investment next year, one organizational strategy might be to reduce marketing costs by 15 percent. This organizational strategy would then become a marketing goal.

The *selection of target markets* is obviously a key step in marketing planning. Management should analyze existing markets in detail and identify potential markets. At this point, management also should decide to what extent, and in what manner, it wants to segment its markets. As part of this step in the planning process, management also should forecast its sales in its various markets.

The Marketing Mix

Management next must *design a strategic marketing mix* that enables the company to satisfy the wants of its target markets and to achieve its marketing goals. The design, and later the operation, of the marketing mix constitutes the bulk of the company's marketing effort.

Marketing mix is the term that is used to describe the combination of the four inputs that constitute the core of an organization's marketing system. These four elements are the product offerings, the price structure, the promotional activities, and the distribution system. While the marketing mix is largely controllable by company management, this mix still is constrained by external environmental forces. The mix also is both influenced and supported by a company's internal nonmarketing resources. Figure 3-7 reflects a company's total marketing system as being a combination of these environmental and internal forces.

The four "ingredients" in the marketing mix are interrelated. Again we see the *systems* concept; decisions in one area usually affect actions in the others. Also, each of the four contains countless variables. A company may market one item or several—related or unrelated. They may be distributed through wholesalers or directly to retailers, and so on. Ultimately, from the multitude of variables, management must select the combination that will (1) best adapt to the environment, (2) satisfy the target markets, and (3) still meet the organizational and marketing goals.

Product   Managing the product ingredient includes planning and developing the right products and/or services to be marketed by the company. Strategies are needed for

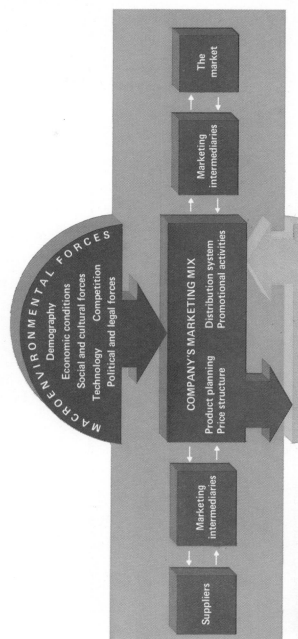

FIGURE 3-7
A company's complete marketing system: a framework of internal resources operating within a set of external forces.

changing existing products, adding new ones, and taking other actions that affect the assortment of products carried. Strategic decisions are also needed regarding branding, packaging, and various other product features.

Price In pricing, management must determine the right base price for its products. It must then decide on strategies concerning discounts, freight payments, and many other price-related variables.

Promotion Promotion is the ingredient used to inform and persuade the market regarding a company's products. Advertising, personal selling, and sales promotion are the major promotional activities.

Distribution Even though marketing intermediaries are primarily a noncontrollable environmental factor, a marketing executive has considerable latitude when working with them. Management's responsibility is (1) to select and manage the trade channels through which the products will reach the right market at the right time and (2) to develop a distribution system for physically handling and transporting the products through these channels.[5]

Nonbusiness firms also need a marketing mix.

NONBUSINESS MARKETING MIX

The concept of a marketing mix is also applicable to nonbusiness and/or nonprofit organizations. To illustrate, the marketing mix for the Denver Symphony Orchestra might include:

- *"Product"*: Concerts of classical, semiclassical, and even "pop" music that provide product benefits of social uplifting, music appreciation, enjoyment, relaxation, and use of leisure time.
- *Price*: Public donations and admission charges.
- *Distribution*: Direct from the orchestra to its market; no intermediaries (middlemen) are used.
- *Promotion*: Advertisements in the media telling about the forthcoming season, or ads for individual concerts; signs outside the concert hall; an advertising campaign to sell season tickets.

Annual Marketing Plans

Periodically, the ongoing strategic marketing planning process in an organization culminates in the preparation of a series of short-term marketing plans. These plans usually cover the period of a year—hence the name "annual marketing plan." However, in some industries it is necessary to prepare these plans for even shorter time periods because of the nature of the product or market. A separate annual plan should be prepared for each product line, major product, brand, or market.

An **annual marketing plan** is the master guide covering a year's marketing activity for the given business unit or product. The plan then becomes the how-to-do-it document that guides executives in each phase of their marketing operations. The plan includes (1) a statement of objectives, (2) the identification of the target markets,

[5]For a historical perspective on the marketing mix, see G. Ray Funkhouser, "Technological Antecedents of the Modern Marketing Mix," *Journal of Macromarketing*, Spring 1984, pp. 17–28.

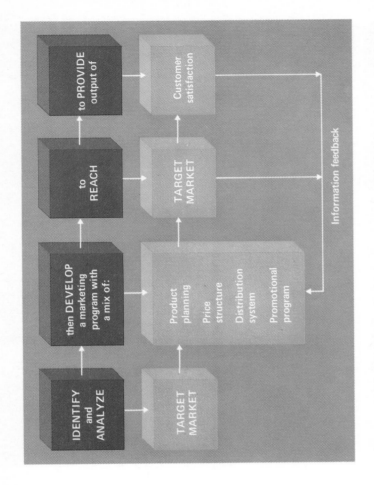

FIGURE 3-8
Marketing in the firm begins and ends with the customers.

(3) the strategies and tactics pertaining to the marketing mix, and (4) information regarding the budgetary support for the marketing activity.

In an annual marketing plan, more attention can be devoted to tactical details than is feasible in longer-range planning. As an example, long-range marketing planning may emphasize the role of personal selling in the promotional mix. The annual plan then might be concerned, for example, with increased college recruiting as a source of sales people.

In conclusion, let's sum up the role of marketing in an individual organization. To fulfill its mission and achieve its goals, a company should start and end its marketing effort with a consideration of its customers and their wants (see Fig. 3-8). Thus, management first should select and analyze its markets. Then, within a framework of the environmental constraints that face the organization, management should develop a marketing program to provide want-satisfaction to those markets. Permeating the planning and operation of this model is the company's marketing information system—a key marketing subsystem intended to aid management in its decision making. The next chapter is devoted to the subjects of marketing information systems and marketing research.

SUMMARY

Within its external and internal environment, a company must develop and operate its marketing system. That is, the organization must *manage* its marketing effort. The management process, as applied to marketing, involves (1) *planning* the company's goals and strategies, (2) *implementing* these plans, and (3) *evaluating* the marketing performance. Executives need to understand the management concepts of objectives, strategies, tactics, and policies.

Strategic planning is a major key to a company's success. With regard to the organizational level on which it is conducted, we find company-wide planning, strategic business unit planning, and strategic marketing planning. Strategic *company* planning is the process of matching an organization's resources with its marketing opportunities over the long run. The organization-wide strategic planning process consists of (1) defining the organization's mission, (2) setting organizational objectives, (3) conducting an organizational portfolio analysis, and (4) designing organizational strategies to achieve the objectives.

Strategic *marketing* planning should be done within the context of the organization's overall strategic planning. The strategic marketing planning process consists of (1) conducting a situation analysis, (2) setting marketing goals, (3) selecting target markets, (4) designing a strategic marketing mix to satisfy those markets and achieve those goals, and (5) preparing an annual marketing plan to guide the tactical operations.

A company's marketing mix is the core of its marketing system. The mix is a combination of the firm's product offerings, price structure, distribution system, and promotional activities.

KEY TERMS AND CONCEPTS ■

Management and administration 40
The management process: planning, implementing, evaluating 40
Basic management terminology: 41
objectives and goals 41
strategies 42
tactics 42
policies 42
Planning 44
Strategic company planning 46
Organizational mission 47

Strategic business unit (SBU) 49
Business portfolio analysis 50
Porter's generic-strategies model 51
Boston Consulting Group's strategic planning matrix 52
Product/market expansion strategies 52
Strategic marketing planning 53
Marketing mix 54
Annual marketing plan 56

QUESTIONS AND PROBLEMS ■

1. Which, if any, of the main topics discussed in this chapter are useful to a small manufacturer or retailer?
2. Explain the relationship among the three main stages of the management process.
3. a. Explain the terms *strategy* and *tactic*, using examples.
   b. What is the difference between a strategy and a policy in marketing management?
4. Explain the difference between organizational objectives and marketing objectives in strategic planning. Give some examples of each.
5. Using a marketing approach (benefits provided or wants satisfied), answer the question, "What business are you in?" for each of the following companies:

a. Holiday Inn.
b. Adidas sports shoes.
c. Apple computers.
d. Universal (movie) Studios.
e. Goodyear Tire and Rubber Co.

6. Using examples, explain the concept of a strategic business unit (SBU).

7. What criteria should an organizational division meet in order to be classified as a strategic business unit?

8. For each of the following Porter generic strategies, give some examples of organizations that might employ the particular strategy.
a. Cost leadership.
b. Differentiation.
c. Focus.

9. For each of the following product/market growth strategies, give some examples (other than those in this chapter) of how a company might employ the particular strategy.
a. Market penetration.
b. Market development.
c. Product development.
d. Diversification.

10. In the situation-analysis stage of the marketing planning process, what are some points that should be analyzed by a manufacturer of backpack equipment for wilderness camping?

11. Explain how the concept of the marketing mix might be applied to:
a. Mothers Against Drunk Drivers (MADD).
b. An art museum.
c. Your school.

4

MARKETING INFORMATION SYSTEMS AND MARKETING RESEARCH

CHAPTER GOALS

A marketing system runs on current, accurate information—about the market, the macroenvironment, and internal and external operations. This chapter is concerned with the sources and uses of such information. After studying this chapter, you should understand:

- Marketing information systems—what they are, why they are needed, and how they are used.
- The difference between a marketing information system and marketing research.
- The procedure in marketing research investigations.
- The current status of marketing research.

Frank Shorter, ex-Olympic marathon winner, was wondering whether to close his sporting goods store on the downtown mall in Boulder, Colorado, and concentrate his efforts on his other store in a nearby major shopping center.

A ski resort wanted to find out how to attract more college students among its skiers. A manufacturer of consumer electronics products needed to decide whether to make its new television product compatible with a videocassette recorder (VCR) or a videodisc player (VDP). A manufacturer of women's dresses was wondering what color would be popular during next year's fall and winter seasons. Holiday Inn wanted to select a location for a new unit in a midwestern college town. A producer of plastic pipe and tubing products planned to add four new sales people to the company's sales force. The sales manager was wondering what would be the two or three best recruiting resources. A regional supermarket chain wanted to know which grocery products, such as coffee, would sell best using end-of-aisle displays.

The above companies all had one thing in common. They needed information to aid them in decision making regarding their stated problems. Some years ago, Marion Harper, Jr., then president of a large advertising agency, said, "To manage a business well is to manage its future; and to manage the future is to manage information." That statement applies today in any organization—business or nonbusiness, profit or nonprofit, domestic or international.

Management in any organization needs information—and lots of it—about potential markets and the environmental forces discussed in Chapter 2. In fact, *one essential requirement for success in strategic marketing planning is information—effectively managed.* Today, a mass of information is available both from external sources and from within a firm. The problem, however, is to sort it out and use it effectively—to manage it. This is the role of a marketing information system. The use of this tool should permeate every phase of a company's marketing program. For this reason, we discuss information management early in this book.

WHAT IS A MARKETING INFORMATION SYSTEM?

A **marketing information system (MkIS)** is an ongoing, future-oriented structure designed to generate, process, store, and later retrieve information to aid decision making in an organization's marketing program.

A marketing information system to some extent resembles a military or diplomatic intelligence operation. It gathers, processes, and stores potentially useful information that exists in open and available form in several locations inside and outside the company. In an MkIS, however, we are *not* suggesting the use of undercover intelligence methods such as industrial espionage or hiring competitors' personnel to learn their secrets. In most cases a company does not need to rely on such clandestine methods. The information a company needs is usually available by socially acceptable means, if the firm will just establish a marketing information system.

A MARKETING INFORMATION SYSTEM IS:

1. The systems concept applied to information handling, to:
   a. determine what data you need for decision making.
   b. generate (gather) this information.
   c. process the data (with the aid of quantitative analytical techniques).
   d. provide for the storage and future retrieval of the data.
2. Future-oriented. It anticipates and prevents problems as well as solving them. It is preventive as well as curative medicine for marketing.
3. Operated on a continuing basis, not a sporadic, intermittent one.
4. Wasted if the information is not used.

A marketing information system is especially characterized by its use of a computer and personnel possessing quantitative analytical capabilities. A modern MkIS is not possible without a computer because of the masses of data to be handled. Fortunately, the wide variety in types and prices of computer hardware and software available today brings an MkIS capability to almost any organization.

NEED FOR A MARKETING INFORMATION SYSTEM

A marketing information system makes it imperative that every firm manage its marketing information as effectively as possible. Let's consider a few of these forces and their relationship to information management.

• *There is a shortening of the time span allotted to an executive for decision making.* Product life cycles frequently are shorter than they used to be. Also, companies are being forced to develop and market new products more quickly than ever before.

• *Marketing activity is becoming more complex and broader in its scope.* Companies are expanding their markets, even to the point of engaging in multinational marketing. Our insights into buyer behavior, while limited, are still sufficient to tell us there is a world of behavioral data we need to acquire and understand.

• *Shortages of energy and other raw materials* mean that we must make more efficient use of our resources and labor power. A company needs to know which of its products are profitable and which ones should be eliminated.

• *Growing consumer discontent* is often intensified because management lacks adequate information about some aspect of its marketing program. Maybe the firm does not realize that its product is not up to consumer expectations or that its middlemen are not performing adequately.

• *The knowledge explosion (the information explosion)* is fantastic. We have more than an adequate supply of information. We simply need to figure out what to do with it—how to manage it. Fortunately, with the continued improvement of computers and other data processing equipment, management has a fast, inexpensive means of processing masses of marketing information.

Today, many environmental forces make it imperative that every firm manage its marketing information as effectively as possible. Let's consider a few of these forces and their relationship to information management.

A marketing information system can help marketers to cope with each of these dynamic forces. Yet, many firms seem to be doing little or nothing toward managing information in a sophisticated manner. Even today, many firms do not have a marketing research department.

FIGURE 4-1
A marketing information system, with two examples of its use.

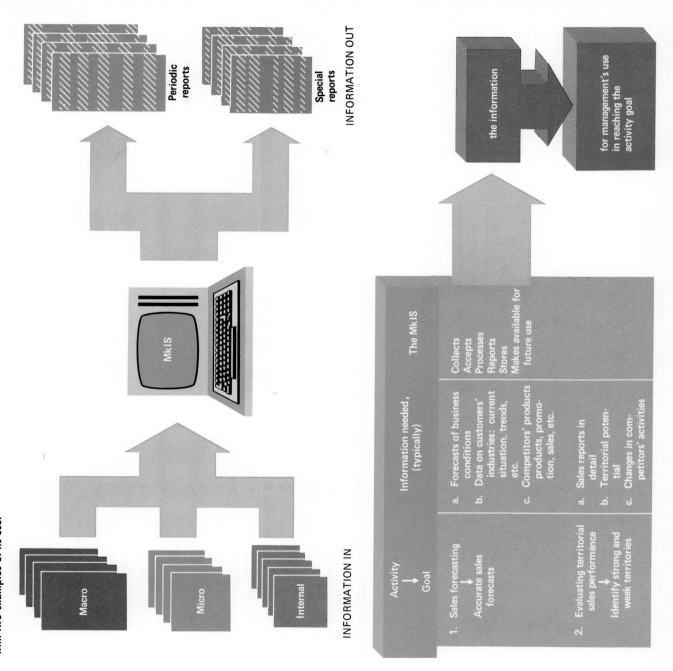

INFORMATION IN

INFORMATION OUT

Periodic reports

Special reports

MkIS

Macro

Micro

Internal

the information

for management's use in reaching the activity goal

Activity → Goal	Information needed, (typically)	The MkIS
1. Sales forecasting Accurate sales forecasts	a. Forecasts of business conditions b. Data on customers' industries: current situation, trends, etc. c. Competitors' products products, promotion, sales, etc.	Collects Accepts Processes Reports Stores Makes available for future use
2. Evaluating territorial sales performance Identify strong and weak territories	a. Sales reports in detail b. Territorial potential c. Changes in competitors' activities	

An organization generates and gathers much information in its day-to-day operations, and much more information is available to it. But unless the company has some system to retrieve and process this information, it is unlikely that it is using its marketing information effectively. Without such a system, information flowing from these sources is frequently lost, distorted, or delayed.

In contrast, a well-designed MkIS can provide a fast, less expensive, and more complete information flow for management decision making. The storage and retrieval capability of an MkIS allows a wider variety of data to be collected and used. Management can continually monitor the performance of products, markets, sales people, and other marketing units in greater detail.

A marketing information system is of obvious value in a large company where information is likely to get lost or distorted as it becomes widely dispersed. However, experience also tells us that integrated information systems can also have beneficial effects on management's performance in small and medium-sized firms. Figure 4-1 illustrates the use of an MkIS in connection with two marketing activities—sales forecasting and the evaluation of territorial sales performance.

BENEFITS AND USES OF AN MkIS ■

RELATIONSHIP BETWEEN MARKETING INFORMATION SYSTEMS AND MARKETING RESEARCH

The relationship between marketing information systems and marketing research is perceived quite differently by various people. Some see an MkIS as simply a logical, computer-based extension of marketing research. (The first marketing information systems were developed in the 1960s, while marketing research as a separate activity predates this by some 40 years.) Others see the two as distinctly different activities, related only to the extent that they both deal with the management of information. Firms without an MkIS will perceive a broader role for their marketing research group. If a company has a formal MkIS, then the marketing research activity is probably treated as just one part of this information system.

Marketing research may be defined as the thorough and objective gathering and analysis of data that pertain to a given problem in marketing. This definition suggests

TABLE 4-1   CONTRASTING CHARACTERISTICS OF MARKETING RESEARCH AND A MARKETING INFORMATION SYSTEM

Marketing research	Marketing information system
1. Emphasizes the handling of external information.	1. Handles both internal and external data.
2. Is concerned with solving problems.	2. Is concerned with preventing as well as solving problems.
3. Operates in a fragmented, intermittent fashion—on a project-to-project basis.	3. Operates continuously—is a system.
4. Tends to focus on past information.	4. Tends to be future-oriented.
5. Need not be computer-based.	5. Is a computer-based process.
6. Is one source of information input for a marketing information system.	6. Includes other subsystems besides marketing research.

a *systematic* activity, thus sounding like the essence of an MkIS. Yet, as traditionally practiced, marketing research has tended to be *unsystematic*. (See Table 4-1 for a comparison of the two activities as they are usually practiced.)

Marketing research tends to be conducted on a project-to-project basis, with each project having a starting point and an end. Projects often seem to deal with unrelated problems on an intermittent, almost "brush-fire" basis. This is in contrast to the continuous information flow in a marketing information system. Marketing research tends to stress the collection of past data to solve problems. Information systems perform future-oriented activities designed to prevent problems from arising.

Parenthetically, we should recognize that many marketing research practitioners would not agree with these distinctions. They would contend that they already are doing much of what we have attributed to MkIS. And they may be correct *if* the firm has no formal MkIS. Then the scope of the marketing research activity is likely to be much broader. It may well include some sales-volume analysis, demand forecasting, and so on.

In firms that have an MkIS, a separate marketing research activity can be extremely valuable. Marketing research projects are a significant source of data for an MkIS. Consequently, at this point we turn to the subject of marketing research. We shall discuss (1) its scope, (2) the typical procedure in a marketing research investigation, (3) the organizational structures typically used for marketing research, and (4) the current status of the field.

■ SCOPE OF MARKETING RESEARCH ACTIVITIES

For about 60 years there has been a steady growth in marketing research departments, reflecting management's recognition of the importance of this activity. In a broad-based study sponsored by the American Marketing Association, 77 percent of the responding companies reported having a formal (consisting of more than one person) marketing research department.

Over half these formal departments had been established during the preceding decade. The broad scope of marketing research activities and the percentage of firms engaging in each are summarized in Table 4-2. The most common activities were determination of market characteristics, measurement of market potentials, market-share analysis, and sales analysis. It is interesting to note the sizable number of firms now engaging in research on corporate responsibility.[1]

■ PROCEDURE IN MARKETING RESEARCH

The general procedure illustrated in Fig. 4-2 is applicable to most marketing research projects. However, some of the steps listed there are not needed in every project. (The numbers in the following section headings correspond to the steps in the research procedure in Fig. 4-2.)

[1]Dik Warren Twedt (ed.), *1983 Survey of Marketing Research*, American Marketing Association, Chicago, 1983. This survey covered 650 firms including manufacturers, retailers, wholesalers, advertising agencies, publishers and broadcasters, banks, and insurance companies.

1: Define the Objective

TABLE 4-2 MARKETING RESEARCH ACTIVITIES OF 600 COMPANIES
Most common activities are determination of market characteristics, measurement of market potentials, market-share analysis, and sales analysis.

Research activity	% engaged in activity
Advertising research:	
Motivation research	47
Copy research	61
Media research	68*
Studies of ad effectiveness	76
Business economics and corporate research:	
Short-range forecasting (up to 1 year)	89
Long-range forecasting (over 1 year)	87
Studies of business trends	91
Pricing studies	83*
Plant- and warehouse-location studies	68*
Acquisition studies	73*
Export and international studies	49*
Corporate-responsibility research:	
Studies of legal constraints on advertising and promotion	46*
Social values and policies studies	39*
Product research:	
New-product acceptance and potential	76
Competitive-product studies	87
Testing of existing products	80
Packaging research (on design or physical characteristics)	65
Sales and market research:	
Measurement of market potentials	97
Market-share analysis	97
Determination of market characteristics	97
Sales analysis	92
Establishment of sales quotas, territories	78*
Distribution-channels studies	71*
Test markets, store audits	59*
Consumer panel operations	63*
Sales-compensation studies	60*

*In more than half these companies, this research activity was conducted in some department other than the marketing research department.
Source: Dik Warren Twedt (ed.), 1983 Survey of Marketing Research, American Marketing Association, Chicago, 1983, p. 41.

Researchers should have a clear idea of what they are trying to accomplish in a research project—that is, what is the goal of the project. Usually the objective is to solve a problem, but this is not always so. Often the purpose is to *define* the problem, or to determine whether the firm even *has* a problem. To illustrate, a manufacturer of commercial air-conditioning equipment had been enjoying a steady increase in sales

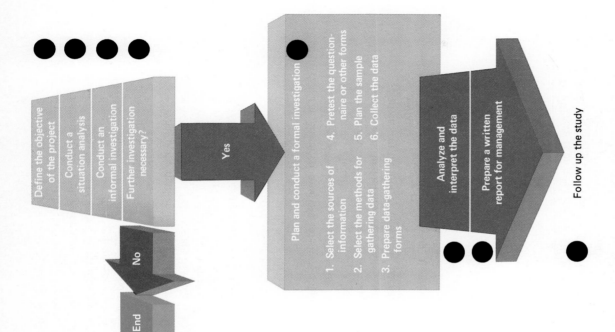

FIGURE 4-2
Procedure in a marketing research investigation.

volume over a period of years. Management decided to make a sales analysis. This research project uncovered the fact that, although the company's volume had been increasing, its share of the market had declined. In this instance, marketing research uncovered a problem that management did not know existed.

The case history of Photo Accessory Company (an actual company but a fictitious name) can be used to illustrate the first three steps in a marketing research project—namely, problem definition, situation analysis, and informal investigation. The Photo Accessory Company was a small manufacturer of camera accessory equipment. Its engineering department developed a rechargeable power cell for use by professional photographers. The prototype was 3 inches thick, 6 inches wide, and 9 inches long.

It weighed 4 pounds. A photographer would hang it from a belt and have a 3-foot wire connecting it to the camera. Approximately 300 flashes were possible before recharging it by plugging it into an electrical wall outlet.

The general problem, as presented to an outside marketing research firm, was to determine whether the company should add this product to its line. A breakdown of the problem into parts that could be handled by research resulted in the following specific questions:

- What is the market demand for such a product?
- What additional features are desired, if any?
- What channels of distribution should be used for such a product?
- What will technology be like in the next 5 years?
- What will the competition be like in the next 5 years?

With this tentative restatement of the problem, the researchers were ready for the next procedural step, the situation analysis.

2: Conduct Situation Analysis

The **situation analysis** involves obtaining information about the company and its business environment by means of library research and extensive interviewing of company officials. The researchers try to get a "feel" for the situation surrounding the problem. They analyze the company, its market, its competition, and the industry in general. In the Photo Accessory case the researchers studied several trade magazine articles in the library and held extensive discussions with company executives and workers.

In the situation analysis, the researchers also try to define the problem more clearly and to develop hypotheses for further testing. In a research project, a **hypothesis** is a tentative supposition or a possible solution to a problem. It is something that is assumed or conceded merely for purposes of argument or action. In a well-run project, each hypothesis should be proved or disproved on the way to fulfilling the project's objectives.

In the Photo Accessory case the situation analysis suggested the following hypotheses:

- There is an adequate market demand for the product.
- Marketing channels should concentrate on selling through traditional retail stores in order to reach the mass market.
- Advancing technology will not quickly make the project obsolete.
- Competition is not a threat to the success of the product.

3 and 4: Conduct Informal Investigation

Having gotten a feel for the problem, the researchers are now ready to conduct an informal investigation. To some extent this step overlaps the preceding one, which involves getting background information from *within* the company or from a library. The **informal investigation** consists of talking to people *outside* the company—middlemen, competitors, advertising agencies, and customers.

The researchers in the Photo Accessory case talked with many people. From their situation analysis plus telephone conversations with officials of the Photo Marketing Trade Association, the researchers developed an estimate of the potential market for the product. This estimate suggested that the market was large enough to warrant further investigation. Next, 15 photographers in three cities were interviewed to get their evaluation of the product itself, plus photographic practices in general. All liked the product, but they did suggest some product modifications.

To investigate channels of distribution, the researchers talked on the telephone with several photo retailers around the country. The consensus was that the retailers would not stock this new product for various reasons. The researchers then visited the annual Photo Marketing trade show to talk with more retailers and to get a line on the competition. Again, the retailers' reaction was negative. Also, the researchers learned that three major competitors—Vivitar, Quantum, and Bogen—soon would introduce rechargeable batteries that would compete directly with Photo Accessory's new product. Furthermore, there was a rumor that the Japanese soon would be entering the market.

The informal investigation is an important step in a research project because it often will determine whether further study is necessary. Decisions on the main problem in a research project frequently are made after the informal investigation is completed. As a matter of fact, at this point Photo Accessory decided not to market its portable power cell.

5: Plan and Conduct Formal Investigation

If the informal investigation has shown that the project is economically feasible, management then determines what additional information is needed. The next step for the researcher is to plan where and how to get the desired data.

SELECT THE SOURCES OF INFORMATION

Primary data, secondary data, or both can be used in an investigation. **Primary data** are original data gathered specifically for the project at hand. **Secondary data** have already been gathered for some other purpose. For example, when researchers stand in a supermarket and observe whether people use shopping lists, they are collecting primary data. When they get information from the Census of Population, they are using a secondary source.

One of the biggest mistakes made in marketing research is to collect primary data before exhausting the information available in secondary sources. Ordinarily, secondary information can be gathered much faster and at far less expense than primary data.

Sources of secondary data   Several excellent, readily available sources of secondary information are at the disposal of a marketing researcher. One such source, of course, is the multitude of records and reports *within* the firm itself. *Outside* the firm the major sources are as follows:[2]

- *Libraries.* Lest we forget, a good library is probably the best single, all-around source of secondary information. It will contain publications from practically all the sources mentioned here.

[2]For an excellent concise and annotated reference list of major secondary sources of business data, see C. R. Goeldner and Laura M. Dirks, "Business Facts: Where to Find Them," *MSU Business Topics,* Summer 1976, pp. 23–36. Also see Lorna M. Daniells, "Sources on Marketing," *Harvard Business Review,* July–August 1982, pp. 40, 42.

- *Government.* The federal government furnishes more marketing data than any other single source. These data are available at very low prices, even though there is a tremendous cost involved in collecting them. Also, the government has access under the law to types of information (company sales and profits, personal income, and the like) that are impossible for a private company to get.

  The *Monthly Catalog of United States Government Publications* lists all federal publications, grouped according to the agency or department that prepared them. But perhaps of more value to a researcher initially are three summary publications put out by the Department of Commerce. The most inclusive of these is the annual *Statistical Abstract of the United States.* The monthly *Survey of Current Business* furnishes data on a wide variety of topics. The third of these summaries is the *County and City Data Book,* which is published about every 3 years. This book contains demographic, economic, and other kinds of information for all countries in the United States, as well as for all cities over 25,000 in population.

  State and local governments provide many sources of information. Tax records, license applications, and other registration systems furnish much of the state and local information.

- *Trade, professional, and business associations.*
- *Private business firms.* Private marketing research firms, advertising agencies, and individual manufacturers or middlemen may be able to provide information needed by a researcher. Companies such as the A.C. Nielsen Company (the largest marketing research firm in the world) conduct various kinds of marketing research. Nielsen, for example, prepares a report showing how many households watched various television programs during a given week. Selling Areas Marketing, Inc., (SAMI) tracks the movement of supermarket products from warehouses to retail food stores.
- *Advertising media.* Many magazines, newspapers, and radio and television stations publish information that marketing researchers may not find available elsewhere. *Sales & Marketing Management* magazine, for example, annually publishes its "Survey of Buying Power." This survey covers the population, retail sales, income, and effective buying power for all states, counties, metropolitan areas, and cities with populations over 10,000.
- *University research organizations.* Most large universities operate research bureaus and publish findings of value to the business community.
- *Foundations.* Nonprofit research foundations and related groups carry out many kinds of research projects. Statistical analyses and reports on special topics are

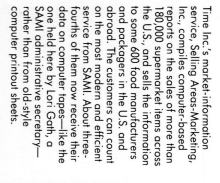

Time Inc.'s market-information service, Selling Areas-Marketing, Inc., compiles computer-based reports on the sales of more than 180,000 supermarket items across the U.S., and sells the information to some 600 food manufacturers and packagers in the U.S. and abroad. The customers can count on the most modern and efficient service from SAMI. About three-fourths of them now receive their data on computer tapes—like the one held here by Lori Gath, a SAMI administrative secretary—rather than from old-style computer printout sheets.

published by such groups as The Conference Board and the American Management Association.

Sources of primary data   After exhausting all reasonable secondary sources of information, researchers may still lack sufficient data. Then they will turn to primary sources and gather the information themselves. In a company research project, for instance, a researcher may interview that firm's sales people, middlemen, or customers to obtain the pertinent market information.

DETERMINE METHODS FOR GATHERING PRIMARY DATA

There are three widely used methods of gathering primary data: survey, observation, and experimentation. Normally, all three are not used on one project. The choice of method will be influenced by the availability of time, money, personnel, and facilities.

Survey method   A **survey** consists of gathering data by interviewing a limited number of people (a sample) selected from a larger group. A survey has the advantage of getting to the original source of information. In fact, this may be the *only* way to find out the opinions or buying intentions of a group.

While interviewing is still the most widely used method of collecting primary data, there may be a trend away from it. Other methods have been improved and their value has been more fully realized. The survey method contains certain inherent limitations. There are opportunities for error in the construction of the survey questionnaire and in the interviewing process. Surveys may be very expensive, and they are time-consuming. Another key weakness is that respondents often cannot or will not give true answers.

The interviewing in a survey may be done by the researcher in person, by telephone, or by mail.

Personal interviews are more flexible than the other two types because interviewers can alter the questions to fit the situation as they see it. They are able to probe more deeply if an answer is not satisfactory. Ordinarily, it is possible to obtain more information by personal interview than by telephone or mail. Also, the interviewer can, by observation, obtain data regarding the respondents' socioeconomic status—their home, neighborhood, and apparent standard of living.

The rising costs and other problems associated with door-to-door interviewing have prompted many market researchers to interview in central locations, typically regional shopping centers. This new technique is called the **shopping mall intercept** method of interviewing.[3] Another currently popular tool for face-to-face interviewing is the **focus group.** In a focus-group interview usually four to ten people meet with the researcher. Open-ended questions are often used to prompt participants into freely discussing the topic. The researcher can ask follow-up questions of the people in order to probe deeper into their attitudes.

In addition to their high cost and time-consuming nature, personal interviews also face the possible limitation that the researcher may introduce personal bias into

In a survey you can collect primary data by personal interviews.

—or by telephone interviews.

—or by a mail questionnaire.

an interview. Sometimes, for example, respondents will answer a question in a way that they perceive the interviewer wants that question answered.

In a **telephone survey**, the respondent is approached by telephone, and the interview is completed at that time. Telephone surveys can usually be conducted more rapidly and at less cost than either personal or mail surveys. Since a few interviewers can make any number of calls from a few central points, this method is quite easy to administer. The use of computer-assisted techniques has broadened the scope of telephone interviewing. These techniques involve automatic random-number dialing, a recorded voice asking the questions, and a machine to record the respondents' answers.

A telephone survey can be timely. For instance, people may be asked whether they are watching television at the moment and, if so, the name of the program and the sponsor. One limitation of the telephone survey is that interviews must be short. Lengthy interviews cannot be conducted satisfactorily over the phone. Also, about 20 percent of the households either have unlisted numbers, have moved since the last directory was printed, or have no telephone at all.

Interviewing by mail involves mailing a questionnaire to potential respondents and having them return the completed form by mail. Since no interviewers are involved, this type of survey is not hampered by interviewer bias or problems connected with the management of interviewers. Mailed questionnaires are more economical than personal interviews and are particularly useful in national surveys. Also, if the questionnaire returns, particularly when the returns are anonymous. If the respondents have characteristics that differentiate them from nonrespondents, the survey results will be invalid.

A major problem with mail questionnaires is the compilation of a good mailing list, especially for a *broad-scale* survey. If the sample can be drawn from a *limited* list, such as property taxpayers in certain counties or subscribers to a certain magazine, the list presents no problem. Another significant limitation concerns the reliability of the questionnaire returns, particularly when the returns are anonymous. If the respondents remain anonymous, they are more likely to give true answers because they do not feel the need to impress the interviewer.

Still another limitation is that typically there is a very low response rate in a mail survey. Some of the more successful inducements to improve the response rate include sending questionnaires by first-class mail, sending follow-up questionnaires, and enclosing incentives—monetary or nonmonetary—with the questionnaires. Using incentives is particularly effective in improving response rates, apparently since people receiving them feel obligated to cooperate.[4]

Observational method In the **observational method**, the data are collected by observing some action of the respondent. No interviews are involved, although an interview may be used as a follow-up to get additional information. For example, if customers are observed buying beer in cans instead of bottles, they may be asked why they prefer that one form of packaging to the other.

Information may be gathered by personal or mechanical observation. In one form

---

[4]For suggestions on increasing the response rate, see Milton M. Pressley, "Try These Tips to Get 50% to 70% Response Rate from Mail Surveys of Commercial Populations," *Marketing News*, Jan. 21, 1983, p. 16.

Let a scanner be your observer.

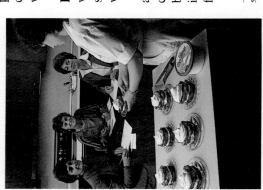

Test your market with a taste test.

of personal observation, the researcher poses as a customer in a store. This technique is useful in getting information about the caliber of the sales people or in determining what brands they push. Mechanical observation is illustrated by an electric cord stretched across a highway to count the number of cars that pass during a certain time period.

The observation method has several merits. It can be highly accurate. Often it removes all doubt about what the consumer does in a given situation. The consumers are unaware that they are being observed, so presumably they act in their usual fashion.

The observation technique reduces interviewer bias. However, the technique is limited in its application. Observation tells *what* happened, but it cannot tell *why*. It cannot delve into motives, attitudes, or opinions.

To overcome the biases inherent in the survey method, some firms are using sophisticated observational techniques that involve a combination of cable TV, electronic scanners in supermarkets, and computers. For example, one marketing research organization (Information Resources Inc.) established a panel of 15,000 participants in six small United States cities. The researchers then mechanically recorded every TV commercial played in the participants' homes and electronically scanned every purchase the participants made in supermarkets. With this observational method—called BehaviorScan—the researchers claim they can accurately predict what products will sell successfully and what television ads will best sell those products.[5]

Experimental method The **experimental method** of gathering primary data involves the establishment of a controlled experiment that simulates the real market situation as much as possible. The theory is that the small-scale experiment will furnish valuable information for designing a large-scale marketing program.

The experimental method may be used in several different ways. In one instance, a firm may manufacture a few units of a product and give them to employees or consumers to try out. Probably the major application of the experimental method has been in market testing. This technique consists of establishing (1) a control market, in which all factors remain constant, and (2) one or more test markets, in which one factor is varied. A firm may be trying to determine whether to change the color of its

[5]Fern Schumer, ''The New Magicians of Market Research,'' *Fortune*, July 25, 1983, pp. 72–74.

package. In city A, the product is marketed in its traditional color. In each of cities B, C, and D, a different color is used. All other factors are kept constant. By measuring sales in the four markets over a period of time, the manufacturer hopes to determine which color is most effective.

The outstanding merit of the experimental method is its realism. It is the only one of the three methods of gathering primary data that simulates an actual market situation.

Two big problems are encountered in market testing: selecting the control and test markets and controlling the variables. It is difficult—though necessary—to select markets that are identical in all significant socioeconomic factors. Some variables are really uncontrollable, and these may upset the comparability of results. Competitors may get wind of the test and try to confuse the picture by suddenly increasing their advertising, for example. Furthermore, the experimental method is expensive; it requires long periods of careful planning and administration.

Because of its inherent limitations, the use of traditional test marketing is declining as faster, less expensive alternatives are being developed. One such method, for example, is to simulate test marketing by using fewer people in a more controlled environment. Another alternative is the computer-based analysis of market information provided by electronic scanners in supermarkets.[6]

PREPARE DATA-GATHERING FORMS

When the interviewing or observation method is used, the researcher must prepare standard forms to record the information. However, the importance of the questionnaire in the survey method and the difficulty of designing it cannot be overemphasized.

SOME TYPICAL ERRORS IN QUESTIONNAIRE DESIGN

- The respondent feels the information requested is none of your business: What is your family's income? How old are you? What percentage of your home mortgage remains to be paid?
- Questions lack a standard of reference: Do you like a large kitchen? (What is meant by "large"?) Do you attend church regularly?
- The respondent does not know the answer: What is your spouse's favorite brand of ice cream?
- The respondent cannot remember and, therefore, guesses: How many calls did you (as a sales rep) make on office supply houses during the past year?
- Questions are asked in improper sequence. Save the tough, embarrassing ones for late in the interview. By then, some rapport ordinarily has been established with the respondent. A "none-of-your-business" question asked too early may destroy the entire interview.

In fact, most of the problems in data collection, whether it is done by personal, mail, or telephone survey, center on the preparation of the questionnaire. Extreme care and skill are needed in designing questionnaires to minimize bias, misunderstanding, and respondent anger.

PRETEST THE QUESTIONNAIRE OR OTHER FORMS

No matter how good a researcher thinks the questionnaire is, it still should be pretested. This process is similar to field-testing a product. In pretesting, a questionnaire is simply tried out on a small number of people similar to those who will be interviewed. Their responses should tell the researcher whether there are any problems with the questionnaire.

PLAN THE SAMPLE

Normally, it is unnecessary to survey every person who could shed light on a given research problem. It is sufficient to survey only some of these people, if their reactions are representative of the entire group. However, before the data can be gathered, the researchers must determine whom they are going to survey. That is, they must plan or establish a sample. Sampling is no stranger to us because we employ it frequently in our everyday activities. We often base our opinion of a person on only one or two conversations with that person. We often take a bite of food before ordering a larger quantity.

The fundamental idea underlying the concept of **sampling** is as follows: If a small number of items (the sample) is selected at random from a larger number of items (called a "universe"), then the sample will have the same characteristics, and in about the same proportion, as the universe. In marketing research, sampling is another procedural step whose importance is difficult to overestimate. Improper sampling is a source of errors in many survey results. In one study, an opinion on student government was derived by interviewing a sample of fraternity and sorority members. With no dormitory students, off-campus residents, or commuting students included, this was obviously a biased (nonrepresentative) sample of student opinion.

One of the first questions asked regarding sampling is: How large should the sample be? To be statistically reliable, a sample must be large enough to be truly representative of the universe or population.

To be statistically reliable, a sample must also be proportionate. That is, all types of units found in the universe must be represented in the sample. Also, these units must appear in the sample in approximately the same proportion as they are found in the universe. Assume that a manufacturer of power lawn mowers wants to know what percentage of families in a certain metropolitan area own this product. Further, assume that one-half the families in the market live in the central city, and the other half in the suburbs. Relatively more families in the suburbs have power mowers than do families in the city. If 80 percent of the sample is made up of suburban dwellers, the percentage of families owning power mowers will be overstated because the sample lacks proportionality.

Several sampling techniques can be used in marketing research. Some of these are quite similar, and some are hardly ever used. For a basic understanding of sampling, we shall consider three types: (1) simple random samples, (2) area samples, and (3) quota samples. The first two are probability (random) samples, and the third is a nonrandom sample. A random sample is one that is selected in such a way that every unit in the predetermined universe has a known and equal chance of being selected.

In a **simple random sample**, each unit in the sample is chosen directly from the universe. Suppose we wished to use a simple random sample to determine department store preferences among people in Denver, Colorado. We would need an accurate and complete listing of all people within the city limits. This would be our universe. Then in some random fashion we would select our sample from this universe.

A widely used variation of the simple random sample is the **area sample.** An area sample may be used where it is not economically feasible to obtain a full list of the universe. In the Denver department store study, for example, one way to conduct an area sample would be first to list all the blocks in the city. Then select a random sample of the blocks. Then every household or every other household in the sample blocks could be interviewed.

A **quota sample** is both nonrandom and stratified (or layered). Randomness is lost because the sample is "forced" to be proportional in some characteristic. Every element in the universe does *not* have an equal chance of being selected. To select a quota sample, the researchers first must decide which characteristic will serve as the basis of the quota. Then they determine in what proportion this characteristic occurs in the universe. The researchers then choose a sample with the same characteristic in the same proportion.

In an actual case—a study of tourists who went to Alaska—the researcher decided to select a quota sample based on the tourists' home state. From secondary sources, the researcher found that 30 percent of the tourists to Alaska came from California, 10 percent from the state of Washington, and 15 percent from the East North Central census region (Illinois, Indiana, Ohio, Michigan, and Wisconsin). The researcher then chose a sample of vacationers in which 30 percent were from California, 10 percent were from Washington, and so forth. The sample was forced to the extent that it was constructed on a nonrandom basis according to the home state of the tourist. That is, not every tourist in Alaska had an equal chance of being included in that sample.

Random sampling has one big advantage: Its accuracy can be measured with mathematical exactness. In quota sampling, much reliance is placed on the judgment of those designing and selecting the samples. There is no mathematical way of measuring the accuracy of the results.

COLLECT THE DATA

The actual collection of primary data in the field—by interviewing, observation, or both—normally is the weakest link in the entire research process. Ordinarily, in all other steps, reasonably well-qualified people are working carefully to ensure the accuracy of the results. The fruits of these labors may be lost if the fieldworkers (data gatherers) are inadequately trained and supervised. The management of fieldworkers is a difficult task because they usually are part-time workers with little job motivation. Also, their work is done where it cannot be observed, often at many widely separated locations.

A myriad of errors may creep into a research project at this point, and poor interviewers only increase this possibility. Bias may be introduced because people in the sample are not at home or refuse to answer. In some instances, fieldworkers are unable to establish rapport with respondents. Or the interviewers revise the wording of a question and thus obtain untrue responses. Finally, some interviewers just plain cheat in one way or another.

6 and 7: Analyze the Data and Prepare a Written Report

The final steps in a marketing research project are to analyze the data, interpret the findings, and submit a written report. Today sophisticated electronic data processing equipment enables a researcher to tabulate and analyze masses of data quickly and inexpensively. The end product of the investigation is the researcher's conclusions and recommendations, submitted in written form.

8: Follow Up the Study

For their own best interests, researchers should follow up each study to determine whether their recommendations are being followed. Too often, the follow-up is omitted. Actually, an analyst's future relations with an organization can depend on this follow-up, whether the analyst works in the organization or for an outside agency. Unless there is a follow-up, the company may not pay much attention to the report. It may be filed and forgotten.

WHO DOES MARKETING RESEARCH? ■

When a firm wishes to carry out a research project, the job can be done by the company's own personnel or by an outside organization.

Within the Company

The American Marketing Association study mentioned earlier indicated a trend toward companies having a separate marketing research department. The manager of this department reports either to the chief marketing executive or directly to top management. When marketing research is done within the company, the researchers are well versed in company procedures and know what information is available. Also, the firm is more apt to use its research facilities fully. On many problems, executives might not bother to call in an outside agency, but they might present the same problems to their own research department.

Outside the Company

A sign of maturity in the marketing research field is that it has already developed many institutions from which a company may seek help. One group of organizations includes research and consulting firms such as the A. C. Nielsen Company or McKinsey and Company. A second group includes, for example, railroads and public utilities that engage in marketing research to promote the services they are selling. A third type of outside organization includes trade associations and university bureaus of business research, which conduct marketing research on common problems faced by a group of companies.

These outside agencies employ highly qualified marketing research specialists. Also, the agencies may bring to a given case the experiences of many other clients who had similar problems.

STATUS OF MARKETING RESEARCH ■

American business is just beginning to realize the potential of marketing research. Significant advances have been made in both quantitative and qualitative research methodology, to the point where researchers are making effective use of the behavioral sciences and mathematics. Still, however, far too many companies are spending dollars on manufacturing research, but only pennies to determine the market opportunities for their products.

Several factors account for this less-than-universal acceptance of marketing research. Unlike the results of a chemical experiment, the results of marketing research cannot always be measured quantitatively. The research director cannot do a given job and then point to x percent increase in sales as a result of that job. Also, if management is not convinced of the value of marketing research, it will not spend the amount of money necessary to do a good job. Good research costs money. Executives may not realize that they cannot always get half as good a job for half the amount of money.

Marketing research cannot predict future market behavior accurately in many cases, yet often that is what is expected of it. In fact, when dealing with consumer behavior, the researcher is hard-pressed to get the truth regarding *present* attitudes or motives, much less those of next year.

Possibly a more fundamental reason for the modest status of marketing research has been the failure of researchers to communicate adequately with management. Admittedly, there are poor researchers and poor research. Moreover, sometimes the mentality of the quick-acting, pragmatic executive may be at odds with the cautious, complex, hedging-all-bets mentality of a marketing researcher. However, researchers, like many manufacturers, are often product-oriented when they should be market-oriented. They concentrate on research methods and techniques, rather than on showing management how these methods can aid in making better marketing decisions. Executives are willing to invest heavily in technical research because they are convinced there is a payoff in this activity. Management is not similarly convinced of a return on investments in marketing research.

Another basic problem is the apparent reluctance of management (1) to treat marketing research as a continuing process and (2) to relate marketing research and decision making in a more systematic fashion. Too often, marketing research is viewed in a fragmented, one-project-at-a-time manner. It is used only when management realizes it has a marketing problem. One way to avoid such a view is to incorporate marketing research as one part of a marketing information system—a system that provides a continuous flow of data concerning the changing marketing environment.[7]

Looking to the future, however, we think the prospects for marketing research are encouraging. As more top marketing executives embrace the concept of strategic marketing planning, we should see a growing respect for marketing research and

---

[7]For some suggestions on how to improve the effectiveness of marketing research departments, see David J. Luck and James R. Krum, *Conditions Conducive to the Effective Use of Marketing Research in the Corporation*, Marketing Science Institute, Cambridge, Mass., 1981. Also see David A. Aaker and George S. Day, "Increasing the Effectiveness of Marketing Research," *California Management Review*, Winter 1980, pp. 59–65.

marketing information systems. The strategic planning process requires the generation and careful analysis of information. Marketing researchers have the particular training, capabilities, and systems techniques that are needed for effective information management.[8]

SUMMARY

For a company to operate successfully today, management must develop an orderly method for gathering and analyzing the mass of information that is relevant to the organization. A marketing information system is such a method. It is a structure designed to generate and process an information flow to aid managerial planning and decision making in a company's marketing program. A marketing information system is a future-oriented, continuously operating, computer-based process. It is designed to handle internal and external data and to prevent problems as well as to solve them.

Marketing research is a major component or subsystem within a marketing information system. It is used in a very wide variety of marketing situations. Typically, in a marketing research study, the problem to be solved is first identified. Then a researcher normally conducts a situation analysis and an informal investigation. If a formal investigation is needed, the researcher decides whether to use secondary or primary sources of information. To gather primary data, the researcher may use the survey, observation, or experimental method. Normally, primary data are gathered by sampling. Then the data are analyzed, and a written report is prepared.

KEY TERMS AND CONCEPTS

Marketing information system 61
Marketing research 64
Situation analysis 68
Hypothesis 68
Informal investigation 68
Primary data 69
Secondary data 69
Survey method 71
Personal interview 71

Shopping mall intercept 71
Focus group 71
Telephone survey 72
Mail questionnaire 72
Observational method 72
Experimental method 73
Pretesting 75
Random sample 76
Quota sample 76

QUESTIONS AND PROBLEMS

1. Why does a company need a marketing information system?
2. How does a marketing information system differ from marketing research?
3. "The marketing information executive—rather than an operating, decision-making executive—should be the one to identify marketing problems, delineate the area to be studied, and design the research projects." Do you agree? Explain.

---

[8]See Linden A. Davis, Jr., "What's Ahead in Marketing Research?" *Journal of Advertising Research,* June 1981, pp. 49–51.

4. A group of wealthy business executives regularly spend some time each winter at a popular ski resort—Aspen, Colorado; Sun Valley, Idaho; Snow Valley, Vermont; or Squaw Valley, California. They were intrigued with the possibility of forming a corporation to develop and operate a large ski resort in the Colorado Rockies. This would be a totally new venture and would be on U.S. Forest Service land. It would be a complete resort with facilities appealing to middle- and upper-income markets. What types of information might they want to have before deciding whether to go ahead with the venture? What sources of information would be used?

5. A manufacturer of a liquid glass cleaner competitive with Windex and Glass Wax wants to determine the amount of the product that he can expect to sell throughout the country. To help him in this project, prepare a report that shows the following information for your home state and, if possible, your home city or county. Carefully identify the source you use for this information, and state other sources that provide this information.

   a. Number of households or families.
   b. Income or buying power per family or per household.
   c. Total retail sales in the most recent year for which you can find reliable data.
   d. Total annual sales of food stores, hardware stores, and drugstores.
   e. Total number of food stores.

6. Explain, with examples, the concepts of a situation analysis and an informal investigation in a marketing research project.

7. Evaluate surveys, observation, and experimentation as methods of gathering primary data in the following projects:

   a. A sporting goods retailer wants to determine college students' brand preferences for skis, tennis rackets, and golf clubs.
   b. A supermarket chain wants to determine shoppers' preferences for the physical layout of fixtures and traffic patterns, particularly around checkout stands.
   c. A manufacturer of conveyor belts wants to know who makes buying decisions for his product among present and prospective users.

8. Carefully evaluate the relative merits of personal, telephone, and mail surveys on the bases of flexibility, amount of information obtained, accuracy, speed, cost, and ease of administration.

9. Explain and differentiate among a random sample, an area sample, and a quota sample.

10. What kind of sample would you use in each of the research projects designed to answer the following questions?

    a. What brand of shoes is most popular among the female students on your campus?
    b. Should the department stores in or near your hometown be open all day on Sundays?
    c. What percentage of the business firms in the large city nearest your campus have automatic sprinkler systems?

1

SIERRA NATIONAL BANK*

Applying the marketing concept

The top management at the Sierra National Bank was trying to figure out why the introduction of the marketing concept had been a failure in the bank. These executives were aware of excellent results from introducing the marketing concept in manufacturing firms. But some of them were beginning to wonder whether different conditions were required for the successful implementation of the marketing concept in the banking business. Sierra's management began a self-analysis to determine where the bank went wrong and what should be done at this stage.

The Sierra National Bank was a large commercial bank with headquarters in San Francisco and branches throughout the state of California. Regional offices, each headed by a vice president, were located in San Diego, Los Angeles, Bakersfield, Sacramento, and Redding. Major policy matters were handled in the head office. At the same time, much authority on loans and other matters was decentralized—that is, delegated to the regional offices. Throughout its history, Sierra's early expansion had come through internal growth and mergers. The bank's growth was satisfactory until the late 1940s, but it really boomed between 1950 and 1970. During that period, the number of branches tripled, and the net profit, assets, and foreign currency holdings more than doubled.

Then through the 1970s and 1980s, Sierra experienced increasing competition from several sources. Other commercial banks and savings and loan associations were becoming more sophisticated and more aggressive in their marketing. Securities brokers such as Merrill Lynch and E. F. Hutton were expanding the financial services that they offered and were advertising excessively. Even product retailers such as Sears, Kroger, and K mart were entering the financial services field.

These winds of change that were blowing through the banking business made Sierra's management realize that it had to do something if it wanted to maintain Sierra's market share and growth patterns. About 2 years ago a few of Sierra's top

*Adapted from a case prepared by Prof. Lionel A. Mitchell, Acadia University.

executives had come into contact with some marketing professors at a business conference. The executives were impressed by what they heard about the marketing concept. They thought that by applying the marketing concept in the bank they could better adapt to their changing environment. Consequently, they decided to introduce the marketing concept on an experimental basis in a few of the branches in the San Francisco Bay Area.

Sierra's main target markets were big businesses and large accounts. Not much attention was given to attracting small depositors and investors. However, management now believed that the bank needed to change its image and outlook. The total population and personal incomes were increasing considerably in California. Sierra needed to change its attitude, approach, and distorted image if it wanted to tap into this potential market.

The responsibility for these changes would be placed in a marketing department, if the executives understood correctly the marketing concept as explained by the professors. The only previous activity conducted by the bank in the field of marketing had been in the area of public relations and advertising. In the late 1950s, the bank had established a separate public relations and advertising department, headed by a manager who reported to one of the top officials (the secretary). This department supplied ink blotters and book covers for students, posters which were displayed at branches, advertising cards for use on public transportation, small information folders for branch disposal, and many similar items. The common characteristic of each of these items was a message from Sierra National—for instance, a message with descriptive pictures telling of the advantages of a savings account or a safety deposit box.

This type of promotion may have been adequate in the beginning, but the bank soon found that it must do a lot more. This led to more intensive promotional activities such as the establishment of student tours, the sponsoring of prizes at regional fairs, student scholarships, and display booths at industrial fairs. Because banking had become more complex and competitive, the bank was outgrowing its public relations and advertising department.

Charles Fleming, who came to Sierra National from the marketing department of a leading consumer goods manufacturing firm, was named to head the new marketing department. He carried the title of assistant general manager of marketing, and he reported directly to Louis Beam, the general manager. Beam indicated to Fleming that he (Fleming) was in complete charge of the marketing department and had full rein to implement any new marketing feature.

As his first objective, the new department head planned a major reorganization designed (1) to upgrade and modernize all services, (2) to handle customer services more efficiently, and (3) to listen to and act upon customers' suggestions and complaints.

The public relations and advertising department was placed under the new marketing department. One of the first projects of the marketing department was to redesign the banking forms, using the new bank logo and colors. The uniforms of porters, messengers, chauffeurs, and mail and service staff were redesigned to reflect the bank's new image. Banking hours were to be extended for customer convenience. Fleming suggested that marketing departments be established in each of the five regional offices.

After 9 months the marketing department's staff numbered 29 people. Most of the proposed projects had been initiated. The public relations and advertising department was virtually absorbed by the marketing department. Research and planning were underway to establish marketing departments in the five regions.

About this time, however, problems began to arise and conflicts developed. Doubts were raised about the many and frequent changes. Many of the changes did not transpire as well as the bank had expected. Mr. Fleming, who was inexperienced in banking matters, had plunged into his job of introducing a marketing orientation into the bank. However, he received little or no cooperation or assistance from the older staff members—that is, the experienced bank personnel. Fleming relied entirely on his previous marketing knowledge and experience. But some of his ideas were considered unorthodox by the banking public as well as by many of the staff, including his subordinates and his superiors. Fleming secretly admitted that he did not care what the staff thought of the new concept—it was a good thing and it would be implemented.

In the meantime, Fleming had a clash with Beam and, in the weeks that followed, Fleming was unable to patch up this relationship. This situation eventually led to Fleming's dismissal from the bank. The marketing department was dissolved as an organizational unit. A new public relations and advertising department was set up to perform the marketing activities, and Peter Hudson was installed as manager of this new department.

QUESTIONS

1. Why did the introducton of the marketing concept fail at Sierra National?
2. Should the introduction of the marketing concept in a service industry be different from that in retailing or manufacturing?
3. If you were Peter Hudson, what approach would you adopt in your new position? Evaluate Peter Hudson's chances of success.

CASE 2

BOOKWORMS, INC.*

Planning a marketing research project ■

Late one August morning, Nancy Klein, co-owner of Bookworms, Inc., sat at her desk near the back wall of a cluttered office. With some irritation, she had just concluded that her nearby calculator could help no more. "What we still need," she thought to herself, "are estimates of demand and market share . . . but at least we have 2 weeks to get them."

Klein's office was located in the rear of Bookworms, Inc., an 1,800-square-foot bookstore specializing in quality paperbacks. The store carried over 10,000 titles and sold more than $520,000 worth of books in 1986. Titles were stocked in 18 categories, ranging from art, biography, and cooking to religion, sports, and travel.

Bookworms, Inc., was located in a small business district across the street from the boundary of Verdoon University (VU). VU currently enrolled about 12,000 under-

*Case prepared by Prof. James E. Nelson, University of Colorado. Used with permission.

graduate and graduate students majoring in the liberal arts, the sciences, and the professions. Despite national trends in enrollment, the VU admissions office had predicted that the number of entering students would grow at about 1 percent per year through the 1980s. The surrounding community, a city of about 350,000 was projected to grow at about twice that rate.

Bookworms, Inc., carried no texts even though many of its customers were VU students. Both Klein and her partner, Susan Berman, felt that the VU bookstore had simply too firm a grip on the textbook market in terms of price, location, and reputation. Bookworms also carried no classical records, as of 2 months ago. Klein recalled with discomfort the $15,000 or so they had lost on the venture. "Another mistake like that and the bank will be running Bookworms," she thought. "And, despite what Susan thinks, the copy service could just be that final mistake."

The idea for a copy service had come from Susan Berman. She had seen the candy store next to Bookworms (under the same roof) go out of business in July. She had immediately asked the building's owner, Ed Anderson, about the future of the 800-square-foot space. Upon learning it was available, she had met with Klein to discuss her idea for the copy service. She had spoken excitedly about the opportunity: "It can't help but make money. I could work there part-time and the rest of the time we could hire students. We could call it 'Copycats' and even use a sign with the same kind of letters as we do in 'Bookworms.' I'm sure we could get Ed to knock the wall out between the two stores, if you think it would be a good idea. Probably we could rent most of the copying equipment, so there's not much risk."

Klein was not so sure. A conversation yesterday with Anderson had disclosed his desire for a 5-year lease (with an option to renew) at $1,000 per month. He had promised to hold the offer open for 2 weeks before attempting to lease the space to anyone else. Representatives from copying-equipment firms had estimated that charges would run between $200 and $2,000 per month, depending on equipment, service, and whether the equipment was bought or leased. The copy service would also incur other fixed costs in terms of utility expenses, interest, insurance, and the like. Further, Bookworms would have to invest a sizable sum in fixtures and inventory (and perhaps equipment). Klein concluded that the service would begin to make a profit at about 20,000 copies per month under best-case assumptions, and at about 60,000 copies per month under worst-case assumptions.

Further informal investigation had identified two major competitors. One was the copy center located in the Krismann Library on the west side of the campus, a mile away. The other was a private firm, Kinko's, located on the south side of the campus, also 1 mile away. Both offered service while you wait, on several machines. The Library's price was about ½ cent per copy higher than Kinko's. Both offered collating, binding, color copying, and other services, all on a 7-day-a-week schedule.

Actually, investigation had discovered that a third major "competitor" consisted of the VU departmental machines scattered throughout the campus. Most faculty and administrative copying was done on these machines, but students were allowed the use of some, at cost. In addition, at least 20 self-service machines could be found in the library and in nearby drugstores, grocery stores, and banks.

Moving aside a stack of books on her desk, Nancy Klein picked up the telephone and dialed her partner. When Berman answered, Klein asked, "Susan, have you any idea how many copies a student might make in a semester? I mean, according to my figures, we would break even somewhere between 20,000 and 60,000 copies per month. I don't know if this is half the market or what.''

"You know, I have no idea," Berman answered. "I suppose when I was going to school I probably made 10 copies a month—for articles, class notes, old tests, and so on."

"Same here," Klein said. "But some graduate students must have done that many each week. You know, I think we ought to do some marketing research before we go much further on this. What do you think?"

"Sure. Only it can't take much time or money. What did you have in mind, Nancy?"

"Well, we could easily interview our customers as they leave the store and ask them how many copies they've made in the past week or so. Of course, we'd have to make sure they were students."

"What about a telephone survey?" Berman asked. "That way we can have a random sample. We would still ask about the number of copies, but now we would know for sure they would be students."

"Or what about interviewing students in the union cafeteria? There's always a good-sized line there around noon, as I remember, and this might be even quicker."

"Boy, I just don't know. Why don't I come in this afternoon and we can talk about it some more?"

"Good idea," Klein responded. "Between the two of us, we should be able to come up with something."

QUESTIONS

1. What sources of information should Klein and Berman use?
2. How should Klein and Berman gather data?
3. What questions should they ask?
4. How should they sample?

CASE 3

THE HARRISONBURG-ROCKINGHAM CHAMBER OF COMMERCE*

Designing a marketing research project

■

The Harrisonburg-Rockingham Chamber of Commerce was a nonprofit organization that was started in 1916 and currently had over 500 members. This Chamber of Commerce served an area in the northwestern part of Virginia, extending from the Blue Ridge mountains to the West Virginia border. Harrisonburg, the largest city in Rockingham County, was the social and economic center for the area. The region's primary industry was agriculture, especially poultry raising. However, improved transportation services had helped to attract new industry over the past few years.

The major goals of the Chamber were as follows: (1) to encourage the growth of existing businesses, (2) to give appropriate assistance to new firms in the area, and (3) to support those civic and cultural activities deemed beneficial to the well-being of the community.

*Case prepared by James Eitler and Laurence Farin, research associates, and Professor Thomas M. Bertsch, all at James Madison University. Reproduced with permission.

Exhibit 1

To: BIAD Research Inc.
From: Rebecca L. Cover, executive vice-president, Harrisonburg-Rockingham Chamber of Commerce
Subject: Research project to determine local residents' opinion of proposed Coors brewery.

This research project is to be used to obtain the opinions of Harrisonburg-Rockingham County residents on three issues of concern to the Chamber of Commerce:

1. What is the general opinion of residents toward the Coors Company locating in the area?
2. What factions can be identified as supporting or not supporting the Coors plant?
3. What is the opinion of residents toward the expansion of business in the area?

This project is a quick, inexpensive, and relatively accurate method for gathering information on local feelings in regard to the proposed Coors plant and entry of new businesses into the area. The recommended study is described in the following paragraphs.

The sample to be studied should be drawn on a quota basis. Pertinent secondary information would be used to determine how to stratify the sample by marital status, age, sex, and education. Hopefully, this information can be obtained from previous studies done by BIAD, or by using federal census data.

Data would be gathered by telephone interviews. Two hundred phone numbers would be selected from area phone books. Each number would be called, and the head of the house would be asked to answer a few questions.

All the information can be determined from answers to preset questions. Two types of questions should be used. The first type would be multiple choice for personal information on age, sex, marital status, income, and area of residence. The second set of questions would consist of (1) a series of opinion-type statements, read by the interviewer, and (2) a five-point response scale ranging from "strongly agree" to "strongly disagree."

Machine tabulation should be used to ensure speed and accuracy. Proper editing for bias should then be done. A preliminary review by Ms. Cover and a BIAD representative could further determine the significance of the results and help in preparation of a report for the Chamber.

The results would be presented first at a meeting of the Board of Directors, and then later to a meeting of the entire membership. The format for the presentation would be the same for both meetings. Through the use of overhead transparencies or drawings, the information would be grouped in columns to show how many people are in favor of the proposed plant and how many are opposed. Respondents would be categorized by occupation and place of residence to see if these factors account for the significant differences in opinion. Ms. Cover and the BIAD representative would explain how the results were obtained and what they feel are the most significant findings. After each presentation they would field questions from the audience to try to clear up any misunderstandings of the results.

Rebecca L. Cover, the executive vice-president, was responsible for the day-to-day operations of the Chamber. She supervised the Chamber's publications, and she gathered all the necessary information herself. Secondary data usually were sufficient to meet the Chamber's information needs. However, she believed that a project using primary data would be needed in connection with a forthcoming industry-location study.

The Adolph Coors Company, a large producer of beer, had selected Rockingham County as one of the possible sites for its new brewery. The announcement was received with great enthusiasm by many members of the Chamber of Commerce. However, there were some people in both the community and the Chamber who felt that the Coors plant would do more harm than good. Most of the anti-Coors advocates were local poultry producers who thought the brewery would take away much of the unskilled labor from the poultry plants. In addition, environmental groups were opposed to Coors, because they believed that the plant would ruin the land and pollute the Shenandoah river.

The pro-Coors supporters stressed the importance of locating a major manufacturer in the area. They pointed out that the new brewery would bring increased tax revenues and a large number of both skilled and unskilled jobs for area residents. The Coors supporters also said that locating the plant in Rockingham County would bring a number of new, supporting industries to the area and increase the revenues for established businesses.

The differences of opinion among members of the Chamber of Commerce were very noticeable. Some members believed Coors should be supported by the Chamber because of the Chamber's commitment to helping business in the area. Others thought that the Chamber should adhere to its policy of the "greatest good for the greatest number." The Board of Directors for the Chamber finally agreed that the opinion of people in the Harrisonburg-Rockingham County area should be the main factor in deciding whether or not to support Coors. The Board requested that Ms. Cover gather information to answer three questions:

1. What is the opinion of citizens in the area toward the building of a Coors plant?
2. Which groups support or oppose the establishment of the Coors plant and why?
3. What should be the stand of the Chamber of Commerce toward expansion of business in the area?

The research study that Rebecca Cover prepared to do is described in Exhibit 1. She had never done a study of this nature before. Consequently, the Chamber hired an outside research firm, BIAD Research Inc., to evaluate Cover's proposed study.

QUESTIONS

Assume that you are the BIAD Research representative who is assigned to review Rebecca Cover's proposed project.

1. Evaluate Cover's proposal.
2. What changes, if any, should be made in the project?

TARGET MARKETS

An analysis of the people and organizations who buy, why they buy, and how they buy.

In Part 1 we stressed the importance of customer orientation in an organization's marketing efforts. We also defined strategic planning as the process of matching an organization's resources with its marketing opportunities. These notions suggest that early in the strategic marketing process, an organization should determine who its potential customers are. Only then can management develop a marketing mix intended to satisfy the wants of these customers. Therefore, in Part 2 we discuss the selection of an organization's intended customers—that is, its target market.

In Chapter 5 we review the concept of a target market, and we discuss the demographic and buying-power dimensions of consumer markets. Chapter 6 is devoted to the buying behavior and the buying process in consumer markets. Chapter 7 covers various aspects of the industrial (or business organizational) market. In Chapter 8 we discuss the concepts of market segmentation and market demand forecasting.

MARKET DEMOGRAPHICS AND BUYING POWER

CHAPTER GOALS

This is the first of four chapters on target markets—ultimate consumers and industrial users. After studying this chapter, you should understand:

- Some fundamentals regarding the selection of target markets.
- The difference between ultimate-consumer markets and industrial-user markets.
- The marketing implications of the distribution and composition of population.
- The influences of consumer-income distribution on marketing.
- Consumer spending patterns and the way they affect marketing.

People *are* different in different parts of the country, and regional differences *do* exist in product preferences and in brand preferences. In soup, for example, cream of mushroom soup is the number 1 seller in California, while people in the Northeast and Midwest prefer chicken noodle soup and tomato soup. In autos, the Southwest is the best market for pickup trucks, vans sell best in the Northwest, and California is a good market for expensive imported cars such as a BMW or Mercedes. Following is a list of cities that are the number 1 market for the stated product. These ratings are based on the per capita purchases of the product.[1]

Product	Number 1 market (on per capita basis)	Product	Number 1 market (on per capita basis)
Antacids and aspirin	Atlanta	Motor oil additives	Oklahoma City
Popcorn	Dallas/Fort Worth	Iced tea	Philadelphia
Vitamins	Denver	Coffee	Pittsburgh
Rat poison	Grand Rapids	Dry cat food	Portland (Oregon)
Shoe polish	Indianapolis	Candy bars and marshmallows	Salt Lake City
Laundry soaps	New York	Meat tenderizers	Savannah
Ketchup	New Orleans	Toothbrushes	Seattle

Why do you suppose that people in Atlanta are such big consumers of aspirin, and why do people in Seattle buy so many toothbrushes? In addition to regional influences, many companies find that the markets for their products are influenced by age, ethnic background, and other demographic factors. (Remember, in Chapter 2 we defined *demography* as the statistical study of human population and its distribution.)

In short, any marketer that hopes to prosper in the challenging decade of the 1990s must be aware of the demographics of that decade. As the editor of *American Demographics* magazine said, "You cannot understand the consumer marketplace today without an appreciation of demographic trends. . . . Demographic characteristics help shape preferences, determine attitudes, and mold values."[2]

---

[1]Thomas Moore, "Different Folks, Different Strokes," *Fortune*, Sept. 16, 1985, p. 65.

[2]Bryant Robey, as quoted in "The Year 2000: A Demographic Profile of Consumer Market," *Marketing News*, May 25, 1984, p. 8.

The demographics of the consumer market is a large part of what we shall be talking about in this chapter. Before an organization develops a marketing program to achieve its marketing goals, management first must select its target market(s). In Chapter 2 we defined a **market** as people or organizations with (1) wants (needs) to satisfy, (2) money to spend, and (3) the willingness to spend it. A **target market** is a group of customers (people or organizations) at whom the seller specifically intends to aim its marketing efforts.

MARKET OPPORTUNITY ANALYSIS

Theoretically, a market opportunity exists any time and any place there is a person or an organization with an unfilled need or want. Realistically, of course, a company's market opportunity is much more restricted. Consequently, selecting a target market requires an appraisal of the market opportunities available to the organization. A market opportunity analysis involves, first, a study of the various environmental forces (as discussed in Chapter 2) that affect a firm's market program. Then the organization must analyze the three components of a market—people (or organizations), their buying power, and their willingness to spend. Analysis of the "people" component involves a study of the geographic distribution and demographic composition of the population. The second component is analyzed through the distribution of consumer income and consumer expenditure patterns. These first two components are discussed more fully later in this chapter. Finally, to determine consumers' "willingness to spend," management must study their buying behavior. This involves the sociological and psychological factors that influence buyer behavior—the topics covered in Chapter 6.

Target-Market Strategy: Market Aggregation or Market Segmentation

In defining the market or markets it will sell to, an organization has its choice of two general approaches. In one, the total market is viewed as a single unit—as one mass, aggregate market. This approach leads to the strategy of *market aggregation*. In the other approach, the total market is seen as being composed of many smaller, homogeneous segments. This approach leads to the strategy of *market segmentation*, in which one or more of these segments are selected as target markets.

Deciding which of these two strategies to adopt is a key step in selecting target markets. We shall discuss market aggregation and segmentation in more detail in Chapter 8, after we have a better understanding of the three components of a market. That is, segmentation decisions are based on the demographic characteristics of the marketplace, plus some understanding of customer buying behavior and the buying process. However, for our discussion of the three market components, it will be helpful at this point to divide the total potential market into two broad categories—ultimate consumers and industrial users.

Ultimate Consumers and Industrial Users

The sole criterion for placement in one or the other of these categories is the customer's *reason for buying*. **Ultimate consumers** buy and/or use products or services for their own personal or household use. They are satisfying strictly nonbusiness wants, and they constitute what is called the "consumer market"—the topic of this chapter and Chapter 6.

Industrial users are business, industrial, or institutional organizations that buy products or services to use in their own businesses or to make other products. A manufacturer that buys chemicals with which to make fertilizer is an industrial user of these chemicals. Farmers who buy the fertilizer to use in commercial farming are industrial users of the fertilizer. (If homeowners buy fertilizer to use on their yards, they are ultimate consumers because they buy it for personal, nonbusiness use.) Supermarkets, hospitals, or paper manufacturers that buy floor wax are industrial users of this product because they use it in a business or institution. Industrial users in total constitute the "industrial market"—the topic of Chapter 7.

The segmentation of all markets into two groups—consumer and industrial—is extremely significant from a marketing point of view because the two markets buy differently. Consequently, the composition of a seller's marketing mix—the products, distribution, pricing, and promotion—will depend upon whether it is directed toward the consumer market or the industrial market.[3]

POPULATION: ITS DISTRIBUTION AND COMPOSITION

According to our definition, people are the main component of a market. Therefore, marketers should analyze the geographic distribution and demographic composition of the population as a first step toward understanding the consumer market.

Total Population

A logical place to start is with an analysis of total population, and here the existence of a "population explosion" becomes evident. The population of the United States did not reach 100 million until 1915. However, it took only another 52 years (until 1967) to reach the 200 million mark. And, by the year 2000, about 270 million people will be living in the United States, even though the birthrate has been declining since the 1960s and is expected to stay at its present low level.

This total market is so large and so diverse in its characteristics that it must be analyzed in segments. Significant shifts are occurring in regional and urban-rural population distribution patterns. Market differences traceable to differences in age, sex, household arrangements, life-styles, and ethnic backgrounds pose real challenges for marketing executives.

Regional Distribution

Figure 5-1 shows the distribution of population in 1985 and its projected growth from 1980 to 2000 by census regions. The biggest markets are in the East North Central, South Atlantic, and Middle Atlantic census regions. These three areas account for a little over one-half of the nation's population. However, the greatest rate of population growth in the latter part of the twentieth century is occurring in the "Sun Belt"—the Southern and Western regions. By the year 2000 the three most populous states will be California, Texas, and Florida, in that order.

The regional distribution of population is important to marketers because people within a given region broadly tend to share the same values, attitudes, and style preferences. However, significant differences do exist among the various regions, because of differences in climate, social customs, and other factors. Thus, bright, warm colors are preferred in Florida and the Southwest, while grays and cooler colors predominate in New England and the Midwest. People in the West are less formal than Easterners, and they spend more time outdoors. Consequently, as the Western population continues to increase, there will be still larger markets for such products as patio furniture, sports clothes, and barbecue equipment.

[3]For a thoughtful analysis which proposes that this traditional distinction between consumer marketing and industrial marketing is not justified, see Edward F. Fern and James R. Brown, ''The Industrial/Consumer Marketing Dichotomy: A Case of Insufficient Justification,'' *Journal of Marketing*, Spring 1984, pp. 68–77.

FIGURE 5-1
Regional distribution of population, 1985, and projected growth, 1980-2000.
The East North Central, South Atlantic, and Middle Atlantic census regions account for the largest part of our total population. However, the Southern and Western regions show a more rapid growth rate. Movement of the population center of the United States is still generally south and westward.

A = 1985% distribution
B = 1980-2000% increases
(U.S. total = 18%)

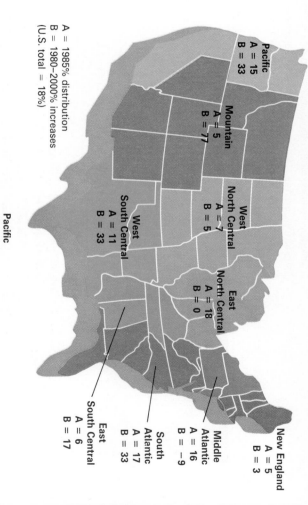

New England
A = 5
B = 3

Middle Atlantic
A = 16
B = -9

South Atlantic
A = 17
B = 33

East South Central
A = 6
B = 17

East North Central
A = 18
B = 0

West South Central
A = 11
B = 33

West North Central
A = 7
B = 5

Mountain
A = 5
B = 77

Pacific
A = 15
B = 33

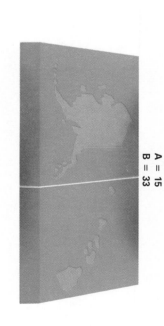

Pacific
A = 15
B = 33

Urban, Rural, and Suburban Distribution

For many years, in the United States there has been a decline in the farm population, and this situation is expected to continue. In 1950, about 1 out of 6 people lived on a farm; in 1980, it was about 1 out of 40. The declining farm population has led some marketing people to underrate the rural market, however. Both as an industrial market for farm equipment and supplies and as a consumer market with increased buying power and a more urbanlike sophistication, the farm market is still big. Sociological patterns (like average family size and local customs) among rural people differ significantly from those of city dwellers. These patterns have considerable influence on buying behavior. Per capita consumption of cosmetics and other beauty aids, for example, is much lower in farm markets than in city markets.

METROPOLITAN STATISTICAL AREAS

As the farm population has shrunk, the urban and suburban population has expanded. In recognition of the urbanization of the American market, the federal government has established a geographic hierarchy of metropolitan areas that (among its many uses) serves as an excellent market-measurement tool. This classification structure consists of three sets of metropolitan areas—Metropolitan Statistical Area (MSA), Primary Metropolitan Statistical Area (PMSA), and Consolidated Metropolitan Statistical Area (CMSA). Together, this metropolitan-area structure accounts for 75 to 80 percent of the nation's population and retail sales. Obviously, for many products, these metropolitan areas present attractive, geographically concentrated target markets with considerable sales potential.

The basic unit in the metropolitan-area structure is the **MSA—Metropolitan Statistical Area**—and the federal government has identified 335 MSAs. A geographical area qualifies to be an MSA in one of two ways: (1) It has a central city of at least 50,000 population, or (2) it has a general urban area of 50,000, with a total metropolitan population of at least 100,000. The boundaries of an MSA are drawn around county lines and may cross state borders. But the counties must be a socially and economically integrated unit, and virtually all employment must be nonagricultural.

A **PMSA—Primary Metropolitan Statistical Area**— conceptually is identical to an MSA. The 78 PMSAs are especially titled and separated out *only* because they are components of the giant urban centers—the CMSAs.

A **CMSA—Consolidated Metropolitan Statistical Area**— is a megalopolis that consists of a group of closely related PMSAs. The center of each Consolidated Metropolitan Area is a very large city such as New York, Los Angeles, Chicago, Philadelphia, etc.

SUBURBAN GROWTH

As the metropolitan areas have been growing, something else has been going on *within* them. The central cities are growing very slowly, and in some cases the older established parts of the cities are actually losing population. The real growth is occurring in the fringe areas of the central cities or in the suburbs outside these cities. For the past 40 years, one of the most significant social and economic trends in the United States has been the shift of population to the suburbs. As middle-income families have moved to the suburbs, the economic, racial, and ethnic composition of many central cities (especially the core areas) has changed considerably. This has changed the nature of the markets in these areas.

The growth of the suburban population has some striking marketing implications. Since a great percentage of suburban people live in single-family residences, there is a vastly expanded market for lawn mowers, lawn furniture, home furnishings, and home repair products. Suburbanites are more likely to want two cars than are city dwellers. They are inclined to spend more leisure time at home, so there is a bigger market for home entertainment and recreation items.

Lately, however, marketing people have noted some countertrends in these rural-urban-suburban population distribution patterns. For example, the *rate* of suburban growth has slowed down considerably, especially in suburbs in the largest metropolitan areas. Don't misunderstand—the suburban population is still growing. It is just that suburbia is not expanding as fast as it did in past years. Another countertrend is the migration of people from the suburbs to "exurbia"—areas just beyond the suburbs. In fact, many of the nation's smaller cities and rural areas are growing faster than the metropolitan areas—the big cities and the suburbs.

Two additional changes in suburban population have marketing implications. One is the changing racial mix in many suburbs, mainly as a result of the in-migration of blacks. The other change is a dramatic decline in married couples' share of suburban households. Along with this is a significant increase in the number of households with single-female parents and other single people living in suburbia.

Age Groups

Analyzing the consumer market by age groups is a useful approach in the marketing of many products. But marketing executives must be aware of the changing nature of the age mix. Looking ahead to the year 2000, we anticipate both a slower growth in population and an aging population. In the mid-1980s, for example, for the first time in our history, the number of people 65 and over exceeded the number of teenagers. And by 1990 the ratio of over-65 people to teenagers will be about 3 to 2.

The *youth* market (roughly grade school ages 5 to 13) carries a three-way marketing impact. First, these children can influence parental purchases. Second, billions of dollars are spent on this group by their parents. Third, these children themselves make purchases of goods and services for their own personal use and satisfaction. Promotional programs are often geared to this market segment. Children's television shows, for instance, are sponsored by cereal, toy, and video-game manufacturers and other advertisers in an effort to develop brand preferences at an early age.

The *teenage* market is recognized as an important one, and yet it has proved to be difficult to reach. The mistake might be in attempting to lump all teenagers into one group. Certainly the 13-to-16 age group is very different from the 17-to-20 age bracket.

Yet marketers must understand teenage consumers because of the size of this market and because its members have a considerable amount of money to spend. It is true that the number of teenagers has declined appreciably since the 1970s. At the same time, going into the 1990s there still will be millions of teenagers with substantial incomes from part-time jobs and two income-earning parents. These youngsters constitute a big market that is pursued by the makers of apparel, cosmetics, autos, stereo records, and other products.[4]

In the 1990s the early *middle-age* population segment (35 to 50) will be an especially large and lucrative market. These people are the products of the post-World War II baby boom and were the rebels of the 1960s and the 1970s. They also were a very big and profitable teenage and young adult market for many companies during those years. Now as they move toward middle age in the 1990s, they are reaching high earning years. Typically, their personal values and life-styles are far different from those found among the people of the same age in previous generations. Already manufacturers are adjusting to these changing demographics. Minnetonka, Colgate, Crest, and other toothpaste makers who had stressed cavity prevention to those people 20 years ago now are producing toothpaste to fight plaque—an adult dental problem. Levi Strauss outfitted the bottom half of the baby boomers' wardrobes 20 years ago. Today this company markets nondenim clothes, office wear, and even blue jeans that are slightly bigger in the hips and seat to accommodate this older and bulging customer.[5]

[4] See Aimée L. Stern, "Companies Target Big-Spending Teens," *Dun's Business Month*, March 1985, p. 48.

[5] See Geoffrey Colvin, "What Will the Baby-Boomers Buy Next?" *Fortune*, Oct. 15, 1984, p. 28.

THE AVERAGE AGE OF OUR POPULATION IS RISING, SO—

- Germaine Monteil cosmetics ads featured a 45-year-old interior designer and mother of three children.
- Sears formed a Mature Outlook, a club that offered discounts to people over 55.
- Wendy's Hamburgers featured three little old ladies in its well-known "Where's the beef?" advertising.
- Johnson & Johnson formulated a hair shampoo, Affinity, for people over 40 and bluntly stated that this shampoo is for brittle, hollowed-out, older hair.
- Gerber, the baby food company, now sells life insurance to older people, using the theme "Gerber now babies the over-50s."
- Levi Strauss markets a three-piece suit and "Levi's for Men" that are more fully cut "to accommodate the guy who has stopped playing football and is now watching it." The clothing is cut "to fit a man's build with a little more room in the seat and thighs."

Source: Adapted in part from Ronald Alsop, "Firms Try New Ways to Tap Over-50 Population," The Wall Street Journal, Aug. 23, 1984. p. 21.

NEW LEE® STONEWASH SEAM JEAN™

Here's a new slant on the soft, easy fit of Stonewash denim—Lee® Seam Jean™ with slanted front pockets and slanted front seams. These jeans know how to head straight for fashion.

THE BRAND THAT FITS.

Young adults are a key market.

At the older end of the age spectrum are two market segments that should not be overlooked. One is the group of people in their fifties and early sixties. This *mature* market is large and financially well off. Its members are at the peak of their earning power and typically no longer have financial responsibility for their children. Thus, this segment is a good target for marketers of high-priced, high-quality products and services.[6]

The other older age group comprises people over 65—a segment that is growing both absolutely and as a percentage of the total population. Manufacturers and middlemen alike are beginning to recognize that people in this age group are logical prospects for small, low-cost housing units, cruises and foreign tours, health products, and cosmetics developed especially for older people. Many firms are also developing promotional programs to appeal to this group because their purchasing power is surprisingly high. Also, the shopping behavior of the over-65 market typically is different from that found in other age segments.[7]

Sex

Sex is an obvious basis for consumer market analysis. Many products are made for use by members of one sex, not both. In many product categories—autos, for example—women and men typically look for different product benefits. Market analysis by sex is also useful because many products have traditionally been purchased by either men only or women only.

However, some of these traditional buying patterns are breaking down, and marketers certainly should be alert to changes involving their products. Not too many years ago, for example, the wife did practically all the grocery shopping for her family, and the husband bought the products and services needed for the automobile. Today, men are frequent food shoppers, and women buy the gas and arrange for repair and maintenance. Many products and activities once considered limited to the male market are now readily accepted by women.

The number of working women (married or single) is increasing dramatically. In the late 1980s well over half of all American women were working outside the home. About three-fourths of women in their twenties were in the labor force, and about one-half of the women with children under 6 years old were working outside the home. By 1990, women will constitute almost one-half of the total United States labor force. These facts are significant to marketers. The life-style and buying behavior of women in the outside labor force are quite different from those of women who do not work away from home.

Family Life Cycle

Frequently, the factor accounting for differences in consumption patterns between two people of the same age and sex is that they are in different life-cycle situations. The concept of the **family life cycle** implies that there are several distinct stages in the life of an ordinary family. A six-stage family cycle, with two alternative stages, is shown in Fig. 5-2. Life-cycle position is also a major determinant of buying behavior. A young couple with two children (the full-nest stage) has quite different needs from

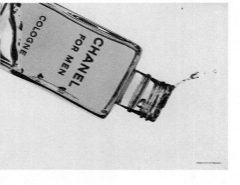

The main market is men, but women may buy it as a gift.

[6]Fabian Linden, "New Money and the Old," *Across the Board*, July–August 1985, pp. 43–49.

[7]See Charles D. Schewe, "Gray America Goes to Market," *Business*, April–June 1985, pp. 3–9. This article also has an excellent bibliography. See also Maria B. Dwight and Harold N. Urman, "Affluent Elderly Is a Unique Segment," *Marketing News*, Aug. 16, 1985, p. 7.

1. Bachelor stage: young, single people

2. Young married couples with no children

3. Full nest I: young married couples with children

ALTERNATIVE STAGES

A. Divorced person without dependent children

B. Young or middle-aged person with dependent children—the single parent.

4. Full nest II: older married couples still with dependent children

5. Empty nest: older married couples with no children living with them

6. Older single people, still working or retired

those of a couple in their mid-fifties with children no longer living at home (the empty-nest stage). A single-parent family (divorced or widowed) with dependent children faces social and economic problems quite different from those of a two-parent family. The financial position and buying behavior of these two families usually are quite different. Typical buying patterns in the various stages are discussed later in this chapter in connection with consumer buying patterns.

FIGURE 5-2
The family life cycle.

Two rapidly growing markets—reflecting our changing life-styles—are called the *singles* and the *mingles*. In 1980 the Census Bureau reported that almost 1 out of every 4 American households consisted of just one person—a **single**. Also, the number of singles households was increasing at a much faster rate than that of family units. Among the reasons for this increase in one-person households are:

- The growing number of working women.
- People marrying at a later age.
- The reduced tendency for single people to live with their parents.
- A rising divorce rate.

The impact that single people of both sexes have on the market is demonstrated by such things as apartments for singles, social clubs for singles, and special tours, cruises, and eating places seeking the patronage of singles. Even in the mundane field of grocery products the growing singles market (including the divorced and widowed) is causing changes by retailers and food processors.[8]

The singles in the 25 to 39 age bracket are especially attractive to marketers because they are such a large group. Also, compared with the population as a whole, this singles group is:

• More affluent.	• More fashion- and appearance-conscious.
• More mobile.	• More active in leisure pursuits.
• More experimental and less conventional.	• More sensitive to social status.

The number of **mingles**—unmarried couples of opposite sex living together—

[8] See Valarie A. Zeithaml, "The New Demographics and Market Fragmentation," *Journal of Marketing,* Summer 1985, pp. 64–75.

Apple and the Apple logo are registered trademarks of Apple Computer Inc.

YOUR CHILD'S FREE GIFT
(A $3.50 value)
This colorful, sturdy Cat in the Hat Bookrack measures 11½″ x 6¼″ x 6½″ and holds up to 15 books.

If not delighted, return the books and keep the bookrack. You owe nothing. But if you keep the books and join the club, you'll receive two delightful new books every four weeks. And you're never obligated to accept any book unless you want to.

So start your child on a more assured, confident future right now. Send no money. Just fill out and mail the order form.

bill you for only $1.95, plus shipping and handling, for all four. And include a Cat in The Hat bookrack, a $3.50 value, free.

One way to reach parents with little kids.

Singles constitute an attractive market.

almost quadrupled between 1970 and 1984, reaching a total of 2 million couples. (The increase was more than *eightfold* for people under 25.) The number of these couples abruptly leveled off in the mid-1980s, and they still represent only a small part (2 percent) of all households. Nevertheless, the social and demographic phenomenon of mingles bears watching by marketers in the future.

Other Demographic Bases for Segmentation

The market for some consumer products is influenced by such factors as education, occupation, religion, or ethnic origin. With an increasing number of people attaining higher levels of **education**, for example, we can expect to see (1) changes in product preferences and (2) buyers with more discriminating taste and higher incomes. **Occupation** may be a more meaningful criterion than income in segmenting some markets. Truck drivers or auto mechanics may earn as much as young retailing executives or college professors. But the buying patterns of the first two are different from those of the second two because of attitudes, interests, and other life-style factors.

For some products, it is quite useful to analyze the population on the basis of **religion** or **ethnic origin**. Religious mores in Utah, for example, affect the markets for tobacco, liquor, and coffee. There is a large market for Polish sausage in some Midwestern areas. People of Mexican descent in the Southwest have some product preferences that are quite different from those of, say, Oriental consumers living on the West Coast.

In some cities ethnic markets are especially large. In fact, minorities—Asians, blacks, Hispanics, and others—constitute over 50 percent of the population in 25 of the nation's largest cities. These cities include Los Angeles, San Antonio, New Orleans, Miami, Atlanta, Baltimore, Washington, D.C., Detroit, and Chicago.

One ethnic group receiving increasing attention because of its large and growing buying potential is the black American market. It contained over 30 million consumers with a combined buying power estimated at more than $100 *billion* in the late 1980s. There is a black consumer market—a *big* market, with plenty of buying power and some individualistic traits that demand the attention of every marketer!

There are distinct differences between the black American and white American markets with regard to socioeconomic characteristics (income, occupation, family structure, education, expenditure patterns, and consumption patterns). To market successfully to black consumers, a company must understand something about their buying behavior and their motivation. Furthermore, this market is not a homogeneous unit any more than any other population segment consisting of 30 million people is. The black market contains subsegments based on income, occupation, geographic location, and so on.[9]

For many products, another ethnic group well worth studying is the 18 million Spanish-speaking (Hispanic) people. This group is large and it is growing at a rapid rate. In fact, by the year 2000, Hispanics are expected to be the largest minority group in the United States, surpassing the blacks in population. The Hispanic market is geographically concentrated in New York City, Miami, California, and the Southwest. This is a relatively accessible market because of its common language, geographic concentration, and relative homogeneity in terms of income. Advertisers in particular may make use of Spanish-language radio stations, television programs, movies, news-

To communicate—speak the language.

[9]For more information on the nature of the black market, see "Special Report—Marketing to Blacks," *Advertising Age*, Dec. 19, 1985, pp. 15ff.

CONSUMER INCOME AND ITS DISTRIBUTION

Nature and Scope of Income

papers, and magazines. At the same time, marketers should be fully aware that this market is not a homogeneous unit, despite its common language. Cubans in Florida have many market characteristics which differ from those of Puerto Ricans in New York. Mexican-Americans in southern Texas are not the same market as Mexican-Americans in southern California.[10]

People alone do not make a market; they must have money to spend. Consequently, income, its distribution, and how it is spent are essential factors in any quantitative market analysis.

What is income? There are so many different concepts of income that it is good to review some definitions. The following outline is actually a "word equation" that shows how the several concepts are related.

National income: Total income from all sources, including employee compensation, corporate profits, and other income

Less: Corporate profits and social security contributions

Plus: Dividends, government transfer payments to persons, and net interest paid by government

Equals:

Personal income: Income from wages, salaries, dividends, rent, interest, businesses and professions, social security, and farming

Less: All personal federal, state, and local taxes

Equals:

Disposable personal income: The amount available for personal consumption expenditures and savings

Less: (1) Essential expenditures for food, clothing, household utilities, and local transportation and (2) fixed expenditures for rent, house mortgage payments, insurance, and installment debt payments

Equals:

Discretionary purchasing power: The amount of disposable personal income that is available after fixed commitments (debt repayments, rent) and essential household needs are taken care of. As compared with disposable personal income, discretionary purchasing power is a better (more sensitive) indicator of consumers' ability to spend for *nonessentials*.

In addition, we hear the terms "money income," "real income," and "psychic income." **Money income** is the amount a person receives in actual cash or checks

---

[10]For more information on the nature of the Hispanic market, see Joel Saegert, Robert J. Hoover, and Mary Tharpe Hilger, "Characteristics of Mexican-American Consumers," *Journal of Consumer Research*, June 1985, pp. 104–109; Madhav Segal and Lionel Sosa, "Marketing to the Hispanic Community," *California Management Review*, Fall 1983, pp. 120–134; and "Marketing to Hispanics—A Special Report," *Advertising Age*, Feb. 27, 1986, pp. 12–13.

One way to use your discretionary income.

for wages, salaries, rents, interest, and dividends. **Real income** is what the money income will buy in goods and services; it is purchasing power. If a person's money income rises 5 percent in 1 year but the cost of purchases increases 8 percent on the average, then real income decreases about 3 percent. **Psychic income** is an intangible, but highly important, income factor related to comfortable climate, a satisfying neighborhood, enjoyment of one's job, and so on. Some people prefer to take less real income so they can live in a part of the country that features a fine climate—greater psychic income.

As measured by income, the American market has grown fantastically during the past three decades. Disposable personal income rose from $350 billion in 1960 to about $2.8 *trillion* in 1985. This is an increase of 700 percent in 25 years (1960) and 300 percent in the past 15 years (1970). Discretionary purchasing power also increased at just a slightly lower rate during the same time periods. Even after allowing for the rise in prices and the increase in total population, the advances in income are very substantial.

Income Distribution

To get full value from an analysis of income, we should study the variations and trends in the distribution of income among regions and among population groups. Regional income data are especially helpful in pinpointing the particular market to which a firm wishes to appeal. Income data on cities and even on sections within cities may indicate the best locations for shopping centers and suburban branches of downtown stores.

The income revolution that has been going on in the United States in recent decades has dramatically changed the profile of household income distribution. (See Table 5.1.) Over the past 25 to 35 years, there has been a tremendous growth in the middle-income and upper-income markets and a decrease in the percentage of low-income groups.

Looking ahead, marketers expect this trend to continue. By 1995, more than one-fourth of the households in the United States are expected to have incomes of $35,000 or more, based on 1980 dollars. The over-$50,000 households alone will increase 67 percent during the 1980s. This anticipated increase in the number of affluent households is the result of several factors. These include (1) the large growth

Marketing Significance of Income Data

TABLE 5-1 DISTRIBUTION OF HOUSEHOLD INCOME, 1980–1995, IN 1982 DOLLARS

Households earning under $10,000 a year are expected to decline as a percent of total households. What are the marketing implications in the projected increase from 16 to 28 percent in the over-$40,000 households?

Annual household income	% of households				% change, 1980–1995
	1980	1985	1990	1995	
Less than $10,000	23	22	21	20	−13
$10,000–$19,999	26	25	22	21	−19
$20,000–$29,999	21	20	19	17	−19
$30,000–$39,999	14	14	14	14	0
$40,000–$49,999	8	9	10	10	+25
$50,000 and over	8	10	14	18	+125
Total	100%	100%	100%	100%	

Source: *American Demographics*, April 1984, p. 50.

in the 25-to-45 age group, (2) the increase in dual-income families, and (3) the wider distribution of inherited wealth.[11] We still shall have low-income families. However, far fewer will be below the poverty level, even though that level (by government definition) is moving up, in recognition of both inflation and our more abundant society.

The declining percentage of families in the poverty bracket, coupled with the sharp increases in the upper-income groups, presages an explosive growth in discretionary purchasing power. And, as discretionary income increases, so too does the demand for items that once were considered luxuries.

The middle-income market is a big market and a growing market, and it has forced many changes in marketing strategy. Many stores that once appealed to low-income groups have traded up to the huge middle-income market. These stores are upgrading the quality of the products they carry and are offering additional services.

In spite of the considerable increase in disposable income in the past 30 years, many households are still in the low-income bracket or find their higher incomes inadequate to fulfill all their wants. Furthermore, many customers are willing to forgo services in order to get lower prices. One consequence of this market feature has been the development of self-service retail outlets and discount houses.[12]

Earlier in this chapter we noted the dramatic increase in the number of working wives. This demographic factor also has had a tremendous impact on family income

[11]See William Lazer, "How Rising Affluence Will Reshape Markets," *American Demographics*, February 1984, pp. 17–21; and "Affluent Market Growing but Elusive," *Marketing News*, Jan. 4, 1985, p. 54.

[12]See Hank Gilman, "Selling to the Poor: Retailers That Target Low-Income Shoppers Are Growing Rapidly," *The Wall Street Journal*, June 24, 1985, p. 1.

levels. Today in the United States, there are substantially more two-income families than families with only one provider. This increase in two-income families has significant marketing and sociological implications. Dual incomes generally enable a family to offset the ravages of inflation. But more than that, two incomes often enable a family to buy within a short time the things that their parents worked years to acquire.

CONSUMER EXPENDITURE PATTERNS

How consumers' income is spent is a major market determinant for most products and services. Consequently, marketers need to study consumer *spending patterns*, as well as the *distribution* of consumer income. Marketers also should be aware of the significant *shifts* in family spending patterns that have occurred over the past two or three decades. Energy costs, inflation, and heavy consumer debt loads have had a major impact on our spending patterns. As examples, let's consider just a few of the changes in spending patterns that have occurred between the 1960s and the late 1980s. Over that time span, families have *increased* the percentage of their total expenditures going for housing, health, and utilities. Spending (as a percentage of total) has *decreased* for food, beverages, clothing, and home expenses (except utilities).

But expenditure patterns are not the same for all families. These patterns vary considerably, depending upon family income, life-cycle stage, and other factors.

Relation to Stage of Family Life Cycle

Consumer expenditure patterns are influenced by the consumer's stage in the life cycle. There are striking contrasts in spending patterns between, say, people in the full-nest stage with very young children and people in the empty-nest stage. Table 5-2 summarizes the behavioral influences and the spending patterns for families in each stage of the cycle. (This table expands the number of stages shown earlier in Fig. 5-2.) Young married couples with no children typically devote large shares of their income to clothing, autos, and recreation. When children start arriving, expenditure patterns shift as many young families buy and furnish a home. Families with teenagers find larger portions of the budget going for food, clothing, and educational needs. Families in the empty-nest stage, especially when the head is still in the labor force, are attractive to marketers. Typically, these families have more discretionary buying power.[13]

Relation to Income Distribution

The size of a family's income is an obvious determinant of how that family spends its income. Consequently, marketers should analyze the expenditure patterns of the various income classes (under $5,000, $10,000 to $15,000, and so on). Some of the findings from Department of Labor studies of consumer expenditures are summarized below. These findings suggest the type of information that marketers might get from analyses of spending patterns by income groups.

- There is a high degree of uniformity in the expenditure patterns of *middle-income* spending units. As we shall note in Chapter 6, however, social-class structure is often a more meaningful criterion for determining expenditure patterns.

[13]For a view of the family life cycle that reflects the growing numbers of single adults, with or without dependent children, see Patrick E. Murphy and William A. Staples, "A Modernized Family Life Cycle," *Journal of Consumer Research*, June 1979, pp. 12–22.

TABLE 5-2 BEHAVIORAL INFLUENCES AND BUYING PATTERNS, BY FAMILY LIFE-CYCLE STAGE

Bachelor stage; young single parent not living at home	Newly married couples; young, no children	Full nest I; youngest child under 6	Full nest II; youngest child 6 or over	Full nest III; older married couples with dependent children	Empty nest I; older married couples, no children living with them, head in labor force	Empty nest II; older married couples, no children living at home, head retired	Solitary survivor, in labor force	Solitary survivor, retired
Few financial burdens. Fashion opinion leaders. Recreation-oriented. Buy: Basic kitchen equipment, basic furniture, cars, equipment for the mating game, vacations.	Better off financially than they will be in near future. Highest purchase rate and highest average purchase of durables. Buy: Cars, refrigerators, stoves, sensible and durable furniture, vacations.	Home purchasing at peak. Liquid assets low. Dissatisfied with financial position and amount of money saved. Interested in new products. Like advertised products. Buy: Washers, dryers, TV sets, baby food, chest rubs and cough medicine, vitamins, dolls, wagons, sleds, skates.	Financial position better. Some wives work. Less influenced by advertising. Buy larger-sized packages, multiple-unit deals. Buy: Many foods, cleaning materials, bicycles, music lessons, pianos.	Financial position still better. Many wives work. Some children get jobs. Hard to influence with advertising. High average purchase of durables. Buy: New, more tasteful furniture, auto travel, nonnecessary appliances, boats, dental services, magazines.	Home ownership at peak. Most satisfied with financial position and money saved. Interested in travel, recreation, self-education. Make gifts and contributions. Not interested in new products. Buy: Vacations, luxuries, home improvements.	Drastic cut in income. Keep home. Buy: Medical appliances, medical care, products which aid health, sleep, and digestion.	Income still good but likely to sell home.	Same medical and product needs as other retired group; drastic cut in income. Special need for attention, affection, and security.

Source: William D. Wells and George Gubar, "Life Cycle Concept in Marketing Research," *Journal of Marketing Research*, November 1966, p. 362.

- For each product category, there is a considerable *absolute* increase in dollars spent as income rises (or, more correctly, as we compare one income group with a higher income group). In other words, people in a given income bracket spend significantly more *dollars* in each product category than those in lower brackets. However, the lower-income households devote a larger *percentage* of their total expenditures to some product categories, such as food. Marketers are probably more concerned with the total *dollars* available from each income group than with the *percentage* share of total expenditures.

- In each successively higher income group, the amount spent for food declines as a *percentage* of total expenditures.
- The *percentage* of expenditures devoted to the total of housing, utilities, and home operation remains reasonably constant in the middle- and high-income brackets.
- Amounts spent for medical and personal care remain a reasonably constant *percentage* of total expenditures, regardless of income.
- The share of expenditures going for automotive products and services tends to increase as incomes increase in low- and middle-income groups. The proportion levels off or drops a bit in higher-income brackets.
- In each successively higher income group (with one exception), a greater share of total family expenditures goes for clothing.

Generalizations such as these provide a broad background against which marketing executives can analyze the market for their particular product or service. People with needs to satisfy and money to spend, however, must be *willing* to spend before we can say a market exists. Consequently, in the next chapter we shall look into consumer motivation and buying behavior—the "willingness-to-buy" factor in our definition of a market.

SUMMARY

A sound marketing program starts with the identification and analysis of the target market for a product or service. A market is people with needs or wants, money to spend, and the willingness to spend it. In preparation for target-market selection, it is helpful first to divide the total market into ultimate-consumer and industrial-user submarkets. The makeup of the population—its distribution and composition—has a major effect on target-market selection. For some products it is useful to analyze population on a regional basis. Another useful division is by urban, suburban, and rural segments. In this context, the bulk of the population is concentrated in metropolitan areas. Moreover, these areas are expanding and joining together in several parts of the country.

The major age groups of the population make up another significant basis for market analysis—young adults, teenagers, the over-65 group, and so on. The stage of the family life cycle influences the market for many products. Other demographic bases for market analysis include education, occupation, religion, and ethnic origin.

Consumer income—especially disposable income and discretionary income—is a meaningful measure of buying power and market potential. The distribution of income affects the market for many products. Income distribution has shifted considerably during the past 25 years. Today, a much greater percentage of families are in the over-$35,000 bracket and a much smaller percentage earn under $10,000. A family's income level and life cycle are, in part, determinants of its spending patterns.

KEY TERMS AND CONCEPTS

Market 92
Target market 92
Market aggregation 92
Market segmentation 92

Ultimate consumers 92
Industrial users 92
Demography 93
Population distribution by regions 93

Urban-suburban-rural distribution 94
Metropolitan Statistical Area (MSA) 94
Primary Metropolitan Statistical Area (PMSA) 95
Consolidated Metropolitan Statistical Area (CMSA) 95
Population distribution by age group 96
Market segmentation by sex 98
Stages in the family life cycle 98
Disposable personal income 102
Discretionary purchasing power 102
Types of income: money, real, psychic 102
Income distribution 103
Expenditure patterns 105

QUESTIONS AND PROBLEMS ■

1. Give several examples of products whose market demand would be particularly affected by each of the following population factors:
   a. Regional distribution.
   b. Marital status.
   c. Sex.
   d. Age.
   e. Urban-rural-suburban distribution.

2. Cite some sectional differences in product preferences caused by factors other than climate.

3. Suppose you are marketing automobiles. How is your marketing mix likely to differ when marketing to each of the following market segments?
   a. High school students.
   b. Husbands.
   c. Blue-collar workers.
   d. Homemakers.
   e. Young single adults.

4. What users' benefits would you stress in advertising each of the following three products to each of the three markets?

   Product
   a. Stereo record player.
   b. Toothpaste.
   c. 10-day Caribbean cruise.
   d. Birthday cards.
   e. Outdoor barbecue grills.

   Market
   a. School teachers.
   b. Retired people.
   c. Working women.

5. Using the demographic and income segmentation bases discussed in this chapter, describe the segment likely to be the best market for:
   a. Snow skis.
   b. Good French wines.
   c. Power hand tools.

6. List three of the major population trends noted in this chapter (for instance, a growing segment of the population is over 65 years of age). Then carefully explain how *each* of the following types of retail stores might be affected by *each* of the trends.
   a. Supermarket.
   b. Sporting goods store.
   c. Drugstore.
   d. Restaurant.

7. In which stage of the life cycle are families likely to be the best prospects for each of the following products or services?
   a. Braces on teeth.
   b. Suntan lotion.
   c. Second car in the family.
   d. Vitamin pills.
   e. Refrigerators.
   f. Life insurance.
   g. Jogging suits.
   h. 46-day Mediterranean cruise.

8. In what ways has the rise in disposable personal income since 1960 influenced the marketing programs of a typical department store? A supermarket?

9. Is psychic income a concept applicable to groups or only to an individual? Can psychic income be measured in a quantitative manner?

10. Give examples of products whose demand is substantially influenced by changes in discretionary purchasing power.

11. Describe some of the effects that (*a*) inflation and (*b*) a recession have on consumers' spending patterns. What can marketers do to adjust to these situations?

6

SOCIAL-GROUP AND PSYCHOLOGICAL INFLUENCES ON BUYER BEHAVIOR

CHAPTER GOALS

In Chapter 5 we discussed the population and buying-power (income) components of a market. In this chapter we consider consumers' *willingness to buy,* as influenced by their motivation, perception, social environment, and psychological forces. After studying this chapter, you should understand:

- The roles of motivation and perception in consumer behavior.
- Culture as an influence on perceptions.
- The influence of social classes on buyer behavior.
- The effects of small reference groups on buyer behavior.
- Family buying behavior.
- The psychological forces that influence buyer behavior, especially the consumer's learning experiences, personality, attitudes and beliefs, and self-concept.
- The decision-making process in buying, especially patronage buying motives and postpurchase behavior (cognitive dissonance).

B ill and Halina Spaulding are a young married couple living in San Francisco. They have no children and both of them are working outside the home. They are an example of young urban professionals. In the course of doing the weekly grocery shopping at a local supermarket late on a Friday afternoon, Bill recently bought a sampler package of Celestial Seasonings Herb Tea. The package consisted of 24 tea bags—4 each of 6 different blends of tea: Red Zinger, Morning Thunder, Roastaroma, Chamomile, Mo's 24, and Mellow Mint. To the casual observer—and perhaps even to Bill himself—this may have been a simple, routine purchase. Yet this seemingly simple buying action was the result of decisions made on several issues. Why purchase Celestial Seasonings instead of Lipton's, Bigelow, or some other brand of herb tea? Why buy herb tea instead of "regular" Ceylon tea? Why buy an assortment instead of a package consisting of only one blend? Why buy tea bags instead of instant tea or a package of unbagged tea leaves? Why shop at that particular store, and why on a Friday instead of a Saturday?

In this chapter we try to shed some light on consumer behavior to help explain buying decisions. First, we consider how our buying behavior is influenced by our motivations and perceptions. Next we discuss how our perceptions are determined to a great extent by our culture and by the various groups of people with whom we associate. Then our focus shifts to the psychological forces that influence our perceptions. In the final section, we tie together these discussions as we examine the decision-making process that we go through when making a purchase.

We have reasonably good quantitative data on the number of people living in each geographic region, what their incomes are, and so on. For some products (snow shovels, oil filters), demographic and economic factors alone may explain why a consumer bought the product. Most consumer purchases, however, are also likely to be influenced by psychological or sociological factors.

We know very little about what goes on in a buyer's mind before, during, and after a purchase. Sometimes the explanation for buyers' behavior is not even discernible to the buyers themselves. To illustrate, buying motives may be grouped on three different levels depending upon the consumers' awareness of them and their willingness to divulge them. At one level, buyers recognize, and are quite willing to talk about, their motives for buying certain products. At a second level, they are aware of their reasons for buying but will not admit them to others. (A man may buy a backyard swimming pool because he feels it adds to his social position in the neighborhood. Or a woman may buy a fur coat to keep up with her peer group. But when questioned about their motives, they offer other reasons that they think will be more socially acceptable.) The most difficult motives to uncover are those at the *third* level, where even the buyers themselves do not know the real factors motivating their buying actions.

Motivation

A purchase is rarely the result of a single motive. Furthermore, various motives may conflict with one another. In buying a new dress, a woman may want to (1) please herself, (2) please her boyfriend, (3) be considered a fashion leader by other women in her social circle, and (4) strive for economy. To do all these things in one purchase is truly a difficult assignment. Also, a person's buying behavior changes over a period of time because of changes in income, changes in life-cycle stage, and other factors.

If we add to this complexity the countless variations occurring because each consumer has a unique personality, our task of understanding consumer behavior may seem an impossible dream. Yet try we must, because an understanding of buyer behavior is critical to the success of a marketing program. Fortunately, marketing people, working with behavioral scientists, have been able to develop some generalizations about what influences consumer buying behavior.

To understand why consumers behave as they do, we first must ask why a person acts at all. The answer is, "Because he or she is motivated." That is, all behavior starts with motivation. A **motive** (or drive) is a stimulated need that an individual seeks to satisfy. Thus hunger, a need for security, and a desire for prestige are examples of motives.

In discussing the behavioral forces that influence consumer buying activity, our model will be as follows: One or more motives within a person trigger behavior toward a goal that is expected to bring satisfaction.

It is important to note that need must be *aroused or stimulated* before it becomes a motive. People sometimes have needs that are dormant and therefore do not activate behavior because these needs are not sufficiently intense. That is, they have not been aroused. The source of this arousal may be internal (we get hungry) or environmental (we see an ad for food). Or just thinking about a need (food) may cause arousal of that need (hunger).

CLASSIFICATION OF MOTIVES

No single classification of motives is generally accepted by psychologists, simply because we do not know enough about human motivation. However, psychologists generally do agree that motives can be grouped into two broad categories. They are (1) aroused **biogenic needs** (such as the needs for food and bodily comfort), which arise from *physiological* states of tension, and (2) aroused **psychogenic needs** (such as the needs for affection and self-respect), which arise from *psychological* states of tension.

A. H. Maslow has formulated a useful theory of motivation. He calls it a "holistic-dynamic" theory because it fuses the points of view of different schools of psychological thought. It also conforms to known clinical, observational, and experimental facts.[1] Maslow identified a hierarchy of five levels of needs, arrayed in the order in which a person seeks to gratify them. This hierarchy is shown in Fig. 6-1.

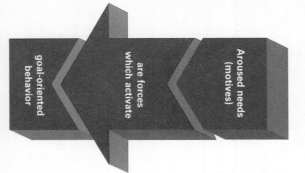

Aroused needs
(motives)

are forces
which activate

goal-oriented
behavior

---

[1] A. H. Maslow, *Motivation and Personality*, Harper & Row, Publishers, Inc., New York, 1954, pp. 80–106.

FIGURE 6-1
Maslow's hierarchy of needs.

Which of Maslow's levels of needs does this ad appeal to?

Maslow contended that people remain at one level until all their needs at that level are satisfied. Then new needs emerge on the next higher level. To illustrate, as long as a person is hungry or thirsty, the physiological (biogenic) needs dominate. Once they have been satisfied, the needs in the safety category become important. When safety needs have been largely gratified, new (and higher-level) needs arise, and so on.

For the relatively few people who move through all five levels, even to fulfilling a need for self-actualization, Maslow identified two additional classes of cognitive needs:

- The need to know and understand.
- The need for aesthetic satisfaction (beauty).

Maslow recognized that in real life there is more flexibility than his model seems to imply. Actually, a normal person is most likely to be working toward need satisfaction on several levels at the same time. And rarely are all needs on a given level ever fully satisfied.

While the Maslow construct has much to offer us, it still leaves some unanswered questions and disagreements. For one thing, there is no consideration of multiple motives for the same behavior. Thus, a teacher may go on a ship's cruise to better her knowledge of foreign countries, to meet new people, and to rest her frazzled nerves. Other problems not fitting our model are (1) identical behavior by several people resulting from quite different motives and (2) quite different behavior resulting from identical motives.

Perception

A motive is an aroused need. It, in turn, acts as a force that *activates* behavior intended to satisfy that aroused need. But what *influences* or *shapes* this behavior? What determines the direction or path this behavior takes? The answer is our perceptions. We define **perception** as the process whereby we receive stimuli (information) through our five senses, we recognize this information, and then we assign a meaning to it. In other words, perception is the meaning we give to stimuli, or the way we interpret stimuli.

This interpretation, or meaning, that we attribute to stimuli—that is, our perceptions—is shaped by our sociocultural environment and by psychological conditions within us. Our behavior, in turn, is determined by what stimuli we respond to and how we interpret those stimuli. That is, our behavior is determined by our perceptions.

Every day an almost infinite number of marketing stimuli exist that conceivably we could be exposed to. In reality, however, a process of **selectivity** that limits our perceptions is occurring continuously. As an illustration, consider that:

- We are exposed to only a portion of all marketing stimuli (products, ads, stores). We cannot read every magazine or visit every store. Or we perceive only part of what we are exposed to. We can read a newspaper and not notice an ad. (This is selective exposure.)
- We may alter information when it is inconsistent with our beliefs or attitudes. Thus, someone may say, "I don't believe smoking is hazardous to my health." (This is selective distortion.)
- We retain only part of what we selectively perceive. We may read an ad but later forget it. (This is selective retention.)
- We act upon only part of what we retain. (This is selective action.)

There are many marketing implications in this selectivity process. To illustrate, if a marketing stimulus—a product or a store—falls outside your range of selective perception, then for you that product or store does not exist. In another situation, a given product stimulus such as a videocassette recorder (VCR) may be perceived quite differently by various consumers. A child perceives a VCR as a source of entertainment. Mother may view it as a baby-sitter, a source of information, and a teacher for her child. Father may view it as an overpriced luxury that prevents him from buying a new outboard motor. (The color TV set was perfectly okay, as he perceived it.)

Marketers cannot afford the expense of unlimited exposure of their marketing stimuli—products, ads, stores, etc. Consequently, they strive for the selective exposure that will fall within the perception range of the target market. This means, for example, carefully selecting the right stores to carry the product or the right magazines to carry the ads. In the case of advertising stimuli, the message must be sufficiently meaningful and strong to survive the customers' selective retention processes. Thus, the seller may run an extra large ad or a color ad placed in a sea of black-and-white ads. In Chrysler's TV commercials, Lee Iacocca (the company's president) came across as a credible, sincere, and consequently persuasive speaker.

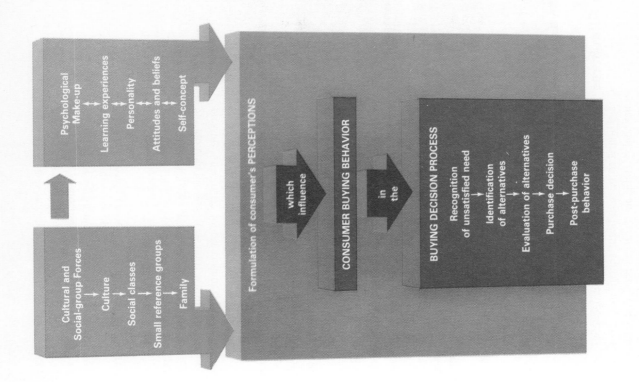

FIGURE 6-2
Sociocultural and psychological forces that influence consumers' buying behavior.

CULTURAL
INFLUENCES

■

**Definition of Culture
and Cultural Influence**

The structure for the remainder of our discussion of consumer buying behavior in this chapter is illustrated in Fig. 6-2. How we perceive things—and how we think, believe, and act—are determined to a great extent by the various groups of people with whom we interrelate. All the social-group influences on consumer buying behavior start with the *culture* in which the consumer lives.

A **culture** is the complex of symbols and artifacts created by a given society and handed down from generation to generation as determinants and regulators of human

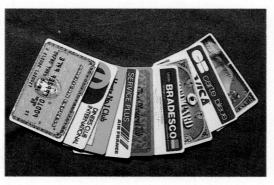

behavior. The symbols may be intangible (attitudes, beliefs, values, languages, religions) or tangible (tools, housing, products, works of art). A culture implies a totally learned and "handed-down" way of life. It does *not* include instinctive biological acts (eating, eliminating body wastes, and sexual relationships) can be culturally established. Thus everybody gets hungry, but what people eat and how they act to satisfy the hunger drive will vary among cultures.

Actually, much of our behavior is culturally determined. Our sociocultural institutions (family, schools, churches, and languages) provide behavioral guidelines. Years ago, Kluckhohn observed: "Culture . . . regulates our lives at every turn. From the moment we are born until we die there is constant conscious and unconscious pressure upon us to follow certain types of behavior that other men have created for us."[2] This concept still holds true today.

Cultural influences do change over time, as old patterns gradually give way to the new. During the past 10 to 25 years in the United States, cultural changes—that is, life-style changes—of far-reaching magnitude have been occurring. Marketing executives must be alert to these changing life-styles so that they can adjust their planning to be in step with, or even a little ahead of, the times. In Chapter 2 we mentioned some of these cultural changes when we discussed social and cultural forces as an environmental factor influencing a company's marketing system. Now at this point we shall simply summarize just a few of the sociocultural changes that significantly affect consumer buying behavior.[3]

- From a thrift and savings ethic to spending freely and buying on credit.
- From a work ethic to self-indulgence and having fun.
- From a husband-dominated family to equality in husband-wife roles; or, in a broader context, the changing role of women.
- From emphasis on *quantity* of goods to emphasis on *quality* of life.
- From self-reliance to reliance on government and other institutions.
- From postponed gratification to immediate gratification.
- A concern about the pollution of our natural environment.
- A concern for safety in our products and in our occupations.
- A concern for the conservation of irreplaceable resources.

Subcultures

Any time there is a culture as heterogeneous as the one in the United States, there are bound to be significant subcultures. These are based upon factors such as race, nationality, religion, or urban-rural distribution. Some of these were recognized in Chapter 5 when we analyzed the demographic market forces. In the 1990s, increasing

---

[2]Clyde Kluckhohn, "The Concept of Culture," in Richard Kluckhohn (ed.), *Culture and Behavior*, The Free Press, New York, 1962, p. 26.

[3]For some major life-style trends and how marketers can react to them, see Ronald D. Michman, "New Directions for Lifestyle Behavior Patterns," *Business Horizons*, July–August 1984, pp. 59–64; and William Lazer, "Turning Changing Consumers into Profitable Market Opportunities," *Sales & Marketing Management*, July 25, 1983, pp. A-30ff.

Cultural Change

attention will be paid to behavioral influences stemming from *racial subcultures*—black, Hispanic, Oriental, American Indian, and others.

Blacks constitute a major racial subculture in the United States. However, we need to recognize that the so-called black market is in reality a series of separate segments based on demographic, economic, psychological, and sociological factors, just as are white markets. The fact that blacks have experienced social constraints in the areas of housing, jobs, and education has influenced their buying behavior.

Hispanics constitute the other large racial subculture in the United States. In fact, population forecasts predict that they will outnumber blacks in this country before the end of this century. Again, there is no such thing as *the* Hispanic market. Instead, this subculture is a series of separate market segments based on differentiating factors, just as in the white and black markets.[4]

In the 1890s immigrants to the United States came largely from Europe. In the 1990s they will come primarily from Asia and Latin America. In West Coast cities we have had concentrations of Chinese and Japanese for over a century. What is new today are the neighborhoods with growing numbers of people from Korea, Vietnam, or Thailand. These new ethnic subcultures will furnish still another set of market segments with different behavioral characteristics that must be understood by firms wishing to sell to these people.

This store is targeting a major subcultural market.

SOCIAL-GROUP INFLUENCES

Consumers' perceptions and buying behavior are also influenced by the social groups to which they belong. These groups include the large social classes and smaller reference groups. The smallest, yet usually the strongest, social-group influence is a person's family.

Influence of Social Class

Social classes do exist in the United States. And people's buying behavior is often more strongly influenced by the class to which they belong, or to which they aspire, than by their income alone. The idea of a social-class structure and the terms *upper*, *middle*, and *lower* class may be repugnant to many Americans. However, the sociologists who identify the class structure and the marketers who use it do not impute value judgments to it. We do not claim that the so-called upper class is superior to, or happier than, the middle class—only that both do exist.

Many years ago two respected sociologists, W. Lloyd Warner and Paul Lunt, directed a study that identified a six-class system within the social structure of a small town.[5] A study made some years later in Chicago, under Professor Warner's direction, concluded that essentially the same social-class structure found in small towns also existed in large metropolitan centers.[6]

[4]For a discussion of black and Hispanic cultural influences on consumer buying behavior, along with a wealth of footnote references, see James F. Engel, Roger D. Blackwell, and Paul W. Miniard, *Consumer Behavior*, 5th ed., Dryden Press, Hinsdale, Ill., 1986, pp. 410–423.

[5]See W. Lloyd Warner and Paul Lunt, *The Social Life of a Modern Community*, Yale University Press, New Haven, Conn., 1941; and W. Lloyd Warner, Marchia Meeker, and Kenneth Eells, *Social Class in America*, Science Research Associates, Inc., Chicago, 1949.

[6]See Pierre Martineau, "Social Classes and Spending Behavior," *Journal of Marketing*, October 1958, pp. 121–130.

During the decades following Warner's studies, we experienced considerable social turbulence in America, particularly in the 1960s and 1970s. Also there have been significant changes in family demographics, income distribution, and personal life-styles. Consequently, it is reasonable to ask whether the concept of a social-class system is relevant or useful to marketing executives in the late 1980s. Clearly the answer is "yes." More recent research shows that a social-class structure still exists today, and it is *not* very different from the earlier one described by Warner.

A social-class structure currently useful to marketing managers is one developed by Richard Coleman and Lee Rainwater, two respected researchers in social-class theory. The placement of people in this structure is determined primarily by their *education, occupation, and type and neighborhood of residence.*[7]

Note that "amount of income" is *not* one of the placement criteria. There may be a general relationship between amount of income and social class—people in the upper classes usually have higher incomes than people in the lower classes. But *within* each social class there typically is a wide range of incomes. Also, the same amount of income may be earned by families in different social classes.

For purposes of marketing planning and analysis, marketing executives and researchers often divide the total consumer market into five social classes. These classes and their characteristics, as adapted from the Warner and Coleman structures previously footnoted, are summarized below. The percentages are only approximations and may vary slightly from one city to another.

SOCIAL CLASSES AND THEIR CHARACTERISTICS

The **upper class**, about 2 percent of the population, includes two groups: (1) the socially prominent "old families" of inherited wealth and (2) the "new rich" of the corporate executives, owners of large businesses, and wealthy professionals. They live in large homes in the best neighborhoods and display a sense of social responsibility. They buy expensive products and services, but they do not conspicuously display their purchases. They patronize exclusive shops.

The **upper-middle class**, about 12 percent of the population, is composed of moderately successful business and professional people, and owners of medium-sized companies. They are well educated, have a strong drive for success, and want their children to do well. Their purchases are more conspicuous than those in the upper class. This class buys status symbols that show their success, yet are socially acceptable. They live well, belong to private clubs, and support the arts and various social causes.

The **lower-middle class**, about 32 percent of the population, consists of the white-collar workers—office workers, most sales people, teachers, technicians, and small-business owners. The **upper-lower class**, about 38 percent of the population, is the blue-collar "working class" of factory workers, semiskilled workers, and service people. Because these two groups together represent America's mass market and thus are so important to most marketers, we have described their characteristics in more detail in the nearby boxed exhibit.

[7]See Richard P. Coleman, "The Continuing Significance of Social Class to Marketing," *Journal of Consumer Research*, December 1983, pp. 265–280.

TWO SOCIAL CLASSES THAT TOGETHER CONSTITUTE "AMERICA'S MASS MARKET"

Middle class (also called the lower-middle class):

This is the white-collar world of office workers, most sales people, teachers, and owners of small businesses. This class is the source of America's work ethic, moral code, and drive "to be better than you are." This is the class that strives for "respectability"—its members want to do the "right thing" and buy "what's popular." They live in well-cared-for homes in middle-level neighborhoods, and they save to send their kids to college. When their incomes increase, they seek a "better home," in a "nicer neighborhood," with "good schools."

They are upwardly mobile as they try to copy people in the upper classes. This "upward gaze" is one feature that distinguishes the middle class from the working class. Other class distinctions are that the middle class is more future-oriented, has broader horizons, and is more self-confident and willing to take risks.

One significant change that has occurred in this class over the past 30 years is that people have "loosened up" quite a bit and are openly enjoying life. They are not as "stuffy" and as totally conformist as in years gone by.

Working class (also called the upper-lower class):

This is the blue-collar world of factory workers, skilled and semiskilled crafts-men, and service workers. These people are "family folk" who depend heavily on the immediate family and relatives for economic and emotional support. The family structure still maintains the traditional sharp division of male-female sex roles and stereotyping. These people, compared to the middle class, will live in a smaller house in a less desirable neighborhood. However, they will have a larger car, more kitchen appliances, and a bigger television set. They spend more on sports—ball games, bowling, hunting, fishing.

Working-class horizons—socially, geographically, and psychologically—are more limited compared with those of the middle class. The working-class locational narrowness shows up in diverse ways—"their neighborhood" is important to them; in sports, they closely follow local teams; in TV news, they prefer local items over national or international events; for autos, they buy American cars; for vacations, they stay at home or go to a nearby resort area. These people, even with good incomes, are cautious and very concerned about security. Yet they tend to be short-run oriented—living for the present.

Source: Adapted from Richard P. Coleman, "The Continuing Significance of Social Class," *Journal of Consumer Research,* December 1983, pp. 270–272.

The **lower-lower class,** about 16 percent of the population, is composed of unskilled workers, the chronically unemployed, unassimilated racial immigrants, and people frequently on welfare. They typically are poorly educated, with low incomes,

Where America's mass market shops.

and live in substandard houses and neighborhoods. They tend to live for the present and often do not purchase wisely. The public tends to differentiate (within this class) between the "working poor" and the "welfare poor."

MARKETING SIGNIFICANCE OF SOCIAL CLASSES

Now let's summarize the basic conclusions from social-class research that are highly significant for marketing:

- A social-class system still does exist in small towns and in large metropolitan centers. And there are substantial differences among classes regarding their buying behavior.
- Far-reaching psychological differences exist among the classes. Thus the classes respond differently to a seller's marketing program. (See the thumbnail sketch of America's mass market in the boxed exhibit.)
- For many products, class membership is a more significant determinant of buyer behavior than is income.

This last point—the relative importance of income versus social class—has generated considerable controversy. There is an old saying that "a rich man is just a poor man with money—and that, given the same amount of money, a poor man would behave exactly like a rich man." Studies of social-class structure have proved that this statement simply is not true. Two people, each earning the same income but belonging to different social classes, will have quite different buying patterns. They will shop at different stores, expect different treatment from sales people, and buy different products and even different brands. Also, when a family's income increases because more family members get a job, this increase almost never results in a change in the family's social class.

A word of caution, however: Buying behavior may very well be different at the various income levels *within* each social class or occupational group. For example, a carpenter's family with an income of $25,000 a year has consumption patterns that are different from those of another carpenter's family whose annual income is $40,000. Thus a more useful basis for market analysis might be some index that combines both social class and income.

Influence of Small Reference Groups

Small-group influence on buyer behavior introduces the concept of reference-group theory, which we borrow from sociology. A **reference group** may be defined as a group of people who influence a person's attitudes, values, and behavior. Each group develops its own standards of behavior that then serve as guides, or "frames of reference," for the individual members. The members share these values and are expected to conform to the group's normative behavioral patterns.

Consumer behavior is influenced by the small groups to which consumers belong or aspire to belong. These groups may include family, fraternal organizations, labor unions, church groups, athletic teams, or a circle of close friends or neighbors. Studies have shown that personal advice in face-to-face groups is much more effective as a behavioral determinant than advertising in newspapers, television, or other mass media. That is, in selecting products or changing brands, we are more likely to be influenced by word-of-mouth advertising from satisfied customers in our reference group. This is true especially when the speaker is considered to be knowledgeable regarding the particular product.

A person may agree with all the standards set by the group or only some of them. Moderate Republicans or Democrats may not agree with *all* the political views of their local party unit. Also, a person does not have to belong to a group to be influenced by it. Young people frequently pattern their dress and other behavior after that of an older group which the younger ones aspire to join.

Another useful finding pertains to the flow of information between and within groups. For years marketers operated in conformity with the "snob appeal" theory. This is the idea that if you can get social leaders and high-income groups to use your products, the mass market will also buy them. The assumption has been that influence follows a *vertical* path, starting at levels of high status and moving downward through successive levels of groups. Contrary to this popular assumption, studies by Katz and Lazarsfeld and by others have emphasized the *horizontal* nature of opinion leadership. Influence emerges on each *level* of the socioeconomic scale, moving from the opinion leaders to their peers.[8]

The proven role of small groups as behavior determinants, plus the concept of horizontal information flow, suggests that a marketer is faced with two key problems. The first is to identify the relevant reference group likely to be used by consumers in a given buying situation. The second is to identify and communicate with two key people in the group—the innovator (early buyer) and the influential person (opinion leader). Every group has a leader—a tastemaker, or **opinion leader**—who influences the decision making of others in the group. The key is for marketers to convince that person of the value of their products or services. The opinion *leader* in one group may be an opinion *follower* in another. Married women with children may be influential in matters concerning food, whereas unmarried women are more likely to influence fashions in clothing and makeup.

Small reference groups influence our buying behavior.

Family Buying Behavior (Buying Habits)

Of all the small groups that we belong to through the years, one group normally exerts the strongest and most enduring influence on our perceptions and behavior. That group is our family.

In addition to understanding *why* people buy, marketers also need to know *when*, *where*, and *how* they buy. We are talking now about consumers' buying *habits*, or overt buying *patterns*, in contrast to their buying *motives* (why they buy). This section on buying habits applies to consumers living alone as well as to families. For families we need to answer an additional question—who does the family buying?

WHEN CONSUMERS BUY

Marketing executives should be able to answer at least three questions about *when* people buy their products or services: During what season do they buy? On what day of the week do they buy? At what time of the day do they buy? If seasonal buying patterns exist, marketing executives should try to extend the buying season. There is obviously little opportunity for extending the buying season for Easter bunnies or

[8]See Elihu Katz and Paul Lazarsfeld, *Personal Influence*, Free Press, New York, 1955, especially p. 325.

Christmas packaging reflects when people buy some products.

One-stop shopping can lead to some interesting product assortments.

Christmas-tree ornaments. But the season for vacations has been shifted to such an extent that winter and other "off-season" vacations are now quite popular.

When people buy may influence the product-planning, pricing, or promotional phases of a firm's marketing program. After-shave lotion and alcoholic beverages often are distinctly packaged at Christmastime because they are purchased for gifts. To smooth the seasonal peaks and valleys in production, a fishing tackle manufacturer may want retailers to buy well in advance of the summer season. To get retailers to do this, the manufacturer may offer them "seasonal datings." This is a pricing strategy whereby retailers take delivery in April but do not have to pay for the merchandise until July.

WHERE CONSUMERS BUY

A firm should consider two factors with respect to where people buy—where the buying decision is made and where the actual purchase occurs. For many products and services the decision to buy is made at home. For others, the decision is often made in whole or in part at the point of purchase. A man shopping in a sporting goods store for golf clubs may see some tennis balls on sale. Knowing he needs some, he decides on the spot to buy them. A woman may decide at home to buy a birthday gift for her husband. But she will wait until she gets to the store before deciding whether it will be a shirt or a book.

A company's promotional program, and its product planning, must be geared to carry the greatest impact at the place where the buying decision is made. If this decision is made in the store, then attention must be devoted to packaging and point-of-purchase display materials, particularly in self-service stores. A shopper may decide at home to buy some cold cereal, but the key decisions regarding which type and which brand may be made at the store.

HOW CONSUMERS BUY

The how part of consumers' buying habits encompasses several areas of behavior and, consequently, many marketing decisions. Long ago, for example, many firms found that consumers prefer to buy such products as pickles, cookies, and butter already packaged. The advantages of cleanliness and ease of handling offset the higher unit price.

The trend toward one-stop shopping has encouraged retailers to add related and even unrelated lines of merchandise to their basic groups of products. The increase of credit-card buying has led many stores to accept Visa or MasterCard credit cards. In the past, these retailers would accept only their own charge-account cards.

WHO DOES THE FAMILY BUYING?

Marketers should treat this question as four separate ones, because each may call for different marketing strategies and tactics. The four questions are:

1. Who influences the buying decision? (This may be a member of the family, or the influence may come from an outside reference group.)
2. Who makes the buying decision?
3. Who makes the actual purchase?
4. Who uses the product?

Four different people may be involved, or only one member may do all four, or there may be some other combination of influences.

For many years, women have done most of the family buying. They still exert substantial influence in buying decisions and do a considerable amount of the actual purchasing. However, men have increasingly entered the family buying picture. Self-service stores are especially appealing to men. Night and Sunday openings in suburban shopping centers also encourage men to play a bigger role in family purchasing.

In recent years, teenagers and young children have become decision makers in family buying, as well as actual purchasers. The amount of money teenagers spend now is substantial enough to be considered in the marketing plans of many manufacturers and middlemen. Even very young children are an influence in buying decisions today because they watch television programs or shop with their parents.

Purchasing decisions are often made jointly by husband and wife (sometimes even the children are included). Young married people are much more likely to make buying decisions on a joint basis than older couples. Apparently the longer a husband and wife live together, the more they feel they can trust each other to act unilaterally.

Who buys a product will influence a firm's marketing policies regarding its product, channels of distribution, and promotion. If children are the key decision makers, as is often the case in purchasing breakfast cereals, then a manufacturer may include some type of premium with the product. In a department store, the men's department is often located on the street floor near a door. This permits men to enter, shop, and leave the store without having to wade through crowds of shoppers. The entire advertising campaign—media, appeals, copy, radio and television programming, and so forth—is affected by whether the target consists of men, women, or children.

Sometimes a little guy can influence a buying decision—especially when there is a premium in the box.

PSYCHOLOGICAL DETERMINANTS OF BUYER BEHAVIOR ■

In discussing the psychological forces in consumer behavior, we shall continue to use the model we set up near the beginning of this chapter. That is, one or more motives within a person trigger behavior toward a goal that is expected to bring satisfaction. This goal-oriented behavior is influenced by the person's perceptions. In this section, we discuss the effects that learning experiences, personality, attitudes and beliefs, and self-concept have on perceptions. (Recall Fig. 6-2.) These psychological variables help to shape a person's life-style and values. The term **psychographics** is being used by many researchers as a collective synonym for these psychological variables and life-style values.[9]

Learning Experiences

As a factor influencing a person's perceptions, **learning** may be defined as changes in behavior resulting from previous experiences. However, also by definition, learning does *not* include behavior changes attributable to instinctive responses, or temporary states of the organism such as hunger or fatigue.[10]

---

[9] No universally accepted definition of the term *psychographics* has as yet been developed. See William D. Wells, "Psychographics: A Critical Review," *Journal of Marketing Research*, May 1975, pp. 196–213.

[10] For a discussion of other definitions of learning, see John F. Hall, *Psychology of Learning*, J. B. Lippincott Company, Philadelphia, 1966, pp. 3–6.

The ability to interpret and predict the consumer's learning process is a real key to understanding buying behavior. Therefore, it is unfortunate that no simple learning theory has emerged as universally workable and acceptable. The principal learning theories described here are (1) stimulus-response (S-R) theories, (2) cognitive theories, and (3) gestalt and field theories.

STIMULUS-RESPONSE THEORIES

These theories were first formulated by psychologists such as Pavlov, Skinner, and Hull on the basis of their laboratory experiments with animals. This school of theorists holds that learning occurs as a person (or animal) (1) responds to some stimulus and (2) is reinforced with need satisfaction for a correct response or penalized for an incorrect one. When the same correct response is repeated in reaction to a given stimulus, behavioral patterns are established.

Today we realize that attitudes and other factors (not just the mechanical stimulus-response) also influence a consumer's response to a given stimulus. Nevertheless, the stimulus-response model, with reinforcement as an essential element, is a useful explanation of the learning process. Four factors—drive, cue, response, and reinforcement—are fundamental to the process. A **drive** (or motive) is a strong stimulus that requires satisfaction—a response of some sort. The **cues** are weaker stimuli that determine the pattern of this response—the "when," "where," and "how" of the response behavior. For instance, a TV commercial or a change in price is a cue that might shape a consumer's behavior in seeking to satisfy an aroused hunger drive. The **response** is simply the behavioral reaction to the cues and drive. **Reinforcement** results when the response is rewarding (satisfying).

If the response is gratifying, a connection between cue and response will be established; that is, a behavioral pattern will be learned. Learning, then, emerges from reinforcement. Continual reinforcement leads to habit or brand loyalty. Once a habitual pattern of behavior is established, it replaces conscious, willful behavior. The stronger the habit, the more difficult it is for a competitive product to break the habit and enter a consumer's learning field. On the other hand, if the original response action is not rewarding, the consumer's mind is open to another set of cues leading to another response. For example, the consumer will buy a substitute product or switch to another brand.

COGNITIVE THEORIES

Cognitive learning theories reject the S-R model as being too mechanistic. In S-R theory, behavior is the result of *only* the degree of reinforcement stemming from a response to some stimulus. No other influences are recognized as intervening in the S-R channel. Proponents of cognitive theory insist that learning is influenced by factors such as attitudes, beliefs, and an insightful understanding of how to achieve a goal. Cognitive theorists believe that a person can use thinking ability to solve a current problem, even if there are no historical precedents in the person's experience. Habitual behavioral patterns, then, are the result of perceptive thinking and goal orientation.

GESTALT AND FIELD THEORIES

Gestalt is a German word which roughly means "configuration," "pattern," or "form." Gestalt psychologists are concerned with the "whole" of a thing—the total scene—

rather than its component parts. They maintain that learning and behavior should be viewed as a total process, in contrast to the individual-element approach in the S-R model.[11]

Field theory, as formulated by Kurt Lewin, is a useful refinement of gestalt psychology.[12] This theory holds that the only determining force accounting for a person's behavior at any given time is that person's psychological "field" at that time. A person's *field* or *life space* may be defined as the totality of facts pertaining to the individual and his or her environment at the time of the behavior. Gestalt psychologists believed that people perceive the whole—their total environment—rather than its parts. Thus, to understand consumers' behavior, we must understand their perception of their environment. These psychologists further postulate that a person's perception of the whole is quite different from what we might expect if each part were considered separately. Thus, looking at the following configuration,

most people will perceive four sets of tracks, or four pairs of lines, but rarely do they perceive eight vertical lines.

Moreover, rather than perceive separate parts, a person will organize them into a whole that is meaningful in light of that person's past experience. Thus, the properties of the *total field* influence people's perceptions of the stimuli in that field. To illustrate, a distinguished-looking man in a white coat can speak in a serious tone in a TV commercial advertising a pain reliever. Many viewers will perceive him as a doctor or a pharmacist, because that is how they interpret the total scene in light of their past experience.

Several field principles, which have applications in marketing, deal with the ways in which properties of stimuli affect our perception of them. The principle of **closure** postulates that we tend to complete (close) figures to make them meaningful. Thus, "13 0" will be "closed" by the viewer to get "B O." A change in spacing (illustrating the principle of **proximity**) can give different results—"1 3 0" will be viewed as the number "130" rather than as two letters.

According to another field principle, marketing messages must be placed in a reasonable **context**—a smartly dressed woman should not be shown painting her house. Ads should also be **simple** in both structure and content. Because of **locational properties,** some items will stand out in a sea of similar-looking products. This principle places a premium on eye-level shelf position in a supermarket, for example. And all parts of a marketing program—price, type of ads, product quality, and the like—must be in **harmony,** that is, consistent with consumers' expectations.

Personality

The study of human personality has given rise to many, sometimes widely divergent, schools of psychological thought. Yet, perhaps because of this multifaceted attention, we still lack even a consensus definition of the term. Attempts to inventory and classify

[11]See K. Koffka, *Principles of Gestalt Psychology,* Harcourt, Brace, & World, Inc., New York, 1935; Wolfgang Kohler, *Gestalt Psychology,* Liveright Publishing Corporation, New York, 1947.

[12]See Kurt Lewin, *A Dynamic Theory of Personality* (1935) and *Principles of Topological Psychology* (1936), McGraw-Hill Book Company, New York.

personality traits have understandably produced many different structures. In this discussion, **personality** is defined as an individual's pattern of traits that are a determinant of behavioral responses. Thus we speak of people having personality traits such as being self-confident, aggressive, shy, domineering, dynamic, secure or insecure, extroverted or introverted, easygoing, friendly, flexible or stubborn, etc.

It is generally agreed that consumers' personality traits do influence their perceptions and buying behavior. Unfortunately, however, there is no agreement as to the nature of this relationship—that is, *how* personality influences behavior. We know that people's personalities are often reflected in the clothes they wear, the brand and type of car they drive (or whether they use a bike or motorcycle instead of a car), the restaurants they eat in, etc. But we don't know how to measure their personality traits in relation to their forms of behavior. These traits are virtually impossible to quantify—how many pounds or square feet of shyness or arrogance do you have? Nor do we know to what extent an excess of one trait can overcome a shortage of another.

PSYCHOANALYTIC THEORIES OF PERSONALITY

The psychoanalytic school of personality, founded by Sigmund Freud and later modified by his followers and critics, has had a tremendous impact on the study of human behavior. Freud contended that there are three parts to the mind—the id, the ego, and the superego. The **id** houses the basic instinctive drives, many of which are antisocial. The **superego** is the conscience, accepting moral standards and directing the instinctive drives into acceptable channels. The id and the superego are sometimes in conflict. The **ego** is the conscious, rational control center that maintains a balance between the uninhibited instincts of the id and the socially oriented, constraining superego.

Freud's behavioral thesis was that we enter the world with certain instinctive biological drives that cannot be satisfied in a socially acceptable fashion. As we learn that we cannot gratify these needs in a direct manner, we develop other, more subtle means of seeking satisfaction. These other means require that the basic drives be repressed, and consequently, inner tensions and frustrations develop. Also, feelings of guilt or shame about these drives cause us to suppress and even sublimate them to the point where they become subconscious. For satisfactions of these drives, we substitute rationalization and socially acceptable behavior. Yet the basic urges are always there. The net result is very complex behavior. Sometimes even we ourselves do not understand why we feel or act as we do.

One significant marketing implication of psychoanalytic theory is that a person's real motive for buying a given product or shopping at a certain store may well be hidden. The research techniques which are adequate for determining demographic and economic data normally prove fruitless in uncovering the real reasons for a person's buying behavior.

Psychoanalytic theory has caused marketers to realize that they must provide buyers with socially acceptable rationalizations for their purchasing. Yet we also can appeal subconsciously to buyers' dreams, hopes, and fears.

Attitudes and Beliefs

An **attitude** may be defined as a person's enduring cognitive evaluation, emotional feeling, or action tendency toward some object or idea. Attitudes involve thought processes as well as emotional feelings, and they vary in intensity. Attitudes influence beliefs, and beliefs influence attitudes. In fact, for the purpose of our generalized, introductory-level discussion of buying behavior, we shall use the two concepts interchangeably. They both reflect value judgments and positive or negative feelings toward a product, service, or brand.

Attitudes and beliefs are strong and direct forces affecting consumers' perceptions and buying behavior. Attitudes significantly influence people's perceptions by selectively screening out any stimuli that conflict with those attitudes. They also can distort the perception of messages and affect the degree of their retention.

Various studies uniformly report a very close relationship between consumers' attitudes and their buying decisions in regard to both the type of product and the brand selection. Surely, then, it is in a marketer's best interests to understand how attitudes are formed, measured, and changed. Attitudes are **formed,** generally speaking, by the information individuals acquire (1) through their past learning experiences with the product or idea or (2) through their relations with their reference groups (family, social and work groups, etc.). The perception of this information is influenced by personality traits.

Attitude **measurement** is far from easy. In limited instances a researcher may simply employ the direct-question, survey technique. The most widely used techniques, however, have been some form of attitude scaling. Respondents may be asked, for instance, to rank several models or products by order of preference. Or they may be asked to rate some item according to a verbal scale ranging from one extreme to another (from ultramodern to very old-fashioned, for example). Many features in a company's marketing program lend themselves to attitude measurement. A seller may measure, for example, what people think about various product features (brand, package, color), middlemen's activities (store hours or location, helpfulness of sales clerks), or promotional activities (advertisements, TV programs).

We need to note that measuring attitudes is *not* the same as measuring buying intentions or forecasting sales. You can have a very favorable attitude toward a product, but never buy it. (One of the authors would love to have a Rolls Royce, but he undoubtedly never will buy one.) Maybe the item is too expensive, or some other reason may block your purchase, regardless of your highly favorable attitude.

It is *extremely* difficult to **change** consumers' attitudes, regardless of marketing critics' opinions to the contrary. As far as attitudes are concerned, to get consumers to buy its product a seller has two choices. The first is to change consumers' attitudes to be consonant with that product. The second is to determine what the consumers' attitudes are and then change the product to match those attitudes. Ordinarily it is much easier to change the product than it is to change the consumers' attitudes.

Nevertheless, in some situations attitudes have been changed in recent years. Consider, for instance, the cultural changes discussed earlier in this chapter. Every one of those situations involved a change in people's attitudes. Consider further how formerly negative attitudes have changed in favor of small cars, yellow tennis balls and oversized racquets, off-season vacations, adults getting their teeth straightened, coed dorms in colleges, the French drinking beer, and women wearing glasses.

The Self-Concept

Another behavior is the self-concept, or self-image. Your **self-image** is the way you see yourself. At the same time, it is the picture you think others have of you. Some psychologists distinguish between (1) the *actual* self-concept (the way you really see yourself) and (2) the *ideal* self-concept (the way you want to be seen or would like

Describe her self-image.

to see yourself). To some extent, the self-image theory is a reflection of other psychological and sociological concepts already discussed. A person's self-image is influenced, for instance, by innate and learned physiological and psychological needs. It is conditioned also by economic factors, demographic factors, and social-group influences.

Studies of actual purchases show that people generally prefer brands and products that are compatible with their own self-concept. There are mixed reports concerning the degree of influence of the actual and ideal self-concepts on brand and product preferences. Some psychologists contend that consumption preferences correspond to a person's *actual* self-image. Others hold that the *ideal* self-image is dominant in consumers' choices.

Perhaps there is no consensus here because in real life we often switch back and forth between our actual and our ideal self-concepts. A middle-aged man may buy some comfortable, but not fashionable, clothing to wear at home on a weekend where he is reflecting his actual self-image. Then later he buys some expensive, high-fashion exercise clothing as he envisions himself (ideal self-image) as a young, active, upwardly mobile guy. Or this same fellow may drive a beat-up pickup truck for his weekend errands (actual self-concept). But he'll drive his new foreign sports car to work where he wants to project a different (ideal) self-image.[13]

[13]For an analytical review of self-concept studies, the research problems connected with these studies, and a comprehensive bibliography, see M. Joseph Sirgy, "Self-Concept in Consumer Behavior: A Critical Review," *Journal of Consumer Research*, December 1982, pp. 287–300.

DECISION-MAKING PROCESS IN BUYING

It is time now to tie together some of our points regarding consumer behavior and to describe the process consumers go through when making purchasing decisions. The process is a problem-solving approach consisting of the following five stages, also shown in the lower half of Fig. 6-2:

1. *Recognition of an unsatisfied need*: A family man needs a new auto.
2. *Identification of alternate ways of achieving satisfaction*: He can buy a sports car or a station wagon.
3. *Evaluation of alternatives*: He considers pros and cons of the two types of auto.
4. *Purchase decision*: He buys a sports car.
5. *Postpurchase behavior*: He wonders if he made the right decision.

Once the process has been started, potential buyers can withdraw at any stage prior to the actual purchase, and some stages can be skipped. A total-stage approach is likely to be used only in certain buying situations—a first-time purchase of a product, for instance, or in buying high-priced, infrequently purchased articles. For many products the purchasing behavior is a routine affair in which the aroused need is satisfied in the usual manner by repurchasing the same brand. That is, past reinforcement in learning experiences leads directly to the buying response-act, and thus the second and third stages are bypassed. However, if something changes appreciably (price, product, services), buyers may reopen the full decision process and consider alternative brands or products.

Recognition of Unsatisfied Need

The process starts when an unsatisfied need (motive) creates inner tension. This may be a biogenic need, aroused internally (the person feels hungry). Or the need may have been dormant until it was aroused by an external stimulus, such as an ad or the sight of the product. Or perhaps dissatisfaction with the present product created the tension.

Once the need has been recognized, often consumers become aware of conflicting or competing uses for their scarce resources of time or money. Let us say that a man has a desire to install a hot tub in the backyard at a cost of $5,000. His wife may remind him that they need new furniture for the living room. Or he may fear that one of his key reference groups would not approve. A person must resolve these conflicts before proceeding. Otherwise, the buying process stops at this point.

Identification of Alternatives

Once a need has been recognized, both product and brand alternatives must be identified. Suppose a woman wants to make her hands feel softer. Some alternative solutions include buying a dishwasher, using rubber gloves, or trying a different detergent or a new hand cream. Or she can get her husband and her kids to wash the dishes and scrub the floors. If one of the product alternatives is selected, then there still are several brand alternatives to choose from.

The search for alternatives is influenced by such factors as (1) what the time and money costs are (not much time is spent buying a hamburger, in comparison with the time spent buying a new winter coat); (2) how much information the consumer already has from past experience and other sources; and (3) the amount of the perceived risk if a wrong selection is made.

Evaluation of Alternatives

Once all the reasonable alternatives have been identified, the consumer must evaluate each one preparatory to making a purchase decision. The criteria that consumers use in their evaluations should be familiar by now. They include past experience and attitudes toward various brands. Consumers also use the opinion of members of their families and other reference groups as guidelines in these evaluations.

Purchase Decisions

After searching and evaluating, the consumer at some point must decide whether or not to buy. If the decision is to buy, the buyer must make a series of decisions regarding brand, price, store, color, and so on.

Anything marketers can do to simplify decision making will be attractive to buyers, because most people find it very hard to make a decision. Sometimes several decision situations can be combined and marketed as one package. A travel agency simplifies travelers' decisions concerning transportation, hotels, and which tours to take by selling a packaged tour.

At this point in the buying process, marketers are trying to determine the consumers' **patronage buying motives.** These are the reasons that a consumer shops at (patronizes) a certain store. These are different from *product buying motives,* which are reasons for buying a certain product. Some of the more important patronage buying motives are:

- Convenience of location.
- Rapidity of service.
- Ease of locating merchandise.
- Uncrowded conditions.
- Price.

- Assortment of merchandise.
- Services offered.
- Attractive store appearance.
- Caliber of sales personnel.

Patronage motives and choice of stores are related to the concept of social-class structure. The *Chicago Tribune* studies of social classes show definitely that people match their own values and expectations with the status of the store. Not all people want to shop at glamorous, high-status stores. Lower-status people know that they will be punished in subtle ways by the clerks and other customers if they go into an exclusive department store. "The clerk treats you like a crumb," was one response.

Postpurchase Behavior

All the steps in the buying process up to this point occur *before* or *during* the time a purchase is made. However, a buyer's feelings *after* the sale are also significant for the marketer. They can influence repeat sales and what the buyer tells others about the product.

Typically, buyers experience some postpurchase anxieties in all but routine purchases. We refer to this state of anxiety as **cognitive dissonance.** The theory is that people strive for internal harmony and consistency among their *cognitions* (knowledge, attitudes, beliefs, values). Any inconsistency in these cognitions is called *dissonance.*

Postpurchase cognitive dissonance occurs because each of the alternatives considered by the consumer usually has both advantages and limitations. Thus, when the purchase decision is finally made, the selected alternative has some drawbacks, while the rejected alternatives each possess some attractive features. That is, *negative* aspects of the item *selected,* and the *positive* qualities of the *rejected* products, create cognitive dissonance in the consumer.

Dissonance typically increases as (1) the dollar value of the purchase increases; (2) the relative attractiveness of the unselected alternatives increases; and (3) the

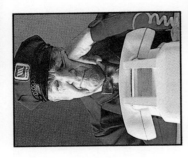

An ad like this can reduce cognitive dissonance.

relative importance of the decision increases (buying a house or car creates more dissonance than buying a candy bar).

To restore internal harmony and minimize discomfort, people will try to reduce their postpurchase anxieties. Thus they are likely to avoid information (such as ads for the rejected products) that is likely to increase dissonance. Prior to making the purchase, they may shop around quite a bit, especially for high-priced, infrequently purchased articles. In this way they seek to minimize postdecision dissonance by spending more time in predecision evaluations.

Some useful generalizations can be developed from the theory. For example, anything sellers can do in their advertising or personal selling to reassure buyers—say, by stressing desirable features of a product—will reduce dissonance. This reduction will reinforce consumers and increase the likelihood of repeat purchases. When the product in question is expensive and infrequently purchased, the sellers' postsale service program can be a significant factor in reducing dissonance.

SUMMARY ■

In Chapter 2 we defined markets as people with money to spend and the willingness to spend it. It is important that marketers understand the "willingness-to-buy" factor—that is, consumer buying behavior. It is also very difficult to interpret consumer behavior, because we do not know what goes on in a person's mind.

The simplified behavioral model we followed is this one: Buying behavior is initiated when aroused needs (motives) create inner tensions that lead to behavior designed to satisfy the needs and thus reduce the tensions. This goal-oriented behavior is shaped by our perceptions. Our perceptions, in turn, are shaped by the cultural, social-group, and psychological forces that constitute a person's frame of reference.

Marketers must be aware of cultural change and of the importance of segmenting the market into subcultures. A social-class structure exists in American society; our society may be categorized into five social classes. And there are significant differences in buying behavior among those classes.

Small reference groups to which we belong, or aspire to belong, also influence our perceptions. Reference groups stress conformity to the behavioral standards set for the groups' members and often enforce these standards. Most groups have opinion leaders. A company's marketing effort should be directed toward identifying and communicating with these leaders. The family is the smallest social group to influence our perceptions, and often it is the most powerful social force affecting buyer behavior. Marketers need to know *who* does the family buying and *when*, *where*, and *how* people buy—that is, the buying habits of consumers.

One of the psychological forces affecting perceptions and buying behavior is a person's learning experience. Three sets of learning theories—the stimulus-response model, cognitive theory, the gestalt and field theory—describe learning and its effect on behavior. Another psychological influence on perceptions is personality, although there is no agreement as to how personality influences behavior. Freudian psychoanalytic theory of personality also has significant marketing implications. Finally, perceptions are also influenced by attitudes and beliefs and by self-image.

Consumers often go through a logical, five-stage process in the course of making a buying decision. First, the unsatisfied need is recognized. Next, the reasonable alternatives are first identified and then evaluated. The actual decision to purchase is then made. (This stage involves patronage buying motives and retail-store image.) In the final stage, postpurchase behavior may involve some cognitive dissonance on the part of the buyer.

■ KEY TERMS AND CONCEPTS

Buyer behavior 111	Learning 123
Motivation 112	Stimulus-response theories 124
Hierarchy of needs 112	Cognitive theories 124
Perception 114	Gestalt and field theories 124
Selectivity in perceptions 114	Personality 125
Culture 115	Psychoanalytic theories 126
Cultural changes 116	Attitudes and beliefs 126
Subcultures 117	Self-concept (self-image) 127
Social-class structure 117	Buying-decision process 129
Small reference group 120	Patronage buying motives 130
Consumer buying habits 120	Cognitive dissonance 130
Psychographics 123	

■ QUESTIONS AND PROBLEMS

1. Which needs in Maslow's hierarchy might be satisfied by each of the following products or services?

   a. Home burglary alarm system.
   b. Pepsi-Cola.
   c. *World Book Encyclopedia.*
   d. Body lotion.
   e. Certified public accountant.
   f. Starting your own business.

2. Explain what is meant by the selectivity process in perception.

3. In social-class research, what are some of the major conclusions that are significant for marketing?

4. Which of the social classes do you associate with each of the following products or activities? In some cases more than one class could be listed, but try to associate each item with only one class.

a. Polo game.
b. Bowling.
c. Pickup truck.
d. *National Geographic* magazine.
e. Major-league baseball game.
f. Bank credit card.
g. Borrowing from a bank.
h. Borrowing from a pawnbroker.
i. Shopping at J. C. Penney.
j. Shopping at K mart.

5. Discuss the concept of a small reference group, explaining the meaning of the concept and its use in marketing.

6. Explain how the factors of *when* and *where* people buy might affect the marketing program for each of the following products:

a. House paint.
b. High-quality sunglasses.
c. Outboard motors.
d. Room air conditioners.

7. Distinguish between *drives* and *cues* in the learning process.

8. Does the Freudian psychoanalytic theory of personality have any practical application in the marketing of:

a. Eye shadow?
b. Electric dishwashers?
c. Outboard motor boats?

9. Select two or three products or brands you are familiar with, and explain what marketing action might be employed to change consumers' attitudes toward these products or brands.

10. Describe the differences you would expect to find in the self-concepts of an insurance sales person and an assembly-line worker in an automobile plant. Give some examples of resultant buying behavior. (Assume that both have the same income.)

11. Following is a series of headliners or slogans taken from advertisements of various retailers. To what patronage motive does each appeal?

a. "Factory-trained mechanics at your service."
b. "We never close."
c. "Nobody but nobody undersells Gimbels."
d. "Where Denver shops with confidence."
e. "We never have missed paying a semiannual dividend since we opened." (Savings and loan association.)
f. "One dollar down, no payments until the steel strike is over."
g. "Most complete department store west of the Mississippi."

12. What causes cognitive dissonance to increase in a buying situation? What can a seller do to decrease the level of dissonance in a given purchase of the seller's product?

7

THE INDUSTRIAL MARKET

CHAPTER GOALS

This chapter is a discussion of the huge market for industrial goods. As you read, try to form a comparison between the industrial market and the consumer market. After studying this chapter, you should understand:

- The nature and importance of the industrial market.

- The major characteristics of industrial market demand.

- The demographic makeup of the industrial market.

- Industrial buying motives, the industrial buying process, and buying patterns of industrial users.

How do you market to industrial users a food and drink sweetener that is 20 times more expensive than saccharin and 50 percent more than sugar? That was the problem faced by the G. D. Searle Company a few years ago when it introduced NutraSweet® brand sweetener. NutraSweet (whose generic name is aspartame) is a natural-protein sweetener—a sugar substitute that is very low in calories and, pound for pound, is 200 times sweeter than sugar. Searle was a pharmaceutical manufacturer with virtually no experience marketing to the food and beverage industries. In fact, NutraSweet was discovered accidentally when a lab chemist spilled a chemical compound in the course of developing another product. In the cleaning-up process, the chemist tasted the substance and found that it tasted like sugar.

In marketing NutraSweet®,* the main strategy adopted by Searle was what we call a "pull" strategy. (This is a combination distribution and promotion strategy which we discuss in more detail in Chapter 18.) Essentially this strategy involves promoting the product to ultimate household consumers with the goal of getting them to ask for sugar-free products sweetened with NutraSweet. Once consumer acceptance was achieved, then Searle could convince food and beverage manufacturers that their products would sell better if sweetened with NutraSweet instead of saccharin or another sugar substitute.

Searle's multimillion-dollar promotion campaign to consumers was a great success. Consequently, even with its much higher competitive price, the company was in a strong position when dealing with food and beverage firms. Searle was able to encourage many food and beverage producers—especially Coca-Cola and Pepsi-Cola—to use NutraSweet as the *only* sweetener in their products. Furthermore, Searle was able to require that the NutraSweet name and symbol (logotype) be placed on the front of food packages. So today you will see the now-familiar red and white peppermint-candy-like swirl and the NutraSweet name on many food and beverage products.[1]

*NutraSweet is a registered trademark of The NutraSweet Company for its brand of sweetening ingredient.

[1] Adapted from "Sweet-Talking the Public," *Newsweek*, Jan. 28, 1985, p. 57; and Peter Petre, "Searle's Big Pitch for a Tiny Ingredient," *Fortune*, Sept. 3, 1984, p. 73.

NutraSweet is an industrial product marketed to industrial users in the industrial market—and these are topics that we'll be talking about in this chapter. The industrial market is big, rich, and widely diversified. It requires the efforts of millions of workers in thousands of different jobs. Firms producing for this market are not criticized for extreme claims in selling or advertising. They are not accused of offering duplicate brands or of paying middlemen exorbitant profits. The market is not a target for widespread complaint, because it is largely unknown to the public.

NATURE AND IMPORTANCE OF THE INDUSTRIAL MARKET

The **industrial market** consists of all industrial users. In Chapter 5 we defined **industrial users** as organizations that buy goods and services for one of the three following purposes:

- *To make other goods and services:* Campbell's buys fresh vegetables to make soup, and Henredon buys wood to make furniture.
- *To resell to other industrial users or to consumers:* Kroger's buys canned tuna fish to sell to consumers, and Western Pipe Supply Company sells lawn sprinkler equipment and supplies to sprinkler contractors.
- *To conduct the organization's operation:* the University of Colorado buys office supplies and electronic office equipment for use in the registrar's office, and the Denver General Hospital buys supplies to use in its surgical operating rooms.

In the industrial market we deal with both consumer products and industrial products. **Industrial marketing,** then, is the marketing of products and services to industrial users, as contrasted to ultimate consumers.

In these definitions we have used the traditional terminology. We should note, however, that the American Marketing Association is now using the term *business marketing* to replace *industrial marketing.* This change is intended to bring a broader, more relevant title to this field that includes all organizations that market directly to other organizations rather than to the ultimate consumer.[2] For this edition of this book, however, we shall continue to use the *industrial* terminology. Until the terminology transition is further along, we believe that business people will be more familiar with the traditional term *industrial* to describe nonconsumer markets and products.

Because the industrial market is largely unknown to the average consumer, we are apt to underrate its significance. Actually, this market is a huge one in terms of its total sales volume and the number of firms involved in it. About 50 percent of all manufactured products are sold to the industrial market. In addition, about 80 percent of all farm products and virtually all minerals and forest and sea products are industrial goods. These are sold to firms for further processing.

The magnitude and complexity of the industrial market are also shown by the many transactions required to produce and market a product. Consider, for example, the industrial marketing transactions and the total sales volume involved in getting a pair of cowhide work shoes to their actual user. First, the cattle are sold through one or two middlemen before reaching a meat-packer. Then the hides are sold to a tanner, who in turn sells the leather to a shoe manufacturer. The shoe manufacturer may sell finished shoes to a shoe wholesaler, who markets the products to retail stores or to factories that supply shoes to their workers. Each sale of the cow, leather, or shoe is another industrial marketing transaction.

In addition, the shoe manufacturer buys metal eyelets, laces, thread, steel safety toe plates, heels and soles, and shoe polish. Consider something as simple as the shoelaces. Other industrial firms must first buy the raw cotton and then spin, weave, dye, and cut it so that it becomes shoestring material. All the manufacturers involved

2See "AMA Restructures the Industrial Marketing Division into Business Marketing Division," *Marketing News,* Aug. 17, 1984, p. 13.

have factories and offices with furniture, machinery, and other equipment—and these also are industrial goods that have to be produced and marketed. Factories also are industrial products, as are the heating and maintenance equipment and supplies required to run them. In short, thousands of industrial products and industrial marketing activities come into play before almost any product—consumer good or industrial good—reaches its final destination.

Another indication of the scope and importance of the industrial market is the following range of industries that make up this market.

- Agriculture, forestry, and fishing.
- Mining and quarrying.
- Contract construction.
- Manufacturing.
- Transportation, communication, and other public utilities.
- Wholesale trade and retail trade.
- Finance, insurance, and real estate.
- Services.
- Government—federal, state, and local.
- Nonbusiness (nonprofit) organizations.

Every retail store and wholesaling establishment is an industrial user. Every bus company, airline, and railroad is part of this market. So is every hotel, restaurant, bank, insurance company, hospital, theater, and school. In all, there are close to 12 million industrial users in the United States. While this is far short of the approximately 250 million consumers, the total sales volume in the industrial market far surpasses total sales to consumers. This difference is due to the very many industrial marketing transactions that take place before a product is sold to its ultimate user.

Sometimes Overlooked Industrial Markets

Four large segments of the industrial market are given special recognition at this point. The reason is that these segments often are underrated and overlooked, because most attention typically is devoted to the manufacturing segment.

THE FARM MARKET

The high level of cash income from the sale of farm products—about $141 billion in 1984—gives farmers, as a group, the purchasing power that makes them a highly attractive market. Moreover, world population forecasts and food shortages in many countries undoubtedly will keep pressure on farmers to increase their output. Companies hoping to sell to this farm market must analyze it carefully and be aware of significant trends. For example, both (1) the proportion of farmers in the total population and (2) the number of farms have been decreasing and probably will continue to decline. Counterbalancing this has been an increase in large corporate farms. Even the surviving "family farms" are tending to expand in size. Farming is becoming more automated and mechanized. This means, of course, that capital investment in farming is increasing. Truly, **agribusiness** is becoming big business in every sense of the word.

As industrial buyers, most farmers—especially the owners of large farms—are quite discerning and well informed. Like any business executive, the farmers are

Products designed for the farm market.

looking for better ways to increase their crop yields, to cut their expenses, and to manage their cash flow. And, as farms become fewer, larger, and more sophisticated, manufacturers must change their distribution and promotion strategies to reach the farm market effectively.

In distribution, for example, producers must recognize the key role played by farm equipment dealers and feed-seed suppliers located in farm communities. Farmers tend to buy locally, where they can get repair service, parts, and supplies from people they know. Even a major capital expenditure for large equipment usually is made through a local dealer. This is unlike the buying behavior of most industrial users, who typically buy large equipment directly from the manufacturer.

When promoting their products, manufacturers should be aware of the high degree of specialization in the farm market. Some producers of fertilizer (International Minerals and Chemical Company is one), for example, will send a sales person directly to a large farm. There, working with the farmer, the sales rep will analyze the soil and determine exactly what fertilizer mix is best for that farm. From that analysis, the manufacturer will prepare, as a special order, the appropriate blend of fertilizers for that particular farm.

On the other side of a farm market exchange transaction, *buying from* farmers sometimes is done on a contract basis. In fact, **contract farming**, while it has existed for a long time, seems to be on the increase in recent years. Under one type of contract-farming arrangement, one firm (a middleman or a manufacturer) agrees to furnish the farmer with supplies and possibly with equipment and working capital to grow a crop. The farmer, in turn, agrees to sell the entire crop to this supplier at some predetermined price. In effect, the farmer is an employee of this supplier. In another type of contract-farming arrangement, the farmer furnishes the supplies and equipment. But a processor (perhaps a canner or freezer of fruits or vegetables) agrees in advance to buy that farmer's entire crop. The price may be set before the growing season, or it may be negotiated at some time during the season. Contract farming also affects the marketing of farm supplies and equipment. Often, it is difficult for the seller to determine who makes a buying decision. Is it the farmer, the contract buyer, or both?

THE RESELLER MARKET

Intermediaries in the American macro marketing system—approximately 400,000 wholesaling middlemen and 2 million retailers—constitute the **reseller market.** This is a large segment of the total industrial market. The basic activity of resellers—unlike any other industrial market segment—involves buying products and services from supplier organizations and reselling these items in essentially the same form to the resellers' customers. In economic terms, resellers create time, place, and possession utilities, rather than form utility.

Resellers also buy many products and services for use in operating their businesses—items such as office supplies and equipment, warehouses, materials-handling equipment, legal services, electrical services, janitorial supplies, etc. However, in these buying activities, resellers are no different essentially from manufacturers, financial institutions, or any other segment of the industrial market.

However, it is their role as buyers for resale that differentiates resellers and attracts special marketing attention from their suppliers. To resell an item, you must please your customer. Usually it is more difficult to determine what will please your outside customers than to find out what will satisfy somebody within your own organization. Thus, buying for resale typically is more difficult and risky than buying for use within a firm.

Consequently, buying for resale, especially in a large reseller's organization, can be a complex, sophisticated procedure. Buying for a supermarket chain, for example, is frequently done by a committee. Department stores may retain resident buyers—independent buying agencies—located in New York or other major market centers. Computerized inventory-control systems are used to minimize overstocking, obsolete merchandise, or out-of-stock conditions.

The retailing and wholesaling institutions that constitute the reseller market are discussed in more detail in Chapters 14 and 15.

THE GOVERNMENT MARKET

The fantastically large government market includes thousands of federal, state, and local units buying for countless government institutions, such as schools, offices, hospitals, and military bases. Spending by the federal government alone accounts for about 20 percent of our gross national product. Spending at the state and local levels accounts for another 10 percent. The government as a buyer is so big and complex, however, that it is difficult to comprehend and deal with. Government procurement processes are different from those in the private sector of the industrial market.

A unique feature of government buying is the **bidding system.** Much government procurement, by law, must be done on a bid basis. That is, the government advertises for bids, stating the product specifications. Then it must accept the lowest bid that meets these specifications. In other buying situations, the government may negotiate a purchase contract with an individual supplier. This marketing practice might be used, for example, when the Department of Defense wants someone to develop and build a new weapons system, and there are no comparable products on which to base bidding specifications.

Many companies make no real effort to sell to the government, preferring not to contend with the red tape. Yet government business can be quite profitable. Dealing

The federal government is a big customer.

with the government to any significant extent, however, usually requires specialized marketing techniques and information.[3]

THE "NONBUSINESS" BUSINESS MARKET

In recent years we have been giving some long-overdue marketing attention to the multibillion-dollar market comprised of so-called nonbusiness or nonprofit organizations. This industrial market segment includes such diverse institutions as churches, colleges and universities, museums, hospitals and other health-care institutions, political parties, labor unions, and charitable organizations. We said "so-called" nonbusiness organizations. Actually each of these institutions really is a business organization. Unfortunately, however, our society (and the institutions themselves) in the past did not perceive of a museum or a hospital as being a business organization. And many people today still feel uncomfortable thinking of their church, school, or political party as being a business organization. Nevertheless, these are business organizations and they have real marketing problems. If you don't think so, just take a look at some of the advertising being done by universities, hospitals, etc., as they try to attract customers.

These organizations also conduct marketing campaigns—albeit under a different name—as they try to attract billions of dollars in contributions. In turn, they spend billions of dollars as they buy products and services to run their operations. Marketing to, and by, these organizations is discussed in more detail in Chapter 22.

[3]See Warren H. Suss, "How to Sell to Uncle Sam," *Harvard Business Review*, November–December 1984, pp. 136–144; and David E. Gumpert and Jeffry A. Timmons, "Penetrating the Government Procurement Maze," *Harvard Business Review*, September–October 1982, pp. 14–23.

CHARACTERISTICS OF INDUSTRIAL MARKET DEMAND

■

Four general demand characteristics help to differentiate the industrial market from the consumer market: (1) demand is derived, (2) demand is inelastic, (3) demand is widely fluctuating, and (4) the market is knowledgeable.

Demand Is Derived

The demand for each industrial good is derived from the demand for the consumer products in which the industrial item is used. The demand for steel depends partially upon the consumer demand for automobiles and refrigerators, for example. The demand for steel also depends upon the demand for butter, baseball gloves, and bongo drums. This is because the tools, machines, and other equipment involved in making these items are made of steel. Thus, as the demand for baseball gloves increases, glove manufacturers may buy more steel sewing machines or filing cabinets.

There are several marketing implications in the fact that industrial market demand is a derived demand. For example, the producer of an industrial product may run an advertising campaign promoting consumer products or services that involve the industrial firm's product. Thus, the Boeing Company ran a series of TV ads to promote consumer air travel. The company figured that a significant increase in consumer air

The demand is derived from people who want a sugar substitute.

Another good place to find what's in NutraSweet.

Over half the food you eat today will contain what's in NutraSweet. It's nothing mysterious. NutraSweet brand sweetener is made from two building blocks of protein (amino acids, in more scientific lingo).

They're just like those found in fruits, vegetables, grains, meats and dairy products. And your body treats them no differently than if they came from a peach or a string bean or a glass of milk.

Which is all the more remarkable considering that NutraSweet tastes just like sugar. That's sweetness you can enjoy. And feel good about.

NutraSweet®

Demand Is Inelastic

travel ultimately would lead to an increase in demand for Boeing airplanes. The manufacturer of NutraSweet, a low-calorie sugar-substitute sweetener, ran a consumer advertising campaign designed to build consumer loyalty for products sweetened with NutraSweet. The idea was that this consumer demand would, in turn, trigger a derived demand for NutraSweet on the part of food and soft-drink processors.

Another significant characteristic of the industrial market is related to the derived-demand feature: The demand for many industrial products is relatively inelastic. That is, the demand for a product responds very little to changes in its price. If the price of buttons for men's jackets should suddenly rise or fall considerably, there would probably be no appreciable change in the demand for buttons. (If you would like to review some of your economics, the concept of elasticity of demand is explained early in Chapter 12.)

This demand is inelastic because the cost of a single part or material is ordinarily a small portion of the total cost of the finished product. The cost of the chemicals in paint is a small part of the price that a consumer pays for paint. The cost of the enamel on a refrigerator is a small part of its retail price. Even the cost of expensive capital equipment, when distributed over thousands of units of a product, becomes a very small part of the unit cost. As a result, when the price of the industrial product changes, there is very little shift in the demand for the related consumer products. If there is no appreciable shift in the demand for the consumer goods, then (by virtue of the derived-demand feature) there is no change in the demand for the industrial product.

From a marketing point of view, there are three factors to consider regarding this inelasticity of industrial demand:

The demand is inelastic for a product like a fan belt.

- The first is the position of an entire industry as contrasted with that of an individual firm. An industry-wide cut in the price of steel belts used in tires will have little effect on the demand for automobile tires. Consequently, it will cause little change in the total demand for steel belts. The pricing policy of an individual firm, however, can substantially alter the demand for that firm's products. If one supplier significantly cuts the price of steel belts, the drop in price may draw a great deal of business away from competitors. The advantage will, of course, be temporary, because competitors will undoubtedly retaliate in some way to recapture their lost business. Nevertheless, in the short run, the demand curve faced by a single firm is much more elastic than the industry's curve.

- The second marketing factor involved here is time. Much of our discussion refers to short-run situations. Over the long run, the demand for a given industrial product is more elastic. If the price of cloth for women's suits is raised, there probably will be no immediate change in the price of the finished garment. However, the increase in the cost of materials could very well be reflected in a $50 rise in suit prices for next year. This rise could then influence the demand for suits, and thus for cloth, a year or more hence.

- The third modifying aspect is the relative importance of a specific industrial product in the cost of the finished good. We may generalize to this extent: The greater the cost of an industrial product as a percentage of the total price of the finished good, the greater the elasticity of demand for this industrial product.

Demand Is Widely Fluctuating

Although the demand for industrial goods does not change much in response to price changes, it is far from steady. In fact, the market demand for most classes of industrial goods fluctuates considerably more than the demand for consumer products. The demand for installations—major plant equipment, factories, etc.—is especially subject to change. Substantial fluctuations also exist in the market for accessory equipment—office furniture and machinery, delivery trucks, and similar products. These tend to accentuate the swings in the demand for industrial raw materials and fabricating parts. This has been exemplified by downturns in the construction and auto industries, which affected the suppliers of lumber, steel, and other materials and parts. One exception to this generalization is found in agricultural products intended for processing. There is a reasonably consistent demand for animals intended for meat products, for fruits and vegetables that will be canned or frozen, and for grains and dairy products.

Fluctuations in the demand for industrial products can influence all aspects of a firm's marketing program. In product planning, they may stimulate a firm to diversify into other products to ease production and marketing problems. Distribution strategies may be affected. Consider a firm's sales force—when demand declines, the sales force must be either trimmed back or maintained at full strength (but at a loss). Rather than try to cope with this problem, a seller may decide to make greater use of wholesalers to reach its market. In its pricing, management may attempt to stem a decline in sales by cutting prices, hoping to attract customers away from competing firms.[4]

Market Is Knowledgeable

Unlike ultimate consumers, typical industrial buyers are usually well informed about what they are buying. They know the relative merits of alternative sources of supply and competitive products. The position of purchasing agent is being upgraded in many firms, and purchasing executives are using sophisticated tools to improve their performance.[5]

These improvements in purchasing skills carry significant marketing implications, then, for the sellers of industrial products. For example, producers of industrial goods place greater emphasis on personal selling than do firms marketing consumer products. Industrial sales people must be carefully selected, properly trained, and adequately compensated. They must give effective sales presentations and furnish satisfactory service both before and after each sale is made. Sales executives are devoting increased effort to the assignment of sales people to key accounts to ensure that these reps are compatible with industrial buyers.

DETERMINANTS OF INDUSTRIAL MARKET DEMAND

To analyze a consumer market, a marketer would study the distribution of population and income and then try to determine the consumers' buying motives and habits. Essentially the same type of analysis can be used by a firm selling to the *industrial* market. The factors affecting the market for industrial products are the number of potential industrial users and their purchasing power, buying motives, and buying

---

[4]See William S. Bishop, John L. Graham, and Michael H. Jones, "Volatility of Derived Demand in Industrial Markets and Its Management Implications," *Journal of Marketing,* Fall 1984, pp. 95–103.

[5]See Richard M. Hill, "Industrial Marketers Should Heed Shift in Purchasing Emphasis with 5 New 'Tools,'" *Marketing News,* June 12, 1981, p. 18. Also see Gregory D. Upah and Monroe M. Bird, "Changes in Industrial Buying: Implications for Industrial Marketers," *Industrial Marketing Management,* April 1980, pp. 117–121.

Number and Types of Industrial Users

habits. In the following discussion we identify several basic *differences* between consumer markets and industrial markets.

TOTAL MARKET

The industrial market contains relatively few buying units when compared with the consumer market. In the United States, there are approximately 12 million industrial users, in contrast to about 250 million consumers divided among more than 85 million households. The industrial market will seem even more limited to most companies, because they sell to only a segment of the total market. A firm selling to manufacturers of metal cans, for example, had only 336 potential customer plants with 20 or more employees, according to *Sales & Marketing Management*'s 1985 Survey of Industrial and Commercial Buying Power.[6] In that same employment-size class, there were only 49 plants making sewing machines and 53 plants producing synthetic rubber. Consequently, marketing executives must try to pinpoint their market carefully by type of industry and geographic location. A firm marketing hard-rock mining equipment is not interested in the total industrial market, or even in all 30,000 firms engaged in mining and quarrying.

One very useful information source developed by the federal government is the **Standard Industrial Classification** (S.I.C.) system, which enables a company to identify relatively small segments of its industrial market.[7] In this system, all types of businesses in the United States are divided into 10 groups. Then a range of two-digit code numbers is assigned to each group as follows:

S.I.C. range	Industry group
01 to 09	Agriculture, forestry, fishing
10 to 14	Mining
15 to 19	Contract construction
20 to 39	Manufacturing
40 to 49	Transportation and other public utilities
50 to 59	Wholesale and retail trade
60 to 67	Finance, insurance, and real estate
70 to 89	Services
90 to 97	Government—federal, state, local, and international
99	Others

A separate two-digit number is assigned to each major industry within each of the above groups. Then, three- and four-digit classification numbers are used to subdivide each major industry into finer segments. Fig. 7.1 illustrates the S.I.C. system as applied to the dairy industry—a segment of the food-products group within the broad category of manufacturing.

[6] "1985 Survey of U.S. Industrial & Commercial Buying Power," *Sales & Marketing Management*, Apr. 22, 1985, pp. 54–57.

[7] For a description of the Standard Industrial Classification system and a complete listing of all S.I.C. numbers and classifications, see *Standard Industrial Classification Manual*, U.S. Government Printing Office, Washington, D.C., 1972 and also *1977 Supplement*. Also see "SIC: The System Explained," *Sales & Marketing Management*, Apr. 22, 1985, pp. 52–53.

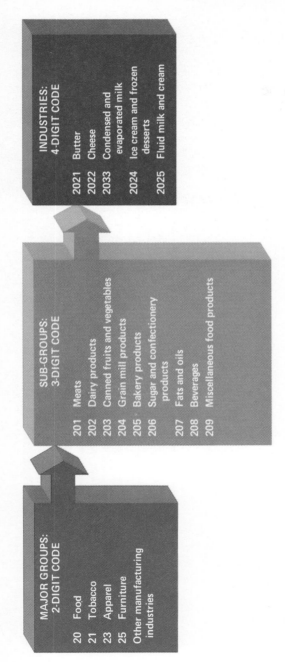

FIGURE 7-1
**Examples of S.I.C. codes.
Dairy-industry segment of food
products.**

The federal government publishes a considerable amount of useful marketing-research information for each four-digit industry classification. These data include the number of establishments, employment, and sales volume—all by geographic area.

One limitation of S.I.C. data is that a multiproduct company is listed in only a single four-digit category. Also, the government's nondisclosure rules prevent revealing information that can identify a given establishment. Consequently, four-digit detail is not available for an industry in a geographic location where this information would identify a certain company.

SIZE OF INDUSTRIAL USERS

While the industrial market may be limited in the total number of buyers, it is large in purchasing power. A relatively small percentage of firms account for the greatest share of the value added to products by manufacturing. Let's look at some examples from the latest available Census of Manufacturers. Less than 2 percent of the firms—those with 500 or more employees—accounted for almost 50 percent of the total dollar value added by manufacturing and for almost 40 percent of the total employment in manufacturing. Firms with fewer than 100 employees accounted for 90 percent of all manufacturing establishments, but they produced only 23 percent of the value added by manufacturing (Table 7-1).

The marketing significance of these facts is that buying power in the industrial market is highly concentrated in a relatively few firms. This market concentration means that sellers have the opportunity to deal directly with industrial users. Middlemen are not so essential as in the consumer market.

These statements are, of course, broad generalizations covering the *total* industrial market. They do not take into account the variation in industrial concentration from one industry to another. In some industries—women's dresses and ready-mix

TABLE 7-1 SIZE DISTRIBUTION OF MANUFACTURING ESTABLISHMENTS IN THE UNITED STATES, 1982, BY NUMBER OF EMPLOYEES

This table shows that buying power in the industrial market is highly concentrated among relatively few firms. Ten percent of the companies—those with 100 or more employees—accounted for 80 percent of the value added by manufacturing. How might this market concentration influence a seller's marketing program?

Number of employees	Number of establishments*	% of firms	% of employees	% of value added
1–4	113,100	33	1	1
5–9	60,100	17	2	2
10–99	140,800	40	25	20
100–499	29,200	8	34	31
500–999	3,300	1	13	15
1,000–2,499	1,400	1	11	14
2,500 or more	500	1	14	17
Total	348,400	100.0%	100.0%	100.0%

*Numbers rounded off.
Source: 1982 Census of Manufacturers.

TABLE 7-2 CONCENTRATION IN THE INDUSTRIAL MARKET

High concentration	← In each industry →	Low concentration
Market share held by 4 largest companies*		**Market share held by 20 largest companies***
Hard-surface floor coverings	99%	Special dies, tools, jigs	13%
Chewing gum	95%	Ready-mix concrete	16%
Household refrigerators, freezers	94%	Commercial printing	16%
Motor vehicles	92%	Women's dresses	17%
Light bulbs	91%	Screw machine products	17%

*Based on value of shipments.
Source: Census of Manufactures, 1982.

REGIONAL CONCENTRATION OF INDUSTRIAL USERS

There is a substantial regional concentration in many of the major industries and among industrial users as a whole. A firm selling products usable in copper mining will find the bulk of its American market in Utah and Arizona. Hat manufacturers are located

concrete, for example—there is a relatively low level of concentration. (See Table 7-2.) Nevertheless, even a so-called low-concentration industry represents far, far more of a concentrated market than anything we could find in the consumer market.

mostly in New England, and a large percentage of American-produced shoes come from New England, St. Louis, and the Southeast.

The eight states constituting the Middle Atlantic and East North Central census regions accounted for almost 50 percent of the total value added by manufacturing in 1982. Just 10 Standard Metropolitan Areas alone accounted for about 25 percent of the total United States value added by manufacturing.

VERTICAL AND HORIZONTAL INDUSTRIAL MARKETS

For effective marketing planning, a company should know whether the market for its products is vertical or horizontal. If an industrial product is usable by virtually all firms in only one or two industries, it has a **vertical** market. For example, some precision instruments are intended only for the marine market, but every boatbuilder or shipbuilder is a potential customer. If the product is usable by many industries, its market is said to be broad, or **horizontal.** Industrial supplies, such as lubricating oils and greases, small motors, and some paper products, may be sold to a wide variety of industries.

A company's marketing program ordinarily is influenced by whether that firm's markets are vertical or horizontal. For example, in a vertical market a product can be tailor-made to meet the specific needs of one industry. In a horizontal market the product must be developed as an all-purpose item. Moreover, advertising and personal selling efforts can be directed more effectively in vertical markets.

Buying Power of Industrial Users

Another determinant of industrial market demand is the purchasing power of industrial users. This can be measured either by the expenditures of industrial users or by their sales volume. Many times, however, such information is not available or is very difficult to estimate. In such cases it is more feasible to use an **activity indicator**— that is, some market factor that is related to income generation and expenditures. Sometimes an activity indicator is a combined indicator of purchasing power and the number of industrial users. Following are examples of activity indicators that might be used to estimate the purchasing power of industrial users.

MEASURES OF MANUFACTURING ACTIVITY

Firms selling to manufacturers might use as market indicators such factors as the number of employees, the number of plants, or the dollar value added by manufacturing. One firm selling work gloves used the number of employees in manufacturing establishments to determine the relative values of various geographic markets. Another company that sold a product that controls stream pollution used two indicators—(1) the number of firms processing wood products (paper mills, plywood mills, and so forth) and (2) the manufacturing value added by these firms.

MEASURES OF MINING ACTIVITY

The number of mines operating, the volume of their output, and the dollar value of the product as it leaves the mine all may indicate the purchasing power of mines. This information can be used by any firm marketing industrial products to mine operators.

MEASURES OF AGRICULTURAL ACTIVITY

A company marketing fertilizer or agricultural equipment can estimate the buying

The number of operating steel mills is a measure of the market for a lot of industrial products.

power of its farm market by studying such indicators as cash farm income, acreage planted, or crop yields. The chemical producer that sells to a fertilizer manufacturer might study the same indices, because the demand for chemicals in this case is derived from the demand for fertilizer.

MEASURES OF CONSTRUCTION ACTIVITY

If an enterprise is marketing building materials, such as lumber, brick, gypsum products, or builders' hardware, its market is dependent upon construction activity. This may be indicated by the number and value of building permits issued or by the number of construction starts by type of housing (single-family residence, apartment, or commercial).

Industrial buying behavior, like consumer buying behavior, is initiated when an aroused need (a motive) is recognized. This leads to goal-oriented activity designed to satisfy the need. Once again, marketing practitioners must try to determine what motivates the buyer.

Buying Motives of Industrial Users

Industrial buying motives, for the most part, are presumed to be rational, and an industrial purchase normally is a methodical, objective undertaking. Industrial buyers are motivated primarily by a desire to maximize their firms' profits. More specifically, their buying goal is to achieve the optimal combination of price, quality, and service in the products they buy. On the other hand, sales people would maintain that some industrial buyers seem to be motivated more toward personal goals that are in conflict with their employers' goals.

Actually, industrial buyers do have two goals—to improve their positions in their firms (self-interest) and to further their company's position (in profits, in acceptance by society). Sometimes these goals are mutually consistent, and sometimes they are in conflict. Obviously, the greater the degree of consistency, the better for both the organization and the individual. When very little mutuality of goals exists, the situation is poor. Probably the more usual situation is to find some overlap of interests, but also a significant area where the buyer's goals do not coincide with those of the firm. In these cases, a seller might appeal to the buyer both on a rational, "what's-good-for-the-firm" basis and on an ego-building basis. Promotional efforts attuned to the buyer's ego are particularly useful when two or more competing sellers are offering essentially the same products, prices, and services.

The Industrial Buying Process

Competition and the complexity of industrial marketing have encouraged companies to focus attention on the *total* buying process. Buying is treated as an ongoing relationship of mutual interest to both buyer and seller. As one example of this approach, researchers in a Marketing Science Institute study developed a framework to explain different types of industrial buying situations.[8] The model for this framework—called a **buy-grid**—is illustrated in Table 7-3. The model reflects two major aspects of the

[8]Patrick J. Robinson, Charles W. Faris, and Yoram Wind, *Industrial Buying and Creative Marketing,* Allyn and Bacon, Boston, 1967. For a different perspective on the buy-grid concept, see Joseph A. Belizzi and Phillip McVey, "How Valid Is the Buy-Grid Model?" *Industrial Marketing Management,* February 1983, pp. 57–62.

TABLE 7-3   THE BUY-GRID FRAMEWORK
Stages in the industrial buying process (buy phases) in relation to buying situations (buy classes)

Buy phases (stages in buying-decision process)	Buy classes		
	New class	Modified rebuy	Straight rebuy
1. Recognize the problem.	Yes	Maybe	No
2. Determine product needs.	Yes	Maybe	No
3. Describe product specifications.	Yes	Yes	Yes
4. Search for suppliers.	Yes	Maybe	No
5. Acquire supplier proposals.	Yes	Maybe	No
6. Select suppliers.	Yes	Maybe	No
7. Select an order routine.	Yes	Maybe	No
8. Evaluate product performance.	Yes	Yes	Yes

Source: Adapted from Patrick J. Robinson, Charles W. Faris, and Yoram Wind, *Industrial Buying and Creative Marketing,* Allyn and Bacon, Inc., Boston, 1967, p. 14.

Buying a Learjet is usually a new-task buying situation.

industrial buying process: (1) the classes of typical buying situations and (2) the sequential steps in the buying process.

Three typical buying situations (called **buy classes**) were identified as follows: new tasks, modified rebuys, and straight rebuys. The **new task** is the most difficult and complex of the three. More people influence the new-task buying-decision process than influence the other two types. The problem is that new-information needs are high, and the evaluation of alternatives is critical. Sellers are given their best opportunity to be heard and to display their creative selling ability in satisfying the buyer's needs.

Straight rebuys—routine purchases with minimal information needs and no real consideration of alternatives—are at the other extreme. Buying decisions are made in the purchasing department, usually from a list of acceptable suppliers. Suppliers, especially those from new firms not on the list, have difficulty getting an audience with the buyer. **Modified rebuys** are somewhere between the other two in terms of time required, information needed, alternatives considered, and other characteristics.

The other major element in the buy-grid reflects the idea that the industrial buying process is a sequence of eight stages, called **buy phases.** The process starts with the recognition of a problem. It ranges through the determination and description of product specifications, the search for an evaluation of alternatives, and the buying act. It ends with postpurchase feedback and evaluation. (This surely is reminiscent of the consumer's buying-decision process outlined in Chapter 6.)

Multiple Buying Influences—The Buying Center

One of the biggest problems in marketing to an industrial user is determining who in the organization buys the product. That is, who influences the buying decision, who determines the product specifications, who makes the buying decision, and who does the actual buying (places the order). In the industrial market, these activities typically involve several people—there is a **multiple buying influence**—particularly in medium-sized and large firms. Even in small companies where the owner-managers make all major decisions, they usually consult with knowledgeable employees before making some purchases.

Understanding the concept of a buying center is helpful in identifying the multiple buying influences and understanding the buying process in industrial organizations. A **buying center** may be defined as all the individuals or groups who are involved in the purchasing decision-making process. Thus a buying center includes the people who play any of the following roles:[9]

This secretary may be a user, influencer, gatekeeper, or all the above.

- **Users:** The people who actually use the product—perhaps a secretary, a production-line worker, or a truck driver.

- **Influencers:** The people who set the specifications and aspects of buying decisions because of their technical expertise, their financial position, or maybe even their political power in the organization.

- **Deciders:** The people who make the actual buying decision regarding the product and the supplier. A purchasing agent may be the decider in a straight rebuy situation. But someone in top management may make the decision regarding whether to buy an expensive computer.

- **Gatekeepers:** The people who control the flow of purchasing information within the organization and between the buying firm and potential vendors. These people may be purchasing agents, secretaries, receptionists, or technical personnel.

- **Buyers:** The people who select the suppliers, arrange the terms of sale, and process the actual purchase orders. Typically, this is the purchasing department's role. But again, if the purchase is an expensive, complex new buy, the buyer's role may be filled by someone in top management.

Several people in an organization may play the same role—for example, there may be several users of the product. Or the same person may occupy more than one role. A secretary may be a user, an influencer, and a gatekeeper in the purchase of an office machine.

The size and composition of a buying center will vary among business organizations. Also, within a given organization, the size and makeup of the buying center will vary depending on the product's expense, complexity, and length of life. The buying center for a straight rebuy of office supplies will be quite different from the center handling the purchase of a building or a fleet of trucks.

It is probably obvious that the variety of people involved in any industrial buying situation, plus the difference among companies, present some real challenges to sales people. As they try to determine "who's on first"—that is, determine who does what in a buying situation—the sales reps often will call on the wrong executives. Even knowing who the decision makers are is not enough—these people may be very difficult to reach.

[9]Frederick E. Webster, Jr., and Yoram Wind, "A General Model for Understanding Organizational Buying Behavior," *Journal of Marketing*, April 1972, pp. 12–19. Also see Webster and Wind, *Organizational Buying Behavior*, Prentice-Hall, Englewood Cliffs, N.J., 1972, especially pp. 75–87, and Thomas V. Bonoma, "Major Sales: Who Really Does the Buying," *Harvard Business Review*, May–June 1982, pp. 111–119.

Buying Patterns of Industrial Users

Overt buying behavior in the *industrial* market differs significantly from *consumer* behavior in several ways. These differences obviously stem from the differences in the products, markets, and buyer-seller relationships.

DIRECT PURCHASE

Direct sale from the producer to the ultimate consumer is rare. In the industrial market, however, direct marketing from the producer to the industrial user is quite common. This is true especially when the order is large and the buyer needs much technical assistance. From a seller's point of view, direct marketing is reasonable, especially when there are relatively few potential buyers, they are big, and they are geographically concentrated.

FREQUENCY OF PURCHASE

In the industrial market, firms buy certain products very infrequently. Large installations are purchased only once in many years. Smaller parts and materials to be used in the manufacture of a product may be ordered on long-term contracts, so that an actual selling opportunity exists only once every year. Even standardized operating supplies, such as office supplies or cleaning products, may be bought only once a month.

Because of this buying pattern, a great burden is placed on the advertising and personal selling programs of industrial sellers. Their advertising must keep the company's name constantly before the market. The sales force must call on potential customers often enough to know when a customer is considering a purchase.

SIZE OF ORDER

The average industrial order is considerably larger than its counterpart in the consumer market. This fact, coupled with the infrequency of purchase, spotlights the importance of each sale in the industrial market. Losing the sale of a pair of shoes to a consumer is not nearly so devastating as losing the sale of 10 airplanes.

LENGTH OF NEGOTIATION PERIOD

The period of negotiation in an industrial sale is usually much longer than in a consumer market sale. Some of the reasons for the extended negotiations are (1) several executives are involved in the buying decision; (2) the sale often involves a large amount of money; (3) the industrial product is often made to order, and considerable discussion is involved in establishing the specifications.

RECIPROCITY ARRANGEMENTS

A highly controversial industrial buying habit is the practice of **reciprocity**—the policy of "I'll buy from you if you'll buy from me." Traditionally, reciprocity was common among firms marketing homogeneous basic industrial products (oil, steel, rubber, paper products, and chemicals). In these industries, price competition generally did not exist, and a firm in one industry was a major supplier to a firm in another industry. Then, through the years, reciprocal selling expanded to a wide variety of industries. Many companies established "trade relations" departments to make effective use of this powerful selling tool.

Today, however, most of these departments have vanished. There has been a significant decline in the practice of reciprocity on a *systematic* basis. This decline has occurred for two reasons—one legal and the other economic. Both the Federal Trade Commission and the Antitrust Division of the Department of Justice have forbidden the use of reciprocity in any systematic manner, particularly in large companies. From an economic point of view, reciprocity may not make sense because the morale of both the sales force and the purchasing department may suffer. Under any circumstances, it is difficult to justify purchasing from customers unless the buyer is getting competitive price, quality, and service from the seller.

DEMAND FOR PRODUCT SERVICING

The user's desire for excellent service is a strong industrial buying motive that may determine buying patterns. Consequently, many sellers emphasize their service as much as their products. Frequently a firm's only attraction is its service, because the product itself is so standardized that it can be purchased from any number of companies.

Sellers must stand ready to furnish services both before and after the sale. A manufacturer of computers may study a customer firm's accounting operations and suggest more effective systems that involve using the seller's products. The manufacturer will also arrange to retrain the present office staffs. After the machines have been installed, other services, such as repairs, may be furnished.

QUALITY AND SUPPLY REQUIREMENTS

Another industrial buying pattern is the user's insistence upon an adequate quantity of uniform-quality products. Variations in the quality of materials going into finished products can cause considerable trouble for manufacturers. They may be faced with costly disruptions in their production processes if the imperfections exceed quality-control limits. Adequate *quantities* are as important as good quality. A work stoppage that is caused by an insufficient supply of material is just as costly as one that is caused by inferior quality of material. In one study of problems faced by purchasing agents for smaller manufacturers, the problem most often reported was sellers failing to deliver on schedule.[10]

Adequacy of supply is a problem especially for sellers and users of raw materials such as agricultural products, metal ores, or forest products. Climatic conditions may disrupt the normal flow of goods—logging camps or mining operations may become snowbound. Agricultural products fluctuate in quality and quantity from one growing season to another. These "acts of God" create managerial problems for both buyers and sellers with respect to warehousing, standardization, and grading.

LEASING INSTEAD OF BUYING

A growing behavioral pattern among firms in the industrial market is that of **leasing** industrial products instead of buying them outright. In the past, this practice was limited to large equipment, such as data processing machines (IBM), packaging equip-

Sometimes it's better to rent than to buy.

[10]Monroe M. Bird, "Small Industrial Buyers Call Late Delivery Worst Problem," *Marketing News,* Apr. 4, 1980, p. 24.

ment (American Can Company), and heavy construction equipment. Today, industrial firms are expanding leasing arrangements to include delivery trucks, sales-force automobiles, machine tools, and other items generally less expensive than major installations.

Leasing has several merits for the firm leasing out its equipment. Total net income—after charging off pertinent repair and maintenance expenses—is often higher than it would be if the unit were sold outright. Also, the market may be expanded to include users who could not afford to buy the product, especially large equipment. Leasing offers an effective method of getting distribution for a new product. Potential users may be more willing to rent a product than to buy it. If they are not satisfied, their expenditure is limited to a few monthly payments.

From the user's point of view, the benefits of leasing may be summarized as follows:

- Leasing allows users to retain their investment capital for other purposes.
- There may be significant tax advantages. Rental payments are totally tax-deductible, and they usually are larger than corresponding depreciation charges on owned products.
- New firms can enter a business with less capital outlay than would be necessary if they had to buy the equipment outright.
- Leased products are usually serviced by lessors; this eliminates one headache associated with ownership.
- Leasing is particularly attractive to users who need the equipment seasonally or sporadically, as in food canning or construction.

SUMMARY

The industrial market consists of organizations that buy goods and services to use in their businesses. It is an extremely large, complex, and important market. It includes a wide variety of industrial users who buy a wide variety of industrial products and services. Industrial market demand may be characterized generally as being derived, inelastic, and widely fluctuating. Industrial buyers usually are quite well informed about what they are buying. Industrial market demand is analyzed by evaluating the same three basic factors as those in the consumer market: (1) the number and kinds of industrial users, (2) their buying power, and (3) their motivation and buying behavior. Industrial buying motives generally are rational, but the purchasing agent's self-interest must also be considered.

The concept of a buying center reflects the multiple buying influences often involved in industrial purchasing decisions. In a typical buying center are people playing the roles of users, influencers, deciders, buyers, and gatekeepers. Buying patterns (habits) of industrial users often are quite different from patterns in the consumer market. In the industrial market, the negotiation period usually is longer, and purchases are made less frequently. Orders are larger, and direct purchases (no middlemen) are more common. Reciprocity arrangements and leasing (rather than product ownership) are quite common in industrial marketing.

KEY TERMS AND CONCEPTS ■

Industrial market 136
Industrial products 136
Industrial marketing 136
Farm market 137–138
Agribusiness 137
Contract farming 138
Reseller market 139
Government market 139
Nonbusiness market 140
Derived demand 141–142
Inelastic demand 142
Standard Industrial Classification (S.I.C.) system 144
Vertical industrial markets 147
Horizontal industrial markets 147
Activity indicators of buying power 147

Buy-grid 148
Buy classes 149
Buy phases 149
Multiple buying influences (buying center): 149–150
  Users 150
  Influencers 150
  Deciders 150
  Buyers 150
  Gatekeepers 150
Direct purchase 151
Reciprocity 151
Leasing products or services 152–153

QUESTIONS AND PROBLEMS ■

1. "About 80 percent of all farm products are industrial goods." Give some examples of farm products that are *consumer* goods.

2. If the demand for most industrial goods is inelastic, why is it that sellers do not raise their prices to maximize their revenues?

3. Why does the demand for industrial goods usually fluctuate more widely than that for consumer goods?

4. What are some marketing implications in the fact that the demand for industrial goods:
   a. fluctuates widely?
   b. is inelastic?
   c. is derived?

5. What are the marketing implications for a seller in the fact that customers are geographically concentrated and limited in number?

6. What differences would you expect to find between the marketing strategies of a company selling to horizontal industrial markets and those of a company selling to vertical industrial markets?

7. Select four of the buy phases in the industrial buying process and explain how the relative importance of each one changes, depending upon whether the buying situation is a new task or a straight rebuy.

8. Select three advertisements for industrial products and identify the buying motives stressed in the ads.

9. What suggestions do you have for industrial sellers to help them determine who influences the buying decision among industrial users?

10. In the buying center in an industrial organization, discuss briefly the role of each of the following:
    a. Influencers.
    b. Buyers.
    c. Gatekeepers.

11. NCR, IBM, Burroughs, and other manufacturers of office machines make a substantial proportion of their sales directly to industrial users. At the same time, wholesalers of office equipment are thriving. Are these two market situations inconsistent? Explain.

8

MARKET SEGMENTATION AND FORECASTING MARKET DEMAND

CHAPTER GOALS

This is the last of four chapters dealing with target markets. We have analyzed the components of consumer and industrial markets. To conclude our discussion of target-market selection, we consider the concepts of market segmentation and demand forecasting. After studying this chapter, you should understand:

- The concept of market segmentation—its meaning, benefits, limitations, and conditions for use.
- The bases for segmenting consumer markets.
- The bases for segmenting industrial markets.
- Target-market strategies—aggregation, concentration, and multiple segmentation.
- The nature and importance of demand forecasting in marketing.
- The major methods used in forecasting market demand.

Traditionally in the United States, women's fashion clothing has been designed for women of medium height and weight—generally in a size range of 8 to 14. Very small women shopped in the junior or girls' department for dresses and often in the boys' department for jeans, parkas, and other sportswear. Large women similarly were ignored by the fashion designers, manufacturers, and retailers. *Very* few retail clothing stores—the Lane Bryant chain was one—catered to large-sized women.

But the times, they have been a'changing. Today clothing designers, manufacturers, and retailers alike finally are recognizing the profit potential in the market segments comprised of very small or very large women. The Fashion Bar, a chain of large, departmentalized specialty stores in Colorado, now has a "Petite" clothing division for women. This division features clothing designed by name fashion designers such as Liz Claiborne, Evan Picone, John Meyer, Koret, Villager, and others. Short Cuts, a specialty store in Boulder, Colorado, features sizes 0 to 12 and "total dressing for the woman 5'4" and under."

At the other end of the size spectrum, there are 30 to 40 million American women who wear a clothing size of 16 or larger. This adds up to a $6 billion annual market segment that firms in the clothing industry finally are starting to serve. Firms are designing and manufacturing fashion apparel for large-sized women. In so doing, these companies recognize that they cannot simply take a size 8 design for a dress and upsize it to a 26. Totally new designs are being developed. In retailing, Macy's and Bloomingdale's department stores now have placed their large-size apparel departments in high-fashion locations in their stores. (Bloomingdale's department formerly was on the budget floor in the basement.)[1]

---

[1]Based in part on Jolie Solomon, "Fashion Industry Courting Large Women, Offering Stylish Clothes in Big Sizes," *The Wall Street Journal,* Sept. 27, 1985, p. 31.

By catering separately to small and large women, the apparel industry in effect is engaging in market segmentation. Not all consumers want to wear the same type of clothing, use the same hair shampoo, or participate in the same recreational activities. Nor do all business firms want to buy the same type of word processors or delivery trucks. At the same time, a marketer usually cannot afford to tailor-make a different product for every single customer. Consequently, some form of market segmentation is the strategy that most marketers adopt as a compromise between the extremes of one product for all and a different product for each customer. A major key to a company's success is its ability to select the most effective location on this segmentation spectrum between the two extremes.

In our discussion of selecting target markets, we have completed the phase of market opportunity analysis in which we analyzed the three components of a market—people or organizations with wants to satisfy, the money to spend, and the willingness to spend it. With this analysis, plus our earlier environmental analysis as a guide, a

GUIDELINES IN MARKET SELECTION ■

There are some general guidelines to follow when selecting target markets. The first one is that the target markets should be compatible with the organization's goals and image. A firm that is marketing high-priced personal computers should not sell through discount chain stores in an effort to reach a mass market.

A second guideline—consistent with our definition of strategic planning—is to match the marketing opportunity with the company's resources. Liggett & Myers followed this guideline when it decided to enter the market for low-cost, unbranded cigarettes. Management decided that it did not want to spend the huge sums for advertising that would be necessary for a new cigarette brand to compete with the established national brands. Consequently, the company introduced and marketed a nonadvertised, "no brand" generic cigarette through supermarkets at a lower price. Thus the company matched its limited marketing-mix resources with its intended market.

Over the long run, a business must generate a profit if it is to continue in existence. This rather obvious, third guideline translates into what is perhaps an obvious market-selection guideline. That is, an organization should consciously seek markets that will generate a sufficient sales volume at a low enough cost to result in a profit. Unfortunately, through the years, companies often overlooked the profit factor in their quest for high-volume markets. The goal often was sales volume alone, not *profitable* sales volume.

Finally, a company ordinarily should seek a market wherein the number of competitors and their size are minimal. An organization should not enter a market that is already saturated with competition unless it has some overriding competitive advantage that will enable it to take customers away from existing firms.

NATURE OF MARKET SEGMENTATION ■

What Is Market Segmentation?

Market segmentation is the process of dividing the total heterogeneous market for a product into several segments, each of which tends to be homogeneous in all signif-

company can start to zero in on its selection of target markets. Two main tasks that remain are to decide on a market segmentation strategy and to estimate the demand in the selected segments. These tasks are discussed in this chapter.[2]

The total market for most types of products is too varied—too heterogeneous—for management to consider it as a single, uniform entity. To speak of the market for vitamin pills, or electric razors, or tractors is to ignore the fact that the total market for each product consists of submarkets that differ significantly from one another. This lack of uniformity may be traced to differences in buying habits, in ways in which the product is used, in motives for buying, or in other factors. Market segmentation takes these differences into account.

[2]For the classic article on market segmentation, and one foundation for much of today's research on the subject, see Wendell R. Smith, "Product Differentiation and Market Segmentation as Alternative Marketing Strategies," *Journal of Marketing,* July 1956, pp. 3–8.

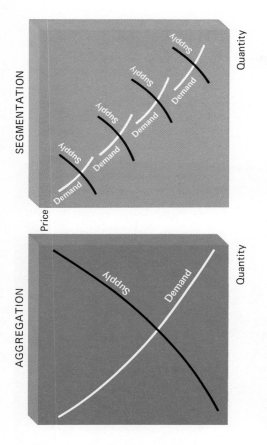

FIGURE 8-1
Demand curves representing market aggregation and market segmentation.
The object of aggregation is to fit the market to the product. Segmentation is an attempt to fit the product to the market.

icant aspects. Management then selects one or more of these market segments as the organization's target market. Finally, a separate marketing mix is developed for each segment or group of segments in this target market.

Market segmentation is the opposite of market aggregation. **Market aggregation** is the strategy whereby an organization treats its total market as a unit—that is, as one mass, aggregate market whose parts are considered to be alike in all major respects. This organization then develops a single marketing mix to reach as many customers as possible in this aggregate market.

In the language of economic theory, in market aggregation the seller assumes there is a single demand curve for its product. In effect, the product is assumed to have a broad market appeal. In contrast, in market segmentation the total market is viewed as a series of demand curves. Each one represents a separate market segment calling for a different product, promotional appeal, or other element in the marketing mix. See Fig. 8-1. Thus, instead of speaking of one aggregate market for personal computers, we can segment this total market into several submarkets. We then will have, for example, a college-student market segment for personal computers. Other submarkets might consist of segments representing homemakers, professors, traveling executives, traveling sales people, small businesses, etc.

Market segmentation is a customer-oriented philosophy and thus is consistent with the marketing concept. We first identify the needs of the customers within a submarket (segment) and then satisfy those needs. Stated another way, in market segmentation we employ a "rifle" approach (separate programs, pinpointed targets) in our marketing activities. In contrast, market aggregation is a "shotgun" approach (one program, broad target).

By tailoring marketing programs to individual market segments, management can do a better marketing job and make more efficient use of marketing resources. A small firm with limited resources might compete very effectively in one or two market segments, whereas the same firm would be buried if it aimed for the total market. By employing the strategy of market segmentation, a company can design products that

Benefits of Market Segmentation

Pheasant Run aims at two market segments.

Limitations of Market Segmentation

really match the market demands. Advertising media can be used more effectively because promotional messages—and the media chosen to present them—can be more specifically aimed toward each segment of the market.

While market segmentation can provide a lot of marketing benefits to an organization, this strategy also has some drawbacks with respect to costs and market coverage. In the first place, market segmentation can be an expensive proposition in both the production and marketing of products. In production, it obviously is less expensive to produce mass quantities of one model and one color than it is to produce a variety of models, colors, and sizes.

Segmentation increases marketing expenses in several ways. Total inventory costs go up because adequate inventories of each style, color, etc., must be maintained. Advertising costs go up because different ads may be required for each market segment. Or some segments may be too small for the seller to make effective use of television or some other advertising medium. Administrative expenses go up when management must plan and implement several different marketing programs.

Conditions for Effective Segmentation

Ideally, management's goal should be to segment its markets in such a way that each segment responds in a homogenous fashion to a given marketing program. Three conditions will help management move toward this goal.

- The basis for segmenting—that is, the characteristics used to categorize customers—must be *measurable*, and the data must be *accessible*. The "desire for ecologically compatible products" may be a characteristic that is useful in segmenting the market for a given product. But data on this characteristic are neither readily accessible nor easily quantified.

- The market segment itself should be *accessible* through existing marketing institutions—middlemen, advertising media, company sales force, and so on—with a minimum of cost and waste. To aid marketers in this regard, some national magazines, such as *Time* and *Sports Illustrated*, publish separate geographical editions. This allows an advertiser to run an ad aimed at, say, a Western segment of the market, without having to pay for exposure in other, nonmarket areas.

- Each segment should be *large enough* to be profitable. In concept, management could treat each single customer as a separate segment. (Actually, this situation may be normal in industrial markets, as when Boeing markets passenger airplanes to commercial airlines.) But in segmenting a consumer market, a firm must not develop too wide a variety of styles, colors, sizes, and prices. Usually, the diseconomies of scale in production and inventory will put reasonable limits on this type of oversegmentation.

BASES FOR MARKET SEGMENTATION ■

In Chapter 5 we discussed the segmentation of the entire United States market into two broad categories—ultimate consumers and industrial users. That was a worthwhile start toward useful segmentation, but it still leaves too broad and heterogeneous a grouping for most products, either consumer or industrial. Consequently, we need to identify some of the widely used bases for further segmenting these two broad markets. We shall start with the consumer market.

Bases for Segmenting Consumer Market

The commonly used bases for segmenting the consumer market may be grouped into the following four broad categories:

- Geographic.
- Demographic.
- Psychographic.
- Behavior toward product (product-related bases).

Table 8-1 summarizes the segmentation bases for the consumer market. Four main categories are shown along with typical subcategories under each of the four. Then for each subcategory there are some examples of typical market segments.

In using these bases to segment markets, we should note two points. First, buying behavior is rarely traceable to only one segmentation factor. Useful segmentation typically is developed by including variables from several bases. To illustrate, the market for a product rarely consists of all the people living in Pacific Coast states or all people over 65. Instead, the segment is more likely to be described with several

TABLE 8-1 SEGMENTATION BASES FOR CONSUMER MARKETS

Segmentation basis	Examples of typical market segments
Geographic:	
Region	New England, Middle Atlantic, and other census regions.
City or MSA size	Under 25,000; 25,000–100,000; 100,000–500,000; 500,000–1,000,000; etc.
Urban-rural	Urban; suburban, exurban, rural.
Climate	Hot, cold, sunny, rainy-cloudy.
Demographic:	
Age	Under 6, 6–12, 13–19, 20–34, 35–49, 50–64, 65 and over.
Sex	Male, female.
Family life cycle	Young single, young married no children, etc.
Education	Grade school only, high school graduate, college graduate.
Occupation	Professional, manager, clerical, craftsman, sales, student, housewife, unemployed.
Religion	Protestant, Catholic, Jewish, other.
Ethnic background	White, black, Oriental. American, Hispanic, Scandinavian, Italian, German, Middle Eastern, etc.
Income	Under $10,000, $10,000–$25,000, $25,000–$35,000, $35,000–$50,000, over $50,000.
Psychographic:	
Social class	Upper class, upper middle, lower middle, upper lower, etc.
Personality	Ambitious, self-confident, aggressive, introverted, extro-verted, sociable, etc.
Life-style	Conservative, liberal, health and fitness oriented, "straight," "swinger," adventuresome.
Behavior toward product (or product-related bases):	
Benefits desired	Examples vary widely depending upon product: appliance: cost, quality, life, repairs, toothpaste: no cavities, plaque control, bright teeth, good taste, low price.
Usage rate	Nonuser, light user, heavy user.

of these variables. Thus a market segment might be families living on the Pacific Coast, with young children, and earning above a certain income. As another example, one clothing manufacturer's target market was affluent young women (income, age, sex).

The other point to observe is the interrelationships among these factors, especially among the demographic factors. For instance, age and life-cycle stage typically are related. Income depends to some degree on age, life-cycle stage, education, and occupation.

GEOGRAPHIC SEGMENTATION

Many organizations segment their market on some geographic basis such as census region, city size, urban-suburban-rural, or climate. Many companies market only in a limited geographic area. Coors Brewery, for example, until recent years limited its distribution to 11 Western states. Since then the company has selected additional geographic market segments in the Midwest and Southeast, but Coors still does not market its beer in all geographic regions. Toys "R" Us, the largest chain of toy stores in the United States, locates its stores only in cities with a population exceeding 250,000. Within these large cities, the company segments further in that it usually places its warehouse-style outlets *away from* busy shopping centers.[3]

DEMOGRAPHIC SEGMENTATION

Probably the most widely used basis for segmenting consumer markets is some demographic factor such as age, sex, income, stage in family life cycle, ethnic background, etc. Again, see Table 8-1. The reason for this is simply that so often consumers' wants or product use are related to some one or more of these factors. Also, most demographic factors can serve as the bases for *operational* market segments, because they meet the conditions for effective segmentation—measurable, accessible, and large enough.

Let's look briefly at a few demographic factors to illustrate how they can serve as segmentation bases.

Age We all are well aware that our needs and wants change as we go through life. In recognition of this fact, countless firms use age categories as a basis for segmenting the markets for their products. Johnson & Johnson markets toys for different ages of children, and the specific age segment is stated on the package. Food manufacturers advertise in *Seventeen* magazine because they recognize the grocery buying power of the teenage market segment. Cosmetic manufacturers market acne creams for teenagers and hair shampoo for people over 40. Attractive women over 40 are featured in cosmetic ads aimed at this age market.

Many companies select large cities as their market segment.

THE FLIP SIDE OF USING ATTRACTIVE WOMEN OVER 40 YEARS OLD AS ROLE MODELS IN ADS—

"The end result of all this is that those of us who failed to look like Brooke Shields at 17 can now fail to look like Victoria Principal at 33, like Linda Evans at 42, and like Sophia Loren at 50."

—*Ellen Goodman, syndicated columnist*

See Hank Gilman, "Founder Lazarus Is a Reason Toys 'R' Us Dominates Its Industry," *The Wall Street Journal*, Nov. 21, 1985, p. 1.

Some traditionally one-sex products now are targeted at both men and women.

Sex For many years sex has been a commonly used segmentation basis for many products such as clothing, shoes, autos, personal care products, and magazines. In recent years, however, there have been some interesting variations on traditional sex-based segmentation. In clothing, for example, several traditionally male products have been redesigned and repositioned for the female segment of the market.[4] Jockey markets a line of Jockey Underwear for Her. Calvin Klein designs a line of men's-style boxer shorts for women. Blue jeans and T-shirts, once for men only, today are unisex items. Some cosmetics and personal care products originally targeted only at the women's market today are also marketed to men. A picture of a man has replaced that of a woman on the label of Nestlé Company's Taster's Choice instant coffee.

PSYCHOGRAPHIC SEGMENTATION

Three common bases for the psychographic segmentation of consumer markets are social-class structure, personality characteristics, and life-styles.

Income Segmenting markets on the basis of income is commonly done by firms selling such products and services as autos, housing, travel, jewelry, and furs. A Rolls Royce or a yacht obviously is intended for a different income market than is a Yugo or a rowboat. Income also typically is combined with some other base in market segmentation. In Chapter 6 we pointed out, for example, that social class may be a better predictor of consumer buying behavior than income alone.

Social class As we observed in Chapter 6, a person's social class has a considerable influence on that person's choice in many product categories. Consequently, many companies will select one or two social classes as target markets and then develop a product and marketing mix to reach those segments.

Personality characteristics *Theoretically*, personality characteristics should form a good basis for segmenting markets. Compulsive people buy differently from cautious consumers. Quiet introverts presumably make product choices different from those made by gregarious, outgoing people. *Realistically*, however, personality character-istics pose some problems that limit their usefulness in practical market segmentation. These characteristics typically are virtually impossible to measure accurately in a quantitative sense. Many studies have been made of consumer attitudes and personality traits in relation to product and brand preferences in a wide variety of product cate-gories. But the results generally have been too limited or inconclusive to be of much practical value when companies want to implement their market segmentation strat-egies.

Nevertheless, it is interesting that many firms in their advertising do appeal to consumers who have certain personality traits. Even though the given market segment is immeasurable, the seller knows that it does exist and hopefully will be attracted by this seller's promotional appeal. Thus we see a brand advertised to consumers who

[4] To help us understand the new segmentation of the women's market, Judith Langer traces the develop-ment of the women's movement through five phases, starting with the traditional premovement phase. See "At Last, Marketers Acknowledge Women's New Role," *Marketing News*, Nov. 8, 1985, p. 45.

"are on the way up," or who are "men of distinction," or who "don't want their family left helpless."

Life-styles   The term *life-style* is a very broad concept and sometimes overlaps personality characteristics. Being cautious, skeptical, ambitious, a workaholic, a copycat—are these personality or life-style traits? Life-styles relate to your activities, interests, and opinions. They reflect how you spend your time and what your beliefs are on various social, economic, and political issues.[5]

There is no commonly accepted terminology of life-style categories for segmenting markets. Researchers often develop a different category terminology to fit the market or product being studied. As an example, one widely respected study of values and life-styles (VALS) segmented consumers into the following nine life-style categories:[6]

[5]See Joseph T. Plummer, "The Concept and Application of Life Style Segmentation," *Journal of Marketing,* January 1974, pp. 33–37.

[6]See Arnold Mitchell, *The Nine American Lifestyles,* Macmillan, New York, 1983. Mitchell was the founding director of the VALS study, an ongoing project sponsored by SRI International, a research firm formerly associated with Stanford University.

Life-style is a basis for segmenting some markets.

Another study used a different nine category titles to segment the over-65 age market on a life-style basis.[7]

- Survivors.
- Sustainers.
- Belongers.
- Emulators.
- Achievers.
- I-Am-Me.
- Experiential.
- Socially conscious.
- Integrated.

Regardless of the impreciseness in terminology, people's life-styles undoubtedly do affect their choice of product types and their brand preferences within these product categories. Marketers are well aware of this and often attempt to segment their markets on a life-style basis. VALS research, for example, convinced the Bank of America that the business people the bank wanted to reach were primarily in the "achiever" segment. A leading home builder in San Antonio, Texas, also targeted in on this market.[8] Many retailers are successful, in part, because they regularly determine the latest consumer life-style trends and then design strategies to reach these market segments.[9]

While it is a valuable marketing tool, life-style segmentation still has some of the same serious limitations ascribed to segmentation based on personality characteristics. It is very difficult to accurately measure the size of the life-style segments in a quantitative manner. Another problem is that a given life-style segment simply might not be accessible at a reasonable cost through a firm's usual distribution system or promotional program.

PRODUCT-RELATED BASES

Some marketers regularly attempt to segment their markets on the basis of a consumer behavioral characteristic related to the product. In this section we shall briefly consider two of these product-related segmentation bases—benefits desired and product usage rate.

Benefits desired   Conceptually it is very logical to segment a market on the basis of the different benefits that customers want from the product. Certainly benefit segmentation is consistent with the idea that a company should be marketing product *benefits* and not simply the physical or chemical characteristics of a product. From the consumers' point of view, they really are buying product *benefits* and not the product itself. That is, a customer wants a smooth surface (the benefit) and not sandpaper (the product).

For benefit segmentation to be effective, two tasks must be accomplished. First, a company must be able to identify the various benefits that people seek in the product or service. To illustrate, in segmenting the market for its ocean cruises, the Viking Steamship Line might identify such benefit segments as (1) the opportunity to meet

---

[7]See Warren A. French and Richard Fox, "Segmenting the Senior Citizen Market," *The Journal of Consumer Marketing*, Winter 1985, pp. 61–74.

[8]Kim Foltz, "Wizards of Marketing," *Newsweek*, July 22, 1985, pp. 42–44.

[9]See Max L. Densmore and Sylvia Kaufman, "How Leading Retailers Stay on Top," *Business*, April–June 1985, pp. 28–35; and Roger D. Blackwell and W. Wayne Talarzyk, "Life-Style Retailing: Competitive Strategies for the 1980s," *Journal of Retailing*, Winter 1983, pp. 7–27.

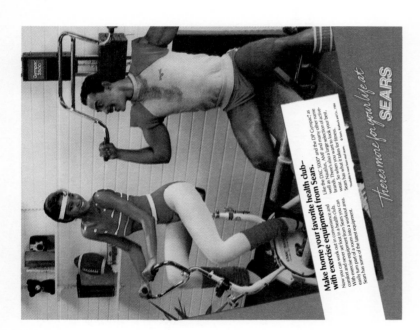

What are the benefit segments for this product?

people, (2) recreation, (3) education, (4) rest and relaxation. In his classic study which originated the concept of benefit segmentation, Russell Haley identified the following benefit segments for toothpaste and the benefits sought by these segments: (1) sensories—flavor and appearance; (2) sociables—brightness of teeth; (3) worriers—decay prevention; (4) independents—low price. Today Haley might add "plaque control" as a fifth benefit segment.[10]

Once these separate benefits are identified, the second task is to describe the demographic and psychographic characteristics of the people in each segment. Then the seller is in a position to launch a product and marketing program to reach a selected target segment.

Usage rate Another product-related basis for market segmentation is the rate at which people use or consume a product. Thus we can have categories for nonusers, light users, medium users, and heavy users. Normally a company is most interested

[10]See Russell J. Haley, "Benefit Segmentation: A Decision Oriented Research Tool," *Journal of Marketing*, July 1963, pp. 30–35. For an update on this classic article and the concept of benefit segmentation, see Haley, "Benefit Segmentation—20 Years Later," *The Journal of Consumer Marketing*, vol. 1, no. 2, 1983, pp. 5–13.

Bases for Segmenting Industrial Market

in the heavy users of its product. The 50 percent of the people who are the "heavy half" of the users of a product typically account for 80 to 90 percent of the total purchases of a given product. The remarkable feature of these usage patterns is that they seem to remain reasonably constant over time. Thus this segmentation base becomes an effective predictor of future buying behavior. Comparable studies in the 1960s and 1980s showed similar patterns in the percentage of total purchases accounted for by the heavy-user half of the market in each product category. Some sample products and percentages of the total market accounted for by the heavy half in 1962 and 1982 were as follows: shampoo, 81 and 79 percent; cake mixes, 85 and 83 percent; beer, 88 and 87 percent; soaps and detergents, 80 and 75 percent.[11]

Sometimes the target market is the nonuser or light user, where the objective is to woo these customers into a higher use category. Once the characteristics of these light users are identified, management can go to them directly with an introductory low-price offer. Or a seller might increase usage rates by promoting (1) new times for a product (baking soda as a deodorant); (2) new times for uses (off-season vacations); or (3) multiple packaging (a six-pack of soft drinks).

Several of the bases that were used to segment the consumer market could also be used to segment the broad industrial market. For example, we can segment industrial markets on a geographical basis. Several industries are geographically concentrated, so any firm selling to these industries could nicely use this segmentation basis. Sellers also can segment on product-related bases such as usage rate or benefits desired.

At this point, let's look at some of the bases that are used solely when segmenting industrial markets. Three in particular that deserve our attention are type of customer, size of customer, and type of buying situation.[12]

TYPE OF CUSTOMER

Any firm that sells to customers in a variety of industries may want to segment this market on the basis of customer types. In the preceding chapter we discussed the Standard Industrial Classification (S.I.C.) code as a very useful tool for identifying industrial target markets. A firm selling to manufacturers of men's clothing, for example, can start out with potential customers included in the two-digit code number 23 for apparel manufacturing. Then the three-digit code 232 identifies potential customers making men's and boys' furnishings. Finally, code number 2321 pinpoints manufacturers of dress shirts and night wear.

A firm selling janitorial supplies or small electric motors would have a broad potential market among many different industries. Management in this firm could segment its market by type of customer and then perhaps decide to sell to firms in only a limited number of these segments.

[11]Victor J. Cook, Jr., and William A. Mindak, "A Search for Constants: The 'Heavy User' Revisited," *The Journal of Consumer Marketing*, vol. 1, no. 4, 1984, pp. 79–81.

[12]For some additional approaches to industrial market segmentation, see Benson P. Shapiro and Thomas V. Bonoma, "How to Segment Industrial Markets," *Harvard Business Review*, May–June 1984, pp. 104–110. See also the companion article by the same authors, "Evaluating Market Segmentation Approaches," *Industrial Marketing Management*, October 1984, pp. 257–268.

Industrial markets can be segmented by type of customer.

SIZE OF CUSTOMER

In this situation size can be measured by such factors as sales volume, number of production facilities, or number of sales offices. Many industrial sellers divide their potential market into large and small accounts, using separate distribution channels to reach each segment. The large-volume accounts, for example, may be sold to directly by the company's sales force. But to reach the smaller accounts, the seller will use a manufacturers' agent or some other form of middleman.

TYPE OF BUYING SITUATION

Again referring back to the preceding chapter, we discussed three types of buying classes—new buy, modified rebuy, and straight rebuy. We also recognized in that discussion that a new buy was significantly different from a straight rebuy in several important respects. Consequently, an industrial seller might well segment its market into these three buy-class categories. Or the seller could at least set up two segments by combining new buy and modified rebuy into one segment. Then different marketing programs would be developed to reach each of these two or three segments.[13]

TARGET-MARKET STRATEGIES ∎

Let's assume that a company is aware of the opportunities for segmenting its market, having analyzed the various segmentation bases in relation to the company's product. Now management is in a position to select one or more segments as its target markets. The company can follow one of three broad strategies in this selection process. The three alternatives are market aggregation, single-segment concentration, and multiple-segment segmentation. See Fig. 8-2.

Market Aggregation

By adopting a strategy of **market aggregation**—also known as a *mass-market* or an *undifferentiated-market* strategy—an organization treats its total market as a single given. This unit is one mass, aggregate market whose parts are considered to be alike in all major respects. Management then develops a single marketing mix to reach as many customers as possible in this aggregate market. That is, the company develops a single product for this mass audience; it develops one pricing structure and one distribution system for its product; and it uses a single promotional program that is aimed at the entire market.

When is an organization likely to adopt the strategy of market aggregation? Generally, when a large group of customers in the total market tends to have the same perception of the product's want-satisfying benefits. Therefore, this strategy often is adopted by firms that are marketing a nondifferentiated, staple product such as gasoline, salt, or sugar. In the eyes of many people, cane sugar is cane sugar, regardless of the brand. All brands of table salt are pretty much alike, and one unleaded gasoline is about the same as another.

Basically, market aggregation is a production-oriented strategy. It enables a com-

Some products are suited for a market-aggregation strategy.

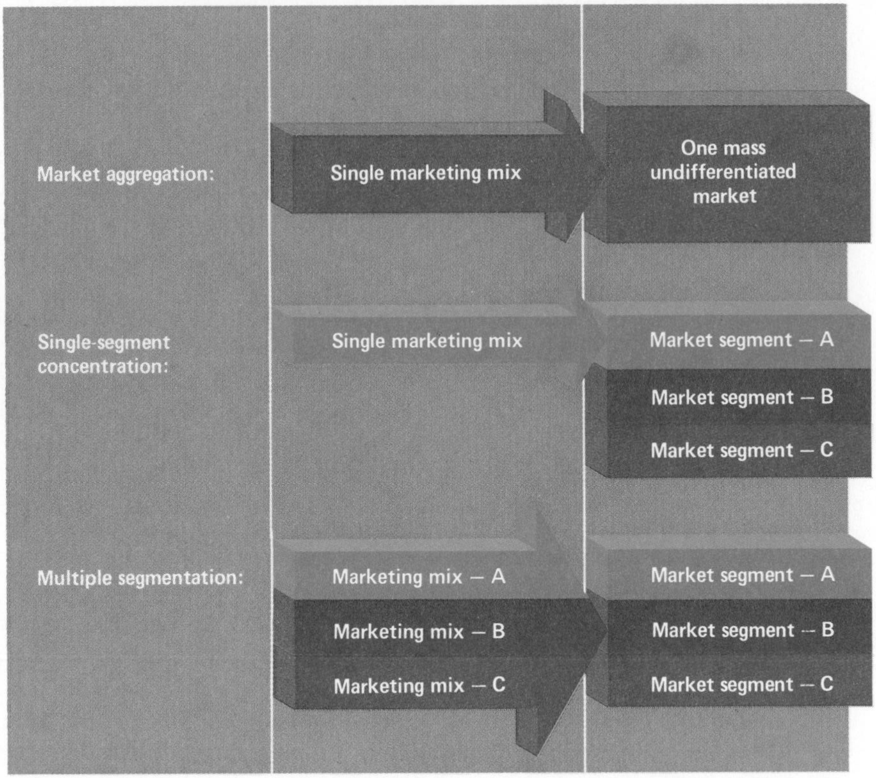

FIGURE 8-2
Alternative target-market strategies.

Market aggregation: Single marketing mix → One mass undifferentiated market

Single-segment concentration: Single marketing mix → Market segment — A / Market segment — B / Market segment — C

Multiple segmentation: Marketing mix — A / Marketing mix — B / Marketing mix — C → Market segment — A / Market segment — B / Market segment — C

pany to maximize its economies of scale in production, physical distribution, and promotion. Producing and marketing one product for one market means longer production runs at lower unit costs. Inventory costs are minimized when there is no (or a very limited) variety of colors and sizes of products. Warehousing and transportation efforts are most efficient when one product is going to one market.

Market aggregation will work only as long as the seller's single marketing mix continues to satisfy enough customers to meet the company's sales and profit expectations. The strategy of marketing aggregation typically is accompanied by the strategy of product differentiation in a company's marketing program. **Product differentiation** is the strategy by which one firm attempts to distinguish its product from competitive brands offered to the same aggregate market. By differentiating its product, an organization hopes to create the impression that its product is better than the competitors' brands. The seller also hopes to engage in nonprice competition and thus avoid or minimize the threat of price competition.

A seller implements this strategy either (1) by changing some superficial feature of the product—the package or color, for example—or (2) by using a promotional appeal that features a differentiating benefit. Crest says that its toothpaste now fights tartar formation on teeth. Morton's claims its salt will pour even in damp, rainy weather. Ocean Spray puts its cranberry-based juices in aseptic packages that keep fresh without refrigeration.

Single-Segment Concentration Strategy

A strategy of **single-segment concentration** involves selecting as the target market one homogeneous segment from within the total market. One marketing mix is then developed to reach this single segment. A small company may want to concentrate on a single market segment, rather than to take on many competitors in a broad market. For example, a Western dude ranch got started by appealing only to guest horseback riders who also enjoyed square dancing. A large cruise-ship company, offering a round-the-world luxury cruise, targets its marketing effort at one market segment—the older, financially well-off people who also have time to travel.

When the manufacturers of foreign automobiles first entered the United States market, they typically targeted a single market segment. The Volkswagen's *Beetle* was intended for the low-priced, small-car market, and in the late 1980s Yugo continues that tradition. Honda originally sold only lower-powered motorcycles, and Mercedes-Benz targeted the high-income market. Today, of course, most of the original foreign car marketers have moved into a multisegment strategy. Only a few, such as Rolls Royce and Ferrari, continue with a concentration strategy.

This strategy enables a company to penetrate one small market in depth and to acquire a reputation as a specialist or an expert in this limited market. A company can enter such a market with limited resources. And as long as the single segment remains a small market, large competitors are likely to leave the single-segment specialist alone. However, if the small market should show signs of becoming a large market, then the big boys may well jump in. This is exactly what happened in the market for herbal teas. Starting in 1971 Celestial Seasonings, a then-small Colorado firm, specialized in this market segment and practically owned the market for close to 10 years. But as herbal teas became more popular, this market segment grew enough to attract major competitors such as the Lipton Tea Company.

The big risk and limitation to a single-segment strategy is that the seller has all its eggs in one basket. If that single segment declines in market potential, the seller can suffer considerably. Also, a seller with a strong name and reputation in one segment may find it very difficult to expand into another segment. Sears, Roebuck was not too successful in its move into the market for expensive furs and diamond rings. Gerber's baby food company was not successful in marketing its food in single-serving quantities to adults. Do you think Volkswagen could successfully market a high-priced car to compete with a top-of-the-line Mercedes or BMW?

Multiple-Segment Strategy

In the strategy of **multiple segmentation,** two or more different groups of potential customers are identified as target-market segments. Then a separate marketing mix is developed to reach each segment. A marketer of personal computers, for example, might identify three separate market segments—college students, small businesses, and homemakers—and then design a different marketing mix to reach each segment. In segmenting the passenger automobile market, General Motors develops separate marketing programs built around its five brands—Chevrolet, Pontiac, Buick, Oldsmobile, and Cadillac. General Motors, in effect, tries to reach the total market for autos, but does so on a segmented basis.

As part of the strategy of multiple segmentation, a company frequently will develop a different variety of the basic product for each segment. However, market segmentation can also be accomplished with no change in the product, but rather with separate marketing programs, each tailored to a given market segment. A producer

FORECASTING MARKET DEMAND

of cosmetics, for instance, can market the identical product to the teenage market and to the 25 to 30 age segment. But the promotional programs for the two markets will be different.

A multiple-segment strategy normally results in a greater sales volume than a single-segment approach. Multiple segmentation also is useful for a company facing a seasonal demand for its product. In England during the summer, several universities market their empty dormitory space to the tourists—another market segment. A firm with excess production capacity may well seek additional market segments to absorb this capacity. Probably the biggest drawback to the multiple-segment strategy is that the unit costs of production and marketing typically increase when multiple segments are targeted.

As the final step in selecting its target markets, a company should forecast the market demand for its product or service. Forecasting market demands means to estimate the sales-volume size of a company's total market and the sales volume expected in each market segment. This step involves estimating the total industry potential for the company's product in the target market. (This industry figure is called the *market potential* for the product.) Then the seller should estimate its share of this total market. (This company figure is called the *sales potential*.)

The key requirement in demand forecasting is the preparation of a sales forecast, usually for a 1-year period. A sales forecast is the foundation of all budgeting and operational planning in all departments of a company—marketing, production, and finance.

Definition of Some Basic Terms

Before we discuss forecasting methods, we need to define several terms, because they often are used loosely in business.

MARKET FACTOR AND MARKET INDEX

A **market factor** is an item or element that (1) exists in a market, (2) may be measured quantitatively, and (3) is related to the demand for a product or service. To illustrate, the "number of cars 3 years old and older" is a market factor underlying the demand for replacement tires. That is, this element affects the number of replacement tires that can be sold. A **market index** is simply a market factor expressed as a percentage, or in some other quantitative form, relative to some base figure. To illustrate, one market factor is "households owning appliance X"; in 1986, the market index for this factor was 132 (relative to 1975 equals 100). An index may also be composed of multiple market factors, such as the number of cars 3 years old and older, population, and disposable personal income

MARKET POTENTIAL AND SALES POTENTIAL

The **market potential** for a product is the total expected sales of that product by all sellers during a stated period of time in a stated market. **Sales potential** (synonymous with **market share**) is the share of a market potential that an individual company expects to achieve.

Thus we may speak of the "market potential" for automatic washing machines, but the "sales potential" (or market share) for one company's brand of machine. In the case of either market potential or sales potential, the market may encompass the entire United States, or even the world. Or it may be a smaller market segmented by income, by geographic area, or on some other basis. For example, we may speak of the *market potential* for washing machines on the Pacific Coast, or the *sales potential* for Whirlpool washers in homes with incomes of $25,000 to $35,000. The market potential and sales potential are the same when a firm has a monopoly in its market, as in the case of some public utilities.

SALES FORECAST

A **sales forecast** may be defined as an estimate of sales (in dollars or product units) during some specified future period of time and under a predetermined marketing plan in the firm. A sales forecast can ordinarily be made more intelligently if the company first determines its market and/or sales potential. However, many firms start their forecasting directly with the sales forecast. See Fig. 8-3.

The sales forecast and the marketing plan   The marketing goals and broad strategies—the core of a marketing plan—must be established before a sales forecast is made. That is, the sales forecast depends upon these predetermined goals and strategies. Certainly, different sales forecasts will result, depending upon whether the marketing goal is (1) to liquidate an excess inventory of product A or (2) to expand the firm's market share by aggressive advertising.

However, once the sales forecast is prepared, it does become the key controlling factor in all *operational* planning throughout the company. The forecast is the basis

---

MARKET SHARE WORKSHEET FOR 1987

Dan's Diaper Deliveries
Los Angeles, CA

Market factor: _____   Number: _____

Base period: _____   Number: _____

Market index: _____ + _____

Market potential @ 6 dozen per child per month:

6 X _____ = _____ dz/mo

Sales projection: _____

Market share: _____ + _____ = _____ dz/mo

FIGURE 8-3
Business application of some of
our definitions.

Methods of Forecasting Demand

of sound budgeting. Financial planning for working-capital requirements, plant utilization, and other needs is based on anticipated sales. The scheduling of all production resources and facilities, such as setting labor needs and purchasing raw materials, depends upon the sales forecast.

Sales-forecasting periods   The most widely used period for sales forecasting is 1 year, although many firms will review annual forecasts on a monthly or quarterly basis. Annual sales forecasts tie in with annual financial planning and reporting, and are often based on estimates of the coming years' general economic conditions.

Forecasts for less than a year may be desirable when activity in the firm's industry is so volatile that it is not feasible to look ahead a full year. As a case in point, many firms engaged in fashion merchandising—producers and retailers alike—prepare a forecast that covers only one fashion season.

A company can forecast its sales by using either of two basic procedures—the "top-down" or the "buildup" approach.

Using the **top-down** (or **breakdown**) approach, management generally would:

1. *start with a forecast of general economic conditions*, as the basis to
2. *determine the industry's total market potential for a product*; then
3. *measure the share of this market the firm is getting*; the measurements in items 2 and 3 form the basis to
4. *forecast the sales of the product*.

In the **buildup** technique, management would generate estimates of future demand in segments of the market or from organizational units (sales people or branches) in the company. Then management would simply add the individual estimates to get one total forecast.

Predictions of future market demand—whether they are sales forecasts or estimates of market potential—may be based on techniques ranging from uninformed guesses to sophisticated statistical methods. Marketing executives do not need to know how to do the statistical computations. However, they should understand enough about a given technique to appreciate its merits and limitations. They should also know when each method is best used, and they should be able to ask intelligent questions regarding the assumptions underlying the method.

Here are some of the commonly used methods of predicting demand.

MARKET-FACTOR ANALYSIS

This method is based on the assumption that the future demand for a product is related to the behavior of certain market factors. If we can determine what these factors are and can measure their relationship to sales activity, we can forecast future sales simply by studying the behavior of the factors.

The key to the successful use of this method lies in the selection of the appropriate market factors. It is also important to minimize the number of market factors used. The greater the number of factors, the greater the chance for erroneous estimates and the more difficult it is to tell how much each factor influences the demand. The two procedures used to translate market-factor behavior into an estimate of future sales are the direct-derivation method and the correlation-analysis technique.

Direct derivation   Let's illustrate the use of this method to estimate *market potential*. Suppose that a manufacturer of automobile tires wants to know the market potential for replacement tires in the United States in 1988. The primary market factor is the number of automobiles on the road. The first step is to estimate how many cars are likely prospects for new tires. Assume (1) that the seller's studies show that the average car is driven about 10,000 miles a year and (2) that the average driver gets about 30,000 miles from a set of four tires. This means that all cars that become 3 years old during 1988 can be considered a part of the potential market for replacement tires during that year. The seller can obtain a reasonably accurate count of the number of cars sold in 1985. (These are the cars that will become 3 years old in 1988.) The information sources are state and county licensing agencies or private organizations. In addition, the seller can determine how many cars will become 6, 9, or 12 years old in 1988. (These ages are multiples of 3. That is, in 1988, a 6-year-old car presumably would be ready for its second set of replacement tires.) The number of cars in these age brackets times 4 (tires per car) should give a fair approximation of the market potential for replacement tires in 1988. We are, of course, dealing in averages. Not all drivers will get 30,000 miles from a set of tires, and not all cars will be driven exactly 10,000 miles per year.

The direct-derivation method has much to recommend it. It is relatively simple and inexpensive to use, and it requires little statistical analysis. It is reasonably easy to understand, so that executives who are not statistics-oriented can follow the method and interpret the results.

Correlation analysis   This technique is a mathematical refinement of the direct-derivation method. When correlation analysis is used, the degree of association between potential sales of the product and the market factor is taken into account. In effect, a correlation analysis measures, on a scale of 0 to 1, the variations between two series of data. Consequently, this method can be used only when a lengthy sales history of the industry or the firm is available, as well as a history of the market factor.

Correlation analysis gives a more exact estimate of market demand, provided that the method is applied correctly. In direct derivation, the correlation measure is implicitly assumed to be 1.00. But rarely does this perfect association exist between a market factor and the sales of a product. Correlation analysis therefore takes the past history into account in predicting the future. It also allows a researcher to incorporate more than one factor into the formula.

There are at least two major limitations to this method. First, as suggested above, a lengthy sales history must be available. To do a really good job, researchers need about 20 periods of sales records. Also, they must assume that approximately the same relationship has existed between the sales and the market factors during this entire period. And, furthermore, they must assume that this relationship will continue in the next sales period. These can be highly unrealistic assumptions. The other major drawback is that very few marketing people understand correlation analysis and can actually do the necessary computations. Thus a statistical staff may be necessary.

SURVEY OF BUYER INTENTIONS

Another commonly used method of forecasting is to survey a sample of potential customers. These people are asked how much of the stated product they would buy

Computers enable you to employ more complex forecasting methods.

Some forecasting starts with talking to prospective customers.

at a given price during a specified future time period. Some firms maintain consumer panels on a continuing basis to act as a sounding board for new-product ideas, prices, and other product features.

A major problem is that of selecting the sample of potential buyers. For many consumer products, a very large, and thus very costly, sample would be needed. Aside from the extremely high cost and large amount of time that this method often entails, there is another very serious limitation. It is one thing for consumers to *intend to buy* a product, but quite another for them to *actually buy* it. Surveys of buying intentions inevitably show an inflated measure of market potential.

Surveys of buying intentions are probably most effective when (1) there are relatively few buyers; (2) these buyers are willing to express their buying intentions; and (3) their past record shows that their follow-up actions are consistent with their stated intentions.

TEST MARKETING

In using this technique, a firm markets its product in a limited geographic area. Then, from this sample, management projects the company's sales potential (market share) over a larger area. Test marketing is frequently used in deciding whether sufficient sales potential exists for a new product. The technique also serves as a basis for evaluating various product features and alternative marketing strategies. The outstanding benefit of test marketing is that it can tell management how many people *actually buy* the product, instead of only how many *say they intend* to buy. If a company can afford the time and money for this method, and can run a valid test, this is the best way of measuring the potential for its product.

These are big ''ifs,'' however. Test marketing is expensive in time and money. Great care is needed to control the test-marketing experiment. A competitor, learning you are test marketing, is usually adept at ''jamming'' your experiment. That is, by unusual promotional or other marketing effort, a competitor can create an artificial situation that distorts your test results. To avoid such test-market ''wars,'' some companies are using simulations of test markets. In effect, these marketers are conducting a test market in a laboratory, rather than in the field.[14]

PAST SALES AND TREND ANALYSIS

A favorite method of forecasting is to base the estimate *entirely* on past sales. This technique is used frequently by retailers whose main goal is to ''beat last year's figures.'' The method consists simply in applying a flat percentage increase to the volume achieved last year or to the average volume of the past few years.

This technique is simple, inexpensive, and easy to apply. For a firm operating in a stable market, where its market share has remained constant for a period of years, past sales alone might be used to predict future volume. On balance, however, the method is highly unreliable.

Trend analysis is a variation of forecasting based on past sales, but it is a bit

[14]For a series of articles on the practical aspects of test marketing, see Aimée L. Stern, ''Test Marketing Enters a New Era,'' *Dun's Business Month*, October 1985, p. 86; and ''Special Report on Test Marketing,'' *Advertising Age*, Feb. 28, 1985, pp. 15–16ff, and Feb. 13, 1986, pp. 11–12ff.

more complicated. It involves either (1) a long-run projection of the sales trend, usually computed by statistical techniques, or (2) a short-run projection (forecasting for only a few months ahead) based upon a seasonal index of sales. The statistical sophistication of long-run trend analysis does not really remove the inherent weakness of basing future estimates only on past sales activity. Short-run trend analysis may be acceptable if the firm's sales follow a reliable seasonal pattern. For example, assume that sales reach 10,000 units in the first quarter (January–March) and, historically, the second quarter is always about 50 percent better. Then we can reasonably forecast sales of 15,000 units in the April–June period.

SALES-FORCE COMPOSITE

This is a buildup method that may be used to forecast sales or to estimate market potential. As used in sales forecasting, it consists of collecting from all sales people and middlemen an estimate of sales in their territories during the forecasting period. The total (the composite) of these separate estimates is the company's sales forecast. This method can be used advantageously if the firm has competent, high-caliber sales people. The method is also useful for firms selling to a market composed of relatively few, but large, customers. Thus, this method would be more applicable to sales of large electrical generators than small general-use motors.

The sales-force composite method takes advantage of the sales people's specialized knowledge of their own market. Also, it should make them more willing to accept their assigned sales quotas. On the other hand, the sales force usually does not have the time or the experience to do the research needed in forecasting future sales.

EXECUTIVE JUDGMENT

This method covers a wide range of possibilities. Basically it consists of obtaining opinions regarding future sales volume from one or more executives. If these are really informed opinions, based on valid measures such as market-factor analysis, then the executive judgment is useful and desirable. Certainly all the previously discussed forecasting methods should be tempered with sound executive judgment. On the other hand, forecasting by executive opinion alone is risky. In some instances, such opinions are simply intuition or guesswork.

This ends our discussion of the consumer and industrial markets. Once a company's executives know their market or markets, they are in a position to capture their desired share of those markets. They have the four components of the marketing mix—product, price, distribution system, and promotion—with which to attain that goal. Each of Parts 3 to 6 is devoted to one of these components.

SUMMARY

Some form of market segmentation is the strategy that most marketers adopt as a compromise between the extremes of an aggregate, undifferentiated market and a different product tailor-made for each customer. Market segmentation is the process of dividing the total heterogeneous market into several homogeneous segments. Then a separate marketing mix is developed for each segment that the seller selects as a target market. Market segmentation is a customer-oriented philosophy that is consistent with the marketing concept.

Marketing segmentation enables a company to make more efficient use of its marketing resources. Also, this strategy allows a small company to compete effectively in one or two segments. The main drawback to market segmentation is that it requires higher production and marketing costs than if a one-product, mass-market strategy were used. The requirements for effective segmentation are that (1) the bases for segmentation be measurable with accessible data; (2) the segments themselves be accessible to existing marketing institutions; and (3) the segments be large enough to be potentially profitable.

The total United States market may be divided into two broad segments—ultimate consumers and industrial users. The four broad categories for further segmenting the consumer market are geographic bases, demographic bases, psychographic bases, and product-related bases. Each of these four typically is further divided into several segments. Firms selling to the industrial market may use several of these same bases for segmentation. In addition, the industrial market may be segmented on the bases of type of customer, size of customer, and type of buying situation. Normally, in either the consumer or industrial market, a seller will use a combination of two or more segmentation bases.

There are three alternative segmentation strategies that a marketer can choose from when selecting a target market. The three are market aggregation, single-segment concentration, or multiple segmentation. Market aggregation involves using one marketing mix to reach a mass, undifferentiated market. In single-segment concentration, a company still uses only one marketing mix, but it is directed at only one segment of the total market. The third alternative involves selecting two or more segments and then developing a separate marketing mix to reach each one.

Before deciding on a target market, the company should forecast the demand in the total market and in each segment under consideration. Demand forecasting involves measuring the industry's market potential, then determining the company's sales potential (market share), and finally preparing a sales forecast. The sales forecast is the foundation of all budgeting and operational planning in all major departments of a company. There are several major methods available for forecasting market demand.

KEY TERMS AND CONCEPTS

Market segmentation 158–159

Market aggregation 159

Conditions for effective segmentation 161

Bases for consumer market segmentation: 161–162

Geographic 163

Demographic 163

Psychographic 164

Product-related 166

Bases for segmenting industrial markets 168–169

Market aggregation strategy 169

Product differentiation 170

Single-segment concentration strategy 171

Multiple-segment strategy 171

Market factor and market index 172

Market potential 172–173

Sales potential (market share) 172–173

Sales forecast 173

Methods of demand forecasting 174–177

QUESTIONS AND PROBLEMS

1. Distinguish between market aggregation and market segmentation.

2. What benefits can a company expect to gain from segmenting its market?

3. Explain, with examples, the conditions required for effective market segmentation.

4. a. Select three demographic segmentation bases and then describe your marketing class in terms of these demographic characteristics.

   b. List six products or services for which your marketing class would be a good market segment. Explain your reasoning in each case.

5. Describe what you believe to be the demographic characteristics of heavy users of:

   a. Dog food.   c. Videocassette recorders.

   b. Ready-to-eat cereal.   d. Pocket calculators.

6. Explain how the concept of benefit segmentation might be applied by the marketing executives for a symphony orchestra or an art museum.

7. How would you segment the market for copying machines such as Xerox or Canon copiers?

8. Explain the similarities and differences between a single-segment and a multiple-segment target-market strategy.

9. How might the following organizations implement the strategy of market segmentation?

   a. Manufacturer of personal   c. Universal Studios (Hollywood movies).
      computers.   d. Producer of laser-disc style of stereo
   b. American Heart Association.   records.

10. Assume that an American company has developed a new type of portable headphone-type cassette player in the general product category of a Sony Walkman. Which of the three target-market strategies should this company adopt?

11. Carefully distinguish between market potential and a sales forecast, using examples of consumer or industrial products.

12. What are some logical market factors that you might use in estimating the market potential for each of the following products?

    a. Central home air conditioners.   d. Sterling flatware.
    b. Electric milking machines.   e. Safety goggles.
    c. Golf clubs.

13. How would you determine the market potential for a textbook written for the beginning course in marketing?

14. Explain the direct-derivation method of sales forecasting, using a product example other than automobile tires. How does this forecasting method differ from the correlation-analysis method?

15. What are some of the problems a researcher faces when using the test-market method for determining market potential or sales potential?

2

HUBBARD MANUFACTURING COMPANY*

Analysis of a market

A little over 2 years ago, Grant Hubbard and his son David were considering purchasing riding lawn mowers for their suburban homes. (A riding mower is the kind you sit on and drive like a small tractor, rather than the kind that you walk behind.) After comparing several competitive models, both men bought the same brand of mower from a local farm equipment dealer. After using their mowers a few times, they were completely dissatisfied.

The men were confident that they could build a better lawn mower than the ones they had purchased. Since they were the owners and operators of an equipment-manufacturing firm, they had both the experience and the facilities to do so. After 2 years of engineering development and manufacturing effort, the Hubbards recently unveiled their new Hubbard riding lawn mower. The men believed they had produced a high-quality, compact mower that would be easy to operate and maintain and that provided for easy bagging of cut grass.

Now that their new mower was available, Grant and David realized that they faced a number of questions concerning the marketing of the product. They especially wanted to determine just what constituted the market for the mower.

The Hubbard Manufacturing Company originally began operations about 35 years ago as a producer of gasoline-powered golf carts. To balance the seasonality of golf-cart sales, Hubbard introduced a small, multipurpose vehicle that could serve as a flatbed truck, a pickup truck, a tractor, a small bulldozer, or a forklift truck.

In the 1960s, Grant Hubbard sold his rights to these products and the company ceased operations. Then, several years later, he started up again—this time to produce a line of evaporative air coolers that could be used in farm tractor cabs, trucks, vans, and recreation vehicles. The sale and distribution of these coolers were handled by another company; Hubbard had no marketing organization. The coolers were the mainstay of the Hubbard Manufacturing Company at the time the riding lawn mower was developed.

*Adapted from case prepared by Daniel Rye, under the direction of Prof. William J. Stanton.

The Hubbard lawn mower was a rotary-type mower, powered by an 8-hp motor with an electric starter. The shipping weight was either 600 or 670 pounds, depending upon whether an optional grass-handling attachment was included. The mower had three wheels—two in front and one in the back. The front wheels provided the drive power and the steering through the use of two independent Eaton hydrostatic transmissions. Two hand-operated levers allowed the driver to control the direction (forward/reverse/turning) and the speed. No shifting was required. The mower had a 36-inch-wide cutting deck that discharged grass clippings to the side.

The Hubbards believed that their unit had several advantages over conventional riding lawn mowers. Compared with competitive models, the Hubbard machine was much more maneuverable, compact, and easy to handle. The controls were easily reached, and the operator did not have to raise or lower the cutting deck. The machine was easy to mount, comfortable to sit on, and safe to ride. A tilt-up body and removable cutting deck made the machine easy to service. Both Grant and David felt that one of the outstanding features was the optional grass-handling system. This is a partially mechanized system for catching and bagging grass clippings and then emptying the clippings into a standard plastic trash bag.

Grant Hubbard expected to sell direct to consumers. The mower would be priced to consumers at $1,895 for the standard model, and at $2,245 for the mower with the grass-handling system included. Freight charges from the factory in Nebraska would be additional.

The Hubbards planned to utilize their existing plant and equipment to manufacture the riding lawn mowers. During the first year, production would be limited to 50 to 100 units. If the mower proved to be successful, production, with the existing manufacturing facilities, could go as high as 1,000 to 1,500 per year.

According to Dave Hubbard, the riding lawn mower industry was very competitive, with a large number of producers. However, a few large manufacturers, such as Toro, Jacobsen, John Deere, and Bolens-FMC, produced most of the riding lawn mowers. These companies marketed a wide assortment of mowers, distributed them nationwide, and spent considerable funds on promotion and on product research and development. Their products generally were of high quality, selling for $1,000 to $2,500 per mower.

In addition, a substantial number of riding lawn mowers were sold by the large general-merchandise chains, such as Sears and Montgomery Ward. These firms sold their mowers under their own private brands, generally at a much lower price than the national (manufacturers') brands.

Many of these competitive models were also priced lower than the Hubbard mower. And the higher-priced mowers typically offered a large assortment of accessories that increased their versatility. Also, the large competitors offered several different models to more closely meet the needs of different market segments.

Grant and Dave Hubbard realized that before they could develop an effective marketing program, they needed an accurate, detailed description of the market for their lawn mower. At first, they believed that their market consisted of (1) the homeowner with a large lawn and (2) the light commercial user. In fact, they intentionally decided *not* to produce a mower with a 30-inch cutting deck, so as to avoid competing with large manufacturers that were targeting on homeowners with small and medium-sized yards.

The Hubbards got some consumer feedback that supported their market contentions. Their new mowers were exhibited recently at the Oklahoma State Fair. Most people who showed an interest in the mower had anywhere from ½ to 5 acres of grass to cut. But Dave wondered whether these responses reflected only a local market condition rather than a broader geographical situation.

Executives from the Decatur Company—the firm that marketed Hubbard's evaporative coolers—wanted to obtain the marketing rights to the new mower. These executives believed that the Hubbard mower would appeal to homeowners with almost any size of yard. Even with the Hubbards' relatively high price, the Decatur people believed that the mower's competitive advantages would appeal to the wide variety of consumers.

Lee Remington, a local farm equipment dealer and a friend of the Hubbards, suggested that the mower be sold only to the industrial market. He felt that users such as golf courses, city parks departments, forest services, and professional lawn-mowing services were good target markets. This type of customer would be willing to pay more for the high-quality Hubbard product. Remington also suggested that marketing to homeowner-consumers would be very difficult and expensive.

Dave Hubbard also wondered whether there were any distinctive qualitative factors or behavioral traits that might characterize his potential market.

QUESTION

What is the market for the Hubbard riding lawn mower in the state where your school is located? Identify this market in some detail, considering quantitative measures as well as any possible qualitative or behavioral dimensions.

CASE 5

MERCURY AIRLINES*

Handling an important customer

Mercury Airlines was one of the major airlines in the United States. Its domestic routes served major cities in most parts of the United States, and its international routes served markets in Canada, Mexico, and the Caribbean. As a basis for its strategic marketing planning for the late 1980s, in the now deregulated airline industry, Mercury was evaluating several phases of its operations. As part of this evaluation, Mercury was analyzing its target markets—especially its major corporate accounts. The vice president of marketing, Vincent Brunswick, was wondering particularly how he should handle one of these accounts—the Crockett Electronics Company.

As was common in the industry, Mercury Airlines relied on travel agents both to promote its business and to sell tickets. Travel agents typically received a commission of 10 percent, based on the price of the tickets they sold. Mercury also had several company sales representatives located in the company's major city markets. In addition, Mercury had contracts with several large corporations whereby Mercury handled the reservations, ticketing, and other arrangements related to the corporation's

*Based on a case prepared by Lisa A. Wengert, under the direction of Prof. William J. Stanton.

business travel. In return, Mercury hoped that the corporation's employees would use Mercury any time they traveled on a route that was serviced by that airline.

Fifteen years ago Mercury entered into one of these contractual relationships with the Crockett Electronics Company, a large corporation located in Chicago, Illinois. This contract established Mercury as the sole company through which Crockett would make its business travel reservations and buy its tickets. Throughout the years Mercury has provided an increasing variety of travel-related services for Crockett. These services included a staff of nine Mercury employees who comprised the "Crockett-Mercury travel desk."

Over the past 8 years, the ticketing activities and telephone volume handled by this travel desk doubled. However, Mercury's percentage of Crockett's travel business did not increase at anywhere near this rate. That is, even though Mercury was providing the reservation and ticketing service, the majority of Crockett's travel was on other airlines.

This trend in the Mercury-Crockett relationship finally was brought to the attention of Vincent Brunswick. He then asked his director of marketing research, Glenda Haines, to investigate the Crockett account in some depth. Brunswick particularly wanted to know to what extent Mercury was losing its share of Crockett's travel business and the reasons for the loss. Brunswick also wanted to find out what it was costing to operate the Crockett-Mercury travel desk.

One phase of the marketing research study involved an analysis of a sample of 2,450 tickets written by the travel desk for Crockett travel during April 1986. Some of the points covered in this ticket analysis were:

1. Revenue generated by the travel desk and the distribution of this revenue between Mercury and other airlines.
2. Mercury's sales performance against competing airlines whose flights departed (a) within ½ hour and (b) within 1 hour of Mercury's flights.
3. Ticket revenue generated by flights to 45 destinations, divided into the following three market groups:
   a. 15 cities classed as major markets for Crockett travel.
   b. 15 cities served by Mercury, but considered to be minor markets for Crockett travel.
   c. 15 minor-market cities *not* served by Mercury.

Some of the findings from this ticket analysis were as follows. (The numbers were rounded off for presentation to company executives.)

1. The 2,450 tickets generated $480,000 in revenue. This represented 37 percent of the $1,300,000 total revenue generated by the Crockett travel desk during that sample month.
2. Only 30 percent of the $480,000 went to Mercury. Sixty percent went to Skyways Airlines, Mercury's major competitor. The remaining 10 percent was divided among nine other airlines. A summary of this sample revenue by airlines, and the monthly total revenue projected from this sample, was tabulated as follows:

Airline	Sample revenue	Market share, in %	Estimated total revenue
Mercury	$144,000	30	$390,000
Skyways	288,000	60	780,000
9 others	48,000	10	130,000
Totals	$480,000	100%	$1,300,000

3. When competitors' flights were scheduled ½ hour before or after a Mercury flight, 57 percent of the flight reservations were booked on Mercury airlines. Mercury was chosen in 50 percent of the cases when competing flights were available within 1 hour of a Mercury departure.

4. The 15 major-market cities generated $370,000 (77 percent) of the sample revenue. In fact, just six of these cities accounted for 55 percent of the total sample revenue.

5. The 30 cities that were classed as minor markets for Crockett travel accounted for $110,000, or 23 percent, of the sample revenue. About 55 percent of this $110,000 came from the 15 cities where Mercury competed. The other 45 percent was generated by Crockett travel to the group of 15 cities *not* served by Mercury.

6. The research report particularly called attention to the subject of Mercury's flight scheduling. The researchers believed that Mercury often lost business—especially to Skyways—simply because Mercury's departure times were not as convenient or desirable as those of the competition.

The following tabulation of cost and revenue data was prepared for April 1986—the same month used for the ticket analysis:

	Revenue	Cost	Cost/Revenue, in %
Total Crockett travel	$1,300,000	$30,000	2.3
Crockett travel on Mercury	390,000	30,000	7.7

The researchers also analyzed the costs of operating the Crockett-Mercury travel desk. The total cost was calculated to be $30,000 per month, or $360,000 for a year. These figures included such direct expenses as the salaries of the people staffing the desk, telephone charges, expenses for ticket stock and printer, and computer charges. The total did not include any charges for office space, utilities, or other overhead costs.

When presenting the research report, Glenda Haines noted that the 7.7 percent cost-revenue ratio did not seem out of line for handling the Crockett travel on Mercury Airlines. Mercury would have had to pay a commission of 10 percent if this business had been handled by travel agencies. At the same time, Haines reminded Brunswick that Mercury received only 30 percent of the total revenue generated by Crockett Company travel.

Brunswick accepted the research report and thanked Haines for her department's efforts and comments. Brunswick realized he had to weigh the benefits of having the Crockett account against the costs of operating the travel desk. In effect, Brunswick had to decide whether to continue handling the Crockett account as is, make some changes in order to increase the account's profitability, or give up the account entirely.

If Brunswick closed the travel desk—in effect, ending the special treatment of the Crockett account—several alternatives would then be opened up for all parties involved. Skyways or some other airline might offer Crockett a deal similar to the

Mercury travel desk, or Crockett might simply give its business to a travel agency. Or Crockett could operate its own travel department. These were only a few of the possibilities.

As Brunswick packed the research report and related data into his briefcase on Friday afternoon, two thoughts occurred to him. First, the Crockett account represented over $15 million in annual airline revenues, and second, it was going to be a long 2-day weekend.

QUESTION

What course of action should Vincent Brunswick adopt concerning the Crockett Electronics Company account?

CASE 6

DRAPER FURNITURE*
Consumer buying behavior
■

Bob and Harriet Draper knew they had to make some basic decisions about a new store soon. Their option for a 10-year lease on some property along Interstate 59 in southwest Birmingham, Alabama, would expire in less than a month. The property would then be available to anyone.

The property seemed ideal for a large furniture store. At least 50,000 households were located within a 10 minute's drive. A 110,000-square-foot building in excellent shape occupied about one-third of the property; the balance could quickly be developed into a parking lot. Prospective customers could see the building easily from I-59 and reach it via an exit ramp (seven blocks away) and frontage road. A 160,000-square-foot furniture "warehouse" operated by a local chain was only a block from the property.

The Drapers considered this last point particularly important. From their experience operating a 60,000-square-foot showroom (about 7 miles away in southeast Birmingham), they knew that most furniture buyers shopped around before making a decision. The proximity of the property to the competing chain would facilitate this shopping behavior. In addition, the chain was known to be a heavy advertiser on television and in newspapers. By attracting large numbers of furniture shoppers, the chain's advertising would also benefit any other furniture store located close by. Indeed, the Drapers had noticed that the chain faced a "next-door" competitor at several of its other locations.

The decisions facing the Drapers primarily centered around consumers. The Drapers knew from industry sources (and their own experience) that about 80 percent of all furniture sales were made to consumers between the ages of 18 and 49. About two-thirds of all furniture sales were made to households of three or more people. Harriet described four segments that she thought were predominant:

Young singles, age 18–34: Younger singles often buy inexpensive new and used furniture; older singles may buy good quality. Many singles buy "scaled-down pieces" to fit apartments and condominiums. Most singles tend to buy pieces as opposed to matched sets.

---

*Case prepared by Prof. James E. Nelson, University of Colorado. Used with permission.

Newlyweds, age 18–29: Newlyweds buy good-quality new furniture, usually for an apartment or condominium. Price is often more important than style; store name is often more important than brand name.

Young families, age 24–34: Young families buy good-quality furniture for their first house. Standard sizes are preferred, although a trend toward scaled-down pieces and sets is apparent. Young families are much like newlyweds in terms of the importance they give to price, style, store name, and brand name.

Older families, age 35–49: Older families often buy replacement furniture of high quality. Frequently only one spouse makes the purchase decision in the store, often placing more confidence in her own judgment than in the sales person's.

Within each segment, Harriet could identify different groups based on things that group considered important in making the purchase. For example, some singles placed a much greater emphasis on style than on price. Others valued free delivery over style, and still others considered price over everything.

All this knowledge would prove helpful in making two basic decisions about the new store. The first decision concerned the types of customers that the store was supposed to attract. The Drapers could seek to attract newlyweds and families (like the competing chain) and offer conventional living room, bedroom, and outdoor furniture. The Drapers thought that these segments accounted for as much as 60 percent of the retail sales of furniture in Birmingham. Alternatively, the Drapers could aim for the young singles market, thought to account for about 20 percent of retail sales. The choice between these two types of customers would have a pronounced impact on furniture lines carried, advertising, and several other aspects of store operation.

The second basic decision concerned the new store's quality and price position. The store could stock and sell medium- to lower-quality furniture at prices established by the competing chain. The chain's stores displayed most merchandise on a bare concrete floor with the balance kept on four-tier shelving (usually in a large room at the rear of the store). The Drapers could easily match this quality position and layout. Or, instead, the Drapers could stock and display merchandise of slightly better quality on a carpeted floor. Prices, of course, then would have to be somewhat higher than the competing chain, but the difference in quality should be readily apparent.

Complicating the two decisions was the image of the Drapers' present store. That operation was primarily aimed at a white-collar mass market, presenting better lines of furniture on a carpeted showroom floor. Harriet thought that the new store should be similar. That is, the new store should carry the same name, merchandise, and sales terms so that consumers would not have to learn about the new store before deciding to visit it. Bob, on the other hand, saw no reason why the new store could not carry another name and operate much differently than the present store.

QUESTIONS

1. How does the buying-decision process for furniture differ between young singles and older families?

2. What should be the target market for the Drapers' new store? Consider the new store's price-quality position in your analysis of this question.

THE PRODUCT

The planning, development, and management of the want-satisfying goods and services that are a company's products

Part 2 was concerned with the selection and identification of target markets in accordance with the firm's marketing goals. The next step in the strategic marketing planning process is to develop a marketing mix that will achieve these goals in the selected target markets. The marketing mix is a strategic combination of four variables—the organization's product, pricing structure, distribution system, and promotional program. Each of these is closely interrelated with the other three variables in the mix.

Part 3, consisting of three chapters, is devoted to the product phase of the marketing mix. In Chapter 9 we define the term *product*, consider the importance of product planning and innovation, and discuss the new-product development process. Chapter 10 deals mainly with product-mix strategies, the management of the product life cycle, and a consideration of style and fashion. Chapter 11 is concerned with branding, packaging, labeling, and other product features.

PRODUCT PLANNING AND DEVELOPMENT

CHAPTER GOALS

This chapter will show you why "building a better mousetrap" is *not* enough to ensure success. After studying this chapter, you should understand:

• The meaning of the word *product* in its fullest sense.

• What a "new" product is.

• The classification of consumer and industrial products.

• The relevance of these product classifications to marketing strategy.

• The importance of product innovation.

• The steps in the product-development process.

• The criteria for adding a product to a company's line.

• The new-product adoption and diffusion processes.

• Organizational structures for new-product planning and development.

For years the Campbell Soup Company was considered to be a successful, but rather stodgy, conservative and production-oriented company. All that changed in 1980 when Gordon McGovern became president. He immediately turned the company into a consumer-driven operation. Nowhere was this more apparent than in his new-product strategies. He split the company into 50 strategic business units divided by such product categories as soup, frozen foods, and beverages. He increased marketing expenditures by 150 percent between 1980 and 1985. During that same 5-year period, Campbell introduced 334 new products—more than any other company in the food industry. Two of those new foods—Prego spaghetti sauces and Le Menu frozen dinners—became superstars, accounting for more than 10 percent of the company's total annual sales. Several other new products also were successful.

On balance, however, by 1985 McGovern decided that the company's emphasis should be switched toward improving product quality and production efficiency in order to hold down operating costs. Some of the product units—Pepperidge Farm and Juice Works (a blend of natural fruit juices), for example—were major disappointments. Campbell has slowed down, but not stopped, its development of new products. In 1985 the company was test-marketing such products as Pepperidge Farm ice cream, granola bread, and a dry-soup mix to compete with Lipton's.[1]

---

[1] Adapted from Francine Schwadel, "Burned by Mistakes, Campbell Soup Co. Is in Throes of Change," *The Wall Street Journal*, Aug. 14, 1985, p. 1.

As the Campbell Soup Company shifts its new-product strategy, two points stand out. First, the president of the company is heavily involved in product innovation, and this is an absolutely essential ingredient for success with new products. Second, the management of the product planning component of the marketing mix (the subject of this and the following two chapters) is a difficult, complex task. And there is no guarantee of success, as witnessed by the large number of product failures.

THE MEANING OF PRODUCT

In a very *narrow* sense, a product is a set of tangible physical attributes assembled in an identifiable form. Each product carries a commonly understood descriptive (or generic) name, such as apples, steel, or baseball bats. Product attributes appealing to consumer motivation or buying patterns play no part in this narrow definition. A Cuisinart and a La Machine are one and the same product—a food processor.

A *broader* interpretation recognizes each *brand* as a separate product. In this sense a Hart Schaffner & Marx man's suit and a Hickey-Freeman man's suit are two different products. Squibb's aspirin and Bayer aspirin are also separate products, even though their only tangible difference may be the brand name on the aspirin tablet. But the brand name suggests a product difference to the consumer, and this brings the concept of consumer want-satisfaction into the definition.

Product itself + Package + Price + Promotion + Service 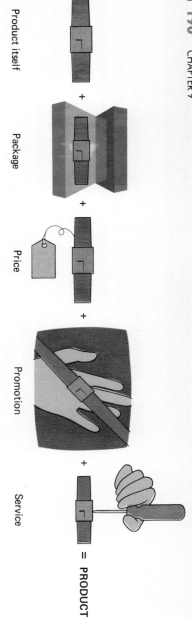 = PRODUCT

Any change in a physical feature (design, color, size, packaging), however minor it may be, creates another product. Each such change provides the seller with an opportunity to use a new set of appeals to reach what essentially may be a new market. Pain relievers (Tylenol, Anacin) in capsule form are a different product from the same brand in tablet form, even though the chemical contents of the tablet and the capsule are identical.

We can broaden this interpretation still further. An RCA television set bought in a discount store on a cash-and-carry basis is a different product from the identical model purchased in a department store. In the department store, the customer pays a higher price for the TV set. But he buys it on credit, has it delivered free of extra charge, and receives other store services. Our concept of a product now includes services accompanying the sale, and we are close to a definition that is valuable to marketing people.

Our definition is as follows: A **product** is a set of tangible and intangible attributes, including packaging, color, price, manufacturer's prestige, retailer's prestige, and manufacturer's and retailer's services.

The key idea in this definition is that the consumers are buying more than a set of physical attributes. Fundamentally, they are buying want-satisfaction. Thus, a wise firm sells **product benefits** rather than just products. As Elmer Wheeler, an author and sales training consultant, said, "Don't sell the steak, sell the sizzle."

Our "Product" May Not Be a Product

Actually the "product" being sold by a company to provide benefits and customer want-satisfaction may not be a physical, tangible article at all. Within our broad definition, a product may be a service, a place, a person, or an idea.

The Holiday Inn product is a service that provides the benefit of a comfortable night's rest at a reasonable price. The Hawaii Visitors Bureau product is a group of tropical islands that provide romance, sun and sand, relaxation, cross-cultural experiences, and other benefits. In a political campaign, the Democratic or Republican party's product is a person (candidate) that the party wants you to buy (vote for). The American Cancer Society is selling the idea and the benefits of not smoking. In Chapters 21 and 22 we discuss in more detail the marketing of nonphysical, intangible products such as services and ideas. But throughout the entire book when we speak of *products*, we intend that the term be used broadly.

What Is a "New" Product?

Just what is a "new" product? Are the new models that auto manufacturers introduce each autumn new products? If a firm adds a wrinkle-remover cream to its assortment

We don't want sandpaper; we want a smooth surface. We don't want a ¼-inch drill; we want a ¼-inch hole. So tell us what your product can do for us—the end benefits. The product itself is only a means to that end.

- Calvin Klein or Jordache blue jeans are not blue jeans. They are a sex symbol and a fashion status symbol.
- Miller's Lite beer isn't a beer. It's a blue-collar macho symbol.
- Visa and American Express cards are not credit cards that let you charge what you buy. They are a security blanket.
- Disneyland, Disneyworld, and Six Flags Over Texas are not simply amusement parks with rides and shows. They are an escape from reality.
- Zales Jewelers is not a chain of jewelry stores. It's a place that takes the risk out of buying diamonds and lets you buy with confidence.

Source: Adapted from Robert H. Bloom, "Product Redefinition Begins with Consumer," *Advertising Age,* Oct. 26, 1981, p. 51.

of women's cosmetics, is this a new product? Or must an item be totally new in concept before we can class it as a *new* product?

Here, we need not seek a very limited definition. Instead, we can recognize several possible categories of new products. What is important, however, is that each separate category may require a quite different marketing program to ensure a reasonable probability of success.

Three recognizable categories of *new products* are as follows:

- Products that are *really* innovative—truly unique. Examples would be a hair restorer or a cancer cure—products for which there is a real need but for which no existing substitutes are considered satisfactory. In this category we can also include products that are quite different from existing products but satisfy the same needs. Thus, microwave ovens compete with conventional ovens and solar power competes with other energy sources.
- Replacements for existing products that are *significantly* different from the existing goods. For many people instant coffee replaced ground coffee and coffee beans; then freeze-dried instant replaced instant coffee. Compact-disc players are replacing conventional stereo records and players. Disc cameras and cordless telephones are replacing some traditional models. In some years annual model changes in autos and new fashions in clothing are different enough to fit into this category.
- Imitative products that are new to a particular company but not new to the market. The company simply wants to capture part of an existing market with a "me-too" product.

Perhaps the key criterion as to whether a given product is new is how the intended market perceives it. If buyers perceive that a given item is significantly different (from

A "product" may be an idea or a social cause.

STILL TO COME

Research and development executives predict that these products and services will be available within the next 25 years:

• Readily available artificial human organs, except the brain.
• A means of speedy transportation without an automobile, perhaps an individual flying machine.
• Drugs to cure or prevent cancer and the common cold.
• A personal telephone, no larger than a cigarette pack, that can be used from any location.
• A pocket-sized personal/business computer that will answer many questions put to it.
• Clothing that can be cleaned by placing it in a "cleaning chamber" for 1 minute.
• A synthetic material to replace wood.

Source: May 1981 newsletter from New Product Development, as reported in "Survey of New Product Developers Offer 25-Year Innovation Forecast," Marketing News, Sept. 4, 1981, p. 4.

competitive goods being replaced) in some characteristic (appearance, performance), then it is a new product.

CLASSIFICATION OF PRODUCTS

Consumer Goods and Industrial Goods

Just as it is necessary to segment markets to improve the marketing programs in many firms, so also it is helpful to separate *products* into homogeneous classifications. First we shall divide all products into two groups—consumer goods and industrial goods—in a classification that parallels our segmentation of the market. Then we shall divide each of these two product categories still further.

Consumer goods are products intended for use by ultimate household consumers for nonbusiness purposes. **Industrial goods** are products intended to be sold primarily for use in producing other goods or for rendering services in a business. The fundamental basis for distinguishing between the two groups is the *ultimate use* for which the product is intended in its present form.

Particular stages in a product's distribution have no effect upon its classification. Cornflakes and children's shoes are classed as consumer products, even if they are in the manufacturer's warehouse or on retailers' shelves, *if ultimately they will be used in their present form by household consumers*. Cornflakes sold to restaurants and other institutions, however, are classed as industrial goods.

Often it is not possible to place a product only in one class or the other. A personal computer may be considered a consumer good if it is purchased by a student or a homemaker for nonbusiness use. But if the computer is bought by a traveling sales representative for business use, it is classed with industrial goods. The manufacturer of such a product recognizes that the product falls into both categories and therefore develops separate marketing programs for the two markets.

The two-way product classification is a useful framework for the strategic planning of marketing operations. Each major class of products ultimately goes to a different type of market and thus requires different marketing methods.

Classification of Consumer Products

The marketing differences between consumer and industrial goods make this two-part classification of products valuable. Yet, the range of consumer goods is still too broad for a single class. Consequently, consumer products are further classified as convenience goods, shopping goods, specialty goods, and unsought goods. (See Table 9-1.) This subdivision is based on consumer *buying habits* rather than on *types of products*.

CONVENIENCE GOODS

The significant characteristics of convenience goods are (1) that the consumer has complete knowledge of the particular product wanted *before* going out to buy it and (2) that the product is purchased with a minimum of effort. Normally, the gain resulting from shopping around to compare price and quality is not considered worth the extra time and effort required. A consumer is willing to accept any of several brands and thus will buy the one that is most accessible. For most buyers, this subclass of goods includes groceries, tobacco products, inexpensive candy, drug sundries, such as toothpaste, and staple hardware items such as light bulbs and batteries.

Convenience goods typically have a low unit price, are not bulky, and are not greatly affected by fad and fashion. Convenience goods usually are purchased frequently, although this is not a necessary characteristic. Items such as Christmas-tree lights or Mother's Day cards are convenience goods for most people, even though they may be bought only once a year.

Marketing considerations A convenience good must be readily accessible when the consumer demand arises, so the manufacturer must secure wide distribution. But, since most retail stores sell only a small volume of the manufacturer's output, it is not economical to sell directly to all retail outlets. Instead, the producer relies on wholesalers to reach part of the retail market.

The promotional strategies of both the manufacturer and the retailer are involved here. Retailers typically carry several brands of a convenience item, so they are not able to promote any single brand. They are not interested in doing much advertising of these articles because many other stores carry them. Thus, any advertising by one retailer may help its competitors. As a result, virtually the entire advertising burden is shifted to the manufacturer.

SHOPPING GOODS

Shopping goods are products for which customers usually wish to compare quality, price, and style in several stores before purchasing. This search continues only as long as the customer believes that the gain from comparing products offsets the additional time and effort required. Examples of shopping goods include women's apparel, furniture, major appliances, and used cars.

Some typical convenience goods.

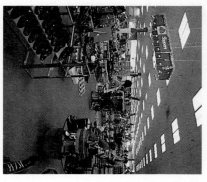

Many people like to shop around for shoes.

For some people an auto is a specialty product.

Marketing considerations The buying habits with shopping goods affect the distribution and promotional strategy of both manufacturers and middlemen. Manufacturers of shopping goods require fewer retail outlets because consumers are willing to look around a bit for what they want. To increase the convenience of comparison shopping, manufacturers try to place their products in stores located near other stores carrying competing items. Similarly, department stores and other retailers who carry primarily shopping goods like to be bunched together.

Manufacturers usually work closely with retailers in the marketing of shopping goods. Since manufacturers use fewer retail outlets, they are more dependent upon those they do select. Retail stores typically buy shopping goods in large quantities. Thus, distribution direct from manufacturer to retailer is common. Finally, store names often are more important to buyers of shopping goods than manufacturers' names. This is true particularly for items such as wearing apparel, where the average customer does not know or care who made the product.

SPECIALTY GOODS

Specialty goods are those products for which consumers have a *strong* brand preference, and are willing to expend considerable time and effort in purchasing them. The consumer is willing to forgo more accessible substitutes in order to procure the wanted brand, even though this may require a significant expenditure of time and effort. Examples of products usually classified as specialty goods include expensive men's suits, stereo sound equipment, health foods, photographic equipment, and, for many people, new automobiles and certain home appliances.

Marketing considerations Since consumers *insist* on a particular brand and are willing to expend considerable effort to find it, manufacturers can afford to use fewer outlets. Ordinarily, the manufacturer deals directly with these retailers. The retailers are extremely important, particularly if the manufacturer uses only one in each area. And, where the franchise to handle the product is a valuable one, the retailer may become quite dependent upon the producer. Thus, they are interdependent; the success of one is closely tied to the success of the other.

Because brand is important and because only a few outlets are used, both the manufacturer and the retailer advertise the product extensively. Often the manufacturer pays some portion of the retailer's advertising costs, and the retailer's name frequently appears in the manufacturer's advertisements.

UNSOUGHT GOODS

The very title of this category suggests a somewhat unusual type of product that does not parallel the three categories already discussed. For this reason we did not try to include unsought goods in Table 9-1.

There are two types of unsought products: (1) new products that the consumer is not yet aware of and (2) products that right now the consumer does not want. For some people, products in the first group might include disc cameras, computers that speak, telephoto telephones, or methanol as a fuel for autos. Examples of the second type of product might include prepaid burial insurance, gravestones, and auto seat belts (for some people).

The title of this product category also suggests that a seller faces a monumental advertising and personal selling job when trying to market these products.

TABLE 9-1   CHARACTERISTICS OF CLASSES OF CONSUMER PRODUCTS AND SOME MARKETING CONSIDERATIONS

Characteristics and marketing considerations	Type of product*		
	Convenience	Shopping	Specialty
Characteristics:			
1. Time and effort devoted by consumer to shopping	Very little	Considerable	Cannot generalize; consumer may go to nearby store and buy with minimum effort or may have to go to distant store and spend much time and effort
2. Time spent planning the purchase	Very little	Considerable	Considerable
3. How soon want is satisfied after it arises	Immediately	Relatively long time	Relatively long time
4. Are price and quality compared?	No	Yes	No
5. Price	Low	High	High
6. Frequency of purchase	Usually frequent	Infrequent	Infrequent
7. Importance	Unimportant	Often very important	Cannot generalize
Marketing considerations:			
1. Length of channel	Long	Short	Short to very short
2. Importance of retailer	Any single store is relatively unimportant	Important	Very important
3. Number of outlets	As many as possible	Few	Few; often only one in a market
4. Stock turnover	High	Lower	Lower
5. Gross margin	Low	High	High
6. Responsibility for advertising	Manufacturer's	Retailer's	Joint responsibility
7. Importance of point-of-purchase display	Very important	Less important	Less important
8. Advertising used	Manufacturer's	Retailer's	Both
9. Brand or store name important	Brand name	Store name	Both
10. Importance of packaging	Very important	Less important	Less important

*Unsought products are not included. See text explanation.

Classification of Industrial Products

As was the case with consumer products, the general category "industrial products" is too broad to use in developing a marketing program. The practices used in marketing the various industrial goods are just too different. Consequently, we separate industrial goods into five categories: raw materials, fabricating materials and parts, installations, accessory equipment, and operating supplies. (See Table 9-2.) This classification is based on the broad *uses* of the product.

RAW MATERIALS

Raw materials are industrial goods that will become part of another physical product. And they have not been processed in any way, except as necessary for economy or protection during physical handling. Raw materials include (1) goods found in their natural state, such as minerals, land, and products of the forests and the seas; and (2) agricultural products, such as wheat, cotton, fruits, vegetables, livestock, and animal products—eggs and raw milk. These two groups of raw materials are marketed quite differently.

Coal is an industrial raw material.

These steel reinforcing bars are classed as fabricating parts.

Marketing considerations The marketing of raw materials in their natural state is influenced by several factors. The supply of these products is limited and cannot be substantially increased. Usually only a few large producers are involved. The products must be carefully graded and, consequently, are highly standardized. Because of their great bulk, their low unit value, and the long distance between producer and industrial user, transportation is an important consideration.

These factors necessitate short channels of distribution and a minimum of physical handling. Frequently, raw materials are marketed directly from producer to industrial user. At most, one intermediary may be used. The limited supply forces users to assure themselves of adequate quantities. Often this is done either (1) by contracting in advance to buy a season's supply of the product or (2) by owning the source of supply. Advertising and other forms of demand stimulation are rarely used. There is very little branding or other product differentiation. Competition is built around price and the assurance that a producer can deliver the product as specified.

Agricultural products used as industrial raw materials are supplied by many small producers located some distance from the markets. The supply is largely controllable by producers, but it cannot be increased or decreased rapidly. The product is perishable and is not produced at a uniform rate throughout the year.

Close attention must be given to transportation and warehousing. Transportation costs are high relative to unit value, and standardization and grading are very important. Because producers are small and numerous, many middlemen and long channels of distribution are needed. Very little promotional activity is involved.

FABRICATING MATERIALS AND PARTS

Fabricating materials and parts are industrial goods that become an actual part of the finished product. They have already been processed to some extent (in contrast to raw materials). Fabricating **materials** will undergo further processing. Examples include pig iron going to steel, yarn being woven into cloth, and flour becoming part of bread. Fabricating **parts** will be assembled with no further change in form. They include such products as zippers on clothing and semiconductor chips in computers.

Marketing considerations Fabricating materials and parts are usually purchased in large quantities. To ensure an adequate, timely supply, a buyer may place an order a year or more in advance. Because of such buying habits, most fabricating products are marketed on a direct-sale basis from producer to user.

Middlemen are used most often where the buyers are small or where they place small fill-in orders for a rapid delivery. Normally, buying decisions are based on the price and the service provided by the seller. Branding is generally unimportant. However, some firms have made successful attempts to pull their products out of obscurity by identifying them with a brand. Talon zippers and the NutraSweet brand of sweetener are notable examples.

INSTALLATIONS

Installations are manufactured industrial products—the long-lived, expensive, major equipment of an industrial user. Examples include large generators in a dam, a factory building, diesel engines for a railroad, blast furnaces for a steel mill, and jet airplanes for an airline. *The differentiating characteristic of installations is that they directly affect the scale of operation in a firm.* Adding 12 new typewriters will not affect the scale of operation at Eastern Airlines, but adding 12 new jet airplanes certainly will. Therefore, the airplanes are classed as installations, but the typewriters are not.

Marketing considerations   The marketing of installations presents a real challenge to management because every single sale is important. Usually no middlemen are involved; sales are made directly from producer to industrial user. Typically, the unit sale is large, and often the product is made to the buyer's detailed specifications. Much presale and postsale servicing is required. A high-caliber sales force is needed to market installations, and often sales engineers are used. Promotional emphasis is on personal selling rather than advertising, although some advertising is used.

ACCESSORY EQUIPMENT

Accessory equipment is used in the production operations of an industrial firm, but it does not have a significant influence on the scale of operations in the firm. Accessory equipment does not become an actual part of the finished product. The life of accessory equipment is shorter than that of installations and longer than that of operating supplies. Examples include cash registers in a retail store, small power tools, forklift trucks, and the typewriters mentioned above.

Marketing considerations   It is difficult to generalize about the distribution policies of firms marketing accessory equipment. In some cases, direct sale is used. This is true particularly where the order is for several units of the product or where the product is of relatively high unit value. A firm which manufactures forklift trucks may sell directly because the price of a single unit is large enough to make this distribution policy profitable. In the main, however, manufacturers of accessory equipment use middlemen. They do so because (1) the market is geographically dispersed, (2) there are many different types of potential users, and (3) individual orders may be relatively small.

OPERATING SUPPLIES

Operating supplies are the "convenience goods" of the industrial field. They are short-lived, low-priced items usually purchased with a minimum of effort. They aid in a firm's operations but do not become a part of the finished product. Examples are lubricating oils, pencils and stationery, registration supplies in a university, heating fuel, and washroom supplies.

Marketing considerations   Like consumer convenience products, industrial operating supplies must be distributed widely. The producing firm makes extensive use of

A blast furnace is an installation in a steel mill.

Forklifts are accessory equipment in a lot of firms.

TABLE 9-2 CLASSES OF INDUSTRIAL PRODUCTS: SOME CHARACTERISTICS AND MARKETING CONSIDERATIONS

Characteristics and marketing considerations	Type of product				
	Raw materials	Fabricating parts and materials	Installations	Accessory equipment	Operating supplies
Example:	Iron ore	Engine blocks	Blast furnaces	Storage racks	Paper clips
Characteristics:					
1. Unit price	Very low	Low	Very high	Medium	Low
2. Length of life	Very short	Depends on final product	Very long	Long	Short
3. Quantities purchased	Large	Large	Very small	Small	Small
4. Frequency of purchase	Frequent delivery; long-term purchase contract	Infrequent purchase, but frequent delivery	Very infrequent	Medium frequency	Frequent
5. Standardization of competitive products	Very much; grading is important	Very much	Very little; custom-made	Little	Much
6. Limits on supply	Limited; supply can be increased slowly or not at all	Usually no problem	No problem	Usually no problem	Usually no problem
Marketing considerations:					
1. Nature of channel	Short; no middlemen	Short; middlemen only for small buyers	Short; no middlemen	Middlemen used	Middlemen used
2. Negotiation period	Hard to generalize	Medium	Long	Medium	Short
3. Price competition	Important	Important	Not important	Not main factor	Important
4. Presale/postsale service	Not important	Important	Very important	Important	Very little
5. Demand stimulation	Very little	Moderate	Sales people very important	Important	Not too important
6. Brand preference	None	Generally low	High	High	Low
7. Advance buying contract	Important; long-term contracts used	Important; long-term contracts used	Not usually used	Not usually used	Not usually used

wholesaling middlemen. This is done because the product is low in unit value, is bought in small quantities, and goes to many users. Price competition is heavy because competitive products are quite standardized and there is little brand insistence.

IMPORTANCE OF PRODUCT INNOVATION

The social and economic justification for the existence of a business is its ability to satisfy its customers. A company meets this basic responsibility to society through its products. In this section we point out some of the reasons why effective new-product planning and development are so important to a company today. Good executive judgment elsewhere cannot offset weaknesses in product planning. A company cannot successfully sell a poor product over the long run.

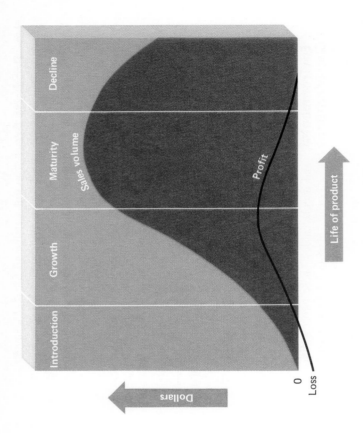

FIGURE 9-1
Typical life cycle of a product—sales and profit curves.
Profit usually starts to decline while a product's sales volume is still increasing. How does the relationship between these curves influence the time at which additional new products should be introduced?

Products Have Life Cycles

Like people, products go through a life cycle. They grow (in sales), then decline, and eventually are replaced. From birth to death, a product's life cycle can generally be divided into four stages—introduction, growth, maturity, and decline. The sales-volume curve in Fig. 9-1 illustrates the typical pattern of sales growth and decline for products as they go through their life cycle. The concept of the product life cycle is discussed in more detail in the next chapter.

Two points related to the life-cycle concept help to explain why product innovation is so important. First, every company's present products will eventually become obsolete as their sales volume and market share are reduced by competitive products. Second, as a product ages, its profit generally declines (as shown in Fig. 9-1). If those products are not changed or replaced, the company's sales volume and profit will be reduced.

Product Is a Basic Profit Determinant

New products are essential for sustaining a company's expected rate of profit. Figure 9-1 illustrates a typical relationship between the sales-volume curve and the profit curve through the life cycle of a product. Note that the profit curve for most new products is negative through most of the introductory stage. Also, the profit curve starts to decline while the sales volume is still ascending. This occurs because a company usually must increase its advertising and selling effort or cut its prices (or do both) to continue its sales growth during the maturity stage in the face of intensifying competition. The introduction of a new product at the proper time will help to maintain the company's desired level of profits.

New Products Are Essential to Growth

A useful watchword for management is to "innovate or die." Truly, an innovating attitude is a philosophy almost paralleling that of the marketing concept. Many companies will get a substantial portion of their sales volume and net profit this year from products that did not exist 5 to 10 years ago. Moreover, various studies have shown that growth industries are those that are oriented to new products.

Increased Consumer Selectivity

In recent years consumers have become more selective in their choice of products. As consumers' disposable income has increased, and as an abundance of products has become available, consumers have fulfilled many of their wants. The big middle-income group is reasonably well fed, clothed, housed, transported, and equipped. If market satiation—in terms of quantity—does exist to some extent, it follows that consumers may be more critical in their appraisal of new products. While the consumer is being increasingly selective, the market is being deluged with products that are imitations or that offer only marginal competitive advantages. This situation may be leading to "product indigestion." The cure is to develop *really* new products—to *innovate*, and not just *imitate*.

Resources and Environmental Considerations

We are finally realizing that the supply of many of our natural resources is limited and irreplaceable. These two conditions clearly point up the importance of careful new-product planning. Environmental factors will increasingly influence product decisions because we simply cannot afford to waste our natural resources or pollute our environment. As a corollary, business must make effective use of its human resources—particularly its scarce scientific and technical talent.

DEVELOPMENT OF NEW PRODUCTS

It has been said that nothing happens until somebody sells something. This is not entirely true. First, there must be something to sell—a product, a service, or an idea— and that "something" must be developed.

The development process for new products should begin with the selection of an explicit new-product strategy. This strategy then can serve as a meaningful guideline throughout the step-by-step development process used for each individual new product.

Selection of New-Product Strategy[2]

The purpose of an effective overall new-product strategy is to identify the strategic role that new products are to play in helping the company achieve its corporate and marketing goals. For example, a new product might be designed to defend a market-share position or to maintain the company's position as a product innovator. In other situations, the product's role might be to meet a specific return-on-investment goal or to establish a position in a new market.

A new product's intended role also will influence the *type* of product to be developed. To illustrate:

---

[2]See *New Products Management for the 1980s*, Booz, Allen & Hamilton, New York, 1982; pp. 10–11. Also see Earl L. Bailey (ed.), *Product-Line Strategies*, The Conference Board, New York, report no. 816, 1982, pp. 6–23.

Company goal

1. To defend a market-share position.
2. To further the company's position as an innovator.

Product strategy

1. Introduce an addition to an existing product line, or revise an existing product.
2. Introduce a *really* new product—not just an extension of an existing one.

Only in recent years have many companies consciously identified new-product strategies as a separate and explicit activity in the development process. Since then, however, there has been a dramatic increase in the efficiency of the development process. To illustrate, a survey by the Booz, Allen & Hamilton management consulting firm reported that in 1968 there were 58 new-product ideas considered for every successful new product introduced. In 1981, only seven new-product ideas were required to generate one successful new product—truly a dramatic improvement in the mortality rate for new-product ideas.[3]

Steps in the Development Process

With the company's new-product strategy as a guide, the development of a new product can proceed through a series of six steps (or stages). (See Fig. 9-2.) During

[3]*New Products Management for the 1980s*, p. 14. For a report on several new-product strategies, and their impact on performance results, see Robert G. Cooper, "Industrial Firms' New Product Strategies," *Journal of Business Research*, April 1985, pp. 107–121; and Robert G. Cooper, "Overall Corporate Strategies for New Product Programs," *Industrial Marketing Management*, August 1985, pp. 175–193.

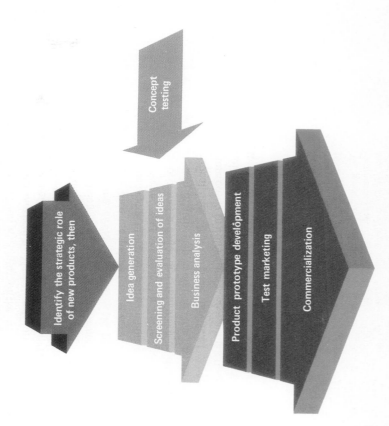

FIGURE 9-2
Major stages in new-product development process.

each stage, management must decide whether to move on to the next stage, abandon the product, or seek additional information.

The first two steps—generating new-product ideas and evaluating them—are tied especially to the overall new-product strategy. This strategy can provide (1) a focus for generating new-product ideas and (2) a criterion for screening and evaluating these ideas.

1. *Generation of new-product ideas.* New-product development starts with an idea. The particular source of ideas is not nearly so important as the company's system for stimulating new ideas and then acknowledging and reviewing them promptly.
2. *Screening and evaluation of ideas.* In this stage, new-product ideas are evaluated to determine which ones warrant further study.
3. *Business analysis.* A new-product idea that survives to this stage is expanded into a concrete business proposal. Management (*a*) identifies product features, (*b*) estimates market demand and the product's profitability, (*c*) establishes a program to develop the product, and (*d*) assigns responsibility for further study of the product's feasibility.

    These first three steps are together referred to as *concept testing.* This is pretesting of the product *idea,* as contrasted to later pretesting of the product itself and its market.[4]

4. *Product development.* The idea-on-paper is converted into a physical product. Pilot models or small quantities are manufactured to designated specifications. Laboratory tests and other necessary technical evaluations are made to determine the production feasibility of the article.
5. *Test marketing.* Market tests, in-use tests, and other commercial experiments in limited geographic areas are conducted to ascertain the feasibility of a full-scale marketing program. In this stage, design and production variables may have to be adjusted as a result of test findings. At this point, management must make a final decision regarding whether or not to market the product commercially.
6. *Commercialization.* Full-scale production and marketing programs are planned, and then the product is launched. Up to this point in the development process, management has virtually complete control over the product. Once the product is "born" and enters its life cycle, however, the external competitive environment becomes a major determinant of its destiny.

    In this six-step evolution, the first three—the idea, or concept, stages—are the critical ones. Not only are they least expensive—each stage becomes progressively more costly in dollars and scarce human resources. But more important, many products fail because either the idea or the timing is wrong—and those three stages are designed to identify such situations.[5]

[4] For a further discussion of concept testing, with an excellent bibliography, see William L. Moore, "Concept Testing," *Journal of Business Research,* September 1982, pp. 279–294; and David A. Schwartz, "Concept Testing *Can Be* Improved—and Here's How to Do It," *Marketing News,* Jan. 6, 1984, p. 22.

[5] For a report on the criteria used in making go/no-go decisions at major stages in the product-development process, see Ilkka A. Ronkainen, "Criteria Changes across Product Development Stages," *Industrial Marketing Management,* August 1985, pp. 171–178.

SUPPLY REQUISITION

American International College

RECEIVED BY: _Y. Cedeño_

Quantity	Dept.	Description	Retail	Cost	Initials
1.	1	1	Fundamentals of marketing	36.95		
2.						
3.						
4.						
5.						
6.						
Total						

INSTRUCTIONS TO DEPARTMENTS:

1. Use only for items stocked in Bookstore. Do not use for text books or items to be purchased on special order.
2. Duplicate will be returned to you from Business Office.
3. Person receiving items to sign in space provided.

Account No.: _____

Department: _Marketing_

Authorized. _K.M._

Date: _9-29-88_

DESK COPY

Companies increasingly are using mathematical models and other quantitative techniques, both during the stages of new-product development and for evaluation once the product has been marketed commercially. To illustrate, PERT (program evaluation and review technique) and CPM (critical path method) are two quantitative tools used in coordinating the many activities in the development process.

Manufacturer's Criteria for New Products

When should a proposed new product be added to a company's existing product assortment? Here are some guidelines that some manufacturers use in answering that question:

- There should be an *adequate market demand*. This is by far the most important criterion to apply to a proposed product. Too often, management begins with a question such as, "Can we use our present sales force?" or "Will the new item fit into our production system?" The basic question is, "Do enough people really want our product?"
- The product must be compatible with current *environmental and social standards*. Do the manufacturing processes heavily pollute air or water (as steel or paper mills do)? Will the use of the finished product be harmful to the environment (as automobiles are)? After being used, is the product harmful to the environment (as DDT and some detergents are)? Does the product have recycling potential?
- The product should fit into the company's present *marketing* structure. The general marketing experience of the company is important here. Bill Blass probably would find it easy to add designer sheets and towels to his clothing line, whereas paint manufacturers would find it quite difficult to add margarine to theirs. More specific questions may also be asked regarding the marketing fit of new products: Can the existing sales force be used? Can the present channels of distribution be used?

McDonald's decided there was a large enough potential market before introducing the new product.

AVON INTRODUCES

WHISPERING COLORS

Bold Fuchsia for your cheeks.

Sun-Drenched Apricot for your cheeks.

Cool Peach for your lips and nails.

Sweet Honey for your nails.

Whispering Blue for your eyes, and more.

Sunny Pink for your nails.

- A new-product idea will be more favorably received by management if the item fits in with existing *production* facilities, labor power, and management capabilities.
- The product should fit from a *financial* standpoint. At least three questions should be asked: Is adequate financing available? Will the new item increase seasonal and cyclical stability in the firm? Are the profit possibilities worthwhile?
- There must be no *legal* objections. Patents must be applied for, labeling and packaging must meet existing regulations, and so on.
- *Management* in the company must have the time and the ability to deal with the new product.
- The product should be in keeping with the *company's image* and objectives. A firm stressing low-priced, high-turnover products normally should not add an item that suggests prestige or status.

It helps when the new product fits in with existing marketing and production facilities.

Middleman's Criteria for New Products

When retailers or wholesalers are considering whether to take on a new product, they should use all the above criteria except those related to production. In addition, a middleman should consider:

- *The relationship with the manufacturer:* The manufacturer's reputation, the possibility of getting exclusive sales rights in a given geographic territory, and the type of promotional and financial help given by the manufacturer.
- *In-store policies and practices:* What type of selling effort is required for the new product? How does the proposed product fit with store policies regarding repair service, alterations (for clothing), credit, and delivery?

NEW-PRODUCT ADOPTION AND DIFFUSION PROCESSES

The opportunity to market a new product successfully is increased if management understands the adoption and the diffusion processes for that product. The **adoption process** is the decision-making activity of *an individual* through which the new product—the innovation—is accepted. The **diffusion** of the new product is the process by which the innovation is spread through a *social system* over time.[6]

Stages in Adoption Process

A prospective user goes through the following six stages during the process of deciding whether to adopt something new:

Stage	Activity in That Stage
Awareness	Individual is exposed to the innovation; becomes a prospect.
Interest	Prospect is interested enough to seek information.
Evaluation	Prospect mentally measures relative merits.
Trial	Prospect adopts the innovation on a limited basis. A consumer buys a small sample; for example, if for some reason (cost or size) an innovation cannot be sampled, the chances of its being adopted will decrease.
Adoption	Prospect decides whether to use the innovation on a full-scale basis.
Postadoption confirmation	The innovation is adopted; then the user continues to seek assurance that the right decision was made.

Adopter Categories

Researchers have identified five categories of individuals, based on the relative time when they adopted a given innovation. Figure 9-3 illustrates the proportion of adopters in each category. The categories are rather arbitrarily partitioned on a time scale to

---

[6]For some foundations of diffusion theory, a review of landmark studies on diffusion of innovation, and extensive bibliographical references, see Everett M. Rogers, *Diffusion of Innovations*, 3d ed., The Free Press, New York, 1983.

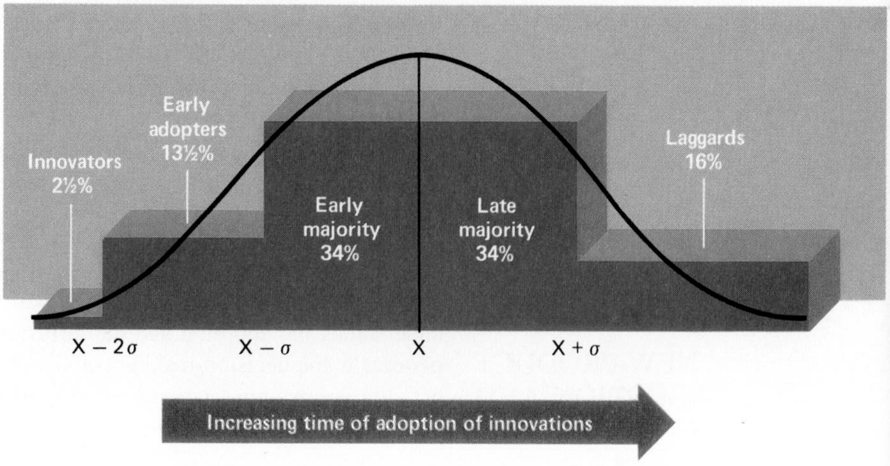

represent unit standard deviations from the average time of adoption. Also, *nonadopters are excluded.*

FIGURE 9-3
Distribution of innovation adopters.

(Figure labels: Innovators 2½%, Early adopters 13½%, Early majority 34%, Late majority 34%, Laggards 16%; axis X − 2σ, X − σ, X, X + σ; Increasing time of adoption of innovations)

INNOVATORS

Innovators, a *venturesome* group, constitute about 2.5 percent of the market and are the first to adopt an innovation. In relation to later adopters, the innovators are likely to be younger, have a higher social status, and be in a better financial position. Innovators also tend to have broader, more cosmopolitan social relationships. They are likely to rely more on impersonal sources of information, rather than on sales people or other word-of-mouth sources.

EARLY ADOPTERS

Early adopters—about 12.5 percent of the market—tend to be a more integrated part of a local social system. That is, whereas innovators are cosmopolites, early adopters are localites. Thus the early-adopter category includes more opinion leaders than any other adopter group. Early adopters are greatly *respected* in their social system. An "agent of change" is a person who is seeking to speed up the diffusion of a given innovation. This change agent will often try to work through the early adopters because they are not too far ahead of others in their peer group. As information sources, sales people are probably used more by the early adopters than by any other category.

EARLY MAJORITY

The more *deliberate* group, the early majority, represents about 34 percent of the market. This group tends to accept an innovation just before the "average" adopter in a social system. This group is a bit above average in social and economic measures. Its members rely quite a bit on advertisements, sales people, and contact with early adopters.

LATE MAJORITY

Representing about another 34 percent of the market, the late majority is a *skeptical* group. Usually its members adopt an innovation in response to an economic necessity or to social pressure from their peers. They rely on their peers—late or early majority—as sources of information. Advertising and personal selling are less effective with this group than is word-of-mouth.

LAGGARDS

This *tradition-bound* group—16 percent of the market—includes those who are the last to adopt an innovation. Laggards are suspicious of innovations and innovators. By the time laggards adopt something new, it may already have been discarded by the innovator group in favor of a newer idea. Laggards are older and are at the low end of the social and economic scales.

At this point we might recall that we are discussing only *adopters* (early or late) of an innovation. For most innovations, there still are many people who are *not* included in our percentages. These are the people who *never do* adopt the innovation—the nonadopters.

Characteristics of Innovations Affecting Adoption Rate

Five characteristics of an innovation, as perceived by individuals, seem to influence the adoption rate.[7] One is **relative advantage**—the degree to which an innovation is superior to preceding ideas. Relative advantage may be reflected in lower cost, higher profitability, or some other measure. Another characteristic is **compatibility**—the degree to which an innovation is consistent with the cultural values and experiences of the adopters.

The degree of **complexity** of an innovation will affect its adoption rate. The more complex an innovation is, the less quickly it will be adopted. The fourth characteristic—**trialability**—is the degree to which the new idea may be sampled on some limited basis. On this point, a central home air-conditioning system is likely to have a slower adoption rate than some new seed or fertilizer, which may be tried on a small plot of ground. Finally, the **observability** of the innovation affects its adoption rate. A weed killer that works on existing weeds will be accepted sooner than a preemergent weed killer. The reason is that the latter—even though it may be a superior product—produces no dead weeds to show to prospective adopters.

ORGANIZING FOR PRODUCT INNOVATION

For new-product programs to be successful, they *must* be supported by a strong and continuing commitment from top management over the long term. Furthermore, this commitment must be maintained even in the face of the failures that are sure to occur in some individual new-product efforts. To effectively implement this commitment to innovation, the new-product programs must be effectively organized.

Types of Organization

There is no "one best" organizational structure for new-product planning and development. In fact, many companies use more than one type of such structures to manage these activities. Four of the most widely used organizational structures for planning and developing new products are:

- *Product-planning committee:* The members usually include the company president

---

[7]Rogers, op. cit., chap. 6.

and executives from major departments—marketing, production, finance, engineering, and research.

• *New-product department:* Generally these units are small, consisting of four or five or even fewer people, and usually the department head reports to the president.

• *Venture team:* A venture team is a small, multidisciplinary group, organizationally segregated from the rest of the firm. It is composed of representatives of engineering, production, finance, and marketing research. The team operates in an entrepreneurial environment, in effect being a separate small business. Typically the group reports directly to top management.

• *Product manager:* We discuss this concept later in this section.

Upon the completion of the development process, responsibility for marketing a new product usually is shifted to another organizational unit. This unit may be an existing department, or a new department established just for this new product. In some cases, the team that developed the product may continue as the management nucleus of a newly established division in the company.

Which of these particular organizational structures is chosen is not the critical point here—each has its strengths and weaknesses. The key point is to make sure that some person or group has the specific organizational responsibilities for new-product development—and is backed by top management. Product innovation is too important an activity to let it be handled in an unorganized, nonchalant fashion, figuring that somehow the job will get done.

At least two risks are involved in the course of organizationally integrating new products into departments now marketing established, mature products. First, the executives involved with ongoing products may have a short-term outlook as they deal with day-to-day problems of existing products. Consequently, they tend to put the new products on the back burner, so to speak. Second, managers of successful existing products often are reluctant to assume the risks involved in marketing new products.[8]

PRODUCT MANAGER

In many companies a product manager—sometimes called a brand manager or a merchandise manager—is the executive responsible for planning related to *new* products as well as to *established* ones. A large company may have several product managers, who report to a top marketing executive. The wealth of discussion in business regarding the product manager's function is some indication of management's interest in this organizational structure.

In many large firms—Procter & Gamble, Pillsbury, and General Foods, for example—the product manager's job is quite broad. This executive is responsible for *planning the complete marketing program* for a brand or group of products. Thus, he or she may be concerned with new-product development as well as the improvement of established products. Responsibilities include setting marketing goals, preparing budgets, and developing plans for advertising and field selling activities. At the other

8 For more on this problem, see Roger C. Bennett and Robert G. Cooper, ''The Product Life Cycle Trap,'' *Business Horizons*, September–October 1984, pp. 7–16.

extreme, some companies limit product managers' activities essentially to the areas of selling and sales promotion.

Probably the biggest problem in the product-manager system is that a company will saddle these executives with great responsibility, yet it will *not* give them the corresponding authority. They must develop the field selling plan, but they have no line authority over the sales force. Product managers do not select advertising agencies, yet they are responsible for developing advertising plans. They have a profit responsibility for their brands, yet they are often denied any control over product costs, prices, or advertising budgets. Their effectiveness depends largely on their ability to influence other executives to cooperate with their plans.

Interestingly enough, there are some indications that the product-manager system may change considerably as we head into the 1990s. The product-manager system was widely adopted and thrived particularly during the period of economic growth and market expansion in the 1950s to 1970s. In the 1980s, however, many industries experienced slow economic growth in maturing markets, coupled with a trend toward strategic planning that stresses centralized managerial control. Because of these environmental forces, one careful study concluded that the product-manager system will be greatly modified in many companies and eventually abolished in some firms.[9]

WHY NEW PRODUCTS FAIL OR SUCCEED ■

Why do some products fail while others succeed? In the various research studies regarding this question, we find some consistently recurring themes. The key reasons typically cited for the failure of new products are as follows.[10]

- *Poor marketing research:* Misjudging what products the market wanted; overestimating potential sales of the new product; and lack of knowledge of buying motives and habits.
- *Technical problems in the new product's design or in its production:* Poor product quality and performance; products that were too complicated; and especially products that did not offer any significant advantage over competing items already on the market.
- *Poor timing in product introduction:* Delays in bringing the product to the market; or, conversely, rushing the product too quickly to the market.
- *Other poor management practices:* Lack of a well-defined new-product strategy; lack of a strong, long-term commitment by top management to new-product development; ineffective organization for new-product development.

Now let's look at the good news. Corrective actions to remedy these deficiencies

---

[9] See Victor P. Buell, "Firms to Modify, Abolish Product Manager Jobs Due to Sluggish Economy, Centralized Planning," *Marketing News*, Mar. 18, 1983, p. 8. For a report on the role of product managers in the strategic planning process, see Thomas J. Cossé and John E. Swan, "Strategic Marketing Planning by Product Managers—Room for Improvement?" *Journal of Marketing*, Summer 1983, pp. 92–102.

[10] See David S. Hopkins, *New-Product Winners and Losers*, The Conference Board, New York, report no. 773, 1980, pp. 12–20. Also see Valerie S. Folkes and Barbara Kotsos, "'Buyers' and Sellers' Explanations for Product Failure: Who Done It?" *Journal of Marketing*, April 1986, pp. 74–80.

have increased the systemization and effectiveness of the new-product development process. Specifically, we can attribute new-product success to these product factors and management characteristics.[11]

- The product satisfies one or more market needs.
- The product is technologically superior, and it enjoys a competitive cost advantage.
- The product is compatible with the company's internal strengths in key functional areas such as selling, distribution, and production.
- Top management makes a long-term commitment to new-product development. The experience thus gained enables management to improve its performance in introducing new products over a period of years.
- Strategies for new products are clearly defined. They enable a company to generate and select new products that specifically meet internal strategic needs and external market needs.
- There are an effective organization and a good management style. The organization structure is consciously established to promote new-product development. The management style encourages new-product development and can adjust to changing new-product opportunities.

One authority on new products observed that in the history of every successful product he studied, he always found at least one of three advantages—a product advantage, a marketing advantage, or a creative advertising advantage.[12] Without at least one of these three, it appeared there simply was no chance for success. Here are some examples of these features as developed by companies you'll probably recognize.

Product advantage: NutraSweet by Searle (tastes more like sugar without the fattening and cavity-causing side effects), Federal Express's Zap Mail (high-quality copies transmitted via satellite within minutes), Pizza Hut's Personal Pan Pizza (individual-sized pizzas served in 5 minutes or less), and Club Med (entire vacation package offered at one up-front price).

Marketing advantage: Tupperware and Avon (products are distributed to customers in their own homes), Bloomingdale's (offers the convenience of catalog shopping as well as physical facilities), and Century 21 Realtors (nationwide computer listings of homes for sale).

Creative advertising advantage: Wendy's Restaurants ("Where's the beef?"), Calvin Klein jeans (Brooke Shields—"Nothing comes between me and my Calvins"), and Nine Lives Cat Food (Morris, the finicky cat). All of these companies developed attention-getting advertisements that greatly increased consumer sales and repositioned the companies as higher in their fields.

SUMMARY

If the first commandment in marketing is "Know thy customer," then the second is "Know thy product." A firm can fulfill its socioeconomic responsibility to satisfy its customers by producing and marketing truly want-satisfying products or services. In

[11] *New Products Management for the 1980s,* pp. 17–23.

[12] Harry W. McMahan, "Alltime Ad Triumphs Reveal Key Success Factors behind Choice of '100 Best,'" *Advertising Age,* Apr. 12, 1976, p. 72.

light of a scarcity of resources and a growing concern for our environment, socially responsible product innovation becomes even more important. The new products or services marketed by a firm are a prime determinant of that company's growth rate, profits, and total marketing program.

To manage their product assortments effectively, marketers should understand the full meaning of the term *product* and the different concepts of what a *new product* is. Products can be classified into two broad categories—consumer products and industrial products. Then each of these two major groups should be further subdivided, because a different marketing program is required for each subgroup.

There are seven steps in the development process for new products, starting with a clear statement of the intended new-product strategy. The early stages in this process are important. If a firm can make an early (and proper) decision to drop a product, a lot of money and labor can be saved. In its decision regarding whether to accept or reject a new product, there are several criteria for a manufacturer or a middleman to consider. The product should fit in with marketing, production, and financial resources. But the key point is that there *must* be an adequate market demand for the product. Management should understand the adoption and diffusion processes for a new product. Adopters of a new product can be divided into five categories, depending upon how quickly they adopt a given innovation. In addition, there usually is a group of nonadopters.

Organizational relationships are typically reported as a major problem in new-product planning and development. Top management must be deeply committed to product innovation and must support this activity in a creative fashion. Most firms that report reasonable success in product innovation seem to use one of these four organizational structures for new-product development: product-planning committee, new-product department, venture team, or product-manager system. Successful products typically have an advantage in at least one of three areas—as a want-satisfying product, in their marketing program, or in their advertising.

KEY TERMS AND CONCEPTS

Product 190
New product 191
Consumer products: 192
  Convenience goods 194
  Shopping goods 194
  Specialty goods 195
  Unsought goods 195
Industrial products: 195
  Raw materials 195
  Fabricating materials and
    parts 196
  Installations 197
  Accessory equipment 197
  Operating supplies 197
Relation of sales volume and
  profit over life of a
  product 199

New-product development process 200
New-product strategy 200
Product-concept testing 202
Test marketing 202
Diffusion of innovation 205
Stages in new-product adoption
  process 205
New-product adopter categories 205
Product manager 208

QUESTIONS AND PROBLEMS

1. In what respects are the products different in each of the following cases?
   a. A Whirlpool dishwasher sold at an appliance store and a similar dishwasher sold by Sears under its Kenmore brand name. Assume Whirlpool makes both dishwashers.
   b. A Sunbeam Mixmaster sold by a leading department store and the same model sold by a discount house.

2. a. Explain the various interpretations of the term *new product*.
   b. Give some examples, other than those stated in this chapter, of products in each of the three new-product categories.

3. "As brand preferences are established with regard to women's ready-to-wear, these items, which traditionally have been considered shopping goods, will move into the specialty-goods category. At the same time, women's clothing is moving into supermarkets and variety stores, thus indicating that some articles are convenience goods." Explain the reasoning involved in these statements. Do you agree that women's clothing is shifting away from the shopping-goods classification? Explain.

4. In what way is the responsibility for advertising a convenience good distributed between the manufacturer and the retailers? A shopping good? A specialty good?

5. Compare the elements of a manufacturer's marketing mix for a convenience good with those of the mix for a specialty good.

6. In which of the five subclassifications of industrial products should each of the following be included? Which products may belong in more than one category?
   a. Trucks.
   b. Medical X-ray equipment.
   c. Typing paper.
   d. Copper wires.
   e. Printing presses.
   f. Nuts and bolts.
   g. Paper clips.
   h. Land.

7. What factors account for the growing importance of product planning?

8. In planning developing new products, how can a firm make sure that it is being socially responsible in regard to scarce resources and our environment?

9. What are some of the questions that management is likely to want answered during the business-analysis stage of new-product development?

10. Assume that the following organizations are considering the following additions to their product lines. In each case, should the proposed product be added?
    a. McDonald's—pizza.
    b. Safeway—automobile tires.
    c. Exxon—personal computers.
    d. Banks—life insurance.
    e. General Motors—outboard boat motors.

11. In the "trial" stage of deciding whether to adopt an innovation, the likelihood of adoption is reduced if the product cannot be sampled because of its cost or size. What are some products that might have these drawbacks? How might these drawbacks be overcome?

12. Describe the people likely to be found in (*a*) the innovator category of adopters and (*b*) the late-majority category.

13. What are some of the problems typically connected with the product-manager organizational structure?

14. Why do so many new products turn out to be failures in the market?

PRODUCT-MIX STRATEGIES

Holiday Inn Crowne Plaza: Raising Service To An Art.

CHAPTER GOALS

At any given time, a firm may be marketing some new products and some older products, while others are being planned and developed. This chapter is concerned with the managing of the entire range of products. After studying this chapter, you should understand:

• The difference between product mix and product line.

• The major product-mix strategies, such as:

a. Expansion.

b. Contraction.

c. Alterations.

d. Positioning.

e. Trading up and trading down.

• A product's life cycle and its management.

• Planning obsolescence, including:

a. Style and fashion.

b. The fashion-adoption process.

The Quaker Oats Company began to market dog food, and the makers of Levi's blue jeans introduced a line of maternity clothes. IBM discontinued producing its small computer—the PCjr—and the Ralston Purina people dumped their tuna-fish-catching and mushroom-raising businesses. The Timex watch company has diversified into health-care products, and the folks at Toys "R" Us have opened a series of Kids "R" Us clothing stores. Coca-Cola changed its 99-year-old formula when the company introduced New Coke. The formulas for Diet Pepsi, Diet Coke, and Diet 7-Up were changed by substituting NutraSweet for saccharin.

Holiday Inns, Inc.* upgraded its hotel service when it opened its Crowne Plaza Hotels, and Marriott moved into the lower-cost motel market with its chain of "Courtyard by Marriott" hotels. The makers of Admiral refrigerators rejuvenated this very mature product by adding new features such as a built-in wine rack and microwave storage trays. The makers of Atari, ColecoVision, and other video games struggled as they saw that market decline in popularity. Several firms began to market personal computers, videocassette recorders, and men's underwear for women as these products became fashionable.

*Holiday Inn and Holiday Inn Crowne Plaza are registered trademarks of Holiday Corporation, its subsidiaries or affiliates. Used by permission of Holiday Inns, Inc.

One common thread permeates this wide variety of product situations. All of these cases involve strategies related to the company's assortment of products and services. The management of that assortment is the topic of this chapter.

PRODUCT MIX AND PRODUCT LINE

A broad group of products, intended for essentially similar uses and possessing reasonably similar physical characteristics, constitutes a **product line**. Wearing apparel is one example of a product line. But in a different context, say, in a small specialty shop, men's furnishings (shirts, ties, and underwear) and men's ready-to-wear (suits, sport jackets, topcoats, and slacks) would each constitute a line. In another context, men's apparel is one line, as contrasted with women's apparel, furniture, or sporting goods. (See Fig. 10-1.)

The **product mix** is the full list of all products offered for sale by a company. The structure of the product mix has dimensions of both breadth and depth. Its *breadth* is measured by the *number* of product lines carried; its *depth*, by the assortment of sizes, colors, and models offered *within* each product line.

MAJOR PRODUCT-MIX STRATEGIES

Several major strategies used by manufacturers and middlemen in managing their product mix are discussed below. A discussion of planned obsolescence as a product strategy, and of fashion as an influence on the product mix, is deferred until later in the chapter.

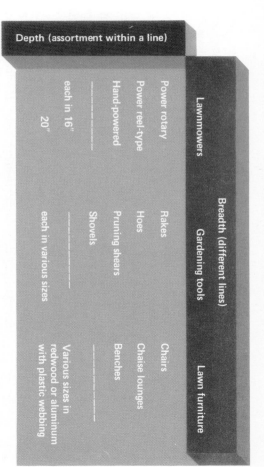

Breadth (different lines)		
Lawnmowers	Gardening tools	Lawn furniture
Power rotary	Rakes	Chairs
Power reel-type	Hoes	Chaise lounges
Hand-powered	Pruning shears	Benches
————	Shovels	————
each in 16"		Various sizes in
20"	each in various sizes	redwood or aluminum
		with plastic webbing

Depth (assortment within a line)

FIGURE 10-1
Product mix—breadth and depth.
Part of the product mix in a lawn and garden store.

Expansion of Product Mix

A firm may elect to expand its present product mix by increasing the number of lines and/or the depth within a line. New lines may be related or unrelated to the present products.

Gerber Products, the leading baby-food marketer, expanded into other baby-oriented products such as pacifiers, car seats, baby wear, toys, and day-care centers. The makers of Budweiser Beer added the LA (low-alcohol) brand to their line in response to the growing public concern over alcohol-related problems. Holiday Inn added Embassy Suites, a chain of all-suite hotels.

Expanding into unrelated lines, Polaroid added security-alarm products, and the Swatch Watch company opened a chain of clothing stores. K mart acquired the Wal-denbook chain of bookstores, and Coca-Cola is now trying to sell movies (Columbia Pictures) like it sells soft drinks.[1]

Contraction of Product Mix

Another product strategy is to thin out the product mix, either by eliminating an entire line or by simplifying the assortment within a line. The shift from fat and long lines to thin and short lines is designed to eliminate low-profit products and to get more

Here we see both breadth and depth in the product mix.

[1]See Myron Magnet, "Coke Tries Selling Movies Like Soda Pop," *Fortune*, Dec. 26, 1983, p. 119.

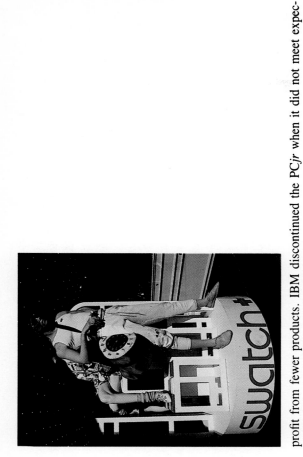

Swatch has expanded into the clothing business.

profit from fewer products. IBM discontinued the PC*jr* when it did not meet expectations in the already saturated personal computer market. After a 6-year stint in the wine business, Coca-Cola sold its Taylor California Cellars and other wine brands when the products did not meet profit expectation. R. J. Reynolds decided to get out of the ocean-shipping and energy-generating businesses and concentrate on cigarettes (Camel), food products (Del Monte, Kentucky Fried Chicken), and drinks (Canada Dry, Heublein liqueurs and wines).

The practice of slimming the product mix has long been recognized as an important product strategy. However, during the past decade it has been used extensively to cope with economic and competitive conditions as well as to retrench from the highly expansionary strategies of earlier years.

Alteration of Existing Products

As an alternative to developing a completely new product, management should take a fresh look at the company's existing products. Often, improving an established product can be more profitable and less risky than developing a completely new one. Most of you are probably familiar with the story of how Coca-Cola altered its existing product when the company came out with New Coke. Whether this move will prove to be a profitable strategy in the long run remains to be seen. However, we know already that the substitution of NutraSweet for saccharin in diet soft drinks (Coke, Pepsi, 7-Up, and others) clearly was a successful alteration.

For some products, *redesigning* is the key to their renaissance. Scott Paper Company produced a redesigned (narrower) paper towel, Scott Towel, Jr., in an effort to carve a new niche in the highly competitive paper-towel market. *Packaging* has been a popular area for product alteration, especially for consumer products. Colgate increased its sales of toothpaste considerably when this product was repackaged in a pump dispenser. Even something as mundane as bread, glue, or cheesecloth can be made more attractive by means of creative packaging and display.

Some strategies involve altering an existing product line.

Positioning the Product

Management's ability to position a product appropriately in the market is a major determinant of company profit. A product's **position** is the image that the product projects in relation to competitive products and to other products marketed by the same company. Unfortunately, the term *product positioning* has no generally accepted definition, so this important concept in product management is loosely applied and difficult to measure.

Marketing executives can choose from a variety of positioning strategies, some of which are as follows. [2]

- *Positioning in relation to a competitor.* For some products (Coca-Cola and Pepsi-Cola, for example), the best position is directly against the competition. For other products, head-to-head positioning is exactly what *not* to do, especially when a competitor has a strong market position. Avis became successful only after it stopped positioning itself directly against Hertz, readily admitted it was number 2, and advertised that it must try harder. The B. F. Goodrich Company, in its advertising, played on the theme, "We are the other guys." This strategy positioned Goodrich away from the more heavily advertised competitive brand of Goodyear tires.

- *Positioning in relation to a target market.* In the face of a declining birthrate,

[2] Adapted from David A. Aaker and J. Gary Shansby, "Positioning Your Product," *Business Horizons,* May–June 1982, pp. 56–58.

This is head-to-head positioning.

Johnson & Johnson repositioned its mild baby shampoo for use by mothers, fathers, and people who must wash their hair frequently. Other reduced-calorie beers were introduced before Miller Lite. However, they typically had been promoted as low-calorie beers and were targeted at diet-conscious consumers who usually drank very little beer. In contrast, Miller Lite was aimed at the male blue-collar worker (a strong beer-drinking market). The new promotional appeal was that Miller Lite is a beer that beer lovers can drink more of because it is less filling.

- *Positioning in relation to a product class.* Sometimes a company's positioning strategy involves associating its product with (or dissassociating it from) a common class of product. The soft drink 7-Up was positioned as an un-cola with no caffeine, to set it apart from Coca-Cola and the other cola drinks. Libby's, Del Monte, Campbell Soups, Kellogg's cereals, and other food processors introduced product lines with one common denominator—no salt (or very little) was added. Thus these items were positioned against the food products that are packed with the conventional (larger) amounts of salt.[3]

- *Positioning by price and quality.* Some retail stores are known for their high-quality merchandise and high prices (Sak's Fifth Avenue, Neiman-Marcus). Positioned at the other end of the price and quality scale are the discount stores such as K mart.

Trying to reposition a company on the price and quality spectrum can be a tricky proposition. In the 1970s, Sears tried to upgrade its fashion and quality image, while at the same time retaining its image of low price and "value for your money." The move was not successful. It served only to blur the company's image, confuse old customers, and reduce the firm's market share. In the 1980s, however, Sears made a more successful attempt to upgrade its image when it positioned itself as "store of the future." The company featured apparel lines backed by Cheryl Tiegs, Johnny Carson, and Diane von Furstenberg. In recent years, both J. C. Penney and K mart also have tried to change their image by upgrading their apparel lines and stressing designer names.

Positioning by quality.

Trading Up and Trading Down

As product strategies, trading up and trading down involve, essentially, an expansion of the product line and a change in product positioning. **Trading up** means adding a higher-priced, prestige product to a line in the hope of increasing the sales of existing lower-priced products. Holiday Inn has added Crowne Plaza Hotels and Embassy Suites (all-suite hotels), two chains of high-rise upscale hotels, which are targeted at more affluent business travelers. In an attempt to erase chronic losses, and to upgrade their image, the Fanny Farmer candy stores have added a line of specialty chocolates. These sell at $8 to $15 per pound (above Russell Stover but below the designer chocolates of Godiva).[4] K mart traded up by adding designer-labeled women's clothing (Gloria Vanderbilt, Jonathan Logan), imported German wines, gourmet pots and pans, and other higher-priced, name-brand merchandise. The company hopes to attract higher-income shoppers without losing its traditional customer base of people who shop K mart as a discount store.

---

[3]For a step-by-step procedure to follow in selecting a positioning strategy, see Aaker and Shansby, op. cit., pp. 58–62; and William D. Neal, "Strategic Product Positioning: A Step-by-Step Guide," *Business*, May–June 1980, pp. 34–42.

[4]Barbara Buell, "Up from $4.95 Fudge: Fanny Farmer Tries to Be a *Chocolatier*," *Business Week*, Dec. 10, 1984, p. 102.

Penney's is trading up.

When a company embarks upon a policy of trading up, at least two avenues are open with respect to promotional emphasis: (1) The seller may continue to depend upon the older, lower-priced product for the bulk of the sales volume and promote it heavily, or (2) the seller may gradually shift promotional emphasis to the new product and expect it to produce the major share of sales volume. In fact, the lower-priced line may be dropped altogether after a transition period.

A company is said to be **trading down** when it adds a lower-priced item to its line of prestige products. The company expects that people who cannot afford the original product will want to buy the new one because it carries some of the status of the higher-priced good. In line with this strategy, in 1985 the Marriott Corporation announced plans to build some 300 "Courtyard by Marriott" hotels—targeted at the midprice market now dominated by chains such as Holiday Inn and Ramada Inn.[5] Quality Inns, a midpriced chain, announced plans to build a series of economy-priced Comfort Inns.

Trading up and trading down are perilous strategies because the new product may simply confuse buyers, so that the net gain is negligible. Nor is any useful purpose served if sales of the new item are generated at the expense of the older products. When *trading down* is used, the new article may permanently hurt the firm's reputation and that of its established high-quality product.

In *trading up*, on the other hand, the seller's major problem is to change the firm's image enough so that new customers will accept the higher-priced product. At the same time, the seller does not want to lose its present customers. The real risk is that the company will lose *both* customer groups through this change in its product positioning. The former customers may become confused because the company has clouded its image; and the new target market may not believe that the company is marketing high-quality merchandise. Many women, for example, will never believe that they can buy high-quality, high-fashion clothing in women's ready-to-wear chain stores. The reason is that these stores have, through the years, projected an image that denotes low-priced merchandise. This is what happened to Sears in the 1970s, as you may recall from our discussion of product positioning. It remains to be seen whether K mart and Penney's can pull off a similar trading-up strategy (and a consequent switch in their product positioning) in the late 1980s.

CONCEPT OF THE PRODUCT LIFE CYCLE

This concept was introduced briefly in Chapter 9. There we noted that products have life cycles that can be divided into four stages: introduction, growth, maturity, and decline. A company's marketing success can be affected considerably by its ability to understand and manage the life cycle of its products. The product life cycle can be illustrated with the sales-volume and profit curves, as in Fig. 10-2. The *shapes* of these curves will vary from product to product. However, the basic shapes and the relationship between the two curves are usually as illustrated. (The relationship between these two curves was explained in Chapter 9 in connection with Fig. 9-1.)

Characteristics of Each Stage

It is quite important that management recognize what part of the life cycle its product is in at any given time. The competitive environment and the resultant marketing strategies ordinarily will differ depending upon the stage.

[5]See Steve Swartz, "How Marriott Changes Hotel Design to Tap Midpriced Market," *The Wall Street Journal*, Sept. 18, 1985, p. 1.

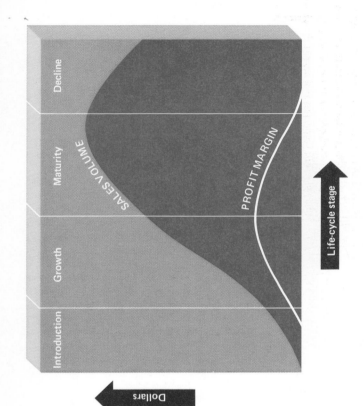

**FIGURE 10-2
Sales-volume curve and profit-margin curve in relationship to a product's life.**
Profit margin usually starts to decline while a product's sales volume is still increasing.

For some markets this product is already in the growth stage; for others it is in the introductory stage.

INTRODUCTION

During the first stage of a product's life cycle, it is launched into the market in a full-scale production and marketing program. It has gone through the embryonic stages of idea evaluation, pilot models, and test marketing. The entire product may be new, like a machine that cleans clothes electronically without using any water. Or the basic product may be well known but have a new feature or accessory that is in the introductory stage—a gas turbine engine in an automobile, for example.

There is a high percentage of product failures in this period. Operations in the introductory period are characterized by high costs, low sales volume, net losses, and limited distribution. In many respects, the pioneering stage is the most risky and expensive one. However, for really new products, there is very little direct competition. The promotional program is designed to stimulate *primary*, rather than *secondary*, demand. That is, the *type of product*, rather than the *seller's brand*, is emphasized.

GROWTH

In the growth, or market-acceptance, stage, both sales and profits rise, often at a rapid rate. Competitors enter the market—in large numbers if the profit outlook is particularly attractive. Sellers shift to a "buy-my-brand" rather than a "try-this-product" promotional strategy. The number of distribution outlets increases, economies of scale are introduced, and prices may come down a bit. Typically profits start to decline near the end of the growth stage.

MATURITY

During the first part of this period, sales continue to increase, but at a decreasing rate. While sales are leveling off, the profits of both the manufacturer and the retailers are declining. Marginal producers are forced to drop out of the market. Price competition becomes increasingly severe. The producer assumes a greater share of the total promotional effort in the fight to retain dealers and the shelf space in their stores. New models are introduced as manufacturers broaden their lines, and trade-in sales become significant.

DECLINE AND POSSIBLE ABANDONMENT

For virtually all products, obsolescence sets in inevitably as new products start their own life cycles and replace the old ones. Cost control becomes increasingly important as demand drops. Advertising declines, and a number of competitors withdraw from the market. Whether the product has to be abandoned, or whether the surviving sellers can continue on a profitable basis, often depends upon management's abilities.

Length of Product Life Cycle

The length of the life cycle varies among products. It will range from a few weeks or a short season (for a fad or a clothing fashion) to several decades (for, say, autos or telephones). In general, however, product life cycles are getting shorter as the years go by. Rapid changes in technology can make a product obsolete. Or, if competitors can quickly introduce a "me-too" version of a popular product, this product may move quickly into the maturity stage.

Figure 10-2 suggests that the life-cycle stages cover nearly equal periods of time. That is *not* the case, however. The stages in any given product's life cycle usually last for *different* periods of time. Also, the duration of each stage will vary among products. Some products take years to pass through the introductory stage, while others are accepted in a few weeks. Moreover, not all products go through all the stages. Some may fail in the introductory stage, and others may not be introduced until the market is in the growth or maturity stage. In virtually all cases, however, decline and possible abandonment are inevitable. This is because (1) the need for the product disappears (as when frozen orange juice generally eliminated the market for juice squeezers); (2) a better or less expensive product is developed to fill the same need (electronic microchips made possible many replacement products); or (3) the people simply grow tired of a product (a clothing style, for example), so it disappears from the market.

Life Cycle Is Related to a Market

When we say a product is in its growth stage, or some other stage, implicitly we are referring to that product's relation to a specific market. That is, a product may be well accepted (growth or maturity stage) in some markets but be in the introductory stage in other markets. Microwave ovens, for example, were in the maturity stage in the airline and industrial in-plant feeding markets while they were still in the introductory stage in most consumer markets.

The definition, or identity, of the product also is involved in this life-cycle–market relationship. To illustrate, computers, broadly defined, are in the growth stage of their life cycle. But personal computers are still in the introductory stage in most consumer markets.

Management of the Product Life Cycle

The shape of a product's sales and profit curves is not predetermined. To a surprising extent, the shape can be controlled by effective managerial action. One key to successful life-cycle management is (1) to predict the shape of the proposed product's cycle even before it is introduced and then, at each stage, (2) to anticipate the marketing requirements of the following stage. The introductory period, for instance, may be shortened by broadening the distribution or by increasing the promotional effort.

MANAGING DURING MATURITY STAGE

A product's life may be extended during the maturity stage of its life cycle if the product is rejuvenated through product modifications, new promotion, or repricing. We find one example of this in the refrigerator industry—an industry considered dull and mature even by some people in it. One company, Admiral, rejuvenated this staid product by adding features that enabled the user to make ice cream, cold soup, and slush drinks. The company also built in a wine rack and microwave storage trays.

The Scott Paper Company brought some new life to a mature product—paper towels—when it brought out a narrower (8¼-inch) towel. Colgate added a plaque-fighting ingredient in a pump dispenser to its toothpaste and enjoyed a substantial increase in sales and market share. Procter & Gamble's new thicker, leak-resistant Blue Ribbon Pampers helped the company to stop its declining sales and market share in the maturity stage of the disposable-diaper market.

MANAGING DURING SALES-DECLINE STAGE

Perhaps it is in the sales-decline stage that a company finds its greatest challenges in life-cycle management. At some point in the product's life, management may have to consider whether to abandon the product. The costs of carrying profitless products go beyond the expenses that show up on financial statements. The real burdens are the insidious costs accruing from managerial time and effort that are diverted to sick products. Unfortunately, management often seems reluctant to discard a product. Sometimes, the reasons are emotional and sentimental.

When sales are declining, management has the following alternatives, some of which are reflected in "A 10-Point Vitality Test . . ." in the nearby box:

• Improve the product in a functional sense, or revitalize it in some manner.
• Make sure that the marketing and production programs are as efficient as possible.
• Streamline the product assortment by pruning out unprofitable sizes and models. Frequently, this tactic will *decrease* sales and *increase* profits.
• "Run out" the product; that is, cut all costs to the bare-minimum level that will optimize profitability over the limited remaining life of the product.

In the final analysis the only reasonable alternative may be simply to abandon the product. Knowing when and how to abandon products successfully may be as important as knowing when and how to introduce new ones. Certainly management should develop a systematic procedure for phasing out its weak products. [6]

Introducing a new feature is one way to rejuvenate a product in the maturity stage.

[6]For a discussion of strategies for reviving declining products and also some ideas for reintroducing abandoned products, see William Lazer, Mushtaq Luqmani, and Zahir Quraeshi, "Product Rejuvenation Strategies," *Business Horizons*, November–December 1984, pp. 21–28; and Mark N. Vamos, "New Life for Madison Avenue's Old-Time Stars," *Business Week*, Apr. 1, 1985, p. 94.

PLANNED OBSOLESCENCE AND FASHION

Nature of Planned Obsolescence

The American consumer seems to be on a constant quest for the "new" but not "too new." The market wants newness—new products, new styles, new colors. However, people want to be moved gently out of their habitual patterns, not shocked out of them. This has led many manufacturers to develop the product strategy of planned obsolescence. Its objective is to make an existing product out of date and thus to increase the market for replacement products.

The term **planned obsolescence** may be used in two ways:

- *Technological or functional obsolescence.* Significant technical improvements result in a more effective product. For instance, pocket calculators made slide rules tech-

---

A 10-POINT VITALITY TEST FOR OLDER PRODUCTS, OR HOW TO GET THAT SALES CURVE TO SLOPE UPWARD AGAIN

1. Does the product have new or extended uses? Sales of Arm & Hammer baking soda increased considerably after the product was promoted as a refrigerator deodorant.

2. Is the product a generic item that can be branded? Sunkist puts its name on oranges and lemons, thus giving a brand identity to a formerly generic item.

3. Is the product category "underadvertised"? Tampons were in this category until International Playtex and Johnson & Johnson started spending large advertising appropriations, particularly on television ads.

4. Is there a broader target market? Procter & Gamble increased the sales of Ivory soap by promoting it for adults, instead of just for babies.

5. Can you turn disadvantages into advantages? The manufacturer of Smucker's jams and jellies advertised: "With a name like Smucker's, it has to be good."

6. Can you build volume and profit by cutting the price? Sales of Tylenol increased considerably after Johnson & Johnson cut Tylenol's price to meet the lower price set by Bristol-Myers' Datril brand.

7. Can you market unused by-products? Lumber companies market sawdust as a form of kitty litter.

8. Can you sell the product in a more compelling way? Procter & Gamble's Pampers disposable diapers were only a moderate success in the market when they were sold as a convenience item for mothers. Sales increased, however, after the advertising theme was changed to say that Pampers kept babies dry and happy.

9. Is there a social trend to exploit? Dannon increased its sales of yogurt tremendously by linking this product to consumers' interest in health foods.

10. Can you expand distribution channels? Hanes Hosiery Company increased its sales of L'eggs panty hose by distributing this product through supermarkets.

Source: Cadwell Davis Savage advertising agency, as reported in The Wall Street Journal, Feb. 18, 1982, p. 25.

nologically obsolete. This type of obsolescence is generally considered to be socially and economically desirable.

• *Style obsolescence.* This is sometimes called "psychological" or "fashion" obsolescence. Superficial characteristics of the product are altered so that the new model is easily differentiated from the previous model. The intent is to make people feel out of date if they continue to use old models.

When people criticize planned obsolescence, they are usually referring to the second interpretation—style obsolescence. In our discussion, planned obsolescence will mean only style obsolescence, unless otherwise stated.

Nature of Style and Fashion

Although the words *style* and *fashion* are often used interchangeably, there is a clear distinction between the two. A **style** is defined as a distinctive manner of construction or presentation in any art, product, or endeavor (singing, playing, behaving). Thus we have styles in automobiles (sedans, station wagons), in bathing suits (one-piece, bikinis), in furniture (Early American, French Provincial), and in dancing, (waltz, rumba).

A **fashion** is any style that is popularly accepted and purchased by several successive groups of people over a reasonably long period of time. Not every style becomes a fashion. To be rated as a fashion, or to be called "fashionable," a style must become popularly accepted.

A **fad** normally does not remain popular as long as a fashion, and it is based on some novelty feature.

Basic styles never change, but fashion is always changing. Fashions are found in all societies, including primitive groups, the great Oriental cultures, and the societies of ancient and medieval Europe.

Origin of Fashion

Fashion is rooted in sociological and psychological factors. Basically, people are conformists. At the same time, they yearn to look, act, and be a *little* different from others. They are not in revolt against custom; they simply wish to be a bit different and still not be accused of bad taste or insensitivity to the code. Fashion discreetly furnishes them the opportunity for self-expression.

Stanley Marcus, president of Neiman-Marcus, once observed:[7]

If, for example, a dictator decreed feminine clothes to be illegal and that all women should wear barrels, it would not result in an era of uniformity, in my opinion. Very shortly, I think you'd find that one ingenious woman would color her barrel with a lipstick, another would pin paper lace doilies on the front of hers, and still another would decorate hers with thumbtacks. *This is a strange human urge toward conformity, but a dislike for complete uniformity.*

Fashion-Adoption Process

The fashion-adoption process reflects the concepts of (1) large-group and small-group influences on consumer buying behavior and (2) the diffusion of innovation, as discussed in Chapters 6 and 9. People usually try to imitate others in the same social stratum or those on the next higher level. They do so by purchasing the fashionable product. This shows up as a wave of buying in that particular social stratum. The **fashion-adoption process** then, is a series of buying waves that arise as the given

[7]Stanley Marcus, "Fashion Merchandising," a Tobé lecture on retail distribution, Harvard Business School, Mar. 10, 1959, pp. 4–5.

FIGURE 10-3
Fashion-adoption processes.

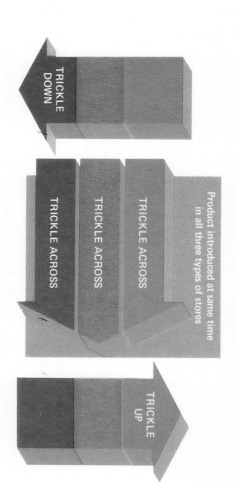

style is popularly accepted in one group, then another and another, until it finally falls out of fashion. This wavelike movement, representing the introduction, rise, popular culmination, and decline of the market's acceptance of a style, is referred to as the **fashion cycle.**

Three theories of fashion adoption are recognized (see Fig. 10-3):

- **Trickle-down,** where a given fashion cycle flows *downward* through several socioeconomic classes.

- **Trickle-across,** where the cycle moves *horizontally* and *simultaneously* within several social classes.

- **Trickle-up,** where the cycle is initiated in lower socioeconomic classes, then later the style becomes popular among higher-income and social groups.

Traditionally, the trickle-down theory has been used as the basic model to explain the fashion-adoption process. As an example, designers of women's apparel first introduce a style to the leaders—the tastemakers who usually are the social leaders in the upper-income brackets. If they accept the style, it quickly appears in leading fashion stores. Soon the middle-income and then the lower-income markets want to

FIGURE 10-3
Fashion-adoption processes.

THE "TRICKLE-UP" PROCESS

Blue jeans, denim jackets, T-shirts, and "soul" food in the 1980s. Years earlier there were popular styles of music we call jazz and the blues. These all have one thing in common. They are styles that *trickled up* in popularity; that is, they were popular first with lower socioeconomic groups. Later, their popularity trickled up as these styles gained wide acceptance among higher-income markets. T-shirts—once the domain of beer-drinking blue-collar workers and radicals—have moved up considerably in social respectability and price. Now they are designed by Yves Saint Laurent, Calvin Klein, Ralph Lauren, and others.

emulate the leaders, and the style is mass-marketed. As its popularity wanes, the style appears in bargain-price stores and finally is no longer considered fashionable.

To illustrate the trickle-across process, let us again use the example of women's apparel. Within a few weeks at the most, at the beginning of the fall season, the same style of dresses appears (1) in small, exclusive dress shops appealing to the upper social class, (2) in large department stores appealing to the middle social class, and (3) in discount houses and low-priced women's ready-to-wear chain stores, where the appeal is to the upper-lower social class. Price and quality mark the differences in the dresses sold on the three levels—*but the style is basically the same. Within each class* the dresses are purchased early in the season by the opinion leaders—the innovators. If the style is accepted, its sales curve rises as it becomes popular with the early adopters, and then with the late adopters. Eventually, sales decline as the style ceases to be popular. This cycle, or flow, is a horizontal movement occurring virtually simultaneously within each of several social strata.

Today the trickle-across concept best reflects the adoption process for most fashions. Granted, there is some flow downward, and obviously there is an upward influence. But market conditions today seem to foster a horizontal flow. By means of modern production, communication, and transportation methods, we can disseminate style information and products so rapidly that all social strata can be reached at about the same time. In the apparel field particularly, manufacturing and marketing programs tend to foster the horizontal movement of fashions. Manufacturers produce a wide *variety* of essentially one style. They also produce various *qualities* of the same basic style so as to appeal to different income groups simultaneously. When an entire cycle may last only one season, sellers cannot afford to wait for style acceptance to trickle down. They must introduce it into many social levels as soon as possible.

Marketing Considerations in Fashion

When a firm's products are subject to the fashion cycle, management must know what stage the cycle is in at all times. Managers must decide at what point to get into the cycle, and when they should get out.

Accurate forecasting is of inestimable value in achieving success in fashion merchandising. This is an extremely difficult task, however, because the forecaster is often dealing with complex sociological and psychological factors. Frequently a retailer or a manufacturer operates largely on intuition and inspiration, tempered by considerable experience.

Some styles remain in fashion for a long time.

The executives also must know what market they are aiming for. Ordinarily, a retailer cannot successfully participate in all stages of the fashion cycle at the same time. A high-grade specialty store selling apparel—whose stocks are displayed in limited numbers without price tags—should get in at the start of a fashion trend. A department store appealing to the middle-income market should plan to enter the cycle in time to mass-market the style as it is climbing to its peak of popularity.

SUMMARY ■

To make the product-planning phase of a company's marketing program most effective, it is imperative that management select appropriate strategies for the company's product mix. One strategy is simply to expand the product mix by increasing the number of lines and/or the depth within a line. An alternative is to prune out the product mix by eliminating an entire line or by simplifying the assortment within a line. Another strategy is to alter the design, packaging, or other features of existing products. Still another is appropriate "positioning" of the product, relative to competing products or to other products sold by the firm. In other strategies, management may elect to trade up or trade down, relative to its existing products.

Executives need to understand the concept of a product's life cycle and the characteristics of each stage in the cycle. The task of managing a product as it moves through its life cycle presents both challenges and opportunities—perhaps most frequently in the sales-decline stage.

An especially controversial product strategy is that of planned obsolescence, built around the concepts of style, fashion, and the fashion cycle. Fashion—essentially a sociological and psychological phenomenon—follows a reasonably predictable pattern. With advances in communications and production, the fashion-adoption process has moved away from the traditional trickle-down pattern. Today the process is better described as trickle-across. There also are some noteworthy examples of fashions trickling up. Style obsolescence, in spite of its critics, is based on consumer psychology.

KEY TERMS AND CONCEPTS ■

Product line 215
Product mix 215
Product-mix breadth and depth 215
Expansion of product mix 216
Contraction of product mix 216
Product alteration 217
Product positioning 217
Trading up/trading down 219
Product life cycle 220
Planned obsolescence 224
Fashion (style) obsolescence 225
Style 225
Fashion 225
Fad 225
Fashion-adoption process 225
Fashion cycle 226
Trickle-down 226
Trickle-across 226
Trickle-up 226

QUESTIONS AND PROBLEMS

1. "It is inconsistent for management to follow concurrently the product-line strategies of *expanding* its product mix and *contracting* its product mix." Discuss.

2. "Trading up and trading down are product strategies closely related to the business cycle. Firms trade up during periods of prosperity and trade down during depressions or recessions." Do you agree? Why?

3. Name some products that you believe are in the introductory stage of their life cycles. Identify the market that considers your examples to be new products.

4. Give examples of products that are in the stage of market decline. In each case, point out whether you think the decline is permanent. What recommendations do you have for rejuvenating the demand for the product?

5. How might a company's pricing strategies differ, depending upon whether its product is in the introductory stage or maturity stage of its life cycle?

6. What advertising strategies are likely to be used when a product is in the growth stage?

7. What products, other than wearing apparel and automobiles, stress fashion and style in marketing? Do styles exist among industrial products?

8. Select a product and trace its marketing as it moves through a complete fashion cycle. Particularly note and explain the changes in the distribution, pricing, and promotion of the product in the various stages of the cycle.

9. Is the trickle-across theory applicable in describing the fashion-adoption process in product lines other than women's apparel? Explain, using examples.

10. Planned obsolescence is criticized as a social and economic waste because we are urged to buy things we do not like and do not need. What is your opinion in this matter? If you object to planned obsolescence, what are your recommendations for correcting the situation?

11. What effects might a recession have on:
    a. Product life cycles?
    b. Planned obsolescence?
    What marketing strategies might a firm employ to counter (or take advantage of) these effects?

CHAPTER

11

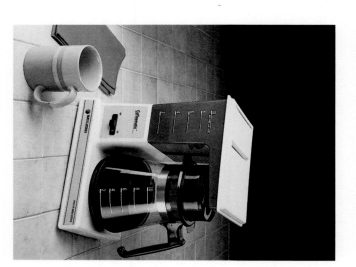

BRANDS, PACKAGING, AND OTHER PRODUCT FEATURES

CHAPTER GOALS

The title of this chapter could be "Product Presentation"—because the way in which a physical product is presented to potential customers is very much a part of the product itself. After studying this chapter, you should understand:

- The nature and importance of brands, including the characteristics of a good brand and the problem of generic brand names.

- Brand strategies of manufacturers and middlemen.

- The "battle of the brands."

- The nature and importance of packaging.

- Major packaging strategies.

- Types of labeling.

- Major legislation regarding packaging and labeling.

- The marketing implications in some other product features—design, color, quality, warranty, and servicing.

"Would you buy a toaster from a drill maker?" This is the question that the Black and Decker Corp. was asking itself, and of course, it was hoping that the answer would be "yes." For many years General Electric had an excellent reputation in the marketing of appliances. Black and Decker's name, on the other hand, was outstanding in the market of power tools. Then in 1984 Black and Decker bought General Electric's small-appliance business. So the question facing Black and Decker's management was whether it could pull off this very major brand transfer—from the basement tool shop to the kitchen and from the industrial market to the consumer market. This case illustrates just how important a company's or a product's brand image is in marketing today.[1]

[1]See Francine Schwadel, "Would You Buy a Toaster from a Drill Maker?" *The Wall Street Journal*, Apr. 19, 1985, p. 25.

In fact, for many products the brand image is all-important. Otherwise, how do you account for some people wanting Bayer aspirin and others preferring Walgreen's brand, when both are physically and chemically the identical product? Some people buy Quaker State motor oil, while others choose Pennzoil. Yet many people contend that there are no significant differences among the well-known brands of motor oils.

Why do some people use certain brands and not others? The buyer's choice may be affected by the package, warranty, color, design, or some other feature of the product. In packaging, for example, Marlboro, Players, and other brands try to increase sales by putting 25 cigarettes into a package, instead of the traditional 20. Colgate and Check-Up brands of toothpaste increased their sales significantly when they marketed this product in a pump-dispenser package. Holiday Inn found that by offering a money-back guarantee, the company gained a second chance with unhappy customers and also improved its own service. Japan's effective use of product quality as a marketing tool is known worldwide. All these product characteristics combined project an image to prospective customers. Consequently, because these product features are such important elements in a company's marketing program, we devote this chapter to them.

INFLUENCES OF PRODUCT FEATURES ON BUSINESS FUNCTIONS

Branding, packaging, and the other product features are interrelated with, and affect, the production and financial functions of a firm as well as other marketing activities. If a product is manufactured in six colors instead of one, the *production* runs are shorter, there are more of them, and therefore they are more costly. A product made in small units and packaged in an attractive wrapper is ordinarily more costly than one put up in large, bulk-packaged units.

Financial risks increase as the variety of sizes and colors is increased. Packaging products in special Christmas containers exposes a company to a financial loss on merchandise that is unsold by December 26. A business that offers a generous warranty—"Double your money back if not entirely satisfied"—has greater financial risks than a firm whose policy is "All sales are final."

Product features are also interrelated with other marketing elements. Products to be sold on a self-service basis must be carefully packaged and labeled to attract the customer at the point of purchase. And, normally, branding increases price rigidity. At the same time, however, well-known brands are most likely to have their prices cut to attract customers to the seller's establishment.

BRANDS

The word *brand* is a comprehensive term, and it includes other, narrower terms. A **brand** is a name, term, symbol, or special design, or some combination of these elements, that is intended to identify the goods or services of one seller or a group of sellers. A brand differentiates one seller's products or services from those of competitors.[2] A brand **name** consists of words, letters, and/or numbers that can be *vocalized*. A brand **mark** is the part of the brand that appears in the form of a symbol, design, or distinctive coloring or lettering. It is recognized by sight but may not be expressed when a person pronounces the brand name. Crest, Coors, and Gillette are brand names. Brand marks are illustrated by the alligator on Izod clothing products or the distinctively lined globe of AT&T. Green Giant (canned and frozen vegetable products) is both a brand name and a brand mark.

The American Marketing Association defines a **trademark** as a brand that is given legal protection because, under the law, it has been appropriated by one seller. Thus *trademark* is essentially a legal term. All trademarks are brands and thus include the words, letters, or numbers that can be pronounced. They may also include a pictorial design (brand mark). Some people erroneously believe that the trademark is only the pictorial part of the brand.

One major method of classifying brands is on the basis of who owns them—producers or middlemen. Sunbeam, Florsheim, Spaulding (athletic products), and Sara Lee are producers' brands, while Allstate, Shurfine, Sysco, Craftsman, and Penncrest are middlemen's brands.

The terms *national* and *private* have been used to describe producer and middleman brand ownership, respectively. However, marketing people prefer the producer-middleman terminology. To say that the brand of a small manufacturer of poultry feed in Birmingham, Alabama, that markets in three states is a *national* brand, while the brands of Penney's or Sears are *private* brands, seems to be stretching the meaning of the terms *national* and *private*.

Importance of Branding

Brands make it easy for consumers to identify products or services. Brands also assure purchasers that they are getting comparable quality when they reorder.

For sellers, brands are something that can be advertised and that will be recog-

Quaker Oats is a brand name. The colonial man is a brand mark. Together they are a brand that is protected as a trademark.

[2] Adapted from *Marketing Definitions: A Glossary of Marketing Terms*, American Marketing Association, Chicago, 1960, p. 8.

nized when displayed on shelves in a store. Branding also helps sellers to control their market because buyers will not confuse one branded product with another. Branding reduces price comparisons because it is hard to compare prices on two items with different brands. Finally, for sellers, branding can add a measure of prestige to otherwise ordinary commodities (Dole tomatoes and pineapples, Sunkist oranges, Morton salt, Chiquita bananas, Domino sugar).

Reasons for Not Branding

The two major responsibilities inherent in brand ownership are (1) to promote the brand and (2) to maintain a consistent quality of output. Many firms do not brand their products because they are unable or unwilling to assume those responsibilities.

Some items are not branded because of the difficulty of differentiating the products of one firm from those of another. Clothespins, nails, and industrial raw materials (coal, cotton, wheat) are examples of goods for which product differentiation (including branding) is generally unknown. The physical nature of some items, such as fresh fruits and vegetables, may discourage branding. However, now that these products are often packaged in typically purchased quantities, brands are being applied to the packages.[3]

Producers frequently do not brand that part of their output that is below their usual quality. Products graded as seconds or imperfects are sold at a cut price and are often distributed through channels different from those used for usual-quality goods.

Selecting a Good Brand Name

Selecting a good brand name is not an easy task. In spite of the acknowledged importance of a brand, it is surprising how few really good brand names there are. In a study made many years ago, it was found that only 12 percent of the names helped sell the product; 36 percent actually hurt sales. The other 52 percent were "nonentities—contributing nothing to the sales appeal of the product." There is no reason to believe that the situation has improved materially since that study was made.

CHARACTERISTICS OF A GOOD BRAND

A good brand should possess as many of the following characteristics as possible. It is extremely difficult, however, to find a brand that has all of them. A brand should:

- Suggest something about the product's characteristics—its benefits, use, or action. Some names that suggest desirable benefits include Beautyrest, Mr. Goodwrench, and Lazy-Boy. Product use and action are suggested by Minute Rice, Dustbuster, Spic and Span, and Reddi-Wip.
- Be easy to pronounce, spell, and remember. Simple, short, one-syllable names such as Tide, Ban, Aim, and Surf are helpful.
- Be distinctive. Brands with names like National, Star, Ideal, or Standard fail on this point.
- Be adaptable to new products that may be added to the product line. An innocuous name such as Kellogg, Lipton, or Ford may serve the purpose better than a highly

[3]See Eleanor J. Tracy, "Here Come Brand-Name Fruits and Veggies," *Fortune*, Feb. 18, 1985, p. 105; and Trish Hall, "Brand-Name Produce Hits Stores—But Will It Really Taste Better?" *The Wall Street Journal*, Sept. 23, 1985, p. 33.

Is this a good brand name?

These brands have been market leaders for a long time.

MANY "GOOD OLE BRANDS" NEVER DIE—THEY JUST STAY AT THE TOP

In an earlier chapter we saw that many new products fail in the market-place. On the other hand, there are brands that remain as market leaders over many years, despite rapid changes in the marketplace, a proliferation of new products, and significant cultural changes. The following list shows the top selling brands in 25 product categories in 1923 and the market position of these brands 60 years later—in 1983.

Product/brand leaders in 1923	Position in 1983	Product/brand leaders in 1923	Position in 1983
Swift Premium bacon	No change	Sherwin-Williams paint	No change
Kellogg's corn flakes	No. 3	Hammermill paper	No change
Eastman Kodak cameras	No change	Prince Albert pipe tobacco	No change
Del Monte canned fruit	No change	Gillette razors	No change
Hershey's chocolates	No. 2	Singer sewing machines	No change
Crisco shortening	No. 2	Manhattan shirts	Among top 5
Carnation canned milk	No change	Coca-Cola soft drinks	No change
Wrigley chewing gum	No change	Campbell's soup	No change
Nabisco biscuits (including Uneeda)	No change	Ivory soap	No change
Eveready flashlight battery	No change	Lipton tea	No change
Gold Medal flour	No change	Goodyear tires	No change
Life Savers mint candies	No change	Palmolive toilet soap	No. 2
		Colgate toothpaste	No. 2

Source: "'Old Standbys' Hold Their Own," *Advertising Age*, Sept. 19, 1983, p. 33.

distinctive name suggestive of product benefits. Frigidaire is an excellent name for a refrigerator and other cold-image products. But when the producer expanded its line of home appliances and added Frigidaire kitchen ranges, the name lost some of its sales appeal.

• Be capable of being registered and legally protected under the Lanham Act and other statutory or common laws.

GENERIC USAGE OF BRAND NAMES

Over a period of years, some brands become so well accepted that the brand name is substituted for the **generic** name of the particular product. Examples of brand names that legally have become generic are linoleum, aspirin, celluloid, cellophane, kerosene, shredded wheat, and nylon. Originally, these were trademarks limited to use by the owner.

A brand name can become generic in several ways. Sometimes the patent on a product expires. There is no simple generic name available, and so the public continues to use the brand name as a generic name. This happened with shredded wheat, nylon, and cellophane. Sometimes a firm just does too good an advertising and selling job with an outstanding brand name. While not yet legally generic, names such as Xerox, Band-Aid, Scotch Tape, and Kleenex are on the borderline. They are outstanding brand names for the original product and have been promoted so well that many people use them generically.

Several strategies can be adopted to prevent the generic use of a brand name. One is to use two names—the brand name in conjunction with the company name (Eastman Kodak), or the brand name together with the generic name (Dacron polyester). Another alternative is to give actual notice to the public that the brand has been copyrighted. The Sony, Sunbeam, and Sunkist companies adopted the drastic alternative of changing the company's name to coincide with that of the brand.

Brand Strategies

MANUFACTURERS' STRATEGIES

Manufacturers must decide whether to brand their products and whether to sell any or all of their output under middlemen's brands.

Marketing entire output under manufacturers' own brands   Companies that market their entire output under their own brands typically are very large, well financed, and well managed. Polaroid, Maytag, and IBM are examples. They typically have broad products lines, well-established distribution systems, and large shares of the market. Probably only a small percentage of manufacturers follow this policy, and their number seems to be decreasing.

Many of the reasons for adopting this policy have already been covered in the section on the importance of branding to the seller. In addition, middlemen often prefer to handle manufacturers' brands, especially when the brands have high consumer acceptance.

Branding of fabricating parts and materials   Some producers of industrial fabricating materials and parts (products used in the further manufacturing of other goods) will brand their products. This strategy is used in the marketing of Dan River cottons, Acrilan fabrics, and many automotive parts—spark plugs, batteries, oil filters, and so on.

Promoting the Nutra-Sweet (fabricating material) helps to sell the final product.

Underlying this strategy is the seller's desire to develop a market preference for its branded part or material. For instance, the G. D. Searle Company wants to build a market situation in which customers will insist on food products sweetened with NutraSweet. In addition, the parts manufacturer wants to persuade the producer of the finished item that using the branded materials will help sell the end product. In our example, the Searle Company hopes to convince food manufacturers that their sales will increase if their products contain NutraSweet.

Certain product characteristics lend themselves to the effective use of this strategy. First, it helps if the product is also a consumer good that is bought for replacement purposes. This factor encourages the branding of Champion spark plugs and Delco batteries, for example. Second, the seller's situation is improved if the item is a major part of the finished product—a television picture tube, for example.

Marketing under middlemen's brands A widespread strategy is for manufacturers to brand part or all of their output with the brands of their middlemen customers. For the manufacturer, this middlemen's-brand business generates additional sales volume and profit dollars. Orders typically are large, payment is prompt, and a manufacturer's working-capital position is improved. Also, manufacturers may utilize their production resources more effectively, including their plant capacities. Furthermore, refusing to sell under a retailer's or wholesaler's brand will not eliminate competition from this source. Many middlemen want to market under their own brands, so if one manufacturer refuses their business, they will simply go to another.

Probably the most serious limitation to marketing under middlemen's brands is that a manufacturer may be at the mercy of the middlemen. This problem grows as the proportion of that producer's output going to middlemen's brands increases.

MIDDLEMEN'S STRATEGIES

The question of whether or not to brand must also be answered by middlemen. There are two usual strategies, as follows:

Carry only manufacturers' brands Most retailers and wholesalers follow this policy because they are not able to take on the dual burdens of promoting a brand and maintaining its quality. Even though manufacturers' brands usually carry lower gross margins, they often have a higher rate of turnover and a better profit possibility.

Carry middlemen's brands along with manufacturers' brands Many large retailers and some large wholesalers have their own brands. Middlemen may find it advantageous to market their own brands for several reasons. First, this strategy increases their control over their market. If customers prefer a given middleman's brand, they can get it only from that middleman's store. Furthermore, middlemen can usually sell their brands at prices below those of manufacturers' brands and still earn higher gross margins. This is possible because middlemen can buy at lower costs. The costs may be lower because (1) manufacturers' advertising and selling costs are not included in their prices, or (2) producers are anxious to get the extra business to keep their plants running in slack seasons. Middlemen have more freedom in pricing products sold under their own labels.

Products carrying a retailer's brand become differentiated products, and this hinders price comparisons that might be unfavorable to that retailer. Also, prices on manufacturers' brands can be cut drastically by competing retail stores. This last point is what has been happening in recent years in the marketing of clothing with designer labels such as Calvin Klein, Halston, Bill Blass, and Ralph Lauren. Some of the large retailers in their upper-priced clothing departments have increased their stocks of apparel carrying the store's brand. These stores (Macy's, Marshall Field, I. Magnin, Neiman-Marcus, Bloomingdale's, for example) have cut back on products with designer brands such as Calvin Klein and the others. The reason for this brand-switching is that many designer-labeled products now are available at much lower prices in stores such as K mart, Target, and other "off-price retailers."[4]

STRATEGIES COMMON TO MANUFACTURERS AND MIDDLEMEN

Manufacturers and middlemen alike must adopt some strategy with respect to branding their product mix and branding for market saturation.

Branding a line of products   At least four different strategies are widely used by firms that sell more than one product.

- The same "family" or "blanket" brand may be placed on all products. This policy is followed by Heinz, Campbell, Libby, and others in the food field, as well as by Westinghouse and General Electric.
- A separate name may be used for each product. This strategy is employed by Procter & Gamble and Lever Brothers.
- A separate family brand may be applied to each grade of product or to each group of similar products. Sears groups its baby items under the Honeysuckle brand and its major home installations (furnaces and building materials) under Homart.
- The company's trade name may be combined with an individual name for the product. Thus there are Johnson's Pledge and Johnson's Glo-Coat, and Kellogg's Rice Krispies and Kellogg's Sugar Corn Pops.

When used wisely, a family-brand strategy has considerable merit. This strategy makes it much simpler and less expensive to introduce new related products to a line. Also, the general prestige of a brand can be spread more easily if it appears on several products rather than on only one. A family brand is best suited for a marketing situation where the products are related in quality, in use, or in some other manner. When Black and Decker, a manufacturer of power tools, purchased General Electric's line of small appliances, the Black and Decker brand was put on those appliances, *but* not immediately. Because of the perceived differences between kitchen products and workroom products, Black and Decker realized it was a risky proposition to switch brands. Consequently, the company mounted a year-long brand-transition campaign before making the change. Also, during those years, Black and Decker introduced

Green Giant gives the "family" brand name to a variety of product.

[4]See Hank Gilman, "Retailers Bet Their Designer Wear Can Lure You Past Calvin Klein," *The Wall Street Journal*, Feb. 1, 1985, p. 17; and "Why Designer Labels Are Fading," *Business Week*, Feb. 21, 1983, p. 70.

Now *this* is a battle of the brands.

The Battle of the Brands

several other housewares products, and this helped in the General Electric–Black and Decker brand transition.[5]

On the other hand, the use of family brands places a greater burden on the brand owner to maintain consistent quality among all products. One bad item can reflect unfavorably, and even disastrously, on all other products carrying the same brand.

Branding for market saturation   Frequently, to increase its degree of market saturation, a firm will employ a multiple-brand strategy. Suppose, for example, that a company has built one type of sales appeal around a given brand. To reach other segments of the market, the company can use other appeals with other brands. Procter & Gamble's two detergents, Tide and Dreft, illustrate this point. Some people feel that if Tide is strong enough to clean soiled work clothes, it cannot be used on lingerie and other fine clothing. For these people, Procter & Gamble has marketed Dreft, a detergent whose image is more gentle than that of Tide. To penetrate the middle-income market, several designers of higher-priced women's apparel have introduced a lower-priced line, usually under a different brand name. Some examples of the original designer label with their "second-tier" brand are Yves St. Laurent (Variation), Ralph Lauren (Classifications), Perry Ellis (Portfolio), Bill Blass (Blassport), and Anne Klein (Anne Klein II).[6]

Middlemen's brands have proved to be eminently successful in competing with manufacturers' brands. However, neither group has demonstrated a convincing competitive superiority over the other in the marketplace. Consequently, the "battle of the brands" shows every indication of continuing and becoming more intense.

About 10 years ago several supermarket chains introduced products sold under their generic names. That is, the products were simply labeled as pork and beans, peanut butter, cottage cheese, paper towels, and so on. These unbranded products generally sell for 30 to 40 percent less than manufacturers' brands and 20 percent less than retailers' brands. While they are the nutritional equivalent of branded products, the generics (graded "standard" in industry terms) may not have the color, size, and appearance of the branded items (graded "fancy"). Most of the chains sell these products completely unbranded—referring to them as "generic" or "generic products" in the store's advertising. In effect, "generic" becomes an unofficial brand name in that it is the identifying name used by the stores and consumers.

Generic products now account for a large enough share of total sales in their respective product lines to be a major factor in the battle of the brands. In the late 1980s the generics' market share leveled off, and even declined, in some product lines. Apparently the low inflation rate had dulled consumers' price sensitivity, and also manufacturers' brands fought back with extensive use of coupons. Nevertheless,

[5] For a discussion of the strategy of using a familiar, established brand on products that are in a product category that is new to a company, see Edward M. Tauber, "Brand Franchise Extension: New Product Benefits from Existing Brand Names," *Business Horizons*, March–April 1981, pp. 36–41. See also Aimée Stern, "New Payoff from Old Brand Names," *Dun's Business Month*, April 1985, p. 42.

[6] See Pamela G. Hollie, "Cheaper Lines by Designers: Offshoots Spur Sales," *New York Times*, July 27, 1985, p. 19-Y.

as we head into the 1990s, generics still are a strong force and in some lines (prescription drugs, for example) are significantly increasing in sales.[7]

Several factors account for the success of middlemen's brands and generic-labeled products. The thin profit margins on manufacturers' brands have encouraged retailers to establish their own labels. The improved quality of retailers' brands has boosted their sales. Consumers have become more sophisticated in their buying and their brand loyalty has declined, so they do consider alternative brands. It is quite generally known that retailers' brands usually are produced by large, well-known manufacturers. Generic labels, with their low-price, no-frills approach, appeal to price-conscious consumers.[8]

Manufacturers do have some effective responses to combat generic labels and retailers' brands. Producers can, for example, devote top priority to product innovation and packaging, an area in which retailers are not as strong. Manufacturers' research and development capacity also enables them to enter the market in the early stages of a product's life cycle, whereas retailer brands typically enter after a product is well established.[9]

Trademark Licensing

An effective branding strategy that has grown by leaps and bounds in recent years is brand (or trademark) licensing. Under this strategy, the owner of a trademark grants permission (a license) to other firms to use the owner's brand name, logotype (distinctive lettering and coloring), and/or character on the licensee's products. To illustrate, Harley-Davidson, the motorcycle manufacturer, has licensed its name to be used by manufacturers of a wine cooler, a $700 gold ring, and polo shirts. Coca-Cola has allowed (licensed) Murjani International to use the Coca-Cola name and distinctive lettering on a line of clothing (blue jeans, sweaters, shirts, jackets). The owner of the trademark characters in the "Peanuts" cartoon strip (Snoopy, Charlie Brown, Lucy, etc.) has licensed the use of these characters on many different products and services. American Greeting Card Company originally created the lovable character, Strawberry Shortcake, *specifically* for licensing purposes. The licensee typically pays a royalty of about 5 percent on the wholesale price of the product that carries the licensed trademark. However, this figure can vary depending upon the perceived strength of the licensor's brand.

Strategy decisions must be made by both parties—the licensor and the licensee.

Even universities are licensing their trademarks.

[7] See "No-Frill Products: 'An Idea Whose Time Has Gone,' " *Business Week*, June 17, 1985, p. 64; and "Generics Grab More of the Drug Action," *Business Week*, May 13, 1985, p. 64.

[8] For some studies on consumers' perceptions and other characteristics of the market for generic products, see Robert E. Wilkes and Humberto Valencia, "A Note on Generic Purchaser Generalizations and Subcultural Variations," *Journal of Marketing*, Summer 1985, pp. 114–120; Isabella C. M. Cunningham, Andrew P. Hardy, and Giovanna Imperia, "Generic Brands versus National Brands and Store Brands," *Journal of Advertising Research*, October–November 1982, pp. 25–32; and Martha R. McEnally and Jon M. Hawes, "The Market for Generic Brand Grocery Products: A Review and Extension," *Journal of Marketing*, Winter 1984, pp. 75–83.

[9] For a review of manufacturer and retailer strategies in the past, regarding generic products, and suggestions for future strategies, now that generics have reached maturity in many product categories, see Brian F. Harris and Roger A. Strang, "Marketing Strategies in the Age of Generics," *Journal of Marketing*, Fall 1985, pp. 70–81.

PACKAGING

Pierre Cardin (a licensor) must ask, "Should we allow other firms to use our designer label?" A manufacturer of eyeglasses (a licensee) must ask, "Do we want to put out a line of high-fashion eyeglasses under the Pierre Cardin name?"

Owners of well-known brands are interested in licensing their trademarks for various reasons. First, it can be very profitable since there is no expense involved on the part of the licensor. Second, there is a promotional benefit, because the licensor's name gets wider circulation far beyond the original trademarked article. Third, licensing can help protect the trademark. If Coca-Cola licenses its brand for use in a variety of product categories, it can block any other company from using that brand legally in those product categories.

For the company receiving the license—the licensee—the strategy is a quick way to gain market recognition and to penetrate a new market. Today there is a high financial cost involved in establishing a new brand name. Even then there is no guarantee of success. It is a lot easier for an unknown firm to gain consumer acceptance of its product if that item carries a well-known brand.

Packaging may be defined as all the activities involved in designing and producing the container or wrapper for a product. There are three reasons for packaging:

- Packaging serves several *safety* and *utilitarian purposes*. It protects a product on its route from the producer to the final customer, and in some cases even while it is being used by the customer. For example, effective packaging can help to prevent ill-intentioned persons from tampering with products. Some protection is provided by "child-proof" closures on containers of medicines and other products that are potentially harmful to children. Also, compared with bulk items, packaged goods generally are more convenient, cleaner, and less susceptible to losses from evaporation, spilling, and spoilage.

- Packaging may *implement a company's marketing program*. Packaging helps to identify a product and thus may prevent substitution of competitive products. At the point of purchase, the package can serve as a silent sales person. Furthermore, the advertising copy on the package will last as long as the product is used in its packaged form. Also, a package may be the only significant way in which a firm can differentiate its product. In the case of convenience goods or industrial operating supplies, for example, most buyers feel that one well-known brand is about as good as another. Marlboro, Players, and Newport cigarettes each tried to further differentiate its brand by packaging its cigarettes in units of 25 rather than the traditional 20.

  Some feature of the package may serve as a sales appeal—a no-drip spout, a reusable jar, or a self-applicator (Gillette's shaving brush with built-in lather, for example). By packaging their toothpaste in a pump dispenser—a product long used in Europe—Colgate and Check-Up brands increased their sales considerably. Crest and Aim later adopted the same type of packaging.

- Management may package its product in such a way as to *increase profit possibilities*. A package may be so attractive that customers will pay more just to get the special package—even though the increase in price exceeds the additional cost of the package. Also, an increase in ease of handling or a reduction in damage losses, due to packaging, will cut marketing costs, again increasing profit.

Importance of Packaging in Marketing

Historically, packaging was a production-oriented activity in most companies, performed mainly to obtain the benefits of protection and convenience. Today, however, the marketing significance of packaging is fully recognized, and packaging is truly a major competitive force in the struggle for markets. The widespread use of self-service selling and automatic vending means that the package must do the selling job at the point of purchase. Shelf space is often at a premium, and it is no simple task for manufacturers even to get their products displayed in a retail outlet. Most retailers are inclined to cater to producers that have used effective packaging.

In addition, the increased use of branding and the public's rising standards in health and sanitation have contributed to the importance of packaging. Safety in packaging has become an especially important marketing and social issue in recent years.

New developments in packaging, occurring rapidly and in a seemingly endless flow, require management's constant attention to packaging design. We see new packaging materials replacing the traditional ones, new shapes, new closures, and other new features (measured portions, metered flow). These all make for increased convenience for consumers and additional selling points for marketers. One new development in packaging that will be particularly interesting to watch in the coming years is the aseptic container—a "paper bottle" made of laminations of paper, aluminum foil, and plastic. Its airtight feature keeps perishables fresh for 5 months without refrigeration, and it costs about one-half as much as cans and 30 percent as much as bottles. Already it is being used to package many different drink products, and its future prospects are exceptionally bright.[10]

Special packaging for use in outer space.

Packaging Strategies

CHANGING THE PACKAGE

In general, management has two reasons for considering a package change—to combat a decrease in sales and to expand a market by attracting new groups of customers. More specifically, a firm may want to correct a poor feature in the existing container, or a company may want to take advantage of new materials. Some companies change their containers to aid in promotional programs. A new package may be used as a major appeal in advertising copy, or because the old container may not show up well in advertisements.

PACKAGING THE PRODUCT LINE

A company must decide whether to develop a family resemblance in the packaging of its several products. **Family packaging** involves the use of identical packages for all products or the use of packages with some common feature. Campbell's Soup, for example, uses virtually identical packaging on its condensed soup products. Management's philosophy concerning family packaging generally parallels its feelings about family branding. When new products are added to a line, promotional values asso-

[10]See '' 'Paper Bottles' Are Coming on Strong,'' *Business Week*, Jan. 16, 1984, p. 56.

Multiple packaging increases sales.

ciated with old products extend to the new ones. On the other hand, family packaging should be used only when the products are related in use and are of similar quality.

REUSE PACKAGING

Another strategy to be considered is reuse packaging. Should the company design and promote a package that can serve other purposes after the original contents have been consumed? Glasses containing cheese can later be used to serve fruit juice. Baby-food jars make great containers for small parts like nuts, bolts, and screws. Reuse packaging also should stimulate repeat purchases as the consumer attempts to acquire a matching set of containers.

MULTIPLE PACKAGING

For many years there has been a trend toward multiple packaging, or the practice of placing several units in one container. Dehydrated soups, motor oil, beer, golf balls, building hardware, candy bars, towels, and countless other products are packaged in multiple units. Test after test has proved that multiple packaging increases total sales of a product.

Criticisms of Packaging

Packaging is in the socioeconomic forefront today because of its relationship to environmental pollution issues. Perhaps the biggest challenge facing packagers is how to dispose of used containers, which are a major contributor to the solid-waste disposal problem. Consumers' desire for convenience (in the form of throw-away containers) conflicts with their desire for a clean environment.

Other socioeconomic criticisms of packaging are:

- Packaging depletes our natural resources. This criticism is offset to some extent as packagers increasingly make use of recycled materials. Another offsetting point is that effective packaging reduces spoilage (another form of resource waste).
- Packaging is excessively expensive. Cosmetic packaging is often cited as an example here. But even in seemingly simple packaging—beer, for example—half the production cost goes for the container. On the other hand, effective packaging reduces transportation costs and losses from product spoilage.
- Health hazards occur from some forms of plastic packaging and some aerosol cans. Government regulations have banned the use of several of these suspect packaging materials.
- Packaging is deceptive. Government regulation plus improvements in business practices regarding packaging have reduced the intensity of this criticism, although it still is heard on occasion.

Truly, marketing executives face some real challenges in satisfying these complaints while at the same time retaining the marketing-effectiveness, consumer-convenience, and product-protection features of packaging.

LABELING

Labeling is another product feature that requires managerial attention. The **label** is the part of a product that carries verbal information about the product or the seller. A label may be part of a package, or it may be a tag attached directly to the product. Obviously there is a close relationship among labeling, packaging, and branding.

Types of Labels

Typically, labels are classified as brand, grade, or descriptive. A **brand label** is simply the brand alone applied to the product or to the package. Thus, some oranges are brand-labeled (stamped) Sunkist or Blue Goose, and some clothes carry the brand label Sanforized. A **grade label** identifies the quality with a letter, number, or word. Canned peaches are grade-labeled A, B, and C, and corn and wheat are grade-labeled 1 and 2. **Descriptive labels** give objective information about the use, construction, care, performance, or other features of the product. On a descriptive label for a can of corn, there will be statements concerning the type of corn (golden sweet), the style (creamed or in niblet kernels), and the can size, number of servings, other ingredients, and nutritional contents.

RELATIVE MERITS

Brand labeling creates very little stir among critics. While it is an acceptable form of labeling, its severe limitation is that it does not supply sufficient information to a buyer. The real fight centers on grade versus descriptive labeling and on whether grade labeling should be made mandatory.

The proponents of grade labeling argue that it is simple, definite, and easy to use. They also point out that if grade labels were used, prices would be more closely related to quality, although grade labeling would not stifle competition. In fact, they believe that grade labeling might increase competition, because consumers would be able to judge products on the basis of both price and known quality.

Those who object to grade labeling point out that a very low score on one grading characteristic can be offset by very high scores on other factors. Companies selling products that score high *within* a given grade would be hurt by grade labeling. These companies could not justify a higher price than that charged for a product that scored very low in the same grade. And some people feel that grades are an inaccurate guide for consumer buying. It is not possible to grade the differences in flavor and taste, or in style and fashion, yet these are the factors that often influence consumer purchases.

Statutory Labeling Requirements

Several of the public's criticisms of marketing have centered on charges of false or misleading packaging and labeling. These criticisms have led to a considerable amount of federal legislation. The Federal Trade Commission Act of 1914 and its Wheeler-Lea amendment (1938) state that unfair competition is illegal. False, misleading, or deceptive labels or packages are specific instances of unfair competition.

In spite of this legislation, consumer discontent with packaging and labeling continues to mount. Consumers have charged, for example, that there are a confusing number of sizes and shapes of packages for a given product. Critics also have claimed that some packages are only partially filled and that some package shapes are deceptive. Also, when contents are measured in odd amounts (such as 6½ ounces), it is very difficult to make unit-price comparisons.

Congress responded with the Fair Packaging and Labeling Act (1966). This law provides for (1) *mandatory* labeling requirements, (2) an opportunity for industry to *voluntarily* adopt packaging standards that will limit the proliferation of weights and measures, and (3) administrative agencies (the Food and Drug Administration and the Federal Trade Commission) with the *discretionary* power to set packaging regulations where deemed necessary.

In the past, the labeling of clothing, furs, and piece goods was often confusing and misleading to the consumer. As a result, three important labeling laws were

The label on this coat must state the generic name of the fur and its country of origin.

passed. The Wool Products Labeling Act (1940) provides that a clothing product containing any wool must be labeled to explain two points clearly: (1) what kind of wool is used (virgin, reprocessed, etc.), and (2) what percentage of each type is included in the product. The Fur Products Labeling Act (1951) requires that in identifying a fur garment, the label must state the generic name of the fur and its country of generic origin. The Textile Fiber Products Identification Act (1958) provides that clothing garments and household textiles, including rugs, must carry the generic description of the fiber content.

The Food and Drug Administration has also established a set of labeling standards for processed foods to ensure full disclosure of their nutritional content. Labels must clearly state the amounts of protein, fat, carbohydrates, and calories contained in the contents of the package. Vitamin and mineral content must be expressed as a percentage of the recommended daily allowance. Also, ingredients must be listed in the order (most to least) in which they are contained in the product.

A 1962 law pertaining to the production and marketing of prescription and nonprescription drugs requires that labels and advertising must prominently state the *generic* name of the drug in addition to the *brand* name. A 1977 law requires that the main ingredients in cosmetics must be disclosed on the label.

The Food and Drug Act of 1906 and its 1938 amendment, the Food, Drug, and Cosmetic Act, are administered by the Food and Drug Administration. These laws provide explicit regulations for labeling drugs, foods, cosmetics, and therapeutic devices. Any conditions for safe use must be included on the label, and items with poisonous content must be so labeled.

OTHER IMAGE-BUILDING FEATURES

A well-rounded program for product planning and development will include a company policy on several additional product attributes: product design, color, quality, guarantee, and servicing.

Product Design

One way to build an image of a product is through its design. In fact, a distinctive design may be the only feature that significantly differentiates a product. Many firms feel that there is considerable glamour and general promotional appeal in product design and the designer's name. In the field of industrial products, *engineering* design has long been recognized as extremely important. Today there is a realization of the marketing value of *appearance* design as well. Office machines and office furniture are examples of industrial products that reflect recent conscious attention to product design, often with good sales results. The marketing significance of design has been recognized for years in the field of consumer products, from big items like automobiles and refrigerators to small products like fountain pens and apparel.

Good design can improve the marketability of a product in many ways. It can make the product easier to operate. It can upgrade the product's quality or durability. It can improve product appearance and reduce manufacturing costs.

Color

Color often is the determining factor in a customer's acceptance or rejection of a product, whether that product is a dress, a table, or an automobile. Color by itself, however, is no selling advantage because many competing firms offer color. The marketing advantage comes in knowing the right color and in knowing when to change colors. If a garment manufacturer or a retail store's fashion coordinator guesses wrong

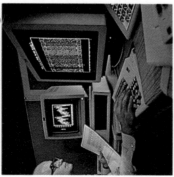

Some companies use a computer to aid in designing a product.

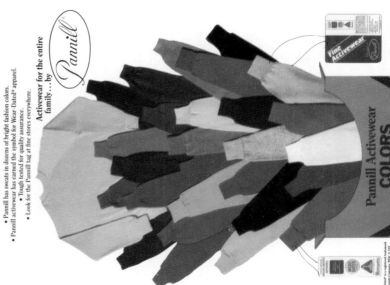

Color me Pannill!

• Pannill has sweats in dozens of bright fashion colors.
• Pannill activewear has earned the symbol for Wear-Dated® apparel.
  • Tough tested for quality assurance.
  • Look for the Pannill tag at fine stores everywhere.

Activewear for the entire family. . . by *Pannill*

One of these colors ought to be fashionable this year.

Product Quality

In recent years, American manufacturers have been increasingly concerned about the quality of their products. And well they should be! For many years, a major consumer complaint has concerned the poor quality of some products—both materials and workmanship. Some foreign products—Japanese cars, for example—have made serious inroads into the American market because these products are perceived as being of better quality than their American counterparts.[12]

The quality of a product is extremely important, but it is probably the most difficult of all the image-building features to define. Users frequently disagree on what constitutes quality in a product, from a cut of meat to a piece of music. Personal tastes are deeply involved. Nevertheless, a marketing executive must make several decisions about product quality. First, the product should reach only that level of quality compatible with the intended use of the item; it need not be any better. In fact, *good* and *poor* are misleading terms. *Correct* and *incorrect* or *right* and *wrong* would be much more appropriate. If a person is making a peach cobbler, grade B or C peaches are the correct quality. They are not necessarily the *best* quality, but they are *right* for the intended use. It is not necessary to pay grade A prices for large, well-formed peaches when these features are destroyed in making the cobbler.[13]

Product Warranty and Product Liability

The general purpose of a warranty is to give buyers some assurance that they will be compensated in case the product does not perform up to reasonable expectations. In years past, courts seemed generally to recognize only *express warranties*—those stated in written or spoken words. Usually these were quite limited in what they covered and seemed mainly to protect the seller from buyers' claims.

But times have changed! Consumer complaints have led to a governmental campaign to protect the consumer in many areas, one of which is product liability. Today, courts and government agencies are broadening the scope of warranty coverage by recognizing the concept of **implied warranty.** This is the idea that a warranty was *intended* by the seller, although not actually stated. Manufacturers are being held responsible, even when the sales contract is between the retailer and the consumer. Warranties are considered to "run with the product." Manufacturers are held liable for product-caused injury, whether or not they are to blame for negligence in manufacturing. It all adds up to "Let the seller beware."

A major legislative reform of consumer product warranty practices is the Magnuson-Moss Consumer Product Warranty Act (1975). This law greatly strengthened

---

[11]See Ronald Alsop, "Color Grows More Important in Catching Consumers' Eyes," *The Wall Street Journal*, Nov. 29, 1984, p. 33.

[12]For a report on American product quality and the task ahead for management, see David A. Garvin, "Quality on the Line," *Harvard Business Review*, September–October 1983, pp. 65–75.

[13]For some suggestions on how quality can be used strategically to position and sell products, see David A. Garvin, "Product Quality: An Important Strategic Weapon," *Business Horizons*, March–April 1984, pp. 40–43.

on what will be the fashionable color in women's clothing, this error can be disastrous.[11]

consumers' rights and increased sellers' responsibilities under product warranties. The law's intent is disarmingly simple—to make warranties strong and understandable so they can protect consumers and aid them in comparing competitive products. Yet the law has created much uncertainty and confusion among business executives as they wait for the FTC to spell out the regulations under the law.

In recent years manufacturers have responded to legislation and consumer complaints by broadening and simplifying their warranties. Many sellers are using their warranties as promotional devices to stimulate purchases by reducing consumers' risks. The effective handling of consumers' complaints related to warranties can be a significant factor in strengthening a company's marketing program.[14]

Another very compelling reason for management to pay special attention to its warranties and product quality is the threat of a costly **product-liability claim.** This is a legal action claiming that an illness, accident, or death resulted from the named product because it was harmful, faulty, or inadequately labeled. Product-liability claims today are a major and growing problem, creating bitter disputes between business groups and consumer advocates. Tens of thousands of suits are filed every year involving alleged defects in a wide variety of products. This product list includes autos, stepladders, asbestos products, tampons, toys, pharmaceuticals, birth-control devices, chain saws, tires, and others. And juries seem inclined to award larger and larger settlements to the plaintiffs.

For most of this decade, Congress has been wrestling with the highly controversial issue of product-liability legislation. It has proven to be difficult to write a law that is considered fair by groups on either side of the issue. Yet everybody recognizes the need for legislation to bring some uniformity to the existing chaos created by the wide variations in state laws, court decisions, and financial settlements.[15]

The Consumer Product Safety Act (1972) is typical of the changed attitude regarding product liability and injurious products. The act created the Consumer Product Safety Commission (CPSC). This commission has authority to establish mandatory safety standards for practically all consumer products. (The CPSC has no authority over autos, food, drugs, tobacco products, and some other products that are covered by separate laws or other agencies.) It can publish information regarding injurious products—naming brands and manufacturers. It can ban the distribution of these products without a court hearing. And top management of offending companies may face criminal—not just civil—charges.

Product Servicing A related problem is that of adequately providing the services guaranteed by the warranty. Product servicing requires management's attention as products become more

---

[14]See John Koten, "Aggressive Use of Warranties Is Benefiting Many Concerns," *The Wall Street Journal,* Apr. 5, 1984, p. 33.

[15]For a good review of the product-liability problem, see Fred W. Morgan, "Marketing and Product Liability: A Review and Update," *Journal of Marketing,* Summer 1982, pp. 69–78. Also see Brad Reid and Ed Timmerman, "Federal Standards for Product Liability Would Help Marketers," *Marketing News,* Apr. 13, 1984, p. 8; "Unfair Products: The Great Debate over Blame and Punishment," *Business Week,* Apr. 30, 1984, p. 96; and "Product-Liability Suits: Why Nobody Is Satisfied," *U.S. News & World Report,* Aug. 19, 1985, p. 49.

complex and consumers grow increasingly dissatisfied and vocal. To cope with these problems, management can consider several courses of action. For instance, a producer can establish several geographically dispersed factory service centers, staff them with well-trained company employees, and strive to make servicing a separate profit-generating activity. Or the producer can shift the main burden to middlemen, compensate them for their efforts, and possibly even train their service people.

Today the provision of adequate product servicing should be high on the list of topics calling for managerial action. A perennial major consumer complaint is that manufacturers and retailers do *not* provide adequate repair service for the products they sell. Oftentimes, the situation is simply that the consumers wish to be *heard*. That is, they simply want someone to listen to them regarding their complaints. In response to this situation, a number of manufacturers have established free (800-number) telephone lines to their customer service departments.

SUMMARY

The management of the various features of a product—its brand, package, labeling, design, color, quality, warranty, and servicing—is an integral part of effective product planning. A *brand* is a means of identifying and differentiating the products or services of an organization. Branding aids sellers in managing their promotional and pricing activities. Brand ownership carries the dual responsibilities of promoting the brand and maintaining a consistent level of quality. Selecting a good brand name—and there are relatively few really good ones—is a difficult task. A good name should suggest a product's benefits, be easy to pronounce and remember, lend itself to product-line additions, and be eligible for legal registration and protection.

Manufacturers must decide whether to brand their products and whether to sell under a middleman's brand. Middlemen must decide whether to carry manufacturers' brands alone or whether to establish their own brands as well. Both groups of sellers must set policies regarding branding of groups of products and branding for market saturation. Customer acceptance of generic-labeled products has heated up the "battle of the brands." Another branding strategy is trademark licensing, which is being employed to an increasing extent by owners of well-known brands. The owner allows the use of (licenses) its name or trademarked character to another firm that is looking for a quick, relatively low-cost way of penetrating a market.

Packaging is becoming increasingly important as sellers recognize the problems, as well as the marketing opportunities, involved in packaging. *Labeling* is a related activity. Marketers should understand the merits and problems of grade labeling and of descriptive labeling. Many consumer criticisms of marketing have involved packaging and labeling, and there are several federal laws regulating these marketing activities.

Companies are now recognizing the marketing value of product *design*—especially appearance design. Two related factors are product *color* and product *quality*. Selecting the right color is a marketing advantage. Projecting the appropriate quality image is essential. In addition, *warranties* and *servicing* require considerable management attention these days because of consumer complaints and governmental regulations in these areas. The prevalence of product-liability claims is a major problem that is getting worse and obviously needs some remedial action by the U.S. Congress.

KEY TERMS AND CONCEPTS

■

Brand 232
Brand name 232
Brand mark 232
Trademark 232
Producer's brand (national brand) 232
Middleman's brand (private brand) 232
Brand names becoming generic names 235
Branding of parts and materials 235
Family (blanket) brands 237
Branding for market saturation 238
Battle of the brands 238
No-name (generic) brands 238

Trademark licensing 239
Packaging 240
Grade label 243
Descriptive label 243
Major labeling laws 243
Product design 244
Product color 245
Product quality 246
Product warranty 246
Product liability 246
Consumer Product Safety Act 247

QUESTIONS AND PROBLEMS

■

1. List five brand names that you think are good ones and five that you consider poor. Explain the reasoning behind your choices.
2. Evaluate each of the following brand names in light of the characteristics of a good brand, indicating the strong and weak points of each name.
   a. Schwinn (bicycles).
   b. Kodak (cameras).
   c. Superior (hand tools).
   d. Hush Puppies (shoes).
   e. Nissan (automobiles).
   f. Whirlpool (appliances).
3. Suggest some brands that are on the verge of becoming generic. What course of action should a company take to protect the separate identity of its brand?
4. Under what conditions would you recommend that a manufacturer brand a product that will be used as a part or material in the production of another product?
5. In which of the following cases should the company adopt the strategy of family branding?
   a. A manufacturer of men's underwear introduces essentially the same products for women.
   b. A manufacturer of women's cosmetics adds a line of men's cosmetics to its product assortment.
   c. A manufacturer of hair-care products introduces a line of portable electric hair dryers.
6. Suppose you are employed by the manufacturer of a well-known brand of snow skis. Your company is planning to add ice skates and water skis to its product line. It has no previous experience with either of these two new products. You are given the assignment of selecting a brand name for the ice skates and water skis. Your main problem is in deciding whether to adopt a family-brand policy. That is, should you use the snow-ski brand for either or both of the new products? Or should you develop separate names for each of the new items? You note that Campbell's (soups) and Heinz (pickle products) use family brands. You also note that Sears and Procter & Gamble generally do the opposite. They use different names for each *group of products* (Sears) or each *separate product* (P&G). What course of action would you recommend? Why?

7. A manufacturer of a well-known brand of ski boots acquired a division of a company that marketed a well-known brand of snow skis. What brand strategy should the new organization adopt? Should all products (skis and boots) now carry the boot brand? Should they carry the ski brand? Is there still some other alternative that you feel would be better?

8. Why do some firms sell an identical product under more than one of their own brands?

9. Assume that a large department-store chain proposed to the manufacturers of Maytag washing machines that Maytag supply the department store with machines carrying the store's brand. What factors should Maytag's management consider in making a decision? If the product were General Foods' Jell-O, to what extent would the situation be different?

10. Give examples of products that are excellently packaged. Mention some that are very poorly packaged.

11. What changes would you recommend in the typical packaging of these products?

a. Coke Classic.   c. Potato chips.

b. Hairspray.   d. Toothpaste.

12. If grade labeling is adopted, what factors should be used as bases for grading the following products?

a. Lipstick.

b. Woolen sweaters.

c. Diet-food products.

13. Give examples of products for which the careful use of the color of the product has increased sales. Can you cite examples to show that poor use of color may hurt a company's marketing program?

14. Explain the relationship between a product warranty on small electric appliances and the manufacturer's distribution system for these products.

15. How would the warranty policies set by a manufacturer of skis differ from those adopted by an automobile manufacturer?

3

CASE 7

FIRST NATIONAL BANK OF WOODBURY*

Adding a new product

Bill Smith, marketing manager for the First National Bank of Woodbury, was wondering whether his bank should offer a bank identification and check guarantee card. Only two weeks ago a proposal regarding the card had been made to the new-product committee. Since then there had been much discussion and very different opinions expressed on whether or not the product should be offered by the First National Bank.

Woodbury was a cosmopolitan community of 250,000 people with an income level considerably above the national average. In the city there were two colleges and one university, the world headquarters and major production facility for a *Fortune* 500 company, and several other manufacturing plants. In the Woodbury market area there were eight financial institutions, with First National Bank being the dominant one. This bank held approximately 45 percent of the accounts and 50 percent of the deposits in the city. In addition to its main office in the downtown area, the First National Bank had six branches located throughout the city.

The proposed new product was a plastic identification and check guarantee card. The card was similar in size and construction to a credit card, but had the photograph of the account holder on the card. The card could be used as identification for check cashing with participating retailers. When the card was used as identification, the bank guaranteed any check for an amount up to $200. To be eligible for this identification card, a person would be required to maintain both a checking account and a savings account with the bank.

The manufacturing process of the card required a Polaroid picture which then was transferred to the card's surface by a patented process. The card also had a magnetic strip on the back side similar to many credit cards.

It was anticipated that within the next two to three years First National Bank would be introducing automatic teller machines. A separate card would be required to access these machines. Bill was concerned that the introduction of two cards within such a short time might generate confusion among the current customers.

*This case was prepared by Prof. Lowell E. Crow, Western Michigan University, and is reproduced with permission.

A second concern was the impact of the card on the retail stores. Several of the major retailers in the area currently had their own check guarantee card which generated consumer loyalty to their stores. Some of First National's executives doubted that the retailers would accept the check guarantee card of First National Bank.

To compound the issue, the operations department had completed a cost study which indicated that the cost of producing the card was approximately $6.50. This cost did not include the floor space requirements nor the time of the First National personnel to gather the consumer information and take the customer's picture.

Fred Sherritt, manager of the mortgage loan department, liked the idea of the card, but only if the customers were charged $5 or $10 for the card. Emily Tilton, the head of customer services, raised some question about the market for the card. She asked whether the primary target market was present customers, or did the bank intend to use the card as a promotional device to attract new customers. She also did not like the idea of requiring the card holder to have both a checking and a savings account at First National. "And one more thing," Emily said, "if we are going to go with this new card, then let's do it right. That means first let's get a catchy name for the card."

Bill Smith realized that the First National Bank was the dominant financial institution in the area. And the bank had always taken the lead in new-product introductions in its market. The new-product committee was to make its recommendation to the board of directors at the next meeting. The committee had asked Bill to give them his recommendations within the next two days.

QUESTIONS

1. Should the First National Bank adopt the proposed check guarantee card?
2. If your decision is "yes," then:
   a. Should there be a charge for the card, and if so, how much?
   b. To whom should the card be promoted?
   c. Should the card holder be required to have both a checking and a savings account at First National?
   d. What should be the name of the card?

PETER RABBIT TOY SHOPPE

Adding a new line of products

Julie Gibson, the founder and owner of the Peter Rabbit Toy Shoppe, was considering the feasibility of expanding into juvenile furniture. The city in which her toy store was located currently had no full-line children's furniture store. Julie felt the time was right and the market was right for Peter Rabbit to add the new line.

The Peter Rabbit Toy Shoppe was located in Hollyglen, a medium-sized shopping center in the Midwestern city of Rockland. Rockland, with a population of about 80,000, was 30 miles from a large city whose population was about 1 million. The store had opened a little over 4 years ago.

Last year Peter Rabbit recorded a net profit of 5 percent on sales of $450,000. Ms. Gibson expected that this year's sales volume would exceed the half-million mark. The main reason for this projected increase was that a major competitor in Rockland had moved to another city. Julie was hoping to capture the market share previously held by this store.

Julie felt that her store was in reasonably good financial condition. Each year Peter Rabbit's earnings were reinvested in the firm. Most of the initial bank loan had been paid-off. Neither Julie nor her husband Kerry, who helped to operate the store, had drawn any salaries since the store opened. If all went well this year, however, Ms. Gibson hoped to start drawing a salary next year.

Peter Rabbit carried only those toys that fitted in with Julie Gibson's philosophy about toys and children. She believed that "toys should be emotionally healthy for children and should be something they are able to love." Thus, for example, her store did not carry toy guns or soldiers.

The line of products that Ms. Gibson was considering adding included a full range of children's furniture and accessories for ages up to 14. The furniture assortment would range from cribs, high chairs, and diapering tables to bunkbeds, desks, and dressers. The accessories would include bedding items, lamps, and wall decorations.

Most of the proposed inventory would reflect the quality image that Peter Rabbit tried to project in its selection of toys. Ms. Gibson intended to carry some expensive, unique items even if they did not sell quickly. She felt that products of this nature would attract the higher-income clientele and perpetuate her desired store image. At the same time, she intended to stock in depth the basic items that would account for the bulk of the sales volume. She also wanted to attract lower-income buyers by carrying some articles that would appeal to that segment. She planned to import from foreign suppliers, as well as buy from American companies. Most of the inventory would carry a markup of 50 percent of the retail selling price—the customary markup in furniture retailing.

To expand into juvenile furniture, Peter Rabbit would have to double its present floor space to 8,000 square feet. The shopping center developers agreed to add this additional floor space by constructing a new building that would be connected with the present Peter Rabbit store. The additional space would rent annually for $20 per square foot. Gibson estimated she would need capital of $150,000 for the new inventory and store furniture and fixtures.

At the present time, no specialty juvenile furniture stores existed in Rockland. Most stores offered only fragmented lines of children's furniture, with no accessories and usually of low quality. To purchase children's furniture, Rockland residents had three options—to buy through a mail-order catalog, to shop at the local discount stores, or to drive to the central city 30 miles away. Since there were no local full-line stores, most people did drive to the larger city.

Julie and Kerry Gibson were reviewing some of the market data they had collected. In 1980 the county in which Rockland was located had a population of about 175,000. The population projections for 1985 and 1990 were approximately 190,000 and 215,000, respectively. In 1980 about 3,000 babies were born in Rockland's county. Rockland itself was largely a middle-income community. There were a large number of young professional people living in the city. The city's economic base was built around a state university, several government laboratories, and private businesses that were mainly in electronics and other light industries.

Looking further at national demographic data, Julie noticed that juvenile furniture sales were directly related to the number of women giving birth to their first child. About one-half of all first-born children were born to parents who had been married

3 years or less. Also, about one-half of all women giving birth were under 25 years of age. In many of the families with young children in Rockland, both parents were working. In the 1980s the birthrate was expected to remain close to the relatively low level of the 1970s. Government agencies had forecast a slowly expanding market for child-related industries in the 1980s.

Kerry Gibson did not think that Peter Rabbit should add the proposed line of juvenile furniture. Although both toys and furniture were intended for the same ultimate users—children—he felt that they were not a compatible combination in the same store. He feared that people would not think of buying good furniture in a toy shop. Furthermore, he was afraid that by adding a line of furniture, Peter Rabbit would blur its image as a high-class toy store.

He questioned whether Peter Rabbit had the executive know-how to buy and market furniture. "Even the company name does not project a satisfactory image for furniture retailing," he said. Both he and Julie also were concerned about their projected cash flow and other financial considerations. Furniture typically was considered a big-ticket item (high unit value), and the average furniture store had a low rate of stock turnover.

QUESTION

Should the Peter Rabbit Toy Shoppe add the proposed line of juvenile furniture?

CASE 9

DEPENDABLE DRUGS*

Brand strategy ■

Two brothers, Ed and Jim Henderson, owned and operated a chain of seven retail drugstores, doing business under the name of Dependable Drugs. From the time they started in business, Ed and Jim had consistently followed the policy of carrying only nationally branded merchandise—that is, well-known manufacturers' brands. In recent months, however, they had come to realize that inflation was making the customers increasingly price-conscious. The brothers also had observed that some supermarket chains had introduced, with apparent success, a line of products being sold without any brand name. These products were simply labeled with the generic name of the article—pork and beans, peanut butter, or paper towels, for example. As a result of these various developments, the Henderson brothers were wondering whether they should add a line of products under their own store name—in effect, their own "private brand."

The Dependable Drugs stores were located in established residential areas and in new suburban shopping centers surrounding a large industrial city on the East Coast. Ed Henderson was a registered pharmacist, and his brother Jim had a degree in business administration.

The first two stores in the Dependable Drugs chain were being successfully operated as full-service businesses when the Henderson brothers acquired them. The other five stores, however, had presented quite a different business situation. These stores were started from scratch as far as location, customers, fixtures, reputation,

*This case was prepared by Prof. Walter F. Rohrs, Wagner College. Used with permission.

and managerial policies were concerned. Consequently, they had presented a series of challenging elements of entrepreneurship not experienced in the first two stores.

Business in the new stores initially was slow, despite elaborate "grand opening" promotional efforts. During succeeding months, the sales volume increased moderately. However, neither the sales volume nor the profit had yet come up to the owners' expectations.

The original store had a large cellar which the company still used as its main storage area. For two reasons, however, this storage area was rapidly becoming overcrowded. First, Dependable Drugs had to buy some products in large amounts in order to obtain the quantity discounts that helped meet the keen price competition. Second, there was a stream of new sizes, colors, and varieties of existing products, plus a flow of new products which the Hendersons felt they had to carry.

The Hendersons believed that their policy of stocking only national (manufacturers') branded merchandise was a good one. With such a policy, they could trade on the general consumer acceptance of national brands as well as the fine reputation of large, well-known organizations. Furthermore, these products typically were heavily advertised and otherwise promoted by the manufacturers.

Over the past several months, clerks in all the Dependable Drugs stores had observed that customers were becoming very price-conscious. In some instances, they even brought in newspaper ads of other local merchants showing nationally branded products at prices considerably lower than those charged by Dependable Drugs. Some customers said they did not mind paying a few cents more at Dependable Drugs, but 15 to 20 percent on an item was just too much. Consequently, the sales of some proprietary (nonprescription) medicines had been declining.

During their recent regular Friday afternoon business meetings, Ed and Jim had been discussing this problem of lost sales caused by intense price competition. They had explored several options, one of which was to market a line of products under their own private brand—the Dependable Drugs brand. At the same time, however, they were uncertain regarding whether or not they should go the private-brand route.

Jim had gathered detailed information and samples from a number of sources which could provide top-grade products under the Dependable Drugs brand. The prices of these products were generally much lower than the prices of similar products carrying the manufacturers' brands. This was the case even though the product-quality specifications on the private-branded merchandise were as good as, or better than, the specifications for the national brands.

Jim and Ed recognized there were advantages to their marketing a group of products under the Dependable Drugs brand. These products could be sold at lower prices than the nationally branded items. Also, by using a private brand, Dependable Drugs largely eliminated price comparisons with competitive products. The Hendersons were impressed by the fact that the large national drug chains, such as Walgreen's, had been marketing under a private brand for years. In fact, the brothers were enthusiastic enough to have selected a brand name—"Double D"—in the event they decided to go the private-brand route.

At the same time, Ed and Jim recognized they were likely to encounter problems with a private brand. Ed pointed out that consumer resistance was likely to be strong, at least in the beginning. He said that strong emotional considerations were involved in the purchase of many drugstore products. Dependable Drugs would have to educate its customers and build consumer confidence in the Double D brand. Store personnel would have to explain to customers that Dependable Drugs' products were, by law, at least the equivalent of the better-known national brands. Ed also stressed that Dependable Drugs would need a carefully planned promotional effort and a strong money-back guarantee of quality.

Both brothers were concerned with the potential warehousing, inventory control, and financing problems that they might face. Already their cellar warehouse often was close to being full. Financing pressures might increase because private-brand suppliers often required large minimum orders.

Jim then raised another question. "Supposing we decide to go the private-brand route," he said, "then we have to consider how extensively we should apply the Double D brand. Do we put it on just a few products where we face the greatest price competition?" Or, do we use our brand over a wider range of products and product lines?"

Ed was wondering if Dependable Drugs could draw on the recent experiences that supermarket chains were having with generic brands. "They started out with only a few items," he observed, "and now they even have generic ice cream, meats, beer, cigarettes, and suntan lotions. Should we follow their expansion policy?"

QUESTIONS

1. Should Dependable Drugs adopt a private-brand policy?
2. If you decision is "yes," what products should carry the Double D brand?
3. Should Dependable Drugs add a line of generic (no-brand) products?

THE PRICE

The development and use of a pricing structure as part of the firm's marketing mix

We are in the process of developing a strategic marketing mix to reach our target markets and achieve our marketing goals. With our product planning completed, we now turn our attention to the pricing ingredient in the marketing mix. In the strategic planning for—and development of—the pricing structure, we face two broad tasks. First, we must determine the base price for a product, including a decision on our pricing objectives. These topics are covered in Chapter 12. Second, we must decide on the strategies (such as discounts) to employ in modifying and applying the base price. These strategies are discussed in Chapter 13.

PRICE DETERMINATION

CHAPTER GOALS

In this chapter we discuss the role of price in the marketing mix—what price is, how it can be used, and how it is set relative to product costs, market demand, and competitive prices. This chapter is somewhat more difficult and quantitative than previous ones. After studying this chapter, you should understand:

- The meaning of price.
- The importance of price in our economy and in an individual firm.
- The major pricing goals.
- The idea of an "expected" price.
- The several types of costs that are incurred in producing and marketing a product.
- The cost-plus method of setting a base price.
- The use of break-even analysis in setting a price.
- Prices established by considering both supply and demand (costs and anticipated revenues).
- Prices established in relation only to the competitive market price.

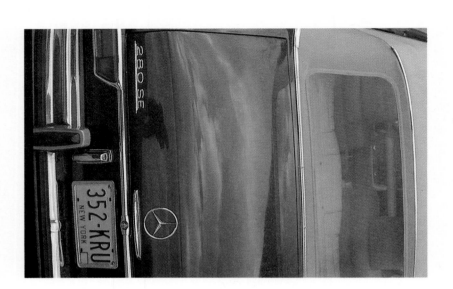

"How much do you think we ought to sell it for?" Procter & Gamble had to answer this question in the course of planning to introduce Liquid Tide and Crest toothpaste in a pump dispenser. This same question is asked by (1) Murjani when it introduces this year's models of Coca-Cola clothes, (2) the business manager of the Denver Symphony Orchestra or the Denver Broncos when pricing season tickets, and (3) surgeons, accountants, and artists when marketing their services. In effect, this question is asked any time an organization introduces a new product or service or considers changing the price on an existing product or service. This question of how much to charge comes up because so often we simply do not have any nice formula or model to follow in setting a price. Pricing still remains an art, not a science, and much intuition sometimes is involved. How else do you account for the fact that several companies increased sales by *raising* their prices? For some autos (Mercedes) and perfumes (Giorgio) it seems like the higher their price is, the more desirable these products become.

Perhaps our opening question would be more accurately worded if we asked, "How much do you think people will pay for this item?" The question then would be in accord with the generalization that *prices are always on trial*. A price is simply an offer or an experiment to test the pulse of the market. If customers accept the offer, then the price is fine. If they reject it, the price usually will be changed quickly, or the product may even be withdrawn from the market. In this chapter we shall discuss some of the major methods used to determine a price—that is, to answer our opening question. Before being concerned with actual price determination, however, executives should understand the meaning and importance of price, and they should decide on their pricing objectives.

MEANING OF PRICE

Undoubtedly, many of the difficulties associated with pricing start with the rather simple fact that often we really do not know what we are talking about. That is, we do not know the meaning of the word *price*, even though it is true that the concept is quite easy to define in familiar terms.

In economic theory, we learn that price, value, and utility are related concepts. **Utility** is the attribute of an item that makes it capable of satisfying human wants. **Value** is the quantitative measure of the worth of a product to attract other products in exchange. We may say the value of a certain hat is three baseball bats or 15 gallons of gasoline. Because our economy is not geared to a slow, ponderous barter system, we use money as a common denominator of value. And we use the term *price* to describe the money value of an item. **Price** is value expressed in terms of dollars and cents, or any other monetary medium of exchange.

Practical problems arise in connection with a definition of price, however, when we try to state simply the price of a product—say, an office desk. Suppose the price

Wonder what the price would be at the orchard if you picked them yourself.

quoted to Helen for an office desk was $525, while Bill paid only $275. At first glance it looks as if Bill got a better deal. Yet, when we get all the facts, we may change our opinion. Helen's desk was delivered to her office, she had a year to pay for it, and it was beautifully finished. Bill bought a partially assembled desk with no finish on it. (He was a do-it-yourself fan.) He had to assemble the drawers and legs and then painstakingly stain, varnish, and hand-rub the entire desk. He arranged for the delivery himself, and he paid cash in full at the time of purchase. Now let us ask who paid the higher price in each case. The answer is not as easy as it seemed at first glance.

This example illustrates how difficult it is to define price in an everyday business situation. Many variables are involved. The definition hinges on the problem of determining exactly what is being sold. This relates to a problem posed in Chapter 9, that of trying to define a product. In pricing, we must consider more than the physical product alone. A seller usually is pricing a combination of the physical product and several services and want-satisfying benefits. Sometimes it is difficult even to define the price of the physical product alone. On one model of automobile, a stated price may include radio, power steering, and power brakes. For another model of the same make of car, these three items may be priced separately.

In summary, price is the value placed on goods and services. **Price** is the amount of money and/or products that are needed to acquire some combination of another product and its accompanying services.

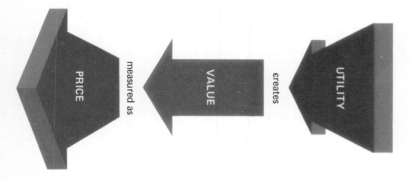

UTILITY → creates → VALUE → measured as → PRICE

THE PRICE IS WHAT YOU PAY FOR WHAT YOU GET

"That which we call a rose by any other name would smell as sweet."
—*Romeo and Juliet*, Act II, Scene 2

Tuition . . . . Education
Interest . . . . Use of money
Rent . . . . Use of living quarters or a piece of equipment for a period of time
Fare . . . . Taxi or bus ride
Fee . . . . Services of a physician or lawyer
Retainer . . . . Lawyer's services over a period of time

Toll . . . . Long-distance phone call or travel on some highways
Salary . . . . Services of an executive or other white-collar worker
Wage . . . . Services of a blue-collar worker
Commission . . . Sales person's services
Honorarium . . . Guest speaker
Dues . . . . Membership in a union or a club

—then in socially undesirable situations, some people pay a price called blackmail, ransom, or bribery.

Source: Suggested, in part, by John T. Mentzer and David J. Schwartz, Marketing Today, 4th ed., Harcourt Brace Jovanovich, San Diego, 1985, p. 599.

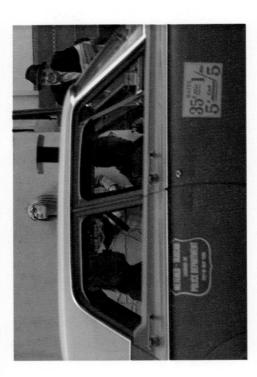

Price—doctors call it a fee and colleges call it tuition.

IMPORTANCE OF PRICE

In the Economy

Pricing is considered by many to be the key activity within the capitalistic system of free enterprise. The market price of a product influences wages, rent, interest, and profits. That is, the price of a product influences the price paid for the factors of production—labor, land, capital, and entrepreneurship. Price thus is a basic regulator of the economic system because it influences the allocation of these factors of production. High wages attract labor, high interest rates attract capital, and so on. As an allocator of scarce resources, price determines what will be produced (supply) and who will get the goods and services that are produced (demand).

Criticism of the American system of reasonably free enterprise, and the public's demand for further restraints on the system, are often triggered by a reaction to price or to pricing policies.

PRICING OBJECTIVES ■

In the Individual Firm

The price of a product or service is a major determinant of the market demand for the item. Price affects the firm's competitive position and its share of the market. As a result, price has a considerable bearing on the company's revenue and net profit.

At the same time, there usually are forces that limit the importance of pricing in a company's marketing program. Differentiated product features or a favorite brand may be more important to consumers than price. In fact, as noted in Chapter 11, one object of branding is to decrease the effect of price on the demand for a product. To put the role of pricing in a company's marketing program in its proper perspective, then, let us say that price is important, but not all-important, in explaining marketing success.

Every marketing task—including (and perhaps, especially) pricing—should be directed toward the achievement of a goal. In other words, management should decide on its pricing objective before determining the price itself. Yet, as logical as this may be, very few firms consciously establish, or explicitly state, their pricing objective.

THE MAIN GOALS IN PRICING ARE:		
Profit-oriented—to:	Sales-oriented—to:	Status quo-oriented—to:
Achieve target return on investment or net sales.	Increase sales.	Stabilize prices.
Maximize profit.	Maintain or increase market share.	Meet competition.

Profit-Oriented Goals

The pricing goal that management selects should be entirely compatible with the goals set for the company and its marketing program. To illustrate, let's assume that the company's goal is to increase its return on investment from the present level of 15 percent to a level of 20 percent at the end of a 3-year period. Then it follows that the pricing goal during this period must be to achieve some stated percentage return on investment. It would not be logical, in this case, to adopt the pricing goal of maintaining the company's market share or of stabilizing prices.

By selecting profit maximization or a target return, management focuses its attention on profit generation. Profit goals may be set either for the short run or for longer periods of time.

ACHIEVE TARGET RETURN

A firm may price its products or services to achieve a certain percentage return on its *investment* or on its *sales*. Such goals are used by both middlemen and manufacturers.

Many retailers and wholesalers use target return on *net sales* as a pricing objective for short-run periods. They set a percentage markup on sales that is large enough to cover anticipated operating costs plus a desired profit for the year. In such cases, the *percentage* of profit may remain constant, but the *dollar* profit will vary according to the number of units sold.

Achieving a target return on *investment* is typically selected as a goal by manufacturers that are leaders in their industry—companies such as General Motors and Alcoa. Target-return pricing is used frequently by industry leaders because they can set their pricing goals more independently of competition than can the smaller firms in the industry.

MAXIMIZE PROFITS

The pricing objective of making as much money as possible is probably followed by a larger number of companies than any other goal. The trouble with this goal is that the term *profit maximization* may have an ugly connotation. It is sometimes connected in the public mind with profiteering, high prices, and monopoly. In economic theory or business practice, however, there is nothing wrong with profit maximization. Theoretically, if profits become unduly high because supply is short in relation to demand, new capital will be attracted into the field. This will increase supply and eventually reduce profits to normal levels. In the marketplace, it is difficult to find many situations where profiteering has existed over an extended period of time. Substitute products are available, purchases are postponable, and competition can increase to keep prices at a reasonable level. Where prices may be unduly high and entry into the field is severely limited, public outrage soon balances the scales. If market conditions and public opinion do not do the job directly, government restraints will soon bring about moderation.

A profit maximization goal is likely to be far more beneficial to a company and to the public if practiced over the *long run*. To do this, however, firms sometimes have to accept short-run losses. A company entering a new geographic market or introducing a new product frequently does best by initially setting low prices to build a large clientele.

The goal should be to maximize profits on *total output* rather than on each single item marketed. A manufacturer may maximize total profits by practically giving away some articles in order to stimulate sales of other goods. Through its sponsored broadcasts and telecasts of athletic events, the Gillette Company frequently promotes razors at very low, profitless prices. Management hopes that once customers acquire Gillette razors, they will become long-term profitable customers for Gillette blades.

Sales-Oriented Goals

In some companies, management's pricing attention is focused on sales volume. In these situations, the pricing goal may be to increase sales volume or to maintain or increase the firm's market share.

INCREASE SALES VOLUME

This pricing goal is usually stated as a percentage increase in sales volume over some period of time, say, 1 year or 3 years. However, to increase sales volume may or may not be consistent with the marketing concept that advocates *profitable* sales volume. Management may decide to increase its volume by discounting or some other aggressive pricing strategy, perhaps incurring a loss. Thus, management is willing to take a short-run loss if the increased sales enable the company to get a foothold in its market.

MAINTAIN OR INCREASE MARKET SHARE

In some companies, both large and small, the major pricing objective is to maintain or increase the share of the market held by the firm. Market share may be a better indicator of corporate health than target return on investment, especially when the total market is growing. Then a firm might be earning a reasonable return. But if management is not aware that the market is expanding, the company may be getting a decreasing share of that market.

Status Quo Goals

Gas stations' pricing goal usually is to meet competition.

These two closely related goals—to stabilize prices and to meet competition—are the least aggressive of any of the pricing goals.

STABILIZE PRICES

Price stabilization often is the goal in industries where a large firm is the price leader and the product is highly standardized—for example, steel, gasoline, copper, or bulk chemicals. A major reason for seeking price stability is to avert price wars. However, adherence to the industry leader's price is not as rigid today as it used to be, especially during periods of sluggish demand. Smaller firms sometimes are cutting below the industry price and are not suffering reprisals from the large firms in the industry.

MEET COMPETITION

Countless firms, regardless of size, consciously price their products simply to meet the competition. In concentrated industries where there is a price leader and where the product is highly standardized, most firms have a follow-the-leader policy.

FACTORS INFLUENCING PRICE DETERMINATION

Knowing their objective, executives then can move to the heart of price management—the actual determination of the base price of a product or service. By **base price** (or list price) we mean the price of one unit of the product at its point of production or resale. This is the price before allowance is made for discounts, freight charges, or any other modification such as those discussed in the next chapter.

The same general procedure is followed in pricing both new and established products. However, the pricing of an established product usually involves little difficulty, because the exact price or a narrow range of prices may be dictated by the market. In the pricing of new products, though, the decisions called for in the pricing process typically are important and difficult.

In the price-determination process, several factors usually influence the final decision. The key factors, however, are as follows:

- Demand for the product.
- Target share of the market.
- Competitive reactions.
- Other parts of the marketing mix—the product, distribution channels, and promotion.

Estimated Demand for the Product

An important step in pricing a product is to estimate the total demand for it. This is easier to do for an established product than for a new one. Two steps in demand estimation are, first, to determine whether there is a price that the market expects and, second, to estimate the sales volume at different prices.

ELASTICITY OF DEMAND
A Review of a Basic Economic Concept

Elasticity of demand refers to the effect that unit-price changes have on the number of units sold and the total revenue. (The total revenue—that is, the total dollar sales volume—equals the unit price times the number of units sold.) We say that the demand is **elastic** when (1) reducing the unit price causes an increase in total revenue or (2) raising the unit price causes a decrease in total revenue. In the first case, the cut in unit price results in a boost in quantity sold and more than offsets the price cut—hence the increase in total revenue.

These situations are illustrated in Fig. 12-A. We start with a situation wherein, at $5 a unit, we sell 100 units and the total revenue equals $500. When we lower the price to $4 a unit, the quantity sold increases to 150 and the resultant total revenue also goes up—to $600. When the unit price is boosted to $6, however, the quantity sold drops off so much (to 70 units) that the total revenue also declines (to $420).

Demand is **inelastic** when (1) a price cut causes total dollar sales volume to decline or (2) a price raise results in an increase in total revenue. In each of these two situations the changes in unit price more than offset the relatively small changes in quantities sold. That is, when the price is cut, the increase in quantity sold is not enough to offset the price cut, so total revenue

goes down. When the unit price is raised, it more than offsets the decline in quantity sold, so total revenue goes up.

In Fig. 12-B, again we start with a unit price of $5, we sell 100 units, and our total revenue is $500. When we lower the unit price to $4, our quantity sold increases to 115. But this is not enough to offset the price cut, so our total revenue declines to $460. When we raise our unit price to $6, our quantity sold falls off to 90. But the price increase more than offsets the drop in quantity sold, so our total revenue goes up to $540.

As a generalization, the industry demand for necessities (salt, sugar, cigarettes, gasoline, telephone service, gas and electric service) tends to be inelastic. If the price of gasoline, for example, goes up or down, say, 10 or 15 cents a gallon, the total number of gallons sold does not change very much. On the other hand, the demand for products purchased with our discretionary income (luxury items, large appliances, furniture, autos) typically is much more elastic. Moreover, the demand for individual brands is much more elastic than is the demand for the broader product category. Thus, the demand for Continental Airlines or Hertz rental cars is far more elastic (price-sensitive) than is the demand for air travel or rented cars in general.

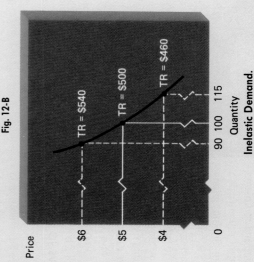

Fig. 12-A

Elastic Demand.

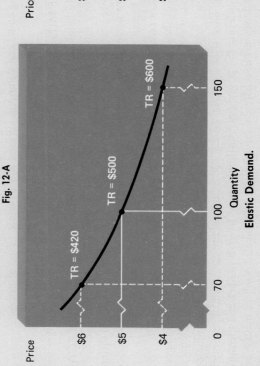

Fig. 12-B

Inelastic Demand.

What is the expected price?

THE "EXPECTED" PRICE

The "expected" price for a product is the price at which customers consciously or unconsciously value it—what they think the product is worth. The expected price usually is expressed as a *range* of prices, rather than as a specific amount. Thus, the expected price might be "between $250 and $300" or "not over $20." Consumers sometimes can be surprisingly shrewd in evaluating a product and its expected price.

A producer must also consider the middlemen's reaction to the price. Middlemen are more likely to give an article favorable treatment in their stores if they approve of its price. Retail or wholesale buyers can frequently examine an item and make an accurate estimate of the selling price that the market will accept.

It is possible to set a price too low. If the price is much lower than what the market expects, sales may be lost. For example, it would probably be a mistake for a well-known cosmetics manufacturer to put a 49-cent price tag on its lipstick or to price its imported perfume at $2.29 an ounce. Either customers will be suspicious of the quality of the product or their self-concepts will not let them buy such low-priced merchandise. More than one seller has raised the price of a product and experienced a considerable increase in sales. This situation is called **inverse demand**—the higher the price, the greater the unit sales. This inverse demand situation usually exists only within a given price range and only at the lower price levels. Once a price rises to some particular point, inverse demand ends and the usual-shaped demand curve takes over. That is, demand then declines as prices rise.

How do sellers determine expected prices? They may submit articles to experienced retailers or wholesalers for appraisal. A manufacturer of industrial products might get price estimates by showing product models or blueprints to engineers working for prospective customers. A third alternative is to survey potential consumers. They may be shown an article and asked what they would pay for it. Often, however, there is a considerable difference between what people say a product is worth and what they will actually pay for it. A more effective approach is to market the product in a few limited test areas. By trying different prices under controlled test-market conditions, the seller can determine at least a reasonable range of prices.

ESTIMATES OF SALES AT VARIOUS PRICES

It is extremely helpful to estimate what the sales volume will be at several different prices. By doing this, the seller is, in effect, determining the demand curve for the product and thus determining its demand elasticity. These estimates of sales at different prices also are useful in determining break-even points—a topic which we discuss later in this chapter.

There are several methods that sellers can use to estimate potential sales at various prices. Some of these methods were suggested in the preceding section on expected prices. Other methods were discussed in the sales forecasting section of Chapter 8. To illustrate, a company can conduct a survey of buyer intentions to determine consumer buying interest at different prices. Or management can conduct test-market experiments, offering the product at a different price in each market and measuring consumer purchases at these different prices. For an established product, management can measure sales of competitors' products, especially when reasonably similar models are offered at different prices.

A seller may be able to design a computerized model that would simulate field

Computers can help a company to estimate the demand for its products.

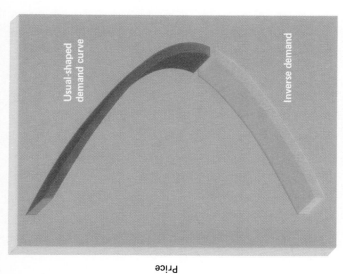

Price

Usual-shaped demand curve

Inverse demand

Quantity sold

selling conditions and sales responses at various prices. Some firms can get these estimates by surveying their wholesalers and retailers. For some industrial products, the sales estimates can be generated by using the sales-force composite method of forecasting.

Target Share of Market

The market share targeted by a company is a major factor to consider in determining the price of a product or service. A company striving to increase its market share may price more aggressively (lower base price, larger discounts) than a firm that wants to maintain its present market share.

The expected share of the market is influenced by present production capacity and ease of competitive entry. It would be a mistake for a firm to aim for a larger share of the market than its plant capacity can sustain. So, if management will not expand its plan (because ease of competitive entry will drive down future profits), then the initial price should be set relatively high.

Competitive Reactions

Present and potential competition is an important influence in determining a base price. Even a new product is distinctive for only a limited time, until the inevitable competition arrives. The threat of *potential* competition is greatest when the field is easy to enter and the profit prospects are encouraging. Competition can also come from three other sources:

- *Directly similar products:* Nike running shoes versus Adidas or New Balance shoes.
- *Available substitutes:* Air freight versus truck or rail freight.
- *Unrelated products seeking the same consumer dollar:* Videocassette recorder (VCR) versus a bicycle or a weekend excursion.

Other Parts of the Marketing Mix

The base price of a product normally is influenced considerably by the other major ingredients in the marketing mix.

You have to consider a competitor's reaction when you set your price.

THE PRODUCT

We have already observed that the price of a product is influenced substantially by whether it is a new item or an older, established one. The importance of the product in its end use must also be considered. To illustrate, there is little price competition among manufacturers of packaging materials or producers of industrial gases, and a stable price structure exists. These industrial products are only an incidental part of the final article, so customers will buy the least expensive product consistent with the required quality. The price of a product is influenced also (1) by whether the product may be leased as well as purchased outright, (2) by whether or not the product may be returned to the seller, and (3) by whether a trade-in is involved.

CHANNELS OF DISTRIBUTION

The channels selected and the types of middlemen used will influence a manufacturer's pricing. A firm selling both through wholesalers and directly to retailers often sets a different factory price for each of these two classes of customers. The price to wholesalers is lower because they perform activities (services) that the manufacturer otherwise would have to perform itself—activities such as providing storage, granting credit to retailers, and selling to small retailers.

PROMOTIONAL METHODS

The promotional methods used, and the extent to which the product is promoted by the manufacturer or middlemen, are still other factors to consider in pricing. If major promotional responsibility is placed upon retailers, they ordinarily will be charged a lower price for a product than if the manufacturer advertises it heavily. Even when a manufacturer promotes heavily, it may want its retailers to use local advertising to tie in with national advertising. Such a decision must be reflected in the manufacturer's price to these retailers.

BASIC METHODS OF SETTING PRICES

In our price-determination discussion we now are at the point where we can talk about setting a *specific* selling price. Most of the approaches used by companies to establish base prices for their products are variations of one of the following methods:

- Prices are based on total cost plus a desired profit. (Break-even analysis is a variation of this method.)
- Prices are based on a balance between estimates of market demand and supply (the costs of production and marketing).
- Prices are based only on competitive market conditions.

COST-PLUS PRICING

Cost-plus pricing means setting the price of one unit of a product equal to the unit's total cost plus the desired profit on the unit. As an example, suppose a contractor figures that the labor and materials required to build and sell 10 houses will cost $750,000, and that the other expenses (office rent, depreciation on equipment, wages of management, and so on) will equal $150,000. On this total cost of $900,000, the

TABLE 12-1 **EXAMPLE OF COST-PLUS PRICING**
Actual results often differ from the original plans because the various types of costs react differently to changes in output.

Costs, selling prices, profit	Number of houses built and sold	
	Planned = 10	Actual = 8
Labor and material costs ($75,000 per house)	$750,000	$600,000
Overhead (fixed) costs	150,000	150,000
Total costs	$900,000	$750,000
Total sales at $99,000 per house	990,000	792,000
Profit: Total	$90,000	$42,000
Per house	$9,000	$5,250
As % of cost	10%	5.6%

contractor desires a profit of 10 percent of cost. The cost plus the profit amount to $990,000, so each of the 10 houses is priced at $99,000.

While this is a very simple and easily applied pricing method, it has one serious limitation. It does not account for the fact that there are different types of costs, and that these costs are affected differently by increases or decreases in output. In our housing example, suppose the contractor built and sold only eight houses at the cost-plus price of $99,000 each. Total sales would be $792,000. Labor and material chargeable to the eight houses would total $600,000 ($75,000 per house). Since the contractor would still incur the full $150,000 in overhead expenses, however, the total cost would be $750,000. This would leave a profit of only $42,000, or $5,250 per house instead of the anticipated $9,000. On a percentage basis, the profit would be only 5.6% of total cost rather than the desired 10 percent. This example of the cost-plus pricing of the houses is summarized in Table 12-1.

The total unit cost of a product is made up of several types of costs. These costs react differently to changes in the quantity produced. Thus, the total unit cost of the product changes as output expands or contracts. A more sophisticated approach to cost-plus pricing takes such changes into consideration.

The cost concepts in the nearby box are important to our discussion. These nine cost concepts and their interrelationships may be studied in Table 12-2 and in Fig. 12-1, which is based on the table.

The interrelationships among the various *average unit* costs is displayed graphically in Fig. 12-1 and explained briefly as follows (again the data come from Table 12-2):

1. The **average fixed cost curve** declines as output increases because the total of the fixed costs is spread over an increasing number of units.
2. The **average variable cost curve** usually is U-shaped. It starts high because average variable costs for the first few units of output usually are high. The variable costs per unit then decline as the company realizes efficiencies in production.

The Cost Concepts

House builders often start with cost-plus pricing.

THE DIFFERENT KINDS OF COSTS

A **fixed cost** is an element, such as rent, executive salaries, or property tax, that remains constant regardless of how many items are produced. Such a cost continues even if production stops completely. It is called a fixed cost because it is difficult to change in the short run (but not in the long run, over several years).

Total fixed cost is the sum of all fixed costs.

Average fixed cost is the total fixed cost divided by the number of units produced. It is the amount of the total fixed cost that is allocated to each unit.

A **variable cost** is an element, such as labor or material cost, that is directly related to production. Variable costs can be controlled in the short run simply by changing the level of production. When production stops, for example, all variable production costs become zero.

Total variable cost is the sum of all variable costs. The more units produced, the higher this cost is.

Average variable cost is the total variable cost divided by the number of units produced. Average variable cost is usually high for the first few units produced. It decreases as production increases, owing to such things as quantity discounts on materials and more efficient use of labor. Beyond some optimum output it increases, owing to crowding of production facilities, overtime pay, etc.

Total cost is the sum of total fixed cost and total variable cost (for a specific quantity produced).

Average total cost is the total cost divided by the number of units produced.

Marginal cost is the cost of producing and selling one more unit; it is the cost of the last unit produced. Usually the marginal cost of the last unit is the same as the variable cost of that unit.

Eventually the average variable cost curve reaches its lowest point, reflecting the optimum output as far as variable costs (not total costs) are concerned. In Fig. 12-1, this point is at six units of output. Beyond that point, the average variable cost rises, reflecting the increase in unit variable costs caused by overcrowded facilities and other inefficiencies. If the variable costs per unit were constant, then the average variable cost curve would be a horizontal line at the level of the constant unit variable cost.

3. The **average total cost curve** is the sum of the first two curves—average fixed cost and average variable cost. It starts high, reflecting the fact that total *fixed* costs are spread over so few units of output. As output increases, the average total cost curve declines, because the unit fixed cost and unit variable cost are decreasing. Eventually, the point of lowest total cost per unit is reached (eight units of output in Fig. 12-1). Beyond that optimum point, diminishing returns set in and the average total cost curve rises.

4. The **marginal cost curve** has a more pronounced U-shape than the other curves in Fig. 12-1. The marginal cost curve slopes downward until the fifth unit of output, at which point the marginal costs start to increase.

TABLE 12-2   COSTS FOR INDIVIDUAL FIRM

Total fixed costs never change, despite increases in quantity. Variable costs are the costs of inputs—materials, labor, power. Their total increases as production quantity rises. Total cost is the sum of all fixed and variable costs. The other measures in the table are simply methods of looking at costs per unit; they always involve dividing a cost by the number of units produced.

(1) Quantity output	(2) Total fixed costs	(3) Total variable costs	(4) Total costs (2) + (3)	(5) Marginal cost per unit	(6) Average fixed cost (2) ÷ (1)	(7) Average variable cost (3) ÷ (1)	(8) Average cost per unit (4) ÷ (1)
0	$256	$ 0	$256		Infinity	$ 0	Infinity
1	256	64	320	$ 64	$256.00	64	$320.00
2	256	84	340	20	128.00	42	170.00
3	256	99	355	15	85.33	33	118.33
4	256	112	368	13	64.00	28	92.00
5	256	125	381	13	51.20	25	76.20
6	256	144	400	19	42.67	24	66.67
7	256	175	431	31	36.57	25	61.57
8	256	224	480	49	32.00	28	60.00
9	256	297	553	73	28.44	33	61.44
10	256	400	656	103	25.60	40	65.60

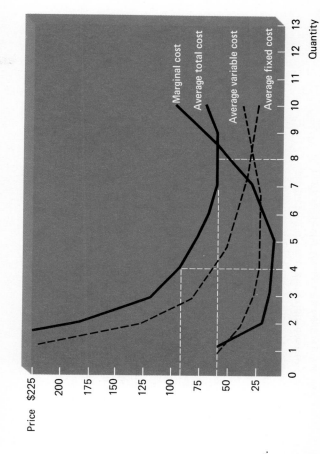

FIGURE 12-1

Unit cost curves for an individual firm.

This figure is based on data in Table 12-2. Here we see how *unit costs change as quantity increases.* Using cost-plus pricing, four units of output would be priced at $92 each, while eight units would sell for $60 each.

Now note the relationship between the marginal cost curve and the average total cost curve. The average total cost curve slopes downward *as long as the marginal cost is less than the average total cost.* Even though the marginal cost increases after the fifth unit, the average total cost continues to slope downward until after the eighth unit. This is so because marginal cost—even when it is going up—is still less than average total cost.

The marginal cost curve and the average total cost curve intersect at the lowest point of the average total cost curve. Beyond that point (the eighth unit in the example), the cost of producing and selling the next unit is higher than the average cost of all units. Therefore, from then on the average total cost rises. The reason for this is that the average variable cost is increasing faster than the average fixed cost is decreasing. Table 12-2 shows that producing the ninth unit reduces average fixed cost by $3.56 (from $32 to $28.44), but causes average variable cost to rise by $5.

Refinements in Cost-Plus Pricing

Once management understands that not all costs react in the same way to output increases or decreases, refinements in cost-plus pricing are possible. Let's assume that the desired profit is included either in the fixed cost or in the variable cost schedule. That is, profit is included as a cost in Table 12-2 and Fig. 12-1. Then management can refer to the table or graph to find the appropriate price, once a decision has been made regarding output quantity. If the executives decide to produce six units in our example, the selling price will be $66.67 per unit. A production run of eight units would be priced at $60 per unit. (Refer to Table 12-2 or Fig. 12-1.)

The user of this pricing method assumes that all the intended output will be produced and sold. If fewer units are produced, each would have to sell for a higher price in order to cover all costs and show a profit. But, obviously, if business is slack and output must be cut, it is not wise to raise the unit price. Thus the difficulty in this pricing approach is that no attention is paid to market demand.

Prices Based on Marginal Costs Only

Another approach to cost-plus pricing is to set a price that will cover only the marginal costs, not the total costs. Refer again to the cost schedules shown in Table 12-2 and Fig. 12-1, and assume that a firm is operating at an output level of six units. Under marginal cost pricing, this firm can accept an order for one unit at $31, instead of the total unit cost of $66.67. The firm is then trying to cover only its variable costs. If the firm can sell for any price over $31—say, $33 or $35—the excess contributes to the payment of fixed costs.

Obviously, not all orders can be priced to cover only variable costs. Marginal cost pricing may be feasible, however, if management wants to keep its labor force employed during a slack season. Marginal cost pricing may also be used when one product is expected to attract business for another. A department store, for example, may price meals in its tearoom at a level that covers only the marginal costs. The reasoning is that this tearoom will bring shoppers to the store, where they will buy other merchandise.

Cost-Plus Pricing by Middlemen

Cost-plus pricing is widely used by retailing and wholesaling middlemen. At least it seems this way at first glance. A retailer, for example, pays a given amount to buy products and have them delivered to the store. Then the retailer adds an amount (a markup) to the acquisition cost. This markup is estimated to be sufficient to cover the store's expenses and still leave a reasonable profit. To simplify pricing and accounting, the retailer may add the same *percentage* markup to every product. This is an average markup that the retailer's experience has shown is large enough to cover the costs and profit for the store. Thus, a clothing store may buy a garment for $30 including freight, and then price the item at $50. The price of $50 reflects a retailer markup of 40 percent based on the selling price, or 66⅔ percent based on the merchandise cost.

Different types of retailers will require different percentage markups because of the nature of the products handled and the services offered. A self-service supermarket has lower costs and thus a lower average markup than a full-service delicatessen. Figure 12-2 shows an example of markup pricing by middlemen. The topic of markups is discussed in more detail in Appendix A.

To what extent is cost-plus pricing truly used by middlemen? At least three significant indications suggest that what seems to be cost-plus pricing is really market-inspired pricing:

1. Most retail prices set by applying average percentage markups are really only price offers. If the merchandise does not sell at the original price, that price will be lowered until it reaches a level at which the merchandise will sell.
2. Many retailers do not use the same markup on all the products they carry. A supermarket will have a markup of 6 to 8 percent on sugar and soap products, 15 to 18 percent on canned fruit and vegetables, and 25 to 30 percent on fresh meats and produce. These different markups for different products definitely reflect competitive considerations and other aspects of the market demand.
3. The middleman usually does not actually set a base price but only adds a percentage to the price that has already been set by the manufacturer. The manufacturer's price is set to allow each middleman to add the customary markup and still sell at a retail price that is competitive. That is, the key price is set by the manufacturer, with an eye on the market.

FIGURE 12-2
Examples of markup pricing by retailers and wholesalers.

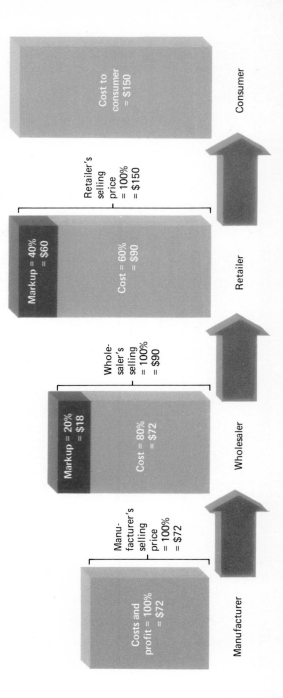

Evaluation of Cost-Plus Pricing

We have emphasized that a firm must be market-oriented and must cater to consumers' wants. Why, then, are we now considering cost-plus pricing? Actually, it provides a good point of departure for our discussion of price determination. Also, cost-plus pricing is mentioned so widely in business that it must be understood. Adherents of cost-plus pricing point to its simplicity and its ease of determination. They say that costs are a known quantity, whereas attempts to estimate demand for pricing purposes are mainly guesswork.

This opinion is questionable on two counts. First, it is doubtful whether adequate, accurate cost data are available. We know a fair amount about cost-volume relationships in production costs, but what we know is still insufficient. Furthermore, our information regarding marketing costs is woefully inadequate. Second, it is indeed difficult to estimate demand—that is, to construct a demand schedule that shows sales volume at various prices. Nevertheless, sales forecasting and other research tools can do a surprisingly good job in this area.

Critics of cost-plus pricing do not say that costs should be disregarded in pricing. Costs should be a determining influence, they maintain, but not the only one. Costs are a floor under a firm's prices. If goods are priced under this floor for a long time, the firm will be forced out of business. But when used by itself, cost-plus pricing is a weak and unrealistic method, because it ignores the influences of competition and market demand.

BREAK-EVEN ANALYSIS

One way to use market demand in price determination, and still consider costs, is to conduct a break-even analysis and determine break-even points. A **break-even point** is that quantity of output at which the sales revenue equals the total costs, *assuming a certain selling price*. Thus, there is a different break-even point for each different selling price. Sales of quantities above the break-even output result in a profit on each additional unit. The further the sales are above the break-even point, the higher the total and unit profits. Sales below the break-even point result in a loss to the seller.

Determining the Break-Even Point

The method of determining the break-even point is illustrated in Table 12-3 and Figs. 12-3 and 12-4. In our hypothetical situation, the company's fixed costs are $250, and

TABLE 12-3 COMPUTATION OF BREAK-EVEN POINT

At each of several prices, we wish to find out how many units must be sold to cover all costs. At a unit price of $100, the sale of each unit contributes $70 to cover the overhead expenses. We must sell about 3.6 units to cover the $250 fixed cost. See Figs. 12-3 and 12-4 for a visual portrayal of the data in this table.

(1) Unit price	(2) Unit variable costs, AVC	(3) Contribution to overhead (1) − (2)	(4) Overhead (total fixed costs)	(5) Break-even point (4) ÷ (3)
$ 60	$30	$ 30	$250	8.3 units
80	30	50	250	5.0 units
100	30	70	250	3.6 units
150	30	120	250	2.1 units

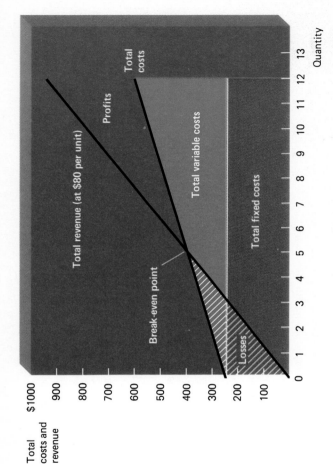

FIGURE 12-3

Break-even chart with selling price of $80 per unit.

Here the break-even point is reached when the company sells five units. Fixed costs, regardless of quantity produced and sold, are $250. The variable cost per unit is $30. If this company sells five units, total cost is $400 (variable cost of 5 × $30, or $150, plus fixed cost of $250). At a selling price of $80, the sale of five units will yield $400 revenue, and costs and revenue will equal each other. At the same price, the sale of each unit above five yields a profit.

its variable costs are constant at $30 a unit. Recall that in our earlier example (Table 12-2, and Fig. 12-1), we assumed that the unit variable costs were *not* constant; they fluctuated. Now, to simplify our break-even analysis, we are assuming that the unit variable costs *are* constant.

Thus the total cost of producing one unit is $280. For five units the total cost is $400 ($30 multiplied by 5, plus $250). In Fig. 12-3 the selling price is $80 a unit. Consequently, every time a unit is sold, $50 is contributed to overhead (fixed costs). That is, the variable costs are $30 per unit, and these costs are incurred in producing each unit. But any revenue over $30 can be used to help cover the fixed costs. At a selling price of $80, the company will break even if five units are sold. This is so because a $50 contribution from each of five units will just cover the total fixed costs of $250.

Stated another way, the variable costs for five units are $150 and the fixed costs are $250, for a total cost of $400. This is equal to the revenue from five units sold at $80 each. So, for an $80 selling price, the break-even volume is five units.

The break-even point may be found with this formula:

$$\text{Break-even point in units} = \frac{\text{total fixed costs}}{\text{unit contribution to overhead}}$$

$$= \frac{\text{total fixed costs}}{\text{selling price} - \text{average variable cost}}$$

It is important to note the assumptions underlying the computations in the preceding paragraph and in Fig. 12-3. First, we assume that total fixed costs are constant. This is true only over a short period of time and within a limited range of output. It is reasonably easy, however, to develop a break-even chart wherein the fixed costs, and consequently the total costs, are stepped up at several intervals. A second assumption in our example is that the variable costs remain constant per unit of output. In the earlier discussion of the cost structure of the firm, we noted that the average variable costs in a firm usually fluctuate.

Another limitation of Fig. 12-3 is that it shows a break-even point only if the unit price is $80. It is highly desirable to compute the break-even points for several different selling prices. Therefore, in Fig. 12-4 the break-even point is determined for four prices—$60, $80, $100, and $150. Figure 12-4 is also based on Table 12-3. If the price is $60, it will take sales of approximately 8.3 units to break even; at $150, only about 2.1 units. Every different selling price will result in a different break-even point. A company could use these break-even points as the basis for setting the selling price—say, by choosing the price that results in the most reasonable break-even point.

Evaluation of Break-Even Analysis

Certainly no one should claim that break-even analysis is the perfect pricing tool. Many of its underlying assumptions are unrealistic in a practical business operation. It assumes that costs are stable (that is, nonfluctuating). Thus, break-even analysis has limited value in companies where the average (unit) cost fluctuates frequently.

The major limitation of break-even analysis as a realistic pricing tool is that it ignores the market demand at the various prices. It is still essentially a tool for cost-plus pricing. The revenue curves in Figs. 12-3 and 12-4 show only what the revenue will be at the different prices *if* (and it is a big if) the given number of units can be sold at these prices. The completed break-even charts show only the amount that must be sold at the stated price to break even. The charts do not tell us whether we *can* actually sell this amount. The amount the market will buy at a given price could well be below the break-even point. For instance, at a selling price of $80 per unit, the break-even point is five units. But competition and/or a volatile market may prevent

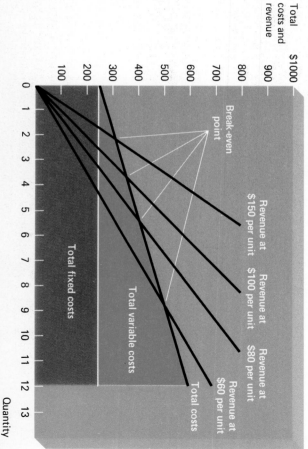

FIGURE 12-4
Break-even chart showing four different selling prices.

Here the company is experimenting with several different prices in order to determine which is the most appropriate. There are four different prices and four break-even points. At a price of $60, the company will start making a profit after it has sold 8.3 units. At the opposite extreme, the break-even point for a price of $150 is about 2.1 units.

Total costs and revenue

$1000
900
800
700
600
500
400
300
200
100
0

Break-even point

Revenue at $150 per unit
Revenue at $100 per unit
Revenue at $80 per unit
Revenue at $60 per unit

Total variable costs
Total fixed costs
Total costs

0 1 2 3 4 5 6 7 8 9 10 11 12 13

Quantity

the company from actually selling those five units. If the company can sell only three or four units, the firm will not break even. It will show a loss.

These limitations, however, should not lead management to dismiss break-even analysis as a pricing tool. Even in its simplest form, break-even analysis is very helpful because, in the short run, many firms are faced with reasonably stable cost and demand structures.

PRICES BASED ON A BALANCE BETWEEN SUPPLY AND DEMAND

Another method of price setting involves balancing demand with costs to determine the best price for profit maximization. This method of price determination is thus best suited for companies whose pricing goal is to maximize profit. However, companies with other pricing goals might use this method in special situations or perhaps to compare prices determined by different methods.

In discussing demand, we should distinguish between the demand curve or schedule facing an individual seller and the one facing the entire industry. Theoretically, when a firm operates in a market of perfect competition, its demand curve is horizontal at the market price. That is, the single seller has no control over the price. And the seller's entire output can be sold at the market price. However, the industry as a whole has a downward-sloping curve. That is, the industry can sell more units at lower prices than at higher prices.

The market situation facing most firms in the United States today is one of monopolistic, or imperfect, competition. This is characterized by product differentiation and nonprice competition. By differentiating its products, an individual firm gains some control over its prices. In effect, each firm becomes a separate "industry"; its product is to some extent unlike any other. Thus an individual firm in monopolistic competition has a downward-sloping demand curve. That is, it will attract some buyers at a high price, but to broaden its market and to sell to more people, it must lower the price.

Determining the Price

To use this pricing method, the price setter must understand the concepts of average and marginal revenue, in addition to average and marginal cost. **Marginal revenue** is the income derived from the sale of the last unit—the marginal unit. **Average revenue** is the unit price at a given level of unit sales. It is calculated by dividing total revenue by the number of units sold. Referring to the hypothetical demand schedule in Table 12-4 we see that the company can sell one unit at $80. To sell two units, it must reduce its price to $75 for each unit. Thus, the company receives an additional $70 (marginal revenue) by selling two units instead of one. The fifth unit brings a marginal revenue of $53. After the sixth unit, however, total revenue declines each time the unit price is lowered to sell an additional unit. Hence, there is a negative marginal revenue.

The price-setting process that involves the balancing of supply and demand is illustrated in the three-part Fig. 12-5. We assume that a firm will continue to produce units as long as the revenue from the last unit sold exceeds the cost of producing this last unit. That is, output continues to increase as long as marginal revenue exceeds marginal cost. At the point where they meet (quantity Q in Fig. 12-5a), output theoretically should cease. Certainly management will not want to sell a unit at a price less than the out-of-pocket (variable) costs of production. Thus the *volume of output is the quantity level at which* **marginal costs equal marginal revenue**, *or quantity Q.*

TABLE 12-4 DEMAND SCHEDULE FOR INDIVIDUAL FIRM

At each market price, a certain quantity of the product will be demanded. Marginal revenue is simply the amount of additional money gained by selling one more unit. In this example, the company no longer gains marginal revenue after it has sold the sixth unit at a price of $60.

Units sold	Unit price (average revenue)	Total revenue	Marginal revenue
1	$80	$ 80	$ 70
2	75	150	66
3	72	216	56
4	68	272	53
5	65	325	35
6	60	360	−10
7	50	350	−30
8	40	320	

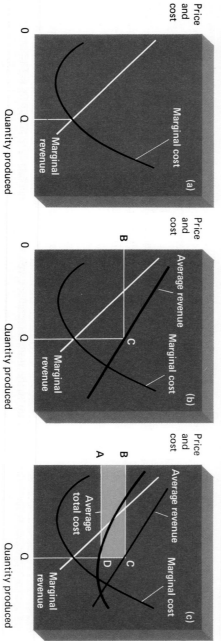

FIGURE 12-5
Price setting and profit maximiza-tion through marginal analysis.

(a) Price and cost / Quantity produced — Marginal cost, Marginal revenue

(b) Price and cost / Quantity produced — Average revenue, Marginal cost, Marginal revenue, B, C

(c) Price and cost / Quantity produced — Average revenue, Marginal cost, Marginal revenue, Average total cost, A, B, C, D

The unit price is determined by locating the point on the average revenue curve that represents an output of Q units. Remember that average revenue represents the unit price. The average revenue curve has been added in Fig. 12-5b. The unit price at which to sell quantity Q is represented by point C. It is the price B in Fig. 12-5b.

The average total (unit) cost curve has been added in Fig. 12-5c. It shows that, for output quantity Q, the average unit cost is represented by point D. This average unit cost is A. Thus, with a price of B and an average unit cost of A, the company enjoys a unit profit given by AB in the future. The total profit is represented by area ABCD (quantity Q times unit profit AB).

Evaluation of Supply-Demand Pricing

Supply and demand analysis as a basis for price setting has enjoyed only limited use. Business people usually claim that better data are needed for plotting the curves exactly. Supply and demand analysis can be used, they feel, to study past price movements, but it cannot serve as a practical basis for setting prices.

On the brighter side, management's knowledge of costs and demand is improving. Data processing equipment is bringing more complete and detailed information to management's attention all the time. Earlier we pointed out that management usually can estimate demand within broad limits, and this is helpful. Also, experienced management in many firms can do a surprisingly accurate job of estimating marginal and average costs and revenues.

Marginal analysis can also have practical value if management will adjust the price in light of some conditions discussed earlier in this chapter. In Fig. 12-5, the price was set at point B. But, in the short run, management may price below B, or even below A, adopting an aggressive pricing strategy to increase its market share, or to discourage competition.

PRICES SET IN RELATION TO MARKET ALONE

Pricing to Meet Competition

Cost-plus pricing is one extreme among pricing methods. At the other end of the scale is a method whereby a firm's prices are set in relation *only* to the market price. The seller's price may be set right at the market price to meet the competition, or it may be set either above or below the market price.

Management may decide to price a product right at the competitive level in several situations. One such situation occurs when the market is highly competitive and the firm's product is not differentiated significantly from competing products. To some extent, this method of pricing reflects market conditions that parallel those found under perfect competition. That is, product differentiation is absent, buyers and sellers are well informed, and the seller has no discernible control over the selling price. Most producers of agricultural products, manufacturers of gray goods in textiles, and small firms producing well-known, standardized products ordinarily use this pricing method.

The sharp drop in revenue that occurs when the price is raised above the prevailing level indicates that the individual seller faces a *kinked demand* (see Fig. 12-6). The prevailing price is at A. If the seller tries to go above that price, the demand for the product drops sharply, as indicated by the flat average revenue curve above point P. At any price above A, then, the demand is highly elastic—that is, total revenue declines. Below price A, the demand is highly inelastic, as represented by the steeply sloping average revenue curve and the negative marginal revenue curve. That is, the total revenue decreases each time the price is reduced to a level below A. The prevailing price is strong. Consequently, a reduction in price by one firm will not increase the firm's unit sales very much—certainly not enough to offset the loss in average revenue.

Up to this point in our discussion of pricing to meet competition, we have observed market situations that involve many sellers. Oddly enough, the same pricing method is often used when the market is dominated by only a few sellers. This type of market is called an **oligopoly.** The demand curve facing an individual seller in an oligopoly is a kinked one, as in Fig. 12-6.

An oligopolist must price at market level to maximize profits. Selling *above* market price will result in a drastic reduction in total revenue because the average

FIGURE 12-6
Kinked demand curve facing manufacturer of product sold at prevailing price (the same type of curve faces individual oligopolist).

The kink occurs at the point representing the prevailing price A. Above A, demand declines rapidly as the price is increased. A price set below A results in very little increase in volume, so revenue is lost. That is, the marginal revenue is negative.

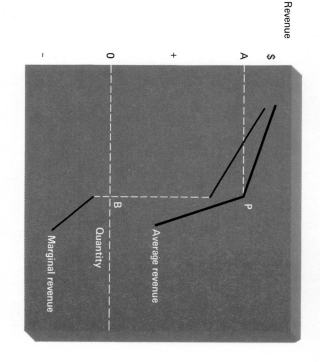

revenue curve is so elastic above point P. If an oligopolist cuts its price *below* the market price, all other members of the oligopoly must respond immediately. Otherwise the price cutter will enjoy a substantial increase in business. Therefore, the competitors do retaliate with comparable price cuts, and the net result is that a new market price is established at a lower level. All members of the oligopoly end up with about the same share of the market that they had before. However, unit revenue is reduced by the amount of the price cut.

Theoretically, oligopolists gain no advantage by cutting their prices. For their own good, they should simply set their prices at a competitive level and leave them

FROM NEW YORK TO CALIFORNIA—OR THE KINKED DEMAND CURVE IN THE REAL WORLD

The type of pricing situation discussed in this section is exactly what has occurred throughout the airline industry in the United States since the industry was deregulated. In an attempt to increase the number of passengers, an airline would cut its price on a heavily traveled route. However, the competitors on this route usually would match that lower fare immediately. As a result, there usually was no significant shift in the market share held by each airline on that route. But another result was that the market price settled at the lower level, and all airlines involved generally lost a lot of money.*

*For some guidelines to strategic pricing in a newly deregulated oligopolistic industry (airlines), see Thomas S. Robertson and Scott Ward, "Management Lessons from Airline Deregulation," *Harvard Business Review,* January–February 1983, pp. 40ff.

there. In reality, price wars often are touched off in an oligopoly because it is not possible to fully control all sellers of the product. In the absence of collusion, every so often some firm will cut its price. Then all others usually will follow to maintain their respective market shares.

Pricing to meet competition is rather simple to do. A firm ascertains what the going price is, and after allowing for customary markups for middlemen, it arrives at its own selling price. To illustrate, a manufacturer of men's dress shoes is aware that retailers want to sell the shoes for $70 ($69.95) a pair. The firm sells directly to retailers, who want an average markup of 40 percent of their selling price. Consequently, after allowing $28 for the retailer's markup, the producer's top price is about $42. This manufacturer then decides whether $42 is enough to cover its costs and still leave it a reasonable profit. Sometimes a manufacturer faces a real squeeze in this regard, particularly when its costs are rising but the market price is holding firm.

Pricing below Competitive Level

A variation of market-based pricing is to set a price at some point *below* the competitive level. This method of pricing is typically used by discount retailers. These stores offer fewer services, and they operate on the principle of low markup and high volume. They typically price nationally advertised brands 10 to 30 percent below the suggested retail list price, or the price actually being charged by full-service retailers. Even full-service retailers may price below the competitive level by eliminating specific services. For example, some gas stations offer a discount to customers who use the self-service pumps or who pay cash instead of using a credit card.

Pricing above Competitive Level

Manufacturers or retailers sometimes set their prices *above* the market level. Usually, above-market pricing works only when the product is distinctive or when the seller has acquired prestige in its field. Most cities have a prestige clothing or jewelry store where price tags are noticeably above the competitive level set by other stores that handle similar products.

Some firms price above the competition.

SUMMARY

In our economy, price is a major regulator because it influences the allocation of scarce resources. In individual companies, price is one important factor in determining marketing success. The problem is that it is difficult to define price. A rather general definition is this: Price is the amount of money (plus possibly some goods or services) needed to acquire, in exchange, some assortment of a product and its accompanying services.

Before setting the base price on a product, management should identify its pricing goal. Major pricing objectives are (1) to earn a target return on investment or on net sales, (2) to maximize profits, (3) to increase sales, (4) to meet competition's prices, of the market, (5) to stabilize prices, and (6) to meet competition's prices.

The key factors that should influence management's decision when setting the base price for a product are (1) demand for the product, (2) desired market share, (3) competitive reactions, (4) other major elements in the marketing mix, and (5) the product's cost.

The major methods used to determine the base price are (1) cost-plus pricing, (2) balancing market demand with product costs (supply), and (3) setting the price in relation only to the market.

For cost-plus pricing to be at all effective, a seller must consider the several types of costs and their different reactions to changes in the quantity produced. A producer usually sets a price to cover total cost. In some cases, however, the best policy may be to set a price that covers marginal cost only. The major weakness in cost-plus pricing is that it completely ignores the market demand. To partially offset this weakness, a company may use break-even analysis as a tool in price setting.

In real-life situations, virtually all price setting is market-inspired to some extent. Consequently, marginal analysis is a useful method for setting a price. Prices are set and output level is determined at the point where marginal cost equals marginal revenue.

For many products, price setting is a relatively easy job because management simply sets the price at the market level established by the competition. Two variations of market-level pricing are to price below or above the competitive level.

KEY TERMS AND CONCEPTS

Price 259

Pricing objectives: 262
  Target return 262
  Maximize profit 263
  Increase sales 263
  Market share 264
  Stabilize prices 264
  Meet competition 264

Base price (list price) 264
Expected price 266
Inverse demand 266

Cost-plus pricing 268
Fixed cost 270
Variable cost 270
Marginal cost 270
Average cost 270
Total cost 270
Prices based on marginal costs 272
Break-even point 274
Marginal revenue 277
Price set at volume of output where marginal cost equals marginal revenue 277
Competitive market price 279

QUESTIONS AND
PROBLEMS

1. Two students paid $2.49 for identical tubes of toothpaste at a leading store. Yet one student complained about paying a much higher price than the other. What might be the basis for this complaint?

2. Explain how a firm's pricing objective may influence the promotional program for a product. Which of the six pricing goals involves the largest, most aggressive promotional campaign?

3. What marketing conditions might logically lead a company to set "meeting competition" as a pricing objective?

4. What is the expected price for each of the following articles? How did you arrive at your estimate in each instance?

   a. A new type of carbonated cola beverage that holds its carbonation long after it has been opened; packaged in 12-ounce (355-ml) and 2-liter bottles.

   b. A nuclear-powered 23-inch table-model television set, guaranteed to run for years without replacement of the original power-generating component; requires no battery or electric wires.

   c. An automatic garage-door opener for residential housing.

5. Name at least five products for which you think an inverse demand exists. For each product, within which price range does this inverse demand exist?

6. In Fig. 12-1, what is the significance of the point where the marginal cost curve intersects the average total cost curve? Explain why the average total cost curve is declining to the left of the intersection point and rising beyond it. Explain how the marginal cost curve can be rising, while the average total cost curve is still declining.

7. In Table 12-2, what is the marginal cost of the seventh unit produced?

8. What are the merits and limitations of the cost-plus method of setting a base price?

9. In a break-even chart, is the total *fixed* cost line always horizontal? Is the total *variable* cost line always straight? Explain?

10. In Table 12-3 and Fig. 12-3, what would be the break-even points at prices of $50 and $90, if the variable costs are $40 per unit and the fixed costs remain at $250?

11. A small manufacturer sold ball-point pens to retailers at $8.40 per dozen. The manufacturing cost was 50 cents for each pen. The expenses, including all selling and administrative costs except advertising, were $19,200. How many dozen must the manufacturer sell to cover these expenses and pay for an advertising campaign costing $6,000?

12. In Fig. 12-5, why would the firm normally stop producing at quantity Q? Why is the price set at B and not at D or A?

13. Are there any stores in your community that generally price above the competitive level? How are they able to do this?

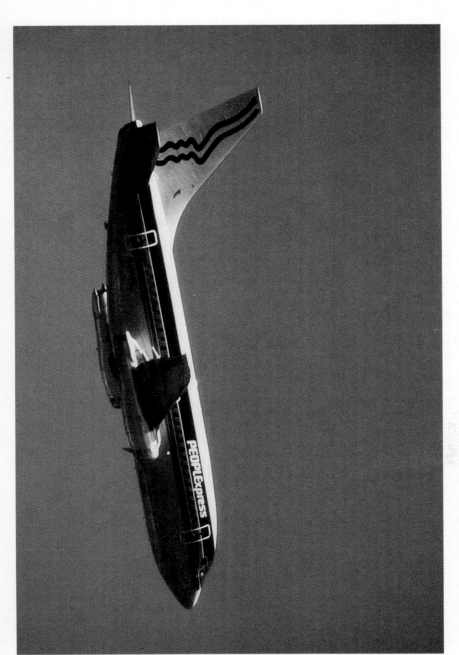

13

PRICING STRATEGIES AND POLICIES

CHAPTER GOALS

This chapter is concerned with the ways in which a base price can (and sometimes must) be modified. After studying this chapter, you should understand:

- Price discounts and allowances.
- Geographic pricing strategies.
- Skimming and penetration pricing strategies.
- One-price and flexible-price strategies.
- Unit pricing.
- Price lining.
- Resale price maintenance.
- "Leader" pricing.
- Psychological pricing.
- Price competition versus nonprice competition.

From time to time throughout the 1980s consumers have benefited from price wars in the newly deregulated airline industry. But the price wars in the late 1980s are quite different from those in the early part of the decade. During the first half of this decade, the airline price wars often spread nationwide and applied to all coach seats on a plane. Typically what would happen was that a low-cost airline such as People Express or Continental would reduce the fare on a popular route such as the transcontinental or the New York to Florida route. Then the competitors on this route would quickly meet the reduced fare with their own price slashes. Little by little, as the airlines tried to keep one jump ahead, these price cuts spread to many other cities.

In recent years, however, the price wars have been conducted in a very different manner. As one financial analyst said—to cut fares, the airlines used to use an ax, but now they use a surgical scalpel. Now, when the low-cost carriers cut their fares on certain routes, the major airlines such as United, American, and Delta react with the strategy of *selective* price cutting. The major carriers limit the number of cities where prices are reduced. The carriers also limit the number of seats and the time periods that are subject to the lower prices. On the less competitive routes, especially on routes not covered by the low-cost carriers, the other airlines sometimes will raise their prices.

With the aid of computer tracking, today the carriers have a much more sophisticated system for controlling their prices. The airlines can tell quickly how many people are traveling at the reduced fares and on what flights. Airlines also are using more imagination and daring in their pricing. In 1985, for example, several airlines offered deep discounts (up to 85 percent) during the 2-day period following Thanksgiving and Christmas.

In conclusion, the airlines are doing a better job of managing price wars. But they still are learning how to compete under deregulation. As a Continental Airlines executive said, "The airlines have less than a decade of pricing freedom and that's put them a couple of thousand years behind most other pricing industries."[1]

[1]Adapted from Jonathan Dahl, "Airlines Use a Scalpel to Cut Fares in the Latest Round of Price Wars," *The Wall Street Journal*, Nov. 26, 1985, p. 33. Also see Kenneth Labich, "Fare Wars: Have the Big Airlines Learned How to Win?" *Fortune*, Oct. 29, 1984, pp. 24–28.

The strategy of engaging in price competition—as the airlines have been doing—is just one of the pricing strategies that we shall discuss in this chapter. In managing the price portion of a company's marketing mix, management first decides on its pricing goal and then sets the base price for a product or service. The next task is to design the appropriate strategies and policies concerning several aspects of the price structure. What kind of discount schedule should be adopted? Will the company occasionally absorb freight costs? In this chapter we shall discuss several pricing topics that require strategy decisions and policy making. We also shall consider some legal aspects of these activities. A company's success in pricing may depend upon management's ability to design creative pricing strategies that reflect a customer orientation, rather than the traditional cost-oriented pricing methodology.

We shall be using the terms *policy* and *strategy* frequently in this chapter. So let's review the meaning of these terms as they were defined in Chapter 3. A **strategy** is a broad plan of action by which an organization intends to reach its goal. A **policy** is a managerial guide to future decision making when a given situation arises. Thus a policy becomes the course of action followed routinely any time a given strategic or tactical situation arises. To illustrate, suppose management adopts the *strategy* of offering certain quantity discounts in order to achieve the goal of a 10 percent increase in sales next year. Then, routinely, every time the company receives an order of a given size, it is company *policy* to grant the customer the prescribed quantity discount.

DISCOUNTS AND ALLOWANCES

Discounts and allowances result in a deduction from the base (or list) price. The deduction may be in the form of a reduced price or some other concession, such as free merchandise or advertising allowances.

Quantity Discounts ■

Quantity discounts are deductions from the list price offered by a seller to encourage customers to buy in larger amounts or to make most of their purchases from that seller. The discounts are based on the size of the purchase, either in dollars or in units.

A **noncumulative** discount is based upon the size of an *individual order* of one or more products. Thus a retailer may sell golf balls at $1 each or at three for $2.50. A manufacturer or wholesaler may set up a quantity discount schedule such as the following, which was used by a manufacturer of industrial adhesives.

Boxes purchased on single order	% discount from list price
1–5	0.0
6–12	2.0
13–25	3.5
Over 25	5.0

Noncumulative quantity discounts are expected to encourage large orders. Many expenses, such as billing, order filling, and the salaries of sales people, are about the same whether the seller receives an order totaling $10 or $500. Consequently, selling expense as a percentage of sales decreases as orders become larger. The seller shares such savings with the purchaser of large quantities.

Cumulative discounts are based on the total volume purchased *over a period of time*. These discounts are advantageous to a seller because they tie customers more closely to that seller. They really are patronage discounts, because the more total business a buyer gives a seller, the greater is the discount. Cumulative discounts are especially useful in the sale of perishable products. These discounts encourage customers to buy fresh supplies frequently so that the merchandise will not grow stale.

Retailers, too, offer quantity discounts.

Quantity discounts can help a manufacturer effect real economies in production as well as in selling. Large orders can result in lower-cost production runs and lower transportation costs. A producer's cumulative discount based on total orders from all the stores in a retail chain may increase orders from that chain substantially. This enables the producer to make much more effective use of production capacity, even though the individual orders are small and do not generate savings in marketing costs.

Trade Discounts

Trade discounts, sometimes called **functional** discounts, are reductions from the list price offered to buyers in payment for marketing functions that they will perform. A manufacturer may quote a retail list price of $400 with trade discounts of 40 percent and 10 percent. This means that the retailer pays the wholesaler $240 ($400 less 40 percent), and the wholesaler pays the manufacturer $216 ($240 less 10 percent). The wholesaler is given the 40 and 10 percent discounts. The wholesaler keeps the 10 percent to cover the costs of the wholesaling functions and passes on the 40 percent discount to the retailers. Note that the 40 and 10 percent discounts do not constitute a total discount of 50 percent off the list price. Each discount percentage in the "chain" is computed on the amount remaining after the preceding percentage has been deducted.

Cash Discounts

A **cash** discount is a deduction granted to buyers for paying their bills within a specified period of time. The discount is computed on the net amount due after first deducting trade and quantity discounts from the base price. Let's say a buyer owes $360 after the other discounts have been granted and is offered terms of 2/10, n/30 on an invoice dated November 8. This buyer may deduct a discount of 2 percent ($7.20) if the bill is paid within 10 days after the date of the invoice (by November 18). Otherwise the entire bill of $360 must be paid in 30 days (by December 8).

Every cash discount includes three elements: (1) the percentage discount itself, (2) the time period during which the discount may be taken, and (3) the time when the bill becomes overdue. (See Fig. 13-1 below.) There are many different terms of

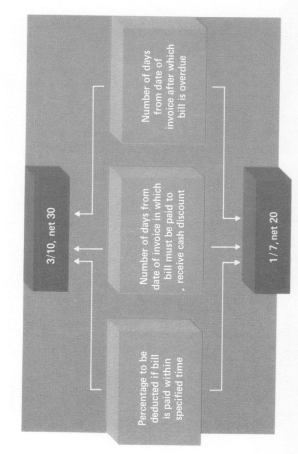

FIGURE 13-1
The parts of a cash discount.
(Source: Don L. James, Bruce J. Walker, and Michael J. Etzel, Retailing Today, 2d ed., Harcourt Brace Jovanovich, Inc., New York, 1981, p. 199)

sale because practically every industry has its own traditional combination of elements.

Normally, most buyers are extremely eager to pay bills in time to earn cash discounts. The discount in a 2/10, n/30 situation may not seem like very much. But management must realize that this 2 percent is earned just for paying 20 days in advance of the date the entire bill is due. If buyers fail to take the cash discount in a 2/10, n/30 situation, they are, in effect, borrowing money at a 36 percent annual rate of interest. (In a 360-day year, there are 18 periods of 20 days. Paying 2 percent for one of these 20-day periods is equivalent to paying 36 percent for an entire year.)

A firm that produces articles, such as air conditioners, that are purchased on a seasonal basis may consider the policy of granting a **seasonal** discount. This is a discount of, say, 5, 10, or 20 percent given to a customer who places an order during the slack season. Off-season orders enable manufacturers to make better use of their production facilities and/or avoid inventory carrying costs.

Forward dating is a variation of both seasonal and cash discounts. A manufacturer of fishing tackle, for example, might seek and fill orders from wholesalers and retailers during the winter months. But the bill would be dated, say, April 1, with terms of 2/10, n/30 offered as of that date. Orders that the seller fills in December and January help to maintain production during the slack season for more efficient operation. The forward-dated bills allow the wholesale or retail buyers to pay their bills after the season has started and some sales revenue has been generated.

Promotional allowances are price reductions granted by a seller in payment for promotional services performed by buyers. To illustrate, a manufacturer of builders' hardware gives a certain quantity of "free goods" to dealers who prominently display its line. Or a clothing manufacturer pays one-half the space charge of a retailer's advertisement that features the manufacturer's product.

The Robinson-Patman Act and Price Discrimination

The discounts and allowances discussed in this section may result in different prices for different customers. Whenever price differentials exist, there is price discrimination. The terms are synonymous. In certain situations, price discrimination is prohibited by the Robinson-Patman Act. This is one of the most important federal laws affecting a company's marketing program.

BACKGROUND OF THE ACT

The Clayton Antitrust Act, which generally outlawed price discrimination, was passed in 1914. Then, during the 1920s and the Depression of the early 1930s, large-scale retailing developed. It was accompanied by the subsequent decline in the competitive position of the small retailer. Some questionable trade practices involving price discrimination were pinpointed as particular sources of the large retailers' competitive advantage. The Clayton Antitrust Act proved inadequate to cope with these practices because of loopholes in this law. Consequently, in 1936, during an era of anti-chain-store feeling, the Robinson-Patman Act was passed to amend Section 2 of the Clayton Antitrust Act.

MAIN PROVISIONS OF THE ACT

The Robinson-Patman Act was intended to curb the practices of large-scale retailers only. It was written in such general terms, however, that through the years it has also become applicable to manufacturers. Not all price differentials are illegal under the

Price
differential
+
Injury to
competition
=
Robinson-Patman
violation

unless
Price
differential
=
Cost
differential

Robinson-Patman Act. Price differentials are unlawfully discriminatory only when their effect *may be* to substantially injure competition. In other words, a price difference is allowed if it does not substantially reduce competition.

Other exceptions and defenses Price differentials are allowable in response to changing conditions that affect the marketability of goods. For example, differentials are allowed in response to seasonal obsolescence, physical deterioration of products, or going-out-of-business sales.

Price differentials may be granted if they do not exceed differences in the cost of manufacture, sale, or delivery of the product. These cost differences may result (1) from differences in the quantity sold or (2) from different methods of sale or delivery of the product. Such differentials are allowable even though there is a reasonable probability of injury to competition. This ''cost proviso'' is a main defense available to firms engaging in differential pricing.

Buyer's liability The Robinson-Patman Act includes an innovation in trade regulation. The buyer is as guilty as the seller if the buyer *knowingly* induces or receives an unlawful price differential. This provision is intended to restrain large-scale buyers from demanding discriminatory prices. Prior to the Robinson-Patman Act, a seller who succumbed and granted the differential could be found guilty, and the pressuring buyer would go free.

In general, the interpretations of this provision have shown that it is largely ineffectual in restraining buyers. From a practical standpoint, it has been difficult to prove that the buyer *knowingly* received an unlawful price differential. The buyer cannot be expected to have access to the seller's accounting records.

Brokerage payments The Robinson-Patman Act tackles the problem of unearned brokerage payments by declaring that it is unlawful to pay or receive brokerage allowances except for services rendered. Essentially, it is illegal for a seller to pay brokerage fees directly to a buyer or to anyone controlled by the buyer.

While interpretations by the courts make the meaning of this section clear, its soundness from a marketing viewpoint is highly questionable. For example, the buyer for a chain of grocery stores may approach a food canner and offer to buy a quantity of canned vegetables. The chain buyer is performing all the services normally provided by a broker working for the seller. Prior to the passage of the Robinson-Patman Act, it was common practice for a seller to grant this buyer the usual brokerage commission. The seller was granting a form of discount to the customers in return for their performance of functions that the seller would otherwise have to provide. This generally is no longer legal.

Promotional allowances Various types of promotional services and facilities are lawful *only* if they are offered to all competing customers on proportionally equal terms. The real problem here is to determine what is meant by ''proportionally equal terms.'' This concept and its practical application are examined in Chapter 18, in connection with a firm's promotional program.

LEGALITY OF QUANTITY DISCOUNTS

Quantity discounts result in different prices to different customers. Consequently, these differential or discriminatory prices are potentially illegal under the Robinson-

Patman Act if the necessary injury to competition can be shown. To justify price differentials stemming from its quantity discount schedule, a firm must rely on the cost defense provided in the act. In a nutshell, quantity discounts are legal if the resultant price differentials do not exceed differences in the cost of manufacturing, selling, or delivering the product.

A study of the quantity discount cases brought under the Robinson-Patman Act indicates that *cumulative* discounts have virtually no chance of being defended. This is because it is not possible to show that the discounts are directly related to differences in costs.

LEGALITY OF TRADE DISCOUNTS

There is no specific statement about trade discounts in either the Clayton Act or the Robinson-Patman Act. Consequently, the legal status of trade discounts is still a little fuzzy. However, three cases brought under the Clayton Act established that separate discounts could be given to separate classes of buyers.[2] That is, one discount could be given to wholesalers and another to retailers as long as all buyers within a given group were offered the same discount. Presumably, trade discounts are legal under the Robinson-Patman Act if they are offered to genuinely different classes of customers in return for services rendered.

GEOGRAPHIC PRICING STRATEGIES

In its pricing, a seller must consider the freight costs involved in shipping the product to the buyer. This consideration grows in importance as freight becomes a larger part of total variable costs. Pricing policies may be established whereby the buyer pays all the freight, the seller bears the entire costs, or the two parties share the expense. The chosen strategy can have an important bearing on (1) the geographic limits of a firm's market, (2) the location of its production facilities, (3) the source of its raw materials, and (4) its competitive strength in various market areas.

F.O.B. Point-of-Production Pricing

In one widely used geographic pricing strategy, the seller quotes the selling price at the factory or at some other point of production. In this situation the buyer pays the entire cost of transportation. This is usually referred to as **f.o.b. mill** or **f.o.b. factory** pricing. Of the four strategies discussed in this section, this is the only one in which the seller does not pay *any* of the freight costs. The seller pays only the cost of loading the shipment aboard the carrier—hence the term **f.o.b.**, or **free on board**.

Under the f.o.b. factory pricing strategy, the seller nets the same amount on each sale of similar quantities. The delivered price to the buyer varies according to the freight charge. The Federal Trade Commission has, in general, considered an f.o.b. mill pricing system nondiscriminatory. However, this pricing strategy has serious economic and marketing implications. In effect, f.o.b. mill pricing tends to establish a geographic monopoly for a given seller, because freight rates prevent distant com-

---

[2]*Mennen Company v. Federal Trade Commission*, 288 Fed. 774 (1923), certiorari denied, 262 U.S. 759 (1923); *Great Atlantic and Pacific Tea Company v. Cream of Wheat Company*, 277 Fed. 46 (1915); *National Biscuit Company v. Federal Trade Commission*, 299 Fed. 733 (1924), certiorari denied, 266 U.S. 613 (1924).

Who will pay the freight charges?

petitors from entering the market. The seller, in turn, is increasingly priced out of more distant markets.

Uniform Delivered Pricing

Under the **uniform delivered pricing** strategy, the same delivered price is quoted to all buyers regardless of their locations. This strategy is sometimes referred to as "postage stamp pricing" because of its similarity to the pricing of first-class mail service. The net revenue to the seller varies, depending upon the shipping cost involved in each sale.

A uniform delivered price is typically used where transportation costs are a small part of the seller's total costs. This strategy is also used by many retailers who feel that "free" delivery is an additional service that strengthens their market position.

Under a uniform delivered price system, buyers located near the seller's factory pay for some of the costs of shipping to more distant locations. Critics of f.o.b. factory pricing are usually in favor of a uniform delivered price. They feel that the freight expense should not be charged to individual customers any more than any other single marketing or production expense.

Zone Delivered Pricing

Under a **zone delivered pricing** strategy, a seller's market is divided into a limited number of broad geographic zones. Then a uniform delivered price is set within each zone. Zone delivered pricing is similar to the system used in pricing parcel post services and long-distance telephone service. A firm that quotes a price and then says "Slightly higher west of the Rockies" is using a two-zone pricing system. The freight charge built into the delivered price is an average of the charges at all points within a zone area.

When adopting this pricing strategy, the seller must walk a neat tightrope to avoid charges of illegal price discrimination. This means that the zone lines must be drawn so that all buyers who compete for a particular market are in the same zone. This condition is almost impossible to meet in the dense market areas of the East and the Midwest.

Freight Absorption Pricing

A **freight absorption pricing** strategy may be adopted to offset some of the competitive disadvantages of f.o.b. factory pricing. With an f.o.b. factory price, a firm is at a price disadvantage when it tries to sell to buyers located in markets nearer to competitors' plants. To penetrate more deeply into such markets, a seller may be willing to absorb some of the freight costs. Thus, seller A will quote to the customer a delivered price equal to (1) A's factory price plus (2) the freight costs that would be charged by the competitive seller located nearest to that customer.

A seller can continue to expand the geographic limits of its market as long as its net revenue after freight absorption is larger than its marginal cost for the units sold. Freight absorption is particularly useful to a firm with excess capacity whose fixed costs per unit of product are high and whose variable costs are low. In these cases, management must constantly seek ways to cover fixed costs, and freight absorption is one answer.

The legality of freight absorption is reasonably clear. The strategy is legal if it is used independently and not in collusion with other firms. Also, it must be used only to meet competition. In fact, if practiced properly, freight absorption can have the effect of strengthening competition because it can break down geographic monopolies.

SKIMMING AND PENETRATION PRICING

When pricing a product, especially a new product, management should consider whether to adopt a skim-the-cream pricing strategy or a penetration pricing strategy.

Skim-the-Cream Pricing

The cream-skimming strategy involves setting a price that is high in the range of expected prices. This strategy is particularly suitable for new products because:

- In the early stages of a product's life cycle, price is less important, competition is minimal, and the product's distinctiveness lends itself to effective marketing.
- This strategy can effectively segment the market on an income basis. At first, the product is marketed to that segment that responds to distinctiveness in a product and is relatively insensitive to price. Later, the seller can lower the price and appeal to market segments that are more sensitive to price.
- The strategy acts as a strong hedge against a possible mistake in setting the price. If the original price is too high and the market does not respond, management can easily lower it. But it is very difficult to raise a price that has proven to be too low to cover costs.
- High initial prices can keep demand within the limits of a company's productive capacity.

Penetration Pricing

In penetration pricing, a low initial price is set to reach the mass market immediately. This strategy can also be employed at a later stage in the product's life cycle. Penetration pricing is likely to be more satisfactory than cream-skimming pricing when the following conditions exist:

- The product has a highly elastic demand.
- Substantial reductions in unit costs can be achieved through large-scale operations.
- The product is expected to face very strong competition soon after it is introduced to the market.

The nature of the potential competition will critically influence management's choice between the two pricing strategies. If competitors can enter a market quickly, and if the market potential for the product is very promising, management probably should adopt a policy of penetration pricing. Low initial pricing may do two things. First, it may discourage other firms from entering the field, because of the anticipated low profit margin. Second, low initial pricing may give the innovator such a strong hold on its share of the market that future competitors cannot cut into it. On the other hand, cream skimming may be more feasible when the market is not large enough to attract big competitors.

ONE-PRICE AND FLEXIBLE-PRICE STRATEGIES

Rather early in its pricing deliberations, management should decide whether to adopt a one-price strategy or a flexible-price strategy. Under a **one-price strategy**, a seller charges the *same* price to all similar customers who buy similar quantities of a product. Under a **flexible-price** (also called a **variable-price**) strategy, similar customers may each pay a *different* price when buying similar quantities of a product.

In the United States, a one-price strategy has been adopted more than variable pricing. Most retailers, for example, typically follow a one-price policy—except in cases where trade-ins are involved, and then flexible pricing abounds. A one-price policy builds customer confidence in a seller, whether at the manufacturing, wholesaling, or retailing level. Weak bargainers need not feel that they are at a competitive disadvantage.

When a flexible pricing policy is followed, often the price is set as a result of buyer-seller bargaining. In automobile retailing—with or without a trade-in—price negotiating (bargaining) is quite common, even though window-sticker prices may suggest a one-price policy. Variable pricing may be used to meet a competitor's price. To meet Japanese competition, Ford and General Motors sold subcompact cars to West Coast dealers at a lower price than was charged to dealers elsewhere in the country. Several airlines (Continental and People Express, for example) have used an aggressive flexible pricing strategy to enter new markets and to increase their market share on existing routes. Their new business comes from two sources—passengers

Open-air markets often engage in flexible pricing.

now flying on other airlines and passengers who would not fly at higher prices. In the second group, especially, the demand for air travel is highly elastic. The trick is to keep the market segment of price-sensitive passengers separate from the business-traveler segment, whose demand is inelastic. Airlines keep these segments apart by placing restrictions on the lower-priced tickets—requiring advance purchases, over-the-weekend stays in destination cities, etc.

A considerable amount of flexible pricing does exist in the United States. On balance, however, a flexible-price strategy is generally less desirable than a one-price strategy. In sales to business firms, but not to consumers, flexible pricing is likely to be in violation of the Robinson-Patman Act. Flexible pricing also may generate considerable ill will when the word gets around that some buyers acquired the product at lower prices.

■ UNIT PRICING

29000	UNSLTD	PEANUTS
UNIT PRICE $2.52 PER LB		RETAIL PRICE $1.89

18200 00902

Unit-pricing shelf labels reduce prices to a common basis.

The universal product code label from a beer six-pack.

Unit pricing is a retail price-information-reporting strategy that, to date, has been employed largely by supermarket chains. The method is, however, adaptable to other types of stores and products. The strategy is a business response to consumer protests concerning the proliferation of package sizes (especially in grocery stores). The practice has made it virtually impossible to compare prices of similar products. Regarding canned beans, for example, Is a can labeled "15½ avoirdupois ounces" for 39 cents a better deal than two "1-pound 1-ounce (482 grams)" cans for 89 cents?

In unit pricing, for each separate product and package size there is a shelf label that states (1) the price of the package and (2) this price expressed in dollars and cents per ounce, pound, pint, or some other standard measure.

Studies covering the early years of unit pricing showed that consumers—especially low-income consumers—were not using unit-pricing data. More recent studies show an increase in the awareness and usage of unit-pricing information. Unfortunately, however, city residents (typically lower-income markets) still use this information significantly less than do suburban residents (typically higher-income consumers).[3]

Increasingly, supermarkets and other retail stores are using electronic scanners at the checkout stands to read the Universal Product Code on products. Many of these retailers are no longer price-marking each individual item in a store. In such situations, unit-pricing shelf signs clearly are important, if not absolutely essential, to provide consumers with price information.

■ PRICE LINING

Price lining is used extensively by retailers of all types of apparel. It consists of selecting a limited number of prices at which a store will sell its merchandise. The Athletic Store, for example, sells several styles of shoes at $19.88 a pair, another group at $29.88, and a third assortment at $39.88.

For the consumer, the main benefit of price lining is that it simplifies buying

[3]See David A. Aaker and Gary T. Ford, "Unit Pricing Ten Years Later: A Replication," *Journal of Marketing*, Winter 1983, pp. 118–122.

This store followed a price-lining strategy.

decisions. From the retailer's point of view, the strategy is advantageous because it helps store owners plan their purchases. A dress buyer, for example, can go into a market looking for dresses that can be retailed for $49.95 or $69.95.

Rising costs can put a real squeeze on price lines, because a company hesitates to change its price line every time costs go up. But if costs increase and prices remain stationary, then profit margins are compressed and the retailer may be forced to seek products with lower costs.

RESALE PRICE MAINTENANCE ■

Some manufacturers want control over the prices at which retailers resell the manufacturers' products. For some producers that follow a policy of providing suggested list prices, the price is just a guide for retailers. These prices often are set by manufacturers at a level that will provide the retailers with their normal markup. To illustrate, a manufacturer sells to a type of store—a hardware store or sporting-goods store, for example—a certain product for which the manufacturer charges $6 a unit. For this product, the manufacturer's suggested retail list price is $10 ($9.95), thus providing these retailers with their normal markup of 40 percent of selling price. Again, this is only a *suggested* resale price. If retailers wish, they can sell below the $9.95 price with absolutely no objections from the manufacturer.

Other manufacturers try very hard to control the retail prices of their products. Normally such a strategy is successful only when a manufacturer sells to a few retailers, and they want very much to carry the product. Nevertheless, the manufacturers keep trying, often approaching the limits of the antitrust laws. Some manufacturers even threaten to cancel a retailer's franchise for price cutting, or they stop shipping products to these retailers.

Obviously these manufacturers are—and have been for many years—in conflict with discount retailers of various types. In the 1980s, however, a phenomenon called *off-price retailing* again called attention to the strategy of resale price maintenance. Off-price retailing—that is, selling well-known brands below the manufacturer's recommended retail price—is discussed in the next chapter. Actually off-price retailing is not a new concept. For decades it has existed in hard goods—appliances, sporting

"Off-price" strategy is popular today in apparel retailing.

goods, etc. In the 1980s, however, the term has been associated with soft goods—especially apparel, accessories, and footwear. The current conflict between manufacturers and retailers involving pricing strategies in the apparel industry has led to court suits and proposed legislation.[4]

Currently a manufacturer no longer can establish a resale price maintenance policy and have it supported by law. For a period of about 45 years (1930 to 1975), a series of state and federal laws permitted manufacturers to legally set the retail prices on their products. The state laws—technically called resale price maintenance laws—became known as *fair-trade laws*. At the federal level, two laws were passed that made it legal for a manufacturer to fair-trade its product in interstate commerce. Without these two laws, a manufacturer could be prosecuted for price fixing (a violation of the Sherman Act) or unfair competition (a violation of the FTC Act).

Resale price maintenance was one of the most controversial of all pricing strategies. The label "fair-trade laws" was a truly strategic choice of titles. Who could argue against fair trade? Opponents used the term *resale price-fixing*, claiming there was nothing fair about fair-trade laws.

The Depression days of the 1930s spawned the state fair-trade laws. The laws were intended to protect small retailers from the onslaught of larger retailers, especially the chain stores. At the peak of their popularity, these laws existed in all states except Vermont, Missouri, and Texas, and the District of Columbia. In 1975 a federal law (Consumer Goods Pricing Act) was passed that, in effect, removed the protection against antitrust prosecution. This ended the use of fair-trade pricing in interstate commerce and thus rendered useless any state fair-trade laws that were still on the books.[5]

LEADER PRICING AND UNFAIR-PRACTICES ACTS

Many firms, primarily retailers, temporarily cut prices on a few items to attract customers. This price and promotional strategy is called **leader pricing**, and the items whose prices are cut are called **loss leaders**. These leader items should be well-known, heavily advertised articles that are purchased frequently. The idea is that customers will come to the store to buy the advertised leader items and then stay to buy other regularly priced merchandise. The net result, the firm hopes, will be increased total sales volume and net profit.

Today, about 25 states have laws (unfair-sales acts, unfair-practices acts) to regulate leader pricing. The states have followed two model laws. Under one model, a reseller is prohibited from selling an item below invoice cost, including freight, plus a stated markup. This markup is usually 2 percent at wholesale and 6 percent at retail. Under the other model law, the minimum price is set at invoice cost, including freight, plus the retailer's or wholesaler's cost of doing business.

[4] See Pat Sloan, "Gloves Off in Off-Price Battle," *Advertising Age*, Oct. 17, 1983, p. 3.
[5] For a discussion of the current and probable future legal status of resale price maintenance, plus some steps that manufacturers can take to avoid legal problems when establishing resale price maintenance programs, see Mary Jane Sheffet and Debra L. Scammon, "Resale Price Maintenance: Is It Safe to Suggest Retail Prices?" *Journal of Marketing*, Fall 1985, pp. 82–91.

Leader pricing in a grocery store.

The general intent of these laws is commendable. They eliminate much of the predatory type of price cutting. However, they still permit firms to use loss leaders as a price and promotional strategy. That is, a retailer can offer an article at a selling price that is below the store's total cost—merchandise cost plus store operating expenses. Yet this selling price still will be *above* the merchandise cost plus a 6 percent markup (the legal minimum), because the store's operating expenses are greater than the 6 percent markup. Unlike the state fair-trade laws, the loss-leader laws do not penalize low-cost retailers or protect high-cost operators. Differentials in retailers' purchase prices can be reflected in their selling prices. And savings resulting from the absence of store services can be passed on to the customers.

A limitation of these laws is that it is difficult or even impossible to determine the cost of doing business for each individual product. It is on this point that some state laws have been declared unconstitutional. Also, the purpose of a business is to make a profit on the *total* operation, and not necessarily on each sale of each product.

PSYCHOLOGICAL PRICING—ODD PRICING

We have already briefly discussed some pricing strategies that might be called **psychological pricing.** For example, there is price lining, prestige pricing above competitive levels, and *raising* a too-low price in order to *increase* sales. At the retail level, another psychological pricing strategy is commonly used. Prices are set at odd amounts, such as 19 cents, 49 cents, and $19.95. Automobiles are priced at $8,995 rather than $9,000, and houses sell for $79,950 instead of $80,000.

In general, retailers believe that pricing items at odd amounts will result in larger sales. Thus, a price of 49 cents or 98 cents will bring greater revenue than a price of 50 cents or $1. There is little concrete evidence to support retailers' belief in the value of odd prices. Various studies have reported inconclusive results. Odd pricing is often avoided in prestige stores or on higher-priced items. Thus expensive men's suits are priced at $450, not $449.95.

PRICE VERSUS NON-PRICE COMPETITION

In the course of developing its marketing program, management has a choice of emphasizing price competition or nonprice competition. This choice can affect various other parts of the firm's marketing system.

Price Competition

In our economy today, there still is a considerable amount of price competition. A firm can effectively engage in price competition by regularly offering prices that are as low as possible. Along with this, the seller usually offers a minimum of services. In their early years, discount houses and chain stores competed in this way. A firm can also use price to compete by (1) changing its prices and (2) reacting to price changes made by a competitor.

PRICE CHANGES BY THE FIRM

Any one of several situations may prompt a firm to change its price. As costs increase, for instance, management may decide to raise the price, rather than to cut quality or aggressively promote the product and still maintain the price. If a company's share of the market is declining because of strong competition, its executives may react initially by *reducing* their price. In the long run, however, their best alternative

Some firms engage in price competition.

may be to improve their own marketing program, rather than to rely on the price cut. *Temporary* price cuts may be used to correct an imbalance in inventory or to introduce a new product.

From the seller's standpoint, the big disadvantage in price cutting is that competitors will retaliate. This is especially true in oligopolistic market situations. The net result can be a price war, and the price may even settle permanently at a lower level. Note that "oligopoly" does not necessarily imply *large* firms. *Oligopoly* means "a few sellers." Thus a neighborhood group of small merchants—barbers, for instance—can constitute an oligopoly. These merchants will try to avoid price competition, because if one reduces prices, all must follow.

REACTION TO COMPETITOR'S PRICE CHANGES

Any firm can assume that its competitors will change prices. Consequently, every firm should be ready with some policy guidelines on how it will react. If a competitor *boosts* prices, a reasonable delay in reacting probably will not be perilous. Advance planning is particularly necessary in case of a competitive price *reduction*, since time is then of the essence.

Airline price wars provide a good illustration of a wrong way and a right way to respond to a competitor's price cuts. In the earlier price wars when an airline cut its prices, competitors typically reacted by reducing fares generally across the board—fly anywhere, anytime, for $99. As a result of this unsound strategy, the airlines suffered heavy financial losses. In recent years, however, the major airlines (American, United, Delta) have adopted a better strategy—that of *selective* price cutting—when low-cost carriers reduce their fares. This newer strategy involves cutting airfares only on certain routes, placing restrictions on the discounted fares, and even raising prices on routes that the low-cost carriers do not fly.

Nonprice Competition

In nonprice competition, sellers maintain stable prices. They attempt to improve their market position by emphasizing other aspects of their marketing programs. Of course, competitive prices still must be taken into consideration, and price changes will occur over time. Nevertheless, in a nonprice competitive situation the emphasis is on something *other than* price.

By using terms familiar in economic theory, we can differentiate nonprice competition from price competition. In price competition, sellers attempt to move up or down their individual demand curves by changing prices. In nonprice competition, sellers attempt to *shift* their demand curves to the right by means of product differentiation, promotional activities, or some other device. This point is illustrated in Fig. 13-2. The demand curve faced by the producer of a given model of skis is DD. At a price of $250, the producer can sell 35,000 pairs a year in a Western ski market. On the basis of price competition alone, sales can be increased to 55,000 if the producer is willing to reduce the price to $230. The demand curve is still DD.

However, the producer is interested in boosting sales without any decrease in selling price. Consequently, the firm embarks upon a promotional program—a form of nonprice competition. Suppose enough new customers are persuaded to buy at the original $250 price so that unit sales increase to 55,000 pairs a year. In effect, the firm's entire demand curve has been shifted to position D'D'.

FIGURE 13-2
Shift in demand curve for skis in a western market.

The use of nonprice competition can shift the demand curve for a product. A company selling skis in a Western market used a promotional program to sell more skis at the same price, thus shifting DD to D'D'. Volume increased from 35,000 to 55,000 units at $250 (point X to point Y). Besides advertising, what other devices might this firm use to shift its demand curve?

Other firms sometimes engage in nonprice competition.

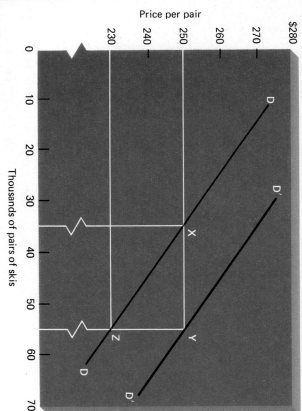

Price per pair

Thousands of pairs of skis

Two of the major methods of nonprice competition are **promotion** and **product differentiation**. In addition, some firms emphasize the **variety and quality of their services**.

Nonprice competition is being used increasingly in marketing. Companies want, at least to some extent, to be the masters of their own destiny. In nonprice competition, a seller's entire advantage is not removed when a competitor decides to undersell. Furthermore, there is little customer loyalty when price is the only feature that distinguishes the seller. Buyers will stick only as long as that seller offers the lowest price.

SUMMARY ■

After deciding on pricing goals and then setting the base (list) price, the next task in pricing is to establish specific strategies in several areas of the pricing structure. One of these areas relates to discounts and allowances—deductions from the list price. Management has the option of offering quantity discounts, trade discounts, cash discounts, and other types of deductions. A producer can pay all the freight (uniform delivered price) or let the buyer pay the freight bill (f.o.b. factory price). Or the two parties can share the cost in some proportion (freight absorption). Any decisions involving discounts or freight allowances must be made in conformity with the Robinson-Patman Act. This is a major law relating to price discrimination and other aspects of a company's marketing program.

When pricing a product, especially a new product, a company should consider whether to use a cream-skimming or a penetration pricing strategy. Management also should decide whether to charge the same price to all similar buyers (one-price strategy) or to adopt a flexible (variable) pricing strategy. Unit pricing—a relatively new development—can affect a company's marketing program. Some firms, especially retailers, have adopted price lining as a marketing strategy. Many retailers use leader pricing to stimulate sales. Odd pricing is a psychological pricing strategy commonly used by retailers.

Another basic decision facing management is whether to engage primarily in price competition or in nonprice competition. Most firms prefer to use promotion, product differentiation, and other nonprice marketing activities, rather than to rely only on price as a sales stimulant.

KEY TERMS AND CONCEPTS

Quantity discount: 286
Noncumulative discount 286
Cumulative discount 286
Trade (functional) discount 287
Cash discount 287
Robinson-Patman Act provisions: 288
Cost defense 289
Buyer's liability 289
f.o.b. factory price 290
Uniform delivered price 291
Zone delivered price 291
Freight absorption 291

Skim-the-cream pricing 292
Penetration pricing 292
One-price strategy 293
Flexible-price strategy 293
Unit pricing 294
Price lining 294
"Off-price" retailing 295
Fair-trade laws 296
Leader pricing 296
Odd pricing 297
Price competition 298
Nonprice competition 299

QUESTIONS AND PROBLEMS

1. Carefully distinguish between cumulative and noncumulative quantity discounts. Which of these two types of quantity discounts has the greater economic and social justification? Why?

2. A manufacturer of appliances quotes a list price of $500 per unit for a certain model of refrigerator and grants trade discounts of 35, 20, and 5 percent. What is the manufacturer's selling price? Who might get these various discounts?

3. Company A sells to all its customers at the same published price. A sales executive finds that company B is offering to sell to one of A's customers at a lower price. Company A then cuts its price to this customer but maintains the original price for all other customers. Is this a violation of the Robinson-Patman Act?

4. Name some products that might logically be sold under a uniform delivered price system.

5. "An f.o.b. point-of-purchase price system is the only geographic price system that is fair to buyers." Discuss.

6. An Eastern firm wants to compete in Western markets, where it is at a significant disadvantage with respect to freight costs. What pricing alternatives can it adopt to overcome the freight differential?

7. For each of the following products, do you recommend that the seller adopt a cream-skinning or a penetration pricing strategy? Support your decision in each instance.

a. Original models of women's dresses styled and manufactured by Dior.

b. A new wonder drug.

c. An exterior house paint that wears twice as long as any competitive brand.

d. A cigarette *totally* free of tar and nicotine.

e. A tablet that converts a gallon of water into a gallon of automotive fuel.

8. Under what marketing conditions is a company likely to use a variable-price strategy? Can you name some firms that employ this strategy, other than when a trade-in is involved?

9. Distinguish between leader pricing and predatory price cutting.

10. How should a manufacturer of prefinished plywood interior wall paneling react if a competitor cuts prices?

11. What factors account for the increased use of nonprice competition?

12. On the basis of the topics covered in this chapter, establish a set of price strategies for the manufacturer of a new glass cleaner that is sold through a broker to supermarkets. The manufacturer sells the product at $10 for a case of a dozen 16-ounce bottles.

13. Suppose you are president of a company that has just developed a camera and film process somewhat comparable to Polaroid's. The camera is designed to be used only with film produced by your firm. The chief marketing executive recommended that the camera be priced relatively low and the film relatively high. The idea was to make it easy to buy the camera, because from then on the customer would have to buy the company's film. The company's chief accountant said "no" to that idea. He wanted to price both camera and film in relation to their full cost plus a reasonable profit. You are mulling over these alternative strategies and also wondering whether there is not a third alternative, better than either of those two. Which pricing strategy would you adopt for the new camera and film?

COLWELL MANUFACTURING COMPANY

Pricing a new product

Two of the marketing executives at the Colwell Manufacturing Company were discussing what the base prices should be for the company's new product line—skylights designed for the residential market. The vice president of marketing, Andrew Burke, proposed that the initial price be set high, thus adopting a skimming strategy. Norman Jamesbury, the general sales manager, argued that the company should enter the market with a penetration pricing strategy. Thus, he wanted to set the base price near the low end of the expected price range.

The Colwell Manufacturing Company was a midwestern firm that specialized in the production of exterior wood doors, door lights, and side lights. Door lights and side lights are products that allow for light to come through part of the doors or through the walls at the sides of the doors. As Burke once put it, "Our goal is to advance the technology and aesthetics of entryway lighting." The company's sales last year were approximately $50 million.

In the past, Colwell had sold primarily in the industrial market. Recently, however, the company had developed a line of skylights for use in new construction and remodeling, but in the *residential* market. In a roof or deck, a skylight is an opening that is covered with a translucent or transparent material such as glass or plastic. The amount of light transmitted will vary with the color of the glass or plastic covering.

The new line of skylights produced by Colwell contained a wide selection of models, shapes, and sizes. The skylights were made of clear Lexan, a polycarbonate plastic material made by General Electric. Lexan is a very durable, weather-resistant material that combines strength, safety, and security, according to Norman Jamesbury. He said, "Our skylights are designed to bring in sunlight, brighten drab areas, and take advantage of the aesthetic and practical benefits of natural light." He also pointed out that the Colwell line had several strong competitive product advantages. "They provide an appealing, low-profile look and are easy to install. Heat loss is minimized and the chances of air or water coming in are virtually zero. Also there is no moisture condensation on our lights."

The channels of distribution to reach the residential market had already been established by competitors who were just beginning to sell to that market. Jamesbury planned to use his own sales force or manufacturers' agents (depending upon the part of the country) to sell to building materials distributors (wholesalers). These distributors, in turn, would sell to building materials dealers who reached the building contractor market and the do-it-yourself market.

In his strategic planning for the new product line, Andrew Burke was at the stage where he had to make some pricing decisions. At this point he called in Norman Jamesbury to discuss the pricing situation. The two men decided first to set the base (list) selling price to building materials wholesalers for one model of skylight—#22 × 22 standard-size, double-glazed (double-domed) unit. Then later they would set the selling prices for all their models and sizes in relation to the price on the standard 22 × 22 unit.

The marketing research done by Colwell people reported that 10 other firms were producing skylights that could be considered competitive with the Colwell line. Competitors' selling prices for a unit comparable to Colwell's 22 × 22 skylight ranged from lows of $27 and $35 to highs of $56 and $60.

Six competitors, including the ones with the lowest and the highest selling price, used acrylic plastic in their skylights, and two firms used Lexan. Burke noted that the two lowest-priced competitors sold on the basis of price alone. Two other firms offered only a limited line of skylights and had weak marketing programs, according to Burke. Another two competitors were selling primarily in the industrial market. Burke believed, interestingly enough, that Colwell's strongest competitor was the company with the highest selling price. All in all, Burke felt that Colwell was in a good competitive position in this new market.

Both men agreed that there was a tremendous market potential for residential skylights. Forecasts made by glazing material suppliers such as General Electric and Eastman Kodak, along with Colwell's own forecasts, indicated that the market would double in the 5-year period from 1982 to 1987. By 1990, Burke expected the market to exceed $100 million a year. He also expected that, by the late 1980s, residential skylights would account for 40 percent of Colwell's sales volume and net profit.

Some of the costs identified with the standard 22 × 22 skylight model were as follows:

Direct materials and labor = $21.50 per unit.

Packaging = $1.25 per unit.

Advertising for the first year = $95,000.

Five delivery trucks = $31,000 each.

When setting their selling price, Burke and Jamesbury both realized that they should consider the elasticity of demand for skylights. However, neither of the executives had any idea or "feel" regarding what the demand elasticity actually was for these products.

They also knew that they had to decide whether to adopt a skimming strategy or a penetration strategy for pricing the skylight. However, they disagreed as to which strategy should be adopted. Burke argued that they should enter the market with a price at the high end of the expected range. He believed that Colwell had a good reputation in the building materials market, an experienced sales force, and a demonstrably better product than the competition. Jamesbury did not disagree with these points. However, he believed that a low entry price would enable Colwell to quickly gain a substantial market share. This way the company could take advantage of decreasing unit costs that would accompany increased output.

QUESTION

What base (list) price should Colwell set for selling one unit of its standard 22 × 22 skylight to building materials wholesalers?

GREEN VALLEY LANDSCAPING COMPANY

Pricing a service in a new company

Last spring, Martin Dixon and Harvey Scully decided to become partners in a lawn-care business. Both had college degrees in horticulture. Eventually they wanted to grow into the business of landscape gardening or landscape architecture—hence their conservative choice of a company name. (Their original idea for a company name was "Marty and Harvey—The Twin Clippers," accompanied by the slogan "You grow it, we mow it.")

However, Marty and Harvey realistically acknowledged that they would have to start out at a more modest level. They also realized that initially most of their business would involve mowing and trimming lawns. Consequently, one of their first concerns was how to price their mowing and trimming services.

The Green Valley Landscaping Company was located in a small city (population 20,000) near Denver, Colorado. The initial services offered by the company included weekly mowing at a grass height of 2½ inches, catching the grass clippings, and trimming the edges of the lawn. As soon as they could become better established, Dixon and Scully intended to provide such services as weed control, fertilizing, aerating, power raking, pruning, laying sod, installing sprinkler systems, and specialized landscape design.

Currently, there were three other lawn-care firms operating in Green Valley's market area. One specialized in liquid fertilizing and offered a mowing service on the side. A second competitor specialized in lawn care for commercial accounts such as apartment complexes. The third firm—Foster's Lawn Service—maintained a variety of accounts, but was not accepting any new business at the present time.

Marty Dixon identified the following four market segments as the best target markets for Green Valley:

- Senior citizens who were physically unable to mow their lawns. Because most of these people were living on a fixed income, price was very important to them.
- People who were too busy to cut their own grass. This segment included households where both the husband and wife were working. Dixon felt that price was important in this market also.
- Higher-income people who could afford more services, who were concerned with the appearance of their yards, and who liked the prestige of having their own lawn service. These people were not very price-conscious.
- Owners of commercial property—office buildings, stores, industrial sites, apartment complexes—that had lawns to maintain. These owners generally expected to pay for lawn-care service.

Dixon and Scully spent $2,500 for tools and equipment. They also bought a used pickup truck for $2,800. They planned to amortize these costs over a 3-year period. Administrative overhead expenses were estimated to be $1,500 a year. Salaries and wages were expected to be $2,300 each month during the April–October growing and operating season. The cost of operating the truck was 25 cents per mile. Other operating expenses (gasoline, oil, equipment maintenance) for mowing and trimming a lawn were estimated to be 40 cents per 1,000 square feet of lawn.

The partners planned to spend $600 on promotion during the first season. They planned to distribute pamphlets to homes in the higher-income areas of the city. They also wanted to run some display ads in the local papers and were considering running a classified ad in a local business directory.

The partners were somewhat at a loss as to (1) what pricing *method* they should use and (2) what general price *level* they should charge for their mowing and trimming service. Marty thought that they should base their charges on a fixed hourly rate. Harvey was in favor of charging at some rate per 1,000 square feet of lawn. Then they wondered whether they should offer some type of discount to stimulate new business. They talked about possibly offering a discount to senior citizens or a referral discount to existing customers who brought them new customers.

The partners next calculated that they needed to charge a minimum of $9 per 1,000 square feet of lawn cutting to cover expenses. They then bid 10 jobs at that price, but landed only 1 of the 10. People whom they contacted in this bidding process generally seemed to think that $9 per 1,000 square feet of lawn was extremely high. Scully said he knew that many people hired neighborhood kids to mow their lawns for $10 to $15. But both men agreed that Green Valley would not compete in what they called "this low-end market."

The men realized they had to charge reasonable prices or they would not land many jobs. On the other hand, there had to be enough profit in the business for them to earn a decent wage and a satisfactory return on their investment. They also believed that the pricing of their mowing and trimming service was going to have a substantial influence on the success of the other services they intended to provide later.

QUESTION

How should Dixon and Scully price their mowing and trimming service?

John Winkleman, president of Winkleman Manufacturing Company, was concerned about the forecast that some of his company's most successful products would experience a declining market share starting next year. He recently had a staff meeting with his managers to discuss the problem.

The Winkleman Manufacturing Company was a major electronics manufacturer in the Pacific Northwest, producing a wide variety of products. The products that currently most concerned Mr. Winkleman were three models of the Series A handheld digital multimeters (DMMs). These multimeters were used to make various types of

*Case prepared by Jim Dooley, under supervision of Professor William L. Weis, Seattle University. Reproduced with permission.

TABLE 1   UNIT SALES FOR DMMs—SERIES A

Model	1986 actual	1987 forecast	% change
1010	37,455	35,500	– 5.5
1020	67,534	61,800	– 8.4
1030	25,602	35,500	+39.0
Totals	130,591	132,800	+ 1.7%

precision measurements of electronic products and product performance where extreme accuracy of measurement was required.

The three multimeters of concern were model numbers 1010, 1020, and 1030. These three models formed a complementary family line. The 1010 was a low-cost unit containing all standard measurement functions and having a basic measurement accuracy of .5%. The 1020 offered identical measurement functions but had an improved basic measurement accuracy of .1%. The top of the line was the 1030. In addition to a basic accuracy of .1%, the 1030 offered several additional features, one being an audible continuity indicator.

As an innovator in the field of DMMs, Winkleman's business flourished over the past few years. Unit sales for 1986 and projections for 1987 are shown in Table 1. But now, with the company's three most successful products in the maturity stage of their life cycle and the industry facing a possible recession, Mr. Winkleman was worried. That is why he had that staff meeting a few weeks ago.

At that meeting he spoke as follows: "Intense competitive pressure is beginning to erode our market share in handhelds. I have documented eleven large orders that have been lost to Backman and Wiston within the past three months. On an annual basis, this amounts to nearly 10,000 units and $1.5 million in lost opportunities. Within the last eighteen months at least sixteen serious competitors have entered the market. Two-thirds of the competitive models already have continuity indicators.

"Our sales for this year (1987) are forecasted to increase only 1.7 percent. According to industry projections, the handheld DMM market will grow 21 percent over the next five years, and I think even that forecast is conservative. Also our next generation of general-purpose, low-cost handheld DMMs is two years away from introduction. In the meantime, it is essential that we do something to retain our profitable position in our traditional channels and markets. At our next meeting I want some ideas from you guys."

At the next meeting, one of the newer management team members, Dave Haug, made the following proposal for tackling the lost-market problem: "What we need is a facelift of our existing product line to hold us over for the next two years. Changes in color, a new decal, some minor case modifications, and, most important, an audible continuity indicator in the 1010 and 1020 should give us two more years of product life. We can call this Series B to retain continuity in switching from the old to the new. By including the Series B features, our decline in 1010/1020 sales could be reversed over the next two years. My discussions with our large-order customers

TABLE 2   PROJECTED DMM SALES, 1987, FOR SERIES A AND B

Model	Unit Price ($)	Series A units	Series B units	Increase Units	Increase %	Series B Sales ($000)	Series B Increase ($000)
1010	139	35,500	40,000	4,500	12.6	5,560	626
1020	179	61,800	66,000	4,200	6.8	11,814	752
1030	219	35,500	36,000	500	1.4	7,884	110
Totals	—	132,800	142,000	9,200	6.9%	$25,258	$1,488

indicate that we could have retained 40–60 percent of our lost orders if our entire handheld line had featured audible continuity.

"My estimate of sales of Series B (as shown in Table 2) has been generated from discussions with our field sales people, distributors, and customers. Sales of Series B (in units) will be 6.9 percent above the current Series A level. This translates into a marginal revenue increase of $1,488,000, assuming the same list prices as for the Series A models.

"Because of current economic conditions in our industry, our market has become very price sensitive. Now I am aware that our normal pricing policy calls for multiplying our factory cost by three to arrive at our selling price. I also am aware that the added factory cost of an audible continuity indicator is $5. But at this time we should *not* add on this cost to our selling price. My analysis indicates that an increase of $5 in selling price would reduce our incremental sales by 20 percent. An increase of $10 in selling price would cut our sales increase by 80 percent.

"Also, remember that we must pay for some nonrecurring engineering costs, which I estimate will be $96,750. This figure will cover such items as updating our operating instruction manual, new dies, decals, engineering labor, and construction of prototype models. These costs must come out of our contribution margin. As you know, we calculate that margin by taking the total dollar sales less our 28 percent discount to distributors less the factory cost for those units. I believe that increasing our prices will reduce our margins significantly, thus hindering our ability to cover the nonrecurring engineering costs, let alone make a profit. Therefore, I propose we go ahead with Series B and hold the line on prices."

Dennis Cambelot, a longtime Winkleman employee, spoke up with the following comment on Dave's proposal:

"Dave, I think this Series B idea shows a lot of potential, but price-wise you are way out of line. We have always added the standard markup to our products. We make quality products and people are willing to pay for quality. The only thing your fancy MBA degree taught you was to be impractical. If you had gotten your experience in the trenches like I did, your pricing theories would not be so conservative, and this company could make more money."

At the close of the meeting, Mr. Winkleman asked that each manager consider the Series B proposal. He especially was interested in getting the managers' reactions to the pricing considerations in Haug's proposal.

QUESTION

What are your recommendations for pricing the Series B models?

DISTRIBUTION

Retailing and wholesaling institutions, the channels of distribution from producer to user, and the physical distribution of a company's products

We are in the process of developing a marketing program to reach the firm's target markets and to achieve the goals established in strategic marketing planning. So far, we have considered the product and the pricing structure in that marketing program. Now we turn our attention to the distribution system—the means for getting the product to the market.

Our discussion of the distribution ingredient in the marketing mix will include three broad topics: (1) the retailing and wholesaling institutional structure used in distribution (Chapters 14 and 15), (2) strategies for selecting and operating channels of distribution (Chapter 16), and (3) physical distribution systems for moving materials and supplies to production facilities and then moving finished products and services to target markets (Chapter 17).

14

RETAILING: MARKETS AND INSTITUTIONS

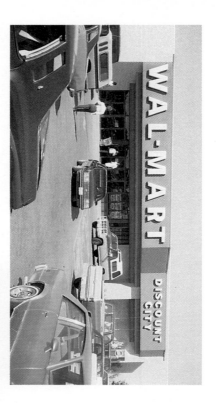

CHAPTER GOALS

The distribution of consumer products begins with the producer and ends with the ultimate consumer. Between the two there usually is at least one middleman—a retailer—who is the subject of this chapter. After studying this chapter, you should understand:

- What a channel of distribution is.
- The functions and importance of middlemen.
- The nature of the retail market.
- The differences between large-scale and small-scale retailing.
- The classification of retailers by:
  a. Product lines carried.
  b. Form of ownership.
- The methods of selling in retailing:
  a. Full-service, in-store.
  b. Supermarket.
  c. Discount.
  d. Nonstore.
- Current trends in retailing.

America has had many successful retail merchants, some of whom became giants in the field over the past century. We are speaking of people like James Cash Penney, Frank W. Woolworth, R. H. Macy, Stanley Marcus, Sebastian S. Kresge (K mart), Julius Rosenwald and General Robert E. Wood (Sears, Roebuck), Marshall Field, A. Montgomery Ward, John Wanamaker, and others. Carrying on that retail tradition are two modern-day merchant princes—Sam M. Walton and Leslie H. Wexner.

Sam Walton is the founder and chief executive officer of Wal-Mart Stores, a chain of highly successful discount department stores located in small towns primarily in the Southwest, South, and Midwest. According to *Forbes* magazine, Walton is one of the wealthiest men in the United States. His company, with headquarters in Bentonville, Arkansas, had a 1984 sales volume of $6.5 billion that placed it as the thirteenth largest retailer in the United States. In 1985 the company had about 800 stores and had opened 115 new stores in that year alone. During the 10-year period ending in 1985, the company enjoyed an annual growth rate of 38 percent in sales and 42 percent in net profit.

In the mid-1980s Walton started a chain of Sam's Wholesale Clubs—a deep-discounting, warehouse-type operation (we'll talk about these clubs later in this chapter). With plans for additional clubs on the drawing board, Wal-Mart was soon expected to become the largest operator of wholesale/warehouse clubs in the United States.

Leslie H. Wexner is the founder and chairman of the board of The Limited. At age 26 in 1963, Wexner started The Limited as one store in Columbus, Ohio, offering a limited selection (hence the company's name) of women's sportswear. By the mid-1980s there were about 600 Limited stores. This chain is the core of a 2,500-store multichain retailing empire under The Limited, Inc. In recent years Wexner added to the original Limited chain by acquiring (1) the 800-store Lerner chain that sells lower-priced women's clothing; (2) the 222-store Lane Bryant chain that specializes in clothes for large women; (3) Victoria's Secret, a chain of lingerie shops; and (4) the Henry Bendel upscale clothing store in New York. Total sales of The Limited, Inc., more than quadrupled from about $300 *million* in 1981 to more than $1.3 *billion* in 1985.[1]

---

[1] Adapted from Todd Mason, "Sam Walton of Wal-Mart: Just Your Basic Homespun Billionaire," *Business Week,* Oct. 14, 1985, p. 142; Wal-Mart's 1985 Annual Report; Brian O'Reilly, "Leslie Wexner Knows What Women Want," *Fortune,* Aug. 19, 1985, p. 154; and Jolie Solomon, "Limited Is a Clothing Retailer on the Move," *The Wall Street Journal,* Oct. 31, 1985, p. 6.

Wal-Mart and The Limited are only two current examples of the fact that the entrepreneurial spirit still prevails in retailing. This is a continually innovating field that provides many entrepreneurial opportunities and executive career opportunities for college graduates. In this chapter we shall discuss the major types of retailing institutions and see where they might fit into the distribution system of a producer's marketing mix.

MIDDLEMEN AND CHANNELS OF DISTRIBUTION

Even before a product is ready for its market, management should determine what methods and routes will be used to get it there. This task involves the establishment of a strategy covering channels of distribution and the physical distribution of the product. Understanding the retailing and wholesaling institutional structure, however, is a prerequisite to doing an effective job of establishing and managing channels of distribution. Consequently, we discuss retailing institutions in this chapter and wholesaling institutions in the next chapter. We begin by defining the terms *middleman* and *channel of distribution*, which we have already used in a more or less intuitive sense.

What Are Middlemen?

A **middleman** is an independent business concern that operates as a link between producers and ultimate consumers or industrial users. Middlemen render services in connection with the purchase and/or sale of products moving from producers to consumers. Middlemen take title to the merchandise as it flows from producer to consumer, or they actively aid in the transfer of ownership.

The essence of middlemen's operations is their active and prominent role in negotiations involving the buying and selling of goods. Their income arises directly from the proceeds of these transactions. Their involvement in the transfer of ownership is what differentiates middlemen from other business institutions, such as banks, insurance companies, and transportation firms. These other institutions help in the marketing process, but they do not take title and are not actively involved in purchase and sale negotiations. A middleman may or may not actually handle the products. Some middlemen store and transport merchandise, while others do not physically handle it at all.

Middlemen are commonly classified on the basis of whether or not they take title to the products involved. **Merchant** middlemen actually take title to the goods they are helping to market. **Agent** middlemen never actually own the goods, but they do actively assist in the transfer of title. Real estate brokers and manufacturers' agents are two examples of agent middlemen. The two major groups of merchant middlemen are wholesalers and retailers. You should note particularly that retailers are merchant middlemen.

What Is a Channel of Distribution?

A **channel of distribution** (sometimes called a **trade channel**) for a product is the route taken by the *title* to the product as it moves from the producer to the ultimate consumer or industrial user. A channel always includes both the producer and the final customer for the product, as well as all middlemen involved in the title transfer. Even though agent middlemen do *not* take actual title to the goods, they are included as part of a distribution channel. Again, this is done because they play such an active role in the transfer of ownership.

A trade channel does *not* include firms such as railroads and banks, which render marketing services but play no major role in negotiating purchases and sales. If a consumer buys apples from the grower at a roadside stand, or if a manufacturer sells a shirt by mail directly to a college student, the channel is from producer to consumer. If the shirt manufacturer sold to a department store that, in turn, sold to the college student, the channel would be producer → retailer → consumer.

Sometimes we need to distinguish between the channel for the *title* to the goods and the channel for the *physical movement* of the goods. Frequently, these routes are partially different. A contractor might order a large load of sand or gravel from a local building supply house. The product would be shipped directly from the sand and gravel producer to the contractor to minimize freight and handling costs. The channel for the title (and for the invoice), however, would be producer → building supply house → contractor.

The channel for a product extends only to the last person who buys it without making any significant change in its form. When its form is altered and another product emerges, a new channel is started. When lumber is milled and then made into furniture, two separate channels are involved. The channel for the *lumber* may be lumber mill → broker → furniture manufacturer. The channel for the *finished furniture* may be furniture manufacturer → retail furniture store → consumer.

How Important Are Middlemen?

Middlemen are very important in many cases—in fact, in virtually *all* cases where consumers are involved. Usually, it simply is not practical for a producer to deal directly with ultimate consumers. Think for a moment how inconvenient it would be if there were no retail middlemen—no drugstores, newspaper stands, supermarkets, or gasoline stations.

There is an old saying in marketing that "you can eliminate the middleman, but you cannot eliminate their functions (activities)." Someone has to perform those activities—if not the middleman, then the producers or the final customers. Middlemen serve as purchasing agents for their customers and as sales specialists for their suppliers (see Fig. 14-1). Middlemen frequently provide various financial services for both their suppliers and their customers. The storage service of middlemen, their bulk-breaking activities (dividing large shipments into smaller quantities for resale), and the market information they provide benefit suppliers and customers alike.

In the next two chapters, we shall discuss the economic services provided by particular types of middlemen—services that justify their existence and demonstrate their importance. For now, let's look at a couple of broad concepts that illustrate the important role of middlemen in our economy.

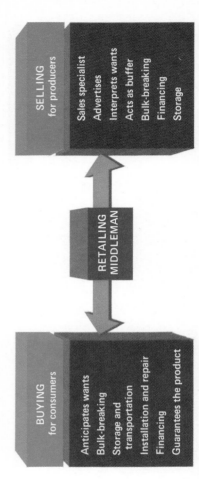

FIGURE 14-1
The retailer provides services for consumers on one hand, and for producers and wholesalers on the other.

NATURE OF RETAIL MARKET

CONCENTRATION, EQUALIZATION, DISPERSION

Frequently, the quantity and assortment of goods produced by a firm are out of balance with the variety and amounts wanted by consumers or industrial users. A business needs paper, pencils, typewriters, and desks. A homeowner wants grass seed, topsoil, fertilizer, a rake, and eventually a lawn mower. No single firm produces all the items either of these users wants. And no producer could afford to sell any of them in the small quantity the user desires. Obviously there is a need for someone to match what various producers turn out with what the final customers want. This is part of the task of middlemen.

The job to be done involves (1) collecting or **concentrating** the outputs of various producers, (2) subdividing these outputs into the amounts desired by customers and then putting the various items together in the assortment wanted (which together are called **equalizing**), and (3) **dispersing** this assortment to consumers or industrial buyers. In a few cases, these concentrating, equalizing, and dispersing tasks are simple enough to be done by the producer and the final customer working closely together. A copper mine may sell directly to a smelting firm; coal producers may sell directly to steel mills. In most cases, however, the producer and the consumer are not able to work out the proper quantity and assortment. A specialist in concentration, equalization, and dispersion is needed, and this is the middleman.

CREATION OF UTILITY

Middlemen aid in the creation of time, place, and possession utilities. In classical economic theory, production is defined as the creation of utility, and several types of utility are recognized. One is **form utility**, which results from chemical or physical changes that make a product more valuable. When lumber is made into furniture or flour into bread, form utility is created. Other utilities are equally valuable to the final user. Furniture located in Grand Rapids, Michigan, in April is of little value to people in Los Angeles who want to give the furniture as Christmas presents. Transporting the furniture from Michigan to California increases its value—**place utility** is added. Storing it from April to December adds another value—**time utility**. Finally, **possession utility** is created when the California families buy the items.

RETAILING

If a supermarket sells some floor wax to a gift-shop operator to polish the shop floor, is this a retail sale? When a gas station advertises that tires are being sold at the wholesale price, is this retailing? Can a wholesaler or manufacturer engage in retailing? Obviously, we need to define the terms *retailing, retail store, retail sales,* and *retailers,* to avoid misunderstandings in later discussions.

Retailing includes all activities directly related to the sale of goods or services to the ultimate consumer for personal, nonbusiness use. While most retailing is done through retail stores, retailing may be done by any institution. A manufacturer selling brushes or cosmetics door to door is engaging in retailing, as is a farmer selling vegetables at a roadside stand. Any firm—manufacturer, wholesaler, or retail store—that sells something to ultimate consumers for their nonbusiness use is making a **retail sale**. This is true regardless of *how* the product is sold (in person or by telephone, mail, or vending machine) or *where* it is sold (in a store or at the consumer's home).

A **retailer** or a **retail store** is a business enterprise whose *primary* function is to sell to ultimate consumers for nonbusiness use. The word *dealer* is generally synonymous with *retailer*. In contrast, a *distributor* is a *wholesaler*.

Note the word *primary* in our definition of a retailer. Actually a manufacturer or a farmer can make a retail sale to a consumer. But a manufacturer's primary function is to make a product, and a farmer's job is to grow a product. So in the common usage of terms, we call a textile mill a manufacturer, even though occasionally that mill may sell towels or sheets directly to an ultimate consumer (a retail sale). People who grow potatoes or raise cattle are called farmers or ranchers, not retailers, even though occasionally they do make a retail sale.

Economic Justification for Retailing

The ease of entry into retailing results in fierce competition and better value for the consumer. Except perhaps in a small town, it is rather difficult to establish an unregulated, monopolistic position in retailing. Certainly large-scale enterprises exist in retailing, and in some markets a relatively few large firms account for most of the business. Yet these giants usually compete with one another, so the consumer still benefits.

To get into retailing is easy. To be forced out is just as easy. Consequently, to survive in retailing, a company must do a satisfactory job in its primary role—catering to the consumer—and in its secondary role—serving producers and wholesalers. This dual responsibility is both the justification for retailing and the key to success in retailing.

Size of Retail Market

There are about 2 million retail stores in the United States, and their total sales volume in 1985 was about $1.4 *trillion* (see Fig. 14-2). In spite of the population boom and rising consumer incomes over the past three decades, there has been no appreciable change in the number of retail stores. The increase in total sales volume, however, has been tremendous—over a fivefold increase from the late 1960s to the mid-1980s. Even if we adjust for the big rise in prices, we find that total retail sales, and per capita retail sales, have gone up considerably. That is, there has simply been a huge increase in the physical volume of merchandise sold at retail.

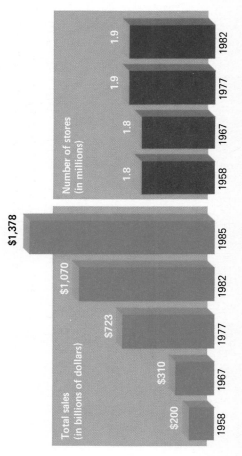

FIGURE 14-2
Total retail trade in the United States, selected years.
Sales volume has increased tremendously. In contrast, note the remarkable stability in the number of retail stores. (*Sources: U.S. Census of Business: Retail Trade, 1982, 1977, 1967; Sales for 1985 from Survey of Current Business, March 1986*)

Costs and Profits of Retailers

Information regarding the costs of retailing is very meager. By gleaning data from several sources, however, we can make some rough generalizations.

TOTAL COSTS AND PROFITS

As nearly as can be estimated, the total average operating expense for all retailers combined is about 25 to 27 percent of retail sales. Wholesaling expenses are estimated at about 8 percent of the *retail* dollar or about 10 to 11 percent of *wholesaling* sales. Thus, retailing costs are about 2½ times the costs of wholesaling, when both are stated as a percentage of sales of the middlemen in question. (See Fig. 14-3.)

The proportionately higher retailing costs are generally related to the expense of dealing directly with the consumer. In comparison with wholesalers' customers, consumers demand more services. The average retail sale is smaller, the rate of merchandise turnover is lower, merchandise is bought in smaller lots, rent is higher, and expenses for furniture and fixtures are greater. And retail sales people cannot be used efficiently because customers do not come into retail stores at a steady rate.

COSTS AND PROFITS BY KIND OF BUSINESS

The expense ratios of retailers vary from one type of store to another. Table 14-1 shows average gross margins as a percentage of sales for different kinds of stores. These margins range from 14 percent for auto dealers to 37 percent for clothing stores. Table 14-1 also shows median net profit (after income taxes) for each type of store.

Retailing Structure in Metropolitan Areas

As we might expect, retail sales and retailer location tend to follow the population. The bulk of retail sales is concentrated in very small land masses—the Metropolitan Statistical Areas. These markets account for about 75 percent of the nation's population and 80 percent of the retail trade.

Within the central city and its adjacent suburbs in a metropolitan area, there are several discernible types of shopping districts. Together, these constitute a retailing structure that should be recognized by marketers. The hub of retailing activity has traditionally been the central downtown shopping district. This is the location of the main units of department stores, major apparel specialty stores, jewelry stores, and other shopping-goods stores.

In the older, larger cities (especially in the East and Midwest), we often find a secondary shopping district with branches of downtown stores. A third type of shop-

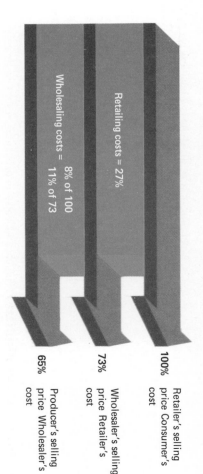

FIGURE 14-3
Average costs of retailing and wholesaling

Retailing costs = 27%

Wholesaling costs = 8% of 100
11% of 73

100% Retailer's selling price Consumer's cost

73% Wholesaler's selling price Retailer's cost

65% Producer's selling price Wholesaler's cost

TABLE 14-1 GROSS MARGIN AND NET PROFIT AS PERCENTAGE OF NET SALES OF SELECTED TYPES OF RETAILERS

Gross margin (net sales minus cost of goods sold) is the amount needed to cover a company's operating expenses and still leave a profit. How do you account for the differences in operating expenses among the various types of retailers?

Line of business	Gross margin %	Net profit % after income taxes
Automobile and truck dealers	14	1.5
Liquor stores	18	n.a.
Grocery stores	21	1.7
Building materials, hardware, and farm equipment:	24	
Building materials		1.9
Hardware		4.1
Gasoline service stations	24	2.1
Drugstores	30	n.a.
Furniture and home-furnishings stores:	35	
Furniture		3.1
Household appliances		3.4
Department stores	37	0.8
Apparel and accessory stores:	37	
Women's ready-to-wear		5.6
Men's and boys' clothing		5.0
Shoe stores		5.2
Jewelry stores		9.5

n.a. = not available.
Source: Gross margins from Cost of Doing Business: Corporations, Dun & Bradstreet, Inc., New York, 1973. Net profit figures from "The Ratios," Dun's Business Month, February 1983, pp. 112, 115.

ping district is a "string-street" development, or a cluster of small, neighborhood stores. None of these three types of shopping districts is planned or controlled for marketing purposes.

During the past decade many cities have made a real effort to revitalize their downtown shopping district. An especially successful venture in this respect has been the development of planned, controlled *downtown* shopping centers—the urban shopping mall. Many cities now have such malls—Faneuil Hall Marketplace in Boston, the Galleria in San Francisco, Nicolet Mall in Minneapolis, Water Tower Place in Chicago, Harborplace in Baltimore, Grand Avenue in Milwaukee, to name just a few. And similar malls are in the planning stages in several other large cities. These malls have restored blighted areas, brought consumers back to the city center, provided excellent shopping for the many people working in downtown areas, and rebuilt an urban tax base.[2]

[2]See "The Shopping Mall Goes Urban," Business Week, Dec. 13, 1982, p. 50; and Cara S. Trager, "Malls Breathe New Life into Cities," Advertising Age, Aug. 9, 1984, p. 13.

The Galleria mall in Houston, Texas helps to revitalize the downtown area.

SUBURBAN SHOPPING CENTERS

Another significant type of shopping district in metropolitan areas is the suburban shopping center—a unit that is planned, developed, and controlled by one organization. These planned centers range from (1) a *neighborhood* center built around a supermarket, through (2) a *community* center featuring a discount store or junior department store, to (3) a *regional* center anchored by a branch of one or more downtown department stores. In the regional center, ideally there is at least one limited-line store to compete with each department in the department stores.

Many of the regional centers are giant-sized; in effect, they are miniature downtowns. These supercenters may have as many as five department stores, plus many small stores and service operations. They also include hotels, banks, office buildings, churches, and theaters. These centers integrate retail, cultural, and commercial activities, all enclosed under one roof. During the past decade the building of giant regional centers slowed considerably as the market for shopping centers became saturated in many parts of the country.

The success of suburban shopping centers lies essentially in their conformity with consumer buying patterns. A wide selection of merchandise is available; stores are open evenings; an informal atmosphere encourages shoppers to dress informally and to bring the children; plenty of free parking space is available. By coordinating their promotional efforts, all stores benefit; one builds traffic for another. Many stores in these centers are too small to do effective, economical advertising on their own. But they can make good use of major advertising media by tying in with the overall shopping-center advertising.

Suburban shopping malls continue to be popular.

Classification of Retailers

To better explain the role of retailing middlemen in the channel structure, we shall classify and discuss retailers on four bases:

1. Size of store, by sales volume.
2. Extent of product lines handled.
3. Form of ownership.
4. Method of operation.

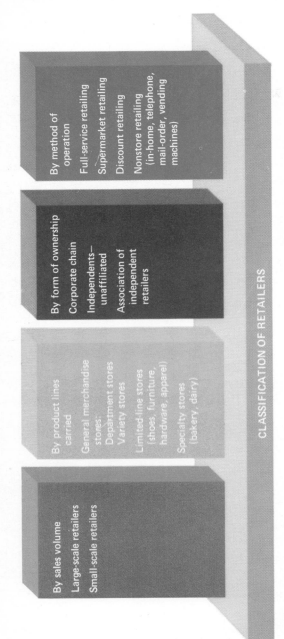

By sales volume	By product lines carried	By form of ownership	By method of operation
Large-scale retailers Small-scale retailers	General merchandise stores: Department stores Variety stores Limited-line stores (shoes, furniture, hardware, apparel) Specialty stores (bakery, dairy)	Corporate chain Independents—unaffiliated Association of independent retailers	Full-service retailing Supermarket retailing Discount retailing Nonstore retailing (in-home, telephone, mail-order, vending machines)

FIGURE 14-4
Retailers may be classed in several ways.

CLASSIFICATION OF RETAILERS

Any given store can be classed according to all four of these bases. We have done this below, using Sears and a neighborhood paint store as examples. See also Fig. 14-4.

Sears	← Classification base →	Paint store
Large General merchandise	1. Size of store 2. Product lines carried	Small Single line of merchandise
Corporate chain Both in-store and mail order; supermarket method and full service depending on product department	3. Form of ownership 4. Method of operation	Independent owner In-store selling; full service

RETAILERS CLASSIFIED BY SALES VOLUME

Sales volume is a useful basis for classifying retail stores, because stores of different sizes (in terms of sales) present different management problems. Buying, promotion, personnel relations, and expense control are influenced significantly by whether a store's sales volume is large or small. And, as you will see, on the basis of store sales volume, retailing is both a small-scale and a large-scale operation.

Quantitative Measurement

Most retail establishments are very small. In 1982, the last available census-data year, about 42 percent of the stores operating the full year had an annual sales volume of less than $100,000. However, these stores accounted for only 2 percent of all retail sales (see Fig. 14-5).

FIGURE 14-5
Distribution of stores and total retail sales, by sales size of store, in United States, 1982.

Although most retailers are small, there is a high degree of concentration in retailing. Forty-two percent of the stores had an annual sales volume under $100,000. Only 2 percent of the stores had annual sales of over $5 million, but these stores accounted for 39 percent of all retail sales.

Source: 1982 Census of Retail Trade, Establishment Size.

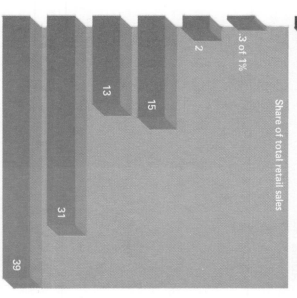

Store size in sales	Percent of stores
Under $25,000	20%
$25,000 – $100,000	22
$100,000 – $500,000	36
$500,000 – $1 million	11
$1 – 5 million	9
Over $5 million	2

Store size in sales	Share of total retail sales
Under $25,000	.3 of 1%
$25,000 – $100,000	2
$100,000 – $500,000	15
$500,000 – $1 million	13
$1 – 5 million	31
Over $5 million	39

At the same time, there is a high degree of concentration in retailing. A small number of establishments account for a substantial share of retail trade. Only 2 percent of all stores had an annual sales volume over $5 million, but they accounted for about 39 percent of total retail sales.

Figure 14-5 still does not tell the full story of large-scale retailing because it represents a tabulation of individual *store* sales and not *company* sales volume. A single company may own many establishments, as in the case of chain stores. When retail sales are analyzed by *companies*, the high degree of concentration becomes even more evident (see Table 14-2). The 1982 Census reported that the 8 largest retailers alone accounted for 9 percent of all retail sales, and the 20 largest firms represented 14 percent of the total sales. The small size of the average net profit among these giants—2 percent of sales in 1984—may surprise people who believe that retailers make high profits. See Table 14-2.

Competitive Positions of Large and Small Retailers

The relative competitive strengths and weaknesses of large and small retailers may be evaluated as follows:

Bases for evaluation	Competitive advantage is generally with:
1. Division of labor and specialization of management.	1. Large-scale retailers. This is their major advantage.
2. Flexibility of operations—merchandise selection, services offered, store design, reflection of owner's personality.	2. Small retailers. This is their biggest advantage.
3. Buying power.	3. Large retailers. They can buy in bigger quantities and thus get lower prices.
4. Effective use of advertising—especially in citywide media.	4. Large retailers. Their markets fit better with media circulation.
5. Development and promotion of retailer's own brand.	5. Large retailers.
6. Feasibility of integrating wholesaling and manufacturing with retailing.	6. Large retailers.
7. Opportunity to experiment with new products and selling methods.	7. Large retailers can better afford the risks and can supply the necessary executive specialists.
8. Cost of operations.	8. Small stores generally have lower expense ratios and lower overhead costs. Large stores pay a price for executive specialization and the large number of employees in non-selling jobs.
9. Financial strength.	9. Large-scale retailers. This advantage also underlies some of the advantages noted above—integration, experimentation, purchase discounts, effective advertising, and executive specialization.
10. Public image and legal considerations.	10. Small merchants enjoy public support and sympathy. But often this same public votes with its pocketbook for (that is, shops at) the big store. Large-scale retailers have been a major target of restrictive legislation.

Improved Position of Small Retailers

With the above evaluation adding up so heavily in favor of large-scale retailing, you might wonder why so many small retailers seem to be succeeding. We find the answer

Now this is a small store . . .

. . . and this is a large one.

TABLE 14-2   WORLDWIDE SALES OF TEN LARGEST RETAILERS IN UNITED STATES, 1984

The total sales of these giant retailers represent a significant share of all retail sales in the United States. Note that the average net profit of these retailers was only 2.1 percent of sales. What are some of the marketing implications of this concentration for a maker of department store merchandise?

Company	Sales (in billions of dollars)	Net profit as % of sales
1. Sears, Roebuck	38.8	3.8
2. K mart	21.1	2.4
3. Safeway Stores	19.6	0.9
4. Kroger	15.9	1.0
5. J. C. Penney	13.5	3.2
6. American Stores	12.1	1.5
7. Southland (7-Eleven)	12.0	1.3
8. Federated Department Stores	9.7	3.4
9. Lucky Stores	9.2	1.0
10. Household International (Ben Franklin, National Car Rental, T. G. & Y. Stores)	8.3	2.8
Total sales volume	$160.2	
Average net profit		2.1%

Source: Fortune, June 10, 1985, pp. 190–191.

in several developments among both large and small firms. One such development has been the voluntary association of retailers in a chainlike form of organization. This gives the individual members the features of specialized management, buying power, and other advantages of scale listed above. A second development has been the expansion of franchising operations in many fields (by Holiday Inn, Avis, and McDonald's hamburgers, for instance). Franchising enables small-scale business people to operate their own businesses under the name and guidance of a large company. This gives some small entrepreneurs the best of both worlds. (Franchising and voluntary associations are discussed later in this chapter.)

Change in the consumer market is another factor working for the smaller retailer. On one hand, huge supermarket-type stores carrying a wide variety of merchandise are catering to consumers' wants. At the same time, small specialty shops are growing in number and apparently doing well, in response to another facet of consumer buying behavior. Small retailers who take advantage of their flexibility can adapt their merchandise lines to their market. They can also establish an individual personality for their stores by means of unusual store layout and design. The relative position of small stores also is improved when large retailers suffer from the usual problems of large-scale operation—retailing or otherwise. High overhead costs, restrictive union contracts, difficulty in motivating sales people, and organizational inflexibilities all limit the competitive position of the large-scale retailer.

RETAILERS CLASSIFIED BY PRODUCT LINE
■

In classifying retailers according to the product lines they carry, we group them into two categories—general merchandise stores and limited-line stores.

General Merchandise Stores

As the name suggests, **general merchandise** stores carry a large variety of product lines, usually with some depth of assortment in each line. Department stores are the type of general merchandise stores with the largest sales volume. Variety stores (Woolworth's, Ben Franklin) are also included in this category.

DEPARTMENT STORES

Department stores are large retailing institutions that carry a *very wide* variety of product lines, including apparel, other soft goods, furniture, and home furnishings. These stores are highly organized business enterprises. Under the merchandising manager are the department buyers. In effect, each department is a business in itself, and the department buyer has considerable autonomy.

In addition to the general advantages and drawbacks of large-scale retailing (specialized management, buying power, and so on), department stores have some other significant merits and limitations. These stores offer a wider variety of products and services than any other type of retail institution where the customer comes to the store. (The mail-order house—a form of nonstore retailing—may carry more lines than a department store.) On the other hand, their operating expenses are considerably higher than those of most other kinds of retail business, running about 35 percent of sales. One of the features of department stores—their many services—contributes significantly to this high operating expense.

A substantial problem confronting department stores has been their location—typically in the heart of the downtown shopping district. The population exodus to the suburbs and the traffic problems downtown have combined to force many department stores to open branches in the suburbs. The big downtown store, with its large investment, high-tax location, and high-cost operations, must be maintained. But it reaps a decreasing share of the total business in the area. Of course, for many years the department stores have been well aware of the "downtown problem." In many cities, working with other downtown merchants, the department stores have spearheaded movements to revitalize the downtown areas. Also, as mentioned earlier, urban shopping malls are revitalizing downtown shopping areas, thus benefiting downtown department stores.

Department stores face strong competition on other fronts as well. Some examples of these challenges are (1) the continued expansion of discount selling; (2) the growth of chains of small specialty apparel stores (The Limited, Petrie Stores, Miller-Wohl); and (3) the development of specialty stores catering to hobbies, sports, and other leisure-time activities.

But department stores are displaying some innovative, aggressive strategies to meet the competitive challenges. To illustrate, stores are using marketing research extensively to determine current purchasing motives, attitudes, and life-styles. Many stores are trying to appeal to a limited number of market segments—especially the

Large stores have set up specialty departments—such as this designer's salon—to compete with the smaller boutiques.

younger, more fashion-conscious groups. These retailers are reducing their merchandise mix—stressing fashion and exclusiveness rather than carrying products in a wide variety of price lines. Many department stores have converted entire floors into groups of specialty shops. Each of these shops features a different line of merchandise, and each has a different decorative display theme or motif. Bargain basements are being revitalized to counter the lower prices in discount stores. Several department stores have adopted programs of selling through warehouses, the mail, and catalog outlets.

Limited-Line Stores

Limited-line stores carry a considerable assortment of goods, but in only one or a few related lines. We identify these stores by the names of the individual products they feature—food stores, shoe stores, furniture stores, hardware stores, and so on.

This identification is still useful for some types of stores—those selling apparel, furniture, or building materials, for instance. For other types, such as food stores and drugstores, however, to include a single type of product in the store name is inaccurate and misleading. This is the result of a major trend toward **scrambled merchandising**—the practice of adding unrelated lines to the products customarily sold in a particular type of store. Moreover, it is a mistake to interpret food store sales, for example, as being equal to total sales of food products. Supermarkets carry many nonfood lines. Food products, in turn, are sold in drugstores, gas stations, and department stores.

The limited-line category also includes what we call **specialty stores**. These are toabcco shops, bakeries, dairy stores, and furriers, for example—stores that typically carry a very limited variety of products. The name "specialty stores" is an unfortunate, and perhaps even misleading, title. Specialty *stores* should *not* be confused with specialty *products*. Actually, specialty shops do *not* often carry specialty products. Using the word *specialty* in describing the store implies only that it carries a limited line of merchandise.

Limited-line stores usually carry an excellent assortment of goods. In the apparel field, they often feature the newest fashions. Frequently they are the exclusive dealers for certain brands in a given market. Because they limit their merchandise to one or a few lines, these stores can often buy in large quantities and thus secure favorable prices.

The name of this store indicates its specialty.

RETAILERS CLASSIFIED BY FORM OF OWNERSHIP

The major store-ownership categories are *independent* stores and *corporate chain* stores. A third group consists of *voluntary associations of independents* that band together in chainlike fashion in order to compete more effectively with corporate chain-store organizations.

Corporate Chain Store

A **corporate chain-store system** is an organization of two or more stores, centrally owned and managed, that generally handle the same lines of products. Technically, two or more units constitute a chain. Today, however, many small-scale merchants have opened two or three units in shopping centers and in newly populated areas. These retailers ordinarily do not think of themselves as chains. Consequently, it might be more meaningful to consider a larger number of units to be a reasonable minimum when categorizing a store as a chain. For instance, 11 or more units (one of several categories used by the Census of Business) is a good definitional basis for discussing chain stores.

Central ownership is the key factor that differentiates corporate chains from voluntary associations of independent wholesalers or retailers. The third element in our definition of a chain-store system is central management. Individual units in a chain have very little autonomy. Buying is highly centralized, and there is considerable standardization in the operating policies of the units in a chain.

IMPORTANCE

Chain-store companies in total have increased their share of the retail market over the past 30 years. The importance of chains varies considerably, however, depending on the type of commodity (see Table 14-3). Chains dominate in the department store business; companies with 11 or more stores account for close to 96 percent of all department store sales. In the variety store field, chains do 79 percent of the business. In the food field, there are several giant firms, yet chains still account for little more than one-half of food store sales.

COMPETITIVE STRENGTHS AND WEAKNESSES

Chain-store organizations are large-scale retailing institutions. As such, they are subject to the general advantages and limitations of all large retailers that we discussed earlier in this chapter. Let's look at a few of these points, especially as they relate to chain stores.

Lower selling prices   Chain stores have traditionally been credited with selling at

TABLE 14-3	CHAINS' SHARE OF TOTAL SALES VOLUME BY KIND OF BUSINESS
	Chains dominate in the department store and variety store fields. For the past 30 years, chains have made their largest gains in drugstores and department stores. How do you account for the growth of department store chains?

Kind of business	% of sales, chains with 11 or more stores
Total retail sales	35
Department stores	96
Variety stores	79
Drugstores	56
Food stores	55
Shoe stores	52
Apparel and accessory stores	41
Auto and home supply stores	21

Source: *Statistical Abstract of the United States, 1985*, p. 783.

lower prices than independents. But the claim of lower prices needs careful scrutiny because it can be misleading. It was probably more justified in the past than it is today. Many independents have pooled their buying power so that, in many instances, they can buy products at the same price as the chains.

It is very difficult to compare the prices of chains with those of independents. The merchandise is often not exactly comparable, because many chains sell items under their own brands. It is difficult to compare the prices of Del Monte peaches with Kroger's or Safeway's brand of peaches. Also, it is not accurate to compare the price of the product sold in a cash-and-carry, no-customer-service store with the price of an identically branded product in a full-service store. The value of services should be included in the comparison.

Multistore feature of chains   Chain stores do not have all their eggs in one basket (or in one store). Even large-scale independent department stores or supermarkets cannot match this advantage of the chains. A multiunit operation has automatically *spread its risks* among many units. Losses in one store can be offset by profits in other units. Multistore organizations can *experiment* quite easily. They can try a new store layout or a new type of merchandise in one store without committing the entire firm.

A chain can make more *effective use of advertising* than even a giant single-unit independent store. To illustrate, a grocery chain may have 25 medium-sized stores blanketing a city. An independent competitor may have one huge supermarket doing 3 to 4 times the business of any single unit of the chain. Yet the chain can use the metropolitan daily newspaper as an advertising medium with much less waste in circulation than the independent can. Many chains can also make effective use of national advertising media.

On the negative side   Standardization, the hallmark of a chain-store system and a major factor in its success, is a mixed blessing. *Standardization also means inflexibility.* Often a chain cannot adjust rapidly to a local market situation. Chains are well aware of this weakness, however, and have consequently given local store managers somewhat greater freedom to act in various situations.

A major competitive factor facing corporate chains is the increased effectiveness of independent retailers and wholesalers that have copied chain-store marketing methods. Independents have adopted self-service methods in many types of stores; they have improved store appearance and layout; they have sought better locations, including suburban shopping centers; they have improved their merchandising practices by eliminating some slow-moving items and keeping fresh stock; and they have improved their accounting and inventory-control systems.

Probably the most effective measure adopted by small independents is their practice of voluntarily associating with wholesalers, manufacturers, or other retailers in some form of contractual franchise system. These associations sometimes resemble a corporate chain so closely that about the only significant difference is that the member stores are not centrally owned.

Franchise Systems Involving Small, Independent Retailers

NATURE AND EXTENT OF FRANCHISE SYSTEMS

In our discussion here, we use a broad interpretation of franchising. It includes any contractual arrangement between *franchisers* (suppliers, that may be manufacturers or wholesalers) and independent *franchisees* (either wholesalers or retailers). The franchiser grants the right to sell certain goods or services in a stated geographic market. The franchiser usually provides equipment, the products or services for sale, and managerial services. In return, the franchisee agrees to market the product or service in a manner established by the supplier. Within this broad definition we find two main types of franchising systems. One is a voluntary association of retailers, and the other is a retailer network sponsored by a producer.

ASSOCIATIONS OF INDEPENDENT RETAILERS

The two main forms of voluntary associations of independent retailers are **voluntary chains** (sponsored by wholesalers) and **retailer cooperative chains** (sponsored by retailers). Both forms have the same basic purpose—namely, to enable independent wholesalers and retailers to meet more effectively the competition from corporate chain stores. By combining the buying power of their many retailer members, these associations can buy at prices competitive with those of the corporate chains.

Some differences between the two groups are as follows:

Voluntary chain	Retailer cooperative chain
1. Sponsored by wholesalers, with a contract between wholesalers and independent retailer members.	1. Sponsored by retailers. They combine to form and operate a wholesale warehouse corporation.
2. Wholesaler provides a wide variety of management services—buying, advertising, store layout, accounting, and inventory control. Retailers agree to buy all (or almost all) their merchandise from wholesaler. Members agree to use common store name and design and to follow common managerial procedures.	2. Services to retailer members are primarily large-scale buying and warehousing operations. Members maintain their separate identities.
3. Most prevalent in grocery field (IGA, Super Valu). These chains also exist in hardware (Ace), auto supplies (Western Auto), and variety stores (Ben Franklin).	3. Quite significant in grocery field (Associated Grocers, Certified Grocers), but not in other lines.

PRODUCER-SPONSORED SYSTEMS

In producer-sponsored systems of franchising, a manufacturer (or other producer) sets up a network of retail outlets by contracting with independent retailers. The contract may cover:

- Only one brand within a department (Hart, Schaffner and Marx suits or Maytag appliances).
- An entire department in a store (Russell Stover candies).

Voluntary chains help small retailers to compete with big stores.

Franchising is one way to help a little guy succeed in business.

- The entire retail outlet (auto dealerships or gas stations, Burger King drive-ins, Midas Mufflers, Hertz auto rentals).

We can distinguish between two concepts in producer-sponsored franchise systems. One features franchising as a form of *exclusive distribution* of a product. This type has existed for years and often involves a large-scale retailer. The other concept is the rise of *entrepreneurship franchising*. This practice is relatively new, and it typically has involved small-scale retailers. Enterprise franchising has especially proliferated in the fast-food industry (Kentucky Fried Chicken, McDonald's hamburgers) and in service industries (recreation, auto rentals, motels, auto repairs).

The concept of a producer franchising an entire retail outlet (as contrasted with a single department or one brand within a department) is not new—automobile manufacturers have done this for decades. What is new, however, is its substantial growth over the past 20 to 30 years and its spreading into many new fields. In addition to fast-food services, today producer-sponsored franchise selling also embraces such products and services as computers, auto mufflers, putting greens, paint, part-time office help, hearing aids, motels, and dance studios.

Competitive advantages Franchising has many economic and social advantages. A producer-sponsored system offers the producer an opportunity for greater control over the pricing, advertising, and selling of its products or services. Franchising also provides suppliers with the means for rapid market expansion and a wide distribution system at a relatively low cost. Franchisees typically put up some of the money. With their own money at stake, they have more incentive and are likely to be more dedicated entrepreneurs.

When the retailers are identified as a group (through a producer's name), then that producer can make effective use of cooperative advertising programs, display materials, and other promotional features. The group buying power enables the independent retailer-members to obtain lower-cost merchandise and a better selection of the latest products. Furthermore, the retailers are able to do a better job of store management because of the administrative services furnished by the sponsor.

In a producer-sponsored network particularly, franchising enables many people to realize their dream of owning their own business. Also, the franchisees' investment is relatively small, and it is easier for them to borrow the necessary funds when big national firms are behind them. They may be independent, small-scale retailers, but they are backed by the buying power, promotional programs, and management know-how of big companies.

Limitations In the authors' opinion, the biggest competitive weakness of all independent retailers, whether affiliated or not, is their assumption that the sole advantage of the chain is its buying power. In fact, the Robinson-Patman Act was based largely on this premise. The real strength of a large-scale institution, however, lies in its superior management personnel and specialized management practices.

Ignorance or disregard of this fact places major limitations on voluntary associations of independents. Too often these retailers reject the management advice given by sponsors. Many retailers think of the association as a buying aid only, and make little use of advertising, accounting, and other association services.

The rapid expansion of producer-sponsored franchising systems during the past 25 years has also brought problems. One is the charge that franchising agreements are grievously one-sided—all in favor of the franchisor. Another threat to continued successful expansion of franchising is the practice whereby the producer-sponsor takes over the ownership of successful units in its franchise system. This, in effect, turns the independent units into a corporate chain system. One unfortunate aspect of this trend is that it reduces the numbers of successful, small, independent entrepreneurs.[3]

RETAILERS CLASSIFIED BY METHOD OF OPERATION

The four types of retailers, classified by method of operation, are listed in Fig. 14-4. The traditional form, *in-store full-service* retailing, is still quite prevalent, although its use has declined considerably over the past 30 years. It probably will continue to be important in retailing high-fashion products and products that require explanation or fitting. The use of the remaining three classes—supermarket, discount, and nonstore retailing (in-home personal selling, telephone selling, mail-order selling, and automatic vending)—has increased considerably during the last two decades.

Supermarket Retailing

It is somewhat difficult to analyze supermarket retailing because there is no universally accepted definition of the term. To some people a supermarket is a *type* of retail store found in the grocery business. To others, the term describes a *method* of retailing and can be used in connection with stores in any product line.

In this discussion, a **supermarket** will be defined as a large-scale departmentized retailing institution offering a variety of merchandise (including groceries, meats, produce, and dairy products). Such a store operates largely on a self-service basis

---

[3]For a report on the current status and future prospects in entrepreneurial franchising, along with a summary of the elements in an ideal franchising program, see Phillip D. White and Albert D. Bates, "Franchising Will Remain Retailing Fixture, but Its Salad Days Have Long Since Gone," *Marketing News*, Feb. 17, 1984, p. 14.

with a minimum of customer services, and features a price appeal and (usually) ample parking space.

DEVELOPMENT OF SUPERMARKETS

Supermarkets, as we know them today, had their start in the Depression days of the early 1930s. They were owned and operated by *independents* attempting to compete with the chain food stores. The supermarket method of food retailing became an immediate success, and the innovation was soon adopted by chain stores as well as other full-service independents. Today, supermarkets are the dominant institution in food retailing. However, the supermarket's average net profit after taxes is only a paper-thin 1 percent of sales.

The rapidly changing competitive environment in grocery retailing in the 1980s has forced conventional supermarkets to make significant changes in order to survive. The number of supermarkets has reached a saturation point in many communities. Also, today a grocery shopper can choose from among warehouse stores, supermarkets combined with general merchandise stores, convenience stores, gourmet shops, ethnic stores, discount supermarkets, and other institutions.

The conventional (or traditional) supermarkets are responding to these competitive pressures in various ways to improve their profits, productivity, and competitive position.[4] Many chains are cutting costs and stressing low prices by offering limited store services, no frills, and generic brands. Many conventional supermarkets are expanding in size and product assortment to become, in effect, superstores—an institution we shall discuss later in this section. These expanded stores often include pharmacies, beauty parlors, restaurants, and automated bank teller machines. Many supermarkets have installed automatic scanners at checkout stands and other technological innovations elsewhere in the store.

At the same time, some of the competitive responses of conventional supermarkets have involved promotional devices such as extra-value coupons, trading stamps, games, and longer store hours. These forms of nonprice competition do, of course, increase operating costs and often the selling prices, but unfortunately not always the profit.

DISCOUNT SUPERMARKETS

The inviting vacancy at the bottom of the supermarket pricing structure has generated discount selling in food and the rise of the *discount supermarket*. This discount food retailer operates with fewer services, no trading stamps, lower gross margins, and lower prices than conventional supermarkets. Most food chains in the United States have converted some or all of their stores to discount operations.

The **warehouse store** (also called a **box store**) is a form of discount supermarket operation that has appeared in recent years. This type of food store offers a limited assortment of brands and commonly used products on a no-frills basis. There is, especially, a limited offering of fresh produce, fresh meats, frozen foods, and other perishable goods. The products are displayed on pallets or shelves in the original packing boxes whose tops or sides have been cut off. To further reduce costs, these

Supermarkets are expanding their product assortment.

[4]See "Special Report on Grocery Marketing," *Advertising Age*, Apr. 18, 1985, pp. 15ff.

stores typically use computerized price-scanning equipment and other labor-saving equipment.[5]

CONVENIENCE STORES

Other innovative competitors of conventional supermarkets are the **convenience stores** (7-Eleven, Li'l General, Minit Markets, Circle K, and others). These stores, interestingly enough, have higher prices and a more limited product assortment and are smaller in size. But they do have longer shopping hours and more convenient locations, and they can provide the fill-in type of merchandise when other food stores are closed. In some ways they are a throwback to the corner grocery store of years past.

In recent years, increasing numbers of convenience stores have been adding gasoline and fast foods to their product assortments. In so doing, these stores provide one-stop shopping for customers. Thus they have become effective competition for gas stations and fast-food chains as well as for conventional supermarkets.

Convenience stores are satisfying customers' wants.

SUPERSTORES

The newest and possibly the toughest innovative competitor of the conventional supermarket is the **superstore**—also called a hypermarket or a super-supermarket. Unlike most modern retailing innovations, the superstore concept did not originate in the United States; it was imported from France.

Supermarkets and the newer superstores are alike in that they both are low-cost, high-volume, limited-service operations. The key difference between the conventional supermarket and the superstore concepts lies in the breadth of consumer needs to be filled. The supermarket strives mainly to fulfill the consumers' needs for food, laundry, and home-cleaning products. The superstore is designed to provide those same products and to fill all other *routine* purchasing needs as well. For example, superstores carry personal-care products, alcoholic beverages and tobacco products, some apparel, low-priced housewares and hardware items, gasoline, consumable lawn and garden products, stationery and sewing supplies, some leisure-time products (books, records, hobby items), and household services (laundry, dry cleaning, shoe repair).

In an effort to boost profits, several supermarket chains are opening new superstores and are expanding existing units into superstore size and product assortment. In general, when compared with conventional supermarkets, we find that the superstore is about double in size, double in customer traffic, and triple in store sales volume. Gross margin and net profit in superstores are higher because they carry more high-margin items in their total product assortment.

Discount Retailing and the Discount House

In this section we really are talking about two things. One is a type of retailing *institution* (the discount house), and the other is a *method* of retail selling that is applicable to almost any type of store. Actually, there is nothing new about discount selling—the practice of selling below the list price. There is also nothing new about discount houses; they have existed in some form for many years. The modern **discount houses** are large stores that are open to the public. They advertise widely, and they carry a reasonably complete selection of wearing apparel and well-known brands of

[5]See "'Super Warehouses' Chomp into the Food Business," *Business Week*, Apr. 16, 1984, p. 72.

Discount retailing continues to change and continues to be popular.

hard goods (appliances, home furnishings, sporting goods, jewelry). They consistently sell below list prices, and they offer a minimum of customer services. Through the years, two major factors led to the success of the modern-day discount houses. Those factors were (1) the traditional high retail markups on appliances and other products that typically are now discounted and (2) the consumers' receptivity to a low-price, limited-service appeal.

RECENT DEVELOPMENTS IN DISCOUNT RETAILING

Discount selling has led to a revision of traditional retailing methods. Manufacturers have altered their channels of distribution to include discounting retailers. Small-scale retailers have been forced to drop discounted products or else to meet the discount-house price by offering fewer services and adopting more efficient marketing methods. Large-scale retailers, such as department stores, have realistically lowered their mark-ups on discounted products and have even dropped some of these items.

The discount houses themselves are changing. Some are upgrading their image to that of "promotional department stores," and some have opened stores in suburban shopping centers. In general, all discounters are trading up in products and services.[6] Today, reasonably expensive, high-fashion women's apparel is carried in a number of large discount department stores. Separate discount department stores have been established by "conventional" retailers such as the May Company (Venture) and Dayton-Hudson (Target and Mervyn's). One discount retailer, K mart, has become the second (to Sears) largest retailer in the United States.

Discount retailers' risks and operating costs do increase, of course, as they add more expensive merchandise, move into fancier buildings and locations, and add more services.

OFF-PRICE RETAILERS

A discounting phenomenon of the 1980s is the so-called off-price retailer—a current name given to stores that sell brand products below the list, or "full," price. This current boom in discounting has occurred principally in shoes and wearing apparel. Industry experts estimate that, by 1990, 10 to 12 percent of apparel and footwear will be sold through off-price outlets. Names such as Syms, Marshall's, Dress Barn, T. J. Maxx, Hit or Miss, and Loehmann's are becoming increasingly well known. In fact, some of the biggest off-price retailers are owned by full-price chain-store organizations.

What is interesting from a historical viewpoint is that the situation in apparel in the 1980s is exactly what occurred in appliances (including television and sound systems) in the 1950s. That is, discount retailers get new products (refrigerators or dresses) from some source and then sell the article below its list price. The full-price (usually high-cost) retailers then scream to the manufacturer, threatening to stop carrying that manufacturer's line if the manufacturer continues to supply the off-price retailers.

Several factors account for the recent growth in off-price retailing. First, there is a large consumer market that is willing to accept limited store services, less con-

[6] See, for example, "K mart: The No. 2 Retailer Starts to Make an Upscale Move—At Last," *Business Week*, June 4, 1984, p. 50.

venient locations, and less attractive stores, if they can buy brand products at greatly reduced prices. Working women especially are interested in fashionable clothing, but at a discount price. Second, manufacturers like the idea of having an outlet for excess inventories. Third, some of the traditional discount houses have upgraded their products and prices so that the price-conscious consumer no longer goes there. Fourth, profit margins generally are good in off-price retailing.

Now the traditional, full-price retailers generally do not object if the off-price stores carry discontinued products or lower-quality products ("seconds" or rejects). Off-price retailers are accepted when they do not advertise much and are not located near the full-price stores. But today most off-price stores are not following those traditional limits. In many off-price apparel stores, as much as 80 to 90 percent of the products are of top quality, purchased early in the fashion season, and advertised heavily. Some off-price stores are even located in shopping malls close to the full-price stores.[7]

WHOLESALE/WAREHOUSE CLUBS

Another innovative discount institution that has developed in recent years is the warehouse club—also called a wholesale club. Actually the idea for this type of middleman was imported from Europe where it has existed for 25 years. A *warehouse club* is both a wholesaler and a retailer. Its target markets are small retailers and a select group of ultimate consumers such as employees of the government, hospitals, schools, and banks. In a typical club format, a small retailer pays a $25 membership fee. Then this retailer can buy, at a substantial discount, products to use in its business or to sell to the public. The ultimate consumers pay no membership fee, but they are charged about 5 percent above the price that the retailer customers pay.

A warehouse club will carry the same variety of goods as a large discount store. But the club will carry only one or two brands and a limited number of sizes and models. So a club may carry 4,000 different items, where a similar-sized discount store will carry 40,000. The clubs generally do no advertising. It is strictly a cash-and-carry business, credit cards are not accepted, and customers handle their own merchandise—even the heavy stuff.

A warehouse club's prices typically are 20 percent to 40 percent below supermarket and discount-store prices. The typical gross margin of a warehouse club—8 to 10 percent—is much less than that of a discount store. The percentage net profit also is less. But the *dollar* profit can be 3 times as high as for other discount retailers, primarily because of the club's huge volume of sales.

The Price Club in San Diego was the first warehouse club in the United States, and other organizations have followed the Price Club model. Warehouse clubs have been spreading throughout the country at a rapid rate. By 1990 warehouse clubs are expected to be a $20 *billion* industry. Already, chains of warehouse clubs are being operated by some of the large discount retailers—Sam's Warehouse Club is a division

[7]For more on off-price retailing, see Jack G. Kaikati, "Don't Discount Off-Price Retailers," *Harvard Business Review*, May–June 1985, pp. 85–92; Liz Murphy, "Off-Price: No Place for the Timid," *Sales & Marketing Management*, Aug. 13, 1984, p. 61; Pat Sloan, "Gloves Off in Off-Price Battle," *Advertising Age*, Oct. 17, 1983, p. 3; and Claudia Ricci, "Discount Business Booms, Pleasing Buyers, Irking Department stores," *The Wall Street Journal*, May 3, 1983, p. 31.

of Wal-Mart Stores and BJ's Warehouse Club is owned by the Zayre discount or-ganization, for example.[8]

Nonstore Retailing

CATALOG SHOWROOMS

The catalog showroom is a form of discount retailing that has expanded considerably in recent years. The showroom features attractive displays of all the merchandise carried in the company's catalog. Customers can examine the products at their leisure. They place orders by filling out order forms and presenting the forms at a desk. Orders are filled immediately from inventory stock in the store's warehouse area. A limited number of sales people are available to help customers with products such as photo-graphic equipment, television sets, and jewelry. Catalog showrooms advertise exten-sively and use their low prices on nationally branded products as their primary selling appeal.

However, in the late 1980s catalog showrooms have run into some rough com-petitive weather. Their no-frills operations no longer enjoy a price advantage as large discounters run price-reduction sales and the warehouse clubs constantly beat the catalog prices. Consequently, several of the catalog-showroom organizations are trying to upgrade their appearance and to encourage shoppers to spend more time in the stores.[9]

There are four broad categories of retailing which for the most part occur away from the regular retail store. The four are in-home personal selling, telephone selling, mail-order selling, and automatic vending. Each one may be used by producers and also by retailers. Producers and retailers alike should be well aware of these nonstore retailing methods, because today they constitute a significant proportion of total retail trade.[10]

IN-HOME PERSONAL SELLING

Door-to-door selling is one of the oldest retailing methods in history. Sometimes it simply involves house-to-house canvassing, without any advance selection of pros-pects. More likely, however, there is an initial contact in a store or by phone, or a mailed-in coupon. **"Party-plan"** selling is also included in this category. A hostess invites some friends to a party. These guests understand that a sales person—say, for a cosmetics or a housewares company—will be making a sales presentation at the party. The sales representative has a larger prospective market under more favorable conditions than if these "guests" were approached individually on a house-to-house basis. And the guests get to do their shopping in a pleasant, friendly atmosphere.

In-home personal selling is used both by producers and by retailers. You probably know of some manufacturing firms that use this method—Avon cosmetics, Electrolux vacuum cleaners, World Book encyclopedias, Tupperware food containers, and Am-

[8]For more on warehouse clubs, see Robert Levy, "Make Way for Warehouse Clubs," *Dun's Business Monthly*, April 1985, p. 76; Arthur Bragg, "Wholesale Clubs: Selling by the Forklift," *Sales & Market-ing Management*, May 13, 1985, p. 69; and "Boom Times in a Bargain Hunter's Paradise," *Business Week*, Mar. 11, 1985, p. 116.

[9]Lee Kimberley Carpenter, "Catalog Showrooms Revamp to Keep Their Identity," *Business Week*, June 10, 1985, p. 117.

[10]In the business world, in-home selling is called *direct selling*, while telephone selling and mail-order selling are called *direct marketing*—an unfortunately confusing use of these terms.

As old as time—yet in-home selling thrives as it adapts to the environment.

way household products, for example. Drapery and home-heating departments in department stores often have their sales people call directly on consumers at their homes.

In-home selling offers consumers the convenience of buying at home, but the merchandise assortment is limited and there is no opportunity to shop and compare products. For the seller, in-home selling allows the most aggressive form of retail selling, as well as the chance to demonstrate a product in the customer's home.

On the negative side, in-home selling is the most expensive form of retailing. Sales-force commissions alone usually run as high as 40 to 50 percent of the retail price. Through the years, this method of selling has acquired a bad reputation because some sales people have been nuisances or even fraudulent. Also, managing a door-to-door sales force is a real problem because good sales people are extremely hard to find and the turnover rate is very high.

TELEPHONE SELLING (TELEMARKETING)

Shopping by telephone is a long-existing method of consumer and industrial buying. And selling by telephone, likewise, has been around a long time as a method of nonstore, in-home retailing. Yet today it is being used more widely than ever. This is partly because consumers are putting higher values on time saving and convenience in shopping. With so many women now in the outside labor force, traditional consumer shopping patterns are changing. At the same time, sellers are finding that telephone selling—or "telemarketing," as they like to call it—is a productive yet low-cost method of selling.[11]

During the 1990s, however, the real growth in this type of in-home buying and selling is expected to involve sophisticated systems of computer- and television-assisted shopping. This "teleshopping" provides the consumer with a two-way com-

---

[11]See Kenneth C. Schneider, "Telemarketing as a Promotional Tool—Its Effects and Side Effects," *Journal of Consumer Marketing*, Winter 1985, pp. 29–39; and Joel Dreyfuss, "Reach Out and Sell Something," *Fortune*, Nov. 26, 1984, p. 127.

Catalog buying is convenient for busy people.

munication channel between home and store.[12] A variation of these nonstore retailing telecommunications systems is the "electronic kiosk" which is being placed in stores and in shopping malls. These kiosks contain interactive computer terminals with video screens that enable a shopper to get information about products in a given store. At some kiosks the consumers can "shop" the store and also place orders and arrange for delivery. Also, some of these kiosks link a customer directly with manufacturers.[13]

MAIL-ORDER SELLING

In addition to ordering merchandise from the traditional catalog, mail-order buying also includes any ordering by mail from an ad or from a direct-mail appeal. Originally designed primarily to reach rural markets, mail-order retailing today is appealing with success to urban buyers. Some of the mail-order houses (Sears, Penney's) are *general merchandise* houses that offer an exceptionally wide variety of product lines. Other mail-order institutions might be termed *specialty* houses in that they limit the number of lines they carry—books, records, garden supplies, or food, for example.

Mail-order retailing enjoys some competitive advantages. Operating costs and prices usually are lower than for in-store retailing. A wide variety of merchandise is

[12]See George P. Moschis, Jac L. Goldstucker, and Thomas J. Stanley, "At-Home Shopping: Will Consumers Let Their Computers Do the Walking?" *Business Horizons,* March–April 1985, pp. 22–29.

[13]See Jeffrey Lener, "Shopping in the 'Storeless Store,' " *Adweek,* June 1985, p. 18; "Electronistore Debuts," *Marketing News,* May 25, 1985, p. 1; and Joel E. Urbany and W. Wayne Talarzyk, "Videotex: Implications for Retailing," *Journal of Retailing,* Fall 1983, pp. 76–92.

offered by general merchandise houses. Also, the consumer can shop at leisure from the catalog and then place an order without the inconvenience of going to a store.

On the other hand, customers must place their orders without actually seeing the merchandise (unless the items are displayed at catalog stores). This disadvantage is counteracted to some extent by liberal return privileges, guarantees, and excellent catalog presentations. Mail-order houses have little flexibility. Catalogs are costly and must be prepared long before they are issued. Price changes and new merchandise offerings can be announced only by issuing supplementary catalogs, which are a weak selling tool.[14]

AUTOMATIC VENDING

Today an amazingly wide variety of products are sold through coin-operated machines that automatically sell merchandise (or services) without the presence of a sales clerk. According to *Vend* magazine, products sold through vending machines account for about 1.5 percent of total retail trade. The bulk of this volume comes from cigarettes, soft drinks, candy, and hot beverages. Such products and others sold through vending machines typically have low unit value and low markups, so they are relatively expensive to sell through stores.

Vending machines can expand a firm's market by reaching customers where and when it is not feasible for stores to do so. In addition, many stores use vending machines as a complementary form of retailing. Another major expanding market for automatic vending is in-plant feeding, that is, the provision of meals for employees of factories and offices.

The outlook for this "robot retailing" is promising, but automatic vending still faces major problems. Operating costs are high, and there is a continual need for machine repair. The prices of automatically vended products are frequently higher than store prices for the same products. Products that can be sold successfully by machine must be well-known, presold brands with a high rate of turnover. They must be reasonably low in unit value, small and uniform in size and weight, and generally of a convenience goods nature. Only a limited amount of processing can be accomplished at the vending machine.

Sometimes these are the only "stores" that are open.

THE FUTURE IN RETAILING

Looking to the 1990s, retailing management faces challenges perhaps unequaled since the Depression of the 1930s. Population increases and economic growth have slowed down considerably. The costs of capital, energy, and other key resources have gone way up. Competition is particularly fierce and consumers are more demanding. Computer technology is affecting many aspects of consumer and retailer behavior. Consumerism and government restrictions affecting retailing are not likely to subside. These environmental forces are shaping several broad, significant trends in retailing.[15]

[14] See James R. Lumpkin and Jon M. Hawes, "Retailing without Stores: An Examination of Catalog Shoppers," *Journal of Business Research*, April 1985, pp. 139–151; "Marketing by Mailbox (It's a Revolution, Folks)," a special report on direct-mail selling, *Sales & Marketing Management*, Jan. 14, 1985, pp. 39ff.

[15] For further discussion of the environmental changes that will affect retailing in the future, see Jagdish N. Sheth, "Emerging Trends for the Retailing Industry," *Journal of Retailing*, Fall 1983, pp. 6–18.

For an in-depth look into the future, see Eleanor G. May, C. William Ress, and Walter J. Salmon, *Future Trends in Retailing*, Marketing Science Institute, Cambridge, Mass., report no. 85–102, 1985. Also see Aimée Stern, "Retailers Restructure," *Dun's Business Month*, February 1986, pp. 28–32.

One of these trends is toward more professional management. Traditionally, store presidents came up through the merchandising ranks and were "good merchants." Today's economic and competitive conditions call for executives with a more rounded managerial capability, along with the traditional merchandising skills. Companies are especially stressing profit performance measures (return on investment, for example) and other internal financial controls. Prior to the mid-1980s, strategic planning generally had not been adopted by retailing executives. However, now there seems to be a growing awareness of the value of this management tool.

Out of dangerously low profit margins is also coming an intensified drive for **increased productivity** in retailing. To this end, virtually all kinds of consumer products are being sold, at least to some extent, on a self-service basis. This permits retailers to reduce their salary and wage cost, which typically is their largest single operating expense. Automated materials-handling systems are helping to cut physical distribution expenses. Computers are making retailers' information systems—for accounting, inventory control, and marketing research—more effective. In fact, better information systems are leading to improved information management in all phases of operations in many retailing organizations.

Another trend is the continuing move toward **scrambled merchandising,** which results in more intense competition among traditionally different types of stores. That is, in the constant search for higher-margin items, one type of store will add products that traditionally were handled by other types of outlets. This forces wholesalers and manufacturers to change their channel systems and retailers to adjust their marketing programs to meet the challenge of scrambled merchandising.

An interesting **polarity in store size and merchandise assortment** is developing in retailing. At one pole are the huge mass-merchandising operations of discount stores and department stores, with their tremendously wide variety of products. At the other pole is the small specialty shop—the boutique type of store. As retailers more carefully identify and segment their markets, these specialty stores and retailers are increasing in numbers and importance.

We can anticipate a considerable increase in nonstore retailing in the coming years. Mail-order selling and telephone selling are expected to expand much faster than in-store selling. The real potential on the horizon for nonstore retailing is in the area of computer-based ordering systems coupled with television.

Changing life-styles—especially among women, who, incidentally, still do most of the shopping—are a major factor stimulating the growth in nonstore retailing. Close to 60 percent of all married women are employed outside the home and have little time to shop. So the timesaving convenience and the product information provided by nonstore retailing are attractive to this growing market segment.

Through the years, many of the evolutionary changes in retailing have followed a cyclical pattern called the **wheel of retailing.** As M. P. McNair has succinctly explained it:[16] "The cycle frequently begins with the bold new concept, the innovation. The innovator has an idea for a new kind of distributive enterprise. At the outset he is ridiculed, condemned as "illegitimate." Bankers and investors are leery of him.

[16]M. P. McNair, "Significant Trends and Developments in the Postwar Period," in A. B. Smith (ed.), *Competitive Distribution in a Free, High-Level Economy and Its Implications for the University,* The University of Pittsburgh Press, Pittsburgh, 1958, pp. 17–18.

But he attracts the public on the basis of a price appeal made possible by the low operating costs inherent in his innovation. As he goes along he trades up, improves the quality of his merchandise, improves the appearance and standing of his store, attains greater responsibility. Then, if he is successful, comes the period of growth, the period when he is taking business away from the established distribution channels that have clung to the old methods. Repeatedly something like this has happened in American distribution. . . .''

''The maturity phase soon tends to be followed by top-heaviness, too great conservatism, a decline in the rate of return on investment, and eventual vulnerability. Vulnerability to what? Vulnerability to the next revolution of the wheel, to the next fellow who has the bright idea and who starts his business on a low-cost basis, slipping in under the umbrella that the old-line institutions have hoisted.''

Several instances of this familiar cycle can be observed in the past 100 years. First the department stores supplanted small retailers in the cities during the late 1800s and early 1900s. In the 1920s, mail-order houses hit their peak. In that same decade the chain stores grew at the expense of independents, particularly in the grocery store field. In the 1930s, the independents retaliated with supermarkets, which proved so successful that the chain stores copied the method. In the 1950s, the discount houses—young innovators—placed tremendous pressure on department stores, which had become staid, mature institutions. By the early 1960s, the discount houses had passed the youthful stage. In the 1970s, we observed substantial growth in warehouse retailing (catalog showrooms, furniture warehouse showrooms) and the spread of supermarket-type retailing. In the 1980s we have seen the expansion of superstores and warehouse clubs, while conventional supermarkets are changing or disappearing. Now we wait to see what will be the innovations of the 1990s—perhaps they will involve automated retailing. Established retailers must be alert to meet the challenge with innovations of their own. Truly, a retailer must be willing to innovate, for the alternative is to die.

SUMMARY
■

Middlemen balance producers' outputs and consumers' wants through the activities of concentration, equalization, and dispersion. They aid considerably in creating time, place, and possession utilities. Truly, one may eliminate middlemen, but not their functions. Middlemen play a significant role in our social and economic system.

Producers and wholesalers of consumer products must understand the retail market before they can intelligently develop distribution strategies. Retailing is selling to people who are buying for personal, nonbusiness reasons. It is easy to get into retailing, but the mortality rate among retail stores is very high. The national average cost of retailing is about 27 percent of the retail selling price. Costs vary considerably, however, among the different types of retailers, and profits (as a percentage of sales) generally are very low. Retailers tend to locate where the market is, mainly in metropolitan areas. In such areas, there are several types of shopping districts such as planned suburban shopping centers and planned urban shopping malls.

We have classified retailers in four ways. First we looked at the competitive positions of large and small retailers. In the second classification (products carried), we examined the positions of department stores and limited-line stores. The third classification (type of ownership) provided an opportunity to discuss corporate chain stores and independents—especially the associations formed by small independents to compete with the large chains. Franchising in its various forms can also be attractive to independent retailers. In the fourth classification (method of operation), we discussed supermarket retailing, discount selling, and the major types of nonstore retailers.

It is obvious that retailing institutions will continue to change in the future (perhaps at an increasing rate). Retailers' success will depend to a great extent upon their ability to adapt to such change.

KEY TERMS AND CONCEPTS ■

Middleman 314
Merchant and agent middleman 314
Channel of distribution 314
Concentration, equalization, and dispersion of middlemen 316
Time and place utilities 316
Retailing 316
Retail sale 316
Retailer 317
Cost of retailing 318
Downtown shopping district 319
Planned suburban shopping center 320
Department store 325
Limited-line store 326
Scrambled merchandising 326
Specialty store 326

Corporate chain store 326
Voluntary chain (wholesaler-sponsored) 329
Retailer cooperative chain 329
Producer-sponsored franchise system 329
Entrepreneurship franchising 330
Supermarket retailing 331
Discount retailing 333
Nonstore retailing: 336
In-home personal selling 336
Telephone selling (telemarketing) 337
Mail-order selling 338
Automatic vending 339
Wheel-of-retailing concept 340

QUESTIONS AND PROBLEMS ■

1. "You can eliminate middlemen, but you cannot eliminate their functions." Discuss.

2. Which of the following institutions are middlemen? Explain.

   a. Avon sales person.
   b. Electrical wholesaler.
   c. Real estate broker.
   d. Railroad.
   e. Auctioneer.
   f. Advertising agency.
   g. Grocery store.
   h. Stockbroker.
   i. Bank.
   j. Radio station.

3. Explain how time and place utility may be created in the marketing of the following products. What business institutions might be involved in creating these utilities?

   a. Sewing machines.
   b. Fresh peaches.
   c. Hydraulic grease racks used in garages and service stations.

4. Explain the terms *retailing*, *a retail sale*, and *a retailer* in light of the following situations:

   a. Avon cosmetics sales person selling door to door.
   b. Farmer selling produce door to door.
   c. Farmer selling produce at a roadside stand.
   d. Sporting goods store selling uniforms to a professional baseball team.

5. How do you account for the wide differences in operating expenses among the various types of retail stores shown in Table 14-1?

6. What is the relationship between the growth and successful development of planned suburban shopping centers and the material you studied in Chapters 5 to 8 regarding the consumer?

7. "Retailing is typically small-scale business." "There is a high degree of concentration in retailing today; the giants control the field." Reconcile these two statements, using facts and figures when appropriate.

8. Of the criteria given in this chapter for evaluating the competitive positions of large-scale and small-scale retailers, which show small stores to be in a stronger position than large-scale retailers? In light of your finding, how do you account for the numerical preponderance of small retailers?

9. What courses of action might small retailers follow to improve their competitive position?

10. What can department stores do to offset their competitive disadvantages?

11. In what ways does a corporate chain (Safeway, A&P, or Sears) differ from a voluntary chain such as IGA?

12. With all the advantages attributed to voluntary associations of independents, why do you suppose some retailers are still unaffiliated?

13. "The only significant competitive advantage that chains have over independents is greater buying power. If buying power can be equalized through antichain legislation or by having the independents join some voluntary association, then independents can compete equally with the chains." Discuss.

14. "The supermarket, with its operating expense ratio of 20 percent, is the most efficient institution in retailing today." Do you agree? In what ways might supermarkets reduce their operating expenses?

15. Name some discount houses in your community or in a nearby large city. Is there a distinction between "discount selling" and a "discount house"?

16. "House-to-house selling is the most efficient form of retail selling because it eliminates wholesalers and retail stores." Discuss.

17. "The factors that accounted for the early growth of mail-order retailing no longer exist, so we may expect a substantial decline in this form of selling." Discuss.

18. The ease of entry into retailing undoubtedly contributes to the high mortality rate among retailers, with the resultant economic waste. Should entry into retailing be restricted? If so, how could this be done?

19. What recommendations do you have for reducing the costs of retailing?

WHOLESALING: MARKETS AND INSTITUTIONS

CHAPTER GOALS

The wholesaling middlemen are the "other" middlemen, the ones that consumers rarely see. After studying this chapter, you should understand:

• The nature and importance of wholesaling:

   a. The meaning of the term *wholesaling*.

   b. The economic justification of wholesaling.

   c. What wholesalers are and how they differ from wholesaling middlemen.

• The major classes of wholesaling middlemen.

• The costs and profits in wholesaling.

• Full-service merchant wholesalers and the services they render.

• The functions of rack jobbers and limited-service wholesalers.

• The several types of agent wholesaling middlemen and the services they provide.

"We want to make people rich." Speaking was the president and chairman of Super Valu Stores, Inc., the nation's largest grocery wholesaler, whose headquarters are in Eden Prairie, a suburb of Minneapolis. And the people he was referring to are the operators of the 2,300 retail supermarkets that are affiliated with Super Valu. They are Super Valu's customers.

When you talk about a grocery wholesaler—or any kind of a wholesaler for that matter—your listeners often have a negative image of your subject. They think of a dreary, multistory building located in a crumby part of town. No way would they want their daughter to marry a wholesaler.

That image of wholesaling might have been true 50 years ago, but not today. At least not today in modern wholesaling establishments located in outlying industrial parks, using modern materials-handling equipment and computerized information systems. These firms are managed by a new breed of executive who is capable of surviving profitably in today's competitive distribution environment. Super Valu is a shining example of just such a modern wholesaling establishment.

According to Super Valu's president, his company is successful in large part because it does two things well. One is the efficient way the company operates its 16 warehouses. The other is the excellent way the company helps its customers to operate their stores. For those retailers, Super Valu provides a wide range of services—including site selection, store design, equipment financing, interior merchandise layout, employee training, promotion planning, advertising copywriting, store insurance, and management counseling.

Super Valu's philosophy is to guide and drive its retail market, rather than simply to supply it. The goal is to make its retailers profitable marketers. And judging by the financial results of the past 10 years, Super Valu is achieving that goal. As the president said, "We've got new perspectives, skilled management, and we know where we're headed." That statement epitomizes the position of today's successful wholesaling middleman.[1]

[1]Bill Saporito, "Super Valu Does Two Things Well," *Fortune*, Apr. 18, 1983, p. 114.

"Let's eliminate the middleman" and "The middleman makes all the profit" are cries that have been echoed by consumers, business people, and legislators through the years. These complaints are most often focused on the wholesaling segment of the distribution structure. Historically, the wholesaler has been a truly powerful figure in American marketing. During the past 25 to 50 years, however, many manufacturers and retailers have made successful attempts to eliminate the wholesaler from their trade channels. Yet wholesaling middlemen continue to be important, and in many cases dominant, in the distribution system for many products.

NATURE AND IMPORTANCE OF WHOLESALING

Wholesaling Broadly Defined

Wholesaling or **wholesale trade** includes the sale, and all activities directly related to the sale, of products or services to those who are buying for business use. Thus, *broadly viewed*, sales made by one manufacturer to another are wholesale transactions, and the selling manufacturer is engaged in wholesaling. A retail variety store is engaged in wholesaling when it sells pencils or envelopes to a restaurant. That is, wholesaling includes sales by any firm to any customer except to an ultimate consumer who is buying for personal, nonbusiness use. Thus, in a broad sense, all sales are either wholesale sales or retail sales. The only real criterion for distinguishing between the two is the purchaser's intended use of the product or service.

The Narrower Definition of Wholesaling

While this general definition of wholesaling is accurate, it is too broad to be useful in (1) understanding the role of wholesaling middlemen and (2) establishing channels of distribution. For analytical convenience, the definition must be limited. We are concerned here with companies that are engaged *primarily* in wholesaling. Therefore, we shall ignore retailers who occasionally make a wholesale sale. We shall also exclude the sales of manufacturers and farmers, because they are primarily engaged in production (creating form utility), and not in wholesaling.

Wholesalers and Wholesaling Middlemen

A **wholesaling middleman** is a firm engaged primarily in wholesaling. The more restrictive term **wholesaler** applies only to *merchant* middlemen engaged in wholesaling activities. (Recall that merchant middlemen are those who take title to the goods they handle.) *Wholesaling middlemen* thus is the all-inclusive term, covering both wholesalers and other wholesaling middlemen, such as agents and brokers, that do not take title to the merchandise. Thus a food broker or a manufacturers' agent is not a wholesaler but, rather, a wholesaling middleman.

Sometimes one hears the terms *jobber* and *distributor*. Although usage varies from trade to trade, in this book these terms are considered synonymous with *wholesaler*. Figure 15-1 shows these distinctions.

Economic Justification of Wholesaling

Most manufacturing companies in the United States are small and specialized. They don't have the capital needed to maintain a sales force large enough to contact the many small retailers who are their customers. Even for manufacturers that have sufficient capital, output often is too small to justify the necessary sales force. On the other hand, most retailers buy in small quantities and have only a limited knowledge of the market and sources of supply. Thus there is a gap between the retailer (buyer) and the producer (seller). The wholesaler can fill this gap by pooling the orders of many retailers and so furnish a market for the small manufacturer. At the same time, the wholesaler is performing a buying service for small retailers.

From a macromarketing point of view, wholesaling brings to the total distribution system the economies of skill, scale, and transactions. Wholesaling middlemen are marketing specialists. Their wholesaling *skills* are efficiently concentrated in a relatively few hands. This saves the duplication of effort that would occur if the many producers had to perform the wholesaling functions themselves. Economies of *scale* result from the specialization of the wholesaling middlemen who performs functions that might otherwise require several small departments run by producing firms. Wholesalers typically can perform the wholesaling functions at an operating-expense per-

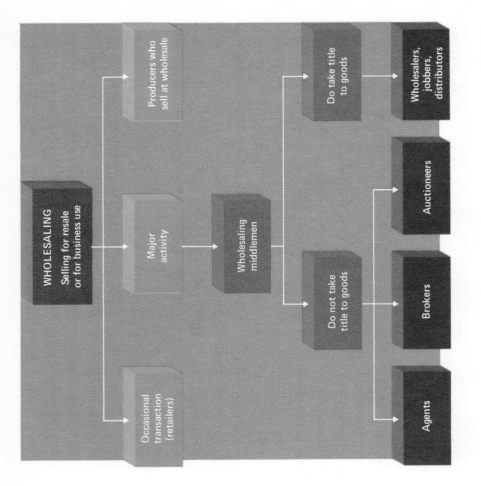

FIGURE 15-1
Wholesaling institutions.
How the general definition of wholesaling leads to our definition of wholesaling middlemen, wholesalers, and agents and brokers.

centage lower than most manufacturers can. *Transaction economies* come into play when wholesaling middlemen are introduced between producers and their customers. Assume four manufacturers want to sell to six retailers. Without a wholesaling middleman, there are 24 transactions. With one wholesaler, the number of transactions is cut to 10. That is, 4 transactions occur when the producers all sell to the wholesaler and another 6 occur when the wholesaler sells to all the retailers (Fig. 15-2).

Size of the Wholesale Market

In 1982 there were about 416,000 wholesaling establishments in the United States, with a total annual sales volume of $1,998 billion. That is almost $2 *trillion!* As table 15-1 shows, the number of establishments has increased substantially over the past three decades. The 1982 total wholesale sales represented an increase of 59 percent over 1977 and 334 percent over 1967. Of course, a substantial part of this increase is traceable to the general rise in prices. But even if each year's wholesale trade were expressed in constant dollars, we would still see a major increase.

Classification of Wholesaling Middlemen

Any attempt to classify wholesaling middlemen in a meaningful way is a precarious project. It is easy to get lost in a maze of categories because, in real life, these middlemen vary greatly in (1) the products they carry, (2) the markets they sell to,

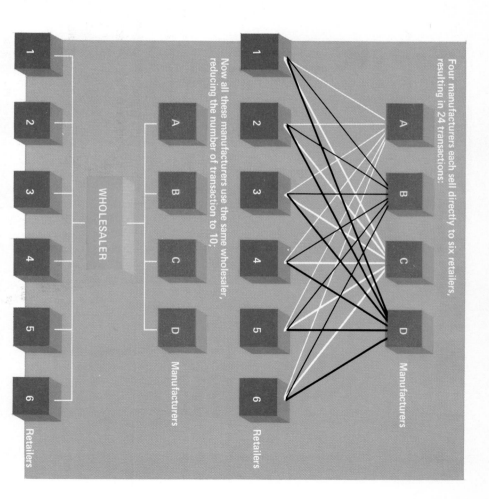

FIGURE 15-2
The economy of transactions in wholesaling.

Four manufacturers each sell directly to six retailers, resulting in 24 transactions:

Now all these manufacturers use the same wholesaler, reducing the number of transaction to 10:

WHOLESALER

Manufacturers

Retailers

TABLE 15-1

TOTAL WHOLESALE TRADE IN UNITED STATES COMPARED WITH RETAIL SALES

Total wholesale sales in 1982 increased 59 percent over 1977 and 334 percent over 1967. How do these figures compare with growth in retail sales?

	Number of wholesaling establishments	Wholesale sales (in billions of dollars)	Retail sales (in billions of dollars)
1982	416,000	1,998	1,066
1977	383,000	1,258	723
1972	370,000	695	459
1967	311,000	460	310
1958	287,000	286	200

Source: U.S. Census of Retail Trade and Wholesale Trade, for respective years.

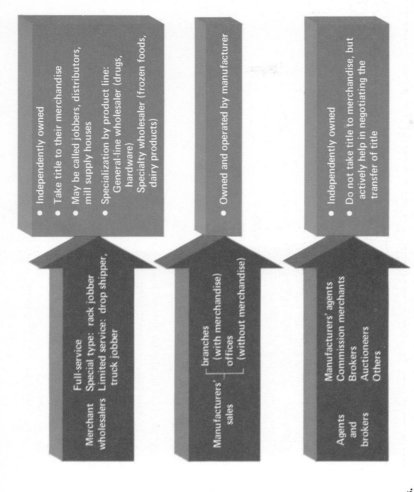

Merchant wholesalers	Full service
	Special type: rack jobber
	Limited service: drop shipper,
	truck jobber
		• Independently owned
		• Take title to their merchandise
		• May be called jobbers, distributors, mill supply houses
		• Specialization by product line:
		  General-line wholesaler (drugs, hardware)
		  Specialty wholesaler (frozen foods, dairy products)

Manufacturers' sales	branches (with merchandise) offices (without merchandise)	• Owned and operated by manufacturer
Agents and brokers	Manufacturers' agents Commission merchants Brokers Auctioneers Others	• Independently owned • Do not take title to merchandise, but actively help in negotiating the transfer of title

FIGURE 15-3
Types of wholesaling institutions.

and (3) the methods of operation they use. To minimize the confusion, we will use the classification scheme shown in Fig. 15-3. There, all wholesaling middlemen are grouped into only three broad categories—merchant wholesalers, manufacturers' sales branches and offices, and agents and brokers. These three groups are the classifications used in the Census of Business, which is the major source of quantitative data covering wholesaling institutions and markets. Later in this chapter we shall discuss merchant wholesalers and agents and brokers in more detail.

MERCHANT WHOLESALERS

These are the firms we usually refer to as wholesalers, jobbers, or industrial distributors. They typically are independently owned, and they take title to the merchandise they handle. They form the largest single segment of wholesaling firms when measured either by sales or by number of establishments. Merchant wholesalers account for 58 percent of the total wholesale trade, and their share of wholesale trade has steadily increased over the past 30 years.

MANUFACTURERS' SALES BRANCHES AND OFFICES

These establishments are owned and operated by manufacturers, but they are physically separated from the manufacturing plants. The distinction between a sales branch and a sales office is that a branch carries merchandise stock and an office does not.

Sales offices support the local effort.

In 1982, sales branches and offices accounted for 31 percent of the total wholesale trade.

AGENTS AND BROKERS

Agents and brokers do *not* take title to the merchandise they handle, but they do actively negotiate the purchase or sale of products for their principals. The main types of agent middlemen are manufacturers' agents, commission merchants (in the marketing of agricultural products), and brokers. As a group, agents and brokers represented 11 percent of total wholesale trade in 1982.

Some other bases used in classifying the wholesaling business are reflected in Fig. 15-3. For example, wholesaling middlemen may be grouped by:

- *Ownership of products:* Merchant wholesalers versus agent middlemen.
- *Ownership of establishment:* Manufacturers' sales branches versus independent merchants and agents.
- *Range of services offered:* Full-service wholesalers versus limited-service firms.
- *Depth and breadth of line carried:* General-line wholesalers (drugs, hardware) versus specialty firms (frozen foods, dairy products).

The quantitative measures shown in Table 15-2 for the three groups of wholesaling middlemen reflect their current status and sales trends. There has been stability among these groups over the past 30 years. The only major change seems to be that merchant wholesalers have increased their market share at the expense of the other two major types of wholesaling establishments. As market potentials have increased in various areas, many manufacturers have established branches in territories once served by agent middlemen.

TABLE 15-2   WHOLESALE TRADE AND PERCENTAGE OF SALES BY TYPE OF OPERATION
Merchant wholesalers have maintained the largest and increasing share of the market—now almost 60 percent. How do you account for the relative decline of agents and brokers?

Type of operation	Number of establishments (in thousands)	1982 sales (in billions of dollars)	% of total sales 1982	% of total sales 1972	% of total sales 1963
United States, total	416	1,998	100	100	100
Merchant wholesalers	338	1,159	58	51	48
Manufacturers' sales offices and branches	38	627	31	37	37
Agents and brokers:	40	212	11	12	15
Manufacturers' agents	22	67	3	3	3
Brokers	7	72	4	3	4
Commission merchants	7	35	2	3	3
Others	4	38	2	3	5

Source: Adapted from U.S. Census of Wholesale Trade, for respective years.

Share of Wholesale Trade

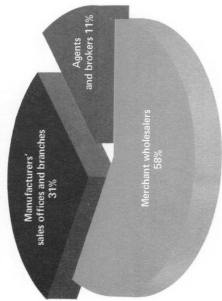

Customers of Wholesaling Middlemen

One might expect that total retail sales would be considerably higher than total wholesale trade, because the retail price of a given product is higher than the wholesale price. Also, many products sold at retail never pass through a wholesaler's establishment and so are excluded from total wholesale sales. Total sales figures belie this particular line of reasoning (see Table 15-1). In each year, the volume of wholesale trade is about 40 percent higher than total retail sales.

TABLE 15-3   SALES OF WHOLESALE ESTABLISHMENTS BY CLASS OF CUSTOMER, SELECTED YEARS
For many years a steadily declining share of merchant wholesalers' sales have been made to retailers. How do you account for this? Who are the main customers of agents and brokers?

TypeType of operation	Year	Total %	Retailers for resale	Industrial, business, or professional users	Other wholesale establishments for resale	Others (mainly export markets)
Merchant wholesalers	1982	100	28	34	25	13
	1972	100	35	42	15	8
	1967	100	39	39	15	8
Manufacturers' sales branches and offices	1982	100	32	39	23	6
	1972	100	36	42	16	6
	1963	100	32	44	19	4
Agents and brokers	1982	100	20	34	37	9
	1972	100	21	42	27	10
	1967	100	18	42	32	8

Source: U.S. Census of Business, Wholesale Trade, for respective years.

Operating Expenses and Profits of Wholesaling Middlemen

The explanation of this seemingly upside-down situation may be found in an analysis of the customers of wholesaling middlemen (Table 15-3). Almost three-quarters of merchant wholesalers' sales are made to customers *other than* retailers. That is, large quantities of *industrial* products are now sold through merchant whole-salers. Moreover, sales by the other types of wholesaling middlemen show this same pattern. Thus, overall, sales to retailers account for less than half of total sales by wholesaling establishments.

Another trend implicit in Table 15-3 is the increase in the percentage of consumer goods sold directly to retailers by producers. Yet, in spite of this increased bypass-ing of the wholesaler, wholesaling is on the upswing—which is indicative of the usefulness of wholesaling to the business world.

The average total operating expenses for all wholesaling middlemen combined has been estimated at about 10 to 11 percent of *wholesale* sales. It has also been estimated that operating expenses of retailers average about 27 percent of *retail* sales. Therefore, on a broad average, the expenses of wholesaling middlemen take about 8 percent of the consumer's dollar. (Recall Fig. 14-3.)

EXPENSES BY TYPE OF OPERATION

Table 15-4 shows operating expenses as a percentage of net sales for the major categories of wholesaling middlemen. Merchant wholesalers have the highest average operating expenses (13 percent), and agents and brokers the lowest (4.5 percent). Sales branches of manufacturers have higher expenses than sales offices—9 percent, compared with 4.5 percent. This is so because branches incur extra costs in handling merchandise stocks.

We should be careful when interpreting these figures. For instance, we should not conclude that agents and brokers are highly efficient and merchant wholesalers

TABLE 15-4	OPERATING EXPENSES AS PERCENTAGE OF NET SALES OF WHOLESALING MIDDLEMEN, BY TYPE OF OPERATION

Merchant wholesalers have the highest operating costs (13 percent). Are they less efficient as a class than agents and brokers, whose expenses are only 4.5 percent of sales?

Type of operation	Operating expenses as % of net sales
Merchant wholesalers, total	13.0
Manufacturers' sales branches (with stocks)	9.1
Manufacturers' sales offices (without stocks)	4.5
Agents and brokers	4.5
Manufacturers' agents	6.6
Brokers	2.9
Commission merchants	5.0

Source: 1982 Census of Wholesale Trade.

inefficient because of the disparity in operating expenses. The cost differentials are traceable to the differences in the services provided by these institutions.

There are tremendous variations in the wholesaling costs for different products. Product considerations such as perishability, value in relation to bulk, special storage requirements, and technical selling needs influence the operating cost ratio. The operating expenses for a general-line grocery wholesaler run about 8 percent of sales, for example, compared with 31 percent for a wholesaler of office machines and equipment.

NET PROFIT

Net operating profit expressed as a percentage of net sales is extremely modest for wholesaling middlemen and is considerably lower than that for retailing middlemen. Wholesalers dealing in 25 product lines were surveyed in 1982.[2] Of these, wholesalers in only 6 product lines reported a median net profit of more than 3 percent of sales. The two highest-profit product lines were furniture and home furnishings (3.8 percent) and chemicals (3.8 percent). Five other groups of wholesalers (handling meat, poultry, tobacco, dairy, and confectionery products) reported less than 1.5 percent profit on net sales.

MERCHANT WHOLESALERS

As we indicated earlier, merchant wholesalers are the wholesaling middlemen that take title to the products they handle, and they account for the largest segment of wholesale trade.

Full-Service Wholesalers

Full-service wholesalers are independent merchant middlemen who generally perform a full range of wholesaling functions. These are the firms that fit the layman's image or stereotype of wholesalers. They may be called simply "wholesalers." Or they may be listed as "distributors," "mill supply houses," "industrial distributors," or "jobbers," depending upon the usage in their line of business. They may handle consumer and/or industrial products, and these goods may be manufactured or nonmanufactured, and imported or exported.

Merchant wholesalers (of manufactured products and farm products) have accounted for about one-half the total wholesale trade for over 30 years. Thus these full-service wholesalers had held their own in the competitive struggles within the distribution system. In fact, their market share has increased slightly, but steadily, over the past three decades. This has occurred in the face of competition from agents and brokers, as well as from direct-selling manufacturers and their sales offices and branches. It is presumed that wholesalers' existence is maintained by the services they render both to their customers and to their producer-suppliers. (See Table 15-5.)

This picture of stability in the full-service wholesaler's share of the market may be a bit misleading. It hides the volatility and shifting competitive positions within various industries. Wholesalers have increased their market share in some industries but have lost ground in other markets where they once dominated.

Full-service wholesalers are a vital link in many distribution channels.

[2] "The Ratios," *Dun's Business Month*, February 1983, pp. 116–117.

TABLE 15-5 WHOLESALERS' SERVICES TO CUSTOMERS AND TO PRODUCER-SUPPLIERS

1. *Buying:* Act as purchasing agents for customers. Anticipate customers' needs and have good knowledge of market and sources of supply. Enable customers to deal with only a few sales people rather than with representatives of many producers.

2. *Selling:* Provide a sales force for producers to reach small retailers and industrial users, at a lower cost than producers would incur to reach these markets. Customers often know and trust their local wholesalers more than distant suppliers.

3. *Dividing, bulk breaking:* Wholesalers buy in carload and truckload lots and then resell in case lots or less, thus providing a saving and a service to customers and producers.

4. *Transportation:* Provide quick, frequent delivery to customers, thus reducing their risks and investment in inventory. Reduce producers' and customers' freight costs by buying in large quantities.

5. *Warehousing:* Provide a service to both customers and suppliers by reducing inventory risks and costs. Wholesalers can warehouse more efficiently than any single customer or producer can do.

6. *Financing:* Grant credit to customers, sometimes for extended periods of time, thus reducing their capital requirements. Producers usually would not offer comparable credit aid to small retailers. Wholesalers also aid producers by ordering well ahead of season and by paying bills on time.

7. *Risk bearing:* We already mentioned some of the ways wholesalers reduce risks for customers and producers. In addition, simply by taking title to products, wholesalers reduce a producer's risk. Losses due to spoilage or fashion obsolescence are then borne by wholesalers.

8. *Market information:* For their customers, wholesalers supply information regarding new products, competitors' activities, special sales by producers, etc.

9. *Management services and advice:* By offering managerial services and advice, especially to retailer customers, wholesalers have significantly strengthened their own position in the market. The existence of full-service wholesalers is dependent upon the economic health and well-being of small retailers. Therefore, by helping the retailers, the wholesalers really help themselves.

Special Types of Merchant Wholesalers

Within the broad category of merchant wholesalers, there are a few subclassifications worth observing because of the special nature of their operations. Their titles reflect either the specialized nature of their work or the limited range of wholesaling services that they offer. (Recall Fig. 15-3.)

RACK JOBBERS

These firms are merchant wholesalers that began to appear about 40 years ago, primarily to supply grocery supermarkets with nonfood items. Since then, rack jobbers have expanded to serve drugstores, hardware stores, and other stores that have instituted the self-service method of retailing. The many general-line wholesalers carrying these nonfood lines could not easily sell to supermarkets for at least three reasons. First, the wholesalers' regular customers, such as drugstores or hardware stores, would complain loudly and probably withdraw their business. Second, too many different wholesalers would have to call on the supermarket to fill all the nonfood lines, and the retailer would object to seeing so many wholesalers. Third, a single supermarket ordinarily orders too small a quantity in any one nonfood line to make it profitable for a wholesaler to service that line.

One rack jobber (or a very few) can furnish all the nonfood items in a supermarket. Rack jobbers furnish the racks or shelves upon which to display the merchandise, and they stock only the fastest-moving brands on these racks. They are responsible for maintaining fully stocked racks, building attractive displays, and price-marking the merchandise. In essence, the retailers merely furnish floor or shelf space and then collect the money as the customers go through the checkout stands.

LIMITED-FUNCTION WHOLESALERS

A small group of merchant wholesalers that have received attention in marketing literature through the years—possibly more attention than their numerical importance merits—are the limited-function wholesalers. These are merchant middlemen who do not perform all the usual wholesaling functions. The activities of most of these wholesalers are concentrated in a few product lines. The major types of limited-function wholesalers are truck jobbers, drop shippers, and retailer cooperative warehouses. The retailer cooperative warehouse was discussed in the preceding chapter.

Truck distributors or jobbers (sometimes still called "wagon jobbers" in memory of the days when they used a horse and wagon) are specialty wholesalers, chiefly in the food field. Each jobber carries a nationally advertised brand of fast-moving and perishable or semiperishable goods, such as candies, dairy products, potato chips, and tobacco products. The unique feature of their method of operation is that they sell and deliver merchandising during their calls. Their competitive advantage lies in their ability to furnish fresh products so frequently that retailers can buy perishable goods in small amounts to minimize the risk of loss. The major limitation of truck jobbers is their high operating cost ratio. This is caused primarily by the small order size and the inefficient use of delivery equipment. A truck is an expensive warehouse.

Drop shippers, sometimes called "desk jobbers," get their name from the fact that the merchandise they sell is delivered from the manufacturer to the customer and is called a "drop shipment." Drop shippers take title to the products but do not physically handle them. They operate almost entirely in coal and coke, lumber, and building materials. These products are typically sold in carload quantities, and freight is high in comparison with their unit value. Thus, it is desirable to minimize the physical handling of the product.

Truck jobbers frequently are used in the distribution channels for perishables.

AGENT WHOLESALING MIDDLEMEN

Agents and brokers (agent middlemen) are distinguished from merchant wholesalers in two important respects: Agent middlemen do *not* take title to the merchandise, and they typically perform fewer services for their clients and principals. (See Table 15-6.) For these reasons, the operating expenses for agents and brokers averaged only 4.5 percent of net sales in 1982, compared with 13 percent for merchant wholesalers. (See Table 15-4.) On the basis of sales volume, the major types of agent middlemen are manufacturers' agents, brokers, and commission merchants. Other types include auction companies, selling agents, import agents, and export agents.

TABLE 15-6   SERVICES PROVIDED BY AGENT WHOLESALING MIDDLEMEN

Services	Manufacturers' agents	Selling agents	Brokers	Commission merchants
Provides buying services	Yes	Yes	Some	Yes
Provides selling services	Yes	Yes	Yes	Yes
Carries inventory stocks	Sometimes	No	No	Yes
Delivers the products	Sometimes	No	No	Yes
Provides market information	Yes	Yes	Yes	Yes
Sets prices and terms of sale	No	Yes	No	No
Grants credit to customers	No	Yes	No	Sometimes
Reduces producers' credit risks	No	Sometimes	No	No
Sells producers' full line	No	Yes	No	No
Has continuing relationship with producer throughout year	Yes	Yes	Sometimes	No
Manufacturer uses own sales force along with agents	Sometimes	No	No	No
Manufacturer uses same agent for entire market	No	Yes	No	No

The relative importance of agents and brokers in wholesale trade has declined over the past 40 years. Their market share has dropped from 17 percent in the early 1950s to 11 percent in 1982. In the wholesaling of agricultural products, agent middlemen are being replaced by merchant wholesalers, or by direct sales to retailers and food processors. In the marketing of manufactured goods, agent middlemen are being supplanted by manufacturers' sales branches and offices. As manufacturers' markets grow in sales potential, it becomes more effective for them to establish their own outlets and sales force in these markets.

Manufacturers' Agents

Manufacturers' agents (frequently called *manufacturers' representatives*) are agents commissioned to sell part or all of a producer's products in particular territories. The agents are independent and are in no way employees of the manufacturers. They have little or no control over the prices and terms of sale; these are established by the manufacturer. Because a manufacturers' agent sells in a limited territory, each producer typically uses several agents. Unlike brokers, manufacturers' agents have continuing, year-round relationships with their principals. Each agent usually represents several noncompeting manufacturers of related products. The agent can pool into one profitable sale the small orders that otherwise would go to several individual manufacturers.

Manufacturers' agents are used extensively in the distribution of many types of consumer and industrial products. The main service offered to manufacturers by these agent middlemen is selling. They seek out and serve markets that manufacturers cannot profitably reach. Furthermore, a manufacturers' agent does not carry nearly so many lines as a full-service wholesaler. Consequently, the agent can offer a higher-caliber, more aggressive selling service. Operating expenses depend upon the product sold and whether the merchandise is stocked. Some representatives operate on a commission as low as 2 percent, while others charge as much as 20 percent. These commissions cover operating expenses and net profit. On an overall basis, the operating expense ratio is about 7 percent for these agents.

There are some limitations to the use of manufacturers' agents. Most agents do not carry merchandise stocks. Also, many agents cannot furnish customers with adequate technical advice or repair service; nor are they equipped to install major products.

Manufacturers' agents are most helpful in three characteristic situations:

• A small firm has a limited number of products and no sales force. Then manufacturers' agents may do all the selling.
• A firm wants to add a new and possibly unrelated line to its existing product mix. But the present sales force either is not experienced in the new line or cannot reach the new market. Then the new line may be given to manufacturers' agents. Thus, a company's own sales force and its agents may cover the same geographic market.
• A firm wishes to enter a new market that is not yet sufficiently developed to warrant the use of its own sales force. Then manufacturers' agents familiar with that market may be used.

Brokers

Brokers are used in selling real estate, securities, and sometimes even fresh celery.

Brokers are agent middlemen whose prime responsibility is to bring buyers and sellers together. They furnish considerable market information regarding prices, products, and general market conditions. Brokers do not physically handle the goods. Nor do they work on a continuing basis with their principals. Most brokers work for sellers, although about 10 percent represent buyers.

Brokers have no authority to set prices. A broker simply negotiates a sale and leaves it up to the seller to accept or reject the buyer's offer. Because of the limited services provided, brokers operate on a very low cost ratio—about 3 percent of net sales.

Brokers are most prevalent in the food field. Their operation is typified by a seafood broker handling the pack from a salmon cannery. The cannery is in operation for possibly 3 months of the year. The canner employs a broker each year (the same one if relationships are mutually satisfactory) to find buyers for the salmon pack. The broker provides information regarding market prices and conditions, and the canner then informs the broker of the desired price. The broker seeks potential buyers among chain stores, wholesalers, and others. When the entire pack has been sold, the agent-principal relationship is discontinued until possibly the following year.

An evolutionary development in the food brokerage field should be noted. Through the years, many brokers have established permanent relationships with some principals. These brokers are now performing activities that would more accurately classify them as manufacturers' agents. They still call themselves "food brokers," however, and they are classed as brokers in the Census of Business.

Commission Merchants

In the marketing of many agricultural products, a widely used middleman is the commission merchant, also called a *commission man* or *commission house.* (The term *commission merchant* is actually a misnomer. This handler is really an agent middleman who, in many transactions, does not take title to the commodities which are handled.)

Auctions are important in the marketing of some products.

The commission method of operation, found mainly in large central markets, may be described briefly as follows: Assemblers in local markets (possibly local produce buyers or grain elevators) consign shipments to commission merchants in central markets. (These firms usually have established working relationships over a period of years.) The commission merchants meet trains or trucks and take charge of the shipments. It is their responsibility to handle and sell the goods. They arrange for any necessary storage, grading, and other services prior to the sale. They find buyers at the best possible prices, make the sales, and arrange for the transfer of shipments. They deduct their commissions, freight charges, and other marketing expenses, and then remit the balance as soon as possible to the local shippers.

Auction Companies

Auction companies provide (1) the auctioneers who do the selling and (2) the physical facilities for displaying the products of sellers. In this way, auction companies help the assembled buyers and sellers to complete their transactions. Auctioneers account for only about 1 percent of total wholesale trade and 7 percent of agent middlemen's sales. Yet they are extremely important in the wholesaling of used cars and some agricultural products (tobacco, livestock, fruit, and furs). Their operating expenses usually are quite low—about 3 percent of the sales they handle.

Selling Agents

A selling agent is an independent middleman who essentially takes the place of a manufacturer's entire marketing department. These agents typically perform more marketing services than any other type of agent middleman does. They also have more control and authority over their clients' marketing programs. A manufacturer will employ one selling agent to market the full output of the firm over its entire market. Although selling agents account for only 1 percent of total wholesale trade, they are quite important in the marketing of textile products and coal. They are also found to some extent in the distribution of apparel, food, lumber, and metal products. Their operating expenses average about 2 percent of sales.

FUTURE OF THE WHOLESALER

In the 1930s, it was frequently forecast that the full-function merchant wholesaler was a dying institution. Statistics in this chapter and elsewhere, however, show that merchant wholesalers have enjoyed a resurgent growth rate during the past 35 years. Today they hold a strong and significant position in the economy.

There are two basic reasons for the comeback of merchant wholesalers. One is a fuller realization of the true economic worth of their services. The other is the general improvement of their management methods and operations. The bandwagon to eliminate the wholesaler proved to be a blessing in disguise. Innumerable firms tried to bypass the wholesaler and came to realize that the net result was unsatisfactory. In many cases, it became evident that the wholesaler was able to provide manufacturers and retailers with better services, and at a lower cost.

Wholesalers are still the controlling force in the channels used by many firms. We must not conclude, however, that only low-cost wholesalers can survive in the competitive market. Even seemingly high-cost wholesalers are thriving. A high operating cost ratio is not necessarily the result of inefficiency. Instead, it is usually the result of providing more and better service.

Wholesalers are admittedly slow to adopt modern business methods and attitudes. However, they are striving to catch up in this respect. Moreover, the already evident trends shaping the future of wholesale distribution suggest that the wholesaler (1) is responsive to the business environment and (2) can effectively adapt to pressures from suppliers and customers for lower-cost distribution.

SUMMARY

Wholesaling is the selling, and all activities directly related to this selling, of products and services to those who are buying (1) to use the items in their business or (2) to resell them. Thus, in a broad sense, all sales are either wholesale sales or retail sales. The difference depends only on the purchaser's purpose in buying. Is it for a business or a nonbusiness use?

On a narrower scale, the definition of wholesaling encompasses only companies that are *primarily* engaged in wholesaling. Excluded are sales by farmers, retailers, manufacturers (except for their sales branches), and other firms usually called producers (in contrast to resellers).

The institutional structure of wholesaling middlemen (the all-inclusive term) may be divided into three groups: (1) merchant wholesalers, (2) manufacturers' sales offices and branches, and (3) agents and brokers. Total operating expenses of all wholesaling middlemen average about 10 to 11 percent of *wholesale* sales and 8 percent of *retail* sales (the consumer's dollar). Net profits in wholesaling average only about 2 percent of sales. About one-third of wholesale sales are made to retailers, and over one-half go to industrial users and other wholesalers.

Merchant wholesalers (also called jobbers or distributors) generally fit the layman's stereotype of a wholesaler. They constitute the largest category of wholesaling middlemen, in both sales volume and number of companies. These middlemen offer the widest range of wholesaling services, and consequently incur the highest operating expenses, of the three major groups of wholesaling middlemen. Merchant wholesalers have consistently accounted for about 50 percent of all wholesale sales over the past 40 years. In spite of persistent attempts to "eliminate the middleman" (namely, the merchant wholesaler), these middlemen continue to grow and thrive, thus attesting to their real economic value in our economy.

The use of agents and brokers has decreased over the years. These middlemen have been replaced in distribution channels by merchant wholesalers and by manufacturers' sales offices and branches. Agent wholesaling middlemen (manufacturers' agents, brokers, and others) remain strong in certain industries, and in geographic areas where the market potential is still too small for a producer's sales force.

KEY TERMS AND CONCEPTS

Wholesaling 346
Wholesaling middleman 346
Wholesaler 346
Manufacturer's sales office 349
Manufacturer's sales branch 349
Distributor 353
Jobber 353
Rack jobber 354

Limited-function wholesaler 355
Agent wholesaling middleman 355
Manufacturers' agent 356
Broker 357
Commission merchant 357
Auction company 358
Selling agent 358

QUESTIONS AND PROBLEMS

1. A large furniture warehouse is located in a major Midwestern city. The following conditions exist with respect to this firm:
   a. All merchandise is purchased directly from manufacturers.
   b. The warehouse is located in the low-rent wholesaling district.
   c. Merchandise remains in original crates; customers use catalogs and swatch books to see what the articles look like and what fabrics are used.
   d. About 90 percent of the customers are ultimate consumers, and they account for 85 percent of the sales volume.
   e. The firm does quite a bit of advertising, pointing out that consumers are buying at wholesale prices.
   f. Crates are not price-marked. Sales people bargain with customers.
   g. Some 10 percent of sales volume comes from sales to furniture stores.
   Is the furniture warehouse a wholesaler? Explain.

2. Which of the following are wholesaling transactions?
   a. Color Tile sells wallpaper to an apartment building contractor and also to the contractor's wife for her home.
   b. General Electric sells small motors to Whirlpool for its washing machines.
   c. A shrimp farmer sells shrimp to a local restaurant.
   d. A family has a friend who is a home decorating consultant. The family orders carpet through the consultant at 50 percent off retail. The carpet is delivered directly to the home.

3. Manufacturers' sales offices and branches have maintained a steadily increasing share of total wholesale trade, while the agents' and brokers' share has declined in each census year since 1948. What conditions account for this fact?

4. How do you account for the substantial variation in operating expenses among the major types of wholesalers shown in Table 15-4?

5. In comparing the operating expense ratio for retailers and for wholesalers in Tables 14-1 and 15-4, we see that wholesalers typically have lower operating expenses. How do you account for this?

6. What activities could full-service wholesalers discontinue in an effort to reduce operating costs?

7. What service does a full-service wholesaler provide for a manufacturer?

8. What types of retailers, other than supermarkets, offer reasonable fields for entry by rack jobbers? Explain.

9. Why would a manufacturing firm prefer to use manufacturers' agents instead of its own company sales force?

10. Why is it that manufacturers' agents often can penetrate a market faster and at a lower cost than a manufacturer's sales force?

11. What is the economic justification for the existence of brokers, especially in light of the few functions they perform?

12. Which type of wholesaling middleman, if any, is most likely to be used by each of the following? Explain your choice in each instance.
    a. A small manufacturer of a liquid glass cleaner to be sold through supermarkets.
    b. A small manufacturer of knives used for hunting, fishing, and camping.
    c. A salmon canner in Alaska packing a high-quality, unbranded product.
    d. A small-tools manufacturing firm that has its own sales force selling to the industrial market and that wishes to add backyard barbecue equipment to its line.
    e. A North Carolina textile mill producing unbranded towels, sheets, pillowcases, and blankets.

13. Looking into the future, which types of wholesaling middlemen do you think will increase in importance, and which ones will decline? Explain.

16

CHANNELS OF DISTRIBUTION: CONFLICT, COOPERATION, AND MANAGEMENT

CHAPTER GOALS

A distribution channel is a system—often with very independent parts that may be in conflict. To work effectively, a distribution channel must be well designed and well managed. After studying this chapter, you should understand:

- The distribution channel as a total system.

- The nature of the conflicts in channels of distribution:
  a. Between manufacturers and wholesalers.
  b. Between manufacturers and retailers.

- Vertical marketing systems.

- The major channels of distribution.

- The factors affecting the selection of a channel.

- The concept of intensity of distribution.

- The choice of individual middlemen.

- The legal considerations in channel management.

What do you think of a channel-of-distribution strategy where manufacturers compete with their own best customers? We call this *dual distribution*. A manufacturer sells through its company-owned retail stores at the same time it is selling to independent retailers who are competing against those company stores. For many years this strategy has been used by Hart, Schaffner & Marx (men's apparel), Florsheim in shoes, and Sherwin-Williams in paints.

What is new in the 1980s is the upsurge in this risky distribution strategy, especially among relatively small, unknown women's apparel manufacturers. These are firms such as Esprit de Corp., Murjani International (featuring a line carrying the Coca-Cola label), Eileen West of San Francisco, and Los Angeles–based Guess?, Cherokee, and L. A. Gear.

Esprit de Corp. provides a good example of a company newly engaged in dual distribution. The company sells through about 2,000 leading department stores and apparel specialty stores. Esprit also opened its first company-owned store in Hong Kong in 1983. Since then it has opened stores in Los Angeles, New Orleans, and Melbourne, Australia, and has plans to open in several other cities. The company also sends glossy mail-order catalogs to its customers. Sales volume in 1985 was about $800 million.

The company is marketing a unique design—a broad and constantly changing line of fashion sportswear and accessories that come in a variety of colors and bold prints. Esprit store sales people project a bright, breezy, upbeat image. None of them chew gum, they all smile, they all have very current, company-paid haircuts. "If she's dull, she's not part of the Esprit life."

Now why would a relatively young and small company engage in this very risky distribution strategy—especially in fashion merchandising where independent retailers traditionally are so well-entrenched? The main reason is that these manufacturers want more control over the ultimate point of sale. Fierce competition exists in the apparel industry—both at the manufacturing and at the retailing level. Many large retailers rely on their own store brands or on big designer names such as Calvin Klein, Halston, or Liz Claiborne. This situation makes it tough for small manufacturers. And the quality of personal selling in conventional retail stores leaves very much to be desired.[1]

[1]"Clothing Makers Go Straight to the Consumer," *Business Week*, Apr. 29, 1985, p. 114; and Joan Kron, "Breaking the Rules: Apparel Firm Makes Profits, Takes Risks by Flouting Traditions," *The Wall Street Journal*, June 11, 1985, p. 1.

The task of choosing and managing a distribution channel often begins with a manufacturer or producer. For that reason, we shall approach our discussion of channel design largely from the vantage point of the producer. As you will see, however, the channel problems faced by middlemen are similar to those of a producer. Furthermore, the control of the channels used by manufacturers and the freedom of choice regarding these channels may actually rest with middlemen.

CONFLICT AND COOPERATING IN DISTRIBUTION CHANNELS

Nature of the Conflicts

A channel of distribution should be treated as a unit—a total system of action. Producers and middlemen alike should understand that each of them is one component of a system designed to efficiently provide want-satisfaction to the final customer. Thus, there is a real need for coordination throughout the channel. A properly operated distribution system is a significant competitive advantage for each firm that is part of that system.

Unfortunately, a trade channel too often is treated as a fragmented assortment of competing, independently operating organizations. Manufacturers may view their own retailers as competitors. Or middlemen may be in conflict with their suppliers, rather than recognizing that the real threat is other middlemen or the distribution systems of other manufacturers. That is, the real competition is between distribution systems of different producers, rather than among the organizational units within one producer's system.

One possible reason why producers have problems with their channels of distribution is that in most organizations nobody is in charge of the channels. There is no executive with the title of "distribution channels manager" in the same sense that there is an advertising manager or a sales manager. In fact, the distribution system is the *only* major element in the marketing mix that typically does not have anyone directly in charge. Perhaps it is time for manufacturers to establish the position of channels manager in their marketing executive structure. The person in this position would be directly responsible for the managerial activities of planning, coordination, and evaluation as they are related to the firm's distribution channels.[2]

The systems concept of distribution suggests a need for cooperation among channel members. Yet power structures do exist in trade channels, and there is a continuous tug-of-war among channel members. At the root of this struggle is institutional change, several examples of which were observed in our study of retailing and wholesaling institutions. It is axiomatic that change begets conflict, and conflict very often results in change.[3]

FIRMS ON THE SAME LEVEL OF DISTRIBUTION

Horizontal conflicts may occur:

- *Between middlemen of the same type:* Hardware store versus hardware store.
- *Between different types of middlemen on the same level:* Hardware store versus paint store.

Competitive conflicts in channels of distribution may involve middlemen on the same level of distribution (horizontal conflict) or firms on different levels of distribution (vertical conflict).

[2] Donald W. Jackson, Jr., and Bruce J. Walker, "The Channel Manager: Marketing's Newest Aide?" *California Management Review*, Winter 1980, pp. 52–58.

[3] For a report on the status of theory and research regarding power and conflict in channels of distribution, see John F. Gaski, "The Theory of Power and Conflict in Channels of Distribution," *Journal of Marketing*, Summer 1984, pp. 9–29.

Motor oil plus flowers plus fresh vegetables equals scrambled merchandising.

Perhaps the main source of horizontal conflict has been the competition caused by **scrambled merchandising**—that is, the practice whereby middlemen diversify their product assortments by adding new, nontraditional merchandise lines. Grocery supermarkets, for example, have added toiletries, drugs, clothing, magazines, small appliances, records, alcoholic beverages, and other nonfood lines. The retailers who traditionally sell these lines have become irritated both at the grocery stores for diversifying and at manufacturers for using these "unorthodox" channels.

Product proliferation, and the resultant crossing of traditional channel lines, may stem from the market, the middleman, or the manufacturer. Consumers (the *market*) prefer convenient, one-stop shopping, so stores broaden their product offerings to satisfy this want. *Middlemen* constantly seek to add new products with higher gross margins or to add new lines in the hope of increasing customer traffic. *Manufacturers* add new types of outlets to expand their markets or to reduce unit production costs. All these efforts toward product or channel expansion only intensify the degree of channel conflict.

FIRMS ON DIFFERENT LEVELS OF DISTRIBUTION

Perhaps the most severe competitive conflicts in distribution systems today are of a vertical nature—that is:

- *Between producer and wholesaler:* Manufacturers may attempt to bypass wholesalers and sell directly to retailers.
- *Between producer and retailer:* Producers compete with retailers by selling from house to house or by selling through their producer-owned retail stores.

The remainder of this section on conflict is devoted to the *vertical* types of conflict.

Who Controls the Channels?

In marketing literature, authors have generally taken a manufacturer-oriented approach to channels of distribution. The implication is that manufacturers are the ones that make the decisions regarding the type of outlet, the number of outlets, and even the selection of individual outlets. This is a one-sided point of view. Actually, middlemen

Large retailers often have control their channels of distribution.

often have considerable freedom to make their own choices in establishing channels. Certainly the name Macy's, Safeway, or Sears means more to consumers than most of the brands sold in these stores. Large retailers today are challenging manufacturers for channel control, just as the manufacturers challenged wholesalers 50 to 60 years ago. Even small retailers may be quite influential in local markets because their prestige may be greater than that of their suppliers.

Actually, the questions of who *is* the channel leader and who *should* be remain largely unsettled. The position that supports leadership by the manufacturer is production-oriented. That is, manufacturers create the new products, and they need increasing sales volumes to derive the benefits of large-scale operations. One can also argue that the retailers should be the leaders under the marketing concept—standing closest to the consumers, knowing their wants, and being their purchasing agents. Perhaps the best answer to the channel-control question is a compromise—a balance of power—rather than domination by any one level of a distribution channel.

During the past 60 years, a significant channel conflict has occurred between the manufacturer and the wholesaler. The conflict stems from manufacturers' attempts to bypass wholesalers and deal directly with retailers. Ordinarily, this battle is between the producers and wholesalers of manufactured *consumer* products. It usually does not involve wholesaling middlemen for industrial products because there is a tradition of direct sale in industrial marketing. Where middlemen *are* used, the need for their services has long been recognized.

HISTORICAL BACKGROUND OF THE CONFLICT

The clash of interests between wholesalers and manufacturers can be best understood by reviewing (1) the position of the wholesaler before 1920, (2) the changing position of the manufacturer over the years, (3) the changing position of the retailers since 1920, and (4) the net effect these changes have had on the wholesalers and manufacturers.

Historically, *wholesalers* occupied a position of major importance in distribution systems. Before 1920, they were dominant because manufacturers and retailers were small and poorly financed. In addition, retailers were widely dispersed over the country. In effect, the wholesaler serves as a sales force for the manufacturer and as a purchasing agent for the retailer.

As a result of the risks they took and the broad scale of their services, the wholesalers had high operating costs. To cover these costs, they needed a high gross margin. Through the nineteenth century and the early part of the twentieth, wholesaler institutions became complacent. These firms did not adjust to changing economic and social conditions.

During the last half of the nineteenth century and the first part of the twentieth, the position of the *manufacturer* changed substantially. Manufacturing became more efficient. They were quick to learn that the best means of achieving increased volume was through a change in marketing methods. Aggressive selling effort, lower prices, product identification through branding, and advertising were recognized as keys to mass markets. Once the manufacturers embarked upon these programs, they balked at giving wholesalers their customary wide margin on sales—sales that the manufacturers' policies were now stimulating.

After World War I, the position of the *retailer* changed considerably. Large-scale retailing institutions developed in great numbers, and retail markets became concentrated in and around metropolitan centers. Large-scale operations entailed increased buying power, well-financed retailers, and better-managed firms. Large-scale retailers thus were economically able to assume many wholesaling functions. All these factors encouraged retailers to purchase their merchandise directly from manufacturers.

Wholesalers were caught between large-scale, direct-buying retailers on the one hand and large-scale, direct-selling manufacturers on the other. The wholesalers saw their importance being reduced. Yet they realized they could not afford to promote aggressively the products of any one manufacturer, and they resented any cut in their discount margin.

THE VIEW FROM EACH SIDE TODAY

When manufacturers prefer to bypass wholesalers and sell directly to retailers or consumers, it is basically because (1) the manufacturers are dissatisfied with the wholesalers' services or (2) the market conditions call for direct sale. The wholesalers, in turn, are often unhappy with the actions of manufacturers. The arguments voiced by each side are summarized in Table 16–1.

COURSES OF ACTION OPEN TO MANUFACTURERS

If manufacturers wish to bypass wholesalers, there are four possible courses of action to choose from. Each of these alternatives places a greater financial burden on manufacturers and adds immeasurably to their management problems. They must operate their own sales force and handle the physical distribution of their products. And direct-selling manufacturers face competition from their former wholesalers, which are now selling competitive products.

• *Sell directly to retailers.* Under certain market and product conditions, selling directly to retailers is a reasonable alternative. An ideal retail *market* for direct selling is one made up of large-scale retailers who buy in large quantities from central buying offices. In addition, it is often profitable to sell directly to specialty stores (shoes, clothing, photographic equipment) that buy large quantities of a limited line of products.

Direct selling is advantageous when the *product* (1) is subject to physical or fashion perishability, (2) carries a high unit price, (3) is custom-made, or (4) requires mechanical servicing and installation.

• *Establish sales offices or branches.* This variation of the first alternative is frequently adopted by a producer with a large sales force that can be managed more effectively on a decentralized basis. For such a sales force to operate profitably, essentially the same market and product conditions are required as for the direct-selling course of action.

• *Sell directly to consumers.* In Chapter 14 we discussed various direct-to-consumer distribution methods. Producers may employ house-to-house or mail-order selling. They may establish their own retail stores or sell directly to consumers at the point of production.

• *Use a missionary sales force.* As a compromise, when manufacturers prefer to use

TABLE 16–1 MANUFACTURERS VERSUS WHOLESALERS: THE CONTROVERSY TODAY

From manufacturers' point of view:

1. Wholesalers fail to promote products aggressively. Wholesalers generally concur with this charge. Since they usually carry thousands of items, it is not possible for their sales forces even to mention each item to a prospective customer, much less try to sell each item.

2. Wholesalers no longer perform the storage services that producers were accustomed to. Improvements in transportation and communication enable wholesalers to carry smaller inventories, thus shifting the storage function back to the manufacturers.

3. Some wholesalers promote their own brands in direct competition with manufacturers' brands.

4. Wholesalers' services cost too much. The manufacturers believe they can do the job at a lower cost. However, this may be a mistaken assumption. Many producers have learned the hard way that bypassing wholesalers may actually increase the cost of marketing or result in poor market coverage.

5. Manufacturers want closer market contact. They want control over their products for a greater part of the route to the final customer.

6. Some products may need rapid physical distribution because they are perishable or are subject to fashion obsolescence, and the producer–retailer channel is faster.

7. Large-scale retailers usually prefer to buy directly from manufacturers.

From wholesalers' point of view:

1. Manufacturers do not understand that the primary obligation of wholesalers is to serve their customers. Serving the manufacturer is only secondary.

2. Manufacturers expect too much. Wholesalers' discounts are not high enough to justify the level of warehousing and promotion expected by producers.

3. Manufacturers skim the cream off the market. That is, they use wholesalers only in the early stages of territorial development or in the least profitable segments of the market. In the concentrated, profitable areas or after a new market has been developed, manufacturers bypass the wholesalers and sell directly to retailers or industrial users. This observation is accurate. However, wholesalers should understand that their real value lies in their being able to reach markets the manufacturers themselves cannot penetrate profitably.

wholesalers but also want aggressive selling, they may employ missionary sales people. Also known as promotional sales people, detail men, or factory representatives, these missionary sales people perform a number of services. Typically, a missionary sales person calls upon a retailer and aggressively promotes the product of the manufacturer. Any orders the sales person secures are passed on to the jobber, who receives the normal commission. Missionary sales people may be used to install point-of-purchase displays in retail stores or to introduce new items to retailers.

COURSES OF ACTION OPEN TO WHOLESALERS

Wholesalers too can adopt measures to improve their competitive position. These alternatives are attempts (1) to improve the wholesaler's efficiency to such a level that neither suppliers nor customers find it profitable to bypass the wholesaler and (2) to tie the retailers to the wholesaler.

- *Improve internal management.* Many wholesalers have modernized their establishments and upgraded the caliber of their management. New, functional, single-story warehouses have been built outside the congested downtown areas, and mechanized materials-handling equipment has been installed. Electronic data processing equipment has streamlined accounting and reduced inventory losses. Many wholesalers have adopted selective selling. That is, less profitable accounts are visited less frequently, and some customers may be solicited only by mail or telephone. These and other innovations have generally lowered operating costs or have given far better service for the same money.

- *Provide management assistance for retailers.* Wholesalers generally realized that anything they can do to improve retailers' operations is really in the wholesalers' interest. They can help retailers improve store layouts and install better accounting and inventory-control systems. They can also help retailers in selecting and promoting their merchandise.

- *Form voluntary chains.* In a voluntary chain (discussed in Chapter 14), a wholesaler enters into a contract with several retailers, agreeing to furnish management services and large-volume buying advantages. In turn, the retailers agree to do all, or almost all, of their buying from the wholesaler.

- *Develop their own brands.* Many large wholesalers have successfully established their own brands. If a wholesaler is connected with a voluntary chain of retailers, the chain provides the wholesaler's brand with a built-in market.

Manufacturer versus Retailer

Today, perhaps even more significant than the conflict between manufacturers and wholesalers is the struggle for channel control that goes on between manufacturers and retailers. A very basic reason for the conflict is this: *"The people who manufacture the goods and the people who move the goods into the hands of the ultimate consumer do not share the same business philosophy and do not talk essentially the same language."*[4] In manufacturing corporations, the executives' point of view is typically characterized as a psychology of *growth*. Their goals are essentially dynamic and evolving. In sharp contrast, the pscyhology of small and medium-sized retailers is essentially *static* in nature. Their goals are well defined and are far more limited than those of manufacturing corporation executives. At some point, the retailer attains (and tends to maintain) a continuously satisfying plateau.

DOMINATION VERSUS COOPERATION

Each group has weapons it can use in its efforts to dominate the other. Manufacturers can use their promotional weapons to build strong consumer preference for their

---

[4]Warren J. Wittreich, ''Misunderstanding the Retailer,'' *Harvard Business Review,* May–June 1962, p. 147.

Some manufacturers own their retail outlets.

products. Legal weapons are available to them in the form of franchise contracts, consignment selling, or outright ownership of retail stores. As a negative method of domination, the manufacturer may refuse to sell to uncooperative retailers.

Retailers are not necessarily unarmed. By advertising effectively or by establishing their own brands, they can develop consumer preferences for their stores. They can either concentrate their purchases with one supplier or spread their buying among many sources, depending upon which strategy is most effective for them. Over the past several years, especially the large ones, have strengthened their position in channels of distribution. Retailers have upgraded the quality of their management, improved their computerized information systems, and generally employed more sophisticated marketing programs. As a result, these retailers have generally become stronger and more independent in distribution systems.

On the other side of the coin, fortunately, channel members seem to realize that the returns from cooperating with one another do outweigh any reasons for conflict. Perhaps manufacturers and retailers alike understand that it is in their own best interests to treat a distribution channel as a total system. They must consider the channel as an extension (forward or backward, as the case may be) of their own internal organizations. To implement this concept, manufacturers should do the sort of things for retailers that they do for their own marketing organizations. That is, manufacturers can provide advertising aids, training for dealer sales people, managerial assistance, and so on. Retailers can reciprocate by carrying adequate inventories, promoting the products, and building consumer goodwill.

Vertical Marketing Systems

Institutional changes in distribution during the past 30 to 40 years have led to the development of vertical marketing systems. These newer vertical marketing systems offer significant economies of scale and increased coordination in distribution. They also eliminate duplication of marketing services. Instead, they enable any given marketing activity to be performed at the most advantageous position in the system.

Vertical marketing systems may be characterized as corporate, administered, or contractual (see Table 16-2). In corporate vertical marketing systems, the production and marketing facilities are owned by the same company. As manufacturers, for example, Benetton (sportswear), Esprit de Corp. (apparel), and Standard Oil (California) each operate a number of their own retail outlets. Many large food chains run some processing facilities. Sears has ownership interests in manufacturing facilities that supply Sears.

In administered vertical marketing systems, the coordination of production and marketing activities is achieved essentially through the domination of one powerful channel member. This type of distribution is exemplified by Corning in ovenware, Gucci in luggage, Rolex in watches, and Coors beer in Western regional markets. The manufacturer's brand and market position are strong enough to get the voluntary cooperation of retailers in matters of advertising, pricing, and store display.

In contractual vertical marketing systems, independent institutions—producers, wholesalers, and retailers—are banded together by contract to achieve the necessary economic size and coordination of effort. Three types of contractual systems can be identified: wholesaler-sponsored voluntary chains, retailer-owned cooperatives, and franchise systems. All three were discussed in Chapter 14.

TABLE 16-2   TYPES OF VERTICAL MARKETING SYSTEMS

Type of system	Control maintained by:	Examples
Corporate	Ownership	Singer sewing machines, Goodyear tires, Benetton (Italian sportswear)
Administered	Economic power	Hartman luggage, General Electric, Coors beer
Contractual: Wholesaler-sponsored voluntary chain	Contract	Western Auto stores, Ben Franklin stores, IGA stores
Retailer-owned cooperative	Stock ownership by retailers	Associated Grocers
Franchise systems	Contract:	
	Manufacturer-sponsored retailers	Ford, Chrysler, and other auto dealers
	Manufacturer-sponsored wholesalers	Coca-Cola and other soft-drink bottlers
	Marketers of services	Wendy's, Midas Muffler, ComputerLand, Holiday Inn, National car rentals

A vertical marketing system through franchising.

Voluntary chains—one way wholesalers can compete.

SELECTING CHANNELS OF DISTRIBUTION

Major Channels of Distribution

With the background of the previous sections, we can now look at the major channels used by producers. Then we can discuss the factors that most influence a company's choice of its trade channels.

Even to describe the major channels is risky because it may suggest an orthodoxy that does not exist. Nevertheless, what follows is an outline of the most frequently used channels for consumer products and industrial goods. Refer to Fig. 16-1 while reading the following section.

DISTRIBUTION OF CONSUMER GOODS

Five channels are widely used in the marketing of consumer products. In each, the manufacturer also has the alternative of using sales branches or sales offices. Ob-

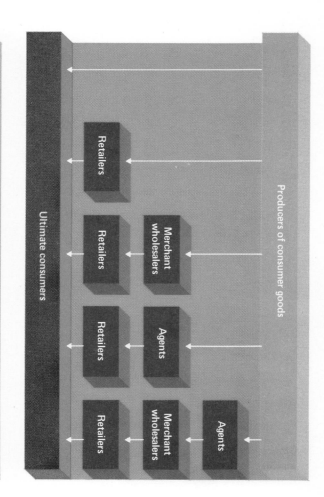

FIGURE 16-1
Major marketing channels available to producers.

viously, our suggestion that there are only five major channels is an oversimplification, but one that seems necessary if we are to discuss this unwieldy subject in a few paragraphs.

- **Producer → consumer.** The shortest, simplest channel of distribution for consumer products is from the producer to the consumer, with no middlemen involved. The producer may sell from house to house or by mail.
- **Producer → retailer → consumer.** Many large retailers buy directly from manufacturers and agricultural producers.

- **Producer → wholesaler → retailer → consumer.** If there is a "traditional" channel for consumer goods, this is it. Small retailers and small manufacturers by the thousands find this channel the only economically feasible choice.
- **Producer → agent → retailer → consumer.** Instead of using wholesalers, many producers prefer to use a manufacturers' agent or some other agent middleman to reach the retail market, especially *large-scale* retailers. For example, a manufacturer of a glass cleaner selected a food broker to reach the grocery store market, including the large chains.
- **Producer → agent → wholesaler → retailer → consumer.** To reach *small* retailers, the producers mentioned in the preceding paragraph often use agent middlemen, who in turn call on wholesalers that sell to small stores.

DISTRIBUTION OF INDUSTRIAL PRODUCTS

Four types of channels are widely used in reaching industrial users. Again, a manufacturer may use a sales branch or a sales office to reach the next institution in the channel. Or two levels of wholesalers may be used in some cases (again see Fig. 16-1).[5]

- **Producer → industrial user.** This direct channel accounts for a greater *dollar* volume of industrial products than any other distribution structure. Manufacturers of large installations, such as airplanes, generators, and heating plants, usually sell directly to users.
- **Producer → industrial distributor → user.** Producers of operating supplies and small accessory equipment frequently use industrial distributors to reach their markets. Manufacturers of building materials and air-conditioning equipment are two examples of firms that make heavy use of the industrial distributor.[6]
- **Producer → agent → user.** Firms without their own marketing departments find this a desirable channel. Also, a company that wants to introduce a new product or enter a new market may prefer to use agents rather than its own sales force.
- **Producer → agent → industrial distributor → user.** This channel is similar to the preceding one. It is used when, for some reason, it is not feasible to sell through agents directly to the industrial user. The unit sale may be too small for direct selling. Or decentralized inventory may be needed to supply users rapidly, in which case the storage services of an industrial distributor are required.

Factors Affecting Choice of Distribution Channels

Because a channel of distribution should be determined by customer buying patterns, the nature of the market is the key factor influencing management's choice of channels. Other major considerations are the product, the middlemen, and the company itself. Basically, when selecting its channels of distribution, a company should follow the criteria of the three C's—channel *control*, market *coverage*, and a *cost* that is consistent with the desired level of customer service.

Some consumer products are distributed without any middlemen.

[5]See Donald M. Jackson, Robert F. Krampf, and Leonard J. Konopa, "Factors That Affect the Length of Industrial Channels," *Industrial Marketing Management*, October 1982, pp. 263–268.

[6]See James D. Hlavacek and Tommy J. McCuistion, "Industrial Distributors—When, Who, and How?" *Harvard Business Review*, March–April 1983, pp. 96–101.

SOME GENERALIZATIONS ABOUT DISTRIBUTION CHANNELS

1. Channel design should begin with the final customer and work backward to the producer, because channels of distribution should be determined by buying habits.

2. The channels finally selected must be totally appropriate to the basic objectives of the firm's marketing program. If management sets as its goal the widest possible distribution of its product line, then obviously an exclusive franchise strategy at the retail level is not appropriate.

3. The channels should provide a firm with access to a predetermined share of the market. A manufacturer of golfing equipment seeking the broadest possible market would make a mistake by using a channel that includes only large department stores and sporting goods stores at the retail level.

4. The channels must be flexible enough so that the use of one channel does not permanently close off another. A manufacturer of small appliances (irons, toasters), for example, distributed only through appliance wholesalers, which in turn distributed to appliance retailers. The company had an offer from a drug chain to buy the products directly from the manufacturer. The appliance retailers threatened to discontinue the line if the manufacturer placed it in drugstores. Subsequently, a competitive manufacturer accepted a similar offer and profited considerably.

5. There is a high degree of interdependence among all firms in the channel for any given product. There can be no weak link in the chain if it is to be successful.

6. Channels of distribution and middlemen are always on trial, and changes occur constantly. Middlemen survive only when their existence is economically sound and socially desirable. Furthermore, new middlemen and channels arise to do new jobs or to do the existing jobs better.*

*For an interesting discussion of 10 conceptual generalizations regarding distribution systems, see Michael M. Pearson, ''Ten Distribution Myths,'' *Business Horizons*, May–June 1981, pp. 17–23. Pearson contends that the 10 points he discusses are commonly accepted assumptions that have not been validated by any quantitative measurements.

MARKET CONSIDERATIONS

Perhaps the most obvious point to consider is whether the product is intended for the consumer or industrial market. If it is going to the industrial market, of course retailers will not be included in the channel. In either case, other significant market variables should be considered:

- **Number of potential customers.** With relatively few potential customers, a manufacturer may use its own sales force to sell directly to consumers or industrial users. For a large number of customers, the manufacturer would more likely use middlemen. A related point is the number of different *industries* to which a firm sells. One company, marketing drilling equipment and supplies only to the oil industry, sold directly to users. A paper products manufacturer, on the other hand, made extensive use of industrial distributors to reach many different industries.

- **Geographic concentration of the market.** Direct sale to the textile or the garment manufacturing industry is feasible because most of the buyers are concentrated in a few geographic areas. Even in the case of a national market, some segments have a higher density rate than others. Sellers may establish sales branches in densely populated markets, but they would use middlemen in the less concentrated markets.
- **Order size.** A food product manufacturer would sell directly to large grocery chains because the large order size and total volume of business make this channel economically desirable. The same manufacturer, however, would use wholesalers to reach the small grocery stores whose orders are usually too small to justify direct sale.

PRODUCT CONSIDERATIONS

- **Unit value.** The unit value of a product affects the amount of funds available for distribution. Thus, the lower the unit value, the longer, usually, are the channels of distribution. However, when products of low unit value are sold in large quantities or are combined with other goods so that the total order is large, shorter channels may be economically feasible.
- **Perishability.** Products subject to physical or fashion perishability must be speeded through their channels. The channels usually are short.
- **Technical nature of a product.** An industrial product that is highly technical is often distributed directly to industrial users. The producer's sales force must provide considerable presale and postsale service; wholesalers normally cannot do this.

Consumer products of a technical nature provide a real distribution challenge for manufacturers. Ordinarily, manufacturers cannot sell the goods directly to the consumer. As much as possible, manufacturers try to sell directly to retailers, but even then the servicing of the product often poses problems.

Perishable products require short distribution channels.

Some manufacturers compete with their own customers.

MIDDLEMEN CONSIDERATIONS

- **Services provided by middlemen.** Each producer should select middlemen that will provide those marketing services that the producer either is unable to provide or cannot economically perform.

- **Availability of desired middlemen.** The middlemen whom a producer desires may not be available. They may be carrying competitive products and may not wish to add another line.

- **Attitude of middlemen toward manufacturers' policies.** Sometimes, manufacturers' choices of channels are limited because their marketing policies are not acceptable to certain types of middlemen. Some retailers or wholesalers, for example, are interested in carrying a line only if they can get an exclusive franchise in a territory.

COMPANY CONSIDERATIONS

- **Financial resources.** A financially strong company needs middlemen less than one that is financially weak. A business with adequate finances can establish its own sales force, grant credit, or warehouse its own products. A financially weak firm would have to use middlemen who could provide these services.

- **Ability of management.** Channel decisions are affected by the marketing experience and ability of the firm's management. Many companies lacking marketing know-how prefer to turn the distribution job over to middlemen.

- **Desire for channel control.** Some producers establish short channels simply because they want to control the distribution of their products, even though the cost of the more direct channel may be higher. By controlling the channel, producers can achieve more aggressive promotion and better control both the freshness of merchandise stocks and the retail prices of their products.

- **Services provided by seller.** Often producers' channel decisions are influenced by the marketing services they can provide in relation to those demanded by middlemen. For example, often a retail chain will not stock a given product unless it is presold through heavy manufacturer advertising.

Use of Multiple Channels of Distribution

A manufacturer is likely to use multiple channels (also called dual distribution) to reach *different* markets when selling:

- The same product (sporting goods, typewriters) to both the consumer and the industrial markets.
- Unrelated products (oleomargarine and paint, or rubber products and plastics).

Dual distribution is also often used to reach a *single* market, but one in which there are differences in (1) the size of the buyers or (2) the densities within parts of the market. A manufacturer of food products will sell directly to large grocery chains but use wholesalers to reach smaller stores. A producer of industrial machinery may use its own sales force to sell directly to users in concentrated markets. But it may employ manufacturers' agents to reach customers in sparsely populated markets.

A significant development in dual distribution (and a source of channel conflict) is the use of competing channel systems to sell the *same* brand to the *same* market. Esprit de Corp. (apparel), Sherwin-Williams (paints), and Goodyear (tires) are examples of manufacturers that distribute through their own retail stores. At the same time, each of these producers reaches its same market by using conventional channels that include independent retailers and possibly wholesalers. Manufacturers may open their own stores (thus creating dual distribution) when they are not satisfied with the market coverage provided by existing retail outlets. Or manufacturers may establish their own stores primarily as testing grounds for new products and marketing techniques.

DETERMINING INTENSITY OF DISTRIBUTION

After selecting their distribution channels, manufacturers should next decide upon the number of middlemen—the intensity of distribution—to be employed at the wholesale and retail levels. There are three strategies to choose from here, but they are not neatly compartmentalized. Instead, they form a continuum, or points on a scale, running from *intensive* distribution to *exclusive* distribution. See Fig. 16-2.

Intensive Distribution

Ordinarily the strategy of intensive distribution is used by manufacturers of consumer convenience goods. Consumers demand immediate satisfaction with this class of product and will not defer purchases to find a particular brand. Retailers often control the extent to which the strategy of intensive distribution can be implemented. For example, a new manufacturer of toothpaste may want distribution in all supermarkets, but the retailers may limit their assortment to the four fastest-selling brands. Intensive distribution places most of the burden of advertising and promotion on the shoulders of the manufacturer. Retailers will not pay to advertise a product that is sold by all their competitors.

Selective Distribution

Selective distribution covers a wide range of distribution intensity. A business that adopts this strategy may have only a few outlets in a particular market. Or it may have a large number but still have something short of intensive distribution. Selective distribution lends itself especially well to consumer shopping and specialty goods and industrial accessory equipment, for which most customers have a brand preference.

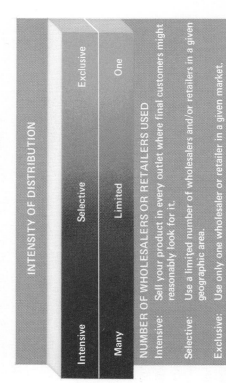

INTENSITY OF DISTRIBUTION

Intensive	Selective	Exclusive
Many	Limited	One

NUMBER OF WHOLESALERS OR RETAILERS USED

Intensive: Sell your product in every outlet where final customers might reasonably look for it.

Selective: Use a limited number of wholesalers and/or retailers in a given geographic area.

Exclusive: Use only one wholesaler or retailer in a given market.

FIGURE 16-2
The intensity-of-distribution continuum.

Cosmetic firms often use selective distribution.

A company may decide to adopt a selective distribution strategy after some experience with intensive distribution. The change usually hinges upon the high cost of intensive distribution or the unsatisfactory performance of some middlemen. Certain customers perennially order in small, unprofitable amounts. Others may be poor credit risks. Eliminating such marginal middlemen may reduce the number of outlets, but it can increase a company's sales volume substantially. Many companies have found this to be the case simply because they were able to do a more thorough selling job with a smaller number of accounts.

Exclusive Distribution

Under an exclusive distribution strategy, the supplier agrees to sell only to a particular wholesaling middleman or retailer in a given market. Under an exclusive distributorship (with a wholesaler) or an exclusive dealership (with a retailer), the middleman is sometimes prohibited from handling a directly competing product line.

Exclusive dealerships are frequently used in the marketing of consumer specialty products such as expensive suits. Producers also often adopt an exclusive distribution strategy when it is essential that the retailer carry a large inventory. This form of distribution is also desirable when the dealer or distributor must furnish installation and repair service. Manufacturers of farm machinery and large construction equipment frequently use exclusive distributorships for this reason.

EVALUATION FROM MANUFACTURER'S STANDPOINT

An exclusive distribution policy helps a manufacturer control the retail segment of its channels. The producer is better able to set the retail prices of its products, and it is in a position to approve advertisements featuring its products. The dealers are more likely to be cooperative and to promote these products aggressively, realizing that their future is tied to the success of the manufacturer.

On the other hand, in using this distribution strategy, a company substantially limits the number of its sales outlets. Also, the producer will suffer if its exclusive dealers don't serve their customers well. Essentially, the manufacturer has all its eggs in one basket in each market. The producer is pretty much dependent on its retailers.

CERRUTI 1881

BARCHETTI, Pittsburgh, PA
WAYNE EDWARDS, Philadelphia, PA
EDUARDO'S, Washington, DC
MAXFIELD, Los Angeles, CA
KILGORE TROUT, Cleveland, OH
CERRUTI 1881, Englewood, NJ
TYRONES, Cedarhurst, NY
L'UOMO, Montreal, Canada
CERRUTI 1881, Newport Beach, CA

NEW YORK OFFICE: 30 WEST 56th STREET · TEL. 212/265-1881

Very exclusive distribution.

EVALUATION FROM RETAILER'S STANDPOINT

A significant advantage of being an exclusive dealer is that the dealer reaps all the benefits of the manufacturer's marketing activities in the particular market.

The main drawback to being an exclusive dealer is that the dealer (retailer) may become too dependent upon the manufacturer. If the producer does a good job with the product, the dealer may prosper. But if the manufacturing firm fails, the dealer is powerless to do anything but sink with it, as far as that product is concerned. Dealership agreements often require the retailer to invest a considerable sum of money in equipment and facilities. If the agreement is then canceled, the retailer stands to lose a major investment. Another hazard is that once the volume has been built up in a market, the manufacturer may add other dealers. The retailer thus is often at the mercy of the manufacturer. It is a one-sided arrangement in this respect, particularly if the brand is strong and the franchise is valuable.

SELECTING AND WORKING WITH INDIVIDUAL MIDDLEMEN

When all is said and done, middlemen can often make or break a manufacturer. Middlemen are the ones who personally contact the final customers—the ultimate consumers or industrial users. Thus the success of manufacturers' distribution efforts depends ultimately upon how well (1) manufacturers select their individual middlemen and then (2) work with these distributors and dealers.

MANUFACTURERS AND MIDDLEMEN: A PERFECT WORKING RELATIONSHIP

The perfect middleman:

1. Has access to the market that the manufacturer wants to reach.
2. Carries adequate stocks of the manufacturer's products and a satisfactory assortment of other products.
3. Has an effective promotional program—advertising, personal selling, and product displays. Promotional demands placed on the manufacturer are in line with what the manufacturer intends to do.
4. Provides services to customers—credit, delivery, installation, and product repair—and honors the product warranty conditions.
5. Pays its bills on time and has capable management.

The perfect manufacturer:

1. Provides a desirable assortment of products—well designed, properly priced, attractively packaged, and delivered on time and in adequate quantities.
2. Builds product demand for these products by advertising them.
3. Furnishes promotional assistance to its middlemen.
4. Provides managerial assistance for its middlemen.
5. Honors product warranties and provides repair and installation service.

The perfect combination:

1. Probably doesn't exist.

When selecting a middleman, the key factor to consider is whether the middleman sells to the market that the manufacturer wants to reach. Then the manufacturer should determine whether the middleman's product mix, promotional activities, and customer service are all compatible with the manufacturer's needs.

There is a community of interests in what each organization—manufacturer and middleman—expects from the other in terms of support for an effective total marketing program. A series of rewards and penalties may be instituted by either party to encourage the other to perform as expected. The major reward for either party is increased profit. Probably the most powerful penalty a manufacturer can impose is to terminate a sales agreement with a dealer. A middleman, in turn, can penalize a manufacturer by not promoting products adequately, by pushing a competitor's products, or ultimately by dropping the manufacturer's line entirely.

LEGAL CONSIDERATIONS IN CHANNEL MANAGEMENT

In various ways, organizations may try to exercise control over the distribution of their product as it moves through the channel. Generally speaking, any attempts to control distribution may be subject to legal constraints. In this section, we shall discuss briefly four control methods that are frequently considered by suppliers (usually manufacturers):

- *Dealer selection.* The manufacturer wants to select its customers, and refuses to sell to some middlemen.
- *Exclusive dealing.* The manufacturer prohibits its dealers from carrying products of the manufacturer's competitors.
- *Tying contracts.* The manufacturer sells a product to a middleman only under the condition that this middleman also buys another (possibly unwanted) product from the manufacturer. Or, at least, the middleman agrees not to buy the other product from any other supplier.
- *Exclusive (closed) territories.* The manufacturer requires each middleman to sell *only* to customers who are located within the middleman's assigned territory.

Each of these four channel-control methods is limited by the Clayton Antitrust Act, the Sherman Antitrust Act, and the Federal Trade Commission Act. None of the four arrangements is illegal by itself. They become illegal only when their effect may be (1) to substantially lessen competition, (2) to tend to create a monopoly, or (3) to be in restraint of trade.[7]

Dealer Selection

The Colgate case in 1919 established the standard that manufacturers have the right to select the middleman to whom they will sell, so long as there is no intent to create a monopoly. However, any decision to *drop* a wholesaler or retailer should be made carefully and in good faith. Generally, it is illegal to drop a middleman for carrying competitors' products or for resisting a tying contract.

Exclusive Dealing

Exclusive-dealing contracts are very likely to be unlawful in either of two situations. One occurs when the manufacturer's sales volume is a substantial part of the total volume in a given market. The reasoning here is that competitors of this manufacturer are shut off from a substantial part of the market. The second likely illegal situation occurs when the contract is between a large manufacturer and a much smaller middleman. The reasoning here is that the supplier's power is inherently coercive, and thus in restraint of trade.

On the other hand, court decisions have also made it clear that exclusive dealing is *not illegal in all cases.* One approved situation occurs when other equivalent products are available in a market or when the manufacturer's competitors have access to equivalent dealers. Then an exclusive contract may be legally acceptable, because competition is not substantially lessened.

---

[7]For some guidelines for manufacturers that want to impose distribution restrictions on their independent middleman, see John F. Cady, "Reasonable Rules and Rules of Reason: Vertical Restrictions on Distributors," *Journal of Marketing*, Summer 1982, pp. 27–37; also see Saul Sands and Robert J. Posch, Jr., "A Checklist of Questions for Firms Considering a Vertical Territorial Distribution Plan," *Journal of Marketing*, Summer 1982, pp. 38–43.

Franchisers typically use some form of tying contract.

Tying Contracts

A supplier is likely to push for a tying agreement when:

- There are shortages of a desired product, and the supplier also wants to push products that are less in demand.
- The supplier grants a franchise (as in fast-food services) and wants the franchisee to purchase all necessary supplies and equipment from this supplier.
- The supplier has exclusive dealers or distributors (in appliances, for example) and wants them to carry a full line of the supplier's products.

In general, tying contracts are likely to be viewed as antitrust violations. As exceptions to this generalization, tying contracts may be acceptable when (1) a new company in trying to enter the market; (2) a supplier wants to maintain a certain level of quality; or (3) an exclusive dealer is required to carry the manufacturer's full line of products, but this middleman is not prohibited from carrying competing products.

Exclusive Territories

Traditionally, the strategy of exclusive (or closed) sales territories has been used by manufacturers in assigning market areas to retail or wholesale middlemen. In some court cases in recent years, however, closed sales territories were ruled illegal on the grounds that they lessen competition and restrain trade. The courts sought to encourage competition among middlemen handling the *same* brand. Exceptions are permitted when a company is small or is a newcomer in the market.

These limitations on closed sales territories are likely to foster vertical marketing systems, where the manufacturer retains ownership of the product until it reaches the final buyer. That is, the manufacturer could either (1) own the retail or wholesale

Other acceptable situations exist (1) when a manufacturer is just getting started in a market and (2) when the manufacturer's share of the total market is so small as to be negligible. In these situations, an exclusive-dealing agreement may actually *strengthen* both that supplier's competitive position and competition in general.

outlet or (2) consign products on an agency basis to the middlemen but retain ownership. In either of these situations, exclusive territories are quite legal.

SUMMARY

With an understanding of the retailing and wholesaling institutional structure as a foundation, marketing executives are in a position to design and manage distribution-channel systems for their companies. These tasks are likely to be easier if executives realize that a trade channel is a living structure that should be developed as a total system. Channel design and management are often a problem, however, because middlemen in the channel are independent organizations, whose goals may conflict with those of the manufacturer.

Conflicts in channels of distribution can occur on the same level of distribution (horizontal conflict) or between different distribution levels (vertical conflict). Probably the most intensive struggle is between producers and wholesalers of manufactured consumer products. Manufacturers may use alternative channels that bypass the wholesalers. Wholesalers, in turn, can strive to improve their efficiency and to provide services for their retailer customers. Manufacturers and retailers are often in conflict, because there are fundamental differences in the goals and business philosophies of the two groups.

To offset the disadvantages of the traditional, fragmented approach to distribution, many firms (producers, wholesalers, and retailers) are developing vertical marketing systems. These systems are typically controlled by means of corporate ownership, economic power, or formal contract.

In establishing channels of distribution, management faces three tasks. The first is to select the basic channel. This choice is influenced by the market, the product, the middlemen, and the company itself. The second step is to determine the intensity of distribution. How many middlemen will be used on each distribution level in a given market? The third step is to select the individual middlemen and then develop a cooperative working relationship with each of them. Throughout the channel-management activity, executives should be aware of the legal constraints affecting their ability to control their product as it goes through the channel.

KEY TERMS AND CONCEPTS

Conflicts on the *same* level of distribution 364
Conflicts between *different* levels of distribution 365
Scrambled merchandising 365
Channel leader 365
Missionary sales people 367
Vertical marketing systems: 370
  Corporate 370
  Administered 370
  Contractual 370

Selection of a channel 371
Dual distribution 376
Intensive distribution 377
Selective distribution 377
Exclusive distribution 378
Exclusive dealing 381
Tying contracts 382
Exclusive (closed) territories 382

QUESTIONS AND PROBLEMS ■

1. "Large manufacturers always control the channels used to reach local markets." Do you agree? In your college community, are there big manufacturers that are unable to tap the local market except through local independent retailers?

2. Explain the role played by each of the following factors in the conflict between manufacturers and wholesalers, particularly in the marketing of consumer products.

   a. Traditional position of the wholesaler before 1920.
   b. Changing position of the manufacturer since the late 1800s.
   c. Changing position of the retailer since 1920.

3. Why is there considerably less friction between manufacturers and wholesalers in the industrial goods field than in the consumer goods field?

4. Explain the reasons why manufacturers are dissatisfied with the performance of wholesalers. Do you agree with the manufacturers' point of view?

5. Why are full-service wholesalers relatively unimportant in the marketing of women's high fashion wearing apparel, furniture, and large electrical equipment?

6. "The use of a missionary sales force is a compromise between the use of the wholesaler and the elimination of the wholesaler." Discuss this idea, showing how missionary sales people can offset manufacturers' objections to wholesalers.

7. "The future of wholesalers depends upon their ability to increase their own efficiency and to furnish managerial aids to their retailers." Discuss, pointing out the alternatives if the wholesaler fails to meet this challenge.

8. Explain, using examples, the differences among the three major types of vertical systems—corporate, administered, contractual. Which is the best kind?

9. Which of the channels illustrated in Fig. 16-1 is most apt to be used for each of the following products? Defend your choice in each case.

   a. Fire insurance.   d. Washing machines.
   b. Single-family residences. e. Hair spray.
   c. Farm hay balers.   f. Men's shoes.

10. "The great majority of industrial sales are made directly from the producer to the industrial user." Explain the reason for this in terms of the nature of the market, then in terms of the product.

11. A small manufacturer of fishing lures is faced with the problem of selecting its channel of distribution. What reasonable alternatives does it have? Consider particularly the nature of its product and the nature of its market.

12. Is a policy of intensive distribution consistent with consumer buying habits for convenience goods? For shopping goods? Is intensive distribution normally used in the marketing of any type of industrial goods?

13. From a manufacturer's viewpoint, what are the competitive advantages of exclusive distribution?

14. What are the drawbacks to exclusive selling from a retailer's point of view? To what extent are these alleviated if the retailer controls the channel for the particular brand?

15. A manufacturer of a well-known brand of men's clothing has been selling directly to one dealer in a Western city for many years. For some time, the market has been large enough to support two retailers very profitably. Yet the present holder of the franchise objects strongly when the manufacturer suggests adding another outlet. What alternatives does the manufacturer have in this situation? What course of action would you recommend?

16. "Manufacturers should always strive to select the lowest-cost channel of distribution." Do you agree? Should they always try to use the middlemen with the lowest operating costs? Explain.

17

MANAGEMENT OF PHYSICAL DISTRIBUTION

CHAPTER GOALS

In the last chapter we set up a distribution channel. In this chapter we physically move the goods through that channel. After studying this chapter, you should understand:

- What physical distribution is.
- The total-system concept of physical distribution.
- The total-cost approach to physical distribution.
- The use of physical distribution to strengthen a marketing program and to reduce marketing costs.
- The five major subsystems within a physical distribution system:
  a. Inventory location and warehousing.
  b. Materials handling.
  c. Inventory control.
  d. Order processing.
  e. Transportation.

The federal government's regulation of transportation carriers largely ended in the early 1980s. Since then, a whole new ball game has been occurring in physical distribution. Many companies are demanding and getting bargain freight rates, on-time delivery guarantees, and specialized new equipment from railroads, trucking lines, barge companies, and other common carriers. Shippers saved over $25 billion in annual freight costs in the mid-1980s. These gains came from lower freight rates and increased physical distribution efficiency.

Today the shippers generally have the upper hand in dealing with the carriers. Houston Lighting and Power Company, for example, negotiated a 26 percent cut in rail freight rates with the Burlington Northern Railroad. General Motors expects to save millions of dollars annually because the Grand Trunk Western Railroad laid 12 miles of track and made other changes to improve General Motors' loading of new autos onto freight cars. Adolph Coors Company was able to expand distribution of its beer into the New England market because the brewer negotiated a 25 percent reduction in rail freight rates.

This story is not entirely sweetness and light, however. Many shippers—some public utilities and agricultural firms, for example—claim that they are captive to a single carrier—usually a single railroad. And, of course, many railroads and trucking companies are complaining loudly about the losses they are incurring.

On balance, however, real operating efficiencies and other savings are occurring in the transportation segment of physical distribution. And the real winner is the consumer. In fact, Professor Bernard LaLonde, an authority on physical distribution, was quoted as saying, "If you listed all the ways that consumers are better off today than in 1980, transportation would be high on the list.[1]

[1]Adapted from Daniel Machalara, "More Companies Push Freight Haulers to Get Better Rates, Service," *The Wall Street Journal*, Dec. 18, 1985, p. 1.

General Motors, Coors, and other companies not specifically named in this story are doing more than negotiating for lower freight rates. These firms generally are developing more effective physical distribution systems to improve their competitive position and to implement their marketing strategy. After a company has established its channels of distribution, then management must arrange for the physical distribution of its products through these channels. **Physical distribution** consists of all the activities concerned with moving the right amount of the right products to the right place at the right time. The term *logistics* also often is used in connection with the movement of materials. Some people distinguish between the two terms—physical distribution and logistics. In this book, however, we treat the two terms as being synonymous.

IMPORTANCE OF PHYSICAL DISTRIBUTION MANAGEMENT

In recent years, American business management has placed increasing emphasis on physical distribution activities. A major reason for all this attention is that physical distribution expenses are quite substantial in many industries. For some products, the largest group of operating expenses comprises those involved in physical distribution. For other products, as much as one-half the wholesale cost is incurred in performing transportation and warehousing activities. The high cost of energy and the high interest rates (which especially affect inventory costs) are additional forces which spotlight the need for efficient physical distribution systems.

> "American management's philosophy typically has been: 'If you're smart enough to make it and aggressive enough to sell it—then any dummy can get it there.' And now we are paying for that philosophy."
>
> —*Bernard J. LaLonde*

Through the years, management has made substantial progress toward reducing production costs. Cost reductions have also been effected in many areas of marketing. Physical distribution is the new (and perhaps the last) major frontier of cost cutting. And the dollars saved in physical distribution have a considerable leverage effect on profit. In a supermarket operation, for instance, the net profit on sales may be 1 percent. Thus, every $1 saved in physical distribution costs has the same effect on profit as an *increase of $100* in sales volume.

Physical Distribution and Customer Service

Perhaps the most important contribution of physical distribution to the total marketing effort in a firm stems from its close relationship to customer service.[2] In a landmark study, it was reported that customer service was considered by top management to be a key element in a company's marketing mix. The surveyed executives stated that the physical distribution function comes closest to their customers' views regarding what constitutes customer service. That is, physical distribution activities constitute the major part of customer service. And effective customer service is not possible without effective physical distribution. Moreover, the study suggested that (1) top management should set customer-service standards in a firm and (2) the physical distribution people should be responsible for maintaining these standards.[3]

---

[2]This paragraph is adapted from Bernard J. LaLonde and Paul H. Zinszer, *Customer Service: Meaning and Measurement*, National Council of Physical Distribution Management, Chicago, 1976, executive summary.

[3]For additional insights on how a firm can better plan its management of customer services, see William B. Wagner and Raymond LaGarce, "Customer Service as a Marketing Strategy," *Industrial Marketing Management*, February 1981, pp. 31–41.

Physical distribution in marketing is essentially a problem in logistics. An army cannot afford to have a battalion in position with guns but no ammunition, or with trucks but no gasoline. By the same token, a private business is in a weak position when it has orders but no merchandise to ship, or when it has a warehouse full of goods in Atlanta but insistent customers in New Orleans. These examples point up the importance of *location* in marketing, especially as regards merchandise. The appropriate assortment of products must be in the right place at the right time to maximize the opportunity for profitable sales.

Physical distribution, then, involves the physical flow of products. **Physical distribution management** is the development and operation of efficient flow systems for products. In its full scope, physical distribution for manufacturers would involve (1) the movement of *finished goods* from the end of the production line to the final customer and (2) the flow of *raw materials* from their source of supply to the production line. Similarly, middlemen would manage the flow of goods *onto* their shelves as well as *from* their shelves to customers' homes or stores.

The task of physical distribution may be divided into five parts—in effect, five subsystems:

● Inventory location and warehousing.
● Materials handling.
● Inventory control.
● Order processing.
● Transportation.

TOTAL-SYSTEM CONCEPT OF PHYSICAL DISTRIBUTION

A decision regarding any one of these parts affects all the others. The location of a warehouse influences the selection of transportation methods and carriers; the decision on carriers influences the optimum size of shipments; and so on. Later in this chapter we shall examine each of these five tasks in more detail.

From time to time in this book, it has been pointed out that marketing is a total system of business action, and not a fragmented series of operations. Nowhere is this idea seen more clearly than in the matter of physical distribution. But it has not always been this way. Traditionally—and unfortunately this is still true in many firms—the activities involved in physical distribution have been fragmented. Managerial responsibility for these activities has been delegated to various units that often have conflicting, and even diametrically opposite, goals. The production department, for instance, sets the production schedule. This group is interested in long production runs to minimize unit manufacturing costs, even though the result may be abnormally high inventory costs. The traffic department looks at the freight rates rather than at the total cost of physical distribution. Thus, carriers with low ton-mile charges are often selected, even though this may mean undue time spent in transit and require larger inventories to fill the long pipelines. The finance department wants a minimum of funds to be tied up in inventories. At the same time, the sales department wants to have a wide assortment of products available at locations near the customers. Under such conditions, it is impossible to optimize the flow of products. However, the systems approach to physical distribution can cut through the problem and result in the effective coordination of these activities.

Shipping costs are low, but total distribution cost may be high.

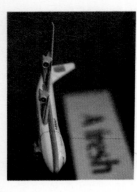

Total distribution cost may be lowered by using high-cost air freight.

In physical distribution, management must deal with a large number of readily measurable variables. Such problems lend themselves nicely to solution by statistical and mathematical techniques. For instance, operations research—a technique involving the use of statistical models and methods—is a particularly helpful tool. It has been used in determining the number and location of warehouses, the optimum size of inventories, and the best transportation routes and methods. Computers are used to rapidly process the large quantities of data needed in these analyses. In our survey treatment in this chapter, however, we shall not be concerned with the quantitative methods used to solve such problems. Instead, we shall discuss the conceptual aspects of physical distribution management.

The Total-Cost Approach

As part of the systems concept, executives should apply a **total-cost approach** to the management of physical distribution. A firm can choose from alternative methods of shipping, of storing, and of handling its products. Administrators should seek the *total set* of alternatives that optimizes the cost-profit relationship for the *entire* physical distribution system, rather than consider the separate costs of individual activities.

Too often, executives attempt to minimize the cost of only one aspect of physical distribution—transportation, for example. They might be upset by the high cost of shipment by air freight. But their efforts to reduce that transportation expense may result in an increase in warehousing expenses that more than offsets the saving in freight costs.

The airlines particularly have been conscious of the total-cost concept. This is so because unit freight rates are appreciably higher for air transportation than for land or sea shipment. A major pharmaceutical company found that the higher costs of air freight were more than offset by the savings from (1) lower inventory costs (2) less insurance and interest expense, (3) lower crating costs, and (4) fewer lost sales due to out-of-stock conditions. The company eliminated all except one warehouse, cut inventories by 50 percent, boosted the rate of stock turnover, and found it could supply markets that had previously been inadequately served.

The point here is *not* that air freight is the best method of transportation. (In fact, the pharmaceutical company later substantially reduced its business with airlines in some parts of the country.) Rather, the idea is that physical distribution should be viewed as a *total* process and its costs analyzed accordingly.

Southland's Major Integrated Operations

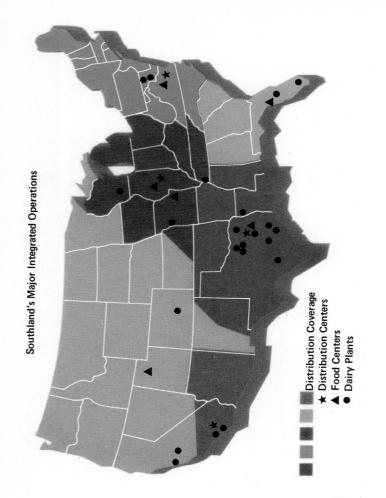

Distribution Coverage
★ Distribution Centers
▲ Food Centers
● Dairy Plants

The distribution centers, dairies, food centers and other supporting operations provide 7-Eleven with better control over product supply and quality

Optimization and Cost Trade-offs

Implicit in the total-cost concept is the idea that management should strive for an optimal balance between total cost and customer services. This is what we call the concept of **optimization** in physical distribution. That is, rather than seek *only* to minimize the total costs of physical distribution, executives should also consider customer want-satisfaction. Actually, it may be necessary to increase physical distribution costs somewhat in order to reach the desired level of customer service.

Achieving this optimal balance leads us to the idea of **cost trade-offs**. To illustrate this concept, let's assume that management wants to minimize both its warehousing expenses and its transportation costs. But these prove to be conflicting goals. In order to accumulate a large enough shipment to get low-cost carload freight rates, the shipper may have to temporarily increase its warehouse stocks. This, in turn, will increase both warehousing and inventory costs. Management then must decide at what point it will trade off its higher warehousing and inventory costs for its lower transportation expenses. In another example, a seller may want to provide quick and frequent deliveries to customers. This seller will have to consider the trade-off between (1) the better service to customers and (2) the higher costs of processing and transporting the small orders.

Trade-off decisions call for careful managerial analysis. In effect, management is seeking that point where there is an even trade-off between (1) the seller's cost and (2) the value received for providing the service.

THE STRATEGIC USE OF PHYSICAL DISTRIBUTION

The strategic use of business logistics may enable a company to strengthen its market position by providing more customer satisfaction and by reducing operating costs. The management of physical distribution can also affect a firm's marketing mix—particularly its product-planning, pricing, and distribution channels. The key here is for executives (1) to understand what their organization is trying to do and then (2) to design an appropriate physical distribution system that will help, and not hinder, the organization in achieving its goals.[4]

Improve Customer Service

A well-run logistics system can improve the distribution service a firm provides its customers—whether they are middlemen or ultimate users. And the level of customer service directly affects demand. This is especially true in the marketing of nondifferentiated products (chemicals, building materials) where effective customer service may be a company's only significant competitive advantage. As regards service, physical distribution systems have generally stressed *spatial* considerations (warehouse location, for example). *Temporal* factors may be equally important. That is, buyers are influenced by service-time and delivery-time differences among suppliers.

Reduce Distribution Costs

Many avenues to cost reductions may be opened by the effective management of a company's physical distribution activities. Effectively managing these activities may lead to simplifications, such as the elimination of unneeded warehouses. Inventories—and their attendant carrying costs and capital investment—may be reduced by consolidating stocks at fewer locations.

Adjust to Differences in Production and Consumption: Create Time and Place Utilities

The economic value of storage (as a key part of warehousing) is the fact that it creates **time utility**. A product may be properly located with respect to its market, but the timing may be such that there is no present demand for it. Management adds precious value to this item simply by holding and properly preserving it in storage until the demand rises. Time utility is created and value is added when bananas are picked green and allowed to ripen in storage, or when meat is aged or tobacco is cured in storage.

Storage is essential to correct imbalances in the timing of production and consumption. An imbalance can come about when there is year-round *consumption* but only seasonal *production*, as in the case of agricultural products. Proper use of warehousing facilities enables a producer to store the seasonal surplus so that it can be marketed long after the harvest has ended.

In other instances, warehousing helps to adjust year-round *production* to seasonal *consumption*, as in the case of skis. Manufacturers prefer to produce on a year-round basis, to operate their plants more efficiently. For this, enough surplus stock must be stored during the off-season to meet the peak-season demand without requiring overtime operation or additional plant capacity.

In an economic sense, the main function of the transportation subsystem in physical distribution is to add value to products through the creation of **place utility**. A

Storing products until they are wanted creates time utility.

[4] For a report on how a well-designed physical distribution system can implement a company's strategic marketing plan, see Roy D. Shapiro, "Get Leverage from Logistics," *Harvard Business Review,* May–June 1984, pp. 119–126.

fine suit hanging on a garment manufacturer's rack in New York City has less value to a retailer in Baltimore than a similar suit displayed in the retailer's store. Transporting the suit from New York to the retailer in Baltimore creates place utility and thus adds value to the product.

Stabilize Prices

Careful management of warehousing and transportation facilities can help to stabilize prices for an individual firm or for an entire industry. If a market is temporarily glutted with a certain product, sellers can store the product until supply and demand conditions are more in balance. This managerial use of warehousing facilities is common in the marketing of agricultural products and other seasonally produced goods. The judicious movement of products from one market to another may (1) enable a seller to avoid a market with depressed prices or (2) allow a seller to take advantage of a market that has a shorter supply and higher prices.

Affect Choice of Channels and Location of Middlemen

Decisions regarding inventory management have an important bearing on a manufacturer's selection of trade channels and the location of middlemen. Logistical considerations may become paramount, for example, when a company decides to decentralize its inventory. Now management must determine (1) how many sites to establish and (2) whether to use wholesalers, its own branch warehouses, or public warehouses. One manufacturer may select merchant wholesalers that perform storage and other warehousing services. Another may prefer to use a combination of manufacturers' agents and public warehouses. These agents can solicit orders and provide aggressive selling, while the ordered products can be physically distributed through the public warehouses.

One point should be kept in mind, however. Rarely are channels selected primarily on the basis of physical distribution considerations. Instead, logistics is only one of several factors to consider. Recall from the previous chapter that the nature of the market and other factors heavily influence channel design.

Ensure Lowest Costs via Traffic Management

Good traffic managers see to it that their companies enjoy the fastest routes and the lowest rates for whatever methods of transportation they use. The pricing of transportation services is one of the most complicated parts of the American business scene. The rate, or tariff, schedule is the carrier's price list. To read one properly is a real art that requires considerable practice. As a simple example of some of the difficulties that are involved, shipping rates vary for different types of goods. Moreover, the classes of goods overlap, so that a particular product may be in two or more classes with different freight rates.

Another service that traffic managers can render their companies is the auditing (checking) of freight bills. This is necessary because carriers sometimes charge a higher rate than the one that should apply. They are not intentionally trying to defraud the shipper. They are simply misinterpreting the complex rate schedule.

Good traffic managers can also negotiate with carriers to get their products reclassified or to get special rates. A company may offer to ship larger quantities on a given carrier if lower rates are granted. Anheuser-Busch, for example, obtained reduced rates from both trucking companies and railroads that netted a $3 million reduction in transportation costs over a 1-year period.

If service and control are key factors for a company, traffic managers should

Southland operates its own "in-house" truck fleet to better serve its 7-Eleven stores.

investigate the possibility of having their own private carrier, especially their own trucking system. With the present relaxed entry regulations, such a carrier could hire itself out to other companies to move their freight as well. The existence of an "in-house" carrier also serves as a powerful bargaining tool in dealing with common carriers for the portion of freight not carried by the private fleet. This strategy (an in-house carrier) has worked well for the Southland Corporation (7-Eleven stores) and for other major shippers.

Benefit from Government Deregulation

In the late 1970s domestic airline, railroad, and trucking industries were largely freed from regulation. The railroad industry had been subject to federal regulations for almost a century, starting with the Interstate Commerce Commission Act in 1887. Airlines and commercial truckers have been regulated in the United States virtually from the beginning of those industries.

Because of this long history of government control, transportation firms experienced some real "cultural shock" once their industry was deregulated. The number of competing firms increased dramatically, especially in the airline and trucking industries. Lightly traveled routes were dropped. Competition intensified considerably on the more profitable routes. Price competition also increased considerably—even to the point sometimes where the carriers were pricing below cost. Many firms suffered financial losses and some even were forced out of business.

But, at the same time, deregulation has provided many strategic marketing opportunities for well-managed firms both within and outside of the deregulated industries. Carriers now have the flexibility to set their rates at levels of service so as to develop new markets. Most important of all, the carriers now can use their rates (that is, their prices) as a marketing tool. The shippers have benefited by being able to shop around for the rates and service levels that best meet their needs.[5]

MAJOR TASKS IN PHYSICAL DISTRIBUTION MANAGEMENT

Inventory Location and Warehousing

An effective physical distribution system is built around five subsystems. There is much interaction and interdependence among these subsystems. Consequently, each of them must be carefully coordinated with the others.

The name of the game in physical distribution is inventory management. Executive judgment must be exercised regarding the size, location, handling, and transporting of inventories. Decision making in these four areas is interrelated. The number and locations of inventory sites, for example, influence inventory size and transportation methods. These interrelationships are often quite complex.

STORAGE VERSUS WAREHOUSING

We should distinguish carefully between these two activities in physical distribution. **Storage** is the marketing activity that involves holding and preserving products from the time of their production until their sale. **Warehousing** embraces storage plus a broad range of functions, such as assembling, dividing (bulk-breaking), and preparing products for reshipping. Warehousing is therefore a broader concept than storage. Storage is more passive by nature; warehousing involves more activity.[6]

INVENTORY: CENTRALIZED OR DISPERSED?

Basic to the inventory-location problem is the company's intended strategy regarding inventory deployment. Is inventory to be heavily concentrated or dispersed throughout the market? Each strategy has its merits and limitations. A centralized inventory can be smaller in total size, can be better controlled, and is more responsive to unusual requests. Efficiency in warehousing and materials handling should be increased. On the other hand, centralizing the stocks often means higher total transportation charges and slower delivery to some segments of the market. Dispersing the inventory presents the other side of the coin on each of these points.

THE DISTRIBUTION-CENTER CONCEPT

An effective inventory-location strategy may be a compromise—the establishment of one or more *distribution centers*. Such centers are planned around markets rather than transportation facilities. The basic idea is to develop under one roof an efficient, fully

Products on pallets are moved by computer-controlled vehicles.

[5]See Lewis M. Schneider, "New Era in Transportation Strategy," *Harvard Business Review,* March–April 1985, pp. 118–126; Thomas S. Robertson and Scott Ward, "Management Lessons from Airline Deregulation," *Harvard Business Review,* January–February 1983, pp. 40–44; and "Shipping by Air Comes of Age in the '80s," *Dun's Business Month,* February 1983, pp. 90–105.

[6]For some guides to improving productivity in warehousing, see Kenneth B. Ackerman and Bernard J. LaLonde, "Making Warehousing More Efficient," *Harvard Business Review,* March–April 1980, pp. 94–102.

Southland's highly automated distribution center provides efficient warehousing services.

integrated system for the flow of products—taking orders, filling them, and delivering them to customers. The **distribution center** is a concept in warehousing that has been adopted by many well-known firms. The Southland Corporation, for example, operates totally from five distribution centers spread evenly across the company's wide market area.

The use of distribution centers has lowered distribution costs by reducing the number of warehouses, cutting excessive inventories, and eliminating out-of-stock conditions. Storage and delivery time have been cut to a minimum. This puts into practice the adage that companies are in business to sell goods, not to store them.

OWNERSHIP AND TYPES OF WAREHOUSES

A firm (manufacturer, wholesaler, or retailer) has the option of operating its own private warehouse or using the services of a public warehouse. **A private warehouse** is more likely to be used if (1) a company moves a large volume of products through a warehouse and (2) there is very little, if any, seasonal fluctuation in this flow. **Public warehouses** offer storage and handling facilities to any interested individual or company. Public warehousing costs are a variable expense. Customers pay only for the space they use, and only when they use it. Additional services typically provided by public warehouses are noted in the box. Major types of public warehousing facilities include:

- *General merchandise warehouses*, which store practically any product that needs to be protected from the weather but has no special temperature, humidity, or handling requirements.
- *Special commodity warehouses*, which are used for particular agricultural products such as grains, wool, cotton, or tobacco.
- *Cold storage warehouses*.

Materials Handling

The selection of the proper equipment to physically handle products is an important aspect of physical distribution management. Proper equipment can minimize losses from breakage, spoilage, and theft. Efficient equipment can reduce handling *costs* as well as the *time* required for handling.

In this discussion of materials-handling equipment, we include the warehouse building itself. Historically, warehouses have been multistory buildings located in congested parts of town. Their operation has been characterized by the use of elevators, chutes, and other highly expensive *vertical* methods of moving products. Modern warehouses are huge one-story structures. They are located in outlying parts of town where land is less expensive and loading platforms are easily accessible to motor trucks and railroad spurs. Forklift trucks, conveyor belts, motor scooters, and other mechanized equipment are used to move merchandise. In some warehouses the order fillers are even equipped with roller skates.

''**Containerization**'' is a cargo-handling system that has gained considerable acceptance in physical distribution. The system involves enclosing a shipment of products in large containers of metal, wood, or some other material. The containers are then transported unopened from the time they leave the shipper until they reach their destination. Thus, containerization minimizes physical handling, which results in reduced damage and allows for more efficient transportation.

BESIDES THE SERVICES MENTIONED BELOW, PUBLIC WAREHOUSES CAN PROVIDE:

A substitute for company warehouses or wholesalers

Public warehouses will provide office and display space, and accept and fill orders for sellers. Manufacturers can ship in carload quantities to a public warehouse, just as they ship to their own branches or wholesalers. Sellers thus have flexibility in their inventory locations. If they wish to change locations, they simply change public warehouses.

Protection through government legislation

Federal and state laws regulate the services of public warehouses. These laws are the guarantee that makes public warehouse receipts acceptable as bank collateral. The laws also curtail abuses by warehouse operators.

Financial services

Warehouse receipts covering stored products may be used as collateral for bank loans.

The field (custodian) warehousing service operates as follows: Assume that some products are stored in the owner's private warehousing facilities. The owner wants to get a bank loan on the merchandise without the expense of moving it to a public warehouse. So the owner leases to a public warehouse company a section of the private warehouse that contains the merchandise in question. (A field warehouse need not be a portion of a regular private warehouse. It can be an office cabinet, locked desk drawer, office safe, open yard, or some other storage facility.) The warehouse company then issues a receipt for the goods, and this receipt serves as collateral for a bank loan. The leased area, in effect, becomes a public warehouse, and the goods cannot be removed until the receipt is redeemed.

Containers provide an efficient materials-handling service.

Inventory Control

A key activity in any physical distribution system is maintaining control over the size and composition of the inventories. Inventory represents a sizable investment for many companies. The goal of inventory control is to minimize both the investment and the fluctuations in inventories, while at the same time filling customers' orders promptly and accurately.

Perhaps the greatest boon to inventory control in recent years has been the improvements in computer technology. These have enabled management to shorten the order-delivery time and to substantially reduce the size of inventories.

Inventory size is determined by balancing market needs and costs. Market demands on inventory can be anticipated through sales forecasts. The more accurate the forecasts, the greater the probability of optimizing inventory size. Inventory costs include (1) acquisition costs, that is, the costs of making or buying the products to put in inventory, and (2) carrying or holding costs—warehousing expenses, interest on investment, losses due to spoilage and pilferage, inventory taxes, and so on.

Inventory size is also influenced considerably by the desired level of customer satisfaction. That is, what percentage of orders does the company expect to fill promptly from inventory on hand? Out-of-stock conditions result in lost sales, loss of goodwill, and sometimes even the loss of customers. Yet, to be able to fill 100 percent of the orders promptly may require an excessively large and costly inventory. Authorities estimate that about 80 percent more inventory is required to fill 95 percent of the orders than to fill only 80 percent.

Management also needs to establish the optimal quantity for reorder when it is time to replenish inventory stocks. Here we introduce the concept of the *economic order quantity* (EOQ). The **economic order quantity** is the volume at which the *economic inventory-carrying cost plus the order-processing cost are at a minimum. Typically, as the order size increases, (1) the inventory-carrying cost goes up (because the average inventory is larger), and (2) the order-processing cost declines (because there are fewer orders).

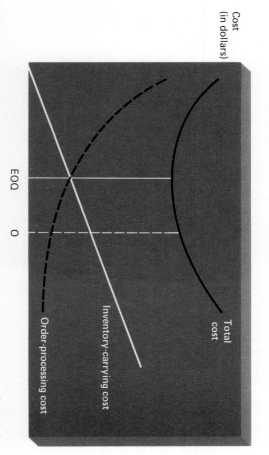

FIGURE 17-1
Economic order quantity.

In Fig. 17-1, point EOQ represents the lowest-cost order quantity. Actually, however, the optimal order quantity often is somewhat different—usually larger—than the EOQ. This situation reflects our earlier discussion of optimization and cost trade-offs. Management should balance its desire for minimum inventory costs with its desired level of customer service. This trade-off may well call for an order quantity that is larger than the EOQ—quantity 0 in Fig. 17-1, for example—in order to provide the desired level of customer service.

A new concept affecting inventory control, purchasing, and production scheduling is the "**just-in-time**" concept. As practiced by Japanese organizations, this concept is attracting increasing attention from top management—not just marketing or physical distribution management—in many American companies. The essence of the concept involves buying in small quantities just in time for use in production and then producing in quantities just in time for sale.

When effectively implemented, this just-in-time concept has many potential benefits. By purchasing in small quantities and maintaining low inventory levels of parts and finished goods, a company can effect dramatic cost savings. Production and delivery schedules can be shortened and made more flexible and reliable. The Japanese have found that quality levels are improved with just-in-time purchasing. When order quantities are small and frequently delivered, a company can more quickly spot and then correct a quality problem.

To be effective, just-in-time purchasing and production scheduling requires very careful managerial monitoring. A high level of cooperation and coordination is called for between suppliers and producers, and then between production and marketing people in the manufacturing firm.[7]

Order Processing

Still another part of the physical distribution system is a set of procedures for handling and filling orders. This should include provision for billing, granting credit, preparing invoices, and collecting past-due accounts. Consumer ill will can result if a company makes mistakes or is slow in filling orders. As information demands become more complex, companies are increasingly turning to computers to implement their order-processing activities.

Transportation

A major part of the physical distribution system in many companies involves the shipping of products to customers. Management must decide on both the form of transportation to use and the particular carriers. In this discussion, we are concerned primarily with *intercity* shipments.

The five major forms of transportation are railroads, trucks, water vessels, pipelines, and airplanes. The relative importance of each, along with some trends in its use, is shown in Table 17-1. Note that the figures reflect *intercity* freight traffic only. Ocean coastal traffic between United States ports is not included. Virtually all farm-to-farm and *intracity* freight movements are made by motor truck. Consequently, the

Computers are increasingly used for inventory control and order processing.

Trucks are by far the primary carrier of *intracity* freight.

[7] For a more detailed discussion of the concept, see Chan K. Hahn, Peter A. Pinto, and Daniel J. Bragg, "'Just-in-Time' Production and Purchasing," *Journal of Purchasing and Materials Management*, Fall 1983, pp. 2–10; and Richard J. Schonberger and Abdolhossein Ansari, "'Just-in-Time' Purchasing Can Improve Quality," *Journal of Purchasing and Materials Management*, Spring 1984, pp. 2–7.

Railroads still are the largest carrier of intercity freight.

TABLE 17-1 DISTRIBUTION OF INTERCITY FREIGHT TRAFFIC IN THE UNITED STATES BY CARRIER

	Ton-miles, 1984 (in billions)	% of total			
		1984	1980	1960	1939
Railroads	936	38	38	44	62
Motor trucks	602	24	22	22	10
Oil pipelines	567	23	24	17	10
Great Lakes	76	3	4	8	14
Rivers and canals	306	12	12	9	4
Air carriers	7	*	—	—	—
Total	2,494	100%	100%	100%	100%

* 3 percent of total
Source: Yearbook of Railroad Facts, Association of American Railroads, Washington, D.C., 1985, p. 32.

figures for water and truck carriers really understate the importance of these methods of transportation by a considerable margin. Nevertheless, Table 17-1 is illuminating. It shows that railroads are still by far the major intercity freight carrier. Although their relative position has declined steadily since 1940, the actual number of ton-miles of freight carried by railroads has increased considerably since that time. The use of motor trucks has expanded phenomenally over the past 40 years.

In Table 17-2, the major transportation methods are compared on the bases of some criteria likely to be used by physical distribution management in the transportation selection process.

TABLE 17-2   COMPARISON OF TRANSPORTATION METHODS

Selection criteria	Transportation method				
	Rail	**Water**	**Highway**	**Pipeline**	**Air**
Speed (door-to-door time)	Medium	Slowest	Fast	Slow	**Fastest**
Cost of transportation	Medium	**Lowest**	High	Low	Highest
Reliability in meeting delivery schedules	Medium	Poor	Good	**Excellent**	Medium
Flexibility (variety of products carried)	**Widest variety**	Widest variety	Medium	Very limited, very inflexible	Somewhat limited
Number of geographic locations served	Very many, but can go only where track is laid	Limited	**Unlimited, very flexible**	Very limited	Many
Products most suitable	Long hauls of carload quantities of bulky products, when freight costs are high in relation to product's value	Bulky, low-value, non-perishable	Short hauls of high-value goods	Oil, natural gas, slurried products	High-value, perishable, where speed of delivery is all-important

SPECIAL SERVICES OFFERED BY RAILROADS

Despite the trend shown in Table 17-1, railroads are still the lowest-cost, most efficient method of transportation for many products and in many marketing situations. To meet the increased competition from other carriers, especially trucks, the railroads have instituted several special services and freight rates.

Carload versus less-than-carload freight rates   Railroads offer substantial savings to firms that ship in carload (c.l.) quantities rather than less-than-carload (l.c.l.) amounts. For many items, the c.l. freight rate is as much as 50 percent less than the l.c.l. rate. This is a tremendous incentive to shippers of large quantities of products—especially minerals, agricultural products, and similar goods for which freight expenses are a significant percentage of total value.

Combined shipments   Long ago the railroads realized that they were vulnerable to competition from other types of carriers when it came to handling l.c.l. shipments. Consequently, the railroads have introduced several measures designed to reduce the cost of l.c.l. shipments and to speed them up. These measures provide for combining into a carload quantity the freight from one or more companies that are shipping products to customers located in one area. The pooled freight can go at carload rates and can be delivered much more rapidly than if its component parts were sent separately in l.c.l. units.

In-transit privileges   Two in-transit privileges offered by railroads are (1) diversion in transit and (2) the opportunity to process some products en route. **Diversion in**

transit allows a seller to start a shipment moving in one direction and to change destination while the car is en route, just as long as the new destination involves no backtracking. The charges are computed on the basis of the through rate or long-haul rate from the point of origin to the ultimate destination, plus a small charge for diversion. This is a valuable service to shippers of perishable products that are subject to price variations from one city to another on any given day. A Washington cooperative can ship Red Delicious apples from Yakima, Washington, to Indianapolis (or they may just be shipped east with no specific destination). Before the shipment reaches Indianapolis, the shipper may hear that market prices are better in Memphis. Consequently, at the appropriate "diversion point" (probably Chicago in this case) the cars will be rerouted to Memphis. The freight charges are determined on the basis of the through rate from Yakima to Memphis.

Under the privilege of **processing in transit,** a shipment of a product is unloaded and processed in some manner while en route. Then it is reloaded and shipped on to its final destination. Wheat may be shipped from Spokane to Minneapolis, where it is made into flour, which is then shipped to Detroit. But the through rate from Spokane to Detroit applies.

Piggyback and fishyback services **Piggyback** service involves carrying truck trailers on railroad flatcars. Products can be loaded on trucks at the seller's shipping dock. The truck *trailer* is later transported by train to the destination city where it is trucked to the buyer's receiving station. This combination service provides (1) more flexibility than railroads alone can offer, (2) lower freight costs than trucks alone, and (3) less handling of the goods.

Fishyback service involves transporting loaded trailers on barges or ships. The trailers may be carried piggyback fashion by railroad to the dock, where they are transferred to the ship. Then, at the other end of the water trip, the trailers are loaded back onto trains for the completion of the haul. In an alternative use of the fishyback service, railroads are not used at all. Merchandise is trucked directly to ports, where the trailer vans are loaded on barges. At the end of the water journey, the vans are trucked to the receiving station.

FREIGHT FORWARDERS

The **freight forwarder** is a specialized marketing institution that has developed through the years to serve firms that ship in l.c.l. quantities. The typical traditional freight forwarder does not own its own transportation equipment, but it does provide a valuable service in physical distribution.

Spurred by the opportunities provided by deregulation in the transportation field, some of the very large freight forwarders have established their own airlines and truck fleets. These firms—Emery and Federal Express, for example—now essentially are integrated as cargo airlines and trucking companies, as well as still providing the traditional freight-forwarding services.

The main function of freight forwarders is to consolidate l.c.l. shipments, or less-than-truckload shipments, from several shippers into carload and truckload quantities. The freight forwarder's operating margin is generally the spread between c.l.

Unloading containers at the end of a piggyback ride.

Freight forwarders provide efficient service for small shippers.

and l.c.l. rates. That is, the shipper pays l.c.l. rates, and the freight forwarder transports the products at c.l. rates. The freight forwarder also picks up the merchandise at the shipper's place of business and arranges for delivery at the buyer's door. The l.c.l. shipper also benefits from the speed and minimum handling associated with c.l. shipments, but does pay l.c.l. rates. Also, freight forwarders provide the small shipper with traffic management services, such as selecting the best transportation methods and routes.

THE FUTURE IN PHYSICAL DISTRIBUTION ■

Executives involved in physical distribution face tremendous challenges and opportunities in the years ahead. These pressures stem both from within their companies and from external environmental forces.

Within most firms there is a need to coordinate physical distribution activities more effectively so that they function as a system. Essentially, this is a problem in organization. If you ask, "Who is in charge of physical distribution?" all too often the answer is, "No one." Instead, managerial responsibility is fragmented among units that may have conflicting goals. Fortunately, there is a trend toward the establishment of a separate department responsible for all physical distribution activities.

It is imperative that *top management* view logistics as one of its prime responsibilities. Physical distribution costs are the largest operating cost in many firms. For countless companies, effective customer service (which involves physical distribution activities primarily) can mean the difference between a strong and a weak marketing position. If these internal conditions are not sufficient incentive to ensure effective management, then certainly the macroenvironmental forces should be.

The federal deregulation of air, rail, and trucking regulations certainly has been a major environmental factor affecting physical distribution in the 1980s. In addition, urban population congestion, high energy costs, and the rising concern for our environment all greatly affect physical distribution management. The entire transportation system in the United States is undergoing substantial changes. Mass urban transportation is getting increasing political attention. Air pollution controls, a national highway speed limit, and soaring fuel costs are altering many traditional patterns in physical distribution. Truly, the 1980s are imposing some formidable challenges for physical distribution executives. But, at the same time, they also are bringing unlimited opportunities for strategic marketing management.

Transportation in the future.

SUMMARY ■

Physical distribution involves the flow of products from supply sources to the firm, and from the company to its customers. Executives who manage physical distribution are responsible for developing and operating efficient flow systems. Their goal is to move the right amount of the right products to the right place at the right time. Physical distribution costs are a substantial part of total operating costs in many firms. Moreover, physical distribution is probably the only remaining source of major cost reductions in many companies.

Physical distribution should be treated as a total system of business action. In the past (and unfortunately even now in too many firms), physical distribution activities have been fragmented operationally and organizationally. Applying the systems concept also means applying the total-cost approach—that is, reducing the cost of the entire system, rather than the costs of individual elements in the system. Thus, management might decide to use expensive air freight if its high cost could be more than offset by savings in warehousing and inventory-carrying costs. However management should *not* strive *only* for the lowest total cost of physical distribution. Instead, the goals should be to effect the best balance between level of customer service and total cost. Sometimes a company can improve its market position by providing a higher level of customer service, even though this means an increase in physical distribution costs.

The actual operation of a physical distribution system requires management's attention and decision making in five areas: (1) inventory location and warehousing, (2) materials handling, (3) inventory control, (4) order processing, and (5) transportation. Again, these areas should not be approached as individual activities, but as subsystems of the whole—the physical distribution system.

KEY TERMS AND CONCEPTS ■

Physical distribution 387
Logistics 387
Systems concept of physical
  distribution 389
Total-cost approach to physical
  distribution 390
Cost trade-offs 391
Time utility 392
Place utility 392
Storage versus warehousing 395
Centralized inventory 395
Inventory dispersal 395
Distribution center 395

Public warehousing 396
Field warehousing 397
Inventory-control systems 398
Economic order quantity (EOQ) 398
Order processing 399
"Just-in-time" concept 399
Transportation methods 399
Carload versus less-than-carload freight
  rates 401
Railroad combined-shipment
  services 401
Railroad in-transit services 401
Freight forwarder 402

QUESTIONS AND PROBLEMS ■

1. In some companies, activities such as processing and shipping orders, maintaining an inventory-control system, and locating inventory stocks throughout the market are treated as separate, fragmented tasks. What are some of the administrative and operational problems that are likely to occur in this type of arrangement?

2. "The goals of a modern physical distribution system in a firm should be to operate at the lowest possible *total* costs." Do you agree?

3. Name some products for which the cost of physical distribution constitutes at least one-half the total price of the goods at the wholesale level. Can you suggest ways of decreasing the physical distribution cost of these products?

4. Explain how marketing managers can use transportation and warehousing facilities to stabilize the prices of their products.

5. "A manufacturer follows an inventory-location strategy of concentration rather than dispersion. This company's inventory size will be smaller, but its transportation and warehousing expenses will be larger, than if its inventory were dispersed." Do you agree? Explain.

6. "The use of public warehouse facilities makes it possible for manufacturers to bypass wholesalers in their channels of distribution." Explain.

7. How are transportation decisions related to packaging policies?

8. Why are l.c.l. shipments so much slower and more costly than c.l. shipments?

9. Assume that a manufacturer must ship in l.c.l. quantities. However, the competitive price structures for this company's products are such that it cannot afford to pay the high l.c.l. freight rates. What alternatives does this firm have regarding the transportation of its products?

10. As a traffic manager of a large distribution center for a retail drugstore chain, determine the best transportation method and route for the shipment of each of the following items to your center. The distribution center is located in the city nearest to your campus. In each case, your company will pay all freight charges, and, unless specifically noted, time is not important. The distribution center has a rail siding and a loading/unloading dock for trucks.

    a. Disposable diapers from Wisconsin. Total shipment weight is 112,000 pounds.

    b. A replacement memory card for your computer, which is now inoperative. Weight of shipment is 3 pounds, and you need this card in a hurry.

    c. Blank payroll checks for your company. (There is a sufficient number of checks on hand for the next 2 paydays.) Shipment weight is 100 pounds.

    d. Ice cream from St. Louis. Total shipment weight is 42,000 pounds.

    e. Shampoo in 12-ounce bottles from Georgia. Total shipment weight is 45,000 pounds.

11. Under what conditions is a company likely to select air freight as the main method of transporting its finished products?

5

REXFORD COMPANY

Selecting a distribution channel to minimize conflict

About 9 months ago, the Rexford Company began to import a new model of vacuum cleaner from West Germany. Rexford's president and owner, Thomas Herff, originally had intended to sell this new product only to the company's existing industrial market. However, the more he thought about it, the more Mr. Herff believed that the vacuum cleaner could also be sold very successfully in the consumer market. The problem was that the Rexford Company had never sold any products to the consumer market. Consequently, Mr. Herff did not know what channels of distribution he should use to reach this market. He also was concerned that, by selling the vacuum cleaner as a consumer product, he might antagonize the middlemen now being used to reach Rexford's industrial market.

The Rexford Company was a Midwestern firm that manufactured and marketed two lines of carpet cleaners for industrial uses. One line consisted of six different models of a steam carpet cleaner, known in the industry as an "extractor." The other product line was a series of vacuum cleaners. Rexford manufactured all these except the new import from Germany.

The extractors consisted of (1) a basic unit (the motor and a bucket containing the cleaning solution), (2) hoses to carry the cleaning solution to the carpet and back, and (3) a series of end-of-hose tools such as brushes, gleaners, and nozzles. Rexford's selling price on these extractors ranged from $1,500 to $11,000.

The vacuums that Rexford manufactured had to be used with one of the extractors, since the extractor contained a bucket which held the debris. The vacuums did not have a bag of their own like most vacuum cleaners. This tended to make the vacuuming a slower process. However, the vacuums were extremely efficient because of the tremendous suction power from the extractors.

The new German import was the usual upright type of vacuum cleaner with a bag attached. However, the vacuum also possessed some unique features which Herff believed would make it one of Rexford's best-selling products. For example, unlike most conventional uprights, the German model had two motors. One powered the vacuum itself and the other operated the brush. The vacuum was lightweight and easy to maintain. Mr. Herff planned to sell the industrial models to distributors for about

$500, but consumer models would be priced much lower. All in all, Mr. Herff was excited about the market prospects for the new vacuum cleaner. He believed it had a great potential in both the industrial and the consumer markets.

The channel of distribution for Rexford's products was from Rexford to industrial distributors to industrial users. The distributors usually were janitorial supply houses. They took an average markup of 15 percent on their cost (Rexford's selling price). Most of the industrial users were janitorial maintenance firms that cleaned carpets in office buildings, schools, hospitals, and hotels and motels. The distributors also sold to building contractors and to companies (other than supermarkets) that rented out carpet-cleaning equipment.

Rexford defined itself strictly as a supplier of steam carpet-cleaning equipment, and therefore the company defined its competition in the same way. It did not consider itself to be competing with companies that sold floor polishers and other carpet-cleaning accessories. Within this definition, most of Rexford's competitors were much larger firms. Yet Tom Herff believed that his company had about 25 percent of the market.

Herff attributed his company's market success to three factors: (1) the variety in its product line, (2) the product design that made the unit easy to use, and (3) the fact that Rexford had its own sales force. Most of the competition used manufacturers' agents. Rexford also used six of these agents, but the company really depended on its own sales force for an effective selling effort.

Rexford had a sales force of 10 people who reported to the sales manager, Terry Fletcher. These sales reps were paid a straight commission of 10 percent of their net sales. The sales people paid their own expenses except for intercity transportation, which was paid by the Rexford Company.

The job of a Rexford sales representative consisted primarily of two sets of activities. The first involved finding distributors (janitorial supply houses) and selling them the Rexford products. The second set of job duties consisted of activities intended to make the distributor's selling effort more effective.

In order to get a distributor to carry the Rexford line, a sales rep often would bring orders to that distributor. This is the way it worked. The sales rep would first go to a janitorial service that cleaned several office buildings. The rep would go through a sales presentation which included a demonstration of the product, and secure an order. The rep then took this order to the distributor. With orders from the final user already secured, it was an easy task to get the distributor to carry the Rexford line.

Once the distributor had agreed to handle Rexford's products, it was the sales rep's job to keep that distributor actively and effectively selling those products. Most of the distributors also carried other brands of carpet cleaners besides Rexford. Consequently, the reps were constantly trying to persuade the distributors to promote the Rexford line over competitors' brands. This meant that the Rexford reps had to make frequent calls on their distributors.

Mr. Herff did not believe there would be any problems in setting up a distribution channel to sell the German vacuum cleaner to the *industrial* market. He planned to have the Rexford sales people sell the machine to Rexford's existing industrial distributors—the janitorial supply houses. These distributors would then sell to the janitorial maintenance firms that would be actual users of the vacuum cleaner.

But to reach the *consumer* market—Mr. Herff realized that was an entirely different situation. One channel of distribution was the traditional channel for home appliances. That is, the Rexford sales force would sell to appliance wholesalers that in turn would sell to retail appliance stores. A variation of this channel would be for Rexford to sell directly to large retailers, such as department stores and discount merchandisers (K mart).

At a meeting to discuss the matter, Terry Fletcher questioned whether the Rexford sales force was sufficiently familiar with the wholesale market for consumer appliances. He also suggested the possibility of using the present wholesale distributors—janitorial supply houses—to sell to appliance retailers.

Edward Jerrold, who was Rexford's director of sales training and also the director of the company's selling seminars for its distributors, then became involved in the discussion. He liked the idea of selling the German vacuum cleaner as a consumer product. However, he wanted to use a trade channel that would not compete with Rexford's existing janitorial supply distributors that were selling to the industrial market.

Jerrold said, "Suppose one of the appliance retailers runs a price special on the new cleaner. Some of the cleaning services and other janitorial maintenance firms that now buy from our distributors then might end up buying at the retail store. Or at least they will question the distributor's price when they see the reduced price at a retail store."

Jerrold continued, "How about this idea—let's get into the consumer market in an indirect way. Let's sell to professional carpet-cleaning firms that clean carpets in private homes. Then, when people at home see the vacuum cleaner in action, a few may buy one at a local store. However, mainly what we'll be doing is to sell to home carpet-cleaning firms that service the consumer market. This business will parallel our sales to janitorial maintenance firms that service the industrial market."

After listening to Ed Jerrold's ideas, Mr. Herff realized that Jerrold had not indicated how their sales people would reach the professional home-cleaning firms. Would Rexford have to increase the size of its sales force and sell directly to these firms, or would Rexford sell through some kind of a distributor? Mr. Herff also wondered what promotional requirements would be needed to support Jerrold's suggested trade channels.

QUESTION

What channel of distribution should the Rexford Company use to sell the German vacuum cleaner in the consumer market?

CASE 14

DIEBOLD EQUIPMENT COMPANY

Changing the channels of distribution

In order for his company to maintain its desired growth rate, Ronald Hewitt wondered if the firm should change its channels of distribution. Ronald Hewitt was the general sales manager for the Diebold Equipment Company. This company manufactured and marketed a line of soft-drink dispensers for top-of-the-counter or under-the-counter installation. These dispensers were the type that mixed concentrated syrup with precooled carbonated water and were designed for operation by a personal attendant.

The basic product unit consisted of (1) a tank for the carbon dioxide (CO_2) gas cylinder and the dry refrigeration unit, (2) a three- or four-flavor dispensing valve and head, and (3) the necessary tubing, regulators, and fittings. A syrup tank was an optional but usually purchased accessory. The product line consisted of seven models, each in a different size and design and each with different features intended for specific markets. Most of the basic models were priced at $900 for a three-flavor unit and $1,000 for a four-flavor dispenser. Syrup tanks were an additional $34 to $43, depending upon their size.

For four of its models, the company marketed the identical dispenser under two brands—the Cummings brand and the Mix-A-Soda name. The other three models were sold only under the Mix-A-Soda name. The Cummings-branded dispensers were sold exclusively to soft-drink bottlers (Pepsi-Cola, 7-Up, Coca-Cola, etc.), and these products carried the trademark decoration of the bottler's franchise. Mix-A-Soda dispensers were sold to independent soft-drink-equipment distributors, and the dispensers did not carry any franchise identification.

The Diebold products had a wide potential market. The soft-drink bottlers themselves sold to a diversified list of users. In addition, the Mix-A-Soda models were ideal for soda fountains, restaurants, bars, and any other place where soft drinks were dispensed over the counter by a personal attendant. Diebold also had one large model designed for volume locations such as stadiums, large drive-in restaurants, schools, and theaters.

To reach its market, the Diebold Company had a small sales organization headed by Ronald Hewitt. Reporting to him were a product training manager, a national accounts manager, and four division managers whose territories covered the United States. The company had no sales force but, instead, used 14 independent manufacturers' agents.

The division managers were responsible for supervising the activities of the manufacturers' agents. These agents were used by Diebold only to sell the Cummings dispensers exclusively to soft-drink bottlers. About 40 percent of the agents' time was devoted to selling the Cummings line. The agents were paid a commission of 6 percent on their sales of Cummings dispensers. The division managers also were responsible for selling the Mix-A-Soda line directly to the independent soft-drink-equipment distributors.

The Diebold Company had enjoyed a satisfactory growth rate during the past 6 years, according to Hewitt. Competition was increasing, however, and annual sales increases were now leveling off. Sales last year totaled $5.4 million. Of this volume, $3.3 million came from Cummings sales made by manufacturers' agents, and $2.1 million came from the division managers' sales of the Mix-A-Soda brand. Selling expenses were 10.6 percent of net sales, and the annual net profit was satisfactory, Hewitt reported.

The slowdown in Diebold's growth rate made Ronald Hewitt wonder whether his company's distribution structure was appropriate for meeting the competitive challenges in today's marketplace. Consequently, he began to examine some alternative channels of distribution. One alternative he considered was that of establishing a company sales force and discontinuing the use of manufacturers' agents. Hewitt had observed that most of Diebold's competitors operated their own sales force.

Hewitt envisioned a staff of 10 sales representatives, plus a field sales manager. To initiate the program, three of the present division managers would become members

CASE 15

PESCO FASTENER CORPORATION*

Evaluating a distribution system

■

of the sales force. The fourth division manager would be promoted to the position of field sales manager. The remaining sales reps would be recruited from among people known in the bottling industry. If qualified reps were not available, a company training program would be instituted to provide the required sales people.

The anticipated increase in sales volume was expected to provide for an improved compensation plan that would induce the division managers to become sales reps. For these experienced people, a proposed compensation plan of salary plus commission was expected to provide a net income of $24,000 a year. This was in addition to all expenses plus the company fringe benefits such as insurance and pension plans. Newly hired, inexperienced sales reps could expect to net about $18,000 per year, plus expenses and fringe benefits.

Hewitt realized that sales volume in some territories might be low for a while. He was so confident that his proposed plan would work, however, that he anticipated having smaller territories and a sales force of 15 reps (a 50 percent increase) in 4 years. He pointed out that 10 company sales people spending 100 percent of their time on Diebold products would be considerably more effective than 14 representatives spending only 40 percent of their time. Furthermore, a direct sales force would be more effective because its training, supervision, and motivation could be directed by company management.

Ron Hewitt's proposal was not favorably received by some of the other managers. The advertising agency executive, George Latrobe, who managed Diebold's advertising program, thought that Hewitt's plan was premature. "I might go for the change in the future," Latrobe said, "but right now I don't think you are big enough or strong enough to pull it off successfully. You are grossly underestimating the cost and difficulty of establishing and operating your own sales force. Furthermore, those manufacturers' agents that you cut loose will no longer be your strong supporters. Instead, they will turn into fierce competitors."

The production manager, Harvey Fraser, tried to calm things down with a compromise. He proposed that Diebold phase in the company sales force little by little. "Let's put company sales reps in territories that now can support them," he suggested. "Let's continue with our manufacturers' agents in low-volume territories. Let's not try to do everything all at once. You are asking for a significant change in our company philosophy as well as changing our distribution system. Changing our company culture will take time."

QUESTION

What changes, if any, should be made in Diebold Company's distribution structure?

The loss of four outstanding manufacturers' agents in less than a year caused the management of the Pesco Fastener Corporation to question its distribution structure. Ed Dutton, the vice president of sales, cited the firm's excellent growth record in defense of the present distribution system. But the company's chief operating executive, Oxford Snaith, believed that the sales growth was attributable primarily to

*Case prepared by Professor John Hess, University of Colorado.

Pesco's broadened product assortment and to the increasing market acceptance of fastener products. Mr. Snaith also noted that the two largest producers in the fastener industry used distribution systems that were substantially different from Pesco's. Consequently, he asked his executive assistant, Ramsey Mills, to make a thorough investigation of Pesco's distribution system.

The Pesco Fastener Corporation, located in eastern Pennsylvania, manufactured stamped metal fasteners. These sheet metal devices replaced nuts, bolts, rivets, screws, and welding in assembly operations. Stamped fasteners often cost only a fraction of other fastening methods, and in many operations they provide speedier and more secure assembly. Pesco produced a wide variety of types and sizes of fasteners for the company's inventory. In addition, custom-designed fasteners accounted for about 30 percent of the company's sales. With sales last year amounting to $27 million, Pesco was the third largest firm in an industry of some 25 producers.

Pesco used four different distribution-channel structures to reach its markets. The first consisted of 12 Pesco sales engineers who worked out of the company's main office. They covered the states in the industrial belt running from Illinois to New York. Last year they accounted for nearly $9 million in sales, and their average commission was 9 percent of sales. These sales engineers each had a territory, and they called directly on medium-sized accounts and also on wholesalers in the territory. When sales to any single account exceeded $30,000 a year, it was taken over as a house account. The sales engineer who had that account was reimbursed $1,500.

The second distribution structure involved five sales people, called field engineers, who handled the house accounts. These sales reps were responsible for selling to all large accounts, and they also provided technical assistance throughout the country to customers with especially knotty problems. The field engineers were paid a straight salary which last year amounted to 4 percent of their direct sales of $9.6 million.

As its third channel structure, Pesco used 26 manufacturers' agents, who last year generated $3.9 million in sales at a commission cost of 7 percent. Each agent had an exclusive territory and worked under the same house-account arrangements as the sales engineers. The agents called on wholesalers and industrial users.

Eight industrial distributors who handled the Pesco line on an exclusive-territory arrangement comprised the fourth segment of Pesco's distribution system. These wholesalers received a full discount on all orders physically handled by them, even if the sale was made by a manufacturers' agent or a sales engineer. A 4 percent override was paid to wholesalers on all orders shipped into their areas, except shipments made to house accounts. Last year, wholesalers handled 40 percent of the orders generated by manufacturers' agents and sales engineers. Wholesalers themselves generated $5.1 million in nonreferred business last year. The average wholesaler carried a fairly deep inventory of some 12 to 15 of the most popular types of fasteners, and 2 to 4 sizes in each type. Wholesalers' territories varied in size from several states to areas less than 100 miles in radius. Most of the distributors' sales reps provided technical service.

Pesco's two major competitors used quite different distribution methods. The industry leader had a vast network of wholesalers, none of whom had an exclusive territory. The wholesalers' markets were segmented by industry—that is, one group served the electronics industry, another the aircraft industry, and so on. The other

SHAPELY SACK COMPANY, INC. *

Physical distribution strategy

The Shapely Sack Company, Inc., produced a large variety of paper sacks that were sold throughout southern Michigan and northern Ohio and Indiana. Shapely was formed in 1947 in response to the demand for nonhygroscopic paper sacks by the then-burgeoning Midwestern concrete industry. Although cement sacks were still the main source of revenue (65 percent of gross sales), Shapely had recently diversified its production. The company currently obtained 30 percent of its revenue from the sales of complete lines of paper sacks to many independent grocery retailers and discount stores in south central Michigan. Shapely recognized its dependence on the production and sale of cement sacks. However, fluctuations in the construction industry prompted Shapely to consider expansion into industries that were relatively more stable.

The sales manager for Shapely had been in contact with representatives of Big Drum Foods, Inc. This was one of the largest and fastest-growing Midwestern supermarket chains, with outlets in Wisconsin, Illinois, and Michigan. Big Drum officials indicated their dissatisfaction with the quality of their present paper goods, and expressed a desire for an offer from Shapely for all or part of their paper sack requirements. These requirements were equivalent to 75 percent of Shapely's present production.

Shapely's president, Jerry Dominic, was very much interested in a contract with Big Drum. Shapely was in an excellent financial position to undertake a large expansion in production capacity. Before making any arrangements with Big Drum, however, Mr. Dominic wanted to be certain that Shapely would be able to meet or exceed Big Drum's requirements while maintaining its high standards of service to present customers.

A committee was organized by Mr. Dominic to provide recommendations on the advisability of taking all, or only selected parts, of Big Drum's business. The committee consisted of a representative from each of the company's functional areas: production, traffic, finance, and sales. Mr. Dominic recognized that the work of the committee did not use wholesalers at all but, instead, depended entirely upon manufacturers' agents and the producer's own sales people. This firm shipped from its three company-owned warehouses.

Pesco's wholesalers were happy with their arrangement. But Mr. Mills thought that the exclusive-distributor system limited distribution unduly and that the override arrangement was too expensive. Pesco's manufacturers' agents and sales engineers also were none too happy with the existing system. Their primary complaint was that the company took over their best accounts as house accounts just when these customers were becoming profitable. The manufacturers' agents also complained that Pesco's territories did not jibe with the agents' own sales areas and that problems of territorial encroachment existed.

QUESTION

What changes, if any, should Pesco make in its distribution system?

*Case prepared by Mr. Gani Browsh, under the supervision of Prof. Bernard J. LaLonde of Ohio State University.

committee would be analytical in nature. Consequently, he appointed to the committee the recent college graduates who would be most proficient with the latest quantitative techniques. The sales manager, because of his established rapport with key executives in Big Drum, was to act as the committee chairman.

As background information to aid the committee in its deliberations, Mr. Dominic provided the following descriptive summary of Shapely's current operations:

1. *Production facilities.* Recently moved into a new plant in Kalamazoo, Michigan; present production—555,000 pounds of paper sacks per week. Plant capacity—693,000 pounds per week. Plant capacity expandable by 20 percent with moderate investment in materials-handling equipment and dock facilities; expandable by an additional 40 percent with heavy investment in new paper-pressing and chemical-treatment equipment.

2. *Warehouse facilities.* Warehouse locations centered in areas of high cement production; Flint, Michigan; Mansfield, Ohio; and Fort Wayne, Indiana. Inventories in warehouses based on 4-week supply; Flint warehouse handles half of plant production. The other warehouses handle one-quarter each. Shipment from plant to warehouses is by company-owned truck, scheduled and supervised by the traffic department. Distribution from the warehouse to the customers is made by public carrier (truck), under the control of the warehouse supervisors.

3. *Supplies.* All raw materials used in the production of paper sacks is received by rail from sources in the upper peninsula of Michigan and from Canada. No difficulty is anticipated in the immediate future in securing whatever quantities of raw materials may be required.

4. *Customer service requirements.* Shapely's reputation is founded upon producing a very high quality product and upon the self-imposed requirement that 100 percent of all orders be filled within 3 days. Within this requirement, Shapely's emphasis is upon the cement aspect of demand, and deliveries to cement firms are made as soon as possible after the receipt of the order. Shapely is presently in the process of enlarging its private fleet of trucks to be able to ensure future performance according to these standards. At present, the number of customers served by the warehouses are as follows:

Flint: 270 cement plants, 412 supermarkets, 115 discount stores. All Michigan customers are served from the Flint warehouse.

Mansfield: 204 cement plants. All Ohio customers are served from the Mansfield warehouse.

Fort Wayne: 197 cement plants. All Indiana customers are served from the Fort Wayne warehouse.

5. *Control.* Reports are made daily by the warehouse superintendents to the company headquarters on the number and sizes of orders received on the previous day. In addition to this telephonic report, which is made to the finance department, the superintendents forward weekly acitivty reports and customer service complaints to the sales department. The sales department then coordinates with the production and traffic departments to ensure that warehouse resupply is adequate.

Prior to the first committee meeting, the sales manager distributed a memorandum. It described the sales and service requirements that Big Drum Foods, Inc. had indicated would form a prior condition to its contracting with Shapely. The following is a description of the geographical characteristics of Big Drum's retail system, and a summary of the conditions mentioned in the memorandum.

Big Drum's outlet system consists of 1,040 supermarkets uniformly dispersed throughout Wisconsin, Illinois, Indiana, and Michigan. Owing in part to Big Drum's "double-bagging" policy, paper sack requirements vary from 350,000 to 430,000 pounds per week, with an average requirement of about 416,000 pounds per week. It is expected that efforts to expand within this region will, in a few years, result in approximately 1,500 outlets, with an anticipated paper sack requirement of about 675,000 pounds per week. Big Drum's present inventory policies require that the stores not fall below a 2-day supply. Unless an individual store is forced to resort to this safety stock prior to its usual delivery date, deliveries are made on a once-a-week basis.

Distribution to the stores can be made directly by the supplier, or through the 21 Big Drum distribution centers. If distribution is to be made directly to the stores, the price at which Shapely is presently selling to grocery outlets would be acceptable. If distribution is to be made through the distribution centers, a substantial price discount would be required.

As the recent college graduate appointed to represent the traffic department, J. R. Kowalski was wondering how he should prepare himself for the first committee meeting. More specifically, he wondered (a) what factors the committee should consider; (b) what additional information would be required; (c) what problems he might encounter within the committee; and (d) in what ways the committee's recommendations might differ from those of on outside consultant in physical distribution.

QUESTION

What specific suggestions would you make to Mr. Kowalski in response to each of the four points he was concerned about?

PROMOTION

The design and management of a marketing subsystem for the purpose of informing and persuading present and potential customers

So far, we have developed three of the four parts of a marketing mix to reach the organization's target markets and achieve its marketing goals. We have considered strategies regarding the product, the pricing structure, and the distribution system. To complete the marketing mix, we now turn to the task of developing a promotional program.

In Chapter 18 we discuss promotion as a communication process, the concepts of the promotional mix and a promotional campaign, and finally, the governmental regulation of promotional activities. Chapter 19 covers the personal selling process and the management of a sales force. Chapter 20 is devoted to the management of advertising and sales promotion.

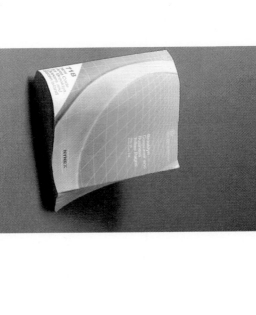

18

THE PROMOTIONAL PROGRAM

CHAPTER GOALS

This chapter is, essentially, a discussion of what promotion is and how it fits into a firm's complete marketing system. After studying this chapter, you should understand:

- Promotion and its relation to selling and nonprice competition.
- Promotion as a communication process.
- The concept of the promotional mix.
- The factors that shape a company's promotional mix.
- The problems and methods involved in determining the promotional appropriation.
- The concept of a promotional campaign.
- Government regulation of promotional activities.

A company's promotional campaign is a coordinated series of promotional activities built around a central idea or focal point that we call the *campaign theme*. The theme is simply the main promotional appeals dressed up in a distinctive, attention-getting form. Frequently the theme is expressed as a slogan. Now just how effective are these theme-slogans? Well, at this point we are listing 15 promotional slogans and are asking you to identify the brand associated with each slogan. The answers are on the next page.

1. When you care enough to send the very best.
2. A diamond is forever.
3. Oh-oh-oh what a feeling!
4. We are number 2, so we try harder.
5. You've come a long way, baby.
6. They melt in your mouth, not in your hands.
7. Reach out and touch someone.
8. The Breakfast of Champions.
9. The champagne of bottled beers.
10. I'd rather fight than switch.
11. You can trust your car to the man who wears the star.
12. Be all you can be.
13. Buy a piece of the Rock.
14. The un-cola drink.
15. Let your fingers do the walking.

Product planning, pricing, and distribution are marketing activities that are performed mainly within the company, or between the company and its marketing "partners." However, in its promotional activities, the firm gets its chance to communicate with potential customers. Chapters 18 to 20 deal with the management of the **promotional mix**—that is, the combination of personal selling, advertising, sales promotion, publicity, and public relations. These are the promotional tools that help an organization to achieve its marketing objectives. The statement that "nothing happens until somebody sells something" expresses rather well the place of promotional activities in today's business scene.

ANSWERS TO PROMOTIONAL THEME-SLOGANS:

1. Hallmark cards.
2. DeBeers Diamonds.
3. Toyota autos.
4. Avis rental cars
5. Virginia Slims cigarettes.
6. M and M candies.
7. A.T.&T.
8. Wheaties.
9. Miller's premium beer.
10. Parliament cigarettes.
11. Texaco products.
12. United States Army.
13. Prudential insurance.
14. 7-Up.
15. Yellow Pages (in telephone directories).

FIGURE 18-1
The role of promotion in the marketing mix.
To reach your target market, coordinate the elements in the promotional mix, and coordinate promotion with the other elements in your marketing mix.

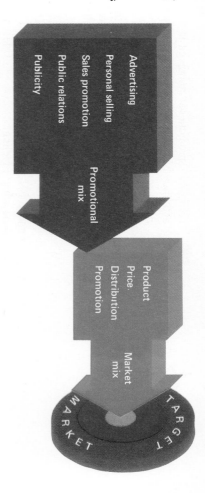

MEANING AND IMPORTANCE OF PROMOTION

Promotion is the element in an organization's marketing mix that is used to inform and persuade the market regarding the organization's products and services. Many people consider the market regarding the organization's products and services. Many is only one of the many components of marketing. We shall treat *selling* and *promotion* as synonymous terms, although promotion is preferred. For many people, *selling* suggests only the transfer of title or only the activities of sales people and does not include advertising or other methods of stimulating demand. In our definition, promotion includes advertising, personal selling, and all other selling tools. Together, they are basic factors in the marketing mix (see Fig. 18-1).

Promotional Methods

The two most widely used methods of promotion are (1) **personal selling** and (2) **advertising**. Other forms of promotion are:

3. **Sales promotion**, which is designed to supplement and coordinate personal selling and advertising efforts. Sales promotion includes such activities as setting up store displays, holding trade shows, and distributing samples, premiums, or "cents-off" coupons.

4. **Publicity**, which is a nonpersonal form of demand stimulation and is not paid for by the person or organization benefiting from it. Typically, publicity takes the

Coupons have become an important part of companies' sales promotion efforts.

form of a favorable news presentation—a "plug"—for a product, service, or organization. The plug is made in print, on radio or television, or in some form of public address. Typically, publicity is part of a firm's public relations effort.

5. **Public relations** which is a planned effort by an organization to influence some group's attitude or opinion toward that organization. The target market of the public relations effort may be any given "public," such as customers, a government agency, or people living near the promoting organization. The firm's public relations department is responsible for a product or for the entire organization.

In addition, there is a group of marketing strategies, discussed in earlier chapters, that are in part promotional. Such strategies as product differentiation, market segmentation, trading up or trading down, and branding belong in this group.

Basic Nature of Promotion

Basically, promotion is an exercise in information, persuasion, and communication. These three are related, because to inform is to persuade, and conversely, a person who is being persuaded is also being informed. And persuasion and information become effective through some form of communication. Many years ago, Prof. Neil Borden pointed up the pervasive nature of persuasion (influence) in our socioeconomic system. He said that "the use of influence in commercial relations is one of the attributes of a free society, just as persuasion and counterpersuasion are exercised freely in many walks of life in our free society—in the home, in the press, in the classroom, in the pulpit, in the courts, in the political forum, in legislative halls, and in government agencies for information."[1]

Promotion and Imperfect Competition

The American marketplace today operates under conditions of imperfect competition. That means there is product differentiation, nonrational buyer behavior, and less-than-complete market information. Under these conditions, promotional activities are essential. That is, a company needs promotion to aid in differentiating its product, to persuade the buyers, and to bring more information into the buying-decision process.

In economic terms, the basic purpose of promotion is to change the location and shape of the demand (revenue) curve for a company's product. (See Fig. 18-2 and recall the discussion of nonprice competition in Chapter 13.) Through the use of promotion, a company hopes to increase a product's sales volume at any given price. It also hopes that promotion will affect the demand elasticity for the product. The intent is to make the demand *inelastic* when the price increases, and *elastic* when the price goes down. In other words, management wants the quantity demanded to decline very little when the price goes up (inelastic demand). However, when the price goes down, management would like sales to increase considerably (elastic demand).

Need for Promotion

Several factors point up the need for promotion today. In the first place, as the distance between producers and consumers increases, and as the number of potential customers grows, the problem of market communication becomes significant.

Once middlemen are introduced into a marketing pattern, it is not enough for a

---

[1] Neil H. Borden, *The Economic Effects of Advertising*, Richard D. Irwin, Inc., Homewood, Ill., 1942, p. 802.

producer to communicate only with the ultimate consumers or industrial users. It becomes essential that the middlemen, too, be informed about products. Wholesalers, in turn, must promote the products to retailers, and retailers must communicate with consumers. In other words, even the most useful and want-satisfying product will be a marketing failure if no one knows it is available. A basic purpose of promotion is to disseminate information—to let potential customers know![1]

The intense competition among different industries, as well as among individual firms within an industry, has placed tremendous pressures on the promotional programs of individual sellers. In our economy of abundance, want-satisfaction has generally replaced the necessity of fulfilling only basic physiological needs. Consequently, customers are more selective in their buying choices, and a good promotional program is needed to reach them.

Oddly enough, promotion is also needed during periods of shortages—the opposite of abundance. During periods of shortages, advertising can stress product conservation and efficient uses of the product. The sales force can direct its efforts toward servicing accounts and helping customers solve their shortage-induced problems.

Any economic recession quickly points up the importance of selling. During such a period, there are no major problems in product planning. Channels remain essentially the same, and the pricing structure is basically unchanged. The key problem is selling. Promotion is needed to maintain the high material standard of living and the high level of employment that we have traditionally enjoyed in this country.

Promotion and Strategic Marketing Planning

In line with the strategic approach to marketing planning, a company should treat all its promotional efforts as a complete subsystem within the total marketing system. This means coordinating sales-force activities, advertising programs, and other promotional efforts. Unfortunately, today in many firms these activities still are fragmented, and advertising managers and sales-force managers often are in conflict.[2]

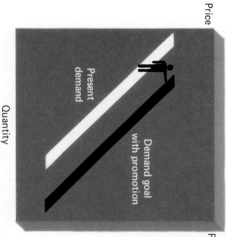

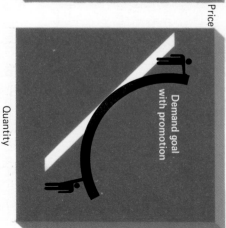

[2]See Alan J. Dubinsky, Thomas E. Barry, and Roger A. Kerin, "The Sales-Advertising Interface in Promotion Planning," *Journal of Advertising*, vol. 10, no. 3 (1981), pp. 35–41.

FIGURE 18-2
The goal of promotion: to change the pattern of demand for a product.
Through promotion a company attempts to (a) shift a product's demand curve to the right and (b) change the shape of the curve.

Price

Quantity
(a)

Present demand

Demand goal with promotion

Price

Quantity
(b)

Demand goal with promotion

As we discuss strategic promotional planning, once again we see the interrelationships among the major elements of the marketing mix. Promotional activities must be coordinated with activities in product planning, pricing, and distribution. Promotion is influenced, for example, by the type of product being marketed and by aspects of pricing strategy. Promotion is especially interrelated with distribution strategy. In fact, promotion should be viewed as a distribution-channel activity. It is a mistake for a manufacturer or a middleman to think of developing a promotional program without considering its interdependency with other organizations in that firm's channel. Each firm in a channel should develop strategies that take into consideration the roles played by other firms in the channel. Each firm should view its promotion as part of a total distribution-channel effort. Such a view then would be consistent with our systems approach to marketing.

Promotion also should be strongly influenced by a firm's strategic marketing plan. Suppose, for example, that a company faces production limitations imposed by materials shortages. This firm's marketing goal is simply to hold onto its present customers and its present market share—at least in the short run. Its strategic marketing planning and the strategic planning for its promotional program would be geared toward attaining that objective. The promotional strategies would be quite different from those of a company where a newly developed technology offered bright prospects for market expansion.

THE COMMUNICATION PROCESS

As noted earlier, promotion is basically an exercise in communication. Executives who understand something of the theory of communication should be able to better manage their firm's promotional program.

The word **communication** is derived from the Latin word *communis*, meaning "common." Thus, when you communicate, you are trying to establish a "commonness" with someone. Through the use of verbal or nonverbal symbols, you as the source send a message through a channel to a receiver, in an effort to share information. Fundamentally, the communication process requires only four elements—a **message**, a **source** of this message, a communication **channel**, and a **receiver**. However, in practice, additional elements come into play. The information that the sending source wants to share must first be **encoded** into transmittable form, *transmitted*, and then *decoded* by the receiver. Another element to be reckoned with is **noise**, which is anything that tends to distort the message at any stage of the system. The final element in the process—**feedback**—tells the sender whether the message was received and how it was perceived by the target. The feedback is also the basis for planning ahead. The sender learns how the communication may be improved by determining how well the message was received. If the message is not understood, then there is no true "commonness" or communication. Thus, **communication** is the verbal and/or nonverbal transmission of information between the sender and the receiver.

These elements constitute a general communications system—a concept that has many practical applications in promotion. In Fig. 18-3 we illustrate a communications system, using as examples some activities in a company's promotional program. The information source may be some marketing executives with ideas to communicate. They will encode these ideas into a transmittable message by putting them in adver-

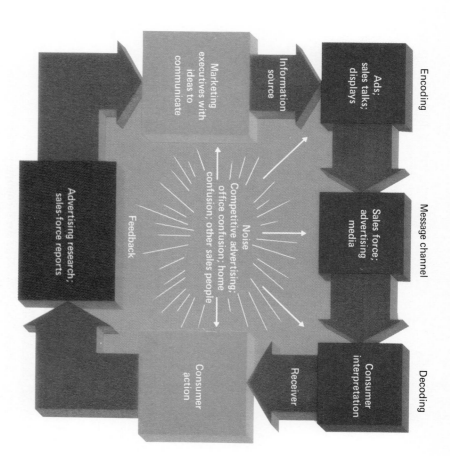

FIGURE 18-3
A marketing communication system illustrating activities in promotional program.

tisements or sales talks. The encoded message is then carried by a sales force or by advertising media (the message channels) to the destination receivers—perhaps various market segments. These consumer-receivers then decode (interpret) the message in light of their individual frames of reference. The closer the decoded message is to its encoded form (assuming it was encoded fully and accurately), the more effective the communication is. By evaluating the receiver's words or actions (feedback), the sender can judge how well the message got through. At various stages in the communication process, the message is subject to interference (noise) from competitors' advertising, confusion in the receivers' homes, or other disturbances.

DETERMINATION OF PROMOTIONAL MIX

Management has to determine what combinations of advertising, personal selling, and other promotional tools will make the most effective promotional program for a company. This is a tough job. Executives simply do not know exactly how much the advertising or any other promotional tool will help achieve the goals of the marketing program.

DO OENOLOGISTS KNOW HOW TO COMMUNICATE—ESPECIALLY WITH THE VAST POTENTIAL MARKET OF PEOPLE WHO KNOW VERY LITTLE ABOUT WINES?

An *oenologist* (also spelled *enologist*) is a specialist in the science and study of wines. Perhaps two oenologists can understand each other. But to the un-initiated outsider, the oenologist's language often seems to be a snobbish jargon that tries to impress us, but really tells us nothing. Consider, for example, the following descriptions of seven French wines displayed at an exhibition at Boulder, Colorado:

1. A sturdy, well-balanced white wine.
2. Fresher and with more grace than wine #1. An underlying soundness and sturdiness. Not fresh like a California wine can be. More serious in tone.
3. A lively rosé.
4. (Same wine as #3, but a vintage from 2 years earlier.) This wine has more color and a more serious rosé (than #3). Exquisite balance and finish,- with a nice complexity.
5. A quiet, subdued, elegant wine. But not for greatness.
6. More forward in bouquet. A big wine. A lasting finish.
7. A wine with an earthy quality. A light vintage with deep tones.

Now you tell us what they—the experts—are talking about. The name of the game in promotion is to communicate. If you cannot inform and persuade us, then you can't sell to us. And with wines, we wonder if the oenologists' message is really coming through.

Factors Influencing Promotional Mix

Four factors should be taken into account in deciding on the promotional mix. They are (1) the amount of money available for promotion, (2) the nature of the market, (3) the nature of the product, and (4) the stage of the product's life cycle.

FUNDS AVAILABLE

Regardless of what may be the most desirable promotional mix, the amount of money available for promotion is the real determinant of the mix. A business with ample funds can make more effective use of advertising than an enterprise with limited financial resources. Small or financially weak companies are likely to rely on personal selling, dealer displays, or joint manufacturer-retailer advertising. Lack of money may even force a company to use a less efficient promotional method. For example, advertising can carry a promotional message to far more people and at a lower cost *per person* than a sales force can. Yet the firm may have to rely on personal selling because it lacks the funds to take advantage of advertising's efficiency.

NATURE OF THE MARKET

As is true in most problem areas in marketing, decisions on the promotional mix will be greatly influenced by the nature of the market. This influence is felt in at least three ways.

- *Geographic scope of the market.* Personal selling may be adequate in a small local market, but as the market broadens geographically, greater stress must be placed on advertising.

- *Type of customers.* The promotional strategy is influenced by whether the organization is aiming its promotion at industrial users, household consumers, or middlemen. To illustrate, a promotional program aimed at retailers will probably include more personal selling than a program designed to attract household consumers. In many situations, the middlemen may strongly influence the promotional strategy used by a manufacturer. Often a retail store will not even stock a product unless the manufacturer agrees to do a certain amount of advertising.

- *Concentration of the market.* The total number of prospective buyers is one consideration. The fewer potential buyers there are, the more effective personal selling is, compared with advertising.

Another consideration is the *number of different types* of potential customers. A market with only one type of customer will call for a different promotional mix from that of a market with many different customer groups. A firm selling large power

To reach customers in a large geographical market requires advertising.

Simple answers to your questions about IBM Personal Computers.

If you're personally interested in personal computers, but want to know more, these definitions, descriptions and details should help.

"Just what is a personal computer, and how can I use it?"

An IBM Personal Computer is a computer designed for a person. It's a tool to help accomplish just about anything a person needs to do with information. It can help you start a small enterprise at home just as surely as it can help a corporate planner solve complex problems.

"Suppose I've never had my hands on a computer. How 'easy' will it be?"

As with any new tool, you'll want to get comfortable with your IBM Personal Computer before getting down to work. The nice thing is that the computer is on your side, interacting with you as you learn. Then you're running programs and feeling good with the results. It becomes clear that you've made a good investment, and you'll probably be telling your friends why they should get one.

"Are IBM Personal Computers simple or sophisticated?"

Both. Our systems have many advanced design features; they are there to make your computer — simple to operate and to help make you more productive. As with a well-designed car, the computer is designed around you, the user.

"What kind of software programs do you have to help me?"

Perhaps the world's largest and most up-to-date library of business programs has been written specifically for the IBM PC family. And among the best

of this software is IBM's Personal Computer Software. A great deal of it is compatible from one system to another or from office to home. You might be interested in help with your writing, filing, graphing, planning or reporting. And if you want to get all your ducks in a row, line them up with the IBM Assistant Series.

You can work with each program individually, or together as a team. There is also software to help you with accounting, inventory and payroll—practically anything, including communications packages to connect you to a company mainframe or outside information services.

"How expensive are they? And what if my needs change?"

With all the quality, power and performance built into IBM Personal Computers including their extraordinary expansion capabilities, you'll find they're surprisingly affordable. All the value doesn't end there, because if your needs change you can always expand or upgrade within the IBM PC family. It's a very extensive, very compatible family of products.

"If I want a demonstration, where do I go and who will show it to me?"

Go to any Authorized IBM Personal Computer Dealer or IBM Product Center, or contact your IBM marketing representative. All have received special training and you should find them quite helpful.

Ask to see the software programs that interest you most, and get your hands on the system yourself. Then you'll begin to see what this tool for modern times can do for you.

For a store near you, call 1-800-447-4700, Dept. HC. In Alaska or Hawaii, 1-800-447-0890.

PERSONAL COMPUTERS

IBM

saws used only by lumber manufacturers may be able to use personal selling effectively. In contrast, a company selling hand tools used by thousands of consumers and virtually all types of industrial firms probably will include liberal portions of advertising in its mix. Personal selling would be prohibitively expensive in reaching the many customers.

Finally, even though a firm sells nationally, it may find its market concentrated in relatively few spots. In this type of market concentration, emphasis on personal selling may be feasible. But it would be unrealistic if the potential customers were widely distributed all over the country.

NATURE OF THE PRODUCT

Consumer products and industrial goods frequently require different strategies. Within the category of consumer goods, a promotional mix is influenced by whether the product is generally considered a convenience, shopping, or specialty item. With regard to industrial goods, installations are not promoted in the same way as operating supplies.

Firms marketing convenience goods will normally rely heavily on manufacturers' advertising in addition to dealer displays. Personal selling plays a relatively minor role. This mix is best because a convenience product is widely distributed and needs no special demonstration or explanation.

In the field of industrial goods, the promotional strategy used to market installations usually features heavy emphasis on personal selling. The unit sales are typically large, products are often made to the customer's specification, and considerable presale and postsale personal service is necessary.

STAGE OF THE PRODUCT'S LIFE CYCLE

Promotional strategies for a product are influenced by the life-cycle stage that a product is in at any given time. Table 18-1 shows how these strategies change as the product moves through its life cycle.

Questions of Basic Promotional Strategy

By asking and then answering six questions regarding promotional strategy, we can set some guidelines for determining a company's promotional mix. The answers are related to the four factors that influence the mix.[3]

WHEN SHOULD PERSONAL SELLING BE THE MAIN INGREDIENT?

Personal selling will ordinarily carry the bulk of the promotional load (1) when the company has insufficient funds with which to carry on an adequate advertising program, (2) when the market is concentrated, or (3) when the personality of a sales person is needed to establish rapport. Personal selling will also be emphasized when the product (4) has a high unit value, (5) requires demonstration, (6) must be fitted to the individual customer's needs, as in the case of securities or insurance, or (7) involves a trade-in.

Selling industrial products requires personal selling.

---

[3]This question approach to promotional strategy was first noted in the writings of Prof. James D. Scott, University of Michigan.

TABLE 18-1   PROMOTIONAL STRATEGY AND PRODUCT LIFE-CYCLE STAGE

Market situation	Promotional strategy
Introductory stage	
Customers do not realize that they want the product, nor do they understand how it will benefit them.	Inform and educate potential customers. Tell them that the product exists, how it might be used, and what want-satisfying benefits it provides. In this stage, a seller must stimulate **primary demand**—the demand for a type of product—as contrasted with **selective demand**—the demand for a particular brand. For example, manufacturers had to sell consumers on the value of microwave kitchen ovens in general before it was feasible to promote Tappan or some other brand.
Growth stage	Normally, heavy emphasis must be placed on personal selling. Trade shows are also used extensively in the promotional mix. Rather than call on customers individually, the company can promote its new product at some type of trade show where prospective customers come to the seller's exhibit. Manufacturers also rely heavily on personal selling to attract middlemen to handle a new product.
Customers are aware of product benefits. The product is selling well, and middlemen want to handle it.	Stimulate selective (brand) demand. Increase the emphasis on advertising. Middlemen share more of the total promotional burden.
Maturity stage	
Competition intensifies and sales level off.	Advertising is used as a tool of persuasion rather than only to provide information. Intense competition forces sellers to devote larger sums to advertising and thus contributes to the declining profits experienced in the maturity stage.
Sales-decline stage	
Sales and profits are declining. New and better products are coming into the market.	All promotional effort should be cut back substantially, except when attempting to revitalize the product.

WHEN SHOULD ADVERTISING BE THE MAIN INGREDIENT?

If the market for the product is widespread, as in the case of a national consumer market, advertising should receive heavy emphasis. Advertising also works best when the seller wishes to inform many people quickly, as in the case of an announcement of new store hours or a special sale.

When to stress advertising and when to stress personal selling: a summary.

Do these greeting cards, hammer, and clothesline meet the criteria for advertising?

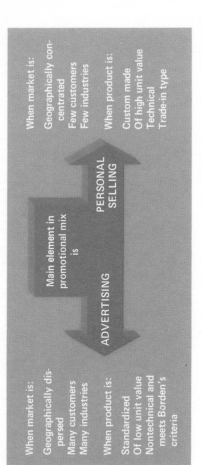

When market is:	When market is:
Geographically dispersed Many customers Many industries	Geographically concentrated Few customers Few industries
When product is:	When product is:
Standardized Of low unit value Nontechnical and meets Borden's criteria	Custom made Of high unit value Technical Trade-in type

Main element in promotional mix is

ADVERTISING   PERSONAL SELLING

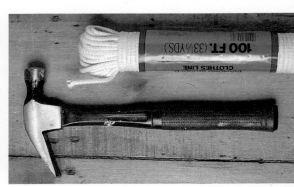

Certainly not every product lends itself to advertising. Many years ago, Prof. Neil Borden identified five criteria that can serve as guides for management in determining the "advertisability" of its product. If all five of these criteria are met, normally there is an excellent opportunity to advertise. However, this ideal situation rarely exists. Ordinarily, a product meets some, but not all, of these conditions. Then the decision on whether to advertise becomes more difficult.

The five criteria are as follows:

- The primary demand trend for the product should be favorable. In spite of public opinion to the contrary, advertising cannot successfully sell a product that people do not want. Nor can advertising reverse a declining primary demand.
- There should be considerable opportunity to differentiate the product. Then it is easier to advertise because the company has something to say. For this reason, automobiles or cosmetics are easier to advertise than salt or sugar. Products that are not easy to differentiate by *brand* may still be advertised by a trade association, such as the Sugar Association or the Pineapple Growers Association.
- The product should have hidden qualities. This condition affords the seller grounds for educating the market through advertising. On this point, a sofa or a mechanical device is easier to advertise than greeting cards.
- Powerful emotional buying motives should exist for the product. Then buying action can be stimulated by appeal to these motives. It is easier to build an effective advertising campaign for Weight Watchers than for an article such as clotheslines or hammers.
- The company must have sufficient funds to support an advertising program adequately.

WHEN SHOULD PROMOTIONAL EFFORTS BY RETAILERS BE STRESSED?

If the product has important qualities that can be judged at the point of purchase, or if it is a highly standardized item, it lends itself to dealer display. So do products that are purchased on impulse. And retailer promotion is particularly important when the retailer is better known in the market than the manufacturer.

WHEN SHOULD MANUFACTURER-RETAILER COOPERATIVE ADVERTISING BE USED?

There are three questions involved here. These queries and some brief answers follow:

- When should a manufacturer list its dealers' names and addresses in advertisements? The retailers' names should be mentioned particularly when the manufacturer employs selective or exclusive distribution policies. It then becomes important to tell the market where the product may be obtained.

- Under what conditions should a manufacturer pay a retailer to mention the manufacturer's product in the retailer's advertisements? The manufacturer may have to pay the retailer's advertising cost just to get the retailer to carry the commodity. Also, the retailer may be in a position to demand payment when the retailer's name has better selling power than the manufacturer's.

- When should a retailer emphasize the manufacturer's product in the store's advertising and display? A retailer should promote the manufacturer's products when the manufacturer's name is very important.

SHOULD MANUFACTURERS USE A "PUSH" OR A "PULL" PROMOTIONAL STRATEGY?

The questions in the two preceding sections involving retailer promotion and cooperative advertising remind us again that promotion is a distribution-channel activity. Consequently, manufacturers may aim their promotion either at middlemen or at end users to help move their products through the channels. Promotion aimed at middlemen is called a "push" strategy, and promotion aimed at end users is referred to as a "pull" strategy. Figure 18-4 illustrates these two strategies.

Using a **push strategy** means that the manufacturer will direct its promotion only at the middlemen who are the next link forward in this manufacturer's distribution channel. Let's take the case of a manufacturer who is selling through wholesalers and

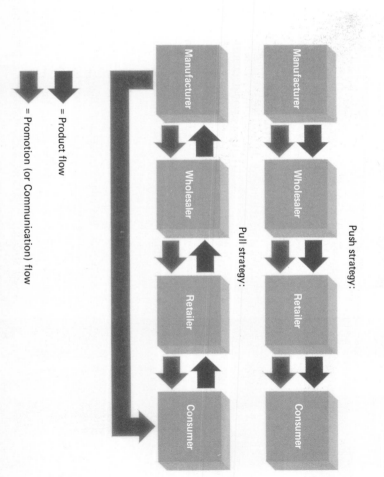

Push strategy:

Manufacturer → Wholesaler → Retailer → Consumer

Pull strategy:

Manufacturer → Wholesaler → Retailer → Consumer

= Promotion (or Communication) flow

= Product flow

FIGURE 18-4
Push and pull promotional strategies.

retailers to reach household consumers. This manufacturer will promote heavily only to the wholesalers. The wholesalers then use a push strategy to the retailers, and the retailers promote to the consumers. A push strategy usually involves the heavy use of personal selling and perhaps sales promotions such as demonstrating the product at trade shows. This promotional strategy is used by a great many manufacturers of industrial products, as well as for various consumer goods.[4]

When a **pull strategy** is used, a manufacturer directs the promotional effort at end users—usually ultimate consumers. The intention is to build up a consumer demand so that these people will ask for the product at retail stores. The retailers, in turn, will demand the product from wholesalers. In effect, the promotion to consumers is designed to *pull* the product through the channels. This strategy typically involves a heavy use of advertising plus possibly various forms of sales promotion such as premiums, free samples, or store demonstrations. Manufacturers of consumer packaged goods often use a pull strategy to get their products stocked on supermarket shelves.

As a practical matter, these push-pull strategies are extremes. Rarely does a company employ one of these strategies exclusively. Most firms—especially those marketing to ultimate consumers—both push and pull their product through the channels. Companies such as Du Pont, IBM, Johnson & Johnson, Eastman Kodak, and Procter & Gamble, for example, advertise heavily to end users. At the same time, these same firms have excellent sales forces which promote their products to wholesalers and large retailers.

SHOULD PROMOTIONAL ACTIVITY BE CONTINUED WHEN DEMAND IS HEAVY OR EXCEEDS CAPACITY?

The answer is a definite "yes." It is important that a manufacturer's name is kept before the public. A market is a dynamic institution, and customer loyalty is a "sometime thing." Old customers leave and new customers must be won. If conditions of high demand persist, they are certain to attract competitors. In any event, the nature of the advertising message may change. When demand is heavy in relation to supply, the advertiser probably will switch to institutional or indirect-action advertising.

Is this a push or pull strategy?

DETERMINATION OF TOTAL PROMOTIONAL APPROPRIATION ■

It is extremely difficult to establish promotional appropriations. Management lacks reliable standards for determining (1) how much to spend on advertising or personal selling in total or (2) how much to spend on specific activities within each area. An even more serious problem is that management normally cannot assess the results of its promotional expenditures. A firm may decide to add 10 sales people or increase its trade-show budget by $200,000 a year. But it cannot determine precisely what increase in sales or profits is to be expected from these moves. Nor can anyone measure with a high degree of certainty the relative values of the two expenditures.

Promotional activities usually are budgeted as current operating expenses, implying that their benefits are used up immediately. Through the years, however, several

---

[4] For a report on the sales and profit impact of various push marketing strategies, see Michael Levy, John Webster, and Roger A. Kerin, "Formulating Push Marketing Strategies: A Method and Application," *Journal of Marketing,* Winter 1983, pp. 25–34.

Methods of Determining Appropriation

There are four basic methods of determining the appropriation for promotion. These methods are frequently discussed in connection with the advertising appropriation alone, but they may also be applied to the total promotional appropriation.

RELATION TO SALES

The promotional appropriation may be related in some way to company income. The expenditures may be set as a percentage of past or anticipated sales. However, some businesses prefer to budget a fixed amount of money per *unit* of past or expected future sales. Manufacturers of products with a high unit value and a low rate of turnover (automobiles or appliances, for example) frequently use the unit method.

This **percentage-of-sales method** is probably the mostly widely used of all those discussed here. It has achieved broad acceptance because it is simple to calculate. It also sets the cost in relation to sales income and thus has the effect of being a variable expense rather than a fixed expenditure.

Actually, the method is unsound and logically inconsistent. By setting promotional expenditures on the basis of past sales, management is saying that promotion is a *result* of sales when, in fact, it is a *cause* of sales. Even when promotion is set as a percentage of *future* sales, this method is logically indefensible. By forecasting *future* sales and then setting the promotional appropriation, management is still considering advertising and personal selling to be a *result* of sales. If sales depend upon promotion, as is truly the case, they cannot be forecast until the promotional appropriation has been determined. Another undesirable result of this method is that it reduces promotional expenditures when sales are declining. And this is just when promotion usually is most needed.

TASK OR OBJECTIVE

A much sounder basis for determining the promotional budget is to decide what tasks the promotional program must accomplish, and then to determine what this will cost. Various forms of this method are widely used today. The *task method* forces management to define realistically the goals of its promotional program.

Sometimes this approach is called the *buildup method* because of the way it operates. For example, as one goal, a company may elect to enter a new geographic market. The executives then decide that this venture will require 10 additional sales people. Compensation and expenses of these people will cost a total of $520,000 per year. Salary for an additional sales supervisor and expenses for ra office and administrative needs will cost $70,000. Thus, in the personal selling part of the promotional mix, an extra $590,000 must be appropriated. Similar estimates can be made for the anticipated cost of advertising, sales promotion, and other promotional tools to be used. Thus the promotional appropriation is *built up* by adding up the costs of the individual promotional tasks needed to reach the goal of entering a new territory.

economists and business executives have proposed that advertising (and presumably other promotional efforts) should be treated as a capital investment. Their reasoning is that the benefits and returns on these investments often (1) are not immediately evident and (2) are spread over several years.

USE OF ALL AVAILABLE FUNDS

A new company frequently plows all available funds into its promotional program. The objective here is to build sales for the first 1 to 5 years. After that period, management expects to earn a profit and be able to budget for promotion in a different manner.

FOLLOW COMPETITION

A weak method of determining the promotional appropriation, but one that is used enough to be noted here, is to match the promotional expenditures of competitors. Sometimes only one competitor is followed. In other cases, management will have access to industry averages through its trade association, and these will become company benchmarks. The system is weak on at least two counts. First, a firm's competitors may be just as much in the dark regarding how to set a promotional budget. Second, one company's promotional goals and strategies may be quite different from those of its competitors, because of differences in the firms' strategic marketing planning.

THE CAMPAIGN CONCEPT: AN EXERCISE IN STRATEGIC PLANNING

In planning the total promotional program for an organization, management should make use of the campaign concept. A **campaign** is a coordinated series of promotional efforts built around a single theme and designed to reach a predetermined goal. In effect, a campaign is an exercise in strategic planning.

Although the term *campaign* is probably thought of most often in connection with advertising, we should apply the campaign concept first to the entire promotional program. Then the total promotional campaign can be subdivided into its advertising, personal selling, and sales promotion components. These subcampaigns can then be planned in more detail, to work toward the program goal.

Many types of promotional campaigns may be conducted by a company, and some may be run concurrently. Geographically, a firm may have a local, regional, or national campaign, depending upon the available funds and objectives. One campaign may be aimed at consumers, and another at wholesalers and retailers. The stage of a product's life cycle may determine whether a pioneering or a competitive campaign will be conducted.

In developing a promotional campaign, a firm should first establish the campaign goal. This goal, and the buying motives of the customers, will determine what selling appeals will be stressed. Assume that the goal of a promotional campaign put on by an airline is to introduce its new jumbo jet service. Then the appeals might be to the customers' desire for speed, a quiet and restful trip, or fine food and courteous service. The same airline might want to increase its plane loadings of air freight. Then the ads and the personal selling might stress speed of delivery, reduction in losses due to spoilage and handling, or convenient schedules.

A campaign revolves around a central idea or focal point. This "theme" permeates all promotional efforts and tends to unify the campaign. A **theme** is simply the promotional appeals dressed up in a distinctive, attention-getting form. It expresses

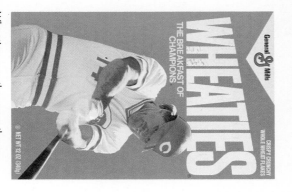

General Mills
WHEATIES
THE BREAKFAST OF CHAMPIONS
CRISPY CRUNCHY
WHOLE WHEAT FLAKES
© NET WT 12 OZ (340g)

Wheaties uses the same theme each year but a different champion.

the product's benefits. Frequently the theme takes the form of a slogan, such as AT&T's "Reach out and touch someone" or the U.S. Army's "Be all you can be." Some companies use the same theme for several campaigns; others develop a different theme for each new campaign.

For a promotional campaign to be successful, the efforts of the participating groups must be coordinated effectively. This means that:

- The *advertising program* will consist of a series of related, well-timed, carefully placed ads that reinforce the personal selling and sales promotional efforts.

- The *personal selling effort* will be coordinated with the advertising program. The sales force will explain and demonstrate the product benefits stressed in the ads. The sales people will also be fully informed about the advertising part of the campaign—the theme, the media used, and the schedule for the appearance of ads. The sales people, in turn, should carry this information to the middlemen so that they can become effective participants in the campaign.

- The *sales promotional devices*, such as point-of-purchase display materials, will be coordinated with the other aspects of the campaign. For each campaign, new display materials must be prepared. They should reflect the ads and appeals used in the current campaign, to maximize the campaign's impact at the point of sale.

- *Physical distribution management* will ensure that adequate stocks of the product are available in all outlets prior to the start of the campaign.

REGULATION OF PROMOTIONAL ACTIVITIES ■

Regulation of promotional activities is authorized in two major pieces of federal legislation: the Federal Trade Commission Act (and its Wheeler-Lea Amendment) and the Robinson-Patman Act. Both laws are administered by the Federal Trade Commission (FTC).

Federal Regulation

Because the primary objective of promotion is to sell something by communicating with a market, promotional activities attract attention. Consequently, abuses by individual firms are easily and quickly noted by the public. This situation in turn soon leads to (1) public demand for correction of the abuses, (2) assurances that they will not be repeated, and (3) general restraints on promotional activities. To answer public demand, regulations have been established by the federal government and most state governments. In addition, many private business organizations have established voluntary guidelines for the direction of their promotional activities. In addition, the advertising industry itself, through the American Association of Advertising Agencies and the National Advertising Review Board, does a considerable amount of self-regulation.

In the 1980s, the FTC has perhaps been less aggressive than it was in the 1970s in policing the advertising business. Nevertheless, the FTC still potentially has plenty of "clout"—particularly where there may be false or deceptive advertising. For example, the commission may require a company to submit test results or other information to prove the company's advertising claims concerning its products. Furthermore, this supporting information may later be made public by the FTC.

In another situation, the FTC may compel a firm to run "corrective advertising"

Warning: The Surgeon General Has Determined That Cigarette Smoking Is Dangerous to Your Health.

This warning will never be seen again.

Instead, these new, more powerful Surgeon General's warnings will now appear:

- SMOKING CAUSES LUNG CANCER, HEART DISEASE, EMPHYSEMA, AND MAY COMPLICATE PREGNANCY.

- SMOKING BY PREGNANT WOMEN MAY RESULT IN FETAL INJURY, PREMATURE BIRTH, AND LOW BIRTH WEIGHT.

- CIGARETTE SMOKE CONTAINS CARBON MONOXIDE.

- QUITTING SMOKING NOW GREATLY REDUCES SERIOUS RISKS TO YOUR HEALTH.

We urge every smoker to consider the seriousness of these new warnings. And rid themselves of the most preventable cause of illness and death in the world today.

American Heart Association

AMERICAN ✝ LUNG ASSOCIATION
The Christmas Seal People ®

AMERICAN CANCER SOCIETY®

Federal regulation has certainly affected the cigarette industry.

to counteract allegedly false ads the company has previously run. Thus, ITT Continental Baking Company had to devote 25 percent of its advertising budget for 1 year to correcting any misunderstanding left in consumers' minds as a result of previous ads for Profile bread. Previous ads had claimed that the use of Profile bread was effective for weight reduction. In fact, the only reason a slice of this bread was lower in calories was that the slices were thinner than those of other breads.[5]

FEDERAL TRADE COMMISSION ACT AND WHEELER-LEA AMENDMENT

The governmental measure that has the broadest influence on promotional messages in interstate commerce is the Federal Trade Commission Act, with its Wheeler-Lea Amendment. The act prohibits unfair methods of competition. And, according to FTC and federal court decisions, clearly one area of unfair competition is false, misleading, or deceptive advertising.

Loopholes in the Federal Trade Commission Act led to the enactment of the Wheeler-Lea Amendment in 1938. With respect to promotion, the amendment considerably strengthened the original act in two ways. First, it specifies that an unfair competitive act violates the law if it injures the *public*, regardless of the effect this practice may have on a *competitor*. Under the original Federal Trade Commission Act, false or misleading advertising had to injure a competitor before a violation could be charged.

[5]For a comprehensive analysis of corrective advertising, including its historical background, the key legal concepts involved, and the managerial issues involved, see William L. Wilkie, Dennis L. McNeill, and Michael B. Mazis, "Marketing's 'Scarlet Letter': The Theory and Practice of Corrective Advertising," *Journal of Marketing*, Spring 1984, pp. 11–31.

The second significant change concerns enforcement of cease-and-desist orders issued by the commission. Under the amendment, such orders *automatically* become effective in 60 days unless the defendant appeals to the federal courts. Previously, a cease-and-desist order could be issued, but if there was no compliance, the commission had the burden of seeking enforcement.

ROBINSON-PATMAN ACT

The Robinson-Patman Act, which was discussed in connection with price strategies, has two sections relating to price discrimination involving promotional allowances. These sections state that a seller must offer promotional services and facilities, or payments for them, on a proportionally equal basis to all competing customers.

Assume that a manufacturer wants to furnish demonstrators, cooperative advertising programs, or any other type of promotional assistance. This promotional device or a comparable one must be made available proportionally to all firms competing in the resale of the product. Generally the courts have accepted the "amount purchased" as a basis for define. "Proportionally equal basis" has sometimes been hard to allocation. Say store A buys $150,000 worth of merchandise per year from a manufacturer and store B purchases $50,000 worth. Then store A may be offered promotional allowances valued at 3 times those offered to store B.

State and Local Regulation

At the state and local levels, we note two types of legislation that regulate promotional activities. The first of these is patterned after the *Printers' Ink* model statute, developed by *Printers' Ink* magazine in 1911 to establish "truth in advertising" in intrastate commerce. Today, almost all states have a *Printers' Ink* statute or one quite similar to it. Several states have established a separate state agency to handle various "consumer defense" activities.

A general type of *local* legislation that affects personal selling goes under the title "Green River" ordinance. This type of legislation is named after the town of Green River, Wyoming, one of the first places to enact such a law. Green River ordinances restrict sales people who represent firms located outside the affected city and who sell door to door or call on business establishments. These laws were supposedly passed to protect local citizens from fraudulent operators. Actually, the measures also serve to insulate local businesses from outside competition.

Regulation by Private Organizations

Several kinds of private organizations also exert considerable control over the promotional practices of business. Many magazines, newspapers, and radio and television stations refuse to accept advertisements they feel are false, misleading, or in bad taste. Some trade associations have established a code of ethics that includes points pertaining to sales-force and advertising activities. Some trade associations regularly censor advertising appearing in their association journals. And Better Business Bureaus located in major cities all over the country are working to control false or misleading promotion.

SUMMARY ◼

Promotion is the fourth major component of a company's total marketing mix (along with product planning, pricing, and distribution). Promotion is synonymous with selling. Its intent is to inform, persuade, and influence people. It is a basic ingredient in nonprice competition, and it is an essential element in modern marketing. The three major forms of promotion are personal selling, advertising, and sales promotion.

The promotional activity in marketing is basically an exercise in communication. Fundamentally, the communication process consists of a source sending a message through a channel to a receiver. Some sort of noise is usually present, which tends to interfere with the transmission of the message. For effective promotion, marketers must understand the makeup of their communication channels and the effects of this noise.

When deciding on the appropriate promotional mix (the combination of advertising, personal selling, and other promotional tools), management should be influenced by four factors: (1) money available, (2) nature of the market, (3) nature of the product, and (4) stage of the product's life cycle. A series of six questions relating to basic promotional strategy can be of help in applying the four factors to develop a promotional mix.

It is difficult to set a dollar figure for the total promotional appropriation, but it must be done. The most commonly used method is to set the appropriation as a percentage of sales. Unfortunately, this is an illogical method. A better approach is to decide what promotional goals are to be achieved, and then figure out how much this will cost. These funds and the promotional efforts of the firm should be coordinated into a campaign built around a single theme and designed to reach a predetermined goal.

As a result of continuous criticism, the federal government has passed regulations affecting promotion. The main federal laws are the Federal Trade Commission Act, its Wheeler-Lea Amendment, and the Robinson-Patman Act. The FTC is charged with administering the federal legislation in this area. Promotional practices also are regulated by state and local legislation, by the activities of private organizations, and by the advertising industry itself.

KEY TERMS AND CONCEPTS ◼

Promotional mix 417
Promotion 418
Selling 418
Advertising 418
Personal selling 418
Sales promotion 418
Publicity 418
Public relations 419
Nonprice competition 419

Using promotion to shift the demand curve 419
Communication process 420
Primary demand 426
Selective demand 426
Push and pull strategies 428
Promotional appropriation 429
Percentage-of-sales method 430
Task or objective method 430

Promotional campaign 431
Campaign theme 431
Federal legislation regulating promotion: 432
   Federal Trade Commission Act 433

Wheeler-Lea Act 433
Robinson-Patman Act 434
State and local legislation regulating promotion 434

QUESTIONS AND PROBLEMS

1. What is the difference between selling and marketing?

2. Explain and illustrate a communication system using the following situations:
   a. A college student trying to sell her father on buying her a new car.
   b. A sales person talking to the college student about buying a car.

3. Explain how the *nature of the market* would affect the promotional mix for the following products:
   a. Contact lenses.
   b. Golf balls.
   c. Plywood.
   d. Colgate toothpaste.
   e. Laser disc record player.
   f. Mainframe computers.

4. Explain how the promotional mix is likely to be affected by the life-cycle stage in which each of the following products is situated.
   a. Television satellite dish.
   b. HBO cable television.
   c. Crest toothpaste.
   d. IBM personal computer.

5. Using Borden's criteria, evaluate the advertisability of each of the following products. Assume that sufficient funds are available in each case.
   a. Automobile tires.
   b. Revlon cosmetics.
   c. Light bulbs.
   d. Sony Walkman.

6. Explain why personal selling is, or is not, likely to be the main ingredient in the promotional mix for each of the following products:
   a. Individual retirement account (IRA).
   b. Tide liquid detergent.
   c. Home swimming pool.
   d. Large order of McDonald's french fries.

7. Explain why retailer promotional efforts should or should not be stressed in the promotional mix for the following:
   a. Levi's 501 Jeans.
   b. Sunkist oranges.
   c. Women's cosmetics.
   d. Bank credit card.

8. Why is the percentage-of-sales method so widely used to determine the promotional appropriation when, in fact, most authorities recognize the task or objective method as the most desirable one?

9. Identify the central idea—the theme—in some current promotional campaigns.

10. Assume you are marketing a liquid that removes creosote (and the danger of fire) from chimneys used for wood-burning stoves. Briefly describe the roles you would assign to advertising, personal selling, sales promotion, and publicity in your promotional campaign.

11. How did the Wheeler-Lea Amendment strengthen the Federal Trade Commission Act?

12. Explain the term *proportionally equal basis* in connection with manufacturers' granting advertising allowances. Consider especially the situations where retailers vary in size.

13. Do you think we need additional legislation to regulate advertising? To regulate personal selling? If so, explain what you would recommend.

Clockwise from top left: Nancy Reck, Jim Hansberger, Helen McVoy, and Greg Finneran

MANAGEMENT OF PERSONAL SELLING

CHAPTER GOALS

In this chapter we look at personal selling from both the sales manager's and the sales person's viewpoint. After studying this chapter, you should understand:

- The importance of personal selling in our economy and in a company's marketing program.
- How sales jobs are different from other jobs.
- The wide variety of sales jobs.
- The steps involved in the selling process—that is, in making a sale.
- The steps involved in staffing and operating a sales force.
- A little about the evaluation of a sales person's performance.

oday's top sales people are well-trained professionals. As the major factors contributing to their success, they list honesty, sincerity, service to customers (both before and after a sale), and long hours of research. Most of the compensation of the top income earners comes from commissions. Let's meet a few of these super salesmen and saleswomen.

Jim Hansberger, 39, has come a long way from his student days at the University of Georgia where he formed a club to invest in the stock market. As a financial consultant at Shearson Lehman/American Express in 1984 (not a good year on Wall Street), he earned in excess of $650,000. He was involved in handling many financial services, mainly for individual customers, including real estate management and retirement plans.

Helen McVoy was a 65-year-old grandmother and plant collector. She also was a national sales director for Mary Kay Cosmetics, earning $375,000 in 1984, largely on commissions from sales made by sales representatives whom she supervised.

Don Wilson, 43, was the top sales representative for New York Life Insurance Company in 1984, earning about $470,000 in commissions. Based in Anchorage, Alaska, Don found his major clients were privately held companies which bought everything from employee benefit programs to estate-planning programs from him.

Dorothy Cole, 33, was a district sales manager for Compaq Computer. Based in Los Angeles in 1984, she had an income in the "high five figures" (something under $100,000). She sold Compaq personal computers (which are IBM-compatible models) to computer chains such as Computerland and Inacomp).

Greg Finneran, 58, was one of 3 M's (Scotch Tape, etc.) most highly paid sales reps in 1984. He was based in New Jersey and sold a line of sandpaper, tape, and window insulation to home-center stores.

Nancy Reck, 30, was a successful sales representative for Xerox, selling Xerox copiers and electronic typewriters door to door to small companies while her husband was in graduate school. Her income in 1984 was estimated at about $50,000, even though she had a low-volume territory of 17 counties in her home state of North Carolina. Since then she was promoted to a new job which was a stepping stone to management.[1]

[1]Adapted from "Meet the Savvy Supersalesmen," *Fortune*, Feb. 4, 1985, pp. 56–62; and "On the Job with a Successful Xerox Saleswoman," *Fortune*, Apr. 30, 1984, pp. 102–109.

Selling is essential to the health and well-being of our economic system, and it probably offers more job opportunities than any other single vocation today. Yet, personal selling is frequently criticized, and it is very hard to attract qualified young people into selling jobs. Truly, the task of managing a sales force is a difficult one. But the level of success in this task often has a direct bearing on the level of success of a company's total marketing program.

NATURE AND IMPORTANCE OF PERSONAL SELLING

In personal selling, Linda Slaby-Baker can tailor a presentation to an individual customer.

The goal of all marketing efforts is to increase profitable sales by offering want-satisfaction to the market over the long run. *Personal selling* is by far the major promotional method or tool used to reach this goal. More than ever, sales people today are a dynamic power in the business world. They are responsible for directly generating more revenue in our economy than workers in any other single vocation. The efforts of sales people have a direct impact on such diverse activities as:

- The success of new products.
- Keeping existing products in strong market positions.
- Constructing manufacturing facilities.
- Opening new businesses and keeping them open.
- Generating sales orders that result in shipping products to customers all over the world.

The number of people employed in advertising is in the *thousands*. In personal selling, the number is in the *millions*. In many companies, personal selling is the largest single operating expense, often equaling 8 to 15 percent of net sales. In contrast, advertising costs average 1 to 3 percent of sales. Expenditures for sales people's salaries, commissions, and travel expenses, the cost of operating sales branches, and the expenses of managing these sales people all add up to a tidy sum.

Relative Merits

Personal selling is the *personal* communication of information to persuade a prospective customer to buy something—a product, service, idea, or something else. This is in contrast to the mass, *impersonal* communication of advertising, sales promotion, and the other promotional tools.

Compared to these other promotional tools, personal selling has the advantage of being *more flexible* in operation. Sales people such as Quaker Oats' Linda Slaby-Baker can tailor their sales presentations to fit the needs and behavior of individual customers. Also, sales people can see the customer's reaction to a particular sales approach and then make the necessary adjustments on the spot. A second merit of personal selling is that usually it can be *focused on prospective customers*, thus minimizing wasted effort. By contrast, in most forms of advertising, much of the cost is devoted to sending the message to people who are in no way real prospects. In personal selling, a company has an opportunity to pinpoint its target market far more effectively than with any other promotional device.

In most instances, a third feature of personal selling is that it *results in the actual sale*. Advertisements can attract attention and arouse desire, but usually they do not arouse buying action or complete the sale.

The major limitation of personal selling is its high cost. It is true that the use of a sales force enables a business to reach its market with a minimum of wasted effort. However, the cost of developing and operating a sales force is high. Another disadvantage is that personal selling is often limited by a company's inability to get the caliber of people needed to do the job. At the retail level, for example, many firms have abandoned their sales forces and shifted to self-service for this very reason. In spite of the great many job opportunities provided in this field, personal selling is frequently criticized, and it is very hard to attract qualified young people into selling jobs.

Role conflict and ambiguity can occur as a sales rep deals with a manager and then with a customer.

Nature of the Sales Job

The sales job of today is quite different from that of years gone by. True, high-pressure selling still exists and may always have a role in some fields, but it is no longer typical. Instead, to implement the marketing concept in a manufacturing firm, for example, we see a new type of sales person—a *territorial manager*. Rather than just push whatever the factory has to sell, our new breed of sales person interprets customers' wants. The sales reps either fill these wants with existing products or relay the wants to the producer so that appropriate new products may be developed. They engage in a *total* selling job—missionary selling, servicing customers, being territorial profit managers, and acting as a mirror of the market as they feed back marketing information. Their job includes selling to new customers, obtaining reorders from existing accounts, selling new products, helping customers find new uses for existing products, and helping customers to use the products properly.

By the very nature of this new position, sales people experience problems—role ambiguity and role conflict. Ambiguity enters into a sales job because the sales people fill so many different roles. They persuade prospective customers, service the accounts, set up displays, expedite orders, coordinate deliveries, gather information, collect on past-due accounts, help solve customers' problems, etc.

In performing these many activities, sales people often encounter role conflict. The reps must identify first with their companies and then with their customers. In so doing, they are subject to conflicts regarding whose position—the company's or the customer's—they are supporting. Also, within the company, several groups with whom sales people interact (credit and production departments, for example) often have differing and even conflicting expectations. The emotional demands stemming from these situations often are great, and they usually must be handled pretty much by the sales people themselves.

Sales Jobs are Different from Other Jobs

Sales jobs usually are quite different from other jobs in several ways:

- Sales people represent their company to the outside world. Consequently, opinions of a company and its products often are formed from impressions left by the sales force. The public ordinarily will not judge a firm by its office or factory workers.

• Other employees usually work under close supervisory control, whereas a sales force typically operates with little or no direct supervision. Moreover, to be successful, sales people often must be creative and persistent and show great initiative—and all of this requires a high degree of motivation.

• Sales people probably need more tact, diplomacy, and social poise than other employees in an organization. Many sales jobs require the sales person to display considerable social intelligence in dealing with buyers.

• Sales people are among the few employees authorized to spend company funds. They spend this money for entertainment, transportation, and their other business expenses.

• Sales jobs frequently require a considerable amount of traveling and much time spent away from home and family. Being in the field puts sales people in enemy territory, so to speak. There they deal with customers who seem determined not to buy the sellers' products. These mental stresses, coupled with the physical demands of long hours and traveling, combine to require a degree of mental toughness and physical stamina rarely demanded in other types of jobs. Selling is hard work!

Sales People as Strategic Planners

Earlier in this chapter we referred to the modern professional sales person as a territorial manager. Truly, today's sales reps may very well do much of the strategic planning for their individual territories. Sales reps may very well do much of the strategic planning for their individual territories. Sales people typically operate with little or no direct supervision. They usually are given a reasonably well defined geographical territory, a product mix, and a price structure. They also may have been through a company training program. They probably are assigned performance goals in the form of a quota.

Within those general guidelines, however, the reps may have to develop their own specific strategies and tactics to reach their goals. They will make their own strategic decisions regarding (1) what target markets they will solicit, (2) how they will deal with each market segment, and (3) what particular products they will push.

Wide Variety of Sales Jobs

No two selling jobs are alike. Even when sales jobs are grouped on some basis, we find that the types of jobs and the requirements needed to fill them cover a wide spectrum. Consider, for example, the job of a Pepsi-Cola driver-sales person who calls in routine fashion on a group of retail stores. That job is in a different world from the job of an IBM computer sales person who sells a system for storing and retrieving information to an automobile manufacturer such as Chrysler. An Avon representative selling cosmetics door to door has a job only remotely related to that of an airplane manufacturer's rep selling executive-type aircraft to large firms.

A useful way to classify the many types of sales jobs is to array them on the basis of the creative skills required in the job, from the simple to the complex. One such classification, developed by Robert McMurry, a noted industrial psychologist, is the following:

1. Positions in which the job is primarily to deliver the product—for example, a *driver-sales person* for soft drinks, milk, or fuel oil. The selling responsibilities, if any, are secondary.

An inside order-taking sales job.

2. Positions in which the sales people are primarily *inside order takers*—for example, retail clerks standing behind counters. Most of the customers have already decided to buy; the sales clerks only serve them. The clerks may sell through suggestion, but ordinarily they cannot do much more.

3. Positions in which the sales people are primarily *outside order takers*, going to the customers in the field—for example, wholesale hardware or office supply sales people who call on retail stores.

4. Positions in which the sales people are not expected to solicit orders. Their job is to build goodwill, perform promotional activities, or provide service for customers. These are the *missionary sales people* for a grocery products manufacturer, for example, or the *detail sales people* for a pharmaceutical firm.

Dorothy Cole is a successful sales rep for Compaq Computer.

5. Positions in which the major emphasis is on the sales person's technical product knowledge—for example, a *sales engineer*.

6. Positions that demand *creative selling of tangible products*, such as vacuum cleaners, airplanes, encyclopedias, or computers. Customers may not be aware of their need for the product. Or they may not realize how the new product can satisfy their wants better than the product they are now using. When the product is of a technical nature, this category may overlap that of the sales engineer.

7. Positions that require *creative selling of intangibles*, such as insurance, advertising services, consulting services, or communication systems. Intangibles are typically difficult to sell because they cannot easily be demonstrated.

TELEMARKETING—THE WAVE OF THE FUTURE IN OUTSIDE SELLING?

The job of outside selling—the kind where the sales person goes to the customer, in contrast to inside (or across-the-counter) selling—is changing dramatically these days. Instead of the traditional in-person sales call, a growing number of sales reps are using the telephone and/or the computer to talk with customers. In effect, outside selling—especially outside *industrial* selling—is going electronic.

The prime factor accounting for this change is the dramatic increase in the cost of keeping sales people on the road. Some companies estimate that their travel expenses—transportation, hotel, and meals—are higher than their sales reps' compensation (salary, commission, and bonus).

Telephone selling, of course, has been used by many companies for decades. What is new today, however, is the innovative use of communication systems involving the telephone, television, and sometimes the computer to aid a company's selling effort and other marketing activities. The term **telemarketing** has been coined to describe these marketing communication systems.

Some companies—Louisiana Oil & Tire Company, for example—have increased sales and reduced costs by taking their field sales people away from their traveling jobs and bringing them into the office. There these reps have been trained to sell by telephone. In effect, personal selling and order taking are being moved from the field to a well-trained inside sales force. The field selling in these firms is shifting to sales promotion work such as instructing customers or providing technical advice and service.

In some companies, telemarketing is making the order-taking sales rep virtually obsolete. For example, American Hospital Supply and some of its customers have a sophisticated mainframe computer capacity so that the buyer's computer can talk to American Hospital's computer. The buyer's computer can determine product availability and shipping dates and, finally, can place an order. No sales people are involved and there is a lot less paperwork. Ford, Chrysler, GM, and American Motors are jointly developing a system whereby a manufacturer and its large suppliers will communicate electronically. This system will eliminate many personal sales calls and a mountain of paperwork.

In Europe, firms in the auto, chemical, steel, and shipbuilding industries are developing electronic communication systems involving manufacturers, suppliers, and even customs agents and shipping agents.

All of the examples cited in this box will save millions and even billions of dollars of personal selling expenses and other communications expenses. Furthermore, these telemarketing processes are expected to increase the operating efficiency and time responsiveness of the participating industries.*

---

*Adapted, in part, from "Rebirth of a Salesman: Willy Loman Goes Electronic," *Business Week*, Feb. 27, 1984, pp. 103–104, and "Detroit Tries to Level a Mountain of Paperwork," *Business Week*, Aug. 26, 1985, p. 94. See also John I. Coppett and Roy Dale Vorhees, "Telemarketing: Supplement to Field Sales," *Industrial Marketing Management*, August 1985, pp. 213–216.

THE STRATEGIC PERSONAL SELLING PROCESS

The personal selling process may be viewed as a logical sequence of actions—called the "5 P's,"—that are taken by a sales person in dealing with a buyer.[2] See Figure 19-1. This process leads, hopefully, to some desired customer action and ends with a follow-up to ensure customer satisfaction. The desired customer action usually is to get that person to buy something. In some cases, however, the desired action may be to get the customer to do some advertising, to display the product, or to reduce the price on the product.

Presale Preparation

In the sequence of events that—it is hoped—will lead to a sale, the first step is to make certain that the sales person is prepared. This means that he or she must be well acquainted with the product, the market, the competition, the techniques of selling—everything that conceivably could pertain to the sale.

Prospecting, or Locating Potential Buyers

The sales person is now ready to locate customers. This second step toward a sale involves drawing up a profile of the ideal prospect. The sales person can examine records of past and present customers in an effort to determine the characteristics of such prospects. From this profile the seller may develop a list of potential buyers. Sellers also may build a list of prospective customers from people who mailed in a coupon or telephoned an 800 number featured in an advertisement.

There are other ways in which sales people can acquire a list of prospects. Their sales manager may prepare a list for them; present customers may suggest new leads; present users may want later or different models of the product. And a little thought will often suggest logical prospects. For instance, sellers of home furnishings or telephone equipment find prospects in the regularly published lists of building permits issued. Sellers of many products find leads among birth or engagement announcements in newspapers.

Preapproach to Individual Prospects

Before calling on prospects, sales people should learn all they can about the persons or companies to whom they hope to sell. They might want to know what products the prospects are now using and the prospects' reactions to these products. Sales people should also try to find out the personal habits and preferences of the prospect.

---

[2]For an in-depth discussion of the personal selling process, see Charles M. Futrell, *ABC's of Selling*, Richard D. Irwin, Inc., Homewood, Ill., 1985.

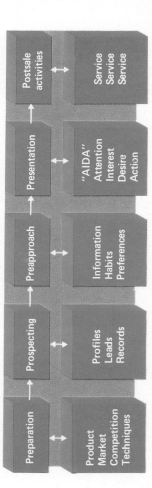

FIGURE 19-1
The personal selling process: the 5 P's.

Presentation—"AIDA"

The actual sales presentation will start with an attempt to attract the prospect's *attention*. The sales person will try to hold the customer's *interest* while building a *desire* for the product. Then the sales person will try to close the sale (*action*). All through the presentation, the sales person must be ready to meet any hidden or expressed objections that the prospect may have.

ATTRACT ATTENTION—THE APPROACH

Several approaches may be used to attract the prospect's attention and start the presentation. The simplest is merely to greet the prospect and state what you are selling. While this is direct, in many situations it is not so effective as other approaches. If the sales person was referred to the prospect by a customer, the right approach might be to start out by mentioning this common acquaintance. Sometimes this is called the "Joe sent me" approach. The sales person might suggest the product benefits by making some startling statement. One sales training consultant often greeted a prospect with the benefit question, "If I can cut your selling costs in half, and at the same time double your sales volume, are you interested?" A fourth approach, which can be effective if the sales person has a new product, is simply to walk in and hand the product to the prospect. While the prospect looks it over, the sales person can start the sales presentation.

HOLD INTEREST AND AROUSE DESIRE

After attracting the prospect's attention, the sales person can hold this interest and stimulate a desire for the product by means of the sales talk itself. There is no common pattern here. Usually, however, a product demonstration is invaluable. Whatever pattern is followed in the talk, the sales person must always show how the product will benefit the prospect.

Many companies insist that their sales people use a "canned" sales talk. That is, all representatives of the firm must give essentially the same presentation. Although many people may feel that this is a poor practice, it has been proved time and again that a canned sales talk can be effective. These presentations ensure that all

Sometimes just getting the prospect to try your product helps to close a sale.

points are covered. They employ tested techniques, and they facilitate the sales training job considerably.

MEET OBJECTIONS AND CLOSE THE SALE

After explaining the product and its benefits, the sales person should try to close the sale and write up an order. As part of the presentation, the sales person may periodically venture a *trial close* to sense the prospect's willingness to buy. By posing some "either-or" questions, a sales person can start to bring the presentation to a head. That is, the sales person may ask, "Would you prefer the gray or the green model?" or "Would you plan to charge this or pay cash?"

The trial close is important because it gives the sales person an indication of how near the prospect is to a decision. A sales person may lose a sale by talking too much. The prospect may be ready to buy at the beginning, and then have a change of mind if the sales person insists on a full presentation. Sometimes sales are lost *simply because the representative fails to ask for the order.*

The trial close also tends to bring out the buyer's objections. A sales person should encourage buyers to state their objections. Then the sales person has an opportunity to answer these objections and to bring out additional product benefits or reemphasize previously stated points.

The toughest objections to answer are those that are unspoken. A sales person must uncover the real objections before hoping to make a sale. Another difficult situation occurs when the prospect wants to "think it over." The sales person must close the sale then and there, or the chances are that it will be lost.

Textbooks on selling discuss different types of sales-closing techniques. The *assumptive close* is probably used as much as any other, and it can be used in a wide variety of selling situations. In this closing technique, the sales person assumes that the customer is going to buy. So it is just a case of settling the details and asking such questions as, "When do you want this delivered?" "Is this a charge sale?" or "What color have you decided upon?"

Postsale Activities

An effective selling job does not end when the order is written up. The final stage of the selling process is a series of postsale services that can build customer goodwill and lay the groundwork for future business. If mechanical installation is necessary, the representative should make certain the job is done properly.

In general, all these activities by the sales person serve to reduce the customer's postdecision anxiety—or cognitive dissonance. The theory of cognitive dissonance holds that after a person has made a buying decision, anxiety (dissonance) will usually occur. This happens because the buyer knows the alternative selected has some disagreeable features, as well as advantages. Consequently, the buyer seeks reassurance that the correct choice was made. Conversely, the buyer wants to avoid anything that suggests that one of the discarded choices really would have been better.

In this final stage of the selling process, it is the sales person's job to minimize the customer's dissonance. The sales person should reassure the customer that the right decision was made by (1) summarizing the product's benefits, (2) repeating why it is better than the discarded alternative choices, and (3) pointing out how satisfied the customer will be with the product's performance.[3]

STRATEGIC SALES-FORCE MANAGEMENT

Management of the personal selling function is simply a matter of applying the three-stage management process (planning, implementing, evaluating) to a sales force and its activities. The process begins when sales executives set their sales goals and do the strategic planning of sales-force activities. This step involves the forecasting of sales, preparation of sales budgets, establishment of sales territories, and setting of quotas for the sales people.

Then the sales force must be organized, staffed, and operated so as to carry out those plans and reach the predetermined goals. The final stage—performance evaluation—includes evaluating the performance of individual sales people, as well as appraising the total sales performance.[4]

Sales-force management strategies are shaped by a company's strategic marketing planning and its overall promotional planning. For example, a firm that relies heavily on personal selling will use different sales-force strategies from those of a company that depends primarily on advertising.

As another illustration, assume that two companies both have the same marketing goal—to increase their sales volume by 30 percent over the next 2 years. But they may plan to use different marketing strategies to reach that goal. Company A's strategy may be to open new geographic markets and sell to new classes of customers. Company B's strategy may be to intensify its coverage of its present markets. These different marketing strategies will call for different strategies in such sales-force management activities as quota setting, training, supervision, and compensation.

OPERATING A SALES FORCE

Most sales executives spend the bulk of their time in staffing and operating their sales forces. Consequently, in this section we shall look briefly at the major tasks that are involved in this managerial activity. These tasks are outlined in Figure 19-2.

Selecting the Sales Force

The key to success in managing a sales force is to select good sales people. In the authors' opinion, *personnel selection* (staffing) is the most important activity in the management process in any organization. This is true whether the organization is a sales force, an athletic team, a college faculty, a political party, or any other group.

[3]For suggestions on how a seller can cultivate and better manage its long-term relationships with its customers, see Theodore Levitt, "After the Sale Is Over . . . ," *Harvard Business Review*, September–October 1983, pp. 87–93.

[4]For an in-depth discussion of sales-force management, see William J. Stanton and Richard H. Buskirk, *Management of the Sales Force*, 7th ed., Richard D. Irwin, Inc., Homewood, Ill., 1987.

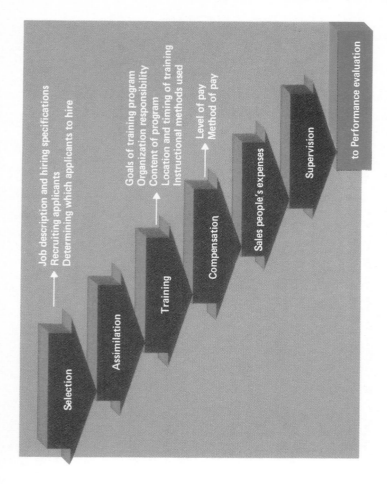

FIGURE 19-2
Staffing and operating a sales force.

Several benefits accrue from having a good sales-personnel selection program. First, it increases a company's chance of getting the type of sales representatives it needs. This is important because there is a shortage of good sales people, and they are hard to find. Second, when running a sales force, a sales manager's performance can be no better than the material he or she has to work with. No matter how well managed a sales force may be, if it is distinctly inferior in quality to that of a competitor, the competitor will win out. Third, a well-selected sales force will be more productive and will build better customer relations than a poorly chosen group.

SCOPE OF SELECTION TASK

The three major steps in sales-force selection are:

1. Determine the number and type of people wanted. This step includes the preparation of a written job description. Management must also determine what specific qualifications are needed to fill the job as it is described.
2. Recruit an adequate number of applicants.
3. Select the qualified persons from among the applicants.

WHAT MAKES A GOOD SALES PERSON?

The key to success in the first step is to establish the proper hiring specifications, just as if the company were purchasing equipment or supplies instead of manpower. To establish these specifications, management must first know what the particular sales job entails. This calls for a detailed job analysis and a written description. It should include specific statements regarding job duties and applicant qualifications. This written description will later be invaluable in training, compensation, and supervision.

Determining the qualifications needed to fill the job is the most difficult part of the selection function. We still really do not know all the characteristics that make a good sales person. We cannot measure to what degree each quality should be present. Nor do we know to what extent an abundance of one can offset the lack of another.[5]

Over the years, many myths have arisen about what traits lead to success in selling. A good sales representative was supposed to be aggressive, extroverted, articulate, well groomed, and endowed with a great physique. Yet in actual fact many outstanding sales people have been mild-mannered and introverted. Other good ones have been somewhat inarticulate and carelessly dressed. Many good sales people are of average or even small size.

The search for the qualities that make a good sales person continues. As one approach, some companies have analyzed the personal histories of their past sales representatives in an effort to determine the traits common to successful (or unsuccessful) performers.

One psychologist, Robert McMurry, who has worked extensively in sales management, concluded that people who are outstanding sales successes inevitably possess these traits:

- A high level of energy.
- Abounding self-confidence.
- A chronic hunger for money, status, and the good things in life.
- A well-established habit of industry.
- The habit of perseverance—each objection or resistance is a challenge.
- A natural tendency to be competitive.

Moreover, McMurry maintained that the key requirement for sales success is an intuitive sensitivity to people. Supersales people are, in effect, constant and habitual "wooers." They have an inherent flair for winning the acceptance of others.

In another approach to the question of what makes a good sales person, Mayer and Greenberg concluded after some years of research that two personality traits are basic to sales success:[6]

- *Empathy:* The ability to identify with customers and their feelings.
- *Ego drive:* The personal need to make a sale, as a measure of self-fulfillment and not just for the money.

RECRUITING APPLICANTS

A planned system for recruiting a sufficient number of applicants is the next step in selection. A good recruiting system has these characteristics:

[5]For a review of research findings regarding factors that are predictive of sales people's performance, see Gilbert A. Churchill, Jr., Neil M. Ford, Steven W. Hartley, and Orville C. Walker, Jr., "The Determinants of Salesperson Performance: A Meta-Analysis," *Journal of Marketing Research*, May 1985, pp. 87–93.

[6]David Mayer and Herbert M. Greenberg, "What Makes a Good Salesman?" *Harvard Business Review*, July–August 1964, pp. 119–125. For an excellent review of recruiting and selecting sales personnel, see James M. Comer and Alan J. Dubinsky, *Managing the Successful Sales Force*, D. C. Heath and Company, Lexington, Mass. 1985, pp. 9–25.

A recruiting ad.

It operates continuously, that is, not only when there are vacancies on the sales force.

- It is systematic, reaching and exploiting all appropriate sources of applicants.
- It provides a continuous flow of qualified applicants in greater numbers than the company can use.

MATCHING APPLICANTS WITH HIRING SPECIFICATIONS

Sales managers should use all available selection tools in their effort to determine which applicants possess the desired qualifications. These tools include application blanks, interviews, references, credit reports, psychological tests, and physical examinations. Probably all companies use application blanks. They serve as records of personal histories and can be used to implement interviewing.

The interview is the other most widely used selection device. Virtually no sales person is hired without at least one personal interview, and it is desirable to have several. Ideally, these should be conducted in different physical settings and by different people. The effect of one person's possible bias is reduced by gathering several opinions. And interviewing in different locations allows interviewers to see how the recruit acts under different conditions. An interview should also help an employer to determine (1) how badly the applicants want the job, (2) whether the company can assure them of the success they want, and (3) whether they will work to their fullest capacity. Patterned interviews are usually considered most desirable because they overcome many weaknesses found in the typical interviewing process. A patterned interview is one that is planned in advance by preparing a list of questions to ask the applicant.

Assimilating New Sales People into the Organization

When sales people are hired, management should pay close attention to the task of integrating them into the company family. Often this step is overlooked entirely. Potential sales people are carefully selected and are wined and dined in order to recruit them into the firm. Then, as soon as they are hired, the honeymoon is over, and they are left to shift for themselves. In such cases, the new people often become discouraged and may even quit. A wise sales manager will recognize that the new people know very little about the details of the job, their fellow workers, or their status in the firm. A vital need exists to maintain open, two-way channels of communication between new sales personnel and management.

Training the Sales Force

Another major aspect of sales-force operation is training. New sales people obviously need careful indoctrination and guidance. But even experienced reps need some training periodically. Setting up a training program involves answering the following questions: In each instance, decisions will be influenced by the kind of training program involved—indoctrination program, refresher course, or some other type.

1. What are the goals of the program? In very general terms, the aim of the program is to increase productivity and stimulate the sales force. In addition, executives must determine what specific ends they wish to reach. For instance, the goal may be to increase sales of high-profit items, or to improve prospecting methods for generating new accounts.

2. Who should do the training? The training program may be conducted by line sales executives, by a company staff-training department, by outside training specialists, or by some combination of the three.

Santo Laquatra, Beecham Products national sales trainer, uses videotaping of role-playing to prepare his sales people.

3. What should be the content of the program? A well-rounded sales training program should cover three general topics: product knowledge, information about company policies, and selling techniques.

4. When and where should training be done? Some companies believe in training new people before they go into the field. Others let new people prove that they have some desire and ability to sell, and then bring them back into the office for intensive training.

   Firms may employ either centralized or decentralized training programs. A centralized program, usually at the home office, may involve a periodic meeting attended by all sales people. A decentralized program may be held in branch offices or during on-the-job training. Decentralized programs generally cost less than centralized programs. The big problem with decentralized programs is that the quality of instruction is often inferior.

5. What instructional methods should be used? The lecture method may be employed to inform trainees about company history and practices. Demonstrations may be used to impart product knowledge or selling techniques. Role playing is an excellent device for training a person in proper selling techniques. On-the-job training may be used in almost any phase of the program.

Compensating the Sales Force

To compensate their sales forces, companies offer both financial and nonfinancial rewards. The *nonfinancial rewards* involve opportunities for advancement, recognition of efforts, and a feeling of belonging. *Financial rewards* may take the form of *direct* monetary payment or of *indirect* monetary payment (paid vacations, pensions, and insurance plans).

Establishing a compensation system really involves decisions concerning both the *level* of compensation and the *method* of compensation. The *level* refers to the total dollar income that a sales person earns over a period of time. The *method* refers to the system or plan by which the sales person will reach the intended level. The level is influenced by the type of person required and the competitive rate of pay for similar positions.

There are three widely used methods of compensating a sales force: straight salary, straight commission, and a combination plan. Today, well over half the firms in the country use some kind of combination plan.

The **straight-salary** plan offers a maximum of security and stability of earnings for a sales person. Management can expect its sales people to perform any reasonable work assignment because they receive the same pay regardless of the task performed. Under a straight salary, the sales reps can consider the customers' best interests, and the reps are less likely to use high-pressure selling tactics.

A commonly stated drawback of the straight-salary plan is that it does not offer adequate incentive. Thus, management has the added burden of motivating and directing the sales people. The pay plan itself does not provide any appreciable direction or control. Also, under this plan, compensation is a fixed cost unrelated to sales revenue. Straight-salary plans typically are used:

- To compensate new sales people or missionary sales people.
- When opening new territories.
- When sales involve a technical product and a lengthy period of negotiation.

A **straight commission** tends to have just the opposite merits and limitations. It provides tremendous incentive for sales people, and the commission costs can be related directly to sales or gross margin. Sales representatives have more freedom in their work, and their level of income is determined largely by their own efforts. On the other hand, it is difficult to control the sales people and to get them to do a fully balanced sales job. It is particularly difficult to get them to perform tasks for which no commission is paid. There is always the danger that they will oversell customers or otherwise incur customer ill will. Straight-commission plans may work well if:

- Great incentive is needed to get the sales.
- Very little nonselling missionary work is required.
- The company is financially weak and must relate its compensation expenses directly to sales or gross margin.
- The company is unable to supervise the sales force.

The ideal combination plan has the best features of both the straight-salary and the straight-commission plans, with as few of their drawbacks as possible. To come close to this ideal, the combination plan must be tailored to the particular firm, product, market, and type of selling.

An important element in the financial affairs of sales people is reimbursement for business expenses they incur in traveling or selling. The importance of sales-force expense control is difficult to overrate. It is essential that sales executives develop a plan both to control these costs and to reimburse the sales people fairly. In principle, sales people should not make or lose money because of their expense accounts. Nor should they forgo any beneficial sales activities because they will not be adequately reimbursed for the attendant expenses.

Supervising the Sales Force

The supervision of a sales force is both difficult and important. It is difficult because sales people often work where they cannot be closely and continually supervised. It is important because supervision serves both as a method of continuation training and as a device to ensure that company policies are being carried out. Still another value of sales-force supervision is that it affords a two-way channel of communication between management and the sales force. Personal supervision by a field supervisor or some other sales executive typically is the most effective supervisory method. Other methods of supervision involve the use of correspondence, reports, and sales meetings.

EVALUATING A SALES PERSON'S PERFORMANCE

Managing a sales force includes the job of evaluating the efforts of the sales people. Until executives know what their sales force is doing, they are in no position to make constructive proposals for improvement. By studying sales people's activities and by establishing standards of performance, management should be able to upgrade the sales force's efforts in general.

Performance analysis can help sales people improve their own efforts. People with poor sales records may know that they are doing something wrong. But they cannot determine what it is if they have no objective standards by which to measure their performance.

Performance evaluation can be of help in determining what should be included in a training program, and it can aid in sales supervision. A supervisor who knows some of the specific strengths and weaknesses of each sales person can do a better job of directing and training. Performance evaluation can also help management decide on salary increases and promotions for individual sales people.

Bases for Evaluation

Both quantitative and qualitative factors should be used as the bases for performance evaluation. The quantitative bases generally have the advantage of being specific and objective. Qualitative factors, unfortunately, require the subjective judgment of the evaluators. For both types of appraisal factors, however, management has the difficult task of setting the standards against which performance can be measured.

AMERICA'S BEST SALES FORCES, AS RATED BY SALES MANAGERS, IN 11 INDUSTRIES

Company	Industry
DuPont	Chemicals
IBM	Computers and office equipment
Marriott	Diversified services
Motorola	Electronics
Pepsi-Cola USA	Food and beverages
Georgia-Pacific	Forest products
Textron	Industrial and farm equipment
Chromalloy American	Metal products
Johnson & Johnson	Pharmaceuticals
Eastman Kodak	Precision instruments
Blue Bell	Textiles and apparel

Rating criteria, in order of importance

1. Reputation among customers.
2. Holding old accounts.
3. Quality of management.
4. Ability to keep top sales people.
5. Opening new accounts.
6. Product/technical knowledge.
7. Meeting sales targets.
8. Quality of training.
9. Innovativeness.
10. Frequency of calls/territory coverage.

Source: Sales & Marketing Management, Dec. 3, 1984, pp. 19–24.

QUANTITATIVE BASES

Sales performance should be evaluated on the basis of both input (or efforts) and output (or results). A person's selling effectiveness is a combination of the two—output as measured by sales volume, gross margin, etc., and input as indicated by call rate, nonselling activities, etc.

Some *output* (result) factors that ordinarily are quite useful as quantitative evaluation bases are:

- Sales volume—by products, customer groups, and territory.
- Sales volume as a percentage of quota or territorial potential.
- Gross margin by product line, customer group, and territory.
- Orders:
  a. Number.

b. Average size (dollar volume).
c. Batting average (number of orders divided by number of calls).
* Accounts:
a. Percentage of accounts sold.
b. Number of new accounts called on and sold.

Some useful *input* (effort) factors to measure are:

* Calls per day (call rate).
* Direct selling expense, in dollars or as a percentage of sales volume.
* Nonselling activities:
a. Advertising displays set up.
b. Number of training sessions held with dealers and/or distributors.

The importance of output factors in a performance evaluation is readily recognized. Sometimes, however, the value of input factors is underestimated. Actually, an analysis of the input factors often is effective in locating trouble spots. If a person's output performance is unsatisfactory, very often the cause lies in the handling of the various input factors over which the sales person has control.

One key to a successful evaluation program is to appraise the sales person's performance on as many different bases as possible. Otherwise, management may be misled. A high daily call rate may look good, but it tells us nothing about how many orders per call are being written up. A high batting average (orders divided by calls) may be camouflaging a low average order size or a high sales volume on low-profit items.

QUALITATIVE BASES

It would be nice if the entire performance evaluation could be based only on quantitative factors. This would minimize the subjectivity and personal bias of the evaluators. Unfortunately, this cannot be done. Many qualitative factors must be considered because they influence a sales person's performance and help in the interpretation of quantitative data. These factors include:

Beecham Products will evaluate this sales rep by using both quantitative and qualitative measures.

- Knowledge of the product, company policies, and the competition.
- Management of the sales person's own time and the preparation for calls.
- Customer relations.
- Personal appearance and health.
- Personality and attitudinal factors, such as:
  - a. Cooperation.
  - b. Resourcefulness.
  - c. Ability to analyze logically and make decisions.

This concludes our coverage of the management of the personal selling effort in a company's promotional mix. In the next chapter we shall consider the other two widely used promotional tools—advertising and sales promotion.

SUMMARY

Personal selling is the major promotional method used in American business—whether measured by people employed, by total expenditures, or by expenses as a percentage of sales. The sales job today is not what it used to be. A new breed of professional sales person has been developing over the past few decades. Today the sales jobs are quite different from other jobs in a company. Also, there are a variety of sales jobs. They range from that of a driver–sales person, through jobs like inside order takers, missionary seller, and sales engineer, to the positions that call for highly creative selling of tangible goods and intangible services.

There are five steps in the actual sale of a product or service. The first three involve presale preparation, prospecting for potential buyers, and preapproaching these prospects. Then a sales person is ready to make a sales presentation. This fourth step involves approaching the customer and creating some customer interest. The actual sales talk may be canned or individually tailored for each prospect. The sales person must be prepared to meet customer objections and then try to close the sale. Finally, postsale activities are needed to satisfy the customer and reduce his or her anxieties concerning the purchase.

Strategic sales-force management involves planning and operating a sales force within the guidelines set by the strategic marketing planning. The tasks involved in staffing and operating a sales force present managerial challenges in several areas. The key to successful sales-force management is to do a good job in selecting the sales people. Then plans must be made for assimilating these new people into the company. Sales training and supervision programs have to be developed. Management needs to set up plans for compensating sales people and reimbursing them for their business expenses.

The final stage in strategic sales-force management is to evaluate the performance of the individual sales people.

KEY TERMS AND CONCEPTS

New type of sales person 441
Classification of sales jobs 442
Telemarketing 444
Presale preparation 445
Prospecting for new customers 445

Preapproach 445
The approach 446
AIDA (Fig. 19-1) 446
Canned sales talk 446
Meeting objections in sales talk 447

Cognitive dissonance 447
Postsale activities 447
Sales-force selection tasks 448
Decisions in sales training 452
Financial compensation 453
Nonfinancial compensation 453

Straight-salary compensation 453
Straight-commission
  compensation 454
Bases for evaluating sales
  people 455

QUESTIONS AND PROBLEMS

1. The cost of a full-page, four-color advertisement in one issue of *Sports Illustrated* magazine is much more than the cost of employing two sales people for a full year. A sales-force executive is urging her company to eliminate a few of these ads and, instead, to hire a few more sales people. This executive believes that one good sales person working for an entire year can sell more than one ad in one issue of *Sports Illustrated*. How would you answer her?

2. "The sales person occupies many roles with many divergent role partners, and this entails heavy emotional demands." Explain.

3. Refer to the seven-way classification of sales jobs in this chapter, and answer the following questions:
   a. In which types of jobs is the sales person most free from close supervision?
   b. Which types are likely to be the highest paid?
   c. Which are likely to involve the most traveling?
   d. For which jobs is a high degree of motivation necessary?

4. What information would you seek as part of your presale preparation to sell each of the following products? In each case, assume you are selling to the users of the product.
   a. Eight-unit apartment complex.
   b. Retail record store.
   c. Minicomputer.
   d. Contributions to the United Way.

5. What are some of the sources you might use to acquire a list of prospects for the following products?
   a. Individual retirement accounts.
   b. Dental X-ray equipment.
   c. Software for personal computers.
   d. Baby furniture and clothes.

6. How should a sales person respond when customers say that the price of a product is too high?

7. "A good selection program is desirable, but not essential. Improper selection of sales people can be counterbalanced by a good training program, by a good compensation system, or by fine supervision." Discuss.

8. What sources should be used for recruiting sales applicants in each of the following firms? Explain your reasoning in each instance.
   a. A Marriott hotel that wants companies to use the hotel's facilities for conventions.
   b. Anway, Avon, or Mary Kay Cosmetics, which are selling directly to consumers.
   c. IBM, which needs sales reps for its large computer division.

9. "It is best to hire experienced sales people because they do not require any training." Discuss.

10. What factors should be considered in determining the *level* of sales compensation?

11. Compare the merits of a straight-salary plan and a straight-commission plan of sales compensation. Name some types of sales jobs in which each plan might be desirable.

12. How might a firm determine whether a sales person is using high-pressure selling tactics that may injure customer relations?

13. How can a sales manager evaluate the ability of sales people to get new business?

CHAPTER

20

MANAGEMENT
OF ADVERTISING,
SALES
PROMOTION,
AND PUBLICITY

CHAPTER GOALS

This chapter is a discussion of nonpersonal selling, as distinguished from the personal selling of the last chapter. After studying this chapter, you should understand:

- The nature of advertising and its importance in our economy and in an individual firm.
- The major types of advertising.
- How to develop an advertising campaign and select the advertising media.
- How to evaluate the effectiveness of advertising.
- Sales promotion—its nature, importance, and services rendered.
- Publicity—its nature, benefits, and relation to public relations.

Spacemaker
APPLIANCE

SUPER GIVEAWAY

55,000 WINNERS!

YOU MAY HAVE ALREADY WON 5
BLACK & DECKER SPACEMAKER™
APPLIANCES

Look inside for YOUR official number

816

MORE VALUABLE COUPONS INSIDE!

Fill out entry form
on reverse side now!

WIN A FREE TRIP TO

THE FAR PAVILIONS

only on HBO

ESCORTED BY M.M. KAYE, AUTHOR OF THE BOOK.

5 GRAND PRIZES:
17-day "Far Pavilions
Tour" trip to India for two.
Pan Am and InnerAsia take
you to the land of dreams
and romance—home of
The Far Pavilions.

500 FIRST PRIZES:
The deluxe hardcover edi-
tion of the international
best-seller, The Far
Pavilions.

DON'T MISS the HBO Premiere
Film "The Far Pavilions."
An epic adventure in three parts.
Premiering April 22, 23, 24.

SEE OFFICIAL RULES FOR DETAILS.
Entries must be received by June 29, 1984.

Sales promotion has grown out of its stepchild status and today is treated as an equal partner with advertising and personal selling in the promotional mix of many organizations. Sweepstakes, contests, and other game promotions have long been successful sales promotion activities directed at ultimate consumers. Today, however, these sales promotional tools are being used increasingly by companies in their promotional activities directed at customers in the industrial (business) market. Sweepstakes, particularly, are getting a heavy play in this business-to-business promotion. Specialists in sweepstakes promotion estimate that by the mid-1990s, sweepstakes directed at business audiences could account for 20 percent of the total sweepstakes market.

Here is what some companies already have done with sweepstakes promotion aimed at business markets:

- Home Box Office aimed its sweepstakes promotion at cable operators, as well as subscribers. Prizes included free vacations and cameo appearances in upcoming film specials.
- Welch Foods targeted grocery retailers with a sweepstakes contest where the prizes were a Hawaii vacation plus $1,000 cash, a barbecue grill, and microwave ovens.
- The Chemical Bank in New York directed its sweepstakes at potential business customers and offered an IBM personal computer as a prize.
- Black & Decker Spacemaker appliance giveaway asked consumers to find out if they had won and gave them product coupons.

Interestingly enough, companies are finding that sweepstakes and contests work even when the respondents are highly paid, highly educated executives. Apparently the idea of "something for nothing" and "free" has a broad appeal—something the airlines have found out with their frequent-flyer promotions. Users of sweepstakes also find that they get a better response when the prizes are business-related—for example, personal computers, attaché cases, or trips that enable the recipient to combine business activities with pleasure.[1] Sweepstakes are just one type of sales promotion, and sales promotion along with advertising and publicity are what we shall be talking about in this chapter.

---

[1]Adapted from Bernie Whalen, "Enter Now, Win Exciting Prizes in Biz-to-Biz Sweeps!" *Collegiate Edition Marketing News*, May 1985, p. 19.

Hunters ordinarily do not use a rifle to hunt ducks. They need a device that reaches a wider area than a rifle without expending additional effort. Thus, duck hunters ordinarily use a shotgun. By the same token, mass communication is needed to reach mass markets at a reasonable cost. Advertising, sales promotion, and publicity are just the tools for this job. It is too costly and time-consuming to try to do the job with sales people alone.

NATURE OF ADVERTISING

Advertising consists of all the activities involved in presenting to a group a nonpersonal, oral or visual, openly sponsor-identified message regarding a product, service, or idea. This message, called an **advertisement**, is disseminated through one or more media and is paid for by the identified sponsor.

We should note some important points in connection with this definition. First, there is a significant distinction between advertising and an advertisement. The advertisement is the message itself. Advertising is a process—it is a series of activities necessary to prepare the message and get it to the intended market. Another point is that the public knows who is behind the advertising because the sponsor is openly identified in the advertisement. Also, payment is made by the sponsor to the media that carry the message. These last two considerations differentiate advertising from propaganda and publicity.

Types of Advertising

An organization's objectives in its advertising program determine, to a great extent, what type of advertising that organization will use. Consequently, marketing executives should understand something about the classifications of the various types of advertising.

PRODUCT AND INSTITUTIONAL ADVERTISING

All advertising may be classed as either product or institutional. In **product advertising**, advertisers are informing or stimulating the market about their products or services. Product advertising is often further subdivided into direct-action and indirect-action advertising. With **direct-action advertising**, sellers are seeking a quick response to their advertisements. An advertisement with a coupon may urge the reader to send immediately for a free sample. **Indirect-action advertising** is designed to stimulate demand over a longer period of time. Such advertising is intended to inform customers that the product exists and to point out its benefits. The idea is that when customers are ready to buy the product, they will look favorably upon the seller's brand.

Institutional advertising is designed either to present information about the advertiser's business or to create a good attitude—build goodwill—toward the organization. This type of advertising is not intended to sell a specific product or service of an advertiser. Two subdivisions of institutional advertising are:

- **Patronage advertising:** Presents information about the advertiser's business. A retail store may advertise its new store hours or a change in its delivery policy, for example.
- **Public service advertising:** Shows the advertiser as a "good citizen." A company's ads may urge the public to support a Red Cross campaign or to drive carefully. Or a manufacturer's ads may tell what the company is doing to reduce the stream pollution caused by its factories.

PRIMARY AND SELECTIVE DEMAND ADVERTISING

Primary-demand advertising is that type which is designed to stimulate the demand for a generic category of a product, such as Colombian coffee, or videocassette recorders. This is in contrast to selective-demand advertising, which is intended to

These public service ads illustrate Bud's commitment to individuals and organizations.

stimulate demand for individual brands such as Chock Full o' Nuts coffee or Sony or Toshiba videocassette recorders.

Typically, primary-demand advertising is to be used in two situations. The first is when a product is in the introductory stages of its life cycle. This is called **pioneering advertising**. An individual firm may run an ad about its new product, explaining the product's benefits, but not emphasizing the brand name. The objective of pioneering primary-demand advertising is to *inform*, and not to *persuade*, the target market. In recent years pioneering primary-demand ads have been run for such products as backyard satellite dishes for TV reception and compact laser discs for stereo sound systems.

The second use of primary-demand advertising is by trade associations to stimulate the demand for their industry's product which is in competition with other product categories. Thus, the National Dairy Association's ads urge us to drink milk, instead of some other beverage. The association doesn't care whose brand of milk we drink, just that we drink milk. The Wool Growers' Association urges us to buy clothing made of wool rather than synthetic fibers.

Selective-demand advertising essentially is competitive advertising—it pits one brand against another. This type of advertising typically is used when a product has gone beyond the introductory stage of its life cycle. The product then is sufficiently well known, and several individual brands are competing for a market share. The

The only alternative to 100% Colombian Coffee.

Colombian coffee uses primary-demand ads and Chock Full o' Nuts coffee uses selective-demand ads to increase sales.

Rolls-Royce uses a quiet form of comparative advertising.

objective of competitive advertising is to *persuade* the potential customers, and it emphasizes the particular benefits of the brand being advertised.

Comparative advertising is one type of selective-demand advertising that has been used for a wide variety of products in recent years. In comparative advertising, the advertiser mentions rival brands by name and flatly states that the advertised brand is better than the other. Thus, General Mills advertises that one bowl of its cereal, Total, carries the equivalent nutritional benefit found in 12 bowls of Nabisco's Shredded Wheat. Tempo advertises that it gives more effective relief for acid stomach than Tums, Rolaids, or Maalox.

Comparative advertising has been especially encouraged by the Federal Trade Commission as a means for stimulating competition and disseminating useful information to consumers. We must state one strong word of caution, however. If you are engaging in comparative advertising, you better be damned sure that what you say about your competition is completely accurate.[2]

COOPERATIVE ADVERTISING

In some situations an effective promotional strategy calls for the use of some form of cooperative advertising. **Vertical cooperative advertising** involves firms on different levels of distribution—such as manufacturers and retailers. In fact, the major type of vertical cooperative advertising is a joint venture between a manufacturer and a retailer. The manufacturer and the retailer share the cost of the retailer's advertising that features the manufacturer's product. The manufacturer of Hickey-Freeman suits, for example, may prepare ads for retail clothing stores, and the stores then pay for the newspaper space that carries these ads.

Another type of vertical cooperative advertising involves an *advertising allowance*—also called a *promotional allowance*. This allowance is an off-invoice or cash discount offered by a manufacturer to a retailer to encourage the retailer to advertise or prominently display the product. This arrangement provides added incentive for the retailer to advertise the manufacturer's product. The producer also benefits from

[2]For some guidelines in the use of comparative advertising, see Bruce Buchanan, "Can You Pass the Comparative Ad Challenge?" *Harvard Business Review*, July-August 1985, pp. 106–113.

the media rate structure which typically has lower prices for advertising placed by local retail firms than for manufacturers' advertising.

Horizontal cooperative advertising involves a group of firms on the same level of distribution—such as a group of retailers. All stores in a suburban shopping center, for example, may run a joint ad weekly in a newspaper. The different businesses in a summer resort area—lodges, stores, restaurants, and marinas—often will participate in joint promotional activities.

Cost of Advertising

Advertising in one form or another is used by virtually all manufacturers and retailers in the country. The importance of advertising may be indicated by its cost.

ADVERTISING EXPENDITURES IN TOTAL AND BY MEDIA

In 1984, total advertising expenditures were about $88 billion—more than 4 times the amount spent in 1970. Table 20-1 shows the relative importance of the major advertising media. For years, newspapers have been the most widely used medium, based upon total advertising dollars invested. Newspapers' and radio's market shares have declined, however, as expenditures for television advertising have increased. About

TABLE 20-1	ADVERTISING EXPENDITURES IN UNITED STATES, BY MEDIA CLASS					

Advertising expenditures reached $88 billion in 1984, an increase of 60 percent over 1980. Newspapers still maintained their first-place position, but do you think that television's share of the total will surpass that of newspapers by 1990?

Media class	1984 Dollars (in billions)	%	1980 %	1970 %	1960 %
Newspapers	23.7	27	28	29	31
Television	19.8	22	21	18	13
Direct mail	13.8	15	14	14	15
Radio	5.8	7	7	7	6
Magazines, including national farm publications	5.1	6	6	7	8
Business papers	2.3	3	3	4	5
Outdoor	.9	1	1	1	2
Miscellaneous*	16.6	19	20	20	20
Total percentage		100%.	100%	100%	100%
Total $ (in billions)	$88.0		$55	$20	$12

*Includes cost of transportation advertising, advertising in weekly newspapers, regional farm publications, point-of-purchase advertising, and other legitimate advertising expenditures not already covered.
Source: 1984 figures from Advertising Age, May 6, 1985, p. 47. 1980 figures from Advertising Age, Mar. 22, 1982, p. 66. Others adapted from Advertising Age, Nov. 17, 1975, p. 40.

TABLE 20-2 TOP-10 NATIONAL ADVERTISERS, 1984, BASED ON TOTAL EXPENDITURES IN UNITED STATES
Procter & Gamble's total is still only 8.5 percent of sales. Note the low percentages for General Motors and Ford.

Company	Advertising expenditures	
	Dollars (in millions)	As % of U.S. sales
1. Procter & Gamble	872	8.5
2. General Motors	764	1.1
3. Sears, Roebuck	747	2.1
4. Beatrice Companies	680	6.9
5. R. J. Reynolds	678	6.6
6. Philip Morris	570	5.7
7. AT&T	563	n.a.
8. Ford Motor Co.	559	1.5
9. K mart	554	2.7
10. McDonald's	480*	18.3

*Represents a 54 percent increase over 1983; worldwide, the company's advertising is 6 percent of sales.
n.a.: Not available.
Source: Advertising Age, Sept. 26, 1985.

85 percent of the expenditures for newspaper advertising goes for local rather than national advertising.

ADVERTISING EXPENDITURES AS PERCENTAGE OF COMPANY SALES

When gauging the importance of advertising, we should measure expenditures against a benchmark rather than simply look at the total. Frequently, advertising expenses are expressed as a percentage of a company's sales. Table 20-2 shows the 10 companies with the largest *dollar* expenditures for advertising. It is interesting to note that some of the largest advertisers dollarwise (GM, Ford) actually devote a *very* small percentage of sales to advertising.

COST OF ADVERTISING VERSUS COST OF PERSONAL SELLING

While we do not have accurate totals for the costs of personal selling, we do know they far surpass advertising expenditures. In manufacturing, only a few industries, such as drugs, toiletries, cleaning products, tobacco, and beverages, have advertising expenditures higher than those for personal selling. In countless companies, advertising runs 1 to 3 percent of net sales. But, in many firms, the expenses of recruiting and operating a sales force run from 8 to 15 percent of sales.

At the wholesale level, advertising costs are very low. Personal selling costs may run 10 to 15 times as high. Even among retailers in total—and this includes those with self-service operations—the cost of personal selling runs substantially higher than advertising.

OBJECTIVES OF ADVERTISING

Fundamentally, the only purpose of advertising is to sell something—a product, a service, or an idea. Stated another way, the real goal of advertising is effective communication. That is, the ultimate effect of advertising should be to modify the attitudes and/or behavior of the receiver of the message.

Specific Objectives

This broad goal of advertising is better reached by setting specific objectives that can be incorporated into individual advertising campaigns. Of course, specific advertising objectives will be determined by the company's overall marketing strategies—especially the strategies related to the firm's promotional program. A few examples of specific goals are as follows:

- Support personal selling. Advertisement may be used to open customers' doors for sales people, and to acquaint prospects with the sellers' company. See Fig. 20-1.
- Reach people inaccessible to the sales force. Sales people may be unable to reach

An ad in this magazine will help reach industrial buyers inaccessible to the sales force.

"I don't know who you are.
I don't know your company.
I don't know your company's product.
I don't know what your company stands for.
I don't know your company's customers.
I don't know your company's record.
I don't know your company's reputation.
Now—what was it you wanted to sell me?"

McGRAW-HILL MAGAZINES
BUSINESS • PROFESSIONAL • TECHNICAL

MORAL: Sales start **before** your salesman calls—with business publication advertising

FIGURE 20-1
(Source: McGraw-Hill Publications)

DEVELOPING AN ADVERTISING CAMPAIGN

top executives, or they may not be certain who makes the buying decisions in a company. In either case, there is a good chance that these executives will read a journal that carries the ads.

- Improve dealer relations.
- Enter a new geographic market or attract a new group of customers.
- Introduce a new product.
- Increase sales of a product. An advertising campaign may be designed to lengthen the season for the product (as has been done in the case of soft drinks); increase the frequency of replacement (as is done in campaigns for spark plugs and light bulbs); increase the variety of product uses; or increase the units of purchase.
- Expand the industry's sales.
- Counteract prejudice or substitution.
- Build goodwill for the company and improve its reputation (a) by rendering a public service through advertising or (b) by telling of the organization behind the product.

Once a company decides to advertise (based on the factors discussed in Chapter 18), management can get on with the job of developing an advertising campaign. An advertising campaign is simply one part of a total promotional campaign—identified in Chapter 18 as an exercise in strategic planning. It is a coordinated series of promotional efforts built around a central theme and designed to reach a specific goal.

Initial Planning

The planning in an *advertising* campaign must be done within the framework of the overall strategic marketing plan and the *promotional* campaign planning. Therefore, at the time the advertising campaign is being planned, presumably management already has made decisions in several areas. For example, the specific promotional goals have been established. Also, management has decided what the central campaign theme will be, and what appeals will be stressed in light of consumer buying motives and habits. The total promotional appropriation has been determined and has been allocated among the various promotional tools. And the role of advertising in the promotional campaign has been determined. Management can now make decisions involving (1) the selection of the advertising media and (2) the creation and production of individual advertisements.

Selecting the Media

Three levels of decision making are required in the selection of advertising media. First, management must determine what general types of media to use. Will newspapers, television, or magazines be used? Second, if magazines are to be used, will they be of the special-interest type (for example, shelter magazines such as *Better Homes and Gardens* or business magazines such as *Business Week*), or of the general-interest type? Finally, the specific medium must be chosen. The company that decides first on radio and then on local stations now must decide what specific station to use in each city. Some of the factors to consider in making media decisions are as follows:

- *Objective of the advertisement.* Media choices are influenced both by the purpose of a specific advertisement and by the goal of an entire campaign. For example, if the goal of the campaign is to generate appointments for sales people, the advertising company will probably use direct mail. If an advertiser wants to place an ad inducing action within a day or two, newspapers or radio may be used.

• *Media circulation.* Media circulation must match the distribution patterns of the product. Consequently, the *geographic* scope of the market will influence the choice of media considerably. Furthermore, media should be selected that will reach the desired *type* of market with a minimum of waste circulation.

Today many media—even national and other large-market media—can be targeted at smaller, specialized market segments. This reduces waste circulation for an advertiser. For example, many national magazines publish regional editions. Trade and professional journals exist in many fields. Large metropolitan newspapers publish suburban editions and regional editions within the big city. Some radio stations specialize in rock, country, or classical music.

• *Requirements of the message.* The medium should fit the message. For example, meat product, floor coverings, and apparel are ordinarily best presented in pictorial form. If the advertiser can use a very brief message, as is possible in advertising salt, beer, or sugar, then billboards may be the best choice.

• *Time and location of buying decision.* The medium should reach prospective customers near the time they make their buying decisions and the places where they make them. For this reason, outdoor advertising often does well for gasoline products. Many grocery store ads are placed in newspapers on Wednesdays or Thursdays in anticipation of heavy weekend buying.

• *Cost of media.* The costs of the advertising media should be considered in relation to (a) the amount of funds available and (b) the circulation of the media. In the first instance, the amount of funds available could rule out television as a choice. Or possibly the advertiser can afford local television but not a national network. On the second count, the advertiser should try to develop some relationships between the cost of the medium and the size of the audience it will reach.

Mary Kay Cosmetics advertises in magazines that prospective customers will read.

CHARACTERISTICS OF MAJOR TYPES OF MEDIA

In the process of selecting the media to use in a campaign, management must consider the advertising characteristics of the main classes of media. The term *characteristics* is carefully chosen instead of *advantages* and *disadvantages*. To illustrate, one characteristic of radio as an advertising medium is that it makes its impression through the ear. For many products, this is an advantage. For products, however, that benefit from a color photograph, this characteristic of radio is a drawback.

Newspapers As an advertising medium, newspapers are flexible and timely. They can be used to cover one city or several urban centers. Ads can be canceled on a few days' notice or inserted on 1 day's notice. Newspapers also give an advertiser an intense coverage of a local market because almost everybody reads newspapers. The local feature also helps in that the ads can be adapted to local social and economic conditions. Circulation costs per prospect are low. On the other hand, the life of a newspaper advertisement is very short.

Magazines Magazines are an excellent medium when high-quality printing and color are desired in an advertisement. Magazines can be used to reach a national market at a relatively low cost per prospect. Through the use of special-interest magazines or regional editions of national magazines, an advertiser can reach a selected audience with a minimum of waste circulation. Magazines are usually read in a leisurely fashion, in contrast to the haste with which other print media are read. This feature is particularly valuable for the advertiser who must present a message at some length. Some of the less favorable characteristics of magazines are their inflexibility and the infrequency with which they reach the market, as compared with other media.

Direct mail Direct mail is probably the most personal and selective of all the media. Because it reaches only the market that the advertiser wishes to contact, there is a minimum of waste circulation. Direct mail is not accompanied by articles or other editorial matter, however, unless the advertiser provides it. That is, most direct mail is pure advertising. As a result, a direct-mail ad creates its own circulation and attracts its own readers. The cost of direct mail per prospect reached is quite high compared with other media. But other media reach many people who are not real prospects and thus have higher waste-circulation costs. A severe limitation of direct mail is the difficulty of getting and maintaining good mailing lists. Direct-mail advertising also suffers from the stigma of being classed as "junk mail."

Radio Radio is enjoying a renaissance as an advertising and cultural medium and as a financial investment. When interest in television soared after World War II, radio audiences (especially for national network radio) declined so much that people were predicting radio's demise. But for the past 10 years or so, this medium has been making a real comeback. Local radio (as contrasted with national networks) is especially strong.

As an advertising medium, radio's big advantage is its relatively low cost. You can reach almost 100 percent of the people with radio. At the same time, with special-interest programming, some segmented target markets can be pinpointed quite effectively.

Where else?
On the radio you can show practically any idea
you've got swimming around.
From a pipe-puffing pike to a bevy of
bebopping barracuda. And no one's ever going to scream
"Holy Mackerel!" when they see the cost.
Get creative and show your stuff with the power
of sound. Then everyone will say:
"I saw it on the radio."

"I SAW IT ON THE RADIO."

Radio advertising can be very creative.

On the other hand, radio makes only an audio impression. So it is useless where visual impact is needed. As with direct mail, radio advertisers must create their own audiences. And the exposure life of a given radio message is extremely short. Also, audience attention often is at a low level, especially when the radio is being used mainly to provide background for driving, studying, or some other activity.

Television Television, the newest and fastest-growing of all major media, is probably also the most versatile. It makes its appeal through both the eye and the ear; products can be demonstrated as well as explained. It offers considerable flexibility in terms of the geographic market covered and the time of message presentation. By making part of its impression through the ear, television can take advantage of the personal, dramatic impact of the spoken word.

On the other hand, television is an extremely expensive medium. The message is not permanently recorded for the message receiver. Thus the prospect who is not reached the first time is lost forever, as far as a particular message is concerned. Television does not lend itself to long advertising copy, nor does it present pictures as clearly as magazines do. As with direct mail and radio, television advertisers must create their own audiences.

Outdoor Outdoor advertising is a flexible, low-cost medium. Because it reaches virtually the entire population, it lends itself nicely to widely used consumer products that require only a brief selling statement. It is excellent for the reminder type of advertising, and it carries the impact of large size and color. There is flexibility in geographic coverage and in the intensity of market coverage within the area. However, unless the advertised product is a widely used consumer good, considerable waste circulation will occur. While the cost of reaching an individual prospect is low, the

Outdoor billboards are great for short messages.

total cost of a national campaign is quite high. There also is considerable public criticism of the clutter and landscape-defacing aspects of outdoor advertising.

Creating the Advertisements

Remember once again that the main purpose of advertising is to sell something and that the ad itself is a sales message. The ad may be a high-pressure sales talk, as in a hard-hitting, direct-action ad. Or it may be a very long-range, low-pressure message, as in an institutional ad. In any case, it is trying to sell something. Consequently, it involves the same kind of selling procedure as sales talks delivered by personal sales people. That is, the ad must first attract attention, and then hold interest long enough to stimulate a desire for the product, service, or idea. Finally, the ad must move the prospect to some kind of action.

Creating an advertisement involves the tasks of writing the copy, selecting the illustrations, preparing the layout, and arranging to have the advertisement reproduced for the selected media.

The **copy** in an advertisement is defined as all the written or spoken material in it. Copy includes the headline, coupons, and advertiser's name and address, as well as the main body of the message. The **illustration** is a powerful feature in a printed advertisement. Probably the main points to consider with respect to illustrations are (1) whether they are the best alternative use of the space and (2) whether they are appropriate in all respects to the ad itself. The **layout** is the physical arrangement of all the elements in an advertisement. A good layout can be an interest-holding device as well as an attention getter. It should lead the reader through the entire advertisement in an orderly fashion.

EVALUATING THE ADVERTISING EFFORT

Importance of Evaluation

As part of the management of its advertising program, a company should carefully evaluate the effectiveness of (1) what has been done and (2) what is planned for the future.

Advertising typically is one of the most highly criticized parts of our marketing system. While advertising has been improved greatly through the years, much still remains to be done. We need to increase the effectiveness of advertising, and we must find better ways to evaluate this effectiveness.

Shrinking profit margins and increasing competition, both foreign and domestic, are forcing management to appraise all its expenditures carefully. Top executives want more proof than they now have that advertising really does pay. They want to know whether dollars spent on advertising are resulting in proportionately as many sales as dollars spent on other activities.

Difficulty of Evaluation

It is very difficult to measure the effectiveness of advertising. One problem is our inability to identify the results of any given advertisement or even an entire campaign. Except in the case of mail-order advertising, we cannot attribute a given unit of sales to any specific advertisement or campaign. By the very nature of the marketing mix, all elements—including advertising—are so intertwined that measurement of any one by itself is impossible. Many factors besides advertising influence sales success.

Essentially, there are only two parts to an advertisement—*what* is said and *how* it is said. The first part deals with product attributes to be explained, and the other is made up of the headlines, illustrations, and layouts. A great deal has been done to improve the manner of presentation (the "how"). This has been possible because research has been able to establish criteria to measure its effectiveness. The most commonly used evaluation methods measure the number of people who saw, read, and remembered the advertisements. But little has been done to aid management in its evaluation of the "what" part of an ad.

Many individual advertisements, and even entire campaigns, do not aim primarily at immediate sales results. For example, some advertisements simply announce new store hours or new service policies. Other institutional advertising is intended to build goodwill or to create a company image. It is very difficult to measure the effectiveness of these kinds of advertising.

Methods Used to Measure Effectiveness

In spite of the difficulties, advertisers do attempt to measure advertising effectiveness simply because they must do so—some knowledge is better than none at all. The effectiveness of an advertisement may be tested before the advertisement is presented to the public, while it is being presented, or after it has completed its run. The sales results test attempts to measure the sales volume stemming *directly* from the advertisement or series of advertisements being tested.

Most other types of tests are *indirect* measurements of effectiveness. One group consists of tests called "readership," "recognition," or "recall" tests. They involve showing respondents part or all of a previously run advertisement. This is done to determine (1) whether the ad was read, (2) what parts in it were remembered, and (3) whether the respondent knows who sponsored it. The theory underlying these tests is this: The greater the number of people who see, read, and remember an advertisement, the greater will be the number who do as the advertisement urges them. Another type of test involves measuring the number of coupons or other forms of inquiries that were received from certain advertisements.

Sometimes marketing people use a consumer panel to appraise a group of advertisements. With respect to radio and television advertising, several techniques are used to measure the size and makeup of program audiences. The theory is that the

The effectiveness of this Sunlight ad can be judged based upon sales, and the numbers of coupons redeemed and Pyrex baking dishes ordered.

number of people who will buy the sponsor's products varies directly with the number who watch or hear the program.

The basic goal of advertising is to sell something—to modify consumer attitudes or behavior. Note, however, that most tests measure effectiveness through some variable other than sales. We should be more concerned with measuring advertising's ability to influence attitudes and behavior than with measuring consumers' recall of given advertisements.

ORGANIZING FOR ADVERTISING

Now let's consider the organization needed to perform and manage the advertising activities in a company. Management has three alternatives. It may (1) develop a company advertising department, (2) use an outside advertising agency, or (3) use both a company department and an advertising agency. Regardless of which alternative is selected, generally the same specialized skills are needed to do the advertising job. Creative people are needed to do the copy writing, generate the illustrative material, and prepare the layouts. Media experts are needed to select the appropriate media, buy the time and space, and arrange for the scheduled appearance of the ads. Managerial skills are needed to plan and administer the entire advertising program.

Within the Company

All these advertising tasks, only some of them, or none of them can be performed within a company department. When advertising is a substantial part of the marketing mix, a company is likely to have its own advertising department. The head of this department should report to the marketing manager, if the company is to implement the marketing concept. Large retailers, for example, often have their own advertising departments and do not use an advertising agency at all.

Advertising Agency

Many companies, especially producers, use an advertising agency to do some or all of the advertising job. An **advertising agency** is an independent company set up to render specialized services in advertising in particular and in marketing in general. Today, the term *agency* is a misnomer. These firms are not agents in the legal sense but, instead, are independent companies.

Advertising agencies employ highly skilled professionals to create ads for products and services.

Many agencies offer a broad range of services. In the field of advertising alone, they plan and execute entire advertising campaigns. In radio and television, some agencies produce the entertainment as well as the commercials. Many of these firms are becoming *marketing* agencies, offering services that heretofore were performed by other outside specialists or by the advertisers themselves.

Why Use Both a Department and an Agency?

Many producers have their own advertising department but also use an advertising agency. The advertising department acts as liaison between agency and company. It approves the agency's plans and advertisements, and has the responsibility of preparing and administering the advertising budget. The department also handles direct-mail advertisements, dealer displays, and other activities not handled by an agency.

Using an agency along with a department has other advantages for a company. The agency usually has more advertising specialists than does the company. Also, a company can benefit from the agency's experience with many other products and clients. An agency often can do more for the same amount of money, because the agency can spread the costs of its staff over many accounts.

NATURE OF SALES PROMOTION

Sales promotion is one of the most loosely used terms in the marketing vocabulary. What, then, is sales promotion? Well, in this book we define **sales promotion** as those promotional activities (other than advertising, personal selling, and publicity) that are intended to stimulate customer demand and to improve middlemen's marketing performance.[3] A list of sales promotion activities is a long one. It includes the use of

---

[3]Adapted from *Marketing Definitions: A Glossary of Marketing Terms*, American Marketing Association, Chicago, Illinois 1960, p. 20. The American Marketing Association also noted that, in the field of retailing, the term *sales promotion* is used to cover "all methods of stimulating customer purchasing including personal selling, advertising, and publicity." Thus, in retailing, *sales promotion* is used in a broad sense. It is virtually synonymous with *promotion*, as that term is used in this book and also by most manufacturers.

For more on this problem of definition, see Ernest F. Cooke, "Defining Sales Promotion Difficult, Important," *Marketing News*, Nov. 8, 1985, p. 35.

IMPORTANCE OF SALES PROMOTION

coupons, premiums, in-store displays, trade shows, free samples, contests for consumers or middlemen, and many other activities that we shall discuss later. These activities may be conducted by producers or by middlemen. Sales promotion by producers may be directed at middlemen or at end users—either household consumers or industrial users. Middlemen direct their sales promotion efforts at the end users—consumer or industrial.

While sales promotion is something separate from advertising and personal selling, all three activities often are interrelated. In contrast, the sales promotion manager of a major oil company once referred to sales promotion as "muddled, misused, and misunderstood." But this situation is changing. As one marketing executive put it, "Sales promotion is moving from being the stepchild to being the Cinderella of marketing."[4] In recent years sales promotion has been the fastest-growing method of promotion, based on percentage increase in annual expenditures. Currently, annual expenditures for sales promotion are estimated to parallel or exceed those for advertising. Sales promotion is also being integrated into the total marketing strategy in many firms. It is being introduced at the inception of a promotion campaign, and not tacked on afterward.

The numbers attached to some of the sales promotion activities are simply mind-boggling. Over 160 *billion* coupons were distributed in 1984, and over 6 *billion* were redeemed by consumers. Experts in the field estimate that close to 400 *billion* coupons will be distributed annually by 1990. *Millions* of people attend trade shows each year, and *billions* of dollars are spent on point-of-purchase displays in retail stores. The number of sweepstakes and the dollar value of their prizes more than tripled from the mid-1970s to the mid-1980s.

Several factors in the marketing environment account for the surging popularity of sales promotion.[5] One is the proliferation of new products and new brands. This leads to a proliferation of sales promotion activities as sellers work hard to get potential customers to try the new items. Of course, the established brands then usually must retaliate with their own promotions. A second environmental factor is the state of the economy. Customers' price sensitivity increases as they worry about the economy,

Traditionally, advertising has been the glamorous promotional tool, attracting much managerial attention in many firms. In contrast, the sales promotion manager of a

---

promotion) furnished by the manufacturer for stores selling Michelin tires may feature a slogan and illustrations from Michelin's current advertising campaign. This effective display then makes the retailers more receptive to talking with the Michelin sales people. Or sales-force prospecting leads may be generated from people who visited the Canon copy-machines exhibit at an office equipment trade show (sales promotion).

motion is to serve as a bridge between advertising and personal selling—to supplement and coordinate efforts in these two areas. For example, an in-store display (sales

[4]See Curt Schleier, "Marketing Image Plots Turnaround," in a special report on sales promotion, *Advertising Age*, Aug. 15, 1985, pp. 15ff.

[5]See John A. Quelch and Kristina Cannon-Bonventre, "Better Marketing at the Point of Purchase," *Harvard Business Review*, November–December 1983, pp. 162–169; and B. G. Yovovich, "Stepping into a New Era," in a special report on sales promotion, *Advertising Age*, Aug. 22, 1983, pp. M-9ff. Also see "Special Report on Sales Promotion," *Advertising Age*, Feb. 6, 1986, pp. 13–14ff.

especially if the economy is faltering. Then promotions, such as coupons, premiums, cents-off deals, and sweepstakes, increase in attractiveness to consumers.

The third factor is the low quality of retail selling. Many retailers use self-service (no sales people) or sales clerks who are inadequately trained and informed. In these situations, sales promotion devices (product displays, informational booklets, etc.) often are the only effective promotional tools available at the point of purchase.

The fourth factor is the growing awareness among sellers that many sales promotion devices (cents-off deals, coupons, free samples, product demonstrations) can generate quick buyer action.

STRATEGIC MANAGEMENT OF SALES PROMOTION

To avoid the label of being "muddled, misused, misunderstood," sales promotion should be included in the company's strategic marketing planning, along with advertising and personal selling. This means establishing sales promotion goals and selecting appropriate strategies. A separate budget should be set up for sales promotion. A wide variety of promotional tools are available to implement the strategic planning. Finally, management should evaluate the sales promotion performance.

One problem that management faces in this situation is that many sales promotion tools are short-run, tactical actions and devices. Coupons, premiums, and contests, for example, are designed to produce immediate (but short-lived) responses. Thus, to manage sales promotion so that it becomes an effective factor in a company's marketing program over the long run requires some real talent.

Determine Sales Promotion Objectives and Strategies

Early in the strategic planning for sales promotion, management should (1) set the goals for the current sales promotion program, (2) select the appropriate strategies, and (3) identify the target markets at which this promotion will be directed.

The following three broad objectives of sales promotion were identified as we discussed the definition of the term:

• To stimulate end-user demand (industrial user or household consumer).
• To improve the marketing performance of middlemen.
• To supplement and coordinate advertising and personal selling activities.

The more specific objectives of sales promotion are much like those for advertising and personal selling. Some examples are as follows:

• *To get consumers to try a new product or an improved model of an established product.* To get consumers to try a new brand of soap or toothpaste, Proctor & Gamble or Lever Brothers may send a free sample through the mail.
• *To attract new customers.* Banks have offered small appliances and other premiums to encourage new customers to open an account.
• *To encourage present customers to use the product or service in greater quantities.* United Airlines, American Airlines, and other large airlines have a "frequent flyer" program to encourage travelers to use the given airline more often.
• *To combat a competitor's promotional activity.* One supermarket chain cuts its prices. The competitors retaliate by offering triple-value coupons, a lottery, or a game such as bingo.

A good display can increase impulse buying by consumers and cooperation by retailers.

- *To increase the amount of impulse buying by consumers.* Supermarkets have increased their sales of candy bars, magazines, and paperback books by placing these products on display at the checkout stands.
- *To get greater cooperation from retailers.* A sporting goods manufacturer gets additional shelf space and other added support from its retailers by providing excellent point-of-purchase displays, by training of the retailers' sales people, and by giving tote bags to consumers.

The specific objectives for a given sales promotion program are derived directly from the objectives and strategies of the total marketing program. The following two case examples illustrate how two different marketing objectives will call for quite different sales promotion objectives, strategies, and tactics.

Case A

	Goal	Strategy
Marketing	Increase sales 10% over last year.	Introduce product into new markets.
Sales promotion	Enter new markets.	Use a pull promotional strategy.

Case B

Marketing	Maintain market share in face of fierce competition.	Improve retailer performance and build dealer goodwill.
Sales promotion	Improve retailer performance and build dealer goodwill.	Use a push promotional strategy.

The Case A pull strategy will call for tactics such as the use of coupons, cash refunds, free samples, and premium gifts. The push strategy in Case B will call for tactics such as training retailers' sales forces, supplying effective point-of-purchase displays, and granting advertising allowances.

Strategic planning also means that a manufacturer must be aware that normally it is dealing with three target markets for its sales promotion efforts. These audiences are the end users (ultimate consumers or industrial users), the middlemen and their sales forces, and the manufacturer's own sales force.

Determining Sales Promotion Budget

Ordinarily the budget for sales promotion should be established in the course of determining the appropriation for the total promotional mix. It is important that the budget for sales promotion be clearly separated from the appropriations for the other major components of the promotional mix. In too many cases, unfortunately, this separation does not occur. Sales promotion often is combined with advertising or public relations for budgetary purposes, or it is included as part of the appropriation labeled "advertising."

Carefully setting a clearly separate budget for sales promotion also will help a company do a better job of managing this activity. And a separate budget will help bring to sales promotion a deserved recognition of its growing importance in many organizations.

Select the Sales Promotion Tools

A key step in sales promotion management is to decide which sales promotion tools to use to help the organization reach its promotional goals. The many types of these activities and devices may be divided into three categories, based upon who is the target audience—end users, middlemen, or the manufacturer's own sales force. See Table 20-3. Frequently the same tool—contests, premiums, or trade shows, for example—may be used to reach more than one audience category.[6]

Some of the factors which influence the choice of promotional tools are as follows:

- *The organization's promotional objectives:* Do we want to use a pull strategy or a push strategy to get middlemen's support?
- *The target market for the promotion:* Are we promoting to ultimate consumers or middlemen?
- *The nature of the product:* Does it lend itself to free samples?
- *The cost of the tool:* Free samples to a wide market are expensive.
- *The current economic conditions:* Coupons, gifts, and cash refund offers are more attractive during periods of recession or inflation.

SALES PROMOTION DIRECTED AT END USERS

The major sales promotion tools directed at ultimate consumers or industrial users by producers and middlemen are listed in Table 20-3. Many of these tools probably are quite familiar to you, but a few words here about some of them still may be useful.

The use of **trading stamps**—which can be redeemed for gifts or cash—as a promotional tool has fluctuated over the years. Today they are used less in product retailing than in the past, but more in the retailing of services, such as by banks and travel agencies. Trading stamps do seem to offer a competitive advantage to the first

---

[6]For a review of several of the sales promotion tools, see Robert J. Kopp, ''Premiums Provide Great Impact, but Little Glamour,'' *Marketing News,* June 7, 1985, p. 12.

TABLE 20-3	**MAJOR SALES PROMOTION TOOLS, GROUPED BY TARGET AUDIENCE**	
End users: consumer or industrial	**Middlemen and their sales forces**	**Producers' own sales force**
Coupons	Trade shows and exhibitions	Sales contests
Cash refunds	Point-of-purchase displays	Sales training manuals
Premiums (gifts)	Free goods	Sales meetings
Free samples	Advertising allowances	Packets with promotional materials
Contests and sweepstakes	Contests for sales people	Demonstration model of product
Trading stamps	Training middlemen's sales force	
Point-of-purchase displays	Product demonstrations	
Product demonstrations	Advertising specialties	
Trade shows and exhibitions		
Advertising specialties		

Cosmetic firms have found gift certificates to be effective in generating sales.

Video displays are popular.

firm that uses them in a given market. When many firms use them, however, this advantage disappears.

Point-of-purchase displays can serve as a silent sales force, especially in a self-service retailing operation. These displays can attract attention, serve as a buying reminder, stimulate impulse buying, and provide useful information in booklets or signs. **Trade shows and exhibitions**—open to consumers—are put on by many industries. Many of you undoubtedly have heard of, or even attended, an auto show, sporting goods show, boat show, travel and resort show, home and garden show, flower show, or art exhibition. These shows are a great way to introduce new products, give product demonstrations, and generally create consumer excitement.

"Advertising specialties" is kind of a miscellaneous category that includes small, inexpensive items given by manufacturers or by middlemen with the company's name on them. Examples include rulers, pens, calendars, ashtrays, caps, key rings, and paperweights.

SALES PROMOTION DIRECTED AT MIDDLEMEN AND THEIR SALES FORCES
Some of the same tools which we just discussed may also be directed at middlemen and their sales forces. (See Table 20-3.) For example, furniture manufacturers and the travel industry periodically will put on a trade show open only to wholesalers and retailers. In addition, some promotional tools are specifically designed for middlemen. For example, many producers spend considerable time and money to **train the sales forces** of their wholesalers and retailers. Producers also provide various forms of advertising allowances for their dealers and distributors.

SALES PROMOTION DIRECTED AT PRODUCERS' OWN SALES FORCES
Again, some of the same promotional tools that a manufacturer aimed at its middlemen's sales forces also can be used for that manufacturer's own sales force. (See Table 20-3.) These tools include **sales contests** and other incentives, and **demonstration models** of the product. In addition, the sales promotion department can prepare visual sales aids for the sales people and **manuals** to be used in company sales training programs.

Evaluate Sales Promotion Performance

As was done for the other major components of the promotional mix, management should also attempt to evaluate the productivity—the effectiveness—of sales promotion.[7] Fortunately, for many types of sales promotion, the evaluation task is much easier and likely to be more accurate than is the case with advertising. For example, a company's sales volume or market share in a given market can be measured before, during, and after a particular sales promotion effort. Assume that the sales were $10 million for the 3-month period before the promotion, $16 million during the 3-month promotion, and $12 million during the 3 months afterward. Then management may assume that the promotion was successful. Sales increased 60 percent during the promotion and settled at a 20 percent increase afterward. If sales had dropped to $4 million after the promotion, management could deduce that the promotion simply had cannibalized sales from a future period. Of course, management also needs to determine whether other factors (competition, economic conditions, etc.) may have accounted for the changes in sales volume.

As other examples, management can examine sales data before and after a training program for retailers' sales forces. When a company exhibits at a trade show, management can measure the sales results coming from leads generated at the show.

PUBLICITY AND PUBLIC RELATIONS ■

Publicity and public relations are the last two major methods of promotion that we shall briefly discuss in connection with an organization's total promotional program. In most organizations these two promotional tools, much as we said about sales promotion, typically are relegated to stepchild status behind personal selling and advertising.

There are three possible reasons for the lack of marketing management's attention to these two areas. First, in most organizational structures, publicity and public relations activities are not even handled by the marketing department. Instead, they are the responsibility of a separate public relations department. Second, the terms are loosely used by both business and the public. There is no generally accepted definition of the two terms, nor a clear-cut distinction between them. Third, only in recent years have many organizations come to realize the tremendous importance of a good public relations and publicity effort. Companies historically told their executives to maintain a low, or even invisible, profile. Now many firms urge their executives to take part in community affairs and to speak out on issues of concern to the company. Companies realize that they need a good public relations program to offset unfavorable, adverse publicity.

Nature and Scope of Publicity and Public Relations

In Chapter 18 we briefly described the essence of publicity and public relations as promotional methods. **Publicity** is any promotional communication regarding an organization and/or its products where the message is *not* paid for by the organization benefiting from it. Usually the publicity communication is either (1) a nonpersonal news story appearing in a mass medium or (2) a promotional "plug" (for a product or organization) that is delivered by a person in a speech or an interview.

[7]See John A. Quelch, "It's Time to Make Trade Promotion More Productive," *Harvard Business Review,* May–June 1983, pp. 130–136; and Thomas V. Bonoma, "Get More Out of Your Trade Shows," *Harvard Business Review,* January–February 1983, pp. 75–83.

Publicity can be used for a wide variety of purposes in a company. Management may use publicity as one means of promoting the products or services marketed by the organization. A company also may publicize its new policies (credit, price discounting), its people (employee achievements, executive promotions, employee civic activities), research and development successes, financial reports, or its progress on pollution control. A company may use publicity to counteract an unfavorable image, unfavorable reports in the media, or an unfavorable news release from other outside organizations. Publicity is part of the broader communication concept that we call public relations.

Public relations is an organization's broad, overall communications effort intended to influence various groups' attitudes toward that organization. Public relations activities typically are designed to build or maintain a favorable image for an organization and a favorable relationship with the organization's various "publics." These publics may be customers, stockholders, employees, unions, environmentalists, the government, people in the local community, or some other group in society.

There obviously is some overlap among publicity, public relations, and advertising, yet we should differentiate among these three activities. Public relations is the strategic image-building communication force in an organization. Publicity is a major tactical tool used to implement the public relations strategy. In this respect, publicity is part of public relations. As an example, one organizational public relations strategy may be to build a better relationship with local environmentalists. The publicity people then implement this strategy by generating news releases explaining what the company is doing to improve the quality of life in the community. In addition, publicity may be involved in promoting individual products or services, whereas public relations typically does not engage in this activity.

Publicity Techniques

Three major communication channels are available for use by an organization in getting its public relations or publicity message to its publics. Different publicity techniques typically are used in each channel. The first channel involves sending a mass communications message through the mass media to reach the intended audience. In using this channel, the public relations or publicity people might prepare a news release or even a longer feature article about the organization. The hope is that the newspapers, the television stations, and other mass media will print or orally report the information. Some companies prepare special tapes or films for publicity purposes.

The second channel involves a personal communication to a group audience. In this situation, an executive or a public relations person might hold a press conference or conduct a tour of the company's physical plant. The people attending might be given a printed or photographic publicity handout. Or someone in the company might make a talk at a civic or professional meeting.

The third channel involves a one-on-one personal communication. In this situation, a company representative, in a lobbying effort, might talk with a legislator or other public official. Or a publicity person might try to get an entertainer to mention the company's new product or put in a plug for a new song or movie.

Benefits and Limitations of Publicity

If the publicity activities in an organization are managed efficiently, they can nicely support and complement the organization's advertising and personal selling efforts.

Publicity normally can be done at a much lower cost than advertising or personal selling, because there are no media space or time costs for conveying the publicity messages. Furthermore, the credibility level of publicity typically is much higher than that of advertising. If I tell you my product is great, you may well be skeptical. But if an independent, objective third party says my product is great, you are more likely to believe it.

A publicity message that appears as a newspaper or magazine article is more likely to be read than if the same message appears in a company ad. Readers can skip the ads entirely, but they are likely to read the news and editorial columns, and this is where the publicity messages come through. Another advantage of publicity is that it can provide more information than an ad can. Also, a company can get out a news release very quickly when some event occurs unexpectedly.

Of course, publicity has its limitations. An organization has little or no control over *what* is said in a newspaper article or television report. In fact, a company has no guarantee at all that its publicity message will even appear in print or on radio or television. The media may decide that the message is not of sufficient interest to publicize it. Furthermore, a company cannot control *when* the message will appear, and there is no opportunity for *repetition* as in ads. It is difficult to plan very far ahead in publicity. How do you prepare in advance for a mine explosion, a radiation leak, or a product recall? Finally, even though there are no immediate time and space costs, publicity is by no means free. Significant expenses are incurred in staffing a publicity department and in preparing and disseminating publicity messages.

SUMMARY

Advertising is the impersonal-selling, mass-communications component in a company's promotional mix. The company has the option of running product or institutional types of advertising. The product ads may call for direct or indirect action. Another useful classification of advertising is primary-demand and selective-demand advertising. This classification features pioneering, competitive, and comparative advertising. Manufacturers and their retail dealers often engage in some form of cooperative advertising. Advertising expenditures are large in total, but the cost of advertising in a firm is only 1 to 3 percent of sales, on the average. This is considerably less than the average cost of personal selling. Most advertising dollars are spent in newspaper media, and second place goes to television.

Management should develop an advertising campaign as part of the firm's total promotional program. The first step here is to set the specific goals for the particular campaign. A major task in developing a campaign is to select the advertising media—both the broad media class and the specific individual media. The selection should be based on the characteristics of the media and the way they fit the product and the market. The advertising message—as communicated to the market through the advertising copy, illustrations, and layout—is an integral part of a campaign.

A particularly important, yet difficult, task in advertising management is to measure (evaluate) the effectiveness of the advertising effort—both the entire campaign and individual ads. Several methods are widely used. Except for the sales results test, the commonly used techniques measure only the extent to which the ad was read or recalled. To operate an advertising program, a firm may use its own advertising department, retain an advertising agency, or combine the two organizational structures.

Sales promotion is the third major promotional tool, and the one used to coordinate and supplement the advertising and personal selling programs. Sales promotion has increased considerably in importance in recent years. Sales promotion should receive the same strategic management that a company gives to its advertising and personal selling programs. This means establishing sales promotion objectives and then selecting appropriate strategies. A separate budget should be set up for sales promotion. To implement its strategic planning, management has a wide variety of promotional tools to select from. Finally, the sales promotion performance should be evaluated.

Publicity and public relations were the final promotional methods that we discussed briefly in this chapter. Publicity is any promotional communication regarding an organization and/or its products where the message is not paid for by the companies benefiting from it. Publicity is part of public relations. Public relations is the broad, overall promotional concept that deals with improving or maintaining an organization's image and its favorable relationships with its various publics. Typically these two promotional activities are handled in a department separate from the marketing department in a firm. Nevertheless, the management process of planning, implementing, and evaluating should be applied to a publicity campaign in the same way as for advertising or personal selling.

KEY TERMS AND CONCEPTS

Advertising 462
An advertisement 462
Product advertising 462
Direct-action advertising 462
Indirect-action advertising 462
Institutional advertising 462
Primary-demand advertising 463
Pioneering advertising 463
Selective-demand advertising 463
Competitive advertising 463
Comparative advertising 464
Cooperative advertising 464

Cost of advertising as a percentage
of sales 466
Advertising campaign 468
Advertising media 468
Advertising copy and layout 472
Sales results test 473
Readership or recall tests 473
Advertising agency 474
Sales promotion 475
Sales promotion tools 479
Publicity 481
Public relations 481

QUESTIONS AND PROBLEMS

1. How do you account for the variation in advertising expenditures as a percentage of sales among the different types of companies in Table 20-2?

2. Several specific objectives of advertising were outlines early in the chapter. Bring to class some advertisements that illustrate at least four of these goals. Or be prepared to describe a current radio or television advertisement that is an attempt to achieve these objectives.

3. Which advertising medium is best for advertising the following products?

   a. Grocery carts.
   b. Hanes women's panty hose.
   c. Toys for children 3 to 5 years old.
   d. Jogging shoes.
   e. Microwave ovens.
   f. Plastic clothespins.

4. Many grocery products manufacturers and candy producers earmark a good portion of their advertising appropriations for use in magazines. Is this a wise choice of media for these firms? Explain.

5. Why do department stores use newspapers so much more than local radio as an advertising medium?

6. Why is it worthwhile to pretest advertisements before they appear in the media? Suggest a procedure for pretesting a magazine ad.

7. What procedures can a firm use to determine how many sales dollars resulted from a given ad or from an entire campaign?

8. Many advertisers on television use program ratings to determine whether to continue the sponsorship of a program. These ratings reflect the number of families that watch the program. Are program ratings a good criterion for evaluating the effectiveness of advertising? Does a high rating indicate that sales volume will also be high? Discuss.

9. If a manufacturing firm finds a good advertising agency, should it discontinue its own advertising department?

10. Visit a supermarket, a clothing store, and a hardware store, and then make a list of all the sales-promotion devices that you observed in each store. Which of these devices do you feel are particularly effective?

11. Is sales promotion effective for selling expensive consumer products such as houses, automobiles, or backyard swimming pools? Is your answer the same for expensive industrial products?

12. Explain how sales promotion can be used to offset weaknesses in personal selling in retail stores.

13. How does publicity differ from advertising?

14. Give a recent example of an organization that encountered unfavorable (negative) publicity. Do you think the organization handled this situation satisfactorily?

15. Give some recent examples of what you consider to be effective publicity campaigns. Explain why you rate these campaigns highly.

6

EAGLE STEEL SUPPLY COMPANY

Promotional program in an expanding market

Everett Allen, president of the Eagle Steel Supply Company, realized that the market for his company's products and services was showing signs of expansion. Consequently, he was wondering what kind of a promotional program his firm should develop (1) to take advantage of the growing market opportunities and (2) to minimize the effects of competition, which was sure to intensify. Located in Detroit, Michigan, the Eagle Company provided Detroit-area industries with custom-made steel products capable of withstanding excessively heavy use in specialized situations.

Basically, Eagle was a service organization. The company did not produce any of the products it sold. Instead, it acted as a liaison between steel users and steel producers in the following manner. During a regular call on a steel user, an Eagle sales person would seek to identify a problem situation that called for a specialty steel product. Or the user company itself—after identifying its need for a high-strength alloyed steel product—might initiate the contact with a specialty steel supplier such as Eagle. The Eagle sales rep would analyze the problem and recommend a particular type of steel.

Eagle then placed an order for this product with a steel manufacturer. There the mill's metallurgists formulated the processes and components which would yield the desired products. Typically, some material (tungsten, manganese, nickel) was mixed with the molten steel to form an alloy that gave the desired flexibility, hardness, or ability to withstand temperature extremes.

Specialty steel products are used in a wide variety of industrial situations involving heavy blows or stresses over long periods of time. For example, alloyed high-strength steel is commonly used in conveyor systems, blast furnaces, and machine parts (gears, bearings, connecting rods, cutting units, etc.). Over the years, there has been an increasing demand for these specialized steel products.

In view of this increasing demand, some people wondered why the major users did not deal directly with the large steel producers, thus bypassing the suppliers such as Eagle. Mr. Allen gave two reasons why the specialty steel suppliers had developed and continued to thrive. First, the major users found that they did not buy this type of product often enough to have a separate procurement facility. However, when the users did need a specialty product, the tasks of determining specifications and procuring the product were complex tasks. Second, the greatly expanded list of steel alloys available meant that considerable expertise was needed to ensure correct product choice.

The Eagle Company's primary market was the heavily industrialized area within a 60-mile radius of Detroit. However, Mr. Allen considered that Eagle's total market extended out 100 miles from Detroit. Within that 100-mile radius, Eagle had a 22 percent market share, according to Mr. Allen. Three other specialty steel suppliers competed with Eagle in this market. Allen estimated that their respective market shares were 30 percent, 28 percent, and 20 percent.

Competition in the specialty steel industry typically was on a nonprice basis, because all steel producers generally maintained comparable prices. Companies competed on their ability to analyze a user's problem and then recommend a steel alloy that would solve the problem at a reasonable cost. Personal relationships which sales people built with their customers also were important.

The Eagle Company had experienced significant ups and downs in its sales history. However, since Everett Allen took over 6 years ago, sales had increased annually to the present level of $2.5 million a year. Net operating profit had increased to 7 percent of sales. Mr. Allen credited much of the sales success to his methods of working with the steel producers. In contrast to previous buying practices, Allen selected only one mill supplier—United States Steel Company. He then maintained intensive written and personal contact with that manufacturer. The net result was that U.S. Steel filled Eagle's orders promptly—sometimes even ahead of orders from other specialty steel firms.

Mr. Allen estimated that the four specialty steel companies could handle only 80 percent of the potential business in the Detroit area, and furthermore, the market was expanding rapidly. Eagle had built a clientele of steady customers in the automotive, cement, and gravel industries. In addition, new users and new uses of specialty steel offered opportunities for market expansion. Local chemical companies and machine parts makers, for instance, were potential customers.

Up to the present time, Eagle's promotional program had consisted primarily of the personal selling efforts of the company's eight sales representatives. No advertising was done at all. In fact, only one of Eagle's three competitors used any advertising, and then only in a very small amount.

With demand outrunning supply in the specialty steel market, Eagle's market prospects looked good. Mr. Allen was smart enough to realize, however, that the current market situation could very well be a short-run phenomenon. Such a market was bound to attract additional competitors and to draw more aggressive, better-trained selling efforts from existing firms. Consequently, he was wondering how he might improve Eagle's promotional efforts in order to capture a satisfactory share of the expanding market.

As one alternative, Mr. Allen considered budgeting $100,000 for an advertising program during the coming year. He consulted a Detroit advertising agency that suggested a program of direct-mail advertising plus placing advertisements in selected trade journals and Detroit newspapers. According to that agency, the proposed advertising program would have several advantages, some of which were:

1. It would make the sales reps' efforts more efficient by using advertising to make the initial customer contact.

2. It would establish company identity and image.
3. It would reach customer personnel now inaccessible to the sales force.

Another alternative was to use the same amount of money to hire, train, and compensate three additional sales people. The total cost per person would be about $40,000, depending on the amount of training the reps needed. If experienced sales reps were hired, then the training costs presumably would be reduced. In that case, any unallocated promotional funds could be used (1) to further train the present sales people and (2) to equip the sales force with better sales tools (catalogs, samples, etc.).

An informal market investigation, which Mr. Allen conducted, revealed the following interesting facts about the purchase decision for specialty steel products:

1. The initial purchase idea comes from the first level of management—a foreman or general foreman—which is in closest contact with a company's problems.
2. Buying decisions for specialty steels are made quickly when a need arises. Then the buyer seeks the assistance of a specialty steel company. The purchase is not a long-range, planned affair.

QUESTION

What promotional program should the Eagle Company use to profitably expand its sales volume?

CONCORD PORTRAIT STUDIOS

Promotional program to enter a new market

The top executives at Concord Portrait Studios realized that many communities were adopting new, or strengthening already existing, consumer-protection laws—especially the ordinances regulating door-to-door selling. As a result of this growing pressure, the executives were reappraising the promotional methods used to support the company's mobile retailing units. Concord Portrait Studios was a company that took photographs of people. The company did its own developing, finishing, and oil-coloring work in five finishing plants.

The company operated a chain of retail outlets in almost every state in the continental United States. About 40 percent of the retail outlets were permanent photographic studios located in medium- and large-sized cities.

The other 60 percent of the retail outlets consisted of traveling, or mobile, units. These traveling units visited small communities for a period of a few days to a few weeks, depending upon the market potential in the town. Some communities were visited only once a year, and others three or four times a year. For these units, the company usually rented office and studio space in a local hotel or motel. The unit's staff included three groups: (1) people to do the promotional work in advance of the unit's visit; (2) one or more photographers; and (3) the clerical help needed to arrange the photographic sittings, show proofs to the customers, take orders, and do the record keeping. The finished portraits were mailed to the customers either prepaid or on a c.o.d. basis.

The quality of the work done by the Concord company was excellent, and the firm enjoyed a good reputation for dependability and responsibility. Operating as it did on a traveling basis, the company was particularly concerned about its reputation in the various towns. Management knew that success depended upon repeat visits and favorable word-of-mouth advertising from past customers. The company's prices were reasonable. In fact, Concord's photographs frequently were priced below those of local competitors. From its inception, the firm had followed a penetration pricing strategy of low unit profit margins, depending upon large sales volume to return a satisfactory total profit. This pricing policy was one of the factors that irritated local photographers in many cities.

Before the photographic crew arrived in a town, the company sent ahead a group of door-to-door sales people who sold introductory offers. This offer was a certificate that sold for $15. The certificate entitled a household to three 8 × 10 color photographs that normally were priced at $30 each. Two requirements accompanied this offer. First, there must be three photographic sittings within 1 year, taken at least 90 days apart. Second, each sitting must involve a different member of the household. In summary, the customer received one photo each for three different people, taken at three different times within a year, and taken at least 90 days apart. Thus, a household received $90 worth of photographs for the $15 certificate.

The sales reps were paid on a straight-commission basis. They also set up appointments for taking the photographs. Of course, when the subject arrived for a sitting, or after the person saw the proofs, the company hoped to increase the original order. Actually, the company lost money if the customer did not buy more than the original $15 order.

The practice of selling certificates on a door-to-door basis had been used successfully for years by the company, and it still was bringing in satisfactory sales volume. Several factors, however, were making the executives wonder whether the method had outlived its usefulness. Except in small towns, it was difficult to reach enough prospects in a short period of time by this method. Also, in many communities people simply were afraid to open their doors to talk to a stranger. As the company had increased in size and prestige, the executives thought that possibly door-to-door selling was damaging the firm's image. One manager stated that this type of selling was all right in the early days, when the firm was starting, but now more socially acceptable methods should be used. In some communities Green River ordinances were hindering the operation of the advance sales people.

The company was considering other promotional methods for entering new markets. Sally Chrosniak, head of the photographic division, said that the company should engage in an intensive campaign of telephone selling to make the introductory offers. Hardy Gallo, the general sales manager, suggested party-plan selling. He was impressed with the success enjoyed by firms selling jewelry, home products, and cosmetics in this manner. The woman giving the home party could be rewarded by portrait photographs of members of her family, or she could select from other prizes. This method would enable one sales person to reach more prospects in a shorter period of time than could be done by approaching them on a door-to-door basis. Local service clubs, garden clubs, church groups, sports clubs, and similar organizations were considered good prospects for party-plan selling. Also, on college campuses, the dormitories and the fraternity and sorority houses were considered excellent market prospects.

The manager of the company's Dallas finishing plant, who had come up through the company ranks as a sales rep and photographer, was inclined toward the extensive use of local newspaper advertising. The advertisements could include the introductory certificate. The use of a newspaper might also earn the newspaper's support if legislative attempts were made to restrict the selling efforts of firms such as Concord. On the other side of the coin, local merchants might put pressure on a newspaper not to accept advertising from an outside company such as Concord.

QUESTIONS

1. What promotional method(s) should Concord use when coming into a community?
2. Should the promotional methods used in towns visited several times a year be different from those used in communities visited only once a year?
3. Should the promotional methods used to enter brand new markets be different from those used in communities where Concord had previously sold?

THE KLOTHES KLOSET

Promotional program for a small retailer

A little over 1 year ago Linda Flambeau and Norma Henderson pooled their resources and opened a small store to sell second-hand goods. After 1 year in business, the store still was operating at a net loss. Given their limited financial resources, Linda and Norma were wondering what kind of promotional program they should adopt in order to increase the store's exposure and to generate more customer traffic.

The two women decided on the name—The Klothes Kloset—hoping that the unusual spelling would attract customer attention. The store was located on a busy street on the north side of Denver, Colorado. The location was considered to be a good one for this type of store.

While the store's primary product line was clothing, the store also carried furniture, shoes, pictures, and some housewares. In fact, The Klothes Kloset would carry any product that a person brought in to be sold, so long as it was in good condition. In addition, Flambeau and Henderson also purchased some articles at rummage sales and garage sales.

All of the articles that the people brought in to be sold were handled on a consignment basis by The Klothes Kloset. When the product was sold, 50 percent of the revenue went to the consignor and 50 percent was retained by the store. Each item was priced by one of the co-owners. If an item was not sold within 1 month, its price was cut in half. If it still was not sold in 3 months, it was donated to charity. Several customers had commented that The Klothes Kloset's prices were lower than those charged by other second-hand stores.

The Klothes Kloset's main competition came from two well-established second-hand stores in North Denver. One of these stores, which had been in business for 25 years, strived to project a more sophisticated image and thus charged higher prices than The Klothes Kloset. The other competitor was located near The Klothes Kloset and had a similar product mix.

In analyzing the store's target market, Henderson determined that the bulk of this market lived within a 2-mile radius of the store. Also, the customers were in the 20- to 40-year age bracket and the lower-middle income bracket, and 80 percent were female. About 70 percent of the customers were Hispanic and 30 percent were Anglos.

The customers were quite particular about the physical condition of the products—demanding that they be in good condition, clean, and currently fashionable.

The store's total sales volume during its first year of operation was $10,500. As is typical in retailing, most of this volume came during the spring and fall seasons. Norma Henderson indicated that they needed a sales volume of $14,400 in order to break even. And this figure obviously did not provide for any salaries to the co-owners. In fact, at the end of the first year, the store had a debt of $700 in consignment fees still owed to people whose goods had been sold.

The women had been spending about $60 a month on advertising. But Henderson said they would be willing to double their advertising expenditure if this would significantly increase customer traffic. Henderson also stated that they would prefer a more steady flow of customers, instead of the present seasonal sales pattern.

The Klothes Kloset's initial promotional effort consisted primarily of three sets of activities. First, Flambeau and Henderson distributed 2,000 flyers to homes in the neighborhood. A coupon, good for a 10 percent discount in the store, was attached to each flyer. Second, the store placed a 3- × 4-inch ad in two small weekly newspapers that were circulated throughout Denver and its surrounding suburbs. One of these papers featured advertising by small, bargain-offering businesses such as The Klothes Kloset. The ad ran for 13 weeks. The other weekly paper was of a more general audience interest, and The Klothes Kloset ad ran for only 2 weeks. Henderson believed that neither of these two series of ads brought in much business.

Third, Linda and Norma distributed business cards to customers and personal friends, and the co-owners also placed brightly colored flags out in front of the store. Norma Henderson felt that these efforts did generate customer traffic.

As the year went along and summer arrived, the women continued to distribute the flyers and business cards, but they stopped the flag display and the newspaper advertising. Sales also dropped during this summer period. This sales decline caused Linda and Norma to sit down and discuss their promotional program.

Linda thought that the store should do more newspaper advertising. Norma, on the other hand, believed they should do more in the way of sales promotion activities such as displaying racks of clothing in front of the store and also restoring the flag display. As Norma said, "We compromised and did both—we put in the displays and we did some more advertising." This time they ran a small (2- × 3-inch) ad weekly in the *North Denver Tribune*, a neighborhood newspaper that was circulated only among North Denver residents. This ad was still running.

During the autumn months of the store's first year, sales increased considerably over the low summer period. But both women agreed that they had a long way to go. As Norma Henderson said, "Neither Linda nor I have ever owned a store before, and neither of us has much of a business background. But we do know that a business like ours has to promote itself if it is going to have a prayer of being successful. Our problem is that we don't know what kind of advertising or other form of promotion we should be using, given our limited amount of money."

QUESTION

What promotional program should be adopted by The Klothes Kloset?

7

MARKETING IN SPECIAL FIELDS

Marketing programs for marketers of services, nonbusiness organizations, and American firms marketing in foreign countries

So far in this book, our discussion has dealt with the *domestic marketing of products by profit-seeking businesses.* Here we rectify that imbalance a bit as we consider strategies in three special areas of marketing. The first is the marketing of intangible services, as contrasted to physical products (Chapter 21). The second is the marketing activity in nonprofit organizations and in organizations that are not usually considered as businesses—hospitals and art museums, for example (Chapter 22). And the third is multinational marketing—that is, the marketing of products and services across national boundaries (Chapter 23).

Strategic marketing planning as applied in these three areas is *fundamentally* the same as we first outlined in Chapter 3 and have been discussing throughout the book. That is, the service, nonprofit, or international organization should first identify its mission. Next, the company should define its overall company goals and its marketing goals. Management then can identify its target markets. Finally, the organization should develop and implement a strategic marketing mix that will reach the target markets and achieve the organization's goals.

However, the results of marketing planning in these special fields often are quite different from those for profit-seeking domestic product marketers. It is these differences—plus the tremendous importance of service, nonprofit, and international organizations in our society and economy—that make these three chapters essential in this book.

MARKETING OF SERVICES

CHAPTER GOALS

The special nature of services—especially their intangibility—leads to special marketing problems. After studying this chapter, you should understand:

- What services are and are not.
- The importance of services in our economy.
- The characteristics of services, and the marketing implications in these characteristics.
- The marketing concept in service marketing.
- A program for the marketing of services.
- The future outlook in service marketing.

You've got the Card.

When you have a question on your bill, it's nice to know someone out there will hear your call.

Would you pay $250 a year for a credit card that serves primarily as a super status symbol in some circles? That is, especially when you can get most of the same financial benefits from two other cards issued by the same company for $45 and $65 a year, respectively. Well, apparently the answer was "yes," in the case of some 60,000 who adopted the Platinum Card when it was initially issued by the American Express Company.

The success of the Platinum Card encouraged the company to move ahead with plans to introduce the Blue Card. This is a revolving-credit card that enables the company to expand its assortment of credit services. Truly, the Travel-Related Services Division of American Express (credit cards, traveler's checks, and other travel services) has been a real success story in the field of service marketing. "The American Express Card—don't leave home without it."

The chairman of the company has stated, "Marketing is our number 1 priority." The company depends upon marketing to generate growth and to enhance the company's image. These twin goals of growth and image-building have been reached, in part, because of effective tie-ins with other projects. For example, in its project Home Town America, the company will donate up to $20,000 for each of at least 150 community projects. One purpose of this commitment is to get people to use their American Express card more often when buying locally. American Express also has used its advertising effectively to attract more women cardholders.

The company so far has been disappointed in the performance of two of its other service divisions—Shearson securities and Fireman's Fund insurance. But the company's basic business—travel-related services—can provide a shining example of the value of marketing in a service organization. This example should be noted especially by the many service firms who have yet to recognize the critical importance of marketing in their operations.[1]

Unfortunately, many service firms simply do not understand what marketing is. They tend to equate marketing with personal selling or advertising, and they have largely ignored the aspects of product development, pricing, and distribution. Looking to the 1990s, however, it is becoming increasingly evident that many organizations in service industries simply must become more marketing oriented if they hope to survive. Service marketing is what we will be talking about in this chapter. The significant differences between service marketing and product marketing, plus the current growth and major importance of services in our economy, are the reasons for having this chapter.[2]

---

[1]Adapted from Kim Foltz, "A Green Giant Is on the Move," *Newsweek*, Oct. 28, 1985, pp. 58–59.

[2]The contributions of Prof. Milton M. Pressley, University of New Orleans, to this chapter when it was being prepared for an earlier edition of this book are again acknowledged. Many of his contributions are retained in this edition.

NATURE AND IMPORTANCE OF SERVICES

Definition and Scope of Field ■

In concept, product marketing and service marketing are essentially the same. In each case, the marketer must select and analyze its target markets. Then a marketing program must be built around the parts of the marketing mix—the product (or service), the price structure, the distribution system, and the promotional program. Moreover, there often are substantial similarities in practice. At the same time, however, the basic characteristics that differentiate services from products usually lead to a quite different marketing program in a service organization. The strategies and tactics used in conventional product marketing often are inappropriate for service marketing.

It is unfortunate that we still do not have general agreement regarding what service marketing encompasses. Here is the definition of services that we shall use in this chapter:

> **Services** are those separately identifiable, essentially intangible activities that provide want-satisfaction, and that are not necessarily tied to the sale of a product or another service. To produce a service may or may not require the use of tangible goods. However, when such use is required, there is no transfer of the title (permanent ownership) to these tangible goods.

Now let's elaborate a bit on that definition, to reduce any possibility of confusion:

- We include such activities as medical care, entertainment, and repair services (but not the medicines or repair parts purchased).
- We *exclude* credit, delivery, and other services that exist only when there is the sale of a product or another service.
- The consumer of a service can take only *temporary* possession or make only *temporary* use of any goods required in the production of the service—a hotel room or a rented car, for example. (An exception here would include such tangible goods as insurance policies, legal papers, or a consultant's reports that supplement but do not comprise the service.) Service organizations are those that do not have as their *principal* aim the production of tangible products that buyers will possess permanently.

The definitional problem will continue. Some statistics on services may be misleading because it is becoming more difficult to separate products and services in our economy. We rarely find situations in which services are marketed without any product involvement whatsoever. Most products are accompanied by services, and most services require supporting products. It is this product-service mix that really is growing in importance in our economy.

We are concerned here primarily with the services marketed by business or professional firms with profit-making motives—commercial services. This is in contrast to services of nonbusiness organizations, such as churches, public schools, and the government. One useful classification of commercial services by industry is given below. No attempt is made to separate these into consumer and industrial services, as we did with products. In fact, most are purchased by both market groups.[3]

- Housing (includes rentals of hotels, motels, apartments, houses, and farms).
- Household operations (includes utilities, house repairs, repairs of equipment in the house, landscaping, and household cleaning).
- Recreation and entertainment (includes rental and repair of equipment used to participate in recreation and entertainment activities; also admission to all entertainment, recreation, and amusement events).
- Personal care (includes laundry, dry cleaning, beauty care).
- Medical and other health care (includes all medical service, dental, nursing, hospitalization, optometry, and other health care).
- Private education.
- Business and other professional services (includes legal, accounting, management consulting, and computer services).
- Insurance, banking, and other financial services (includes personal and business insurance, credit and loan service, investment counseling, and tax service).
- Transportation (includes freight and passenger service on common carriers, automobile repairs and rentals).
- Communications (includes telephone, telegraph, computer, and specialized business communication services).

Importance of Services

The United States has moved beyond the industrial economy stage to the point where it has become the world's first service economy. Almost three-fourths of the nonfarm labor force is employed in service industries, and over two-thirds of the nation's gross national product is accounted for by services. Also, service jobs typically hold up better during a recession than do jobs in industries producing tangible products.

About one-half of consumer expenditures are for the purchase of services. Furthermore, projections to 1990 indicate that services will attract an even larger share of consumer spending and employment. Unfortunately, one feature of the service economy boom is that the prices of most services have been going up at a considerably faster rate than the prices of most products. You are undoubtedly aware of this if you have had your car or TV set repaired, had your shoes half-soled, or paid a medical bill in recent years.

When we say that services account for close to one-half of *consumer expenditures*, we still grossly understate the economic importance of services. These figures do not include the vast amounts spent for *business and industrial services*. By all indications, spending for business services has increased even more rapidly than spending for consumer services.

Now this is a product . . .

. . . and this is a service.

[3]For a series of five classification schemes, each of which separates services into clusters that share certain marketing characteristics, see Christopher H. Lovelock, "Classifying Services to Gain Strategic Marketing Insights," *Journal of Marketing*, Summer 1983, pp. 9–20. This article also includes a summary of several service-classification schemes proposed by other authors.

Part of the boom in services marketing.

To understand the reasons for the boom in *consumer services*, we must understand what has been happening in our economy during the past 40 years. The long period of general prosperity has meant higher incomes, increased leisure time, and an overall rise in living standards. In the early stages of a period such as this, people first expend their rising incomes on goods. This was particularly true after World War II, when there was a huge backlog of product demand. Products were denied to consumers in the 1930s because of the Depression, and in the early 1940s because of the war. Then, as the years go by, the average consumer becomes sated with goods. Consumers increasingly turn to services that heretofore they either could not afford or did not desire—services such as travel, education, personal grooming, and medical care.

The growth of *business services* may be attributed to the fact that business has become increasingly complex, specialized, and competitive. As a consequence, management has been forced to call in experts to provide services in research, taxation, advertising, labor relations, and a host of other areas.

The rate of growth has not been uniform for all categories of consumer services. As disposable personal incomes have increased and life-styles have changed, the demand for some services has grown relatively faster than for others. Projections into the 1990s suggest that high growth rates in jobs and spending will occur especially in the health-care industry, auto repairs, banking and finance fields, and leisure-time industries.

To capitalize on the emerging service economy, many product *manufacturers* have diversified into services. Some product *retailers* have done likewise. Sears, Roebuck now has some 40 nonmerchandise offerings, including an insurance company (Allstate), an income tax counseling firm, a car-rental agency, a securities broker (Dean Witter), a real estate agency (Coldwell-Banker), and a credit-card firm (Discover). Montgomery Ward and other department stores now house law and dental offices that provide services for customers. Broadway department stores, headquartered on the West Coast, also market home cleaning, insurance, income tax counseling, and driving lessons.

Characteristics of Services

The special nature of services stems from several distinctive characteristics. These characteristics create special marketing challenges and opportunities. They also often

result in strategic marketing programs that are substantially different from those found in product marketing.

INTANGIBILITY

Since services are essentially intangible, it is impossible for customers to sample—to taste, feel, see, hear, or smell—services *before* they buy them. This feature of services places some strain on a marketing organization. The burden falls mainly on a company's promotional program. The sales force and the advertising department must concentrate on the *benefits* to be derived from the service, rather than emphasizing the service itself. An insurance company thus may promote service benefits such as guaranteed payment of a child's college expenses, or a retirement income of so many dollars per month. The telephone companies tell us how business users can cut selling costs by using long-distance calling.[4]

INSEPARABILITY

Services often cannot be separated from the person of the seller. Moreover, some services must be created and dispensed simultaneously. For example, dentists create and dispense almost all their services at the same time.

From a marketing standpoint, inseparability frequently means that direct sale is the only possible channel of distribution, and a seller's services cannot be sold in very many markets. This characteristic also limits the scale of operation in a firm. One person can repair only so many autos in a day or treat only so many medical patients.

As an exception to the inseparability feature, the service may be sold by a person who is representing the creator-seller. A travel agent, insurance broker, or rental agent, for instance, may represent and help promote the service that will be sold by the institution producing it.

HETEROGENEITY

It is impossible for a service industry, or even an individual seller of services, to standardize output. Each "unit" of the service is somewhat different from other "units" of the same service. For example, an airline does not give the same quality of service on each trip. All repair jobs a mechanic does on automobiles are not of equal quality. An added complication is the fact that it is often difficult to judge the quality of a service. (Of course, we can say the same for some products.) It is particularly difficult to forecast the quality in advance of buying a service. A person pays to see a ball game without knowing whether it will be an exciting one, well worth the price of admission, or a dull performance.

Service companies should therefore pay particular attention to the "product-planning" stage of their marketing programs. From the beginning, management must do all it can to ensure consistency of quality and to maintain high levels of quality control.[5]

You win some and you lose some—the quality is different, game to game.

[4]For suggestions on how to offset the marketing problems created by intangibility in services (and also in products), see Theodore Levitt, "Marketing Intangible Products and Product Intangibles," *Harvard Business Review*, May–June 1981, pp. 94–102. See also Betsy D. Gelb, "How Marketers of Intangibles Can Raise the Odds for Consumer Satisfaction," *The Journal of Consumer Marketing*, Spring 1985, pp. 55–61.

[5]See Leonard L. Berry, Valarie A. Zeithaml, and A. Parasuraman, "Quality Counts in Services, Too," *Business Horizons*, May–June 1985, pp. 44–52.

There is no tomorrow for selling seats to this game.

THE MARKETING CONCEPT AND SERVICE MARKETING

PERISHABILITY AND FLUCTUATING DEMAND

Services are highly perishable, and they cannot be stored. Unused electric power, empty seats in a stadium, and idle mechanics in a garage all represent business that is lost forever. Furthermore, the market of services fluctuates considerably by season, by day of the week, and by hour of the day. Many ski lifts lie idle all summer, and golf courses in some areas go unused in the winter. The use of city buses fluctuates greatly during the day.

There are some notable exceptions to this generalization regarding the perishability and storage of services. In health and life insurance, for example, the service is purchased. Then it is held by the insurance company (the seller) until needed by the buyer or the beneficiary. This holding constitutes a type of storage.

The combination of perishability and fluctuating demand offers product-planning, pricing, and promotion challenges to service company executives. Some organizations have developed new uses for idle plant capacity during off-seasons. Thus, during the summer, several ski resorts operate their ski lifts for hikers and sightseers who want access to higher elevations. Advertising and creative pricing are also used to stimulate demand during slack periods. Hotels offer lower prices and family packages for weekends. Telephone companies offer lower rates during nights and weekends. In some college towns, apartment rates are lowered in the summer.

The growth in services has generally *not* been due to marketing developments in service industries, but rather to the maturation of our economy and our rising standards of living. Traditionally, executives in our service companies have *not* been marketing-oriented. They have lagged behind sellers of products in accepting the marketing concept, and have generally been slow in adopting marketing techniques. Marketing management in service firms has not been especially creative. Innovations in service marketing have come typically from product-associated companies.

We can identify some of the reasons for this lack of marketing orientation. No doubt, the intangibility of services creates more difficult marketing challenges for service sellers than for product sellers. In many service industries—particularly professional services—the sellers think of themselves as producers or creators, and not as marketers, of the service. They are proud of their ability to repair a car, diagnose an illness, or give a good haircut. They do not think of themselves as business people.

The all-encompassing reason, however, is that top management does not yet understand (1) what marketing is or (2) its importance to a company's success. These executives seem to equate marketing with selling, and they fail to consider other parts of the marketing system. They also do not effectively coordinate their marketing activities. Many service firms lack an executive whose sole responsibility is marketing—the counterpart of the vice president of marketing in a goods-producing company.[6]

There are, of course, exceptions to these negative generalizations. Some extremely successful service firms have adopted modern marketing techniques. The success of such organizations as Holiday Inn, Avis, People Express Airlines, and Federal Express is traceable in large part to their marketing orientation.

The banking industry provides an interesting example of a service industry that was not marketing-oriented in the past but has, in recent years, been struggling to make the transition to modern times. For years, commercial banks made customers feel that they should be honored to have their money in a checking account with no interest, but with a service charge. And savings accounts earned very low interest rates. Banks were marble mausoleums, and bankers were the "black-hatted and caped villains" of song and story.

Most banks are striving to change those images because the market situation in banking has changed appreciably. There has been a considerable degree of government deregulation affecting the banking industry. As a result, commercial banks are encountering intensified competition from other commercial banks, from savings and loan institutions, and from financial institutions outside the banking industry. To meet these challenges, many banks finally started to do a little marketing. In fact, some banks moved aggressively to shorten the transition period by pirating marketing executives from consumer product companies such as Sara Lee and Ford. Banks have established marketing departments, conduct sales training programs, and engage in marketing research. They are running hard-sell "product" ads, expanding their service (product) mix, and sending their employees to bank-marketing executive development programs.

Banks are making concerted efforts to attract retail (consumer) and wholesale (commercial) business. Buildings and internal layouts are now designed to project an image of warmth, friendliness, and informality. Drive-in service and bank credit cards have been initiated for consumer convenience (and, incidentally, additional revenues). Other new services include insurance, personal financial counseling, payment of customers' monthly bills, 24-hour outside deposit and withdrawal facilities, and electronic

Some service firms really have a marketing orientation.

[6]For some reports on professional services—an industry that traditionally has been *very* nonmarketing-oriented, but that is slowly changing its ways—see Paul N. Bloom, "Effective Marketing for Professional Services," *Harvard Business Review,* September–October 1984, pp. 102–110; and Doris C. Van Doren, Louise W. Smith, and Ronald J. Biglin, "The Challenges of Professional Services Marketing," *The Journal of Consumer Marketing,* Spring 1985, pp. 19–27.

banking in supermarkets. Who knows—perhaps the next step will be to offer full-service banking during evening hours and on weekends.[7]

Because of the characteristics of services (intangibility, etc.), the task of developing a total marketing program in a service industry is often uniquely challenging. However, as in product marketing, management first should define its marketing goals and select its target markets. Then management must design and implement marketing-mix strategies to reach its markets and fulfill its marketing goals.[8]

A STRATEGIC PROGRAM FOR THE MARKETING OF SERVICES

Target-Market Analysis

The task of analyzing a firm's target markets is essentially the same, whether the firm is selling a product or a service. Marketers of services should understand the components of population and income—the demographic factors—as they affect the market for the services. In addition, marketers must try to determine, for each market segment, why customers buy the given service. That is, what are their buying *motives*? Also, sellers must determine the buying patterns for their services—when, where, and how do customers buy, who does the buying, and who makes the buying decisions? The psychological determinants of buying behavior—attitudes, perceptions, personality, etc.—are as pertinent in the marketing of services as in product marketing. In

Disney's target market is children of all ages up to 80.

[7]See Leonard L. Berry, Charles M. Futrell, and Michael R. Bowers, *Bankers Who Sell: Improving Selling Effectiveness in Banking*, Dow Jones-Irwin, Homewood, Ill., 1985.

[8]See Valarie A. Zeithaml, A. Parasuraman, and Leonard L. Berry, "Problems and Strategies in Services Marketing," *Journal of Marketing*, Spring 1985, pp. 33–46.

like manner, the sociological factors of social-class structure and small-group influences are market determinants for services. The fundamentals of the adoption and diffusion of product innovation are also relevant in the marketing of services.

Some of the trends pointed out in Chapters 5 to 8 are particularly worth watching because they carry considerable influence in the marketing of services. As an example, increases in disposable income and discretionary buying power mean a growing market for medical care, insurance, and transportation services. Shorter working hours have resulted in increases in leisure time. More leisure time plus greater income mean increased markets for recreation and entertainment services.

Market segmentation strategies can be adopted by service marketers equally as well as by product marketers. Many examples attest to this fact. We find apartment rental complexes for students, for single people, and for the over-65 crowd. Some car repair shops target their services at owners of foreign cars. Limited-service motel chains cater to the economy-minded market segment, while all-suite hotels seek to attract families and business travelers.

Planning and Developing the Service

New services are just as important to a service company as new products are to a product-marketing firm. Similarly, the improvement of existing services and the elimination of unwanted, unprofitable services are also key goals.

Product planning and development has its counterpart in the marketing program of a service industry. Management must select appropriate strategies regarding (1) what services will be offered, (2) what will be the length and breadth of the service mix offered, and (3) what, if anything, needs to be done in the way of service attributes such as branding or providing guarantees.[9]

The high perishability, fluctuating demand, and inability to store services make product planning critically important to service marketers. A service industry can expand or contract its "product mix," alter existing services, and trade up or down. The reasons for these moves are familiar. The company may want to increase its total volume, reduce seasonal fluctuations in volume, or cater to changing buyer patterns such as the desire for one-stop shopping. Some large banks, for example, have expanded their computer-based cash-management programs into a worldwide network that provides financial information services. Insurance firms that formerly specialized in fire-casualty-auto policies now have added the more profitable line of life insurance policies. Dry cleaners have expanded into laundry services, mothproofing, storage, dyeing, and clothing alterations and repairs. Some service firms have effectively expanded their mix by working jointly with companies selling related services. For instance, automobile-rental firms have arrangements with airlines and hotels so that when customers fly to their destination, a reserved car and hotel room are waiting.

In some respects, "product" planning is easier for services than for products. Packaging, color, labeling, and style are virtually nonexistent in service marketing. However, in other respects—branding and standardization of quality, for instance—service industries have greater problems. Branding is difficult because consistency of quality is hard to maintain and because the brand cannot be physically attached to a service.

This dry cleaner even sells clothes.

[9]For a model that management can follow in service (product) development, see G. Lynn Shostack, "Designing Services That Deliver," *Harvard Business Review*, January–February 1984, pp. 133–139.

Pricing of Services

Standardization of *quality* in a service is an extremely important goal, difficult as it may be. In some fields, such as beauty care, medical care, and some of the recreation industries, no attempt is made to mass-produce the service. Instead, the sellers offer custom service as required by each customer. Even in these cases, however, the customer wants consistent quality.

It is extremely important for an organization to *design* and *manage* its service quality in such a way that the customers are satisfied. Unfortunately, in many service organizations (transportation firms and retail stores, for example), the people who are actually involved with the customers often are among the lowest-paid employees in those organizations.

In the marketing of services, nowhere is there a greater need for managerial creativity and skill than in the area of pricing. Earlier, we noted that services are extremely perishable; they usually cannot be stored, and the demand often fluctuates considerably. All these features carry significant pricing implications. To further complicate the situation, customers may perform some services themselves (auto and household repair, for example).

These considerations suggest that the elasticity of demand for a service should influence the price set by the seller. Interestingly enough, sellers often do recognize inelastic demand. Then they charge higher prices. But they fail to act in opposite fashion when faced with an elastic demand—even though a lower price would increase unit sales, total revenue, utilization of facilities, and probably net profit.

Certainly, perfect competition does not apply to any extent, if at all, in the pricing of services. Because of the heterogeneity and the difficulty of standardizing quality, most services are highly differentiated. Also, it is virtually impossible to have complete market information. Further, in any given market, such as a neighborhood, often there are geographic limits within which a buyer will seek a service. Consequently, there are not a large number of sellers. The heavy capital investment required to produce some services (transportation, communications, medical care) often limits considerably the freedom of entry.

Nevertheless, in recent years price competition in many service areas has increased considerably—going through three identifiable phases.[10] In the first phase, price is barely mentioned in the organization's advertising. For example, a health maintenance organization (HMO) will run an ad explaining its services, but not dwelling much on price. In the second phase, the seller uses a market segmentation strategy to target a given market at a specific price. To illustrate, a law firm will prominently feature its low prices when it advertises its services related to a divorce case or the preparation of a will. The third phase involves out-and-out price competition as firms stress comparative prices in their advertising. The airlines and long-distance phone companies, for example, have engaged extensively in price-comparative advertising.

The *basic* methods of price determination now used for services are generally the same as those for products. Cost-plus pricing is used for regulated service industries. It is also used for repair services where the main ingredient is direct labor and the customer is charged on an hourly basis. For other services (rentals, entertainment,

_____
[10]This paragraph is adapted from Stephen W. Brown, "New Patterns Are Emerging in Services Marketing Sector," *Marketing News*, June 7, 1985, p. 2.

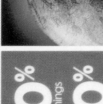
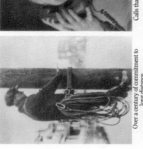

Over a century of commitment to long distance.

Calls that sound as close as you feel.

Calling anywhere, anytime.

40% Evenings

60% Nights & Weekends

Guaranteed discounts.

Only AT&T has over 35,000 operators to give you any help you may need.

Only AT&T offers calling to over 250 countries and faraway locations worldwide.

AT&T puts it all on the line for you.

AT&T makes sure you have all the long distance services you need.

Our operators are there for you to call upon 24 hours a day. To help with collect or person-to-person calls, and to give immediate credit for wrong numbers.

Because AT&T has over 100 years of experience providing quality long distance service, you know your calls will sound as close as next door.

And that's not all. You get savings along with all these services. Dial direct state-to-state Sunday-Friday from 5pm-11pm, and you'll save 40%.

All weekend till 5pm Sunday and every night from 11pm till 8am, save 60%. (Different discounts apply to Alaska.)

Plus, AT&T has special programs and plans to help make your long distance dollar go even further. Who says you can't have it all?

Reach out and touch someone.®

The more you hear the better we sound.℠

© 1985 AT&T Communications.

AT&T

Service firms also engage in discount pricing.

legal counseling, management consulting), prices are determined primarily by market demand and competition.

Many of the pricing strategies discussed in Chapter 13 are applicable to service marketing. Quantity discounts, for example, are used by car-rental agencies. The daily rates are lower if you agree to rent the car for a week or a month at a time. Cash discounts are offered when insurance premiums are paid annually instead of quarterly. Doctors and management consultants can use a variable-price policy. Geographic pricing policies may be involved, although the variable here is time, not freight charges. Mechanics will charge more if they must go out of town, and a doctor will charge more for house calls than for office calls.

Channels of Distribution for Services

Traditionally, most services have been sold directly from producer to consumer or industrial user. No middlemen are used when the service cannot be separated from the seller or when the service is created and marketed simultaneously. For example,

Promoting the Service

public utilities, medical care, and repair services are typically sold without middlemen. Not using middlemen does limit the geographic markets that service sellers can reach. But it also enables the sellers to personalize their services and to get quick, detailed customer feedback.

The only other frequently used channel includes one agent middleman. Some type of agent or broker is often used in the marketing of securities, travel arrangements, entertainment, and housing rentals. Sometimes dealers are trained in the production of the service and then are franchised to sell it. This is the case with the Sanitone dry-cleaning process and Holiday Inn motels.

In recent years, some firms have realized that the characteristic of inseparability is not an insurmountable limitation to a seller's distribution system. With a little imagination in management, a service marketer can broaden its distribution considerably. Let's look at some examples, starting with location.

The location of the service seller or the seller's agent should be conveniently accessible to customers, because many services cannot be delivered. Many motels and restaurants have gone out of business when a new highway bypassed their location, thus drawing away the customer traffic. On the other hand, banks have increased their business by installing 24-hour automated "tellers" and by setting up tellers' windows for drive-in customers. Dental centers, small medical centers, chiropractors, and optometrists all have opened offices in shopping-center malls. The retail-store locations for dental centers have been especially successful, and the idea is expanding to all sections of the country. They offer convenience of location and are open long hours, and typically their fees are considerably below the fees charged in a conventional dentist's office.[11]

The use of intermediaries is another way to broaden distribution. Some banks have arranged for companies to deposit employees' paychecks directly into their bank accounts. The employer thus becomes an intermediary in distributing the bank's service. Insurance firms have expanded their distribution by setting up vending machines in airports.

The characteristic of intangibility means that physical distribution problems are basically eliminated for most service producers. For example, other than supportive supplies, accountants have no physical inventory to store or handle. However, not all service producers are free from physical distribution problems. For example, a chain of equipment rental stores would have to contend with inventory problems. Sometimes hotels and resorts have a surplus of rooms (inventory), which can result in an unprofitable operation.

Personal selling, advertising, and other forms of promotion are used extensively in the marketing of services. However, it is especially difficult to build a promotional program around intangible service benefits. It is so much easier to sell something that can be seen, felt, and demonstrated.

Personal selling is essential when developing close relationships between the

[11]For an analysis of the difference between the retailing of services and the retailing of products, and for suggestions on the strategic changes needed when a product retailer expands into services retailing, see J. Patrick Kelly and William R. George, "Strategic Management Issues for the Retailing of Services," *Journal of Retailing*, Summer 1982, pp. 26–43.

Sometimes you promote a concept.

buyer and seller. While point-of-purchase displays of the *services* offered are often impossible, displays of the *results* of using the service can be effective. Many service firms, especially in the recreation-entertainment field, benefit considerably from free publicity. Sports coverage by newspapers, radio, and television helps in this matter, as do newspaper reviews of movies, plays, and concerts. Travel sections in newspapers have helped sell transportation, housing, and other services related to the travel industry.

For years, of course, advertising has been used extensively in many service fields—housing, household operation, transportation, recreation, and insurance, for example. What *is* new is the use of advertising by firms in professional-service industries—lawyers, accountants, and physicians, among others. Previously, the professional associations in these fields had prohibited advertising on the ground that it is unethical. These associations still try to limit and control the advertising. However, several court and regulatory-agency decisions make it clear that prohibiting a professional firm from advertising is restraint of trade and thus a violation of the antitrust statutes.

As an indirect type of promotion, physicians, lawyers, and insurance agents may participate actively in community affairs as a means of getting their names before the public. Service firms (banks, utilities, railroads) may advertise to attract new industry. They know that anything that helps the community grow will automatically mean an expanded market for them.

A promotional program in a service company should have three major goals. The first is to portray the service benefits in as appealing a manner as possible. The second is to differentiate its offerings from those of competitors. And the third is to build a good reputation. Because the firm is marketing intangibles, reputation is critical.

Advertising campaigns can stress the dependability of the service—its consistent high quality. Ads can also emphasize the courteous, friendly, efficient service.[12]

FUTURE OUTLOOK IN SERVICE MARKETING

The Changing Service Environment

The boom in the service economy in the 1980s has been accompanied by a significant increase in competition in many of the service industries. This competition has been stimulated by several factors. One is the reduction in government regulation in some industries—airlines, trucking, and banking, for example. Court decisions have increased competition by sanctioning advertising in the medical, legal, and other professions. New techniques have opened new service fields—in solar energy and information processing, for example. Technological advances have also brought automation and other "industrial" features to formerly all-hand-labor service fields. Chain-store types of organizations are replacing the small-scale independent in many fields, including health care, auto repairs, beauty shops, dental service, and real estate brokerage. Increases in the supply of some service providers (doctors and lawyers, for example) finally are bringing some competition to previously protected fields.

Need for Increased Productivity

The boom has also been accompanied by a deterioration in the quality of many services. In general, service industries have been plagued by poor management, inefficiency, and low productivity. This inefficiency—and the need to increase productivity—is probably the biggest problem facing service industries in general. The productivity problem also has significant implications for the health of the total economy. Service industries are very labor-intensive compared with manufacturing. Consequently, wage increases in the service sector of the economy have a significant impact on price levels and inflation.

Perhaps the key to increasing efficiency in service industries is for management to adopt a manufacturing attitude.[13] The concept of providing a service traditionally conjured visions of personal ministration and attendance on others. To improve performance meant simply to try harder, but essentially to continue performing a task in the same old way. In contrast, the idea of manufacturing benefits (or efficiently producing them) enables us to focus on new performance methods. We can apply manufacturing technology and organization changes to the task at hand—but all this at a price of less humanism.

Four manufacturing strategies being applied in service industries to increase productivity are mechanization, assembly-line standardization, specialization, and organizational consolidation. The use of *mechanization* to implement hand labor has increased per-worker output in laundry and dry cleaning, for example. Machines have increased service output in commercial dishwashing and floor sanding. *Assembly-line* technology has proven fruitful in such diverse service fields as (1) fast-food retailing (Wendy's hamburgers) and (2) mass physical examinations for corporations and labor unions, using mobile health units and automated test equipment.

Assembly-line production is not limited to factories.

[12]See William R. George and Leonard L. Berry, "Guidelines for the Advertising of Services," *Business Horizons,* July–August 1981, pp. 52–56.

[13]Theodore Levitt, "Production-Line Approach to Service," *Harvard Business Review,* September–October 1972, pp. 41–52; also see Levitt, "The Industrialization of Service," *Harvard Business Review,* September–October 1976, pp. 63–74.

Several service firms have made labor more productive by *specialization* of effort. The medical field abounds with specialists. Auto repair firms specialize in brakes, transmissions, or mufflers. *Consolidation* as a means of improving productivity is being practiced when a major airline adds hotels to its service mix. The development of chain organizations (Ramada Inn, Howard Johnson) is another useful form of consolidation in service firms.

Prospects for Growth

There is every reason to believe that services will continue to take an increasing share of the consumer dollar, just as they have done generally over the past 40 years. This forecast seems reasonable even in the face of periods of economic decline. History shows that the demand for services is less sensitive to economic fluctuations than the demand for products. The demand for *business* services should also continue to expand as business becomes more complex and as management further recognizes its need for business-service specialists. In the field of *professional* services, especially, the use of marketing programs is expected to expand considerably during the coming decade. This expansion will occur as physicians, lawyers, etc., come to understand and appreciate the social and economic benefits they can derive from an effective marketing program.[14]

We should temper these optimistic forecasts with some caution, however, because forces both external and internal to service industries could limit growth in these fields. Perhaps the most obvious *external* factor is the customers' alternative of performing a service themselves. Another growth deterrent comes from product manufacturers that produce goods with features that decrease our reliance on service industries. Wash-and-wear shirts are used instead of those that require commercial laundry service, for example, and television sets substitute for commercial entertainment.

Internal barriers to future growth in service industries are (1) the small size of the average service firm; (2) the shortage of people with specialized skills—physicians, for instance; and (3) the limited competition in many service industries—transportation, medicine, communication. These barriers limit internal price competition and sometimes limit entry into the field. But perhaps the overriding internal growth deterrents are (1) the little emphasis on research and development in many service fields, and (2) the general failure to recognize the importance of marketing in every business.

SUMMARY

Services are those separately identifiable, essentially intangible activities that provide want-satisfaction, and that are not necessarily tied to the sale of a product or another service. In the broadest sense, product marketing and service marketing are the same. In actual practice, however, significant differences do exist between product marketing and service marketing.

Service marketing is also worth special attention because of its scope—about half of what we spend goes for services, and about two-thirds of nongovernmental jobs are in the service field. Not only are services of considerable importance in our economy today, but the prospects are that the service sector will continue to grow

[14]See Ed Bean, "Doctors Find a Dose of Marketing Can Cure Pain of Sluggish Practice," *The Wall Street Journal,* Mar. 15, 1985, p. 25.

faster than the product sector of the economy. Services generally are intangible, inseparable from the seller, heterogeneous, and highly perishable, and they have a widely fluctuating demand. Each of these distinctive characteristics has several marketing implications.

Unfortunately, the growth in services has not been matched by service management's understanding or acceptance of the marketing concept. Service organizations have been slow to adopt marketing programs and techniques that, in product marketing, have brought satisfaction to consumers and profits to producers. The development of a program for the marketing of services parallels that for products but takes into account the special character of services.

Probably the biggest problem facing service industries, as we look to their continued growth, is the need to increase productivity. Perhaps the answer lies in adopting processes that have proven successful in increasing output and efficiency in the production of goods. One cost of "industrialization" services, however, will be an increase in the impersonalization of these services.

KEY TERMS AND CONCEPTS

Services 496
Business services 496
Importance of services 497
Service characteristics:
  Intangibility 499
  Inseparability 499
  Heterogeneity 499
  Perishability 500
  Fluctuating demand 500

Marketing concept in relation to service marketing 500
Manufacturing process applied to services:
  Mechanization 508
  Assembly-line technology 508
  Specialization 509
  Organizational consolidation 509

QUESTIONS AND PROBLEMS

1. How do you account for the substantial increase in expenditures for services relative to expenditures for products in the last 40 years?

2. What are some of the marketing implications in the fact that services possess the characteristic of intangibility?

3. Why are middlemen rarely used in the marketing programs of service firms?

4. Services are highly perishable and are often subject to fluctuations in demand. In marketing its services, how can a company offset these factors?

5. Cite some examples of service marketers that seem to be customer-oriented, and describe what these firms have done in this vein.

6. "Traditionally, marketers of services have *not* been marketing-oriented." Do you agree? If so, how do you account for this deficiency?

7. Present a brief analysis of the market for each of the following service firms. Make use of the components of a market as discussed in Chapters 5 to 8.
   a. Hospital in your city.
   b. Marriott hotel near large airport.
   c. Indoor tennis club.
   d. Savings and loan association.

8. What are some of the ways in which each of the following service firms might expand its line?
   a. Certified public accountant (CPA).
   b. Hairstyling salon.
   c. Bank.

9. Explain the importance of demand elasticity in the pricing of services.

10. "Personal selling should be the main ingredient in the promotional mix for a marketer of services." Do you agree? Discuss.

11. Present in brief form a marketing program for each of the following services. Your presentation should start with a description of the target market you have selected for the service. Then explain how you would plan, price, promote, and distribute the service.
    a. A disc jockey for private parties in the community.
    b. Your electric company.
    c. Household cleaning.

CHAPTER

22

MARKETING IN NONBUSINESS ORGANIZATIONS

PACIFIC OUTDOOR

Face it.

You belong
in the
San Diego Zoo

Dejos
ITALIAN RESTAURANT
LONDON

Russian
& Soviet
Painting

CHAPTER GOALS

In this chapter, we apply many of the concepts and techniques of modern marketing to private, nonbusiness, not-for-profit organizations. After studying this chapter, you should understand:

- The exchange concept as applied to nonbusiness organizations.

- The wide range of nonbusiness organizations.

- The importance of marketing in nonbusiness organizations.

- The concept of contributor markets and client markets.

- The attitudes of nonbusiness organizations toward marketing.

- How market analysis and the marketing mix apply in nonbusiness marketing.

- The status of marketing programs in nonbusiness organizations.

To spread its incoming-patient load more evenly over the week, one Western hospital used a lottery-style drawing to encourage people to enter on Friday or Saturday. (The first prize was an ocean cruise.) Several private and public universities have conducted advertising campaigns and other promotional activities to stem the decline in enrollments. Many museums, symphony orchestras, and social agencies (Girl Scouts, YMCA) use the same techniques to reverse declining contributions or declining memberships. Candidates for political office use advertising campaigns to solicit votes and use survey-research techniques to determine public opinions and preferences. Many religious organizations regularly use advertising, personal selling, and other marketing techniques to add to their membership and to increase contributions. Even some zoos advertise to boost attendance.

Three common threads run through all these real-life situations. First, the organizations are all *nonbusiness* groups, as the term *business* is generally used. Second, they are all *nonprofit* organizations—that is, profit is *not* an intended organizational goal. And third, in each situation, *marketing activities* were used to solve key problems.

NATURE AND SCOPE OF NONBUSINESS MARKETING

Nonbusiness Organizations

Basically, the marketing fundamentals for nonbusiness, nonprofit organizations are the same as for the business sector. That is, we want to develop a marketing program strategically planned around a product or service that is effectively priced, promoted, and distributed to satisfy wants in a predetermined market. However, there are important differences in the *implementation* of the marketing program and in nonbusiness management's *understanding* of and *attitudes* toward marketing. The differences tend to limit the marketing activities of nonbusiness, nonprofit organizations, even though these organizations need effective marketing so much.[1]

Organizations may be classified in several different ways. For our purposes, however, three classification bases apply:

- *Private versus public (government)-owned and -operated.* Most organizations clearly fit in one category or the other, but there are borderline cases. For example, a state university is partially supported by nongovernment funds such as tuition and private donations. A private university, on the other hand, may be partially funded by government grants.
- *Profit-seeking versus not-for-profit.*
- *Business versus nonbusiness.* Most organizations are easy to categorize on this basis.

[1]For an analysis of these differences in one field of nonbusiness marketing—social-cause marketing—see Paul N. Bloom and William D. Novelli, ''Problems and Challenges in Social Marketing,'' *Journal of Marketing*, Spring 1981, pp. 79–88; and Jeffrey A. Barach, ''Applying Marketing Principles to Social Causes,'' *Business Horizons*, July–August 1984, pp. 65–69. Many of the generalizations developed in these articles are equally applicable to marketing in other nonbusiness fields.

The Exchange Concept and Nonbusiness Marketing

In some cases, however, the distinction gets fuzzy. Physicians may consider themselves as professionals rather than as business "organizations." A musician may say, "I am an artist," and consider a lucrative performance contract as secondary to the music. But both are really in business.

In this chapter our discussion will be limited to marketing in organizations that are understood to be private, not-for-profit, nonbusiness units. Most nonbusiness, nonprofit organizations will market *services*, rather than tangible products. Consequently, many of the ideas in Chapter 21 are relevant here.

TYPES OF NONBUSINESS ORGANIZATIONS

Private, not-for-profit, nonbusiness organizations number in the thousands and cover a very wide range of activities. The following list of organizational groupings may give you some idea of this broad spectrum.

- *Educational:* Private grade schools, high schools, colleges, universities.
- *Cultural:* Museums, zoos, symphony orchestras, opera and theater groups.
- *Religious:* Churches, synagogues, temples, mosques.
- *Charitable and philanthropic:* Welfare groups (Salvation Army, United Fund, Red Cross), research foundations, fund-raising groups.
- *Social cause:* Organizations dealing with family planning, civil rights, stopping smoking, preventing heart disease, environmental concerns, those for or against abortion, or for or against nuclear energy.
- *Social:* Fraternal organizations, civic clubs.
- *Health care:* Hospitals, nursing homes, health research organizations (American Cancer Society, American Health Association), HMOs (health maintenance organizations).
- *Political:* Political parties, individual politicians. [2]

In Chapter 1, marketing was broadly defined as an exchange intended to satisfy the wants of all parties involved in the exchange. And marketing consists of all activities designed to facilitate such exchanges. To include a discussion of marketing in nonbusiness organizations is certainly consistent with this broad, exchange-concept definition of marketing. For nonbusiness organizations are also involved in exchanges.

As an example, the Levi Strauss Company, a business organization, sells to you, through a middleman, a pair of blue jeans in exchange for some money. In a similar vein, your local hospital, a nonbusiness organization, may provide you with health

[2] For a sample of reports on marketing programs in some of the above areas, see Steve Swartz, "Colleges Take to the Silver Screen to Lure Top High-School Seniors," *The Wall Street Journal*, May 17, 1985, p. 27; Liz Murphy, "Market or Perish! (marketing by colleges)," *Sales & Marketing Management*, May 13, 1985, p. 50; Janice R. Nall and Parks B. Dimsdale, "Civic Group (Chamber of Commerce) Adopts Marketing Technique," *Marketing News*, June 21, 1985, p. 13; "Medical/Health Services Marketing," a report consisting of several articles, *Marketing News*, Jan. 18, 1985, pp. 7–14; Lynn T. Legum and William R. George, "Analysis of Marketing Management Practices of Dance Companies," *Journal of the Academy of Marketing Science*, Winter 1981, pp. 15–26; and Imran S. Currim, Charles B. Weinberg, and Dick R. Wittink, "Design of Subscription Programs for a Performing Arts Series," *Journal of Consumer Research*, June 1981, pp. 67–75.

Even hospitals are looking for customers these days.

care in exchange for some money. Your college, another nonbusiness organization, offers an education service to you in exchange for your money and/or your labor.

Markets Involved in Nonbusiness Marketing

A major difference between business and nonbusiness marketing involves the groups that the particular organization must deal with. Business executives have traditionally defined their basic markets as being made up of their present and potential customers. They have thus directed their marketing efforts primarily toward this one group. In contrast, most nonbusiness, nonprofit organizations are involved with *two major markets* in their marketing effort. One of these groups consists of the **contributors** (of money, labor, services, or materials) to the organization. Here the nonbusiness organization's task is that of "resource attraction."

The other major target market is the organization's **clients**—the recipients of the organization's money and/or services. This recipient market is much like that of the customers of a business company. However, nonbusiness organizations—such as churches, Girl Scout units, nursing homes, symphony orchestras, or universities—are unlikely to refer to their client-recipients as customers. Instead, these organizations will use such terms as *parishioners, members, patients, audience, or students.*

This distinction between business and nonbusiness marketing, based on the major markets involved, is significant for this reason: A nonbusiness organization must develop two separate marketing programs—one looking "back" at its contributors, and the other looking "forward" at its clients. Moreover, like businesses, nonbusiness organizations also are involved with several publics in addition to their main markets. A private university, for example, must deal with government agencies, environmentalists, mass media, its faculty and staff, and the local community.

Importance of Nonbusiness Marketing

The attention that is finally being devoted to nonbusiness marketing is long overdue and definitely needed. Thousands of these organizations handle billions of dollars and affect millions of people. Often the operation of these organizations is admittedly inefficient. Empty beds in hospitals and empty classrooms constitute a waste of resources we can ill afford. Often a large part of the money collected by a nonbusiness

Social causes are marketing today—the same as profit-seeking firms.

If you've got your health, you've got it all

Get regular cancer checkups.

AMERICAN CANCER SOCIETY

organization goes to cover its administrative expenses, rather than to serve the intended markets. Then there is a dual social and economic loss—donors' gifts are wasted, and clients are not served efficiently.

The importance of marketing also shows up when nonbusiness organizations fail to do an effective marketing job. Then the result may be additional social and economic costs and wastes. If the death rate from smoking rises because the American Cancer Society and other organizations cannot persuade people of the harm of smoking, we all lose. When antilitter organizations fail to convince people to control their solid-waste disposal, we all lose. When good museums or good symphony orchestras must cease operating because of lack of contributions and/or lack of attendance, there again are social and economic losses.

By developing an effective marketing program, a nonbusiness organization can increase immeasurably its chances of (1) satisfactorily serving both its contributor and its client markets and (2) improving the overall efficiency of its operations.

NONBUSINESS ATTITUDE TOWARD MARKETING ∎

Generally speaking, people in most nonbusiness organizations do not realize that they are "running a business" and should employ business management techniques. It is true that making a profit is *not* the goal of these organizations. Nevertheless, they do need to identify their goals, plan strategies and tactics to reach these goals, effectively execute their plans, and evaluate their performance. Yet only very recently have many nonbusiness organizations started to employ accounting systems, financial controls, personnel management and labor relations, and other business management techniques.

Unfortunately, the acceptance of business management techniques does not often include the use of planned marketing programs. Nonbusiness organizations generally do not seem at all comfortable with marketing. To most of these groups, marketing is limited to some form of promotion, such as advertising or personal selling. These organizations rarely understand the concept of a total marketing program.

Many nonbusiness organizations may speak about marketing and even believe they are practicing it. Unfortunately, in many cases they still have a strong production orientation, or at best, a selling orientation. These organizations tend to select—on their own—the products or services that they *think* their customers want (or should want). Then they decide on how to distribute or sell these products. Only at the end

When business and nonbusiness organizations cooperate, both can win.

BUSINESS + NONBUSINESS MARKETING EFFORT = PUBLIC BENEFIT

When business and nonbusiness organizations combine their marketing efforts, the results can be of considerable public benefit. In recent years profit-seeking and not-for-profit organizations have joined together in raising sales and contributions through their product offerings. Examples include Glad Bags and Easter Seals; the record album "We Are the World," sung by a number of American rock stars (USA for Africa), which raised millions of dollars for African food relief; and Jerry Lewis and 7-Eleven's Muscular Dystrophy fundraisers.

With approximately 1.8 million children reported missing in the United States each year, child safety has become a major national concern. Numerous corporations are cooperating with nonbusiness organizations. Operation: Home Free, which is cosponsored by the Dallas-based Trailways Corporation and the International Association of Chiefs of Police, provides runaways with free transportation home. General Mills, Wendy's, and Southland (7-Eleven stores) are working with the National Crime Prevention Council to build child-safety promotions around the McGruff ("Take a bite out of crime") character. These promotions are working. Trailways has provided several thousand children tickets to ride home. General Mills offered a Children's Safety Kit free for four proofs of purchase from seven of their cereals. They received 40,000 responses in about 4½ months.

DEVELOPING A STRATEGIC PROGRAM FOR NONBUSINESS MARKETING

of the process do these groups get involved in analyzing their markets. This really is *not* a marketing orientation.[3]

In many cases, the people working in nonbusiness organizations tend to have a negative attitude toward marketing. They are apt to think that having a marketing program—and using the term *marketing*—is demeaning and in bad taste. They even seem to feel that it is unethical to use marketing in their organizations.

Perhaps the choice of words is important. The governing body in a church, for example, will not object to "informational notices" (don't call it "advertising") in newspapers or in the Yellow Pages regarding church activities. When church members go to foreign lands to bring new members into the fold, the churches don't call this activity "personal selling." Instead, it is called "missionary work."

Nonbusiness organizations in general seem to face a dilemma. On the one hand, they generally are unaware of what marketing is all about, or they may even have a negative attitude toward it. Yet, on the other hand, these organizations generally are badly in need of an effective marketing program. Now, taking this latter stand that marketing is needed for an organization's well-being, let's discuss the development of a marketing program for such an organization.[4]

The basic structure for planning and developing a marketing program is the same in any organization—private or public, business or nonbusiness, profit or not-for-profit. That is, first we identify and analyze the target markets, and then we develop a strategic marketing mix that will provide want-satisfaction to those markets. Throughout, we use marketing research to help in our decision making.

Target-Market Analysis

We really are talking about planning and developing two major marketing programs, one for the contributor market and one for the client market. It is important to pinpoint each market in some detail. Market pinpointing means using market segmentation. A broad (nonsegmented) appeal to the *donor* market is likely to result in a low return. Trying to be all things to all people in the *client* market is likely to result in being "nothing to nobody" and going broke in the process.

The possible bases for market segmentation for nonbusiness groups are generally the same as those discussed in Chapter 8. In trying to reach its *contributor* market, for example, an organization may segment its appeals by age groups, geographic place of residence, record of past donations, or size of past donations. In effect, segmentation analysis is needed to identify the characteristics of those who donate to the particular organization. Some psychographic (life-style) research may be used to iden-

[3]For some insights on developing a true marketing orientation, see Stephen W. Brown, "Two Challenges Demand Immediate Attention from Healthcare Marketers," *Marketing News*, Jan. 18, 1985, p. 10; "Hospital Hospitality," *Newsweek*, Feb. 11, 1985, p. 78; and Alan R. Andreasen, "Nonprofits: Check Your Attention to Customers," *Harvard Business Review*, May–June 1982, pp. 105–110.

[4]For suggestions on improving the marketing programs in the health-care industry, see Peter M. Sanchez, "Health Care Marketing at the Crossroads," *Journal of Health Care Marketing*, Spring 1984, pp. 37–43; and Lucy Z. Martin, "Marketing Traps: 13 Tips on How *Not* to Proceed (in health-care marketing)," *Hospital Forum*, March–April 1985, p. 27.

One way to reach a target market.

tify contributors on the basis of *why* they donate their money, labor, or materials. People give to nonbusiness organizations for various reasons: (1) They sincerely believe in the organization's work; (2) giving makes them feel good; (3) contributions are tax-deductible; (4) contributing adds to their status in their reference group; or (5) their religious beliefs stimulate giving.

Many nonbusiness organizations typically segment their *client* markets, although they probably do not refer to this technique as market segmentation. For example, since the Great Depression, the Democratic party has developed separate appeals to such market segments as organized labor, low-income groups, Southern Democrats, Catholics, Jews, and urban dwellers in Northeastern industrial centers. Country clubs develop separate programs for golfers, tennis players, swimmers, and card players. Private colleges may segment prospective students on the basis of high school grade-point average or area of study (technical, liberal arts, professional).

A decision to employ market segmentation means that the nonbusiness organization must tailor all or part of its marketing program to reach each segment—be it donor or client. Thus the service offering and the promotion may have to be adapted to each major segment.

Careful market analysis requires sophisticated marketing research to identify the various markets. This poses a problem, because most nonbusiness organizations simply are not familiar with marketing research. Fortunately, there are encouraging prospects in this area. Political parties and individual politicians, for example, are frequent users of opinion polls to determine voters' preferences on candidates and issues. Segmentation research also has been used to identify the characteristics of various market segments attending art museums and presentations of the performing arts (opera, concerts, theaters).[5]

[5]See John E. Robbins and Stephanie S. Robbins, "Museum Marketing: Identification of High, Moderate, and Low Attendee Segments," *Journal of the Academy of Marketing Science,* Winter 1981, pp. 66–76; and Margery Steinberg, George Miaoulis, and David Lloyd, "Benefit Segmentation Strategies for the Performing Arts," in *1982 Educators' Conference Proceedings,* American Marketing Association, Chicago, 1982, pp. 289–293.

Product Planning

Like a profit-seeking business firm, a nonbusiness organization must decide (1) what products it will offer, (2) what will be the nature of its product mix, and (3) what, if anything, it will do about product attributes such as branding and labeling. In nonbusiness marketing, again, the organization needs two sets of product strategies—one for its contributor market and one for its client market.

PRODUCT OFFERING

In most nonbusiness organizations, the "product offering" to clients typically is a service, an idea, a person (in politics), or a cause. In the case of foundations and charitable organizations, the product offering often is a cash grant—a form of tangible product. Other nonbusiness organizations may offer such tangible products as food and clothing, printed materials, or birth control devices. However, in such cases, the tangible products are incidental to the main services provided by the organization.

The key to determining what its product offering will be is for the organization to decide (1) what "business" it is in and (2) what client markets it wants to reach. If a church views its mission only as providing religious services, its product offering will be relatively limited. On the other hand, if this church views its mission more broadly, it will offer more services to more markets. The church may then provide family counseling services, day-care services for children, religious education courses, and social activities for single people.

Planning the product offering to the contributor market is an even more difficult task. The organization asks people to donate their money or their time to a cause. The money or time is the price that contributors pay for the organization's "product." What is it they are getting for this price? The benefits they receive in return for their donations must be clearly identified.

PRODUCT-MIX STRATEGIES

Several of the product-mix strategies discussed in Chapter 10 can be employed in nonbusiness marketing. Consider, for instance, the strategy of *expanding the product line.* Symphony orchestras have broadened their lines by offering concerts appealing to children or popular-music concerts appealing to teenagers and college-age people. Universities broadened their mix when they added adult night courses, off-campus extension programs, and concentrated between-semester courses. Hospital chains are adding their own health insurance programs, nursing homes, and home health services.[6]

The strategy of *product differentiation* has been employed by several hospitals. These all provide basically the same health services. But to increase sales volume (number of patients), each hospital's services were differentiated by superficial features. One hospital introduced a bicycle repair class. Another hospital operated a day-care service for the elderly, while a third hospital provides a taxi service for people who have been drinking.[7]

[6]See John W. Wilson, "Hospital Chains Struggle to Stay in the Pink," *Business Week*, Jan. 14, 1985, p. 112.

[7]Laralyn Sasaki, "Hospitals Offer Unconventional Services in Hopes of Attracting Future Patients," *The Wall Street Journal*, Aug. 1, 1985, p. 21.

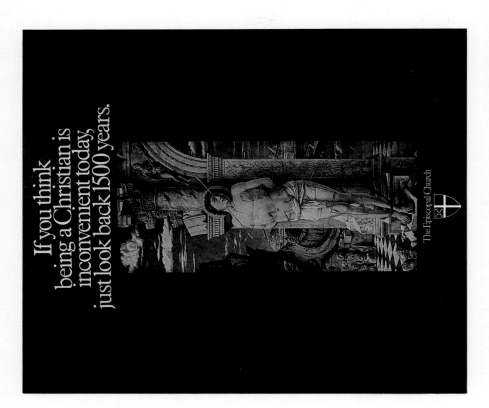

If you think
being a Christian is
inconvenient today,
just look back 1500 years.

The Episcopal Church

Churches offer various services.

A nonbusiness brand.

The *product-life-cycle* concept can be applied to nonbusiness marketing. The March-of-Dimes Foundation was started many years ago to fight poliomyelitis (infantile paralysis) and to care for its victims. After the introductory stage, this organization went through its growth stage and reached maturity, partially through the support of President Franklin Roosevelt, who himself was a polio victim. Later, the foundation entered the decline stage when the Salk vaccine effectively eradicated this dreaded disease. But rather than close shop (abandon the product, in life-cycle terms), the polio foundation changed its name to the National Foundation. It also shifted its emphasis to the treatment and prevention of birth defects in children. In effect, the foundation rejuvenated its services and started another life cycle by altering its product mix.

PRODUCT ATTRIBUTES

Nonbusiness groups generally have not done much in the way of using product strategies such as branding and labeling. The little that has been done in this area, however, suggests that a nonbusiness organization can make its marketing more effective by emphasizing product attributes. For many years, colleges and universities have used

Price Determination

Admission price is up to the consumer.

nicknames (a form of brand name) primarily for their athletic teams, but also to identify their students and alumni. Most colleges and universities have school colors—another product attribute that helps increase the market's recognition and identification of the school.

Among health-research organizations, the Lung Association (formerly the Tuberculosis Association) has registered as a trademark its double-barred Christmas-seal cross. The trademarks of the Girl Scouts, Boy Scouts, YMCA, and Salvation Army are recognized and remembered by many people.

Pricing in many nonbusiness organizations is quite different from pricing in a business firm. First, pricing becomes less important when profit making is not an organizational goal. Also, many nonbusiness groups believe there are *no* client-market pricing considerations in their marketing because there is no charge to the client. The organization's basic function is to help those who cannot afford to pay.

Actually, the products or services received by the clients rarely are free—that is, without a price of some kind. True, the price may not be a monetary charge. Often, however, the client pays a charge—in the form of travel and waiting time, and perhaps degrading treatment—that a money-paying client-customer would not incur for the same service. Poor children who have to wear donated, second-hand clothes certainly are paying a price if their classmates ridicule these clothes. Alcoholics Anonymous and some drug rehabilitation organizations which provide "free" services do exact a price. They require active participation by their clients, and often a very strongly expressed resolve by clients to help themselves.

Some nonbusiness groups *do* face the same general pricing problems we discussed in Chapters 12 and 13. Museums and opera companies must decide on admission prices; fraternal organizations must set a schedule for dues; and colleges must determine how much to charge for tuition. These and other not-for-profit organizations typically face a cash-management problem, the same as in profit-seeking firms. Not-for-profit firms still must generate enough revenue from some source to cover all their operating revenues. This organization still must price its offerings in such a way that the operating revenues come in at the targeted loss figure. Let's take the case of a private school as an illustration. This school's total operating costs are budgeted at $10 million for next year. The school is expecting to generate $7 million in tuition revenue, leaving a loss of $3 million to be covered by gifts and other grants. Now the school must set its price (tuition) in such a way as to generate enough revenue to meet its $7 million target. Basically this is the same situation that a profit-seeking firm faces when pricing to meet a predetermined profit target. Essentially, not-for-profit organizations must (1) determine the base price for their product offering and (2) establish pricing strategies in several areas of their pricing structure.

SETTING THE BASE PRICE

Here again we are faced with two market situations—pricing in the contributor market and pricing in the client market.

When dealing with the contributor market, nonbusiness organizations really do not set the price of the donation. That price is set by contributors when they decide how much they are willing to pay for the benefits they expect to receive in return for their gifts. However, the organization may suggest a price. A charitable organization, for example, may suggest that you donate 1 day's pay or that you donate your time for 1 day a month.

Some of our discussion regarding the pricing of services (Chapter 21) is appropriate to the client market—for example, in pricing admissions to museums, concerts, or college athletic contests. But for most nonbusiness organizations, the basic pricing methods used by business firms—cost-plus, balance of supply and demand, market alone—simply are not appropriate. Many organizations know they cannot cover their costs with prices charged to client markets. The difference between anticipated revenues and costs must be made up by contributions.

As yet, we simply have not developed any real guidelines—any methodology—for much of our nonbusiness pricing. A major problem here is that most nonbusiness organizations simply do not know the cost of the products and services they offer in their client markets.

PRICING STRATEGIES

Some of the pricing strategies discussed in Chapter 13 are also applicable in nonbusiness marketing. Discount strategies have widespread use, for example. Some museums offer discount prices to students and to senior citizens. A season ticket for some opera companies or symphony orchestras costs less per performance than tickets purchased on an individual-performance basis. This is a form of quantity discount.

Considerations regarding one price versus variable price also are strategies applicable in nonbusiness marketing. Most charity hospitals charge according to the patient's ability to pay—a variable-price strategy. A one-price strategy typically is followed by private universities. That is, all students pay the same tuition (in cash or its equivalent in scholarship or hours of labor) for a full load of coursework.

Distribution System

Setting up a distribution system in a nonbusiness organization involves two main tasks. One is to establish channels of distribution back to the contributor market and forward to the client market. The other task, usually the more important one, is to set up a physical distribution system to reach these two sets of publics.

CHANNELS OF DISTRIBUTION

The channels of distribution used in nonbusiness marketing ordinarily are quite simple and short. The nonbusiness organization usually deals directly with its two major publics. That is, no middlemen are used.

When an intermediary is used, ordinarily it is an agent middleman. For instance, to generate increased contributions, a political party or a university may employ an outside fund-raising organization. To reach potential customers, admission tickets to operas or athletic contests may be sold through independent ticket agencies. In some cities the National Crime Prevention Council effectively uses the local police personnel as middlemen. They distribute youth-crime-prevention literature and programs to schools and to the general public.[8]

---

[8]For an analysis of the role of an office manager as an intermediary between physicians and patients in a physician's office, see Nabil Y. Razzouk and Stephen W. Brown, "The Distinctive Marketing Roles of Physician Office Managers and Staff," *Journal of Health Care Marketing*, Spring 1984, pp. 9–18.

Some nonprofit organizations have established a separate marketing program whereby they serve as a retailer of products that are related to the organization's primary service. Thus we see art museums selling prints of paintings, colleges selling many products through the college bookstore, post offices selling stamps to collectors, Planned Parenthood selling or giving away contraceptives, etc. Across-the-counter and/or mail-order methods of retail selling may be used in these situations.[9]

PHYSICAL DISTRIBUTION

The main goal in physical distribution is for the nonbusiness organization to locate itself so as to serve both its contributors and its clients most effectively. The organization should be as accessible to its contributors as possible. That is, if you want people to give you money, make this giving as easy and convenient as possible. Let them pay by check, by payroll deduction, on the installment plan, or even by credit

[9] See Christopher H. Lovelock and Charles B. Weinberg, "Retailing Strategies for Public and Nonprofit Organizations," *Journal of Retailing*, Fall 1983, pp. 93–115.

Physical distribution: Bring the service to the market.

card. If the donor is contributing used products, collect them at the donor's residence or at some other choice location. Don't force the donor to haul the stuff across town to a central depository.

Location is also critically important in dealing with client markets. Thus, universities set up branches around the state and offer correspondence courses. The Salvation Army generally locates its stores in low-income neighborhoods. Health-care organizations provide mobile units for lung X-rays, blood-pressure tests, and inoculations. Big-city museums arrange for portable exhibits to be taken to small towns. [10]

Promotion Program

Promotion is the part of the marketing mix that many nonbusiness organizations are most familiar with and most adept at. They have regularly used advertising, personal selling, and sales promotion—often very aggressively and effectively—to communicate with both their contributors and their clients. The problem is that these organizations have not integrated their promotional mix into a total marketing program. In fact, many nonbusiness groups believe that promotion and marketing are one and the same thing. Obviously, this lack of understanding of what marketing is all about has been a major drawback to these organizations. [11]

ADVERTISING

Advertising is used extensively to reach the donor market. Many nonbusiness organizations conduct an annual campaign to collect funds. Mass media (newspapers, magazines, television, radio) frequently are used in these efforts. The media are also

[10] For some examples of physical distribution decisions in several nonbusiness fields, see J. Richard Jones and Philip D. Cooper, ''The Integration of a Logistical Decision-Making Framework into Nonprofit Marketing,'' *Journal of the Academy of Marketing Science,* Winter 1981, pp. 28–39.

[11] For suggestions on how a hospital can use promotion effectively in its marketing program to balance the demand for, and supply of, its services, see Minette E. Drumwright and Ivan R. Vernon, ''Synchromarketing: A New Concept for Hospital Administrators,'' *Journal of Health Care Marketing,* Spring 1984, pp. 45–50.

The health-care professions are advertising these days.

I really like
my new pearls,
but I just love
my new smile.

Let your inner self shine through, adorned by the beauty of a radiant smile. Leading cosmetic dentists applying the very latest advances in technology and technique, can beautify your smile with amazingly natural artistry. Expertly applied veneer capping is comfortable, stress-free, and your transformation can be complete in only two short visits. We want you to be as beautiful and confident as you know you can be and to

love your smile.

Cosmetic Dentistry Associates

Dr. Philip Kozlow
Dr. Lynn Tenney

used more selectively to solicit funds. Direct mail can be especially effective in reaching segmented donor markets such as past contributors, religious or ethnic groups related to the organizations, or college alumni. Media such as alumni magazines and foreign-language newspapers can also be used to pinpoint donor market segments.

Nonbusiness groups also can use advertising to communicate with client markets. To offset declining enrollments, colleges and universities have run ads in a variety of media. To increase their membership and attendance, a growing number of churches are using increasingly aggressive advertising in print media and on radio and TV.[12] Hospitals are beginning to advertise to fill their empty beds. Ever since the military draft was abolished, the Army has heavily used advertising, and increasingly television advertising, to attract recruits into the all-volunteer force. The total advertising budget for the armed services in 1984 was $155 million.

In some situations, a nonbusiness organization can reach both its contributor and its client markets with the same ad. The American Heart Association, the American

[12]See Ronald Alsop, ''Advertisers Promote Religion in a Splashy and Secular Style,'' *The Wall Street Journal*, Nov. 21, 1985, p. 33.

Cancer Society, or the Lung Association might advertise, asking you to contribute to its annual campaign. In the same ad, it might urge you to watch your diet, quit smoking, or get a medical checkup.

PERSONAL SELLING

Personal selling is frequently used in fund-raising efforts. Sometimes a door-to-door campaign is used. At Christmastime, Salvation Army volunteers, dressed as Santa Claus, collect donations in the downtown areas of many cities. And potential large donors often are approached by sales people.

Many nonbusiness organizations also use personal selling to reach their client public. These personal representatives may not be called salesmen or saleswomen, but that is exactly what they are. For centuries, missionaries of countless religious organizations have recruited new members by personal contact—personal selling. Personal selling also is used to recruit new members for fraternal organizations (YMCA, Girl Scouts, Elks). Colleges send "sales people" (admission officers, alumni, current students) to talk to high school students, their parents, and their counselors.

Using sales representatives to reach either contributors or clients poses some management problems for a nonbusiness organization. In effect, the organization has to manage a sales force, including recruiting, training, compensating, supervising, and evaluating performance. Unfortunately, not many nonbusiness organizations think in these terms, nor are they as yet qualified to do this management job.

SALES PROMOTION

Nonbusiness organizations also have long recognized the value of sales promotion to reach their markets. Many organizations have exhibits (including donation boxes) in local stores and shopping centers and at sporting events. Usually, these organizations are not charged for the use of this space.[13]

Personal selling can be effective for nonbusiness organizations.

IMPLEMENTATION OF MARKETING

Interest and Research in the Field

In this final section we discuss briefly three topics that will affect the future development of marketing in nonbusiness organizations.

If nonbusiness marketing is to have a future, it is important that the people in nonbusiness organizations understand fully (1) what marketing is and (2) what it can do for their organization. Fortunately, in recent years, people in many different nonbusiness fields have displayed a growing interest in marketing. Books on the topic of nonbusiness or nonprofit marketing are appearing.[14] Several general marketing text-

[13]For an example of how telemarketing can be used in a hospital's promotional mix, see John C. Hafer, "'Telemarketing' Hospital Services: Benefits, Pitfalls, and the Planning Process," *Journal of Health Care Marketing*, Spring 1984, pp. 29–35.

[14]Philip Kotler, *Marketing for Nonprofit Organizations*, 2d ed., Prentice-Hall, Inc.. Englewood Cliffs, N.J., 1982; and Christopher H. Lovelock and Charles B. Weinberg, *Marketing for Public and Nonprofit Managers*, John Wiley & Sons, New York, 1984.

books, such as this one, devote all or part of a chapter to nonbusiness marketing. Doctoral dissertations and many journal articles are appearing on this subject, and special sessions at professional marketing meetings are being devoted to nonbusiness marketing.

Just a few years ago, research in nonbusiness was initiated mainly by academicians and other people outside the nonbusiness field being studied. Now the marketing research is being generated by people working within various nonbusiness fields. This is a healthy sign for the future.

Measuring Performance

A real managerial challenge for the future is to come up with some valid means of measuring the marketing performance of a nonbusiness organization. At present, this is very difficult, if not impossible, for many of these organizations. A private business can evaluate its performance by using such quantitative measures as net profit, sales volume, or market share. For most nonbusiness organizations, however, there are no corresponding quantitative measures.

Nonbusiness organizations can measure the contributions they receive, but that evaluates only their fund-raising abilities. It does not measure the services rendered to their clients. How do you quantitatively evaluate the performance of, say, the Red Cross? Perhaps by the number of people they house and feed after a disaster, or by the number of people they train in first aid and lifesaving techniques.

Churches, museums, and YMCAs can count their attendance, but how can we measure the services they provide for their clients? In another area, how does the American Cancer Society or the American Heart Association measure its performance? By the decline in death rates from cancer and heart diseases? Perhaps, but such a decline may be due in part to several factors other than the work of these health-research organizations. These are not easy questions to answer.

Managing the Marketing Effort

As stressed throughout this chapter, nonbusiness organizations typically are unfamiliar with marketing, even though they practice some marketing under different names. The marketing activities that they do perform (usually promotion) are not well coordinated, and the people in charge have other duties and titles. In a university, for example, personal selling may be managed by the director of admissions, and advertising may be done through an office of public information. Nowhere in the university will you find anyone with the title of sales manager or advertising manager.

To establish a more formal marketing structure, the organization may set up a group of people to determine where the organization wants to go regarding its marketing effort.[15] These groups can define the organization's marketing goals and identify marketing strategies to reach these goals. Decisions can be made regarding the development of an internal marketing department. The groups working on such studies should include people with marketing expertise.

As a formal marketing structure develops, the organization may create a new middle-management executive position. Such a position might carry the title of director of marketing. Typically, this will be a staff position—perhaps located in the organization's planning department—with little or no line-operating authority. Even-

[15]This organization approach is adapted from Philip Kotler, ''Strategies for Introducing Marketing into Nonprofit Organizations,'' *Journal of Marketing*, January 1979, pp. 41–44.

tually, as a sign of marketing maturity, our nonbusiness organization will establish a top-level marketing executive position. This will be a line-operating position comparable to that of the vice president of marketing in a business firm.

SUMMARY ■

The marketing fundamentals apply to private, nonprofit, nonbusiness organizations as well as to firms in the business sector. But the development and implementation of a strategic marketing program are quite different in nonbusiness fields.

The nonbusiness field includes thousands of organizations spanning educational, cultural, religious, charitable, social, health-care, and political activities. Because of the large amounts of money and numbers of people involved in these organizations, marketing is quite important. Yet many people in nonbusiness organizations tend to be opposed to marketing. They really do not understand what marketing is or what it can do for their organizations.

Most nonbusiness organizations must deal with two major groups (markets)—the *contributors* to the organization and the *client-recipients* of the organization's money or services. Consequently, a nonbusiness organization must develop two separate marketing programs—one to attract resources from contributors and one to serve its clients.

In developing its marketing programs, a nonbusiness organization first must identify and analyze its markets. The use of market segmentation is especially helpful at this stage. Then the organization is ready to develop its strategic marketing mix. The product offering will be determined largely by deciding what business the organization is in and what client markets it wants to reach. Product-mix strategies, such as expansion of mix or product differentiation, may well be used. Pricing in many nonbusiness organizations is quite different from the usual price determination in a business firm. Channels of distribution typically are quite simple in nonbusiness marketing. The main distribution problem is to physically locate the organization so as to serve both its contributors and its clients. In promotion, many nonbusiness organizations have used advertising, personal selling, and other tools extensively, often aggressively, and often quite effectively.

Interest and research in nonbusiness marketing are growing. Both should be of help in implementing nonbusiness marketing programs in the future. Two important problems still to be solved are those of (1) measuring performance in a nonbusiness organization and (2) developing an internal structure to manage the nonbusiness marketing effort.

KEY TERMS AND CONCEPTS ■

Private versus public organizations 513

Profit versus not-for-profit organizations 513

Business versus nonbusiness organizations 513

Exchange concept in nonbusiness marketing 514

Contributor (donor) markets 515

Client (recipient) markets 515

Importance of nonbusiness marketing 515

The antimarketing attitude 517

Market segmentation in nonbusiness organizations 518

The marketing mix in nonbusiness organizations:

Product offering 520	Promotion 525
Pricing 522	Measuring marketing performance in nonbusiness organizations 528
Distribution 523	Managing a marketing program in nonbusiness organizations 528

QUESTIONS AND PROBLEMS ■

1. Are *nonbusiness organizations* and *nonprofit organizations* synonymous terms? If not,
   a. Name some nonbusiness organizations in which profit making is a major goal.
   b. Name some business organizations that are intentionally nonprofit.
2. Distinguish between business and nonbusiness organizations.
3. In this chapter, it is noted that many people in nonbusiness organizations have a negative attitude toward marketing. What suggestions do you have for changing this attitude so that these people will appreciate the value of marketing for their organizations?
4. Identify the various segments of the contributor market for your school.
5. Identify the client markets for:
   a. Your school.   c. Your church or other place of worship.
   b. The United Way.   d. Police department in your city.
6. What are some target markets (publics), other than contributors or clients, for each of the following organizations?
   a. Girl Scouts.
   b. Community hospital.
   c. Your school.
7. What benefits do contributors derive from gifts to:
   a. The Red Cross.   c. A symphony orchestra.
   b. The Boy Scouts.   d. A candidate for the U.S. presidency.
8. What is the product offering of:
   a. A political candidate.
   b. A family-planning organization.
   c. An organization opposed to nuclear energy.
9. A financial consultant for a private university suggested a change in the school's pricing methods. He recommended that the school discontinue its present one-price policy, under which all full-time students pay the same tuition. Instead, he recommended that the tuition vary by department within the university. In this way, students majoring in high-cost fields of study, such as engineering or a laboratory science, would pay higher tuition than students in lower-cost fields, such as English or history. Should the school adopt this recommendation?
10. Explain how the concept of the marketing mix (product, price, distribution, promotion) is applicable to the marketing of the following social causes:
    a. The use of returnable bottles, instead of the throwaway type.
    b. The prevention of heart ailments.
    c. A campaign against smoking.
    d. Obeying the 55-mile-per-hour speed limit.

11. How would you measure the marketing performance of each of the following?
    a. A church.   c. The Republican Party.
    b. Your school.   d. A group in favor of gun control.
12. The performance of a charitable organization may be measured as the percentage of contributions that is distributed among its clients. Explain why you think this is or isn't an effective measure of marketing performance.
13. Assume that your college or university wants to hire a director of marketing. Prepare a job description for this position, indicating its scope, activities, location within the school's administration, and responsibilities.

23

INTERNATIONAL MARKETING

CHAPTER GOALS

As you will see, international marketing entails more than simply marketing in a foreign language. After studying this chapter, you should understand:

- The importance of international marketing to American producers.
- Managerial orientations toward multinational operations.
- Major organizational structures for operating in foreign markets.
- The nature and problems of international marketing research.
- The importance of recognizing cultural and environmental differences in various foreign markets.
- International marketing programs—product planning, pricing, distribution, and advertising.
- The factors affecting balance of trade between countries.

This chapter opener is a little different from the ones we have presented in previous chapters. This time we are using a short, two-part quiz to introduce you to the topic—international marketing. The answers are on the next page.

Part A: In which of the following companies is the majority owner a foreign (non-United States) firm?

1. Sony (electronics).
2. Benetton (apparel).
3. Heineken (beer).
4. Volkswagen (autos).
5. Bic (pens).

6. Honda (autos).
7. Gucci (handbags).
8. Lipton (teas, soups).
9. Adidas (shoes).
10. Fiat (autos).

Part B. In which of the following firms is the majority owner a United States company?

1. Nestlé (candy).
2. Shell Oil (gasoline).
3. Miles Laboratories (Alka-Seltzer).
4. Liggett Group (cigarettes—L & M, Lark, Eve; Alpo dog food).
5. Lever Bros. (soap—Lux, Wisk; toothpaste—Close Up).

6. Timex (watches).
7. Norelco (electronics).
8. BATUS (cigarettes; stores—Saks Fifth Ave., Marshall Field).
9. Great Atlantic & Pacific Tea Co. (A&P supermarkets).
10. Seagram's (liquor, wine).

There is no disputing the fact that international trade significantly affects the political and economic health of virtually all nations—the industrialized nations as well as the developing countries in the so-called Third World. As we move through the 1980s, however, import quotas and other forms of international trade restrictions are a growing threat to international marketing in several countries. And there is increasing trade friction among the Western European nations, Japan, and the United States. Any growth in trade protectionism is extremely unfortunate. History clearly tells us of the damage that national economies can suffer from trade restrictions and trade wars.

Marketing fundamentals are universally applicable. Whether a firm sells in Toledo or Timbuktu, its marketing program should be built around a good product or service, properly priced, promoted, and distributed to a market that has been carefully selected. However, the strategies used in implementing the marketing programs in foreign countries often are quite different from domestic marketing strategies. Furthermore, for the firm that is interested in international marketing, management must make strategic decisions regarding (1) the company's degree of involvement in international marketing and (2) the organizational structure for operating in each foreign market.

DOMESTIC MARKETING AND INTERNATIONAL MARKETING

Answers to *Part A:* All 10 companies are foreign-owned. The owner's home country is as follows:

1. Japan.
2. Italy.
3. Netherlands.
4. West Germany.
5. France.
6. Japan.
7. Italy.
8. England-Netherlands.
9. West Germany.
10. Italy.

Answers to *Part B:* None of the 10 companies are American-owned. The majority owner's country in each case is as follows:

1. Switzerland.
2. England-Netherlands.
3. West Germany (Bayer Co.).
4. England.
5. England-Netherlands (Unilever Co.).
6. Norway.
7. Netherlands (Phillips Co.).
8. England (BAT Industries).
9. West Germany (Tengelmann Co.).
10. Canada.

Different strategies are needed in foreign markets primarily because those markets exist in a different set of environments. Recall that a company operates its marketing program within the economic, political, and cultural environment of each of its markets—foreign or domestic. And none of these environments is controllable by the firm. What complicates international marketing is the fact that these environments—particularly the cultural environment—often consist of elements very unfamiliar to American marketing executives. A further complication is the tendency for people to use their own cultural values as a frame of reference when in a foreign environment.[1]

IMPORTANCE OF INTERNATIONAL MARKETING

Sales and profits in foreign markets are a significant part of the lifeblood of many American companies. Many large American firms earn more than half their after-tax profits from overseas production and marketing operations. Moreover, there seems to be a growing awareness of international marketing opportunities among companies in the United States. As domestic markets become saturated, American producers—even those with no previous international experience—now look to foreign markets.

Foreign markets can be outlets for surplus productive capacity, as well as sources of wider profit margins and higher returns on investment. Some parts of the world

[1]For an expansion of this thesis and a more complete treatment of international marketing using the environmental approach, see Philip R. Cateora, *International Marketing*, 6th ed., Richard D. Irwin, Inc., Homewood, Ill., 1987.

WHY GO INTERNATIONAL

Eleven reasons why American firms are likely to become more export-minded over the next 10 years:

1. To escape from recessions in the domestic market.
2. To counter adverse demographic changes (like declining birth rates).
3. To export technology to less-developed nations.
4. To increase their political influence.
5. To keep up with or to escape competition.
6. To enjoy economies of scale in production.
7. To extend a product's life cycle.
8. To dispose of inventories.
9. To enjoy tax advantages.
10. To create research opportunities (by testing products in foreign markets).
11. To establish a progressive image.

Source: Douglass G. Norvell and Sion Raveed, "Eleven Reasons for Firms to 'Go International,'" *Marketing News,* Oct. 17, 1980, pp. 1–2.

markets—huge and expanding—offer greater growth opportunities than the domestic market.

International marketing is a two-way street, however. The same expanding foreign markets that offer fine growth opportunities for American firms also have their own producers. These foreign firms are providing substantial competition both in the United States and abroad. American consumers have responded favorably, for example, to Japanese radio-TV products (Sony), motorcycles (Yamaha), cameras (Canon, Nikon), and autos (Nissan, Toyota). We buy Italian shoes, German autos, Dutch electric razors (Norelco), French wines, Austrian skis, Swiss watches, and so on.

Especially strong competition is coming from Japan and the companies in the European Community (EC), more popularly known as the Common Market. This is a group of 12 Western European nations that have banded together in a multinational economic union. Competitive challenges are also being encountered from countries in other multinational economic organizations. (See the nearby box.)

A relatively new competitive factor has been the rise of multinational firms headquartered in developing countries (the so-called Third World). The petroleum-exporting countries (members of OPEC) have received the greatest amount of publicity. However, in many industries, significant competition in international markets has come from firms based in such developing nations as Brazil, Korea, and Taiwan. Furthermore, companies in the developing nations, which are usually strongly supported by their government, are likely to have a growing impact in international business.

Imports are big business.

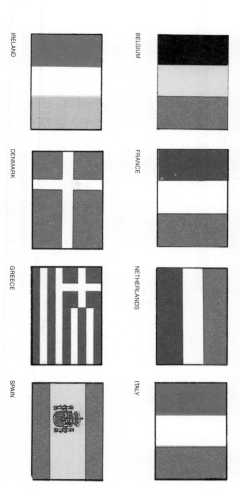

Some members of the European Common Market.

BELGIUM

FRANCE

NETHERLANDS

ITALY

IRELAND

DENMARK

GREECE

SPAIN

The Changing Scene

As we approach the 1990s, there still are excellent marketing opportunities for United States companies in multinational operations. Several situations make international marketing much tougher for American firms than it was from 1945 to 1975. Perhaps the most significant occurrence has been the market entry of foreign companies that are producing a wide variety of high-quality, relatively low-priced products. The high value of the American dollar in relation to foreign currencies also has had a negative effect on American firms. *But* the scene has changed. The strong dollar has resulted in a lowering of the price on competitive imports into the United States, while raising the price of American exports in foreign countries.

Another major change has been the shift in international investment patterns that has taken on significant proportions in the 1980s. Previously, the pattern was for American firms to invest abroad. There even was a fear that American firms would eventually own much of Europe's industry. Today, it is the other way around. The pattern now is for foreign companies to invest in the United States. (See the box "More Over, McDonald's.") These firms are attracted by our political stability, our economic growth potential, and less government regulation than in Europe. The investment alternatives for foreign companies are either to build production facilities in the United States or to acquire existing American firms.

MOVE OVER, McDONALD'S—YOSHINOYA HAS ARRIVED WITH GYUDON.

In Denver, Colorado, and in California, Yoshinoya (Japan) operates Beef Bowl fast-food outlets serving gyudon—thin slices of beef over a mound of rice. Elsewhere in the United States foreign companies are also operating:

Macon, Ga.: YKK (Japan) produces zippers.
Smyrna, Tenn.: Nissan assembles autos.
Lincoln, Neb.: Kawasaki builds motorcycles.
San Diego, Calif.: Sony manufactures color TV sets.
Greenville, S.C.: Michelin makes radial tires.
Chesapeake, Va.: Volvo assembles automobiles.
Walworth, Wis.: Kikkoman Foods makes soy sauce.
Canton, Ohio: Massey-Ferguson (Canada) builds tractors.
Auburn, N.Y.: Kyoei Steel Co. built a steel mill.
Geismar, La.: BASF (Germany) owns a petrochemical plant.
Marysville, Ohio: Honda assembles autos.

In addition, foreign companies and individuals have invested in farmland in Kansas, Arkansas, and Illinois; mansions and electronics plants in California; banks and hotels in Georgia; office buildings in New York City, Boston, and Houston; condominiums in Florida; shopping centers in Texas; and much, much more.

Honda assembles their autos in Ohio.

STRUCTURES FOR OPERATING IN FOREIGN MARKETS

Once a company has decided to market in foreign countries, management must select an organizational structure for operating in those markets. There are four distinct methods of entering a foreign market. Each represents successively greater international involvement, leading ultimately to a truly multinational operation. The same firm may use more than one of these operating methods at the same time. To illustrate, it may export products to one country, establish a licensing arrangement in another, and build a manufacturing plant in a third. See Fig. 23-1.[2]

---

[2]For suggestions regarding special types of intermediaries that small business firms can use to help them enter and develop foreign markets, see John J. Brasch, "Using Export Specialists to Develop Overseas Sales," *Harvard Business Review*, May–June 1981, pp. 6–8; and S. Tamer Cavusgil and Richard A. Yanzito, "Consulting Services and Trade Co-ops Can Assist Small Firms in Exporting," *Marketing News*, Oct. 17, 1980, p. 1

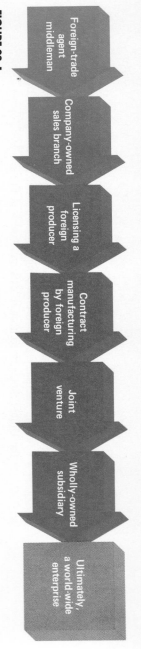

FIGURE 23-1
Structures for operating in a foreign market.

Foreign-trade agent middleman → Company-owned sales branch → Licensing a foreign producer → Contract manufacturing by foreign producer → Joint venture → Wholly-owned subsidiary → Ultimately, a world-wide enterprise

The simplest way of operating in foreign markets is by exporting through **export-import agent middlemen.** Very little risk or investment is involved. Also, little time or effort is required on the part of the exporting producer. On the other hand, the exporter has little or no control over its agent middlemen. Furthermore, these middlemen generally are little or no control over its agent middlemen, and normally they do not generate a large sales volume.

To counteract some of these deficiencies, management can move to the second stage—exporting through **company sales branches** or other sales subsidiaries located in foreign markets. Bypassing the export-import agent middlemen enables a company (1) to promote its products more aggressively, (2) to develop its foreign markets more effectively, and (3) to control its sales effort more completely. Of course, management now has the time- and money-consuming task of managing a sales force. The difficulty here is that these sales people are either (1) foreign nationals unfamiliar with the product and the company's marketing practices or (2) American sales people unfamiliar with the market.

As foreign markets expand, management may enter licensing arrangements whereby foreign manufacturers produce the goods. **Licensing** means granting to another producer—for a fee or royalty payment—the right to use one's production process, patents, trademarks, or other assets. **Contract manufacturing** is related to licensing. An American marketer, such as a retail-chain organization, simply contracts with a foreign producer to supply the products that the American firm will market in that producer's country.

Licensing offers manufacturers a flexible arrangement with a minimal investment. Yet they still can enjoy the advantages of their patents, research, and know-how. Through licensing or contract manufacturing, producers can enter a market that might otherwise be closed to them because of exchange restrictions, import quotas, or prohibitive tariffs. At the same time, by licensing, manufacturers may be building future competitors. A licensee may learn all it can from the manufacturer, and then proceed independently when the licensing agreement expires.[3]

In the fourth method, the company builds or otherwise acquires its own production facilities in a foreign country. The structure can be a *joint venture* or a *wholly-owned foreign subsidiary*. A **joint venture** is a partnership arrangement in which the foreign operation is owned in part by the American company and in part by a foreign company. The foreign ownership share may be any percentage—more than, less than, or exactly 50 percent. Obviously, when the controlling interest is owned by foreign nationals, the American firm has no real control over any of the marketing or pro-

[3]For a discussion of conditions under which licensing may be the preferred strategy for operating in a foreign market, see Farok J. Contractor, "The Role of Licensing in International Strategy," *Columbia Journal of World Business*, Winter 1981, pp. 73–83.

duction activities. At the same time, a joint venture may be the only structure (other than licensing) through which an American firm is allowed to enter a given foreign market.[4]

Wholly-owned subsidiaries in foreign markets are commonly used by companies that have evolved to an advanced stage of international business. With a wholly-owned foreign subsidiary, a company has maximun control over its marketing program and production operations. This type of international structure, however, requires a substantial investment of money, labor, and managerial attention.

This leads us to the final evolutionary stage—one reached by very few companies as yet. This is the stage of the true multinational corporation—the **worldwide enterprise.** Both the foreign and the domestic operations are integrated, and are no longer separately identified. The regional sales office in Atlanta is basically the same as the one in Athens (Greece, that is—not Georgia or Ohio). Business opportunities abroad are viewed in the same way as those in the United States. That is, opportunities in the United States are no longer automatically considered to be better. A true multinational firm does *not* view itself as an American firm (Ford Motor Company), or a Swiss firm (Nestlé), or a Dutch firm (Shell Oil) that happens to have plants and markets in a foreign country. In a true worldwide enterprise, the strategic marketing planning is done on a global basis.[5]

Kentucky Fried Chicken did much marketing research before taking its business to Japan.

A STRATEGIC PROGRAM FOR INTERNATIONAL MARKETING

International Marketing Research

Firms that have been very successful in marketing in the United States have no assurance whatsoever that their success will be duplicated in foreign markets. A key to satisfactory performance overseas lies in gauging which domestic marketing strategies and tactics should be transferred directly to foreign markets, which ones modified, and which ones not used at all. In other words, foreign markets, too, present the need for strategic marketing planning.

A marketing information system would seem to be even more essential in foreign markets than in the domestic market because the risks are so much greater. Yet, in practice, only limited funds are invested in marketing research in foreign countries. The basic reason for this disparity is that the costs, relative to the value received, are greater abroad than at home. This situation arises because environmental conditions in foreign markets often have a negative influence on some of the basic elements of marketing research.

Fundamental to marketing research is the idea that problems should be solved in a *systematic, analytical* manner. Unfortunately, an orderly, rational approach runs counter to the instincts of many people throughout the world. In many cultures, the people are guided by intuition, emotional reaction, or tradition. None of these is particularly conducive to the scientific approach. A second element in marketing

[4]For an analysis of the merits and limitations of a joint venture as a structure for entering and operating in foreign markets, see F. Kingston Berlew, "The Joint Venture—A Way into Foreign Markets," *Harvard Business Review,* July–August 1984, pp. 48ff.

[5]See Thomas Hout, Michael E. Porter, and Eileen Rudden, "How Global Companies Win Out," *Harvard Business Review,* September–October 1982, pp. 98–108.

McDonald's uses different menus in different countries.

Analysis of Foreign Markets

research—*customer information*—depends upon the willingness of people to respond accurately when researchers pose questions involving attitudes or buying habits. In many societies, suspicion of strangers, distrust of government, and an individualism which holds that these things are "none of your business" all serve to compound the problems of gathering information.

The scarcity of *reliable statistical data* may be the single biggest problem in some foreign markets. Figures on population, personal income, and production may be only crude estimates. Few studies have been made on such things as buying habits or media coverage. In the design of a research project, the lack of reliable data makes it very difficult to select a meaningful sample. In the design of a research project, the lack of reliable data makes it very difficult to select a meaningful sample. Lack of uniformity makes intercountry comparisons very unreliable.[6]

Nowhere in international marketing is the influence of the cultural and economic environments seen more clearly than in an analysis of market demand. Market demand throughout the world is determined by population, economic ability to buy, and buying behavior. Also, human wants and needs have a universal similarity. People need food, clothing, and shelter. They seek a better life in terms of lighter work loads, more leisure time, and social recognition and acceptance. But at about this point, the similarities in foreign and domestic markets end, and the differences in cultural and economic environments must be considered.

When analyzing consumers' *economic ability to buy* in a given foreign market, management may study the (1) distribution of income, (2) rate of growth of buying power, and (3) extent of available consumer financing. In the emerging economies, large portions of the population have very low incomes. A much different income-distribution pattern—with resulting differences in marketing programs—is found in the industrialized markets of Western Europe. In those countries there are large groups of working classes and a big middle-income market. Thus, many of the products commonly in demand in Belgium or the Netherlands would find very small markets in many African or Asian countries. In Asia, Japan is an exception, of course. Rising incomes in Japan have generated huge markets for travel, sports, and other leisure-time activities. In response, shops in London, Paris, and Rome now display window signs saying "Japanese is spoken here."[7]

Here are some cultural elements that can influence a company's marketing program. The importance of specific elements in marketing varies from country to country.

- *Family.* In some countries the family is an extremely close-knit unit, whereas in other nations the family members usually act more independently. Each of these two situations requires a different type of promotion, and perhaps even different types of products.

- *Other social groups and institutions.* Some cultural differences are illustrated in the boxed material on the next two pages.

- *Educational system.* The educational system affects the literacy rate, which in turn influences advertising, branding, and labeling. The brand may become all-important

---

[6]For sources of secondary data on foreign markets, see Cateora, op. cit., ch. 9.

[7]For some guidelines in determining foreign market opportunities and potential, see S. Tamer Cavusgil, "Guidelines for Export Market Research," *Business Horizons,* November–December 1985, pp. 27–33.

MARKETING PROBLEMS MAY BE CREATED BY CULTURAL DIFFERENCES

Body language:

Standing with your hands on your hips is a gesture of defiance in Indonesia.

Carrying on a conversation with your hands in your pockets makes a poor impression in France, Belgium, Finland, and Sweden.

When you shake your head from side to side, that means "yes" in Bulgaria and Sri Lanka.

Crossing your legs to expose the sole of your shoe is really taboo in Muslim countries. In fact, to call a person a "shoe" is a deep insult.

Physical contact:

Patting a child on the head is a grave offense in Thailand or Singapore, since the head is sacred.

In an Oriental culture, touching another person is considered an invasion of privacy, while in Southern European countries and in Arabic countries it is a sign of warmth and friendship.

Promptness:

Be on time when invited for dinner in Denmark or in China.

In Latin countries your host or business appointment would be surprised if you arrived at the appointed hour.

Eating:

It is rude to leave anything on your plate when eating in Norway, Malaysia, or Singapore.

In Egypt it is rude not to leave something.

Other social customs:

In Sweden nudity and sexual permissiveness are quite all right, but drinking is really frowned on.

In Spain there is a really negative attitude toward life insurance. By receiving insurance benefits, a wife feels that she is profiting from her husband's death.

Retailers in Taiwan really believe in scrambled merchandising. Here are some product combinations found in small shops: luggage and soap; fresh donuts and playing cards; purses, blankets, and toothpaste; dresses, soap, and table lamps.

Source: Adapted in part from Alice Farrard, "Foreign Faux Pas," *Travel & Leisure,* October 1985, p. 164; and in part from authors' personal observations.

if the potential customers cannot read and must recognize the article by the picture on the label.

- *Language differences.* Language differences also pose problems. Literal translations of American advertising copy or brand names may result in ridicule of, or even enmity toward, American products. Even some English words have different meanings in England and the United States.

- *Religion.* Religion is a major influence on value systems and behavioral patterns.

BEWARE WHEN BEARING GIFTS IN FOREIGN LANDS—AND WATCH IT WHEN IT COMES TO THE COLOR

Brazil: Purple is a death color. Scotch is more popular than bourbon.

England: Apparel and soap are considered a bit too personal. White lilies suggest death, but other flowers are okay.

France: Yellow flowers suggest infidelity, and chrysanthemums are strictly for funerals. Do not give cutlery.

Hong Kong: White is for funerals, but red is popular in all Chinese-speaking areas.

Italy: Red roses are for your favorite woman. Generally, you don't give hand-kerchiefs.

Mexico: Yellow flowers are a sign of death.

Russia: Knives and forks are a friendship-cutter.

Saudia Arabia: Give nothing to another person's wife, and don't give anything alcoholic to anyone.

Taiwan: Knives may wound a friendship. Don't give a clock because the word for "clock" sounds like the one for "terminate."

West Germany: If you give cutlery, ask for a coin in payment so you won't cut the friendship. A gift of red roses to a woman means you really care for her.

Source: *Business Week,* Dec. 6, 1976, pp. 91–92.

A few examples illustrate how buying habits are influenced by cultural elements. One-stop shopping is unknown in most parts of the world. In many foreign markets people buy in small units, sometimes literally on a meal-to-meal basis. Also, they buy in small specialty stores. To buy food for a weekend, a *hausfrau* (housewife) in West Germany may visit the chocolate store, the dairy store, the meat market, the fish market, a dry-grocery store, the greengrocer, the bakery, the coffee market, and possibly some other specialty food stores. While this may seem to be an inefficient use of her time, we must recognize that a shopping trip is more than just a chore to be done as fast as possible. It is a major part of her social life. She will visit with her friends and neighbors in these shops. Shopping in this fashion is simply a foreign version of the American bridge club or neighborhood coffee break. In Japan and in

Western European countries some of these traditional shopping patterns are changing, however. Supermarkets now account for a significant and increasing percentage of the retail trade in many of those countries.

> In France, if you want bread, go to a boulangerie. If you want some pastry, however, you don't go to a bread store. You go to a pâtisserie. Fresh meat you get in a boucherie. If you want sausage or smoked meats, your best bet is a charcuterie. But if you want good fish, try a poissonerie. Canned peaches you can get in an épicerie. But for fresh peaches, you are better off shopping at the fresh fruit and vegetable store (and I forgot the French word for that place).

So far in this chapter, we have stressed the significant environmental differences that exist between and within foreign countries. On the horizon, however, we can see a trend toward standardization of tastes, wants, and habits, especially in the Western European countries. Travel, television, and trade are proving to be effective homogenizers of European culture. But—and this should be well understood—a German is still a German, and a Swede is still a Swede. In Europe's uncommon market, there is no such thing as a Mr. and Mrs. European—yet. However, the old order is changing, and we can see increasingly cosmopolitan demands. Pizzerias do business in Germany, lasagna is sold in a Stockholm supermarket. British fish-and-chips are wanted on the Continent, and whisky sales are large in France.

Most companies would not think of entering a domestic market without careful and often extensive product planning. Yet an American firm typically enters a foreign market with essentially the same product it sells in the United States. Even when a product is changed expressly for an international market, modification is apt to be minor. A producer may convert an appliance for use with 220-volt electrical systems, or paint and package a product to protect it against a destructive tropical climate, for example.

A key question today in product planning involves the extent to which a company can market the same product in several different countries. Theodore Levitt asserts, "Well-managed companies have moved from emphasis on customizing items to offering globally standardized products that are advanced, functional, reliable—and low-priced."[8] While this assertion obviously cannot be applied to all products, or to all international markets, certainly the situation has changed over the past 20 to 30 years. As we just indicated a couple of paragraphs above, international communications is reducing the cultural differences that exist among some markets.

Product Planning for International Markets

Catering to local buying habits.

---

[8]Theodore Levitt, "The Globalization of Markets," *Harvard Business Review*, May–June 1983, pp. 92–102.

For some products in some markets there is a strong common demand. One survey identified eight product categories that were highly in demand in eight major markets spread around the world. These eight markets and products were as follows:[9]

Markets

Australia	France
Brazil	Germany
Britain	Japan
Canada	South Africa

Products

Personal computers	Beer and low-alcohol
Video equipment	beverages
Healthful food	Convenience foods
Physical fitness clothing	Toys
and equipment	Financial services

Nevertheless, the above lists still leave a lot of products and markets to be accounted for. For example, undoubtedly many products have to be especially adapted for markets in a less-developed country (LDC). And by the year 2000 these countries are expected to contain 80 percent of the world's population.[10]

In short, any marketer would be well-advised to study carefully the cultural and economic environment of any market—foreign or domestic—before planning products for that particular market. In Europe, as an example, a 6-cubic-foot refrigerator is the most popular size, in contrast to the larger units preferred in the United States. True, the cost difference and the existence of smaller kitchens in Europe are decision factors. However, the basic reasons for the Europeans' choice lie in the cultural behavior patterns of the consumers. As noted earlier, to many European housewives a food-shopping trip is a social event. They go daily and thus do not buy the large quantities that must be stored for several days in the refrigerator. Also, if they have no car, they walk to the store. Because of this, they cannot carry large quantities. As yet, frozen foods are not purchased to any great extent, so large freezer space for storage is not needed.

Warren Keegan has identified five alternative strategies for adapting a product and its promotion (communication message) to a foreign market:[11]

- *One product, one message—worldwide.* This strategy is appropriate when the same product and the same promotional appeals can be used effectively in all countries and cultures. Pepsi-Cola and Coca-Cola have used this alternative successfully. On balance, however, there probably are more market failures than successes with this approach.

- *Same product, but modified communications.* This strategy is practical when the same product can be used to fill different needs in foreign markets. Outboard motors that are used for recreation in the United States may be used for commercial fishing or transportation abroad. In this instance, the foreign advertising copy would be quite different, depending upon the product use being promoted.

9 Carolyn Hulse, "Popular Categories Cross Cultural Boundaries," *Advertising Age*, Dec. 24, 1984, pp. 17, 26.

10 See John S. Hill and Richard R. Still, "Adapting Products to LDC Tastes," *Harvard Business Review*, March–April 1984, pp. 92–101.

11 The discussion of these strategies is adapted from Warren J. Keegan, "Multinational Product Planning: Strategic Alternatives," *Journal of Marketing*, January 1969, pp. 58–62.

- *Product adaptation, communications extension.* With this strategy, essentially the same promotional message is used abroad as at home, but the product is changed to meet local conditions. To illustrate, a soap formula is changed to adapt to local water conditions, appliances are altered for different voltage requirements, and packaging changes are made for different climates.
- *Dual adaptation.* Both the product and the message are changed to fit the foreign market.
- *Product invention.* A company develops a new product in response to foreign market demands. For markets with low buying power, one firm "invented backward" by developing an inexpensive, hand-operated washing machine with the tumbling action of an automatic machine.

Branding and labeling are especially important in foreign marketing.[12] As suggested earlier, the brand picture may be the only part of the product that a consumer can recognize. Foreign consumers' preference for American products often overcomes their nationalistic feelings. So in many instances a company can use the same brand that is used in the domestic market.

Pricing in International Markets

In earlier chapters, we recognized that determining the base price and formulating pricing strategies are complex tasks, often involving trial-and-error decision making. These tasks become even more complex in international marketing. An exporter faces variables such as currency conversion, a variety of bases for price quotations, and often a lack of control of middlemen's pricing.

Cost-plus pricing is probably used to a greater extent in export marketing than at home. Consequently, foreign prices usually are considerably higher than domestic prices for the same product. This is because of additional physical distribution ex-

Branding and labeling are especially important in many countries.

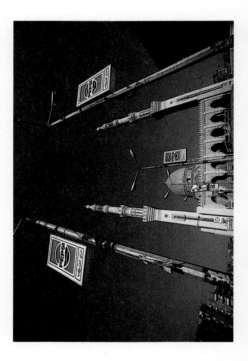

One product, one message—worldwide.

---

[12]For a report on whether consumers in several foreign markets have the same perceptions of a given product's value, thus allowing market segments to cross national boaundaries, see Petr Chadraba and Robert O'Keefe, "Cross-National Product Value Perceptions," *Journal of Business Research*, December 1981, pp. 329–337.

penses, tariffs, and other export costs. At the retail level price bargaining is quite prevalent in many foreign markets—especially in Asia, Africa, and South America.[13]

Sometimes a firm's foreign price is *lower* than its domestic price. The price may be lowered to meet foreign competition or to dispose of outmoded products. Sometimes companies engage in the practice of **"dumping"**—that is, selling products in foreign markets at prices below the prices charged for these goods in their home market. Through the years, the surplus production of some raw materials has led to government control of world market prices. For example, individual governments have tried to stabilize the prices of coffee, nitrates, sugar, and rubber. Also, the governments of several countries have established joint agreements covering the prices of such commodities as oil, tin, potash, and cocoa.

Foreign middlemen often are not aggressive in their pricing strategies. They prefer to maintain high unit margins and low sales volume, rather than develop large sales volume by means of lower prices and smaller margins per unit sold. In fact, there is considerable price rigidity in many foreign markets. In some cases, the inflexibility stems from agreements among firms which tend to restrain independent pricing. The rigidity also sometimes results from price-control legislation that prevents retailers from cutting prices at their own discretion.

Combinations among manufacturers and middlemen are tolerated to a far greater extent in many foreign countries than in the United States. This occurs even when the avowed purpose of the combinations is to restrain trade and reduce competition. Recognizing this, Congress passed the Webb-Pomerene Act in 1918. This law allows American firms to join in a trade combination in a foreign country without being charged with violation of American antitrust laws.

Probably the best known of these international marketing combinations is the cartel. A **cartel** is a group of companies that produce similar products and that have combined to restrain competition in manufacturing and marketing. Cartels exist to varying degrees in steel and aluminum, fertilizers, electrical products, petroleum products, rayon, dyes, and sulfur.

Another area of pricing practices peculiar to foreign trade relates to price quotations. With respect to shipping, insurance, and related export charges, the three following bases of price quotations are used extensively in foreign trade:

- F.O.B. (*free on board*): The f.o.b. point is usually the inland point of departure, or the port of shipment. The buyer pays all shipping charges beyond the f.o.b. point.

- F.A.S. (*free alongside ship, at port of export*): The seller pays all charges to deliver the goods to the dock within reach of the ship's tackle, but not on board. All shipping activities, costs, and risk from that point are the responsibility of the buyer.

- C.I.F. (*cost, insurance, freight at a given point of destination*): The seller pays all costs up to the arrival of the shipment at the foreign port.

[13]For a report on price bargaining by consumers in 10 developing countries, and the conclusion that buyer satisfaction was lower toward retailers that bargain than for retailers that used a fixed-price policy, see Laurence Jacobs, Reginald Worthley, and Charles Keown, "Perceived Buyer Satisfaction and Selling Pressure versus Pricing Policy: A Comparative Study of Retailers in Ten Developing Countries," *Journal of Business Research*, March 1984, pp. 63–74.

Prices may be quoted in United States dollars or in the currency of the foreign buyer. Here we become involved in problems of foreign exchange and conversion of currencies. As a general rule, a firm engaged in foreign trade—whether it is exporting or importing—prefers to have the price quoted in its own national currency. Risks from fluctuations in foreign exchange then are shifted to the other party in the transaction. One way to get around currency problems, especially when dealing with Eastern European or developing nations, is through a barter arrangement in which there is no exchange of money.[14]

DEVALUATION AS AN INTERNATIONAL PRICING STRATEGY

To devalue a nation's currency means to reduce its worth relative to the currencies of other nations. Then, products priced in the devalued currency cost less when purchased with other currencies. The effect is the same as reducing the prices of all the exported products of the devaluing nation. With lower international prices, more of these exported products will be purchased, and the devaluing nation will then export more goods. This leads first to a better balance-of-payments position and increased production, and then to increased domestic investment and employment, and a stronger economy.

International Distribution Systems

Understanding the environment in a foreign market helps in understanding the distribution system, because these marketing institutions result from their environment. The perceptive, and thus usually successful, retailers, for example, will capitalize on environmental change by introducing innovations that anticipate trends in the environment. In fact, several European retailers have done a good job of innovating. Within a relatively few years, they have moved from the stage of "mom and pop" stores to a variety of retailing concepts as advanced as anything in the United States. These innovative retailers simply leapfrogged several stages of institutional development. In mass retailing, the *hypermarché* in France and the *verbrauchermarkt* in Germany are huge self-service superstores operating very profitably and at much lower gross margins than similar American stores.

MIDDLEMEN IN FOREIGN MARKETING

Four groups of middlemen operating in foreign trade consist of (1) American foreign trade middlemen, (2) foreign trade middlemen located abroad, (3) wholesalers and retailers operating within foreign markets, and (4) manufacturers' sales branches and offices located in foreign countries.

For an American producer, the main outlets abroad for manufactured goods are foreign *agents and distributors*. These are firms that act as sales representatives for

---

[14]See Robert E. Weigand, "International Trade without Money," *Harvard Business Review*, November–December 1977, pp. 26ff.; and by same author, "Barters and Buy-Backs: Let Western Firms Beware!" *Business Horizons*, June 1980, pp. 54–61.

American firms in foreign markets. Agents and distributors differ primarily in two respects: Agents do not take title to the goods, and they normally do not carry inventory stocks. These two types of middlemen are so important in the distribution system that often a manufacturer will grant them exclusive territorial rights. They perform a wide variety of services, including personal selling, advertising, providing market and credit information, making repairs, settling disputes, and collecting on invoices. In addition, distributors perform the functions of warehousing and bulk breaking.

CHANNELS OF DISTRIBUTION

The main distribution problem when marketing in a foreign country is to decide whether or not to engage in direct selling and, if so, to what extent. Middlemen operating *within* foreign countries are, in general, less aggressive and perform fewer marketing services than their American counterparts: The foreign marketing situation, however, usually argues against bypassing these foreign middlemen. Often the demand is too small to warrant the establishment of a sales office or branch. Also, in many foreign countries, knowledge of the market may be more important than knowledge of the product, even for high-technology products. And sometimes government controls preclude the use of an American sales organization abroad. Thus, the middlemen in foreign countries ordinarily are a part of the channel structure.

When foreign middlemen are used, the American seller usually advertises extensively and furnishes point-of-purchase display materials to strengthen the efforts of the middlemen. If the product requires mechanical servicing or installation, the American manufacturer must provide reliable repair service. This means training local middlemen, sending in American service representatives, or doing both.[15]

PHYSICAL DISTRIBUTION

In foreign marketing, various aspects of physical distribution are quite different from anything found on the domestic scene. Generally, physical distribution expenses account for a much larger share of the final selling price in foreign markets than in domestic markets. Packing requirements, for example, are more exacting for foreign shipment. Problems caused by humidity, pilferage, breakage, and inadequate marking of shipments must be considered. Requirements regarding commercial shipping documents and governmental documents complicate the paperwork in foreign shipping. Marine insurance and the traffic management of international shipments are specialized fields. They involve institutions that are not ordinarily used in domestic marketing.

BRIBERY IN INTERNATIONAL DISTRIBUTION

Bribes, kickbacks, and sometimes extortion payments are facts of life in many international (and sometimes even in domestic) distribution systems. Bribery apparently has existed to varying degrees in buying and selling since time immemorial. However, bribery is not limited to marketing. It is found in many other areas of human interaction. It can start with parents' bribing their children—"If you kids are good today, we'll take you to the park tomorrow."

[15]For suggestions regarding the selection of qualified distributors in foreign markets, see S. Tamer Cavusgil, "Exporters Wrestle with Market and Distributor Selection Problems in Penetrating New Markets," *Marketing News*, Dec. 23, 1983, p. 10.

HOW ABOUT OPENING GROCERY SUPERMARKETS IN LESS-DEVELOPED NATIONS?

Supply-side problems—operating the stores

1. Self-service does not work well because the products are not prepackaged, standardized, and graded.

2. Branding, the preselling of products, and mass advertising are in their infancy in many Third World countries.

3. Store equipment is expensive, and the skilled and semiskilled labor needed in supermarkets is costly.

4. Supermarkets must use the same channels of distribution and pay about the same prices as small stores. So the supermarkets cannot offer significantly lower prices or enjoy the economies of scale.

5. The small retailers have considerable political influence, which they use against supermarkets.

Demand-side problems—consumer buying behavior

1. Consumers—especially the low-income ones—must shop daily because they lack refrigeration and storage space.

2. Supermarkets do not provide the easy credit terms and friendly personal relationships found in small stores.

3. Travel costs to reach the supermarkets are high.

4. Product variety and shopping convenience—major benefits provided by a supermarket—generally are not important to shoppers in these countries.

5. Consumers do not perceive that supermarket products are of higher quality.

6. Direct cost savings (through lower prices) are too small to be important to shoppers.

I guess the answer to the opening question is, "No, thanks." But do you think we would do any better if we opened 7-Eleven type of convenience stores in these countries?

Source: Arieh Goldman, "Transfer of a Retailing Technology into the Less Developed Countries," *Journal of Retailing,* Summer 1981, pp. 5–29.

Safeway goes overseas.

Bribery is so implanted in many cultures that special slang words are used to designate it. In Latin America, it is called the *mordida* (small bite). It is *dash* in West Africa and *baksheesh* in the Middle East. The French call it *pot de vin* (jug of wine). In Italy there is *la bustarella* (the little envelope) left on a bureaucrat's desk to cut the red tape. In Chicago, we use *a little grease.*

Bribery in marketing became an international scandal in the mid-1970s. Subsequent political sensitivity in the United States resulted in several companies' establishing written ethical guidelines. Also, in 1977 Congress passed the Foreign Corrupt

Practices Act (FCPA). This is a far-reaching and restrictive law that limits considerably the competitive position of United States in international trade.

What complicates this situation is the fact that bribery is not a sharply defined activity. Sometimes the lines are blurred between a bribe, a gift to show appreciation, a reasonable commission for services rendered, and a "facilitating" payment to grease the channel of distribution. Realistically, in some foreign markets, a seller must pay a facilitating fee or commission to an agent in order to get in touch with prospective buyers. Without paying such fees to those agents, there is simply no effective access to those markets.

Now many sellers fear that the FCPA forbids such fees. The net result is that American firms have lost considerable business to companies in Japan and Western Europe that do not operate under similar legal or cultural restrictions. In fact, Congress is continually being urged to amend the FCPA to enable American firms to be more competitive.

Advertising in Foreign Markets

Rather than discuss promotion in its entirety, we limit our discussion to advertising as being illustrative of the strategic problems in international promotion. Advertising is selected because it is probably used by more firms in international marketing than either a company sales force or any sales promotion technique. Many companies without their own international sales force (they use foreign trade middlemen) do advertise internationally.

A controversial issue in international advertising is the extent to which advertising can be standardized in foreign markets. In years gone by, the consensus was that a separate program (copy, appeals, and media) had to be tailored for each country, or even for regions within a country. While nobody is recommending complete uniformity, today there is much support for the idea of commonality in international ad campaigns. Many companies are using basically the same appeals, theme, copy, and layout in all their international advertising—particularly in the Western European countries. Such standardization of advertising is spurred by the increase in international communications. Hordes of Europeans travel from one country to another while

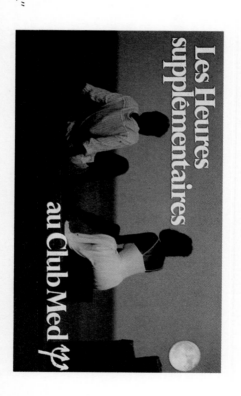

Club Med's new worldwide strategy emphasizes more conservative life-styles. This ad stresses "Overtime at Club Med."

on vacation. Many radio and TV broadcasts from one country reach audiences in another country. The circulation of many European magazines and newspapers crosses national borders.

Perhaps the issue comes down to this point: The goal of advertising is essentially the same at home and abroad, namely, to communicate information and persuasive appeals effectively. It is only the media strategy and the specific messages that must be tuned to each country's cultural, economic, and political environment. For some products, the appeals are sufficiently universal and the market is sufficiently homogeneous to permit the use of uniform advertising in several countries. In general, however, each country has its own national identity and characteristics that must be recognized when advertising in the given country.[16]

ATTITUDE OF FOREIGN MARKETS AND GOVERNMENTS TOWARD ADVERTISING

In many countries, the traditionally negative attitude toward marketing in general and toward advertising in particular is a hardship for American firms. The "build a better mousetrap" theory still prevails to a great extent throughout Europe and the rest of the world. Some foreign consumers feel that a product is of dubious value if it has to be advertised. People in many foreign countries object particularly to American hard-sell advertising.

The extent of active consumer discontent and government regulation of advertising does vary considerably from one country to another. Both these forces do exist, however, and many countries have stringent laws regulating advertising. Where the government regulates the use of radio and television for advertising and where newspapers are government-controlled, this too affects their use as advertising media.

In the late 1980s, however, the winds of change (or at least slight breezes) are blowing through advertising in Western Europe. The growth of private and satellite-beamed cable TV stations is generating pressure to permit commercial advertising on state-owned TV stations. The United Kingdom now allows accountants and lawyers (but still not physicians) to advertise. Carrefour, the largest superstore (*hypermarche*) in France, began to run comparative-price ads, even though French law is unclear on the legality of this strategy.[17]

CHOICE OF MEDIA

Essentially the same types of advertising media are available in foreign countries as in the United States, with the exception of television in some markets. Some print media, such as *Time* and *Reader's Digest*, which are published in the Untied States, are also published abroad in foreign languages.

PREPARATION OF ADVERTISEMENTS

Most of the mistakes in writing copy and preparing individual advertisements may be traced to lack of intimate knowledge of the foreign market. The wrong color or a poor

---

[16]For more on the concept of global advertising, including some words of caution on the idea, see Anne B. Fisher, "The Ad Biz Gloms onto 'Global,'" *Fortune*, Nov. 12, 1984, p. 77.

[17]See Laurel Wentz, "Ad Pressure Mounts for European TV," *Advertising Age*, Feb. 11, 1985, p. 3; Sean Milmo, "U.K. Opens Ads to Professions," *Advertising Age*, Sept. 24, 1984, p. 60; and Phil Hill, "Carrefour Starts Comparative Fight in France," *Advertising Age*, Dec. 26, 1983, p. 12.

INTERNATIONAL TRADE BALANCES

choice of words can completely nullify an otherwise good ad. Illustrations are of prime importance in many markets because of illiteracy. They are, of course, effective in all markets, but they must be accurate, believable, and in accord with local cultures. The translation of advertising copy into the appropriate foreign language—especially for radio—is a major problem. Here the advertiser especially needs someone both adept and current (an expatriate often will not do) in the idioms, dialects, and other nuances of the foreign language.

To conclude this chapter, let's move from the micro level of international marketing in the individual firm to the macro level of international trade in the total economy. To maintain equilibrium in our balance of international payments, we need to generate a substantial favorable balance of *merchandise* trade. That is, our exports of products and services must greatly exceed our imports. This is needed to offset the negative balances stemming from our expenditures in four areas: (1) huge imports of high-priced oil, (2) our overseas military forces, (3) foreign aid, and (4) American tourist travel abroad. Up to about 1970, the United States generally had a sufficiently large favorable balance of product trade. But since then, this favorable balance of product trade has declined to the point where it is not sufficient to offset the outpayments from the United States. Table 23-1 illustrates the impact that imports have had on the American market in 12 product categories over the period from 1972 to 1984. This situation has had serious economic and political repercussions in the United States and internationally.

What has caused this substantial decline in our merchandise trade balance? In recent years a very major factor has been the *high value of the United States dollar* in relation to the currencies of our trading partners. The result of this situation has

TABLE 23-1 IMPORTS' SHARE OF THE UNITED STATES MARKET FOR SELECTED PRODUCTS, 1972 AND 1984

Foreign-made products accounted for one-half or more of the sales of dolls, zinc, radios and TV sets, and shoes in the United States.

Product	Imports' market share, in % 1972	1984	Product	Imports' market share, in % 1972	1984
Blowers and fans	4	29	Precious metal jewelry	5	25
Paper products	10	20	Primary zinc	28	52
Costume jewelry	10	29	Printing machinery	9	23
Dolls	22	55	Radios and TV sets	35	58
Computer equipment	0	14	Semiconductors	12	31
Lighting fixtures	4	17	Shoes	17	50

Source: Adapted from *Business Week*, Oct. 7, 1985, p. 94.

TABLE 23-2 HOURLY PAY LEVELS IN MANUFACTURING INDUSTRIES IN SELECTED COUNTRIES, AS PERCENTAGE OF UNITED STATES AVERAGE PAY, 1981–1984

United States wage rates increased in relation to every country except Taiwan and Korea.

Country	% of U.S. pay 1981	% of U.S. pay 1984	Country	% of U.S. pay 1981	% of U.S. pay 1984
West Germany	97	75	Ireland	51	42
Sweden	108	72	Spain	51	37
Netherlands	91	67	Taiwan	14	15
Italy	68	58	Mexico	34	13
France	75	56	South Korea	10	10
Japan	57	50	Brazil	17	9
Britain	65	46			

Source: Bureau of Labor Statistics, as reported in Alfred L. Malabre, Jr., "Gap between U.S., Foreign Wages Widens," *The Wall Street Journal,* July 17, 1985, p. 6.

been to make American exports very high priced in foreign trade. At the same time, foreign-made products are relatively inexpensive when imported and sold in the United States. Another factor contributing to the high cost of American products in world trade is the *high wage rates in the United States* relative to other countries. See Table 23-2.

However, the high value of the dollar and the high wage rates still don't get to the heart of America's trade problem. Actually, in the late 1970s the dollar was abnormally *low* in value—to the point where Europeans were very critical. They were clamoring for the United States to do something to raise the dollar's value. Yet, during those same years, the United States was also running an *unfavorable* (negative) balance in product trade.

Regarding the high-wage argument, the United States for decades has had wage rates substantially higher than the pay for similar jobs in most other countries. Yet up to the 1970s the United States still enjoyed a very favorable balance of product trade, in spite of its high wage rates. In fact, during the past 10 to 15 years the wage rates in many countries have been catching up with the United States. And some countries even surpassed the United States in some years. Yet, interestingly enough, this is the same time period which the United States has been running especially large product trade deficits.

So the root causes of America's trade problems would seem to lie somewhere other than in the high value of the dollar or the high labor costs. More fundamentally, five other factors affect our balance of trade.

- **High price of oil.** The balance-of-trade problem in the United States was compounded considerably in the mid-1970s by the dramatic (fourfold) increase in the price of oil. Even at those high prices, oil imports continued to increase both in total barrels and as a percentage of all oil used in the United States.
- **Productivity gains.** For about 20 years the United States has had one of the lowest

Foreign technology is a competitive factor in the auto market.

TABLE 23-3 PRODUCTIVITY GAINS IN MANUFACTURING AND CHANGES IN LABOR COSTS, IN SELECTED COUNTRIES, 1984

The United States had the lowest productivity gain among the seven countries, and five of the other six countries reduced their labor costs more than the United States did.

Country	Productivity gain, in %	Change in labor cost, in %
Japan	9.5	− 5.7
Sweden	6.8	+ 2.3
Italy	6.3	− 10.1
France	5.0	− 9.5
West Germany	4.7	− 11.2
Britain	3.9	− 8.4
United States	3.5	+ 0.1

Source: U.S. Labor Department, as reported in Alfred L. Malabre, Jr., "Gap between U.S., Foreign Wages Widens," *The Wall Street Journal*, July 17, 1985, p. 6.

rates of annual productivity increases among industrialized countries in the free world. In 1984, for example, the manufacturing output per worker-hour (productivity) in the United States increased only 3.5 percent—the lowest rate among seven nations. In contrast, the productivity gain that year in Japan was 9.5 percent; in Sweden it was 6.8 percent; and in Italy, 6.5 percent. See Table 23-3. To widen the gap further, five of the other six countries (in Table 23-3) experienced a significant decline in labor costs as compared with the United States. During the decade of the 1970s the same general disadvantageous (for the United States) situation prevailed regarding productivity gains.

- **State of technology.** The "technology gap" between the United States and other major industrial countries is narrowing. The United States does not enjoy the same differential advantages in this area as it did prior to the 1970s.

- **Government policies.** Government policies in foreign countries aid the export trade of those countries, more so than in America. As a case in point, domestic prices and export prices in the United States have increased at about the same rate over the past 10 to 15 years. In many foreign countries, however, the prices on exported products have not risen nearly as much as domestic prices. The question is, how are these countries able to keep down the prices on the products they export? The answer often is found in the government policies of those countries.

One such government policy stimulating exports is to *nationalize* or *subsidize* industries that cannot compete internationally on a private basis. Thus many countries have a national airline (Lufthansa, Air France, Alitalia, SAS, KLM) that is owned wholly or in part by the government. Similar situations exist in the steel, commercial aircraft, computer, and jet-engine industries. These subsidies often enable foreign producers to sell their products in the United States at prices lower than the prices of our domestic products. Sometimes exporters simply "dump" excess products in foreign markets at prices much lower than these goods would sell for at home.

The *tax structure* is another aspect of government policy that can play a significant role in international trade. Some countries impose substantial tariffs or other border taxes (as high as 30 to 40 percent) on imports of some products. Some foreign countries derive substantial revenue from indirect taxes, such as the value-added tax. These taxes are rebated when products are exported, so the products reach the United States at a lower price. In the United States, on the other hand, the main source of revenue is the income tax, which is *not* rebated for exports. So the American product is shipped abroad at a price including income tax. Then, when it reaches the foreign border, the foreign taxes are further added on. Thus the selling price of American goods in the foreign country ends up pretty high, compared with the price of a foreign product being marketed in the United States.

Government policies in many foreign countries protect domestic firms against competition from foreign imports. In Japan, for example, *import quotas*, *regulatory standards*, and *customs delays* serve to severely limit imports that would compete with Japanese industries.

At the same time, various government policies in the United States work against American companies, even though the stated policy of our government is to encourage our export trade. Antitrust and antibribery laws have resulted in the loss of much business to foreign competitors. The Foreign Corrupt Practices Act, for example, is based on good intentions. In actual practice, however, it has cost American firms a lot of business because other countries do not follow our standards. In another area, the United States is the only industrialized nation that taxes its citizens who work in foreign countries. Other United States export trade restrictions stem from policies in such areas as human rights and Russia's involvement in Poland and Afghanistan.

On the other hand, the Export Trading Company Act (1982) is a governmental effort more in the direction of supporting American companies in their foreign trade activities. This Act is an attempt to provide the legal framework for American export management companies to emulate the tremendous international marketing successes of the Japanese trading companies. This law provides complete immunity from U.S. antitrust laws for those domestic competitors who wish to participate in a joint trading company venture. By the mid–1980s, however, the concept of American trading companies still was in the developmental stage. These cooperative ventures still had not really fulfilled the expectations of business or government.[18]

● **Relative marketing capabilities.** Foreign manufacturers (especially those in Western Europe and Japan) have improved their marketing skills over the past 25 years. These producers now are aggressively and effectively competing with American firms. By being highly innovative in their product planning and by being more customer-oriented in their marketing programs, many foreign producers have been quite successful in multinational marketing.

It's tougher when you have to compete against nationalized airlines.

Some American companies have successfully penetrated foreign markets.

[18]For a discussion of American trading companies and the Export Trading Company Act, including an analysis of the type of services that export management companies currently provide for domestic producers, see Daniel C. Bello and Nicholas C. Williamson, ''The American Export Trading Company: Designing a New International Marketing Institution,'' *Journal of Marketing*, Fall 1985, pp. 60–69.

In a negative marketing sense, American companies attempting to enter foreign markets may be hampered by a country's archaic, expensive internal distribution system. In Japan, for example, a lengthy, multilevel, and very expensive distribution system is built into the culture. And it is likely to remain, because it provides jobs for many people. And, while this system is expensive for foreign marketers and extremely difficult (if not impossible) to bypass, it is also the same one that the Japanese have to use. In Japan and other countries, another significant cultural roadblock is that the people simply do not want foreigners of any kind to enter their society.[19]

At the same time, many American firms have not done an effective marketing job abroad. Too often, we have lacked the skill, the patience, and even the interest needed for export trade.

SUMMARY

Many United States companies derive a substantial share of their total sales and profits from foreign marketing operations. These multinational marketing ventures were especially profitable between World War II and the early 1970s. Since then, the situation has changed. International marketing opportunities are still abundant, but it is much more difficult and challenging to capitalize on these opportunities. Competition from foreign producers, especially firms in Japan and Western Europe, has intensified greatly.

In terms of organizational structure, the simplest way to operate in a foreign market is by exporting through foreign trade middlemen. The next stage is to export through company sales branches located in foreign countries. More sophisticated structures involve licensing a foreign manufacturer, engaging in a joint venture, or forming a wholly-owned subsidiary.

To develop an international marketing program, a company follows basically the same procedure as it uses for domestic programs. But each step along the way involves problems and operating methods that may be different for each country, and that must take into account the foreign market environment. Marketing research is more limited overseas. Product planning, pricing, distribution, and advertising all require modification based on cultures and custom—the marketing environment.

A nation's balance of international trade is of significant importance to that nation's economy. In recent years, the United States' balance of trade has been affected by the strong United States dollar, productivity in industry, policies for foreign governments, and the technological and marketing capabilities of other countries.

KEY TERMS AND CONCEPTS

Multinational economic organizations 536
"Licensing" a foreign manufacturer 538
Contract manufacturing 538
Joint venture 538
Wholly-owned foreign subsidiary 539

---

[19]For further discussion about marketing in Japan, see William Lazer, Shoji Murata, and Hiroshi Kosaka, "Japanese Marketing: Towards a Better Understanding," *Journal of Marketing*, Spring 1985, pp. 69–81; E. S. Browning, "U.S. Firms Trying to Do Business in Japan Face Government Market, Cultural Barriers," *The Wall Street Journal*, July 8, 1985, p. 14; and "Fighting Back: It Can Work," *Business Week*, Aug. 26, 1985, pp. 62–68.

Cultural differences as they affect marketing 540

Strategies for matching product and marketing communication 544

Dumping 546

Cartel 546

Pricing terms: f.o.b., f.a.s., c.i.f. 546

Currency devaluation 547

American foreign trade middlemen 547

Foreign trade middlemen located abroad 547

International balance of trade 552

QUESTIONS AND PROBLEMS

∎

1. Report on export marketing activities of companies in the state where your school is located. Consider such topics as the following. What products are exported? How many jobs are created by export marketing? What is the dollar value of exports? How does this figure compare with the value of foreign-made goods imported into the state?

2. A United States luggage-manufacturing company with annual sales over $40 million has decided to market its products in Western Europe. Evaluate the alternative structures this company should consider.

3. Select one product—manufactured or nonmanufactured—for export, and select the country to which you would like to export it. Then prepare an analysis of the market for this product in the selected country. Be sure to include the sources of information you used.

4. If there are foreign students on your campus, interview some of them to determine how their native buying habits differ from ours. Consider such patterns as when, where, and how people in their country buy. Who makes the family buying decisions?

5. Many countries unfortunately have a low literacy rate. In what ways might a company adjust its marketing program to overcome this problem?

6. Why should special attention be devoted to labeling and branding when American products are sold in foreign markets?

7. If an American company used foreign middlemen, it must usually stand ready to supply them with financial, technical, and promotional help. If this is the case, why is it not customary to bypass these middlemen and deal directly with the ultimate foreign buyers?

8. Why do American exporters normally prefer to have prices quoted in United States dollars? Why should foreign importers prefer that quotations be in the currency of their country?

9. "Prices of American products are always higher in foreign countries than at home because of the additional risks, expenses of physical distribution, and extra middlemen involved." Discuss.

10. Study the advertisements in the foreign newspapers and magazines available in your college or city library. Particularly note the advertisements for American products, and compare these with the advertisements of the same products in American newspapers and magazines. In what respect do the foreign ads differ from the domestic ads? Are there significant similarities?

11. Are United States manufacturers being priced out of world markets because of their high cost structures?

DATACORP OF VIRGINIA, INC. *

Marketing strategy in a service organization

In a meeting with his departmental managers, the president of DataCorp was wondering what marketing strategies they should adopt in order (1) to prevent any further loss of customers and (2) to replace the customers already lost. DataCorp of Virginia, Inc., was an organization that provided computerized banking services for small, independent banks. Founded in 1968 and located in Harrisonburg, Virginia, DataCorp currently served 18 banks in Virginia, West Virginia, and Maryland. Although the company was a subsidiary of the Rockingham National Bank, DataCorp's separate business philosophy was to provide service and flexibility for the independent banker.

DataCorp provided an assortment of computer services related to the following banking activities:

Savings

Installment loans

Commercial loans

Customer information file

Certificates of deposit

Automated clearing house;

paperless entry processing

Deposit system

Payroll

Amortization schedules

Depreciation schedules

General ledger

Stockholder accounting

DataCorp currently was preparing to introduce a new service that would enable the company to expand its geographic market by using telephone lines. This new service thus enabled DataCorp to reach almost anywhere and also to cut the delivery time for reports from hours to minutes.

According to the president, DataCorp was continually striving to improve its computer services, its operational reliability, and its systems flexibility. In order to compete in the field, DataCorp tried to provide the most current and useful data

*Case prepared by Sharon Gutschick and Sue Hicks, research associates, and Professor Thomas Bertsch, all at James Madison University. Reproduced with permission.

processing aids available. One big advantage for DataCorp, as opposed to in-house systems and competing data processing companies, was that it used IBM equipment and frequently updated its software systems.

The client relations department was one of nine departments in DataCorp and served as the primary company interface with all client-users (customers). This department was responsible for user training, development of user manuals, and day-to-day problem solving involving users. In addition, this department was responsible for all marketing activities including marketing research, sales to new clients, and expanding sales to existing clients.

When DataCorp first started out, the managers knew many bankers in Virginia as a result of their association with Rockingham National Bank, the parent company. Prospecting was done by making phone calls to bankers in order to set up appointments with their bank.

In connection with expanding its market area, management currently was using a direct marketing approach. Brochures were sent to banks to get them familiar with the DataCorp name and its data processing services. The banks were contacted shortly after the brochure was received to set up an appointment. A slide presentation was shown during the meeting to explain the data processing procedure. Once a bank became a customer of DataCorp, the client relations department took over the account.

The time it actually took to sell the services to an bank ranged from six months to a year. During this period, some competitors or technological changes might interfere with the sale. However, the effort and risk were worthwhile, because an established account provided a contribution to gross profit of between $5,000 and $15,000. Once the sale had been made, it took a considerable amount of time to adapt the actual work for processing. This also was a problem, because some less sophisticated data processing alternatives available to the prospective clients required less time to implement.

The president made many of the "sales" calls involved in obtaining new clients. But he was having a difficult time physically getting to them, because they now were spread out over three states—Virginia, Maryland, and West Virginia. He emphasized seeing the bank presidents himself, because he either knew them personally or had been referred to them by other bank presidents.

Some of DataCorp's customers, mainly small community banks, had merged with other banks or bank holding companies. A merger typically resulted in a change of data processing suppliers for some of the participating banks. DataCorp felt the impact of this form of competition more than any other.

Holding companies created a similar problem for DataCorp by purchasing banks and dominating their decisions concerning which data processing systems and services to use. So far, holding companies had not been a major problem for DataCorp, but they were expected to be an increasing cause of lost sales.

In the changing banking environment, the trend was toward bigger, regional-sized banks, which tended to smother the small community banks. The result was a diminishing number of small community banks, which were the major customers for DataCorp.

Another problem was that some banks previously served by companies such as DataCorp were going to in-house systems. The reasons for changing to in-house systems were apparently lower costs, easier access, and more convenience. However, those banks which had gone to in-house systems were having numerous problems, including a much-higher-than-expected cost of running the equipment and a lack of technically skilled personnel. Some banks that were previous customers of DataCorp and other services found themselves in trouble and were turning back to the use of outside services.

Technological changes can have an incredibly fast effect on the marketability of computer services. Consequently, the people of DataCorp were cautious about the future, and sales forecasts were frequently revised. However, management was sure that DataCorp could continue to thrive because of the marketing efforts of the staff and the daily contact with clients.

QUESTION

What changes in marketing strategy should DataCorp adopt in order to:

a. Slow down the loss of customers?

b. Replace lost customers with new accounts?

CASE 21

HOOVER FURNITURE RENTAL COMPANY*

Competitive strategy in a service firm

■

"I've been in this business for 10 years, but I have never seen competition as rough as it has been for the past 8 or 10 months. Those guys are either offering price concessions, or throwing in extra services, or spending a bundle on special promotions. I just don't know how they can afford such programs. But I do know this—we darned well better come up with a good competitive strategy or else we'll get killed in this market." These words were spoken by Joanna Keuffel, the owner and president of the Hoover Furniture Rental Company, to two of her executives.

The Hoover Furniture Rental Company was one of six furniture rental firms in a Midwestern metropolitan area with a population of about 1 million people. According to Ms. Keuffel, the company had an excellent reputation and was known for its good service and high-quality furniture. Hoover was the only locally owned and operated company of the six. The other five rental firms were branches of large national companies.

The Hoover Company was started about 12 years ago and had grown steadily since then. From time to time the company expanded its warehouse space and its inventory of rental furniture. Last year the gross rental income was about $1.2 million. The company had attracted over 800 new customers last year, over and above about 400 customers who had started renting from Hoover prior to last year.

The company primarily rented furniture for home use. Its stock included a full line of living room, dining room, and bedroom furniture. Lamps and paintings also were available for renting. In addition, Hoover offered a line of office furniture including several styles of desks, filing cabinets, chairs, and credenzas. The company did not carry home appliances or accessories such as dishes or linens.

Ms. Keuffel estimated that 75 percent of the furniture rental market were apartment dwellers—either condominium owners or apartment renters. The other 25 percent were home dwellers (again owners or renters) and industrial users. Industry research

*Adapted from case prepared by Michelle Stark, under the direction of Prof. William J. Stanton.

showed that furniture renters came from a broad spectrum of the population. The age range was from about 18 to 80. Two particularly good market segments were (1) people being transferred in their jobs—especially if the transfer to a given city was only a temporary move—and (2) people with limited financial resources who did not have enough capital to buy a lot of furniture.

It was generally recognized in the industry that the best way to reach the bulk of this market was through the owners or managers of the buildings. This approach was especially important in the case of apartments and condominium complexes, where one manager controlled the access to many separate housing units.

Consequently, the general promotional technique was for a representative of a furniture rental firm to contact the building manager. The furniture rep (1) explained the services offered by the rental firm, (2) left promotional brochures to be given to prospective renters, and (3) encouraged the manager to refer the housing tenants or owners to the rep's company for their furniture needs.

Beyond that general strategy, however, the different rental firms employed a variety of pricing, services, and promotional strategies. For example, some of Hoover's competitors were paying a commission to building managers for each referral they made. Obviously, this was a significant inducement for a building manager to direct potential furniture renters to the commission-paying firm.

Another strategy was for the apartment complex to set aside one "show" apartment, which a rental firm would then completely furnish at no cost to the owners of the complex. Ms. Keuffel pointed out that this amounted to removing an entire set of household furniture from inventory for an unknown period of time, and sending two employees and a truck to deliver it, set it up, and eventually pick it up—all without receiving any revenue.

Still another promotional strategy was a form of exclusive dealing. The furniture rental company agreed to provide, *free of charge*, the furniture for an office, a party room, or perhaps the manager's apartment. In return, the manager agreed to refer prospective renters only to that furniture company. The manager would not even display any literature from other rental firms.

Ms. Keuffel then noted that several pricing or promotional strategies were used when the rental company dealt directly with the renting customers. In one case, for example, after a customer had the rental furniture for 24 months, the company offered the customer an option to buy this furniture. If the customer wanted to continue renting, the company replaced the old furniture with new pieces at no increase in rental charges.

Also, a variety of competitive policies were employed regarding a security deposit. Some companies did not collect any such deposit. Others collected a deposit, but if the damage exceeded this deposit, the company did not charge for the extra damage.

One major competitor offered special deals to institutions and other industrial users. One of these industrial users, for example, was a company that rented furnished condominiums that it owned. Rather than buy the furniture, the owner of this company rented it for all the apartments. The furniture rental firm offered him a particularly attractive package deal for renting the furniture. For one price, the owner had his choice of all the offerings of the furniture rental company—whether the furniture was new or used, expensive or inexpensive.

Keuffel pointed out that the Hoover Company also engaged in variations of some of these practices. However, her company never had gone to the extreme measures adopted by some of her competitors. For example, Hoover offered package deals to industrial users, but not like the lavish (her word) deals offered by some firms. Hoover offered an option to buy after 30 months of rental. But Hoover did not offer to replace the 30-month rented furniture with new pieces. This company required a substantial security deposit and charged for delivering the furniture. It provided no free furniture for "show" apartments, no commissions for referrals, and no free furniture for building managers.

For some time now, Joanna Keuffel had been aware that the national chains operating in her market were becoming more aggressive in their marketing efforts. She believed that some of them were actually losing money in the local market. However, because they were national chain organizations, their risks were geographically spread. They could recoup in other markets whatever they might be losing in Hoover's market.

The Hoover Company had never engaged in any formal strategic planning. Keuffel felt that this was typical of most small, relatively new firms. However, she believed that the time had come for Hoover to consciously develop a marketing strategy of its own, if the company hoped to continue to operate successfully in the existing competitive environment.

QUESTION

What pricing, service, and promotional strategies should be adopted by the Hoover Company?

CASE 22

VALLEY COLLEGE*

A single-sex institution with enrollment problems

Rod Payne was appointed vice president and dean of Valley College about a year ago. During his first year, Rod, an experienced administrator, concluded that the college had some long-range problems which he should address. A few of the problems were clear-cut, but some seemed rather murky.

Valley College was founded about 1850 by local citizens who were convinced of the importance of religious education for women. Although still affiliated with its founding religious group, the school had never been sectarian, and it emphasized the importance of a liberal arts education. Since its founding, the campus had been located in a medium-sized metropolitan area in the Eastern part of the country.

Concerning the current status of the school, Rod had provided the following comments to a visiting admissions officer: "Valley is a well-established women's college; what is now referred to as a 'single-sex' institution. We have an ongoing commitment to women's higher education and this was reaffirmed by the trustees at their last meeting. The current enrollment is about 650 students. And we are naturally anxious to add to that number, to utilize our staff and plant more fully and to give us a firmer financial base for our existing programs. We have most of the problems of

---

*Case prepared by Prof. Eugene H. Fram, Rochester Institution of Technology. Used with permission.

a small private college, along with a few problems that seem to be unique to women's institutions."

One of the problems was the fact that some students were really not academically motivated. Rod was familiar with other small urban women's colleges, and he observed that the problem was more intense than usual at Valley. In the back of his mind was the notion that perhaps the program offerings were not what they should be. Currently, the school offered programs in the following fields of study:

Art and Art history
Biology
Chemistry
Comparative literature
Cooperative nursing
Drama and Speech
Economics
Education (elementary and secondary)
English
Environmental studies
Fine arts

Foreign language and literature
History
Mathematics
Medical technology
Music
Philosophy
Physics
Politics
Psychology
Religion
Sociology and Anthropology

The Valley College admissions officer had conducted a survey of first-year applicants who had been accepted by Valley last year, but who had enrolled at another school. The major reason for selecting another school was a "better program offering."

As the result of his experience during his first year at the school, Rod had concluded that the parental dependency of the student body was rather strong. This observation was supported by the fact that the majority of the students came from homes within a 75-mile radius of the college.

Rod, as dean, had deep concerns about the future of the institution. The faculty, however, did not share the intensity of Rod's concern. Most of the faculty knew that the school's plant and faculty were being used only to about 70 percent of their capacity. But the faculty were involved with their academic specialties, and they viewed this as only a modest problem. In addition, they were somewhat content with the programs offered, especially in view of their commitment to a fully liberal arts education tradition.

Another concern was that the school was not meeting the needs of the more mature student or potential student by offering continuing education courses. This was due in part to a faculty apathy toward these types of programs, and in part to the fact that the college had little experience and no tradition in this area.

One administrator even wondered if perhaps it was time for Valley College to become a coeducational institution—that is, to accept male students.

QUESTIONS

1. What course(s) of action should Valley College take to increase its enrollment?
2. How can the college identify and fill the needs of the more mature women students through continuing education?

3. How can the faculty be persuaded that continuing education is very much in keeping with the nature of the college and probably essential to its future success?

CASE 23

COOPER SUPPLY COMPANY

Distribution channel to reach a foreign market

"You know as well as I do, Ralph, that customers in Saudi Arabia, especially ARAMCO, have been our bread and butter for over 10 years. That's why I'm concerned about this new statement on procurement policy that we just received from ARAMCO. Now the Saudi government may or may not have been behind this new policy. In any case, I think we damned well better come up with the appropriate channel-of-distribution decision that will enable us to comply with this new policy. That is, if we want to continue to compete in the Saudi Arabian market." These words were spoken by Frank Broderick, the senior sales rep in the Cooper Supply Company, in a conversation with Ralph Karras the company's vice president of sales.

The Cooper Supply Company was a large independent distributor (wholesaler) of electrical supplies. The company had its main office and warehouse in Philadelphia, Pennsylvania, and a smaller office and warehouse in Houston, Texas. Since its founding in 1930, the company grew slowly but steadily until 1973, when its sales volume reached $12 million. About 25 percent of this volume was in export business, primarily to large oil companies.

Then in the mid-1970s the price of oil increased dramatically, thus stimulating the exploration and drilling for oil. This situation sharply increased the demand for products carried by Cooper Supply Company. Consequently, since 1973 Cooper's sales had increased considerably. By 1986 the company's annual sales volume was $50 million and its net profit was $5 million. Almost one-half of this business came from export sales to companies in Saudi Arabia.

Cooper Supply carried a wide variety of electrical supplies and small electrical equipment. "We represent the finest names in the industrial electrical supply and equipment industry," Karras said. "And we got there because of our reputation for honesty and integrity in an industry that often is laced with payoffs, price fixing, and price cutting."

One particular group of products was classed as explosion-proof, hazardous-application products. This type of product accounted for 50 percent of Cooper's total sales and about 80 percent of its export sales volume. These items were intended for use in hazardous environments where toxic or inflammable particles or fumes might be in the atmosphere. This class of product permitted the safe transfer of electricity without the danger of igniting volatile gases or particles.

These products included switches, circuit breakers, telephones, lighting equipment, receptacles, timers, and thermostats. Cooper also carried a complete line of these products in the non-explosion-proof category. Other products distributed by Cooper included batteries, flashlights, light bulbs, wire, conduit, transformers, fans, and electric welders.

The large number of competitors, plus the fact that an essentially similar product could be supplied by several manufacturers, made electrical supply wholesaling an intensely competitive industry with the resultant low profit margins. However, as Ralph Karras pointed out, "Typically, export customers will pay higher prices which makes the export business more lucrative and obviously very important to us. Of course, the export business is a lot more complicated and risky than is domestic selling.''

Many of Cooper's customers preferred to deal with only one electrical goods supplier in order to reduce procurement costs and also to give the buyer some influence with the supplier. Cooper easily adapted to this industrial buying pattern by being able to handle a customer's total electrical supply needs. Cooper sold to firms in a variety of industries including railroads, utilities, manufacturing, engineering, construction, federal and state government, and petroleum.

Many of Cooper's petroleum accounts were large oil companies that bought electrical merchandise in the United States for use in their foreign operations. In fact, sales to one customer alone, the Arabian-American Oil Company (ARAMCO) accounted for 30 percent ($15 million) of Cooper's sales in 1986.

ARAMCO was jointly owned by Exxon, Texaco, and Standard Oil of California, each with a 28⅓ percent interest, and Mobil with a 15 percent interest. Because the ARAMCO account was so important to the Cooper Company, Frank Broderick was greatly concerned about ARAMCO's recently issued statement regarding its procurement policy. In effect, the statement said that, starting the first of next year, all ARAMCO purchase orders exceeding $50,000 would be placed either (a) through a Saudi Arabian national or (b) through agents or companies based in Saudi Arabia. That is, ARAMCO would no longer place orders directly with Cooper or other foreign-based suppliers.

The reason stated for the new policy was ARAMCO's dissatisfaction with the situation in which so much capital was leaving Saudi Arabia without adequately benefiting the country. In view of this line of reasoning, Broderick also believed that other large Cooper customers in Saudi Arabia would soon adopt a similar purchasing policy.

Despite its rapid growth since the mid-1970s, Cooper Supply still had only 10 outside sales reps and another 10 who comprised the inside sales force. The outside sales people called on customers' offices in the United States, even though many of the orders were shipped to foreign locations. The inside sales force handled all inquiries, mail orders, and telephone orders. Ralph Karras preferred to limit the size of his sales force. He wanted Cooper Supply to retain the image of being a medium-sized company that offered personalized service and quick delivery in competition with its larger competitors.

Several weeks before receiving ARAMCO's statement, Karras had received a proposal from a Saudi Arabian agent offering to represent Cooper Supply in Saudi Arabia. Karras responded to the agent's letter, saying that Cooper would study the proposal and reply within a reasonable period of time. In fact, Karras had been wondering how to respond to the Saudi's proposal when he (Karras) received the ARAMCO notice.

The proposed agency agreement was to cover a period of 3 years, and was subject to renewal in 3-year time segments. The agent would receive a commission of 2 percent on all orders shipped to Saudi Arabia. This commission was to be paid even if the agent had not been instrumental in soliciting the business or obtaining the order. In return, the agent would (1) supply local sales people in Saudi Arabia, (2) provide contacts with potential customers, and (3) use its good reputation to solicit inquiries and orders for Cooper Supply. The agent also enclosed supporting letters of recommendation from ARAMCO and Saudi government officials who approved of this agent.

Ralph Karras was discussing the agent's proposal and the ARAMCO statement with Frank Broderick. Broderick pointed out that Cooper's annual sales to ARAMCO alone amounted to $15 million, and another $8 to $10 million came from sales to other Saudi Arabian construction projects. On the ARAMCO sales alone the agent's 2 percent commission would amount to $300,000. "And that assumes that the agent can sell at least as much as we've been selling to ARAMCO from our United States offices," Broderick stated.

"I don't like this agent's deal at all," Frank continued. "We tie ourselves up in an exclusive-agency contract for 3 years. That makes us vulnerable if the guy turns out to be ineffective. Competition could kill us during that period. I think we simply ought to open our own sales office in Saudi land—either in Riyadh or in Jiddah. In that way we'd have our own people on the scene. We would avoid paying an agent's commission. We would get better market coverage and still be operating within the terms of the new ARAMCO policy."

"Frank, I'm a little leery of the financial and personnel commitment involved in establishing our own sales office over there," countered Karras. "Salaries and expenses could cost us a bundle, and with no guarantee of success. Maybe we can open an office some time in the future, but for now this agency proposal maybe is our best bet. The guy comes highly recommended, and his 2 percent fee won't put our bids above competitive level. And he will know the territory better than we do. As you well know, the hardest part of obtaining business over there is to make the initial contact—that is, to obtain inquiries from prospective accounts."

"I really don't know which way to go," concluded Karras. "Maybe there is a better alternative that we are overlooking. All I do know is that we have to do something and do it soon."

QUESTION

What channel of distribution should the Cooper Supply Company use to reach the Saudi Arabian market?

IMPLEMENTING
AND
EVALUATING
THE
MARKETING
EFFORT

Implementing a company's marketing
program, evaluating the marketing
performance of a company, and
appraising the role of marketing
in our society

Up to this point in the book, we have
dealt primarily with the selection of target markets and with the development
and management of the four segments
of the marketing mix in an individual
organization.

Now it is time to tie things together—to take an overview of the
firm's *total* marketing program, thus integrating the separate elements of the
marketing mix. Our approach in Part 8
will be to apply the *implementation* and
evaluation aspects of the management
process to the *total* marketing program.
Marketing implementation and evaluation in the individual firm are covered in
Chapter 23. Then in Chapter 24 we appraise the current position of marketing
in the American socioeconomic system.

24

MARKETING IMPLEMENTATION AND PERFORMANCE EVALUATION

CHAPTER GOALS

This chapter is concerned with two parts of the management of a company's total marketing program—implementation and evaluation. After studying this chapter, you should understand:

- The importance of the implementation stage in the management process.
- The relationship among strategic planning, implementation, and performance evaluation.
- Organizational structures typically used to implement marketing effort.
- Importance of good selection.
- Significance of delegation, coordination, motivation, and communication in the implementation process.
- The concept of a marketing audit as a complete evaluation program.
- The meaning of misdirected marketing effort.
- Sales-volume analysis.
- Marketing cost analysis.

managed good, but boy did they play bad.'' This title from an article many years ago in *Sports Illustrated* may not be excellent grammar, but it surely communicates its message. The coaches (management) of the Denver Broncos professional football team prepare a strategic plan—called a game plan—for every one of its games. When the Broncos win a game, often the coaches will say that the team executed well. If the team loses the game, you will hear that the team failed to execute. That is, the team had a strategic plan but failed to carry it out—to execute it or implement it.

Then a day or two later the coaches will study the game films in great detail. In effect, management is evaluating the team's performance as well as the performance of each individual player. This same process of planning, implementing, and performance evaluating can occur in any competitive situation, including marketing by an organization.

In Chapter 3 we defined the management process in marketing as planning, implementing, and evaluating the marketing effort in an organization. See Fig. 24-1, which is a repeat of Fig. 3-1. Most of this book has dealt with the *planning* of a marketing program. We discussed the selection of target markets and the strategic design of a program to deliver want-satisfaction to those markets. This program was built around the components of a strategic marketing mix—the product, price structure, distribution system, and promotional program.

Now we are ready to devote a chapter to the implementation and evaluation stages of the management process in marketing. The implementation stage is the operational stage—the stage during which an organization attempts to carry out (that is, implement or execute) its strategic plan.

At the end of an operating period (or even during the period), management needs to evaluate the organization's performance. In this way management can determine

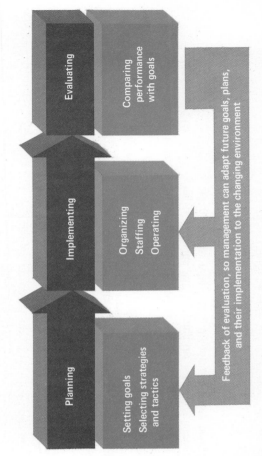

FIGURE 24-1

The management process in marketing systems.

Plans are implemented, and performance results are evaluated to provide information used to plan for the future. The process is continuous and allows for adapting to changes in the environment.

how effectively the organization is achieving the goals set in the strategic planning phase of the management process.

IMPLEMENTATION AND PLANNING INTERRELATIONSHIPS

Obviously there is a close relationship between planning and implementation in the management process. Without planning, a company's operational activities—its implementation—can go off in any direction like an unguided missile. At this point, however, we focus on implementation simply because it ordinarily receives so little attention. Much has been written about strategic planning, but very little has been said about *implementing* these strategies.

No matter how good the strategic planning may be in an organization, it is virtually useless if these plans are not carried out in action—that is, aren't implemented or executed. Stated another way, good planning cannot overcome poor implementation, but effective implementation very often can overcome poor planning or inappropriate strategies.

MARKETING IMPLEMENTATION

In the 1970s and on into the early 1980s, there was a tremendous interest in strategic planning, sparked primarily by some of the leading management consulting firms. Then as we progressed through the 1980s, disenchantment with strategic planning really set in. This cooling off occurred as many companies came to realize that strategic *planning* alone was not enough to ensure a company's success. *These plans had to be effectively implemented.* Management began to realize that the planners were great at telling us *what* to do—that is, designing a strategy. But the planners often came up short with *how* to do it—that is, how to implement the strategy. [1]

"Too often these hot-shot planners could not sell a pair of shoes to a guy who is standing barefooted on a very hot sidewalk with a $50 bill in his hand."

Organizing for Implementation Activities

The implementation stage in the marketing management process includes three broad areas of activity. They are (1) organizing for the marketing effort; (2) staffing this organization; and (3) directing the operational efforts of these people as they carry out the strategic plans.

The first major activity in implementing a company's strategic planning is to organize the people who will be doing the actual implementation work. We must establish an organizational relationship among marketing and the other major functional areas in

[1] See Walter Kiechel III, "Corporate Strategists Under Fire," *Fortune*, Dec. 27, 1982, pp. 34–39; and "The Future Catches Up with a Strategic Planner," *Business Week*, June 27, 1983.

a firm. And, within the marketing department, we must decide on the form of organization that will most effectively aid our implementation efforts.

COMPANY-WIDE ORGANIZATION

In Chapter 1 we stated that one of the three foundation stones of the marketing concept was to organizationally coordinate all marketing activities. In firms that are production-oriented or sales-oriented, typically we find that marketing activities are fragmented. A sales force is quite separate from advertising; physical distribution is handled in the production department; sales training may be under the personnel department, etc.

In a marketing-oriented enterprise all marketing activities are coordinated under one chief marketing executive who typically is at the vice presidential level. This executive reports directly to the president and is on an equal organizational footing with the chief executives in finance, production, and the other major functional areas of the firm. See Fig. 24-2. Under the chief marketing executive, the marketing activities may be grouped into line activities and staff activities. In most firms the chief line activity is personal selling. The supporting staff activities include advertising, marketing research, sales promotion, sales analysis, sales training, and others.

ORGANIZATION WITHIN THE MARKETING DEPARTMENT

Within the marketing department—especially in medium-sized or large firms—the sales force frequently is specialized in some organizational fashion. This is done in order to implement more effectively the company's strategic planning. One of three forms of organizational specialization of line authority typically is adopted. The sales

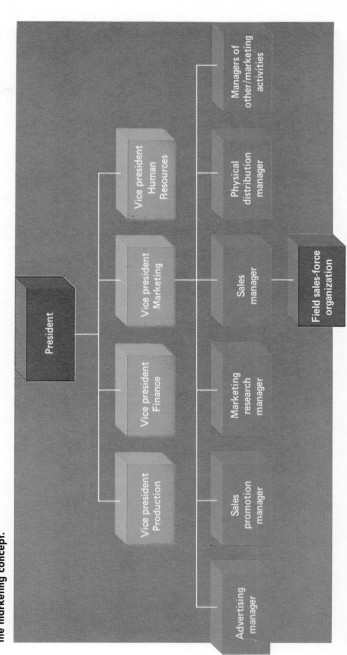

FIGURE 24-2
Company organization embracing the marketing concept.

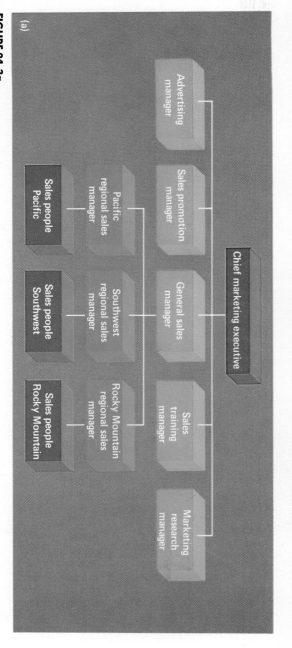

(a)

FIGURE 24-3a
Sales organization specialized by geographic territories.

force may be organized by geographical territory, by product line, or by customer type. In very large companies, sometimes other marketing activities such as advertising or sales promotion also are organizationally specialized in one of these same three categories.

Geographical specialization Probably the most widely used method of specializing selling activities is to organize a sales force on the basis of geographical territories. Under this type of organization, each sales person is assigned a specific geographical area—called a *territory*—in which to sell. Several sales people representing contiguous territories typically are placed under a territorial sales executive who reports directly to the general sales manager. These territorial executives usually are called *district* or *regional* sales managers. See Fig. 24-3a.

A territorial organization usually ensures better implementation of sales strategies in each local market and better control over the sales force. Customers can be serviced quickly and effectively, and local sales reps can respond better to competitors' actions in a given territory.

Product specialization Another commonly used basis for organizing a sales force is some form of product specialization. To illustrate, a company may divide all of its products into three lines. Then one group of sales reps will sell only the products in line A. All sales people in group A will report to a sales manager for product A, who in turn will report to a general sales manager.

This type of organization is especially well suited for companies that are marketing:

- A variety of complex technical products—electronics.
- Dissimilar or unrelated products—luggage, folding chairs, and toy building blocks.
- Many thousands of items—hardware wholesale.

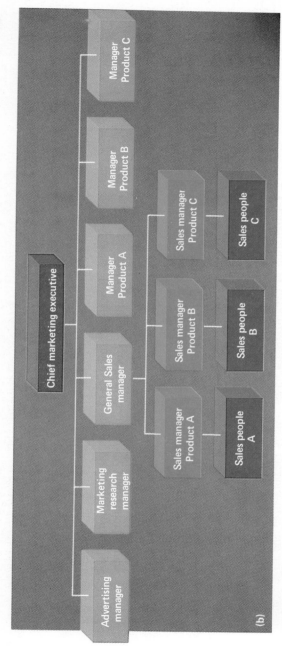

FIGURE 24-3b
Sales organization specialized by product.

The main advantage of this form of organization is the specialized attention each product line can get from the sales force. A potential drawback may occur if more than one sales rep from a company calls on the same customer. This duplication of effort not only is costly but also may irritate the customers.

A variation of product specialization is the use of the product-manager concept that we discussed back in Chapter 9. These people each are given the responsibility of planning and developing a marketing program for a separate group of products. They report to the chief marketing executive. Typically a product manager has no

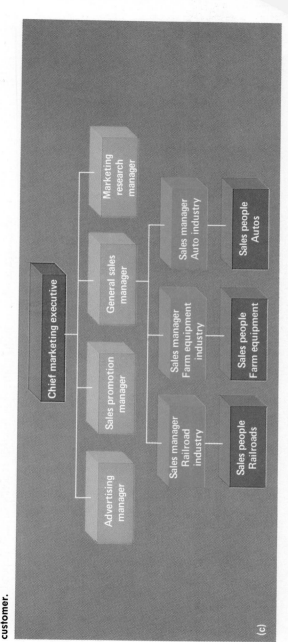

FIGURE 24-3c
Sales organization specialized by customer.

direct authority over a sales force, but acts only in an advisory relationship with the sales force and the line sales executives. See Fig. 24-3b.

Customer specialization   Many companies today have divided their sales departments on the basis of type of customer. Customers may be grouped either by type of industry or by channel of distribution. Thus, an oil company may divide its markets into such industry customer groups as the railroads, auto manufacturers, farm equipment producers, etc. See Fig. 24-3c. A firm that specializes its sales operations by channel of distribution may have one sales force selling to wholesalers and another that deals directly with large retailers.

As more companies fully implement the marketing concept, customer-specialization organization is likely to increase. Certainly the basis of customer specialization is commensurate with the customer-oriented philosophy that underlies the marketing concept. That is, the organizational emphasis is on the customers and markets rather than on products.

Combination of organizational bases   Many medium-sized and large companies typically combine a territorial sales organization structure with one of either product or customer specialization. Thus, a hardware wholesaler operating out of a home base in Chicago may establish geographical sales districts for its sales reps. This same sales force also may be divided on a product basis. Consequently, in the one sales district that covers Eastern Iowa and Northwestern Illinois, there may be two or three of this company's sales reps. Each of these people will be selling a different group of this wholesaler's products.

Staffing the Organization

A key step in implementing strategic planning in an organization is to staff the organization—that is, to select the people who will be doing the actual implementation work. *Of all the specific stages in the management process, in your authors' opinion, selection of people is the most important.* We strongly believe this to be true regardless of what organization is being staffed. A football coach's success depends to a great extent upon his ability to recruit the right players. A political party's success depends upon its ability to select the candidate who will attract the most votes. Your career success will depend in great measure upon your ability to pick the right organization (and people) to work with. A sales manager's success depends to a great extent upon the sales people whom the manager selects. Those of you who now are single will learn that your happiness and success in life depends to a great degree upon the person whom you select as a lifetime mate.

Yes, selection is critically important in *any* organization! And that's why it is such a tragedy that most people do a lousy job in recruiting and selection. Most of us don't know how to pick people—to judge people for the position being filled.

Now let's come back more specifically to the task of implementing a strategic marketing program and the selection of the people who do this job. In most marketing organizations the implementation task is done largely by the sales force. So let's identify the reasons why it is important to have a good program for selecting sales people.

- Good sales people are often hard to find—that is, there is a scarcity of qualified recruits.

- Within limits, any manager is no better than the people working under him. And managers are judged by the way their subordinates perform.
- A good selection job makes other managerial tasks easier. Well-selected workers are easier to train, supervise, and motivate.
- Good selection typically reduces the turnover rate with all its attendant costs.
- In summary, well-selected sales people will do a better job of carrying out management's strategic plans.

Managing the Marketing Operations

The third broad activity included in the implementation stage of the management process involves actually directing and operating a marketing program. This activity is the guts of the entire implementation process. This is where these strategic plans are actually carried out. This is where the revenue-generating activity occurs in the firm. This is where management directs the efforts of the people who earlier were selected and organized.

The guidelines for operating the marketing-mix components (product, price, distribution, promotion) are probably pretty well set by virtue of the strategic marketing plan. Now it is up to the operating executives in the marketing department to follow these guidelines in practice. The key to success in this stage depends upon how well the executives have put into practice four concepts involving people and the management of these people. These four concepts are delegation, coordination, motivation, and communication.

DELEGATION

Very often much of an executive's success is measured by his or her ability to delegate authority and responsibility in an effective manner. Executives who try to do everything themselves—who for some reason are reluctant to delegate—invariably fail to maximize the potential of their programs or their subordinates in the company.

COORDINATION

Effective coordination will bring about a synergy in the organization whereby the people working together will accomplish more than if they go off on their own in a rudderless fashion. Sales peoples' efforts should be coordinated with the media advertising activities. New-product introduction needs to be coordinated with the physical distribution of this product and the middlemen must be prepared to handle the new product.

MOTIVATION

The success enjoyed by a leader of people in any field—athletics, education, politics, the military, business—is greatly dependent upon that leader's ability to motivate his or her people. Here we can consider economic motivation in the form of monetary payments as well as psychological motivation in the form of nonmonetary rewards.

COMMUNICATION

Finally, all these implementation activities will come together in an effective manner only if the executives involved do an effective job of communicating with their workers. In early chapters we spoke often about effectively communicating with our markets. Now we are concerned with doing a good job of internal communication. It is imperative that an organization maintain open communication channels both upward and downward in the company's hierarchy. Management must communicate with the sales people, and these reps must have an open channel to communicate upward to management. Unfortunately, often it is easier to say these things than to do them. Companies spend untold sums of money to improve the communication abilities of their executives, but the workers often still misunderstand management's messages. Yet this is no reason to stop trying. We all must continue to try to improve our abilities to send and to receive the intended messages through the channels in a communication system.[2]

EVALUATING MARKETING PERFORMANCE

As soon as possible after a firm's plans have been set in operation, the process of evaluation should begin. Without evaluation, management cannot tell whether its plan is working and what the reasons are for success or failure. Planning and evaluation thus are interrelated activities. Evaluation logically follows planning and the execution of the plan. That is, planning sets forth what *should be* done, and evaluation shows what *really was* done. Sometimes a circular relationship exists: Plans are made, they are put into action, the operational results are evaluated, and new plans are prepared on the basis of this appraisal. See Fig. 24-4.

Previously we have discussed evaluation as it relates to individual parts of a marketing program—the product-planning process, the performance of the sales force, and the effectiveness of the advertising program, for instance. At this point, let's look at the evaluation of the *total marketing effort*.

The Marketing Audit: A Total Evaluation Program

A marketing audit is the essential element of a total evaluation program.[3] An audit implies a review and an evaluation of some activity. Thus, a **marketing audit** is a systematic, comprehensive, periodic review and evaluation of the marketing function in an organization—its marketing goals, strategies, and performance.

Obviously, a complete audit is an extensive and difficult project. But the rewards from a marketing audit can be great. Management can identify its problem areas in marketing. By reviewing its strategies, the firm is likely to keep abreast of its changing marketing environment. Successes can also be analyzed, so the company can capitalize on its strong points. The audit can spot lack of coordination in the marketing program, outdated strategies, or unrealistic goals. The audit allows management to correctly anticipate future situations. It is intended for "prognosis as well as diagnosis. . . . It is the practice of preventive as well as curative marketing medicine."[4]

FIGURE 24-4
The circular relationship among management tasks.

EVALUATION

PLANNING

IMPLEMENTATION

---

[2]For some guidelines to aid in identifying implementation difficulties and some suggestions for remedying them, see Thomas V. Bonoma, "Making Your Marketing Strategy Work," *Harvard Business Review*, March–April 1984, pp. 69–76.

[3]See *Analyzing and Improving Marketing Performance*: "Marketing Audits" in Theory and Practice, American Management Association, Management Report no. 32, New York, 1959; see especially Abe Schuchman, "The Marketing Audit: Its Nature, Purpose, and Problems," pp. 11–19; and Alfred R. Oxenfeldt, "The Marketing Audit as a Total Evaluation Program," pp. 25–36.

[4]Schuchman, ibid., p. 14.

Misdirected Marketing Effort

One of the primary benefits of evaluation activities is that they can help correct misdirected or misplaced marketing effort.

THE "80-20" PRINCIPLE

A company does not enjoy the same rate of net profit on every individual sale. In most firms a large proportion of the orders, customers, territories, or products account for only a small share of the profit. This relationship between selling units and profit has been characterized as the "80-20" principle. That is, 80 percent of the orders, customers, territories, or products contribute only 20 percent of the sales or profit. Conversely, 20 percent of these selling units account for 80 percent of the volume or profit. The 80-20 figure is used simply to epitomize the misplacement of marketing efforts. Actually, of course, the percentage split varies from one situation to another.

The basic reason for the 80-20 situation is that almost every marketing program includes some misdirected effort. Marketing efforts and costs are proportional to the *number* of territories, customers, or products, rather than to their actual sales volume or profit. For example, in a department store, approximately the same order-filling, billing, and delivery expenses are involved whether a mink coat or a necktie is sold. Or a manufacturer may assign one sales person to each territory. Yet there may be substantial differences in the potential volume and profit from the various territories. In each case, the marketing effort (cost) is not in line with the potential return.

REASONS FOR MISDIRECTED MARKETING EFFORT

Many executives are unaware of the misdirected marketing effort in their firms. They do not know what percentage of total sales and profit comes from a given product line or customer group. Frequently executives cannot uncover their misdirection of effort because they lack sufficiently detailed information. The analogy of an iceberg in an open sea has been used to illustrate this situation. Only a small part of an iceberg is visible above the surface of the water, and the submerged 90 percent is the dangerous part. The figures representing total sales or total costs on an operating statement are like the visible part of an iceberg. The detailed figures representing sales, costs, and other performance measures for each territory or product correspond to the important and dangerous submerged segment.

The dangerous part lies beneath the surface.

Computers are a big help in the evaluation process.

Total sales or costs as presented on an operating statement are too general to be useful in evaluation. In fact, the total figures are often inconclusive and misleading. More than one company has shown satisfactory overall sales and profit figures. But when these totals were subdivided by territory or products, serious weaknesses were discovered. A manufacturer of rubber products showed an overall annual increase of 12 percent in sales and 9 percent in net profit on one product line one year. But management wasn't satisfied with this "tip of the iceberg." When it analyzed the figures more closely, it found that the sales change within territories ranged from an increase of 19 percent to a decrease of 3 percent. In some territories, profits increased as much as 14 percent, and in others, they were down 20 percent.

An even more important cause of misplaced marketing effort is the fact that executives must make decisions based on inadequate knowledge of the exact nature of marketing costs. In other words, management lacks knowledge of (1) the disproportionate spread of marketing effort; (2) reliable standards for determining what should be spent on marketing; and (3) what results should be expected from these expenditures.

As an illustration, a company may spend $250,000 more on advertising this year than last year. But management ordinarily cannot state what the resultant increase in sales volume or profit should be. Nor do the executives know what would have happened if they had spent the same amount on (1) new-product development, (2) management training seminars for middlemen, or (3) some other aspect of the marketing program.[5]

The Evaluation Process

The evaluation process—whether in the form of a complete marketing audit or only an appraisal of individual components of the marketing program—is essentially a three-stage task. In the evaluation process, management's job is as follows:

1. Find out *what* happened—get the facts; compare actual results with budgeted goals to determine where they differ.
2. Find out *why* it happened—determine what specific factors in the marketing program accounted for the results.
3. Decide *what to do* about it—plan the next period's program and activities so as to improve on unsatisfactory performance and capitalize on the things that were done well.

One effective way to evaluate a total marketing program is to analyze the performance results. To do this, two useful tools are available—the sales-volume analysis and the marketing cost analysis. These tools are illustrated in the next two sections.

Our discussion of sales-volume and marketing cost analyses is built around the Great Western Company (GW)—a hypothetical firm that markets office furniture. This company's 13-state Western market is divided into four sales districts, each with seven or eight sales people and a district sales manager. The company sells to office equipment wholesalers and directly to large industrial users. Great Western's products

[5] For some ideas on how to correct an 80-20 situation of misdirected marketing effort, see Alan J. Dubinsky and Richard W. Hansen, "Improving Marketing Productivity: The 80/20 Principle Revisited," *California Management Review*, Fall 1982, pp. 96–105.

mix is divided into four groups—desks, chairs, filing equipment, and accessories (wastebaskets, desk sets, etc.). Some of these products are manufactured by Great Western, and some are purchased from other firms.

ANALYSIS OF SALES VOLUME

A **sales-volume analysis** is a detailed study of the "net sales" section of a company's profit and loss statement (its operating statement). Management should analyze its *total* sales volume, and its volume by *product lines* and by *market segments* (territories, customer groups). These sales should be compared with company goals and with industry sales.

Sales Results versus Sales Goals

We start with an analysis of Great Western's total sales volume, as shown in Table 24-1. The company's annual sales doubled (from $18 million to $36 million) during the 10-year period ending in 1986. Furthermore, they increased each year over the preceding year, with the exception of 1983. In most of these years the company met or surpassed its planned sales goals. Thus far, the company's situation is very encouraging. When industry sales figures are introduced for comparison, however, the picture changes. But let's hold the industry-comparison analysis until the next section.

A study of total sales volume alone is usually insufficient, and maybe even misleading, because of the workings of the iceberg principle. To learn what is going on in the "submerged" segments of the market, we need to analyze sales volume by market segments—sales territories, for example.

Table 24-2 is a summary of the planned sales goals and the actual sales results in Great Western's four sales districts. A key measurement figure is the *performance percentage*—the actual sales divided by the sales goal. A performance percentage of 100 means that the district did exactly what was expected of it. Thus, from the table

TABLE 24-1	ANNUAL SALES VOLUME OF GREAT WESTERN COMPANY, INDUSTRY VOLUME, AND COMPANY'S SHARE IN 13-STATE MARKET

Year	Company volume (in millions of dollars)	Industry volume in company's market (in millions of dollars)	Company's percentage share of market
1986	36.0	300	12.0
1985	34.7	275	12.6
1984	33.1	255	13.0
1983	30.4	220	13.8
1982	31.7	235	13.5
1981	28.0	200	14.0
1980	24.5	170	14.4
1979	22.5	155	14.5
1978	21.8	150	14.8
1977	18.0	120	15.0

TABLE 24-2   DISTRICT SALES VOLUME IN GREAT WESTERN COMPANY, 1986

District	Sales goals (in millions of dollars)	Actual sales (in millions of dollars)	Performance percentage (actual ÷ goal)	Dollar variation (in millions)
A	10.8	12.5	116	+1.7
B	9.0	9.6	107	+ .6
C	7.6	7.7	101	+ .1
D	8.6	6.2	72	−2.4
Total	$36.0	$36.0		

we see that B and C did just a little better than was expected. District A passed its goal by a wide margin, but district D was quite a disappointment.

So far in our evaluation process, we know a little about *what* happened in GW'S districts. Now management has to figure out *why* it happened, and what should be done about it. These are the difficult steps in evaluation. In the GW situation, the executives need to determine why district D did so poorly. The fault may lie in some aspect of the marketing program, or competition may be especially strong there. They also should find out what accounts for district A's success, and whether this information can be used in the other regions.

This brief examination of two aspects of sales-volume analysis shows how this evaluation tool may be used. In a real business situation, GW's executives should go *much* further. They should analyze their sales volume by individual territories within districts and by product lines. Then they should carry their territorial analysis further by examining volume by product line and customer group *within* each territory. For instance, even though district A did well overall, the iceberg principle may be at work *within* the district. The fine *total* performance in district A may be covering up weaknesses in an individual product line or territory.

Comparing a company's sales results with its goal certainly is a useful form of performance evaluation. But it does not tell how the company is doing relative to its competitors. We need to compare the company's sales with the industry's sales. In effect, we should analyze, preferably in some detail, the company's share of the market. That is, we should analyze its market share in total, and also by product line and market segment.

Probably the major obstacle encountered in market-share analysis is in obtaining the industry sales information in total, and in the desired detail. Trade associations and government agencies are excellent sources for industry sales-volume statistics in many fields.

The Great Western situation is a good example of the usefulness of market-share analysis. Recall from Table 24-1 that GW's total sales doubled over a 10-year period, with annual increases in 9 of those years. *But*, during this decade, the industry's annual sales increased from $120 million to $300 million (a 250 percent increase). Thus, the company's share of this market actually *declined* from 15 to 12 percent.

Market-Share Analysis

Although the company's annual sales increased 100 percent, its market share declined 20 percent.

The next step is to determine *why* Great Western's market position declined. The number of possible causes is almost limitless, and this is what makes management's task so difficult. A weakness in almost any aspect of Great Western's product line, distribution system, pricing structure, or promotional program may have contributed to the loss of market share. It may be that the real culprit is competition. There may be new competitors in the market who were attracted by the rapid growth rates. Or competitor's marketing programs may be more effective than Great Western's.

MARKETING COST ANALYSIS

An analysis of sales volume is quite useful in evaluating and controlling a company's marketing effort. A volume analysis, however, does not tell us anything about the *profitability* of this effort. Management needs to conduct a marketing cost analysis to determine the relative profitability of its territories, product lines, or other marketing units. A marketing cost analysis is a detailed study of the operating expense section of a company's profit and loss statement. As part of this analysis, management may establish budgetary goals, and then study the variations between budgeted costs and actual expenses.

Types of Marketing Cost Analyses

A company's marketing costs may be analyzed:

1. As they appear in the ledger accounts and on the profit and loss statement.
2. After they are grouped into functional (also called activity) classifications.
3. After these activity costs have been allocated to territories, products, or other marketing units.

ANALYSIS OF LEDGER EXPENSES

The simplest and least expensive marketing cost analysis is a study of the "object of expenditure" costs as they appear in the firm's profit and loss statement. These figures, in turn, come from the company's accounting ledger records. The simplified operating statement for the Great Western Company on the left side of Table 24-3 is the model we shall use in this discussion.

The procedure is simply to analyze each cost item (salaries, media space, etc.) in some detail. We can compare this period's total with the totals for similar periods in the past, and observe the trends. We can compare actual results with budgeted expense goals. We should also compute each expense as a percentage of net sales. Then, if possible, we should compare these expense ratios with industry figures, which are often available through trade associations.

ANALYSIS OF FUNCTIONAL EXPENSES

For more effective control of marketing costs, they should be allocated among the various marketing functions, such as advertising or warehousing. Then management can analyze the expenses of each of these activities.

The procedure here is to select the appropriate groups, and then to allocate each ledger expense among those activities. (See the expense distribution sheet on the right-

TABLE 24-3 PROFIT AND LOSS STATEMENT AND DISTRIBUTION OF NATURAL EXPENSES TO ACTIVITY COST GROUPS, GREAT WESTERN COMPANY, 1986

Profit and loss statement ($000)		Expense distribution sheet ($000)				
		Activity (functional) cost groups				
		Personal selling	Advertising	Warehousing and shipping	Order processing	Marketing administration
Net sales	$36,000					
Cost of goods sold	23,400					
Gross margin	12,600					
Operating expenses:						
Salaries and commissions	$2,710	$1,200	$ 240	$ 420	$280	$ 570
Travel and entertainment	1,440	1,040				400
Media space	1,480		1,480			
Supplies	440	60	35	240	70	35
Property taxes	130	16	5	60	30	19
Freight out	3,500			3,500		
Total expenses	9,700	$2,316	$1,760	$4,220	$380	$1,024
Net profit	$2,900					

hand side of Table 24-3.) In our Great Western example, we have decided on five activity cost groups. Some items, such as the cost of media space, can be apportioned directly to one activity (advertising). For other expenses, the cost can be prorated only after management has established some reasonable basis for allocation. Property taxes, for instance, may be allocated according to the proportion of the total floor space that is occupied by each department. Thus, the warehouse accounts for 46 percent of the total area (square feet) of floor space in the firm, so the warehousing-shipping function is charged with $60,000 (46 percent) of the property taxes.

A functional cost analysis gives executives more information than they can get from an analysis of ledger accounts alone. Also, an analysis of activity expenses in total provides an excellent starting point for management to analyze costs by territories, products, or other marketing units.

ANALYSIS OF FUNCTIONAL COSTS BY MARKET SEGMENTS

The third and most beneficial type of marketing cost analysis is a study of the costs and profitability of each segment of the market. Common practice in this type of analysis is to divide the market by territories, products, customer groups, or order sizes. Cost analysis by market segment enables management to pinpoint trouble spots much more effectively than does an analysis of either ledger-account expenses or activity costs.

By combining a sales-volume analysis with a marketing cost study, a researcher can prepare a complete operating statement for each of the product or market segments. These individual statements can then be analyzed to determine the effectiveness of the marketing program as related to each of those segments.

TABLE 24-4   ALLOCATION OF ACTIVITY COSTS TO SALES DISTRICTS, GREAT WESTERN COMPANY, 1986

Activity	Personal selling	Advertising	Warehousing and shipping	Order processing	Marketing administration
		Allocation scheme			
Allocation basis	Direct expense to each district	Number of pages of advertising	Number of orders to be shipped	Number of invoice lines	Equally among districts
Total activity cost	$2,316,000	$1,760,000	$4,220,000	$380,000	$1,024,000
Number of allocation units		88 pages	10,550 orders	126,667 lines	4 districts
Cost per allocation unit		$20,000	$400	$3	$256,000
		Allocation of costs			
District A < units / cost	$650,000	27 pages / $540,000	3,300 orders / $1,320,000	46,000 lines / $138,000	one / $256,000
District B < units / cost	$606,000	19 pages / $380,000	2,850 orders / $1,140,000	33,000 lines / $99,000	one / $256,000
District C < units / cost	$540,000	22 pages / $440,000	2,300 orders / $1,920,000	26,667 lines / $80,000	one / $256,000
District D < units / cost	$520,000	20 pages / $400,000	2,100 orders / $840,000	21,000 lines / $63,000	one / $256,000

The procedure for making a cost analysis by market segments is similar to that used to analyze functional (activity) expenses. The total of each activity cost (in the right-hand part of Table 24-3) is prorated on some basis to each product or market segment being studied. Let's walk through an example of a cost analysis, by sales districts, for the Great Western Company, as shown in Tables 24-4 and 24-5.

First, for each of the five GW activities, we select an allocation basis for distributing the cost of that activity among the four districts. (See the top part of Table 24-4.) Then we determine the number of allocation "units" that make up each activity cost, and we find the cost per unit. This completes the allocation scheme, which tells us how to allocate costs to the four districts:

- Personal selling activity expenses pose no problem because they are direct expenses, chargeable to the district in which they are incurred.
- We allocate advertising expenses on the basis of the number of the pages of advertising that were run in each district. Great Western purchased the equivalent of 88 pages of advertising during the year, at an average cost of $20,000 per page ($1,760,000 ÷ 88).
- Warehousing and shipping expenses are allocated on the basis of the number of orders shipped. Since 10,550 orders were shipped during the year at a total activity cost of $4,220,000, the cost per order is $400.
- Order-processing expenses are allocated according to the number of invoice lines typed during the year. Since there were 126,667 lines, then the cost per line is $3.
- The marketing administration—a totally indirect expense—is divided equally among the four districts, with each district being allocated $256,000.

The final step is to calculate the amount of each activity cost to be allocated to each district. The results are shown in the bottom part of Table 24-4. We see that $650,000 of personal selling expenses were charged directly to district A, $606,000 to district B, and similarly to districts C and D. Regarding advertising, the equivalent of 27 pages of advertising was run in district A, so that district is charged with $520,000 (27 pages × $20,000 per page). Similar calculations provide advertising activity cost allocations of $380,000 to district B, $440,000 to district C, and $400,000 to D.

Regarding warehousing and shipping expenses, 3,300 orders were shipped to customers in district A, at a unit allocation cost of $400 per order, for a total allocated cost of $1,320,000. Warehousing and shipping charges are allocated to the other three districts as shown in Table 24-4.

To allocate order-processing expenses, management determined that 46,000 invoice lines went to customers in district A. At $3 per line (the cost per allocation unit), district A is charged with $138,000. Allocations to the other districts are shown in Table 24-4. Finally, each district is charged with $256,000 for marketing administration expenses.

After the activity costs have been allocated among the four districts, we can prepare a profit and loss statement for each district. These statements are shown in Table 24-5. The sales volume for each district is determined from the sales-volume analysis (Table 24-2). The cost of goods sold and gross margin for each district is obtained by assuming that the company gross margin of 35 percent ($12,600,000 ÷ $36,000,000) was maintained in each district.

Table 24-5 now shows, for each district, what the company profit and loss statement shows for the overall company operations. For example, we note that district

TABLE 24-5 PROFIT AND LOSS STATEMENTS FOR SALES DISTRICTS ($000), GREAT WESTERN COMPANY, 1986

	Total	District A	District B	District C	District D
Net sales	$36,000	$12,500	$9,600	$7,700	$6,200
Cost of goods sold	23,400	8,125	6,240	5,005	4,030
Gross margin	12,600	4,375	3,360	2,695	2,170
Operating expenses:					
Personal selling	2,316	650	606	540	520
Advertising	1,760	540	380	440	400
Warehousing and shipping	4,220	1,320	1,140	920	840
Order processing, billing	380	138	99	80	63
Marketing administration	1,024	256	256	256	256
Total expenses	9,700	2,904	2,481	2,236	2,079
Net profit (in dollars)	$ 2,900	$ 1,471	$ 879	$ 459	$ 91
(as percentage of sales)	8.1%	11.8%	9.2%	6.0%	1.5%

A's net profit was 11.8 percent of sales ($1,471,000 ÷ $12,500,000 = 11.8 percent). In sharp contrast, district D did rather poorly, earning a net profit of only 1.5 percent of net sales ($91,000 ÷ $6,200,000 = 1.5 percent).

At this point in our performance evaluation, we have completed the ''what happened'' stage. The next stage is to determine *why* the results are as depicted in Table 24-5. As we indicated earlier, it is extremely difficult to pinpoint the answer to this question. In district D, for example, the sales force obtained only about two-thirds as many orders as in district A (2,100 versus 3,300). Was this because of poor selling ability, poor sales training, more severe competition in district D, or some other reason among a multitude of possibilities?

After a performance evaluation has determined *why* the district results came out as they did, management can move to the third stage in its evaluation process. That final stage is, *what should management do about the situation?* This stage will be discussed briefly after we have reviewed two major problem areas in marketing cost analysis.

Problems Involved in Cost Analysis

Marketing cost analysis can be expensive in time, money, and manpower. In particular, the task of allocating costs is often quite difficult.

ALLOCATING COSTS

The problem of allocating costs becomes most evident when activity cost totals must be apportioned among individual territories, products, or other marketing units.

Operating costs can be divided into direct and indirect expenses. (These are sometimes called ''separable'' and ''common'' expenses.) Direct, or separable, expenses are those incurred totally in connection with one market segment or one unit of the sales organization. Thus the salary and travel expenses of the sales representative in territory A are direct expenses for that territory. The cost of newspaper space to advertise product C is a *direct* cost of marketing that product. The task of allocating direct expenses is easy. They can be charged in their entirety to the marketing unit for which they were incurred.

The allocation problem arises in connection with indirect, or common, costs. These expenses are incurred jointly for more than one marketing unit. Therefore they cannot be charged totally to one market segment.

Within the category of indirect expenses, some costs are *partially* indirect and some are *totally* indirect. Order filling and shipping, for example, are *partially* indirect costs. They would *decrease* if some of the territories or products were eliminated. They would *increase* if new products or territories were added. On the other hand, marketing administrative expenses are *totally* indirect. The cost of the chief marketing executive's staff and office would remain about the same, whether or not the number of territories or product lines was changed.

Any method selected for allocating indirect expenses has obvious weaknesses that can distort the results and mislead management. Two commonly used allocation methods are to divide these costs (1) equally among the marketing units being studied (territories, for instance) or (2) in proportion to the sales volume in each marketing unit. But each method gives a different result for the total costs for each marketing unit.

Warehousing costs typically are partially indirect.

FULL-COST VERSUS CONTRIBUTION-MARGIN CONTROVERSY

In a marketing cost analysis, two ways of allocating indirect expenses are (1) the contribution-margin (also called contribution-to-overhead) method and (2) the full-cost method. A real controversy exists regarding which of these two approaches is better for managerial control purposes.

In the **contribution-margin approach**, only the direct expenses are allocated to each marketing unit being analyzed. These are the costs which presumably would be eliminated if that marketing unit were eliminated. When these direct expenses are deducted from the gross margin of the marketing unit, the remainder is the amount which that unit is contributing to cover total indirect expenses (or overhead).

In the **full-cost approach**, all expenses—direct and indirect—are allocated among the marketing units under study. By allocating *all* costs, management can determine the net profit of each territory, product, or other marketing unit.

For any given marketing unit, these two methods can be summarized as follows:

Contribution margin		**Full cost**	
	Sales $		Sales $
less	Cost of goods sold	*less*	Cost of goods sold
equals	Gross margin	*equals*	Gross margin
less	Direct expenses	*less*	Direct expenses
equals	Contribution-margin (the amount available to cover overhead expenses plus a profit)	*less*	Indirect expenses
		equals	Net profit

Proponents of the *full-cost* approach contend that the purpose of a marketing cost study is to determine the net profitability of the units being studied. They feel that the contribution-margin approach does not fulfill this purpose. The advocates of the full-cost approach point out that management may be deluding itself with the contribution-margin approach. A given territory or product may be showing a contribution to overhead. Yet, after the indirect costs are allocated, this product or territory may actually have a net loss. In effect, say the full-cost people, the contribution-margin approach is the iceberg principle in action. That is, the visible tip of the iceberg (the contribution margin) looks good, while the submerged part may be hiding a net loss.

Contribution-margin supporters contend that it is not possible to accurately apportion indirect costs among product or market segments. Furthermore, items such as administrative costs are not all related to any one territory or product. Therefore the marketing units should not bear any of these costs. These advocates also point out that a full-cost analysis may show that a product or territory has a net loss, whereas this unit may be contributing something to overhead. Some executives might recommend that the losing product or territory be eliminated. But they are overlooking the fact that the unit's contribution to overhead would then have to be borne by other units. Under the contribution-margin approach, there would be no question about keeping this unit as long as no better alternative could be discovered.

Use of Findings from Combined Volume and Cost Analysis

So far in our discussion of marketing cost analysis, we have been dealing generally with the first stage in the evaluation process. That is, we have been finding out *what happened*. To conclude this section, let's look at some examples of how management might use the results from a combined sales-volume analysis and a marketing cost analysis.

TERRITORIAL DECISIONS

Once management knows the net profit (or contribution to overhead) of the territories in relation to their potential, there are several possibilities for managerial action. The executives may decide to adjust (expand or contract) territories to bring them into line with current sales potential. Or territorial problems may stem from weaknesses in the distribution system, and changes in channels of distribution may be needed. Some firms that have been using manufacturers' agents may find it advisable to establish their own sales forces in growing markets. Intensive competition may be the cause of unprofitable volume in some districts, and changes in the promotional program may be advisable.

Of course, a losing territory might be abandoned completely. An abandoned region may have been contributing something to overhead, however, even though a net loss was shown. Management must recognize that this contribution must now be carried by the remaining territories.

PRODUCT DECISIONS

When the relative profitability of each product or group of products is known, a product line may be simplified by eliminating unprofitable models, sizes, or colors. The sales people's compensation plan may be altered to encourage the sale of high-margin items. Channels of distribution may be altered. Instead of selling all its products directly to industrial users, for example, a machine tools manufacturer shifted to industrial distributors for standard products of low unit value. The company thereby improved the profitability of these products.

In the final analysis, management may decide to discontinue a product. Before this is done, however, consideration must be given to the effect this will have on other items in the line. Often a low-volume or unprofitable product must be carried simply to round out the line. Customers expect a seller to carry the article. If it is not available, the seller may lose sales of other products.

DECISIONS ON CUSTOMER CLASSES AND ORDER SIZES

By combining a volume analysis with a cost study, executives can determine the relative profitability of each group of customers. If one group shows a substandard net profit, changes in the pricing structure for these accounts may be required. Or perhaps accounts that have been sold directly should be turned over to middlemen.

A common problem plaguing many firms today is that of the **small order.** Many orders are below the break-even point. The revenue from each of these orders is actually less than the allocated expenses. This is true because several costs, such as billing or direct selling, are the same whether the order amounts to $10 or $10,000. Management's immediate reaction may be that no order below the break-even point should be accepted. Or small-volume accounts should be dropped from the customer list. Actually, such decisions may be harmful. Management should determine first *why* certain accounts are small-order problems and then adopt procedures to correct the situation. Proper handling can very often turn a losing account into a satisfactory one. A small-order handling charge, which customers would willingly pay, might change the profit situation entirely.

SUMMARY

The management process in marketing may be defined as the planning, implementation, and evaluation of the marketing effort in an organization. The implementation stage is the operational stage in which an organization attempts to carry out its strategic planning. Strategic planning is virtually useless in an organization if these plans are not implemented effectively.

The implementation stage includes three broad areas of activity—organizing, staffing, and operating. In organizing, the company first should coordinate all marketing activities into one department whose chief executive reports directly to the president. Then, within the marketing department, the company may utilize some form of organizational specialization based on geographical territories, products, or customer types. Regarding staffing, your authors' philosophy is that selecting people is the most important step in the entire management process. To operate an organization effectively, management needs to do a good job in delegation, coordination, motivation, and communication.

The evaluation stage in the management process involves measuring performance results against predetermined goals. Evaluation enables management to determine the effectiveness of its implementation efforts and to plan future corrective action where necessary.

A marketing audit is extremely important in a total marketing evaluation program. Most companies are victims of at least some misdirected marketing effort. That is, the 80-20 situation and the iceberg principle are at work in most firms. This is so because marketing efforts (costs) are expended in relation to the *number* of marketing units rather than to their profit potential. Fundamentally, companies do not know how much they should be spending for marketing activities, or what results they should get from these expenditures.

Two useful tools for controlling these misdirected marketing efforts are a sales-volume analysis and a marketing cost analysis. Given appropriately detailed analyses, management can study its sales volume and marketing costs by product lines and by market segments (sales territories, customer groups). One major problem in marketing cost analysis is that of allocating costs—especially indirect costs—to the various marketing units. But the findings from these analyses are extremely helpful in shaping decisions regarding several aspects of a company's marketing program.

KEY TERMS AND CONCEPTS

Implementation (in the management process) 570
Organizational structures for implementing strategic planning 570
Importance of good selection 574
Delegating authority and responsibility 575
Coordinating marketing activities 575
Motivating people 575
Communicating inside a company 575
Marketing audit 576
Misdirected marketing effort 577
80-20 principle 577

Iceberg principle 577

Sales-volume analysis 579

Market-share analysis 580

Marketing cost analysis 581

Direct costs 585

Indirect costs 585

Full-cost versus contribution-margin
    allocation 586

QUESTIONS AND PROBLEMS

∎

1. Explain the relationship among planning, implementation, and evaluation in the management process.

2. "Good implementation in an organization can overcome poor planning, but good planning cannot overcome poor implementation." Explain, using examples.

3. How is the organizational placement of marketing activities likely to be different in a marketing-oriented firm as contrasted with a production-oriented firm?

4. What benefits can a company expect to gain by organizing its sales force by geographical territories?

5. Give some examples of companies that are likely to organize their sales force by product groups.

6. What are some of the reasons why this book's authors believe that selecting people is such an important aspect of the management process?

7. Why is effective delegation of authority and responsibility so important in operating a marketing program?

8. Give some examples of how advertising and personal selling activities might be coordinated in a company's marketing department.

9. A sales-volume analysis by territories indicates that the sales of a manufacturer of roofing materials have increased 12 percent a year for the past 3 years in the territory comprising South Carolina, Georgia, and Florida. Does this indicate conclusively that the company's sales-volume performance is satisfactory in that region?

10. A manufacturer found that one product accounted for 35 to 45 percent of the company's total sales in all but 2 of the 18 territories. In each of those two territories, this product accounted for only 15 percent of the company's volume. What factors might account for the relatively low sales of this article in the two districts?

11. Explain how the results of a territorial sales-volume analysis may influence a firm's promotional program.

12. What effects may a sales-volume analysis by products have on training, supervising, and compensating the sales force?

13. "Firms should discontinue selling losing products." Discuss.

14. Should a company discontinue selling to an unprofitable customer? Why or why not? If not, then what steps might the company take to make the account a profitable one?

25

MARKETING: SOCIETAL APPRAISAL AND PROSPECT

CHAPTER GOALS

We have looked at marketing within the individual *firm* and within our *economic system*. Now, in this final chapter, we shall look more closely at the place of marketing within our *social system*. After studying this chapter, you should understand:

- The major criticisms of marketing and the phenomenon of consumerism.
- Some basic yardsticks for evaluating these criticisms and our marketing system in general.
- Government and business responses to consumer discontent.
- The emerging societal orientation in marketing and the social responsibilities of marketing management.
- Some forces that will shape marketing in the next 10 years.
- The broadened, socially responsive marketing concept.

n recent years certain marketing activities in two industries—beer and cigarettes—have been creating quite a bit of controversy. In the marketing of beer, the controversy centers around the extensive promotion aimed at the lucrative college-student market. Brewers sponsor rock concerts, intramurals, and other events to promote their product. Beer advertising appears in printed programs and on scoreboards at campus athletic events, as well as on the radio and TV broadcasts of those events. Yet, at the same time, many people feel that the excess use of alcohol by students is a major problem on many campuses.

Regarding the marketing of cigarettes, the sales of this product are stagnant or declining in many industrialized countries. But in developing (Third World) countries, cigarettes are enjoying a strong growth market, thanks in part to the extensive advertising and other promotions by cigarette producers. This heavy promotion is occurring even though the product is dangerous to one's health and expenditures for cigarettes are a drain on the limited income of ill-fed consumers.

Many people are critical of these industry practices—saying that they are the sort of unethical, socially irresponsible marketing behavior that ultimately leads to government regulation. What do you think? Or would you first like to study this chapter before stating your opinion?[1]

---

[1]Adapted from Johnnie L. Roberts, "Controversy Is Rising over Beer Promotions on College Campuses," *The Wall Street Journal*, Jan. 30, 1985, p. 6; and Steve Mufson, "Cigarette Companies Develop Third World as a Growth Market," *The Wall Street Journal*, July 5, 1985, p. 1.

In the first two chapters of this book, we touched on the broader, societal dimension of marketing and examined briefly the role of marketing in the total economy. For the most part, however, we have approached marketing from the viewpoint of the firm, as we discussed the problems facing an individual producer or middleman in managing its marketing activities. Now in this final chapter, we will once again look at marketing from a broader, societal perspective.

First we shall appraise our marketing system by examining (1) the criticisms of the system, (2) the phenomenon of consumerism, and (3) the responses to these criticisms. Then we shall consider some of the societal aspects of marketing management, including a broadened view of the marketing concept.

BASIS FOR EVALUATING OUR MARKETING SYSTEM

The present-day economic system of the United States is a reasonably free market system, but an *imperfect* one. Price is the prime determinant of resource allocation. We call our system "imperfect" because it is not composed of the elements basic to the theoretical model of perfect competition. Those elements are great numbers of well-informed buyers and sellers, always acting rationally. Each is so small that one individual's activities have no appreciable influence on total supply, demand, or price. Another imperfection is the structural rigidity of our system. Also, in the interest of

Now here is a satisfied customer!

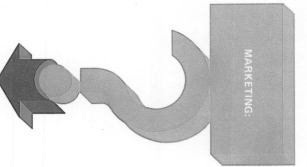

MARKETING:

Does it satisfy consumers' wants—as consumers themselves define or express those wants?

CRITICISMS OF MARKETING

What Are the Criticisms?

the general welfare, the various levels of government often act so as to decrease the free play of market forces.

We shall appraise the American marketing system, using this imperfect economic system as our frame of reference. Before we engage in this evaluation, however, we need to agree on what is the *objective* of the system. Throughout this book we have stressed the philosophy of the marketing concept. The goal of the marketing concept is to develop a customer orientation on the part of management. In line with this philosophy, *it seems reasonable to establish as our objective the satisfaction of consumers' wants as they are expressed by the consumers themselves.* Then marketing should be appraised on the basis of how well it achieves this goal, that is, how effectively it satisfies consumers' wants. We grant that this is not everyone's idea of the ultimate goal. Some feel that consumers do not know what is good for them—that some group (usually the government) should take over the responsibility for setting standards. Others believe that the social and economic goals should be to build the country's military defenses, to promote the growth of its underdeveloped segments, or to clean up the environment.

Regardless of how worthy these or other goals may be, our basis for evaluating our marketing system will be: *Does it satisfy consumers' wants—as consumers themselves define or express those wants?*

For many years, critics of our marketing system have raised a variety of thought-provoking questions and have generated numerous lively discussions. Let us examine their criticisms, try to determine the true nature of these charges, and consider one key question: Does marketing cost too much?

We can summarize the major charges against marketing by grouping them in relation to the components of the marketing mix—product, price structure, distribution system, and promotional activities.

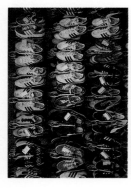

Some people object to the proliferation of products.

THE PRODUCT

Critics allege that many products are of poor quality or are unsafe. Parts fall off cars, zippers jam, food products are adulterated, commuter trains run late, wash-and-wear clothing really needs ironing, appliances do not perform as advertised, etc., etc. Also, these products are backed up by confusing and worthless warranties, and repair service is inadequate. Packaging is deceptive, and labels do not carry sufficient information concerning product contents, operating instructions, or care of the product.

Furthermore, heavily promoted product improvements are often trivial. Planned style obsolescence encourages consumers to get rid of products before they are physically worn out. Moreover, too many different types of goods, and too many different brands of each type, are produced. As a result, the buyer is confused and unable to make accurate buying decisions, and much production capacity is wasted in unnecessary duplication.

PRICE STRUCTURE

We hear that prices are too high, or too inflexible, or that they are controlled by the large firms in an industry. Some people feel that price competition has been largely replaced by nonprice competition.

DISTRIBUTION SYSTEM

Probably the main objection to the distribution system is that it is unnecessarily complex and includes too many middlemen. This is a two-part charge—there are too many different types of middlemen, and too many of each type.

PROMOTIONAL ACTIVITIES

The strongest and most bitter indictments against marketing are in the area of promotional activities—especially in personal selling and advertising. Most of the complaints about personal selling are aimed at the retail level. We find that both consumers and business people often are disenchanted with the poor quality of retail selling. Objections are also voiced against the poor services offered by many retailers.

The general criticisms of advertising may be divided into two groups—social and economic. From a *social* point of view, advertising is charged with overemphasizing our material standard of living and underemphasizing our cultural and moral values. Advertising also is charged with manipulating people—making them want to buy things they should not have, cannot afford, and do not need.

A major social criticism of advertising today, and one that has some justification, is that advertising is often false, deceptive, or in bad taste. Exaggerations, overuse of sex and fear appeals, inane claims, excessive numbers of commercials on radio and television, and poor choice of the placement of commercials are examples of this criticism. As with most criticisms in marketing, this one applies to a small segment of advertising. The main offenders are advertisers of a limited number of consumer goods, and the advertising medium causing most of the furor is television. The charge of misleading and offensive advertising is rarely made against advertisers of industrial products or companies that advertise consumer products in trade journals. Most retail display advertising is not subject to this charge, nor is most classified advertising in newspapers and magazines.

Would you criticize this ad?

The *economic* criticisms of advertising have taken an interesting turn in recent years. We still hear that advertising costs too much—that it increases the cost of marketing and therefore raises the prices of products. Recently, however, the economic charge drawing the most interest is that advertising leads to restraint of competition, economic concentration, and monopoly.

The line of reasoning behind the economic-concentration complaint goes something like this. (1) The big companies can afford to spend much on advertising to differentiate their products, and thus they are able to acquire a large share of the market; (2) in this way, advertising creates a barrier to market entry by new or smaller firms; (3) a high level of market concentration then results; (4) the firms enjoying this protected position can charge high prices, which in turn lead to high profits.

The refutation of the economic-concentration charge was carefully spelled out in a study by Prof. Jules Backman.[2] He concluded that there is no relationship between advertising intensity and high economic concentration. Nor does there seem to be any link between advertising intensity and (1) price increases or (2) high profit rates.

[2]Jules Backman, *Advertising and Competition,* New York University Press, 1967.

Advertising is highly competitive, Backman states, not anticompetitive. In fact, in recent years the Federal Trade Commission has actually *encouraged* professional people (physicians, dentists, lawyers, and optometrists, for example) to advertise in order to *increase* price competition in those fields.

Understanding the True Nature of Criticisms

In evaluating the charges against marketing, we should be careful to recognize the differences in the nature of the various points. We should understand what fundamentally is being criticized. In a company, is it the marketing department or some other department that is the cause of the complaints? In the economy, is it the marketing system or the general economic system that is being criticized? It is also helpful to know when the critics (1) are misinformed, (2) are unaware of the services performed by the marketing system, or (3) are trying to impose their own value judgments on consumers. That is, the critics may not agree that the goal of the marketing system should be consumer want-satisfaction, as the consumers *themselves* define and express their wants.

In some cases, the criticisms of marketing are fully warranted. They point out weaknesses and inefficiencies in the system and call for improvement. By most people's standards, there are instances of deceptive packaging and of misleading and objectionable advertising. There are weaknesses in marketing, just as there are in any system developed and operated by human beings.

The real key to the evaluation of our marketing system lies in the answers to two fundamental questions. First, is the present system of marketing achieving its goal (that is, satisfying consumers' wants as the consumers themselves express those wants) better than any other known alternative could? The answer is an unqualified ''yes.'' Second, is constant effort being devoted to improving the system and increasing its efficiency? Generally speaking, the answer to this question is also a strong ''yes.''

Progress sometimes may seem slow. Companies that operate in a socially undesirable manner even over a short period of time are harmful. Price fixing and objectionable advertising are intolerable and inexcusable. Instances of this nature, though widely publicized, are few relative to the totality of marketing effort. In essence, we are saying that weaknesses exist in marketing and that a continuing effort must be devoted to their elimination. However, at the same time, we should not overlook the improvements in marketing and consumer want-satisfaction over the years. The way to correct existing weaknesses is not to destroy or heavily regulate the existing system.

Does Marketing Cost Too Much?

Many of the censures of marketing can be summarized in the general criticism that marketing costs too much. However, the question of whether marketing costs too much should be analyzed and answered from two points of view. The first is within the *macro* context of our total socioeconomic system, and the second is within the *micro* context of an individual organization.

IN OUR SOCIOECONOMIC SYSTEM

It is estimated that the total cost of marketing for all products is about 50 percent of the final price paid by ultimate consumers. Admittedly, marketing costs are a substantial proportion of the total sales value of all products. However, the question of whether marketing costs too much is somewhat academic, because we do not have

Today we demand services and conveniences—like "free" parking—but that adds to the cost of marketing.

sufficient information to make comparisons. Even if we had accurate data on marketing costs, we would still have no objective criteria for determining whether these expenses are too high or not high enough. As we noted in Chapter 24, we have not yet developed adequate tools for measuring the return (output) that is derived from a given marketing expenditure (input). To say that marketing costs are too high implies that one or more of the following situations prevail: (1) Marketing institutions are enjoying abnormally high profits; (2) more services are being provided than consumers and business people demand; (3) marketing activities are performed in a grossly inefficient manner; (4) consumption is declining; and (5) total costs (production plus marketing) are increasing. Actually, there is no reasonable evidence that any of these conditions exist.

Total marketing costs have indeed risen substantially over the past 100 years. At the same time, careful studies indicate that these costs have been leveling off for the past three or four decades. Still, it is important that we understand the reasons for this increase in marketing expenses. Certainly it would be a mistake simply to jump to the conclusion that the cost increase indicates growing inefficiencies in marketing.

Actually, the rise in marketing expense is traceable to several factors, some of which are external environmental influences. As an example, one reason for the increase in the number of people employed in marketing relative to production is simply that the workweek in marketing has been shortened relative to that in production. In the latter part of the nineteenth century, people employed in wholesaling and retailing worked about 66 hours a week. Those employed in production worked about 52. Today, both groups work about 40. This shift toward equality has meant that relatively more employees were added in marketing.

Another factor is that consumers are demanding more services and more marketing refinements today than in the past. Consumers today demand credit, delivery, free parking, attractive stores, merchandise return privileges, and other services. A related point is the rise in consumer demand for products emphasizing style. And consumers want merchandise assortments covering considerable breadth and depth. Certainly we could cut marketing costs substantially if consumers would buy on a cash-and-carry basis in stores displaying small quantities of standardized merchandise in boxes.

It is a mistake to study the trend in marketing costs alone. A total-cost approach should be adopted. In many instances, a firm can reduce its *total* costs by increasing its *marketing* costs. To illustrate, an increase in advertising expenditures may so expand a firm's market that the unit *production* cost can be reduced more than the *marketing* costs have increased. Thus, the net effect is to reduce total expenses. In another situation, production economies can result when a company locates near sources of raw materials or low-cost power. Yet *marketing* costs (transportation) may be increased in the new location.

It is understandable that productivity in marketing may never match the level attained in manufacturing or agriculture. Marketing offers far fewer opportunities for mechanization. It is one thing to control the input and output of machines. But it is quite another problem when the activity largely involves dealing with people. Until a better system for satisfying consumer wants is proposed, however, we shall continue with the existing system. Its benefits in both the private and public sectors of our economy are bounteous by almost any measure used. American business must continue to improve the efficiency of marketing and to seek accurate measures of its cost. Most important of all, business must explain to the American public the essential role marketing plays in our economy.

IN AN INDIVIDUAL ORGANIZATION

Unquestionably, in some individual firms, marketing *does* cost too much. In firms that market inefficiently or that are production-oriented in their management and operations, marketing probably costs too much. The high rate of mortality among retail businesses attests, in part, to their inefficiencies in marketing. A high rate of new-product failure raises the cost of marketing in a firm.

Marketing costs undoubtedly are too high—that is, marketing efficiency is too low—in firms that:

- Do not carry a product mix that customers want.
- Use obsolete distribution channels.
- Are totally cost-oriented (ignore demand) in their pricing.
- Cannot manage a sales force effectively.
- Waste money with ineffective advertising.

Fortunately, in many firms, marketing does *not* cost too much. These firms have strategically planned and implemented the customer-oriented type of marketing program that has been discussed and advocated throughout this book.

CONSUMERISM: A CRITICISM OF OUR MARKETING SYSTEM

Meaning and Scope of Consumerism

"Consumerism" became a significant social movement in the 1960s, and it shows every indication of continuing to grow in the years ahead. In this section we discuss what consumerism is and why it came to be. Then, in the following section, we consider the responses of government and business to this phenomenon.

We may define consumerism as both (1) a consumer protest against the perceived injustices in exchange relationships and (2) efforts to remedy those injustices. Consumers clearly feel, in exchange relationships between buyers and sellers, that the balance of power lies with the sellers. Consumerism is an expression of this opinion, and an attempt to achieve a more equal balance of power between buyers and sellers.

SCOPE OF CONSUMERISM

Consumerism today includes three broad areas of consumer dissatisfaction and remedial efforts. The original, and still the major, focus of consumerism involves discontent with direct buyer-seller exchange relationships between consumers and business firms.

The second area of discontent extends beyond business. Consumerism extends to *all* organizations with which there is an exchange relationship. Therefore, consumerism involves such diverse organizations as hospitals, schools, and government agencies (police departments, tax assessors, street maintenance departments, etc.).

The third area of consumerism involves the *indirect* impact that an exchange relationship between two social units (a person, a business, etc.) has on a third social

Parents want toys that are safe.

Consumers want to know what they are eating.

unit. Consumer Jones may buy steel from mill A. But in producing the steel for that exchange, the mill pollutes the river used by consumer Smith for fishing and swimming. Smith becomes upset and protests. In other words, an exchange between two people or groups has created a problem for a third person or group.

CONSUMERISM YESTERDAY AND TODAY

Consumerism really is not a new phenomenon. In the early 1900s and again during the Great Depression in the 1930s, there was a "consumer movement." Efforts were made to protect the consumer from harmful products and from false and misleading advertising.

The movement that began in the 1960s, however, is different in three ways from earlier consumer movements. First, today's consumerism is occurring in a setting of higher incomes and largely fills subsistence needs, in contrast to the harsher economic conditions which surrounded earlier movements. Second, the consumer-movement legislation since the 1960s has been intended first and foremost to protect the consumer's interests. Emphasis in earlier legislation was placed on the protection of competition and competitors.

Third, today's consumerism is much more likely to continue to grow, because it has generated an institutional structure to support it. Government agencies have been established to administer the consumer-oriented laws and to protect consumer interests. The social sensitivity of many businesses has increased, and various consumer- and environment-oriented organizations have developed.

Why did consumerism take hold in the 1960s, when the factors of social and economic discontent (pollution, unsafe products, and others) had been with us for some time? It just so happened that a series of issues converged in the mid-1960s to touch off the "social conflagration" that we call consumerism.

BROAD CULTURAL CHANGES

Two broad cultural changes occurred to provide the setting for consumerism. The first was a dramatic shift in the goals of American consumers as we entered a more advanced stage of cultural and economic development. In the decades preceding the 1960s, our emphasis was on improving our material standard of living. Today, with our materialistic needs more or less satisfied, we are more sensitive to social and environmental needs. The second cultural change underlying consumerism was the active role of young people. Compared with previous generations, today's young people are better educated, more articulate, and more inclined (less afraid) to speak out and take action.

CONSUMER DISCONTENTS AND FRUSTRATIONS

This changing cultural setting converged with a series of highly flammable issues that generated much consumer discontent and frustration. There were economic discontent (inflation), social discontent (racial conflict, the Vietnam war), and ecological discontent (pollution, diminishing quality of life).

In the business area, discontent was focused on the marketing system as people perceived that their consumer rights were being violated. (In a presidential message, John F. Kennedy stated that consumers had the right to safety, to be informed, to

Conditions Leading to Consumerism

choose, and to be heard.) Consumers were frustrated and indignant because of unfulfilled promises and expectations. Nobody seemed willing to listen to the consumers' complaints or to do anything about them. "We can't get past the computer to deal with real people."

Consumerism in the 1980s

Many people thought that consumerism would decline, and even disappear, once the initial interest and support burned out. On the contrary, however, the fires of consumerism have continued to burn in the 1980s, although in a different form than in the 1960s and 1970s. Instead of marching in the streets, today more people are working within the existing political, legal, and social systems in order to bring about change.

One reason why consumerism will not disappear is that many consumer demands of earlier years are now set in legislation. Also, in spite of the remedial progress of the past 20 years, the major areas of consumer discontent today are substantially the same as they were then.

In their research on consumerism, Paul Bloom and Stephen Greyser concluded that consumerism is in the maturity stage of its product life cycle—but, again, showing no signs of decline. Originally, the consumerism "industry" consisted of a few organizations interested primarily in generating regulatory legislation. This industry has evolved into "an enormous web of organizations and institutions, each trying to serve the interests of consumers with its own distinctive set of offerings or brands."[3]

RESPONSES TO THESE CRITICISMS

Significant action-oriented efforts to remedy the conditions leading to consumerism have come from the consumers themselves, from government activities, and from business organizations.

Responses of Consumers and Consumer Organizations

Consumers have reacted in a wide variety of ways to vent their frustrations and to correct what they consider to be injustices. Reactions have ranged from refusing to buy a product or shop at a certain store to burning and looting business establishments. Consumers as a group are more active politically than ever before. They support consumer-oriented candidates. They write letters to editors, legislators, and business executives.

Consumers are becoming better organized in their social and economic protests. In recent years, many *local* organizations, such as church groups, the Parent-Teachers Association, and student groups have become involved in consumer issues. Several *national* organizations have actively supported consumers' interests. Some of these

[3]Paul N. Bloom and Stephen A. Greyser, *Exploring the Future of Consumerism*, Marketing Science Institute, Cambridge, Mass., report no. 81–102, p. 7. For the essence of this report, see the authors' article, "The Maturing of Consumerism," *Harvard Business Review*, November-December 1981, pp. 130–139.

For an excellent group of papers dealing with current issues in consumerism and future prospects for the consumer movement, its organizations, and the social environment of marketing, see Paul N. Bloom (ed.), *Consumerism and Beyond: Research Perspectives on the Future Social Environment*, Marketing Science Institute, Cambridge, Mass., report no. 82–102, 1982.

Government seeks to protect consumers.

Government Responses

organizations are multi-issue groups (Common Cause, National Consumers' League), while others are special-interest groups (American Association of Retired Persons). Some organizations deal primarily with buyer-seller exchange relationships (Consumers Union), while others support broader environmental causes (Sierra Club, Audubon Society).

Generally, however, consumer groups are simply too diverse in their interests to generate much effective *uniform* action.

Today it is politically popular to support consumerism. Almost all the states and many cities have created some kind of office for consumer affairs.

LEGISLATION

For the first time, state and federal legislatures have passed laws whose primary purpose is to aid the consumer. A significant group of these new laws is designed to protect the consumers' "right to safety"—especially in situations where they cannot judge the risk themselves. Thus, we have the auto-safety law, the toy-safety law, and laws regulating textiles, tires, food, drugs, cigarettes, cleaning fluid, and many other products. Perhaps the most significant product-safety law is the Consumer Product Safety Act (1972), which we discussed in Chapter 11 in connection with product liability.

Another series of federal law supports the consumers' "right to be informed." These measures help in such areas as (1) reducing the confusion and deception in packaging and labeling (Fair Packaging and Labeling Act), (2) identifying the ingredients and nutritional content in food products, (3) interpreting the price per unit

This space contributed as a public service.

3 column (6 7/16" w. x 5 1/4" d.)

(ounce, pint, pound) of food products (unit-pricing laws), and (4) determining the true rate of interest (Truth-in-Lending Act).

At the state legislative level, there also has been considerable interest in consumer-support laws. Almost all states and several cities now have some form of "cooling-off" law affecting door-to-door selling. This law provides for a cooling-off period (usually 3 days) during which the buyer can cancel the contract, return any merchandise, and obtain a full refund. In effect, you can say "no" to the company even after you have said "yes" to its sales person.

GOVERNMENT REGULATORY AGENCIES

The strengthened and expanded role of regulatory agencies involved in consumer affairs has been a significant government response in the consumer movement. New agencies have been established—the Environmental Protection Agency and the Consumer Product Safety Commission, for example. Existing agencies such as the Food and Drug Administration (FDA) and the Federal Trade Commission (FTC) have been given expanded powers and have become more aggressive in their activities.

EFFECTIVENESS OF GOVERNMENT ACTION

How effective have governmental efforts been in improving the consumer's position? The consumer's answer might start with that cigarette slogan, "You've come a long way, baby," and then would add, "but you still have a long way to go." Just as consumerism started with unrealized expectations from *business* performance, now the consumer is experiencing unrealized expectations from *government's* performance. Although the consumers' position has been greatly improved, the pace of improvement is still too slow to satisfy many consumer advocates. However, even with this criticism, many consumers still have decidedly more confidence in government-enforced action than in voluntary business efforts.

In recent years, the cry for more government regulation and consumer protection has been subsiding. Consumers, economists, and even federal legislators are questioning the value of federal health, safety, and other regulations. Soaring costs are being imposed on business. And the regulations of the FDA, FTC, OSHA (Occupational Safety and Health Administration), EPA, and other federal regulatory bodies increase these costs. Knowledgeable people outside business are joining business leaders in asking whether the benefits are worth the costs. Often today, the answer is "no." Consequently, for the first time in years, movements are afoot in Congress to place some limitations on the FTC, OSHA, and other such agencies.[4]

Certainly government regulations protecting consumers' interests are not going to be eliminated. But the regulators are likely to be forced to take a more responsible, realistic, cost-benefit approach than often has been taken in the past.

Business Responses   Business apathy, resistance, or token efforts in response to consumerism simply increase the probability of more government regulation. It is as simple as this today:

---

[4]For a thoughtful, questioning update on the effectiveness and threats in the current government regulation of advertising, see J. J. Boddewyn, "Advertising Regulation: Fiddling with the FTC while the World Burns," *Business Horizons*, May–June 1985, pp. 32–40.

Consumerism is sufficiently entrenched and well organized so that consumer complaints will be answered. The only question is: answered by whom—business or government? If business cannot or will not do the job, the only alternative is additional government intervention.

POSITIVE RESPONSES OF INDIVIDUAL FIRMS

There is a growing executive awareness of the dangers accompanying a negative response to consumerism. Consequently, we are seeing an increasing number of positive and substantive responses to consumer problems.

Here are just a few examples of how individual firms are responding to consumerism.

- *Better communication with consumers.* Many firms have responded positively to the consumers' "right to be heard." Whirlpool (appliances) Corporation established a 24-hour "cool line." This enabled customers to call free of charge from anywhere in the country to register a complaint, ask about service, or get product-usage information. Other firms (Scott lawn products, Black & Decker, Pan Am Airways, Nabisco, Johnson & Johnson, Pillsbury) have speeded up and otherwise improved their responses to consumers' written inquiries or complaints.[5]

- *More and better information for consumers.* Point-of-sale information has been improved by a number of firms. Manufacturers are publishing instructional booklets on the use and care of their products. In many instances, labeling is more informative now than it was in the past. Many supermarkets, even where not required to do so by law, have instituted unit pricing.

- *Product improvements.* Companies have introduced many product-safety changes and pollution-reduction measures. Warranties have been simplified and strengthened. Nutritional elements have been added to some foods.

- *More carefully prepared advertising.* Many advertisers are extremely cautious in approving agency-prepared ads, in sharp contrast to past practices. Advertisers are involving their legal departments in the approval process. They are very sensitive to the FTC's right to demand substantiation of claims. The advertising industry is doing a more effective self-regulation job than ever before.[6]

ORGANIZING FOR EFFECTIVE RESPONSE

Many firms have made organizational changes to implement their response programs. Most of these moves have been directed toward establishing an "ombudsman" position—sometimes a high-level executive and sometimes a separate department of consumer affairs. The responsibilities of this position or department typically are (1) to serve as a listening post for consumer inquiries and complaints, and to see that

[5]For a report on the benefits that many companies are realizing through improved customer service and communication with customers, see "Making Service a Potent Marketing Tool," *Business Week,* June 11, 1984, p. 164.

[6]See Priscilla A. La Barbera, "Advertising Self-Regulation: An Evaluation," *MSU Business Topics,* Summer 1980, pp. 55–63.

Chainsaws now have safety bars.

they are answered; (2) to represent the consumers' interests when policies and programs are being formulated; and (3) to ensure that the firm maintains the necessary degree of societal orientation in its planning.

The ombudsman position or department must be an independent unit, preferably reporting directly to the chief executive. Placing the consumer affairs group in the marketing department is ordinarily a mistake. When profit or competitive crises arise, marketing executives too often do not place the consumer's interests foremost in their decision making.

Experience so far shows that consumers' reactions to consumer affairs representatives are mixed. Some programs get high ratings, and others are looked upon simply as "paper consumerism" and "corporate hypocrisy."[7]

TRADE ASSOCIATION RESPONSES

Many trade associations have actively responded to consumerism by setting industry standards, stimulating consumer education, and promoting research among the association members. Of course, trade associations have not been neglecting their time-honored activity as congressional lobbyists. In that role they are viewed (1) by business people as seekers of moderation in government antibusiness legislation, but (2) by consumer advocates as negative defense mechanisms striving to defang consumer-oriented legislation.

LIMITATIONS TO BUSINESS SELF-REGULATION

Generally speaking, the efforts at self-regulation by business people have not been too successful, at least not in the eyes of consumer advocates. Many of the business responses already noted have come only as a result of government prodding.

If an industry depends upon the *voluntary* compliance of its members in meeting industry standards, the results are likely to be ineffective. For self-regulation to have any real chance of success, an industry must be able to *force* its members to comply with industry standards. The problem is, however, that any enforcement measure strong enough to be effective (a boycott against an offender, for example) is likely to be a restraint-of-trade violation of the Sherman Antitrust Act. One reasonable solution here is some form of industry and government cooperation whereby the industry sets its own standards. Then, once these standards have been accepted by the government, they are enforced by the government.

BUSINESS DISCONTENT WITH CONSUMER FRAUD

Discontent is not a one-way street. In growing measure, what might be called a "reverse consumerism" is developing. That is, business people are increasingly concerned and vocal about consumer-initiated fraud against business. Shoplifting, fraud-

---

[7]For a disturbing study showing that as consumer complaints increase in an organization, the consumer affairs function is increasingly isolated from marketing decision making, see Claes Fornell and Robert A. Westbrook, "The Vicious Circle of Consumer Complaints," *Journal of Marketing*, Summer 1984, pp. 68–78. To complete this vicious circle, as the isolation of the consumer affairs department increases, so does the number of complaints increase.

ulent redemption of coupons, fraudulent cashing of checks, and other consumer abuses, especially against retailers, are costing businesses billions of dollars each year.[8]

A SOCIETAL ORIENTATION IN MARKETING

Out of consumerism and our changing consumer goals has emerged a new approach to marketing—a societal orientation. (This point was discussed briefly in Chapter 1.) This new approach—societal marketing—is both a broadening and a logical extension of the managerial systems approach to marketing.

Societal Marketing and Managerial Marketing

Societal marketing is a broadening, but not a replacement, of managerial marketing. In societal marketing, we still must develop a marketing program to plan, price, promote, and distribute products and services to satisfy consumers' wants. But we must also consider the societal consequences of this marketing program. In managerial marketing, for example, we are concerned with marketing automobiles to people. In societal marketing, in addition, we worry about the societal aspects of auto production and use—air pollution and traffic congestion.[9]

Conflicts in Consumer Goals

The consumers' shift to socially oriented goals is not proving to be easy to implement. As consumers, we have not abandoned our desire for things—but we have complicated our wants with a social concern. Here is the difference, possibly oversimplified, between pre-1970s goals and today's goals. Then, we wanted big cars that would go fast. We paid little attention to air pollution, traffic congestion, depleting oil resources, and polluted streams from mills making steel for autos. Now, we still want autos, but we also want clean air, no traffic jams, clean water, and no dependence on foreign oil resources. Certainly the former goal—a desire for autos only—was much easier to achieve, because the element of *conflict in goals* was largely absent.

The greater the number of target markets (publics) a company must deal with, the more difficult it becomes to satisfy them all. Often, the goals of the different markets are in conflict. One group may want a mill closed because it pollutes the air and water. But another of the target markets wants it kept open because it provides jobs.

Perhaps a key point to keep in mind is that we are dealing with consumers—human beings—with all their attendant contradictions and self-interests. Thus we cry out for safer autos; but, given the chance, a large percentage of people do not use their seat belts. We want more energy-generating facilities, but we won't allow anyone to build an oil refinery or a power plant in our town.

We want the convenience of disposable packaging, but we also want no litter.

---

[8] See Robert E. Wilkes, "Fraudulent Behavior by Consumers," *Journal of Marketing*, October 1978, pp. 67–75; this article reports on consumer attitudes and rationale involving 15 fraud situations and the extent of consumer participation in these situations.

[9] For a very thoughtful, but also very provocative, notion that societal marketing is an erroneous and counterproductive idea—that "for marketers to attempt to serve the best interests of society is not only undemocratic but dangerous as well"—see John F. Gaski, "Dangerous Territory: The Societal Marketing Concept Revisited," *Business Horizons*, July–August 1985, pp. 42–47.

Social Responsibilities of Marketing Management

A recurring theme in this chapter has been the broadened perspectives in marketing. Continuing in this vein, we now shall focus on the social responsibilities of marketing executives, both in concept and in practice.

WHAT IS SOCIAL RESPONSIBILITY?

Marketing executives have a threefold responsibility—to their firms, to their workers, and to their customers. For their firms, their job is to provide a satisfactory net profit over the long run. For their employees, their responsibility is to provide a good working environment. For their customers, the executive's job is to market want-satisfying goods and services at the lowest reasonable cost.

The substance of social responsibility is much broader, however. It emphasizes the effect of executive actions on the entire social system. Without this broader viewpoint, personal and institutional acts tend to be separated. Marketing executives can lead model personal lives, but they continue to justify their company's pollution of a river because there is no direct personal involvement. To them, river pollution is a public problem to be solved by governmental action.

The concept of social responsibility, however, requires executives to consider their acts within the framework of the whole social system. And the concept implies that executives are responsible for the effects of their acts anywhere in that system. Executives must realize (1) that business does not exist in isolation in our society and (2) that a healthy business system cannot exist within a sick society.[10]

REASONS FOR CONCERN ABOUT SOCIAL RESPONSIBILITY

Marketing executives should have a high degree of social responsibility simply because it is the morally correct thing to do. While this is simple and beautiful in concept, it is far more difficult to put into operation. Let's look at four points that have a more pragmatic flavor—four practical reasons for social responsibility in business.

To reverse declining public confidence in business   The image of business is tarnished—at least in the eyes of many people. To compound the consumerism problem facing business in the 1970s, there were revelations of political bribery, payoffs to agents in foreign markets, illegal and unethical gifts, and a few other unsavory practices. Opinion polls (Harris, Gallup, and Opinion Research, for example) showed that the public's confidence in business leadership had reached a low point. (Some of these same polls also reported a very low opinion of several other institutions—Congress, government agencies, labor unions, education, and the news media, for example.)

Now the question is, How do we reverse this decline in public confidence? Business leaders must demonstrate in convincing fashion that they are aware of, and will *really* fulfill, their social responsibility. A cosmetic, lip-service treatment will only worsen an already bad situation. Companies must set high ethical standards and then enforce them. Failure to act in this fashion will lead inevitably to further government intervention. Indeed, most of the governmental limitations placed on mar-

---

[10]This and the preceding paragraph adapted from Keith Davis, "Understanding the Social Responsibility Puzzle," *Business Horizons*, Winter 1967, p. 46.

SOME COMPANIES HAVE ACTED IN A SOCIALLY RESPONSIBLE MANNER; SOME HAVE NOT

Firestone Tire and Rubber Company

Firestone's 500 series of steel-belted radial tires were involved in the death of 34 people and hundreds of accidents. The company received thousands of consumer complaints regarding the 500 series tires. The federal government said the tire was particularly susceptible to blowouts, tread separations, and other potentially dangerous faults.

The company's response was to lay the blame on the users of the tire—charging that the tire failures were due to consumer neglect and abuse. The company also tried to block the investigations of the tire and sought a court injunction against the release of a survey of tire owners conducted by the National Highway Traffic Safety Administration (NHTSA). The company continued in various ways to delay and generally to "stonewall" the NHTSA investigations. The federal government finally forced Firestone to recall about 13 million of its radial tires.

Ford Motor Company

Ford Motor Company's Pinto automobile had a gasoline tank that was prone to explode and catch fire when the car was hit hard in the rear end. The car was involved in the burn deaths of several people who otherwise would not have been seriously injured in the accident.

For about 8 years the company lobbied against a particular safety standard for motor vehicles that would have required the redesign of the gas tank on the Pinto. The company's successful delaying tactics included (1) inundating the government with technical data that would take the government years to examine, (2) asserting that the drivers, not the cars, were the problem, and (3) asserting that automobile fires were not a major problem. After many years, the company stopped the production of the Pinto.

Johnson & Johnson

In mid-1982, Tylenol, marketed by a division of the Johnson & Johnson Company, was the leading brand of nonaspirin pain reliever. Tylenol's sales accounted for about 17 percent of Johnson & Johnson's net profit. Then tragedy struck. Seven people died after taking Tylenol capsules that had been poisoned. Apparently the poison had been injected into a random assortment of capsules some time after the product had been shipped from the factory.

But history does repeat itself (unfortunately, in some cases). In early 1986 the same tragedy involving Tylenol occurred again. One person was killed and another package in a nearby store was found to be poisoned. This second incident occurred even though the company had been using a new, tamper-resistant package.

On both occasions—1982 and 1986—Johnson & Johnson's response was speedy and thorough, even though the company itself appeared blameless. Within a few days after the poisonings, the company recalled millions of bottles of the capsules. The company was also quite open in its contacts with the media and the public. Toll-free telephone lines were set up to handle over 350,000 calls. Executives appeared on national television, and they talked with the press and the public. All this was done, incidentally, by a company whose former policy was for its executives to stay out of the public eye—that is, to maintain a low public profile. In 1982 the company charged off $100 million as a recall expense, and the company will likely have a similar or larger recall expense after the 1986 calamity.

After the 1982 case, the company ultimately recaptured much, if not all, of its former market share. At this writing (early 1986), it remains to be seen whether Johnson & Johnson again can regain its former market share. This time the company faces especially strong competition from brands that contain ibuprofen, a newly developed, effective pain reliever.

Source: Elizabeth Gatewood and Archie B. Carroll, "The Anatomy of Corporate Social Response: The Rely, Firestone 500, and Pinto Cases," *Business Horizons,* September–October 1981, pp. 9–16; and news articles.

keting throughout the years have been the result of management's failure to live up to its social responsibilities. Moreover, once some form of governmental control has been established, it is rarely removed.

Price of economic freedom and flexibility   Marketing executives must act in a socially desirable manner in order to justify the privilege of operating in our relatively free economic system. No worthwhile privilege or freedom comes without a price. Our economic freedoms sometimes have a high price, just as our precious political freedoms do. Moreover, it is very much in management's self-interest to be concerned with social problems, for these problems affect both the firm and its customers. Also, a concern for the quality of life may very well lead to change, and this change may present opportunities for new business.

The power-responsibility equation   The concept that social power begets social responsibility helps to explain why business executives have a major responsibility to society. Marketing executives do wield a great deal of social power as they influence markets and speak out on matters of economic policy. In business, we see many practical applications of the idea of a reasonable balance between power and responsibility. A management axiom holds that authority and responsibility should be matched. Since responsibility is tied to power, we may reason that the avoidance of social responsibility will lead to an erosion of social power. That is, "In the long run, those who do not use power in a way that society considers responsible will tend to lose it."[11]

Marketing department represents company   Procter & Gamble put this point nicely in an annual report that is paraphrased here: "When a Procter & Gamble sales person walks into a customer's place of business—whether calling on an individual store or keeping an appointment at the headquarters of a large group of stores—that sales person not only represents Procter & Gamble, but in a very real sense, that person is Procter & Gamble."[12]

For marketers who are genuinely interested in working to solve major social problems, there are opportunities for action both within their firms and in their communities. This entire book has been devoted to developing a consumer-oriented, socially responsible marketing program in the firm. In the community, marketing can play an active role in such areas as:

- Hiring and training disadvantaged people.
- Contributing to education and the arts.
- Urban renewal.
- Removing discrimination against women, old people, and minority groups.

[11] Keith Davis and William C. Frederick, *Business and Society*, 5th ed., McGraw-Hill Book Company, New York, 1984, p. 34.

[12] For an empirical survey that (1) identifies the nature and extent of ethical problems confronting marketing managers and (2) examines the effectiveness of top management in reducing these ethical problems, see Lawrence B. Chonko and Shelby D. Hunt, "Ethics and Marketing Management: An Empirical Examination," *Journal of Business Research*, August 1985, pp. 339–359.

- Reducing the marketing problems of low-income consumers.
- Reducing environmental pollution.

In the next section we shall discuss briefly some practical examples of marketing's involvement in the last of these problem areas. But first, note that marketing executives should let the public know about their social-action programs and accomplishments. With all the criticism being heaped on business today, it is not enough just to *do* some good in the social arena. Business executives must start to *tell* people about it instead of hiding their light under a bushel. In the past, many executives went out of their way to maintain a low profile. Now they are urged to be more visible in their community and in the public media. They should explain what they are doing to improve the quality of life, as well as the standard of living.

REDUCING ENVIRONMENTAL POLLUTION

One of the major social problems facing us today is the pollution of our physical environment. Our ecology—the relationship of people to their environment—is being disturbed, and in some cases seriously, by air, water, or noise pollution.

Who are the polluters? Marketing has contributed to the pollution problem. By stimulating a demand for products and by satisfying consumers' wants, marketing has helped to build mountains of solid wastes. Making and using these products pollutes air and water. Promotional efforts in marketing have generated a "throwaway" society and have contributed to a "no-deposit, no-return" behavioral pattern.

However, our ecological problems are far more complex than many people realize. Marketing alone did not cause pollution. Production technology is responsible for air and water pollution from steel mills, chemical plants, paper mills, oil refineries, and utility power plants. Cattle-feed lots and various mining operations contribute their share of wastes. Various government agencies have inadequate control over their own pollution-producing operations—and yet, the critics of business want the government to control pollution. Selfish consumer behavior adds to the problem. We want clean air, but we won't pay to tune up our auto engines. As a group, we demand highway beautification, but as individuals, we toss trash out the car window and often leave picnic grounds a shambles.

We are dealing with a complex assortment of technological, economic, and even cultural and psychological factors. Furthermore, contrary to the belief held by many critics, pollution is *not* restricted to capitalistic economies and big business. Pollution is a by-product of any industrialized urban society, whether it is capitalistic, socialistic, or communistic.

Marketing's contribution to pollution reduction Because of the complexity of ecological problems, effective solutions require cooperation from producers, marketers, and consumers, with the government serving as a coordinating and enforcement agency. The costs of pollution reduction and control are enormously high. Prices will have to be increased to pay for these efforts.

Just as marketing alone did not cause pollution, so too marketing alone cannot cure it. But marketing can and does contribute to the "solution of pollution." To do so is simply a part of our social responsibility. Moreover, there are many profitable

Redemption centers are one action program for reducing pollution.

business opportunities in pollution abatement. Pollution reduction is *not* limited to shut-down-the mill, don't-drive-your-car, and return-that-bottle type of negative alternatives. Some illustrations of positive efforts by marketers revolve around product planning, channels of distribution, and promotion.

The major polluting industries and many of the lesser culprits provide golden market opportunities for new pollution-control products. A little innovative thinking also helps. As we run out of land for garbage dumps, some cities are generating electricity by using solid wastes for fuel. Marketing is also challenged to develop products that will *not* contribute to solid-waste matter. The disposal of solid wastes is a monumental problem, and one way to cope with it is not to accumulate so much waste in the first place. Thus, biodegradable or recyclable products, and returnable or reusable containers, are desirable.

The key in recycling is to develop a distribution system that will move waste products from consumers back to a producer who can use them in manufacturing new products. Marketing's challenge is to find the incentive needed to stimulate the consumer to start this reverse-channel movement. Marketers can use their skills in persuasion to urge consumers to conserve our natural resources by using them in a less wasteful manner. Promotion also can be used to impress upon consumers the seriousness of our pollution and waste-disposal problems.

∎ **BROADENING THE
MARKETING CONCEPT**

In Chapter 1 we introduced the idea of broadening the marketing concept to make it more relevant and useful in today's social and economic environment. Now we are at the end of this book and you are about to finish your course in marketing. As the final section of this book, we return to what has been our guiding philosophy throughout the entire book—namely, the marketing concept. We especially need to review the marketing concept to determine whether it is compatible with a societally oriented marketing perspective.

The philosophy of the marketing concept holds that a company should (1) develop an integrated marketing program (2) to generate profitable sales volume (3) by satisfying consumers' wants. The fact that consumerism exists in the United States today

Air pollution in the District of Columbia: How do we satisfy two markets—auto users and people who want clean air?

means that the marketing concept has to some extent failed. The customer-orientation theme in the marketing concept implies that business should find out what the consumers want, and then try to satisfy those wants profitably. Consequently, carried to their logical extremes, consumerism and the marketing concept are mutually exclusive; if one exists, the other does not. Yet most business people probably would claim that they are consumer-oriented. They look on in wounded surprise at the wave of consumer discontent engulfing them.

Okay, then, what went wrong? Is it simply that the marketing concept has outlived its usefulness and is not compatible with today's societal orientation in marketing? In your authors' opinion, there is nothing wrong with the marketing concept that a broader interpretation won't cure. It is as viable as it ever was. It is quite compatible with a societal orientation to marketing and with a marketing executive's social responsibility.

However, three things did occur that have hurt the credibility of the marketing concept. The first was that too many marketing executives, while professing wholehearted agreement and support of the philosophy, were in actual practice giving it only token implementation. In some cases, these executives were simply too production- or engineering-oriented to fully comprehend the idea of customer orientation. In other cases, short-run crises have forced operating executives to put their self-interest ahead of consumer satisfaction.

The two other factors affecting the implementation of the marketing concept revolve around the narrow interpretation of consumer want-satisfaction. Who is a consumer, and what is meant by want-satisfaction? The answers to both these questions have been too narrow and too short-run-oriented. Most human beings—whether in the role of producer or consumer—tend to be short-run-oriented in most situations. We fail to see the long-run implications of our actions. Thus, I may want certain foods, and be satisfied when marketers cater to these wants. But these foods may be fattening, and thus bad for me, so there is a negative personal effect on me in the long run.

If the goal is defined as consumer want-satisfaction *in the long run*, then the marketing concept is more in line with the societal perspective of marketing. Of course, the problem of goal conflict crops up here again. To sell me the fattening foods is contrary to society's view of socially desirable want-satisfaction. But non-fattening food (while socially desirable and healthy for me) is just not what I want. So the marketer of this food loses my business. My short-run wants and long-run interests conflict.

Besides extending the *time* dimension in the marketing concept, we need to extend its *breadth*. To view only the direct buyers of a company's product as being the consumers—a view generally held in the past—is too narrow a dimension. We must broaden our definition of target markets to include other groups affected by the direct buyer-seller exchange. Thus, someone may buy an auto and be satisfied with it. But the negative social effects of pollution and traffic congestion from the auto displease other groups. In the broader context, we have not generated customer satisfaction and thus have not successfully implemented the marketing concept.

In summary, the marketing concept can be compatible with a societal perspective of marketing if we define the marketing concept as follows:

THE BROADENED MARKETING CONCEPT IS:

A philosophy whereby a company strives:
- to develop an integrated marketing program
- that generates long-run profitable sales volume
- by satisfying the long-run wants of:
  - product-buying customers and
  - the other parts of society affected by the firm's activities.

SUMMARY

In this final chapter, we appraised marketing from a broad, societal perspective, in contrast to the individual-company approach followed in the preceding chapters of this book. When evaluating our marketing system, the key point to recognize is the socioeconomic yardstick we used as the basis for the appraisal. We evaluated marketing on the basis of its ability to satisfy consumers' wants *as consumers themselves define or express those wants*. We reviewed some of the common criticisms of marketing, structuring this review around the four components of the marketing mix. Several aspects of the complex question "Does marketing cost too much?" were discussed.

Then we moved to the topic of consumerism. Consumerism is a protest against perceived business injustices, combined with the efforts to remedy these situations. Actually, consumerism is not limited to business alone. It also includes consumers' relations with government and other public organizations in our society. We have experienced consumer movements in the past, but the current one is significantly different in several respects. Consumerism, as we know it today, stemmed from some broad cultural changes and from consumer discontents and frustrations.

Consumers, individually and in consumer organizations, have responded to perceived injustices. The government, through legislation and the actions of regulatory agencies, also has responded to consumers' cries. Some companies have resisted consumerism, and others have come up with token or apathetic responses. However, there also have been strong positive responses from a significant number of companies and from trade associations. The current consumer movement shows every indication of continuing into the future.

There is an emerging societal orientation in marketing, and a growing social responsibility on the part of marketing management, for some very practical reasons. A societal orientation is needed to build the public's confidence in business and to justify the privilege of operating in our economic system. A socially responsible attitude is needed if business is to retain its social power. Perhaps the overriding reason for operating in a socially responsible manner is that the alternative is further government intervention. This would be unfortunate, because business people are best qualified to solve our social problems.

Finally, in line with this emerging societal orientation in marketing, we broadened our definition of the marketing concept. Our broadened restatement now makes the marketing concept a responsive philosophy that will be compatible with the social and economic environment of the coming decade.

KEY TERMS AND CONCEPTS ■

Basis for evaluating our marketing system 591
Criticisms of marketing 592
Consumerism 597
Scope of consumerism 597
Causes of consumerism 598
Consumer affairs department in a firm 602

Self-regulation by business 602
Societal marketing 604
Social responsibility of marketing management 605
The broadened marketing concept 609

QUESTIONS AND PROBLEMS ■

1. Some people feel that too much power is concentrated in big business in the United States and that large firms should be broken up. Yet these same people will drive a General Motors car, buy groceries at a large chain supermarket, buy Sears appliances, wash with a brand of Procter & Gamble soap, and brush their teeth with the leading brand of toothpaste. How do you reconcile the behavior of these people with their opinion concerning big business?

2. "Middlemen make unfairly high profits." Do you agree?

3. Some people believe that there are too many fast-food outlets in their communities. Suggest a method for reducing the number of these retailers. How many should be eliminated in your college community?

4. Evaluate the following criticisms of advertising:
   a. It creates a false sense of values.
   b. It costs too much.
   c. It is in bad taste.
   d. It is false, misleading, and deceptive.
   e. It tends to create monopolies.

5. What proposals do you have for regulating advertising?

6. What specific recommendations do you have for reducing the costs of marketing?

7. What information do you think should be included in advertisements for each of the following products or services?
   a. Snack foods.
   b. Jogging shoes.
   c. Nursing homes.
   d. Credit cards.

8. What suggestions do you have for an appliance manufacturing company that wants to improve the servicing of its products? An automobile manufacturing company?

9. What is the social and economic justification for "paternalistic" laws—like auto seat-belt regulations—that require us to do something because the government says it is in our best interest?

10. What proposals do you have for resolving some of the consumer goal-conflict situations discussed in this chapter?

11. You are vice president of marketing in a company heavily involved in outdoor advertising. Your company owns billboards and handles the outdoor advertising for many manufacturers. Currently, in your state legislature there is a bill pending

that would eliminate all outdoor advertising on all state and federal highways in your state. Several key members of the committee considering the bill have received major campaign contributions from your company over the years. Should you tell them that your firm will cut off further financial support if they approve the bill? Assume they do approve the bill. Then what position should your company take at the next election when these legislators seek your campaign contributions?

PEERLESS CHOCOLATE COMPANY*

Designing a strategic marketing mix

Joseph van der Steen had just inherited the Peerless Chocolate Company, a family candy business in downtown Baltimore, Maryland. While Mr. van der Steen had only limited experience in the Peerless Candy kitchens, he did have a business degree with a major in marketing. Consequently, he decided, after a detailed evaluation of Peerless and counseling with his accountant, to keep the business and build on the reputation and capital established by his forebears.

The company had a tradition of selling in a limited volume to a select group of customers. Joseph's grandfather had built a loyal following among those who would pay a premium price for beautiful and authentic, old-fashioned, hand-dipped chocolates. All ingredients were natural—real butter and chocolate, fresh-ground vanilla and other flavors, authentic maple sugar, and so on. All nutmeats were of premium quality. Recipes and package designs were virtually unchanged since the family moved from Holland to Baltimore in 1855.

The candy kitchens and production facilities were located very near the center of the older downtown area, which had been bypassed by urban renewal. The building and equipment were sturdy, spotless, and in excellent condition according to time-honored family tradition. The small staff was expert and loyal.

Current production ran from 700 pounds per week in July to a high of 1,200 pounds per week in December. Capacity was estimated to be 2,000 pounds per week. (But, to reach this level, one or two unskilled workers would have to be added for packing, stock control, and cleaning duties.) Demand had remained relatively stable over the past couple of years despite significant price increases caused by the increasing cost of sugar, chocolate, and packaging supplies.

In 1985 the company's sales volume was about $478,000. The cost of goods sold accounted for almost 80 percent of sales, and the net profit before taxes was $23,400.

Peerless sold its candy only to retail customers, and only from the company's

*Case prepared by Prof. Richard J. Jeffries, Catonsville Community College, and Prof. Ernest F. Cooke, Loyola College (Maryland). Used with permission.

retail store in the candy-kitchen building. Last month (November 1985), Mr. van der Steen did a little marketing research by interviewing 87 customers. He learned that all but 5 were regular, repeat customers, and that 22 were business people buying several packages for business gifts.

The family had never advertised in any media; it had depended entirely on word-of-mouth and careful maintenance of customer goodwill. Some investments had been made in packaging, but the basic package designs were virtually unchanged since the turn of the century. They featured Dutch village scenes in pastel colors and Victorian-type faces.

In the course of planning the first formal marketing program that Peerless had ever developed, Mr. van der Steen reviewed the competitive situation facing his company. A one-pound box of the Whitman Sampler sold for $5.75 at Drugfair (a chain drug store) and for $5.17 at Grant's (a chain supermarket). A one-pound box of Russell Stover's assorted chocolates sold for $4.95 at Drugfair and $5.35 at Hecht's (a department store). One pound of Godiva chocolates sold for $19.50 to $23.00 at Hecht's and at Woodward and Lothrop (a department store in Washington, D.C.). The difference in price for the Godiva chocolates apparently was due to a difference in packaging. These three brands were distributed nationally. There were numerous other brands of the Peerless type of candy, most of which sold for under $8.00 a pound while a few brands were over $15.00 a pound. The Peerless type of candy was sold in many different sizes, ranging from 2-ounce "samples" to 5-pound boxes. The price per pound decreased as the package size got larger.

Mr. van der Steen had learned something about strategic marketing planning in his college marketing courses, and he wanted to put some of that knowledge to work immediately. He estimated that, with a good marketing plan, he could boost sales in 1986 to an average of 2,000 pounds per week. At the current retail price of $9.95 per pound, this meant a sales volume of $1 million for the year. This was about twice as much as the 1985 sales volume.

To reach his objective of doubling his company's sales volume in 12 months, van der Steen realized he would need an effective marketing plan. Part of this plan would involve ways of filling in what he called the company's "summer sales valley." He did decide early that the company would work with a promotional budget of $75,000 for 1986.

QUESTIONS

Assume that you have been hired as a marketing consultant by Mr. van der Steen to design a strategic marketing plan for Peerless Chocolates. As part of this plan:

1. Indicate what target markets Peerless should select.
2. Design, in some detail, a marketing mix to reach these markets.

MARKETING ARITHMETIC

Marketing involves people—customers, middlemen, and producers. Much of the business activity of these people, however, is quantified in some manner. Consequently, some knowledge of the rudiments of business arithmetic is essential for decision making in many areas of marketing. Since most students taking this course have already had a beginning course in accounting, this appendix is intended as a review. It contains discussions of three accounting concepts that are useful in marketing: (1) the operating statement, (2) markups, and (3) analytical ratios. Another useful concept—discounts and terms of sale—was reviewed in Chapter 13 in connection with price policies.

THE OPERATING STATEMENT

An operating statement—often called a *profit and loss statement* or an *income and expense statement*—is one of the two main financial statements prepared by a company. The other is the balance sheet. An **operating statement** is a summary picture of the firm's income and expenses—its operations—over a period of time. In contrast, a **balance sheet** shows the assets, liabilities, and net worth of a company at a given time, for example, at the close of business on December 31, 1987.

The operating statement shows whether the business earned a net profit or suffered a net loss during the period covered. It is an orderly summary of the income and expense items that resulted in this net profit or loss.

An operating statement can cover any selected period of time. To fulfill income tax requirements, virtually all firms prepare a statement covering operations during the calendar or fiscal year. In addition, it is common for businesses to prepare monthly, quarterly, or semiannual operating statements.

Table A-1 is an example of an operating statement for a wholesaler or retailer. The main difference between the operating statement of a middleman and that of a manufacturer is in the cost-of-goods-sold section. A manufacturer shows the cost of goods *manufactured*, whereas the middleman's statement shows net *purchases*.

TABLE A-1 **ALPHA-BETA COMPANY, OPERATING STATEMENT, FOR YEAR ENDING DECEMBER 31, 1986**

Gross sales			$87,000
Less: Sales returns and allowances	$ 5,500		
Cash discounts allowed	1,500	7,000	
Net sales			$80,000
Cost of goods sold:			
Beginning inventory, January 1 (at cost)		18,000	
Gross purchases	49,300		
Less: Cash discounts taken on purchases	900		
Net purchases	48,400		
Plus: Freight in	1,600		
Net purchases (at delivered cost)		50,000	
Cost of goods available for sale		68,000	
Less: Ending inventory, December 31 (at cost)		20,000	
Cost of goods sold			48,000
Gross margin			32,000
Expenses:			
Sales-force salaries and commissions		$11,000	
Advertising		2,400	
Office supplies		250	
Taxes (except income tax)		125	
Telephone and telegraph		250	
Delivery expenses		175	
Rent		800	
Heat, light, and power		300	
Depreciation		100	
Insurance		150	
Interest		150	
Bad debts		300	
Administrative salaries		7,500	
Office salaries		3,500	
Miscellaneous expenses		200	
Total expenses			27,200
Net profit			$ 4,800

Major Sections

From one point of view, the essence of business is very simple. A company buys or makes a product and then sells it for a higher price. Out of the sales revenue, the seller hopes to cover the cost of the merchandise and the seller's own expenses and have something left over, which is called *net profit*. These relationships form the skeleton of an operating statement. That is, *sales minus cost of goods sold equals gross margin; then gross margin minus expenses equals net profit*. An example based on Table A-1 is as follows:

	Sales	$80,000
less	Cost of goods sold	– 48,000
equals	Gross margin	32,000
less	Expenses	– 27,200
equals	Net profit	$ 4,800

SALES

The first line in an operating statement records the gross sales—the total amount sold by the company. From this figure, the company deducts its sales returns and sales allowances. From gross sales, the company also deducts the discounts that are granted to company employees when they purchase merchandise or services.

In virtually every firm at some time during an operating period, customers will want to return or exchange merchandise. In a *sales return*, the customer is refunded the full purchase price in cash or credit. In a *sales allowance*, the customer keeps the merchandise, but is given a reduction from the selling price because of some dissatisfaction. The income from the sale of returned merchandise is included in a company's gross sales, so returns and allowances must be deducted to get net sales.

NET SALES

This is the most important figure in the sales section of the statement. It represents the net amount of sales revenue, out of which the company will pay for the products and all its expenses. The net sales figure is also the one upon which many operating ratios are based. It is called 100 percent (of itself), and the other items are then expressed as a percentage of net sales.

COST OF GOODS SOLD

From net sales, we must deduct the cost of the merchandise that was sold, as we work toward discovering the firm's net profit. In determining the cost of goods sold in a retail or wholesale operation, we start with the value of any merchandise on hand at the beginning of the period. To this we add the net cost of what was purchased during the period. From this total we deduct the value of whatever remains unsold at the end of the period. In Table A-1 the firm started with an inventory worth $18,000, and it purchased goods that cost $50,000. Thus the firm had a total of $68,000 worth of goods available for sale. If all were sold, the cost of goods sold would have been $68,000. At the end of the year, however, there was still $20,000 worth of merchandise on hand. Thus, during the year, the company sold goods that cost $48,000.

In the preceding paragraph, we spoke of merchandise "valued at" a certain figure or "worth" a stated amount. Actually, the problem of inventory valuation is complicated and sometimes controversial. The usual rule of thumb is to value inventories at cost or market, whichever is lower. The actual application of this rule may be difficult. Assume that a store buys six footballs at $2 each and the next week buys six more at $2.50 each. The company places all 12, jumbled, in a basket display for sale. Then one is sold, but there is no marking to indicate whether its cost was $2 or $2.50. Thus the inventory value of the remaining 11 balls may be $25 or $24.50. If we multiply this situation by thousands of purchases and sales, we may begin to see the depth of the problem.

TABLE A-2 COST-OF-GOODS-SOLD SECTION OF AN OPERATING STATEMENT FOR A MANUFACTURER

Beginning inventory of finished goods (at cost)			$18,000
Cost of goods manufactured:			
Beginning inventory, goods in process		$24,000	
Plus: Raw materials	$20,000		
Direct labor	15,000		
Overhead	13,000		
		48,000	
Total goods in process		72,000	
Less: Ending inventory, goods in process		22,000	
Cost of goods manufactured			50,000
Cost of goods available for sale			68,000
Less: Ending inventory, finished goods (at cost)			20,000
Cost of goods sold			$48,000

A figure that deserves some comment is the *net cost of delivered purchases.* A company starts with its gross purchases at billed cost. Then it must deduct any purchases that were returned or any purchase allowances received. The company should also deduct any discounts taken for payment of the bill within a specified period of time. Deducting purchase returns and allowances and purchase discounts gives the net cost of the purchases. Then freight charges paid by the buyer (called "freight in") are added to net purchases to determine the net cost of *delivered* purchases.

In a manufacturing concern, the cost-of-goods-sold section has a slightly different form. Instead of determining the cost of goods *purchased,* the company determines the cost of goods *manufactured.* (See Table A-2.) Cost of goods manufactured ($50,000) is added to the beginning inventory ($18,000) to ascertain the total goods available for sale ($68,000). Then, after the ending inventory of finished goods has been deducted ($20,000), the result is the cost of goods sold ($48,000).

To find the cost of goods *manufactured,* a company starts with the value of goods partially completed (beginning inventory of goods in process—$24,000). To this beginning inventory figure is added the cost of raw materials, direct labor, and factory overhead expenses incurred during the period ($48,000). The resulting figure is the total goods in process during the period ($72,000). By deducting the value of goods still in process at the end of the period ($22,000), management finds the cost of goods manufactured during that span of time ($50,000).

GROSS MARGIN

Gross margin is determined simply by subtracting cost of goods sold from net sales. Gross margin, sometimes called *gross profit,* is one of the key figures in the entire marketing program. When we say that a certain store has a "margin" of 30 percent, we are referring to the gross margin.

EXPENSES

Operating expenses are deducted from gross margin to determine the net profit. The operating expense section includes marketing, administrative, and possibly some miscellaneous expense items. It does not, of course, include the cost of goods purchased or manufactured, since these costs have already been deducted.

NET PROFIT

Net profit is the difference between gross margin and total expenses. A negative net profit is, of course, a loss.

MARKUPS

Many retailers and wholesalers use markup percentages to determine the selling price of an article. Normally the selling price must exceed the cost of the merchandise by an amount sufficient to cover the operating expenses and still leave the desired profit. The difference between the selling price of an item and its cost is the **markup,** sometimes referred to as the ''mark-on.''

Typically, markups are expressed in percentages rather than dollars. A markup may be expressed as a percentage of either the cost or the selling price. Therefore, we must first determine which will be the *base* for the markup. That is, when we speak of a 40 percent markup, do we mean 40 percent of the *cost* or of the *selling price?*

To determine the markup percentage when it is based on *cost*, we use the following formula:

$$\text{Markup \%} = \frac{\text{dollar markup}}{\text{cost}}$$

When the markup is based on *selling price*, the formula to use is:

$$\text{Markup \%} = \frac{\text{dollar markup}}{\text{selling price}}$$

It is important that all interested parties understand which base is being used in a given situation. Otherwise, there can be a considerable misunderstanding. To illustrate, suppose Mr. A runs a clothing store and claims he needs a 66⅔ percent markup to make a small net profit. Ms. B, who runs a competitive store, says she needs only a 40 percent markup and that A must be inefficient or a big profiteer. Actually, both merchants are using identical markups, but they are using different bases. Each seller buys hats at $6 apiece and sets the selling price at $10. This is a markup of $4 per hat. Mr. A is expressing his markup as a percentage of cost—hence, the 66⅔ percent figure ($4 ÷ $6 = .67, or 66⅔ percent). Ms. B is basing her markup on the selling price ($4 ÷ $10 = .4, or 40 percent). It would be a mistake for Mr. A to try to get by on B's 40 percent markup, as long as A uses cost as his base. To illustrate, if Mr. A used the 40 percent markup, *but based it on cost*, the markup would be only $2.40. And the selling price would be only $8.40. This $2.40 markup, averaged over the entire hat department, would not enable A to cover his usual expenses and make a profit.

Unless otherwise indicated, markup percentages are always stated as percentage of selling price.

Markup Based on Selling Price

The following diagram should help you understand the various relationships between selling price, cost, and markup. It can be used to compute these figures regardless of whether the markup is stated in percentages or dollars, and whether the percentages are based on selling price or cost:

	Dollars	Percentage
Selling price		
less Cost		
equals Markup		

As an example, suppose a merchant buys an article for $90 and knows the markup based on selling price must be 40 percent. What is the selling price? By filling in the known information in the diagram, we obtain:

	Dollars	Percentage
Selling price		100
less Cost	90	
equals Markup		40

The percentage representing cost must then be 60 percent. Thus the $90 cost is 60 percent of the selling price. The selling price is then $150. [That is, $90 equals 60 percent of the selling price. Then $90 is divided by .6 (or 60 percent) to get the selling price of $150.]

A common situation facing merchants is to have competition set a ceiling on selling prices. Or possibly the sellers must buy an item to fit into one of their price lines. Then they want to know the maximum amount they can pay for an item and still get their normal markup. For instance, assume that the selling price of an article is set at $60 (by competition or by the $59.95 price line). The retailer's normal markup is 35 percent. What is the most that the retailer should pay for this article? Again, let's fill in what we know in the diagram:

	Dollars	Percentage
Selling price	60	100
less Cost		
equals Markup		35

The dollar markup is $21 (35 percent of $60). So, by a simple subtraction we find that the maximum cost the merchant will want to pay is $39.

Series of Markups

It should be clearly understood that markups are figured on the selling price at *each level of business* in a channel of distribution. A manufacturer applies a markup to determine its selling price. The manufacturer's selling price then becomes the whole-saler's cost. Then the wholesaler must determine its own selling price by applying its usual markup percentage based on its—the wholesaler's—selling price. The same procedure is carried on by the retailer, whose cost is the wholesaler's selling price. The following computations should illustrate this point:

Producer's cost $ 7 \
Producer's selling price $10 }   **Producer's markup = $3, or 30%**

| Wholesaler's cost | $10 |
| Wholesaler's selling price | $12 |

Wholesaler's markup = $2, or 16⅔%

| Retailer's cost | $12 |
| Retailer's selling price | $20 |

Retailer's markup = $8, or 40%

Markup Based on Cost

If a firm is used to dealing in markups based on cost—and sometimes this is done among wholesalers—the same diagrammatic approach may be employed that was used above. The only change is that cost will equal 100 percent. Then the selling price will be 100 percent plus the markup based on cost. As an example, assume that a firm bought an article for $70 and wants a 20 percent markup based on cost. The markup in dollars is $14 (20 percent of $70). The selling price is $84 ($70 plus $14):

		Dollars	Percentage
	Selling price	84	120
less	Cost	70	100
equals	Markup	14	20

A marketing executive should understand the relationship between markups on cost and markups on selling price. For instance, if a product costs $6 and sells for $10, there is a $4 markup. This is a 40 percent markup based on selling price, but a 66⅔ percent markup based on cost. The following diagram may be helpful in understanding these relationships and in converting from one base to another.

If selling price = 100%

$$\$10 = 100\% \begin{cases} 60\% \rightarrow \\ 40\% \rightarrow \end{cases} \begin{matrix} \textbf{Cost} = \textbf{\$6.00} \\ \textbf{Markup} = \textbf{\$4.00} \end{matrix} \begin{matrix} \leftarrow 100\% \\ \leftarrow 66\frac{2}{3}\% \end{matrix} \Big\} \ \$10 = 166\frac{2}{3}\%$$

If cost = 100%

The relationships between the two bases are expressed in the following formulas:

(1) % markup on selling price = $\dfrac{\% \text{ markup on cost}}{100\% + \% \text{ markup on cost}}$

(2) % markup on cost = $\dfrac{\% \text{ markup on selling price}}{100\% - \% \text{ markup on selling price}}$

To illustrate the use of these formulas, let us assume that a retailer has a markup of 25 percent on *cost*. This retailer then wants to know what the corresponding figure is, based on selling price. In formula 1 we get:

$$\frac{25\%}{100\% + 25\%} = \frac{25\%}{125\%} = .2, \text{ or } 20\%$$

A markup of 33⅓ percent based on *selling price* converts to 50 percent based on cost, according to formula 2:

$$\frac{33\frac{1}{3}\%}{100\% - 33\frac{1}{3}\%} = \frac{33\frac{1}{3}\%}{66\frac{2}{3}\%} = .5, \text{ or } 50\%$$

The markup is closely related to the gross margin. Recall that gross margin is equal to net sales minus cost of goods sold. Looking below the gross margin on an

ANALYTICAL RATIOS

operating statement, we find that gross margin equals operating expenses plus net profit. Normally, the initial markup in a company, department, or product line must be set a little higher than the overall gross margin desired for the selling unit. The reason for this is that, ordinarily, some reductions will be incurred before all the articles are sold. For one reason or another, some items will not sell at the original price. They will have to be marked down, that is, reduced in price from the original level. Some pilferage and other shortages also may occur.

From a study of the operating statement, management can develop several ratios that are useful in evaluating the results of its marketing program. In most cases, net sales is used as the base (100 percent). In fact, unless it is specifically mentioned to the contrary, all ratios reflecting gross margin, net profit, or any operating expense are stated as a percentage of net sales.

Gross Margin Percentage

This is the ratio of gross margin to net sales. In Table A-1, the gross margin percentage is \$32,000 ÷ \$80,000, or 40 percent.

Net Profit Percentage

This ratio is computed by dividing net profit by net sales. In Table A-1, the ratio is \$4,800 ÷ \$80,000, or 6 percent. This percentage may be computed either before or after federal income taxes are deducted, but the result should be labeled to show which it is.

Operating Expense Percentage

When total operating expenses are divided by net sales, the result is the operating expense ratio. In Table A-1, the ratio is \$27,200 ÷ \$80,000, or 34 percent. In similar fashion, we may determine the expense ratio for any given cost. Thus we note in Table A-1 that the rent expense was 1 percent, advertising was 3 percent, and sales-force salaries and commissions were 13.75 percent.

Rate of Stockturn

Management often measures the efficiency of its marketing operations by means of the **stockturn rate**. This figure represents the number of times the average inventory is "turned over," or sold, during the period under study. The rate is computed on either a cost or a selling-price basis. That is, both the numerator and the denominator of the ratio fraction must be expressed in the same terms, either cost or selling price.

On a *cost* basis, the formula for stockturn rate is as follows:

$$\text{Rate of stockturn} = \frac{\text{cost of goods sold}}{\text{average inventory at cost}}$$

The average inventory is determined by adding the beginning and ending inventories and dividing the result by 2. In Table A-1, the average inventory is (\$18,000 + \$20,000) ÷ 2 = \$19,000. The stockturn rate then is \$48,000 ÷ \$19,000, or 2.5. Because inventories usually are abnormally low at the first of the year in anticipation of taking physical inventory, this average may not be representative. Consequently, some companies find their average inventory by adding the book inventories at the beginning of each month, and then dividing this sum by 12.

Now let's assume the inventory is recorded on a *selling-price* basis, as is done in most large retail organizations. Then the stockturn rate equals net sales divided by average inventory at selling price. Sometimes the stockturn rate is computed by dividing the number of *units* sold by the average inventory expressed in *units*.

Wholesale and retail trade associations in many types of businesses publish figures showing the average rate of stockturn for their members. A firm with a low rate of stockturn is likely to be spending too much on storage and inventory. Also, the company runs a higher risk of obsolescence or spoilage. If the stockturn rate gets too high, this may indicate that the company maintains too low an average inventory. Often, a firm in this situation is operating on a hand-to-mouth buying system. In addition to incurring high handling and billing costs, the company is liable to be out of stock on some items.

Markdown Percentage

Sometimes retailers are unable to sell articles at the originally stated prices, and they reduce these prices to move the goods. A **markdown** is a reduction from the original selling price. Management frequently finds it very helpful to determine the markdown percentage. Then management analyzes the size and number of markdowns and the reasons for them. Retailers, particularly, make extensive use of markdown analysis.

Markdowns are expressed as a percentage of net sales and *not* as a percentage of the original selling price. To illustrate, assume that a retailer purchased a hat for $6 and marked it up 40 percent to sell for $10. The hat did not sell at that price, so it was marked down to $8. Now the seller may advertise a price cut of 20 percent. Yet, according to our rule, this $2 markdown is 25 percent *of the $8 selling price.*

Markdown percentage is computed by dividing total dollar markdowns by total net sales during a given period of time. Two important points should be noted here. First, the markdown percentage is computed in this fashion, whether the markdown items were sold or are still in the store. Second, the percentage is computed with respect to total net sales, and not only in connection with sales of marked-down articles. As an example, assume that a retailer buys 10 hats at $6 each and prices them to sell at $10. Five hats are sold at $10. The other five are marked down to $8, and three are sold at the lower price. Total sales are $74, and the total markdowns are $10. The retailer has a markdown ratio of $10 ÷ $74, or 13.5 percent.

Markdowns do not appear on the profit and loss statement because they occur *before* an article is sold. The first item on an operating statement is gross sales. That figure reflects the actual selling price, which may be the selling price after a markdown has been taken.

Return on Investment

A commonly used measure of managerial performance and the operating success of a company is its rate of return on investment. We use both the balance sheet and the operating statement as sources of information. The formula for calculating return on investment (ROI) is as follows:

$$\text{ROI} = \frac{\text{net profit}}{\text{sales}} \times \frac{\text{sales}}{\text{investment}}$$

Two questions may quickly come to mind. First, what do we mean by "investment"? Second, why do we need two fractions? It would seem that the "sales" component in each fraction would cancel out, leaving net profit divided by investment as the meaningful ratio.

To answer the first query, consider a firm whose operating statement shows annual sales of $1,000,000 and a net profit of $50,000. At the end of the year, the balance sheet reports:

Assets	$600,000	Liabilities	$200,000
		Capital stock	$300,000
		Retained earnings	100,000
	$600,000		400,000
			$600,000

Now, is the investment $400,000 or $600,000? Certainly the ROI will depend upon which figure we use. The answer depends upon whether we are talking to the stockholders or to the company executives. The stockholders are more interested in the return on what they have invested—in this case, $400,000. The ROI calculation then is:

$$ROI = \frac{\text{net profit } \$50,000}{\text{sales } \$1,000,000} \times \frac{\text{sales } \$1,000,000}{\text{investment } \$400,000} = 12\frac{1}{2}\%$$

Management, on the other hand, is more concerned with the total investment, as represented by the total assets ($600,000). This is the amount that the executives must manage, regardless of whether the assets were acquired by stockholders' investment, retained earnings, or loans from outside sources. Within this context the ROI computation becomes:

$$ROI = \frac{\text{net profit } \$50,000}{\text{sales } \$1,000,000} \times \frac{\text{sales } \$1,000,000}{\text{investment } \$600,000} = 8\frac{1}{3}\%$$

Regarding the second question, we use two fractions because we are dealing with two separate elements—the rate of profit on sales and the rate of capital turnover. Management really should determine each rate separately and then multiply the two. The rate of profit on sales is influenced by marketing considerations—sales volume, price, product mix, advertising effort. The capital turnover is a financial consideration not directly involved with costs or profits—only sales volume and assets managed.

To illustrate, assume that our company's profits doubled with the same sales volume and investment because management operated an excellent marketing program this year. In effect, we doubled our profit rate with the same capital turnover:

$$ROI = \frac{\text{net profit } \$100,000}{\text{sales } \$1,000,000} \times \frac{\text{sales } \$1,000,000}{\text{investment } \$600,000} = 16\frac{2}{3}\%$$

$$10\% \times 1.67 = 16\frac{2}{3}\%$$

As expected, this $16\frac{2}{3}$ percent is twice the ROI calculated above.

Now assume that we earned our original profit of $50,000 but that we did it with an investment reduced to $500,000. We cut the size of our average inventory, and we closed some branch offices. By increasing our capital turnover from 1.67 to 2, we raise the ROI from $8\frac{1}{3}$ percent to 10 percent, even though sales volume and profits remain unchanged:

$$\text{ROI} = \frac{\$50,000}{\$1,000,000} \times \frac{\$1,000,000}{\$500,000} = 10\%$$

$$= \mathbf{5\%} \times \mathbf{2} = \mathbf{10\%}$$

Assume now that we increase our sales volume—let us say we double it—but do not increase our profit or investment. That is, the cost-profit squeeze is bringing us "profitless prosperity." The following interesting results occur:

$$\text{ROI} = \frac{\$50,000}{\$2,000,000} \times \frac{\$2,000,000}{\$600,000} = 8\frac{1}{3}\%$$

$$= \mathbf{2\frac{1}{2}\%} \times \mathbf{3.33} = \mathbf{8\frac{1}{3}\%}$$

The profit rate was cut in half, but this was offset by a doubling of the capital turnover rate, leaving the ROI unchanged.

QUESTIONS AND PROBLEMS

1. Construct an operating statement from the following data, and compute the gross-margin percentage:

Purchases at billed cost	$15,000
Net sales	30,000
Sales returns and allowances	200
Cash discounts given	300
Cash discounts earned	100
Rent	1,500
Salaries	6,000
Opening inventory at cost	10,000
Advertising	600
Other expenses	2,000
Closing inventory at cost	7,500

2. Prepare a retail operating statement from the following data and compute the markdown percentage:

Rent	$ 9,000
Closing inventory at cost	28,000
Sales returns	6,500
Gross margin as percentage of sales	35
Cash discounts allowed	2,000
Salaries	34,000
Markdowns	4,000
Other operating expenses	15,000
Opening inventory at cost	35,000
Gross sales	232,500
Advertising	5,500
Freight in	3,500

3. What percentage markups on cost correspond to the following percentages of markup on selling price?
   a. 20 percent.   c. 50 percent.
   b. 37½ percent.   d. 66⅔ percent.

4. What percentage markups on selling price correspond to the following percentages of markup on cost?

   a. 20 percent.
   b. 33⅓ percent.
   c. 50 percent.
   d. 300 percent.

5. A hardware store bought a gross (12 dozen) of hammers, paying $302.40 for the lot. The retailer estimated operating expenses for this product to be 35 percent of sales, and wanted a net profit of 5 percent of sales. The retailer expected no markdowns. What retail selling price should be set for each hammer?

6. Competition in a certain line of sporting goods pretty well limits the selling price on a certain item to $25. If the store owner feels a markup of 35 percent is needed to cover expenses and return a reasonable profit, what is the most the owner can pay for this item?

7. A retailer with annual net sales of $2 million maintains a markup of 66⅔ percent based on cost. Expenses average 35 percent. What are the retailer's gross margin and net profit in dollars?

8. A company has a stockturn rate of five times a year, a sales volume of $600,000, and a gross margin of 25 percent. What is the average inventory at cost?

9. A store has an average inventory of $30,000 at retail and a markup of 50 percent based on cost, and a stockturn rate of five times a year. If the company maintains a markup of 50 percent based on cost, what are the annual sales volume and the cost of goods sold?

10. From the following data, compute the gross margin percentage and the operating expense ratio:

    Stockturn rate = 9
    Average inventory at selling price = $45,000
    Net profit = $20,000
    Cost of goods sold = $350,000

11. A ski shop sold 50 pairs of skis at $90 a pair, after taking a 10 percent markdown. All the skis were originally purchased at the same price and had been marked up 60 percent on cost. What was the gross margin on the 50 pairs of skis?

12. A men's clothing store bought 200 suits at $90 each. The suits were marked up 40 percent. Eighty were sold at that price. The remaining suits were each marked down 20 percent from the original selling price, and then they were sold. Compute the sales volume and the markdown percentage.

13. An appliance retailer sold 60 radios at $30 each after taking markdowns equal to 20 percent of the actual selling price. Originally all the radios had been purchased at the same price and were marked up 50 percent on cost. What was the gross margin percentage earned in this situation?

14. An appliance manufacturer produced a line of small appliances advertised to sell at $30. The manufacturer planned for wholesalers to receive a 20 percent markup, and retailers a 33⅓ percent markup. Total manufacturing costs were $12 per unit. What did retailers pay for the product? What were the manufacturer's selling price and percentage markup?

15. A housewares manufacturer produces an article at a full cost of $1.80. It is sold through a manufacturers' agent directly to large retailers. The agent receives a 20 percent commission on sales, the retailers earn a margin of 30 percent, and

the manufacturer plans a net profit of 10 percent on the selling price. What is the retail price of this article?

16. A manufacturer suggests a retail selling price of $400 on an item and grants a chain discount of 40-10-10. What is the manufacturer's selling price? (Chain discounts are discussed in Chapter 13.)

17. A building materials manufacturer sold a quantity of a product to a wholesaler for $350, and the wholesaler in turn sold to a lumberyard. The wholesaler's normal markup was 15 percent, and the retailer usually priced the item to include a 30 percent markup. What is the selling price to consumers?

18. From the following data, calculate the return on investment, based on a definition of *investment* that is useful for evaluating managerial performance:

Net sales	$800,000	Markup	35%
Gross margin	$280,000	Average inventory	$ 75,000
Total assets	$200,000	Retained earnings	$ 60,000
Cost of goods sold	$520,000	Operating expenses	$240,000
Liabilities	$ 40,000		

B

CAREERS IN MARKETING

Jobs leading to careers in marketing—what are they, where are they, and how do you get one? That's what this appendix is all about. For the past few months, your main concern probably has been to learn enough about marketing to get a good grade in the course. As you studied the various marketing activities, however, at one point or another you might have thought, "I'd like a job like that." Or, as you read about various organizations (manufacturers, retailers, service firms, etc.), you might have said, "I think I'd like to work for an outfit like that." Now perhaps you can devote more attention to the career opportunities that exist in the broad field of marketing.

CHOOSING A CAREER

One of the most significant decisions you will ever make is your choice of a career. Your career decision will have an important influence on your future happiness, self-fulfillment, and well-being. Yet, unfortunately, career decisions often seem to be based on insufficient information, analysis, and evaluation of alternatives.

One key to a wise career decision is to get as much information about as wide a variety of career alternatives as is reasonably possible. By broadening your search, you may discover some interesting fields that you knew nothing about or that you had gross misconceptions about.

At this point, let's look briefly at three key areas that you should analyze in some detail in the course of career selection.

What Do You Want from a Career?

Perhaps this question would be better worded if we asked, "What do you want out of life?" or "What is important to you in life?" To answer these broad questions, you first must answer several more limited ones, such as the following:

Are you looking for a career with high financial rewards?
How important is the social prestige of the career?
Do you want your career to be the main thing in your life?
Or do you see a career only as the means of financing leisure-time activities?

How important are the climate and other aspects of the physical environment in which you live?

That is, would you take less money and a less prestigious job in order to live in a pleasant environment?

Would you prefer to work for a large company or a small organization?

Would you prefer living and working in a small town or in a major urban center?

Another way to approach the key questions in this section is to identify—in writing—your goals in life. Identify both your short-term goals (3 to 5 years from now) and your long-term goals (10 years or more).

Still another approach is to state your self-concept in some detail. By describing yourself as you see yourself, you may be able to identify various careers that would (or would not) fit your self-image.

What Do You Have to Offer?

Here you have to identify in some detail your strong and weak points. Why would anyone want to hire you? What are your qualifications? What experience—work, education, extracurricular activities—do you have that might be attractive to prospective employers?

A key point to recognize is whether you are more interested in people or in things. In the field of marketing, for example, a people-oriented person might be attracted to a career in personal selling and sales management. A things-oriented person might prefer a job in advertising, marketing research, or physical distribution.

Career Factors to Consider

There are several major factors that you should consider when evaluating a job or career in any given field. To some extent, these issues reflect the first two general topics already discussed in this section.

Will you be happy in your work? This is a key factor to consider when evaluating any career. Remember—normally, half or more of your waking hours will be spent at work, commuting to and from work, or doing job-related work at home. So you should look for the job and career that you will enjoy during that big chunk of your waking time.

Also keep in mind that many (and maybe most) of the people in our society do not seem to be happy with their jobs. We speak of "Blue Monday" (the wonderful weekend is finished and I have to go back to work). The saying TGIF (Thank God It's Friday) did not enter our vocabulary because people love their work.

Does the career fit your self-image? Are the job and career in line with your goals, dreams, and aspirations? Will they satisfy you? Will you be proud to tell people about your job? Will your spouse (and someday your teenage children) be proud of you in that career?

What demands (pressures) are associated with the career? Some people thrive on pressure. They constantly seek new challenges in their work. Other people look for a more tranquil work experience. They do not want a job with constant demands, deadlines to meet, and heavy pressures.

WHAT ARE THE JOBS?

Financial considerations How does the starting salary compare with those of other jobs? Consider what the job is likely to pay after you have been there 3 to 5 years. Some engineering jobs, for example, have high starting salaries, but you soon hit a salary ceiling. In contrast, some marketing jobs have lower starting salaries, but no upper limits.

Opportunities for promotion You should evaluate the promotion patterns in a job or in a firm. Try to find out how long it normally takes to reach a given executive level. Study the backgrounds of the presidents in a number of large companies. Did they come up through engineering, the legal department, sales or marketing, accounting, or some other area?

Travel considerations Some jobs involve a considerable amount of travel whether you are an entry-level worker or an executive. Other jobs are strictly in-house, with no travel at all.

Job or career "transportability" Are there similar jobs in many other geographic areas? If you and your spouse both are career-oriented, what will happen, say, to you if your spouse is transferred to another city? Can you also move to that new city and get a job similar to your present job? One nice thing about such careers as teaching, retailing, nursing, and personal selling is that generally these jobs exist in considerable numbers in many different locations.

Qualifications needed Determine what qualifications are needed to enter (and later to prosper in) a given field. Then review your own background to see whether there is a close fit between the job requirements and your qualifications.

Supply and demand situation Determine generally how many job openings currently exist in a given field, as compared with the supply of qualified applicants. At the same time, study the future prospects regarding this supply and demand condition. Determine whether a present shortage of workers, or overcrowding in a field, is a temporary situation, or whether it is likely to exist for several years.

Back in the first chapter, we noted that about one-quarter to one-third of all civilian jobs are in the field of marketing. These jobs cover a wide range of activities. Furthermore, this variety of jobs also covers a wide range of qualifications and aptitudes. Jobs in personal selling, for example, call for a set of qualifications that are different from those in marketing research. A person likely to be successful in advertising may not be a good prospect in physical distribution. Consequently, the personal qualifications and aptitudes of different individuals make them candidates for different types of marketing jobs.

In this section we shall briefly describe the major jobs in marketing, grouping them by the title of the job or the activity.

Personal Selling

By far, sales jobs are the most numerous of all the jobs in marketing. Personal selling jobs (1) cover a wide variety of activities, (2) are found in a wide variety of organizations, and (3) carry a wide variety of titles.

You can get some idea of the wide variety of sales jobs by reviewing the seven-part classification of sales jobs back in Chapter 19. Consider the following people: a driver–sales person for Coca-Cola; a sales clerk in a department store; a sales engineer providing technical assistance in the sales of hydraulic valves; a representative for Boeing selling a fleet of airplanes; a marketing consultant selling his or her services. All these people are engaged in personal selling, but each sales job is different from the others.

Sales jobs of one sort or another are available in virtually every locality. This means you can pretty well pick the area where you would like to live, and still get involved in personal selling.

There are opportunities to earn a *very* high income in personal selling. This is especially true when the compensation plan is straight commission, or is a combination of salary plus a significant incentive element.

A sales job is the most common entry-level position in marketing. Furthermore, a sales job is a widely used stepping-stone to a management position. Many companies recruit people for sales jobs with the intention of promoting some or all of these people into management positions. Personal selling and sales management jobs are also a good route to the top in a firm. This is so because it is relatively easy to measure a person's performance and productivity in selling. Sales results are highly visible.

A sales job is different from other jobs in several significant ways.[1] (1) Sales people represent their company to customers and to the public in general. The public ordinarily does not judge a firm by its factory or office personnel. (2) Outside sales people (those who go to the customers, in contrast to those in situations where the customers come to the seller) operate with very little or no direct personal supervision and stimulation. These jobs frequently require a considerable amount of creativity, persistency, and self-motivation. (3) Because of the customer contacts, sales jobs require more tact and social intelligence than do other jobs on the same level in an organization. (4) Sales people are authorized to spend company money in connection with their travel, entertainment, and other business expenses. (5) Sales jobs frequently involve traveling and require much time away from home and family. (6) Unfortunately, personal selling jobs generally rate low in social status and prestige.

All in all, selling is hard work, but the potential rewards are immense. Certainly no other job contributes as much to the success of an organization. Remember—nothing happens until somebody sells something!

Advertising

As in personal selling, so also in advertising are there many different types of jobs in a wide variety of organizations. However, not nearly so many people are employed in advertising as in personal selling.

Advertising jobs are available in three broad types of organizations. First there

---

[1]Adapted from William J. Stanton and Richard H. Buskirk, *Management of the Sales Force*, 6th ed., Richard D. Irwin, Inc., Homewood, Ill., 1983, pp. 15–17.

are jobs with the *advertisers*. Many of these organizations—manufacturers, retailers, marketers of services—prepare and place their own ads. In some cases, the advertising department is a big operation in these firms. Then there are careers with the various *media* (newspapers, TV stations, magazines, etc.) that carry the ads. And, finally, there are the many jobs with *advertising agencies* which specialize in creating and producing individual ads and entire campaigns.

Jobs in advertising encompass a variety of aptitudes and interests—artistic, creative, managerial, research, and sales, for example. There is a real opportunity for the artistic or creative type of person. Agencies and advertising departments need copywriters, artists, photographers, layout designers, printing experts, and others to create and produce the ads.

An account executive is a key position in advertising agencies. People in this position are the liaison between the agency and its clients (the advertisers). Account executives coordinate the agency's efforts with the clients' marketing programs.

Another group of advertising jobs involves buying and selling the media time and space. Advertisers and agencies also often need people who can conduct consumer behavior studies and other types of marketing research.

Sales Promotion

The main function of sales promotion is to tie together the activities outlined in Table 4-2 in personal selling and advertising. Effective sales promotion requires imagination and creativity, coupled with a sound foundation in marketing fundamentals.

One group of sales promotion activities involves retailer in-store displays and window displays—planning and creating them. Another area of sales promotion jobs involves direct-mail advertising programs. Still another area deals with trade shows and other company exhibits. Sales promotion activities also include the development and management of premium giveaways, contests, product sampling, and other types of promotion.

Marketing Research

Marketing research jobs cover the broad range of activities outlined in Table 4-2 in Chapter 4. People are hired for marketing research jobs by manufacturers, retailers, service marketers, government agencies, and other types of organizations. There also are a large number of specialized marketing research companies. Generally, however, there are fewer jobs in marketing research than in personal selling or in advertising.

Marketing research people are problem solvers. They collect and analyze masses of information. Consequently, they need an aptitude for methodical, analytical types of work. Typically, some quantitative skills are needed. It helps if you understand statistics and feel comfortable using a computer.

Purchasing

The opposite of selling is buying, and here there are a lot of good jobs. Every retail organization needs people to buy the merchandise that is to be sold. Frequently the route to the top in retailing is through the buying (also called merchandising) division of the business. Large retailers have many positions for buyers and assistant buyers. Typically, each merchandise department has a buyer. Consequently, you have a chance to work with the particular products that interest you.

There also are centralized buying offices that buy for several different stores. These resident buying offices typically are in New York City and a few other large cities.

The purchasing agent is the industrial market counterpart of the retail-store buyer. Virtually all firms in the industrial market have purchasing departments. People in these departments buy for the production, office, and sales departments in their firms.

Retail buyers and industrial purchasing agents need many of the same skills. They must be able to analyze markets, determine merchandise needs, and negotiate with sellers. It also helps if you have some knowledge of credit, finance, and physical distribution.

Product/Brand Management

In Chapter 9, we discussed briefly the position of product manager in connection with the organizational structure for new-product planning and development. Product managers (sometimes called brand managers) are responsible for planning and directing the entire marketing program for a given product or a group of products.

Early on, product managers are concerned with the packaging, labeling, and other aspects of the product itself. Product managers also are responsible for doing the necessary marketing research to identify the market. They plan the advertising, personal selling, and sales promotional programs for their products. Product managers also are concerned with the pricing, physical distribution, and legal aspects of the product. All in all, being a product manager is almost like running your own business.

Typically, the job of product manager is a staff position in the organization, rather than a line operating position. Thus, the product manager often has much responsibility for a product's performance. But this person does not have commensurate authority to see that his or her directives and plans are put into effect.

Physical Distribution

A large number of jobs exist in this field, and the prospects are even brighter as we look ahead to the 1990s. More and more firms are expected to adopt the systems approach in physical distribution to control the huge expenses involved in materials movement and warehousing.

Manufacturers, retailers, and all other product-handling firms have jobs that involve two stages of physical distribution. First, the product must be moved to the firm for processing or resale. Then the finished products must be distributed to the markets. These physical distribution tasks involve jobs in transportation management, warehousing, and inventory control.

In addition, the many transportation carriers and warehousing firms also provide a variety of jobs that may interest you.

Public Relations

The public relations department in an organization is the connecting link between that organization and its various publics. The department especially must deal with, or go through, the news media to reach these publics. Public relations people must be especially good in communications. In fact, frequently these people have educational backgrounds in communications or journalism, rather than in marketing.

In essence, the job of public relations is to project the desired company image to the public. More specifically, public relations people are responsible for telling the public about the company—its products, community activities, social programs, environmental improvement activities, labor policies, views regarding controversial issues, and so on. The company's position must be stated in clear, understandable, and above all, believable fashion.

Consumer Affairs and Protection

This broad area encompasses several activities that provide job and career opportunities. Many of these jobs are an outgrowth of the consumer movement discussed in Chapter 25. Many companies, for example, have a consumer affairs department to handle consumer complaints. Several federal and state agencies are set up to keep watch on business firms and to provide information and assistance to consumers. Grocery products manufacturers and gas and electric companies regularly hire home economists to aid consumers in product use. Government and private product-testing agencies hire people to test products for safety, durability, and other features.

Other Career Areas

In this brief appendix, it is not possible to list all the careers stemming from marketing. We have, however, covered the major activity areas. You may get additional career ideas from the next section, which deals with the organizations that provide these career opportunities.

Types of Organizations

WHERE ARE THE JOBS?

Literally millions of organizations provide jobs and career opportunities in marketing. The organizations can be grouped into the following categories.

In this section, we briefly describe the various companies, institutions, and other organizations that provide jobs in marketing. This section also includes comments on jobs in international marketing and comparison of job opportunities in large versus small organizations.

MANUFACTURING

Most manufacturing firms provide career opportunities in all the activities discussed in the previous section. In their promotional mix, some manufacturers stress personal selling, while others rely more on advertising. Even small companies offer job opportunities in most of the categories we've covered previously.

Large manufacturers typically have good training programs, and many of them come to college campuses as part of their job recruiting programs. Starting salaries typically are higher in manufacturing firms than in retailing and the other organizations described below.

RETAILING

Retailing firms provide more marketing jobs by far than does any other organizational category. Yet careers in retailing typically are not well understood by college students. These students tend to equate retailing with clerking in a department store or filling shelves in a supermarket. Students often perceive that retail pay is low and that retail work hours include a lot of evenings and weekends.

Actually, a career in retailing offers many attractive features. There are opportunities for very fast advancement for those who display real ability. Two factors account for these opportunities: (1) There simply is a shortage of qualified people in retailing; and (2) performance results, such as sales and profits, are quickly and highly visible. So, if you can produce, management will generally note this fact in a hurry. While the starting pay in many stores is lower than in manufacturing, the compensation in higher-level retailing jobs typically is very good. There are good retailing jobs in virtually every geographic location. Yet, once you are in a job, there is very little travel involved. And, generally speaking, retailing offers you a better opportunity than any other field to go into business for yourself.

Perhaps the main attractions in retailing are less tangible. Retailing can be an exciting field. You constantly are involved with people—customers, suppliers, and other workers. And there are challenges as a merchandise buyer, especially that of finding out what will sell well—what the customers really want.

Of course, retailing is not all fun and games. The hours can be long, and the work is hard. Retailers often can get so involved with their store and their career that they have little time for anything else. Also, the store mortality rate in retailing is high. Competition is fierce, and many stores do not have the financial backing or the managerial abilities needed to survive.

It is easier to get a job or start a career in retailing than in many other fields. In large stores, there are jobs involving personnel management, accounting controls, and store operations (receiving, credit, and customer service departments). However, the lifeblood of retailing is the buying and selling of merchandise or services. Consequently, the more numerous and better-paying positions are those of buyer and above in the merchandising end of the business. For many people, the goal is to be a store manager.

WHOLESALING

Career opportunities in wholesaling generally are less well understood and appreciated than those in retailing or manufacturing. Wholesaling firms typically do not recruit on college campuses, and they generally have a low profile with students.

Yet the opportunities are there. Merchant wholesalers of consumer products and industrial distributors both provide many jobs in buying, personal selling, marketing research, and physical distribution. Manufacturers' agents, brokers, and the other agent middlemen discussed in Chapter 15 also offer jobs and careers. Wholesaling middlemen are increasing in numbers and in sales volume, and their future is promising.

SERVICE MARKETING

The broad array of service industries listed in Chapter 21 provides a bonanza of job and career opportunities in marketing. Many of these firms really are retailers of services. Consequently, it is likely that jobs and careers will open up in really large numbers over the next several years. And recall the wide variety of nonbusiness organizations—hospitals, museums, schools, religious organizations, foundations, charities, political parties, and all the others. Truly, these are new opportunities for marketing careers that were nonexistent up to just a few years ago.

NONBUSINESS ORGANIZATIONS

As indicated in Chapter 22, nonbusiness organizations are just beginning to realize that marketing is the key to success. Consequently, it is likely that jobs and careers in many nonbusiness organizations will open up in really large numbers over the next

GOVERNMENT

Countless federal and state government organizations hire people for marketing positions. Here we include the major cabinet departments—agriculture, defense, human services, energy, and the others. We also include all the regulatory agencies. Government organizations employ people in buying, marketing research, public relations, physical distribution, consumer affairs and protection, and even advertising and sales promotion. Sometimes students tend to overlook the many marketing career opportunities with the government.

Careers in International Marketing

Some students like to travel, and they want to work at least part of the time in foreign countries. They may be interested in careers in international marketing, and they may even major in international business in college. Typically, however, companies do not hire college graduates and assign them to jobs in international marketing. Normally, people are hired for entry-level positions in the domestic divisions of a company's operations. Then, after some years of experience with the firm, an employee may have an opportunity to move into the firm's international divisions.

Usually the only students hired for entry-level positions in international marketing are (1) M.B.A.s from schools with big international programs or (2) foreign students who are hired by American firms to work in the student's home country.

Large versus Small Companies

Should you go to work for a large company or a small firm? Or should you go into business for yourself upon graduation? For over a decade now, more and more students have been saying that they want to work for a small company. They feel there is more freedom of action, more rapid advancement, and less restraint on their life-styles in the smaller firms.

Perhaps so, and certainly no one should discourage you from a career in small business. *But* your authors typically recommend to students (who ask for advice) that they start their careers in a big company. Then, after some years, they can move into a smaller firm. There are three reasons for this recommendation.

• A large firm is more likely to have a good training program in your chosen field of activity. Most students have little or no practical marketing experience. Consequently, the very fine training programs provided by most large manufacturers, retailers, and major service marketers are critically important to your career.

• You can learn something about how a big company operates. After all, when you go into a smaller firm, the large companies will be your competitors. So the more you know about them, the better able you will be to compete with them.

• After working a while for a big company, you may change your mind and decide to stay with the larger firm after all. On the other hand, let's say that you want to go to a small company after you have worked a few years in a big firm. At that time it will be relatively easy to move from a large company to a smaller one. If you start in a small firm, however, and later want to move into big business, it is not so easy to make such a move.

We have discussed (albeit briefly) the various career fields and the major types of organizations that hire people in these fields. Now let's take a brief look at how you might go about getting a job with one of these organizations.

HOW TO GET A JOB

This entire book and your entire course have been designed to teach you the fundamentals involved in developing and managing a marketing program. These fundamentals are applicable regardless of whether you are marketing a product, service, idea, or place. They are equally applicable (1) to large and small organizations, (2) to domestic and international marketing, and (3) to business and nonbusiness organizations.

Now let's see whether we can apply these fundamentals to a program designed to market *YOU*. In other words, we shall now discuss a marketing approach that you can use to get a job and to get started on a career. Here, we are talking about a *marketing* career. This same approach, however, can be used in seeking jobs and careers in any field.

Identify and Analyze the Market

The first step in building a marketing program is to identify and analyze the market. In this case, the market is your future employer. Right now, you don't know exactly who that target market is. So you must research several possible markets, and then eventually narrow down your choice. In effect, we are talking about "choosing a career." Much of what we discussed in the first section of this appendix is applicable here.

The first thing you should do is get as much information as you can regarding various career opportunities in marketing. For information sources, you might start with one or two professors whom you know reasonably well. Then try the placement office in your school, or wherever the jobs are listed. Many companies prepare recruiting brochures for students, explaining the company and its career opportunities.

Newspapers and business journals are another good information source. *The Wall Street Journal* and the business sections of large-city newspapers can be useful. Journals such as *Business Week, Marketing News, Advertising Age,* and the trade publications in many individual industries are helpful. Sometimes, looking carefully through *Moody's Manual of Investments,* Standard and Poor's *Register,* or even a series of company annual reports can give you ideas of firms you might like to work for. You should exchange information with other students who also are in the job market.

In summary, learn all you can about various firms and industries. Then, from this information search, zero in on the few companies that are your leading choices. You will then be ready to develop the marketing mix that will be effective in marketing yourself to your target markets.

In this case, the "product" you are planning and developing is yourself and your services. You want to make yourself as attractive as possible to your market—that is, prospective employers.

Start your product planning by listing in some detail your strong and weak points. These will lead into another list—your qualifications and achievements. This self-analysis is something we discussed in the first section of this chapter in connection with choosing a career.

When you are considering your qualifications, it may help to group them into broad categories such as these:

- Education—schools attended, degree earned, grade point average, major subjects.
- Work experience—part-time and full-time.

- Honors and awards.
- Extracurricular activities.
- Hobbies.
- Organizations—membership, offices, committees.

Later we will discuss the presentation of your qualifications in a personal data sheet.

An important aspect of product planning is product differentiation. How can you differentiate yourself from all the other college grads? What did you do that was different, unusual, or exceptional?

Another part of product planning is packaging. When you go for an interview, be sure that the external package looks attractive. People do judge you by your appearance, just as you judge products by the way they look. This means paying attention to what you wear. Are your shoes shined and your fingernails clean? Is your hair well groomed? A good impression starts with prospective employers' first look at you—their first meeting with you.

The Price

"What salary do you want?" "How much do you think we should pay you?" These are a couple of questions a prospective employer may ask you in a job interview. These questions may throw you if you have not done some thinking in advance regarding the price you want for your services.

As part of your marketing program, find out what the market price is for people entering your field. Talk with placement officers, career counselors, professors, and other students who are in the job market. From these sources, you should get a pretty good idea of starting salaries in entry-level positions. Use this information to decide on at least a range of salaries for yourself, *before* the interview.

Distribution Channel

There are only a few major channels you are likely to use in marketing yourself to prospective employers. The simplest channel is your placement office, assuming there is one on your campus. Most colleges, through their placement offices, play host to companies that send job recruiters to do on-campus interviewing.

Another channel is help-wanted ads in business journals, trade journals, newspapers, and other sources. Perhaps the most difficult, but often the most rewarding, channel is going directly to firms in which you are especially interested. That is, knock on doors or write letters seeking a job interview. Many employers look favorably on people who display this kind of initiative in their job search.

Promotion
Communication

Other than planning and developing an excellent product, the most important ingredient in your marketing mix is a good promotion (or communication) program. Your promotional mix will consist primarily of written communications (a form of advertising) and interviewing (a form of personal selling).

Frequently, your first contact with a prospective employer is a cover letter in which you state briefly why you are writing to that company and what you have to offer. You enclose a personal résumé, and you request an appointment for an interview.

COVER LETTER

In the opening paragraph of your cover letter, you should indicate why you want to work for the firm. Mention a couple of key points regarding the firm—points that you learned from your research. In the second paragraph, you can present a few highlights of your own experience or personality that make you an attractive prospect. In the third paragraph, state that you are enclosing your résumé, and request an appointment for an interview, even suggesting some times or dates.

RÉSUMÉ

A résumé (also called a personal data sheet) is really a brief history of yourself. You can start with some biographical information such as your name, address, phone number, age, marital status, and physical condition. Then divide the résumé into sections, including education, work experience, and activities that were listed above in the product section.

The final section of your résumé should be your references. Some writers suggest that you simply say "References furnished upon request." We, however, strongly suggest that you list your references by name, also giving their titles and addresses. Make it as easy as possible for the prospective employer to check your references.

It is difficult to overstate the value of a good cover letter and a distinctive résumé. They are critically important elements in your job search. They certainly are two of the most important ads you will ever write.

INTERVIEW

Rarely is anyone hired without one or more interviews. In some cases, as when job recruiters visit your campus, the interview is your initial contact with the firm. In other situations, the interviews come as a result of your letter of introduction and résumé.

The interview is an experience in personal selling—in this case, you are selling yourself. People are often uncomfortable and uptight in interviews, especially their first few interviews. As a result, one good idea is to start by interviewing with companies that you are not especially interested in working for. In effect, these are practice interviews, so if you blow one, there is no great loss. These practice interviews also will help you later in handling the tough questions that sometimes are asked. These are questions such as "Why should we hire you?" "Why do you think you are good enough to work for us?" "What kind of a job do you expect to have in five years?"

Your conduct in an interview often determines whether or not you get the job. So be on your toes—be honest in your answers, and try to look relaxed and confident (even though you may not feel that way). Make sure your clothing, grooming, and general appearance are very much in line with the standards of the particular employer.

After the interviews with the company have been completed, write a letter to the interviewers. Thank them for the opportunity to meet them, and state that you hope you will hear from them soon regarding the job.

CONCLUSION—A PERSONAL NOTE

∎

As we said at the beginning of this appendix, choosing a career is one of the most important decisions you will ever make in your life. Certainly, looking for a job upon graduation can be a very exciting experience and yet at times a difficult and worrisome one. We hope that this brief appendix has furnished some ideas that will be helpful in your job search and career decision-making process. But most of all, we hope that you can find a career in which you will be happy.

William J. Stanton
Charles M. Futrell

accessory equipment In the industrial market, capital goods used in the operation of an industrial firm. Accessory equipment is shorter-lived than installations and does not materially affect the scale of operations in a company.

administered vertical marketing system A distribution system in which channel control is maintained through the economic power of one firm in the channel.

adoption curve The distribution curve showing when various groups adopt an innovation.

adoption process The stages that an individual goes through in deciding whether or not to accept an innovation.

advertisement The nonpersonal message in advertising that is disseminated through media and is paid for by the identified sponsor.

advertising The activities involved in presenting a paid, sponsor-identified, nonpersonal message about an organization and/or its products, services, or ideas.

advertising agency An independent company set up to provide specialized advertising services to advertisers and to the advertising media.

advertising appropriation The amount of money allocated for an organization's advertising program for a specific period of time.

advertising media The vehicles (newspapers, radio, television, etc.) that carry the advertising message (the advertisement) to the intended market.

agent middleman An independent business that does not take title to goods but actively assists in the transfer of title.

agents and brokers A broad category of wholesaling middlemen that do not take title to products. The category includes manufacturers' agents, selling agents, commission merchants, auctioneers, brokers, and others.

agribusiness The business side of farming. Usually involves large, highly mechanized farming operations.

AIDA The sales presentation stage of the personal selling process. Consists of steps to attract Attention, hold Interest, arouse Desire, and generate buyer Action by meeting the buyer's objections and closing the sale.

annual marketing plan A master plan covering a year's marketing operations. It is one part—one time segment—of the ongoing strategic marketing planning process.

area sample A statistical sample that is selected at random from a list of geographic areas.

attitude A person's enduring cognitive evaluation, feeling, or action tendency toward some object, idea, or person.

auction company An independent agent wholesaling middleman that (1) provides the physical facilities for displaying prod-

ucts to be sold, and (2) does the selling in an auction.

automatic vending The nonstore, nonpersonal selling and delivery of products through coin-operated vending machines.

balance of trade In international business, the difference between the value of a nation's imports and its exports. If exports exceed imports, the country has a favorable balance of trade. When imports exceed exports, there is an unfavorable trade balance.

base price The price of one unit of a product at its point of production or resale. Also called *list price*.

battle of the brands Market competition between manufacturers' brands and middlemen's (store) brands. In recent years, "no-brand" (generic) brands have entered this competitive struggle.

benefit segmentation A basis for segmenting a market. A total market is divided into segments based on the customers' perceptions of the various benefits provided by a product.

blanket branding A strategy used for branding a group of products. Also called *family branding*.

box store A low-cost, low-price, low-service, no-frills supermarket. Offers a limited assortment of staple food products displayed in their original packing boxes. Also called a *warehouse store*.

brand A name, term, symbol, special design, or some combination of these elements that identifies the product or service of one seller.

brand manager A product manager responsible for one or more brands.

brand mark The part of a brand that appears in the form of a symbol, picture, design, or distinctive color.

brand name The part of a brand that can be vocalized—words, letters, and/or numbers.

breadth of product mix The number of product lines offered for sale by a firm.

break bulk To divide a large quantity of a product into smaller units for resale to the next customer in the distribution channel. This is usually done by middlemen.

break-even point The level of output at which revenues equal costs.

broker An independent agent wholesaling middleman whose main function is to bring buyer and seller together and to furnish market information.

business portfolio analysis An evaluation to determine the present status and future roles of a company's strategic business units (SBUs).

buy classes Three typical buying situations in the industrial market—namely, new task, modified rebuy, and straight rebuy.

buyer's market A situation in which the supply of a product or service greatly exceeds the demand for it.

buying center All the people who participate in the buying-decision process.

buying decision-making process The steps that a buyer goes through in the course of deciding whether to purchase a given item.

campaign In promotion or advertising, a coordinated series of promotional efforts built around a theme and designed to reach some goal.

canned sales talk A form of sales presentation consisting of a company-provided speech that a sales representative is supposed to deliver verbatim during a sales call.

carload rate (c.l.) The freight rate for shipping a carload of a given product.

cartel A group of companies that have banded together to regulate competition in the production and marketing of a given product.

cash discount A deduction from list price for paying a bill within a specified period of time.

catalog showroom A retail store that displays the merchandise in a showroom, takes orders out of a catalog, and fills these orders from inventories stored on the premises.

chain store One in a group of retail stores that carry the same type of merchandise. Corporate chain stores are centrally owned and managed. Voluntary chains are an association of independently owned stores.

channel captain The firm (producer or middleman) that controls a given distribution channel.

channel conflicts Friction in a channel of distribution occurring because the channel members are independent, profit-seeking organizations often operating with conflicting goals. Conflict may occur among middlemen on the same level of distribution (horizontal conflict) or among firms on different levels (vertical conflict).

channel of distribution The route that a product, and/or the title to the product, takes as it moves to its market. A channel includes the producer, the consumer or industrial user, and any middlemen involved in this route.

Clayton Antitrust Act (1914) A federal law prohibiting price discrimination that may injure competition. Restricts exclusive dealing, tying contracts, and interlocking boards of directors.

closing In personal selling, the stage in the selling process when the sales person gets the buyer to agree to make the purchase.

cognitive dissonance Postpurchase anxiety often experienced by buyers.

cognitive theory of learning A refinement of the stimulus-response theory of learning; Learning is not a mechanistic process but is influenced by mental (thought) processes.

COMECON An economic union comprising Russia and other Eastern European communist nations.

commission merchant An independent agent wholesaling middleman used primarily in the marketing of agricultural products. This middleman physically handles the seller's products in central markets and has authority regarding prices and terms of sale.

commission plan A method of compensating a sales force whereby a sales person is paid for a unit of accomplishment (measured as sales volume, gross margin, or a nonselling activity). It provides much incentive for a sales rep, but little security or stability of income.

communication process A system by which an information source (sender) transmits a message to a receiver.

community shopping center A shopping center that is larger than a neighborhood center but smaller than a regional center. Usually includes one or two department stores or discount stores, along with a number of shopping-goods stores and specialty stores.

company planning Setting broad company goals and then deciding on company strategies to reach these goals. See *strategic planning.*

comparative advertising Ads compare the advertiser's brand with those of specifically named competitors.

concentration In distribution, an activity of middlemen in which the outputs of various producers are brought together. These outputs then are equalized with the market demand and later dispersed to markets.

concept testing The first three stages in the new-product development process—pretesting of the product idea, in contrast to later pretesting of the product itself and the market.

consumer goods Products intended for use by ultimate, household consumers for personal, nonbusiness purposes.

consumerism A protest by consumers against perceived injustices in marketing, and the efforts to remedy these injustices.

containerization A cargo-handling system in physical distribution that involves enclosing a shipment in some form of container. The container is sealed after loading and is not opened until it reaches its destination.

contractual vertical marketing system A distribution system in which control is exercised through contracts signed by the producer and/or middlemen members of the channel.

contribution-margin approach In marketing cost analysis, an accounting approach in which only direct expenses are allocated to the marketing units being studied. A unit's gross margin minus its direct costs equal that unit's contribution to covering the company's indirect expenses (overhead).

convenience goods A class of consumer products that people buy frequently and with the least possible time and effort.

convenience store A type of retail outlet that stresses its accessible location, long shopping hours, and the quickness and ease of shopping there.

cooperative advertising Two or more firms share the cost of an ad. When firms are on the same level of distribution (a group of retailers), we call this *horizontal* cooperative advertising. When producers and middlemen share the costs, we call this *vertical* cooperative advertising.

cooperative vertical marketing system A distribution system wherein control is maintained by one company (usually a manufacturer) owning the other (retailing and/or wholesaling) firms in the channel.

correlation analysis A form of the market-factor method of sales forecasting, more mathematically exact than the direct-derivation method.

cost of goods sold A major section in an operating statement, showing calculations to determine the cost of products sold during the period covered by the statement.

cost-plus pricing A major method of price determination. The price of a unit of a product is set at a level equal to the unit's total cost plus a desired profit on the unit.

cues Stimuli, weaker than drives, that determine the pattern of responses to satisfy a motive.

culture The symbols and artifacts created by people and handed down from generation to generation as determinants and regulators of human behavior in a given society.

cumulative quantity discount A discount based on the total volume purchased over a period of time.

dealer Same as a *retailer*.

decline stage of the product life cycle The stage when sales and profits decline sharply. Management must decide whether to abandon the product or to rejuvenate it in this stage.

demography The statistical study of human population and its distribution characteristics.

department store A large retailing institution that carries a very wide variety of product lines, including apparel, furniture, and home furnishings.

depth of product line The assortment within a product line.

derived demand A situation in which the demand for one product is dependent upon the demand for another product. Found in the industrial market, where the industrial demand is derived from the demand for consumer products.

descriptive label A label that gives information regarding the use, care, performance, or other features of a product.

desk jobber Same as a *drop shipper*.

devaluation of currency Reduction in the value of one country's currency in relation to the value of the currencies of other nations.

diffusion of innovation A process by which an innovation is communicated within social systems over time.

direct-action advertising Advertising that is designed to get a quick response from the potential customer.

direct derivation A relatively simple form of the market-factor method of sales forecasting.

direct expenses Expenses incurred totally in connection with one market segment or one unit (product, territory) of the company's marketing organization. Also called *separable costs*.

direct mail An advertising medium whereby the advertiser contacts prospective customers by sending some form of advertisement through the mail.

direct selling A vague term that may mean selling directly from producer to consumer without any middleman; or it may mean selling from producer direct to a retailer, thus bypassing wholesaling middlemen. Also called *direct marketing* or *direct distribution*.

discount house A general-merchandise retailer featuring self-service and prices that are below list prices or regularly advertised prices.

discount in pricing A reduction from the list price. Usually offered to buyers for buying in quantity, paying in cash, or performing marketing services for the seller.

discount retailing The practice of selling below the list price or regularly advertised price.

discretionary buying power The amount of disposable income remaining after fixed expenses and household needs are paid for.

dispersion In distribution, the middlemen's activities that distribute the correct amount of a product to its market.

disposable personal income Income remaining after personal taxes are paid.

distribution The channel structure (institutions and activities) used to transfer products and services from an organization to its markets.

distribution center A large warehousing center that implements a company's inventory-location strategy.

distributor Same as a *wholesaler*.

diversion in transit A railroad rate concession allowing a shipper to change the destination of its carload-rate rail shipment while the shipment is in transit. The seller pays the carload rate from origin to final destination.

drive A strong stimulus that requires satisfaction. Same as a *motive*.

drop shipper A limited-function wholesaler that does not physically handle the product. Also called a *desk jobber*.

dumping Selling products in foreign markets below the prices that these goods are sold for in their home markets.

early adopters The second group (following the innovators) to adopt something new. This group includes the opinion leaders, is respected, and has much influence on its peers.

early majority A more deliberate group of innovation adopters that adopts just before the "average" adopter.

economic order quantity (EOQ) A concept in the inventory-control phase of the physical distribution system that identifies the optimum quantity to reorder when replenishing inventory stocks.

economy of abundance An economy that produces and consumes far beyond its subsistence needs.

ego In Freudian psychology, the rational control center in our minds that maintains a balance between (1) the uninhibited instincts of the id and (2) the socially oriented, constraining superego.

80-20 principle A term describing the situation in which a large proportion of a company's marketing units (products, territories, customers) accounts for a small share of the company's volume or profit, and vice versa.

elastic demand A price-volume relationship, such that a change of one unit on the price scale results in a change of more than one unit on the volume scale. That is, when the price is decreased, the volume increases to the point where there is an increase in total revenue. When the price is increased, demand declines and so does total revenue.

EOQ See *economic order quantity*.

equalization In distribution, the activity of middlemen that balances the output of

producers with the demands of consumers and industrial users.

European Community (EC) Perhaps better known as the Common Market, an economic union of 12 Western European nations (Belgium, France, West Germany, Luxembourg, Netherlands, Italy, Great Britain, Ireland, Denmark, Greece, Spain, and Portugal).

European Free Trade Association (EFTA) An economic union of six Western European nations (Norway, Sweden, Finland, Austria, Switzerland, and Iceland).

exchange (in marketing) The voluntary act of offering a person something of value in order to acquire something of value in return.

exclusive dealing The practice by which a manufacturer prohibits its retailers from carrying products that are competitive with that manufacturer's products.

exclusive distribution The practice in which a manufacturer uses only one wholesaler or retailer in a given market.

exclusive territories The practice by which a manufacturer requires each middleman to sell only within that middleman's assigned geographic area.

executive judgment A sales forecasting method based on estimates made by the firm's executives. Also called *jury of executive opinion*.

"expected" price The price at which customers consciously or unconsciously value a product; what customers think a product is worth.

experimental method A method of gathering primary data in a survey by establishing a controlled experiment that simulates the real market situation.

export-import agent middlemen Middlemen specializing in international marketing. They may be brokers, selling agents, or manufacturers' agents.

fabricating materials Industrial goods that have received some processing and will undergo further processing as they become a part of another product.

fabricating parts Industrial goods that have

already been processed to some extent and will be assembled in their present form (with no further change) as part of another product.

facilitating agencies Organizations that aid in a product's distribution, but they do not take title to the products or directly aid in the transfer of title. They include such organizations as transportation agencies, insurance companies, and financial institutions, as distinguished from retailing and wholesaling middlemen.

fad A short-lived fashion that is usually based on some novelty feature.

fair-trade laws The laws that formerly (up to 1975) allowed manufacturers to legally set retail prices for their products.

family branding A branding strategy in which a group of products is given a single brand. Also called *blanket branding*.

family life cycle The series of life stages that a family goes through, starting with young single people and progressing through married stages with young and then older children, and ending with older married and single people.

family packaging The use of packages with similar appearance for a group of products.

fashion A style that is popularly accepted by groups of people over a reasonably long period of time.

fashion-adoption process The process by which a style becomes popular in a market; similar to diffusion of innovation. Three theories of fashion adoption are trickle-down, trickle-across, and trickle-up.

fashion cycle Wavelike movements representing the introduction, rise, popular acceptance, and decline in popularity of a given style.

Federal Trade Commission (FTC) A five-person federal agency that administers various laws designed to foster competition and protect the consumer from unfair competition.

Federal Trade Commission Act (1914) A federal law prohibiting unfair competition and establishing the Federal Trade Commission.

feedback In the communication process, the element that tells the sender whether and how the message was received.

field (custodian) warehousing A form of public warehousing that provides a financial service for a seller.

fishyback freight service The service of transporting loaded truck trailers or railroad freight cars on barges or ships.

fixed cost A constant cost regardless of how many items are produced or sold.

F.O.B. (free on board) pricing A geographic pricing strategy whereby the buyer pays all freight charges from the F.O.B. location to the destination.

focus-group interview Interviewing 5 to 10 people who are gathered together as a group in an informal setting.

form utility The utility that is created when a product is produced.

forward dating A combination of a seasonal discount and a cash discount. The buyer places an order and receives shipment during the off-season, but does not have to pay the bill until after the season has started and some sales income has been generated.

franchise system A system wherein one organization (the franchisor) grants a number of independent operators (franchisees) the right to sell the franchisor's products or services, in exchange for meeting certain conditions laid down by the franchisor.

freight absorption A geographic pricing strategy whereby the seller pays for (absorbs) some of the freight charges in order to penetrate more distant markets.

freight forwarder A specialized transportation agency that consolidates less-than-carload or less-than-truckload shipments into carload or truckload quantities. Provides door-to-door shipping service.

full-cost approach In a marketing cost analysis, an accounting approach wherein all expenses—direct and indirect—are allocated to the marketing units being analyzed.

full-function wholesaler A merchant wholesaling middleman that performs all the usual wholesaling activities.

functional (activity) costs The grouping of operating expenses into categories that represent the major marketing activities. In a marketing cost analysis, the ledger expenses are allocated to these various activity categories.

functional discount Same as a *trade discount.*

generic product A product that is packaged in a plain label and is sold with no advertising and without a brand name. The product goes by its generic name, such as "tomatoes" or "paper towels."

generic use of brand names General reference to a product by its brand name—aspirin, cellophane, kerosene, zipper, for example—rather than its *generic name.* The owners of these brands no longer have exclusive use of the brand name.

gestalt theory of learning The theory stating that, in learning, people sense the "whole" of a thing rather than its component parts.

grade label Identification of the quality (grade) of a product by means of a letter, number, or word.

"Green River" ordinances Municipal laws designed to regulate door-to-door selling.

gross margin Net sales minus cost of goods sold. Also called *gross profit.*

growth stage of the product life cycle The stage when sales continue to increase, and profits increase, peak, and start to decline.

horizontal industrial market A situation where a given product is usable in a very wide variety of industries.

horizontal information flow A theory which holds that people take their cues from opinion leaders in their own social class.

human-orientation stage An emerging stage of marketing management that stresses quality of life rather than material standard of living.

hypermarket A very large retail store that sells a very wide variety of products intended to satisfy all of a consumer's routine needs. Also known as a *superstore* or a *super-supermarket.*

iceberg principle The concept that uses the analogy of an iceberg to represent a company's situation. Analyzing only total sales and costs is like looking at the tip of an iceberg and can be misleading.

id In Freudian psychology, the part of the that houses the basic instinctive drives, many of which are antisocial.

image utility The emotional or psychological value in a product or service, usually derived from its reputation or social standing.

imperfect competition Same as *monopolistic competition.*

impulse buying Purchasing without planning the purchase in advance.

indirect-action advertising Advertising that is designed to stimulate demand slowly over a long period of time.

indirect expenses Costs that are incurred jointly for more than one marketing unit (product, territory, market). Also called *common costs.*

industrial buying process The series of steps which an industrial user goes through when deciding whether or not to buy a given industrial product.

industrial distributor A full-service merchant wholesaler that handles industrial goods and sells to industrial users.

industrial marketing The marketing of industrial goods to industrial users.

industrial products Products intended for use in producing other goods or in rendering services in a business.

industrial users People or organizations who buy products to use in their own businesses or as aids in making other products.

inelastic demand A price-volume relationship such that a change of one unit on the price scale results in a change of less than one unit on the volume scale. That is, when the price is increased, the volume demanded goes down but total revenue increases. When the price is decreased, the volume goes up, but not enough to offset the price increase; so the net result is a decrease in total revenue.

informal investigation The stage in a marketing research study that involves informal talks with people outside the company being studied.

in-home retailing Retail selling in the customer's home. A personal sales representative may or may not be involved. In-home retailing includes door-to-door selling, party-plan selling, and selling by television and computer.

innovation Anything that is perceived by a person as being new.

innovators The first group—a venturesome group—of people to adopt something new (product, service, idea, etc.).

installations Long-lived, expensive, major industrial capital goods that directly affect the scale of operation of an industrial user.

institutional advertising Advertising designed to generate an attitude toward a company, rather than toward a specific product marketed by that company.

intensity of distribution The number of middlemen used by a producer at the retailing and wholesaling levels of distribution.

intensive distribution A manufacturer sells its product in every outlet where a customer might reasonably look for it. Also known as *mass distribution*.

introduction stage of the product life cycle The stage in which a product is launched into its market with a full-scale production and marketing program. In this stage, sales are low and losses usually are incurred.

inventory stockturn rate The number of times that a company's average inventory is sold during a year.

inverse demand A price-volume relationship such that the higher the price, the greater are the unit sales. Thus, an increase in price results in an increase in unit sales volume.

jobber Same as a *wholesaler*.

joint venture An operational structure for international marketing in which a firm that wishes to market in a foreign country

forms a partnership with an individual firm in the host country.

jury of executive opinion A sales forecasting method based on estimates made by a firm's executives.

"just-in-time" (inventory-control system) The process of buying parts and supplies in small quantities "just in time" for use in production.

kinked demand curve The type or shape of demand curve existing (1) when prices are determined entirely by market demand or (2) when a "customary" price prevails for a given product. The kink occurs at the level of the market price.

label The part of the product that carries information about the product or the seller.

laggards Tradition-bound people who are the last to adopt an innovation.

late majority The skeptical group of innovation adopters who adopt a new idea late in the game.

leader pricing Temporary price cuts on well-known items. The price cut is made with the idea that these "specials" (loss leaders) will attract customers to the store.

learning Changes in behavior resulting from previous experiences.

leasing A growing behavioral pattern in the industrial market (as well as in the consumer market) of renting a product rather than buying it outright.

ledger expenses A company's operating expenses as they appear in the usual accounting system. Also called "natural" expenses and "object-of-expenditure" costs.

less-than-carload rate (l.c.l.) A railroad freight rate for shipping a quantity that is less than a carload. This rate is higher than the carload rate.

licensing An arrangement whereby one firm sells to another firm (for a fee or royalty) the right to use the first company's patents or manufacturing processes. This is a common method of entering a foreign market: A company grants (licenses) manufacturing rights to a firm in the foreign country.

limited-function wholesaler A merchant

wholesaling middleman that performs a limited number of the usual wholesaling functions.

limited-line store A retailing institution that carries an assortment of products, but in only one or a few related product lines.

list price The official price as stated in a catalog or on a price list. The price of one unit of a product at the point of production or resale. The price before any discounts or other reductions. Also known as *base price*.

local (retail) advertising Advertising that is placed by retailers.

long-range planning Planning that covers a period of 3, 5, or 10 years, or even longer.

loss leaders See *leader pricing*.

lower-lower class The social class that includes unskilled laborers and workers in nonrespectable jobs.

lower-middle class The social class that includes white-collar workers, such as teachers, sales people, small-business owners, and office workers.

lower-upper class The social class that includes the socially prominent, newly rich people in a community.

mail interview The method of gathering data in a survey by means of a questionnaire mailed to respondents and, when completed, returned by mail.

mail-order selling A type of nonstore, nonpersonal retail or wholesale selling in which the customer mails in an order that is then delivered by mail or other parcel-delivery system.

mall-intercept interview Personal interview conducted in a shopping-center mall.

management The process of planning, implementing, and evaluating the efforts of a group of people toward a common goal. In this book, the terms *management* and *administration* are used synonymously.

management process Activities involved in planning, implementing, and evaluating a program.

manufacturers' agent An independent agent wholesaling middleman that sells part or all of a manufacturer's product mix in an assigned geographic territory. The agent sells related but noncompeting products from several manufacturers.

manufacturer's brand A brand owned by a manufacturer or other producer. Also called a *national brand.*

marginal analysis A major method of setting a base price. Involves balancing marginal revenue and marginal cost to determine the best price for profit maximization.

marginal cost The cost of producing and selling one more unit; that is, the cost of the last unit produced or sold.

marginal revenue The income derived from the sale of the last unit—the marginal unit.

markdown A reduction from the original retail selling price, usually made because the store was unable to sell the product at the original price.

market People or organizations with wants to satisfy, money to spend, and the willingness to spend it.

market aggregation A marketing strategy in which an organization treats its entire market as if that market were homogeneous.

market-based pricing A pricing strategy in which a company sets the price of its product only in relation to the competitive market price. The firms' costs have no influence at all on this price.

market factor An item that is related to the demand for a product.

market-factor analysis A sales forecasting method based on the assumption that future demand for a product is related to the behavior of certain market factors.

market index A market factor expressed in quantitative form relative to some base figure.

market potential Total expected industry sales for a product in a given market over a certain time period.

market segmentation The process of dividing the total market into one or more parts (submarkets or segments), each of which tends to be homogeneous in all significant aspects.

market segmentation (with multiple seg-
ments) A segmentation strategy that involves identifying two or more different groups of customers as target-market segments. The seller then develops a different marketing mix to reach each segment.

market segmentation (with a single segment) A segmentation strategy involving the selection of one homogeneous group of customers within the total market. The seller develops one marketing mix to reach this single segment.

market share One company's percentage share of the total industry sales in a given market.

marketing (macro societal dimension) Any exchange intended to satisfy human wants or needs.

marketing (micro organizational definition) Total system of activities designed to plan, price, promote, and distribute want-satisfying goods and services to markets.

marketing audit A total evaluation program consisting of a systematic, objective, comprehensive review of all aspects of an organization's marketing function. An evaluation of the company's goals, policies, results, organization, personnel, and practices.

marketing concept A philosophy of business based on customer orientation, profitable sales volume, and organizational coordination.

marketing cost analysis A detailed study of the operating expense section of a company's profit and loss statement.

marketing information system (MkIS) An ongoing, organized system for gathering and processing information to aid in marketing decision making.

marketing mix A combination of the four elements—product, pricing structure, distribution system, promotional activities—that constitute the core of an organization's marketing system.

marketing plan See *annual marketing plan.*

marketing planning Setting goals and strategies for the marketing effort in an organization. See *strategic marketing planning.*

marketing research The systematic gathering and analysis of information relevant to a problem in marketing.

marketing system A regularly interacting group of ideas forming a unified whole. These items include the organization that is doing the marketing, the thing that is being marketed, the target market, marketing intermediaries helping in the exchange, and environmental constraints.

markup The dollar amount that is added to the acquisition cost of a product to determine the selling price.

markup percentage The dollar markup expressed as a percentage of either the selling price or the cost of the product.

maturity stage of the product life cycle The stage wherein sales increase, peak, and start to decline. Profits decline throughout this stage.

merchandise manager An executive position commonly found in retailing. See *product manager.*

merchant middleman An independent business that takes title to the product it is helping to market.

message In communication, the information sent from the source to the receiver.

middleman The business organization that is the link between producers and consumers or industrial users. Renders services in connection with the purchase and/or sale of products as they move from producer to their ultimate market. Either takes title to the products or actively aids in the transfer of title.

middleman's brand A brand owned by a retailer or a wholesaler. Also called a *private brand.*

misdirected marketing effort A marketing effort (cost) that is expended in relation to the number of marketing units (products, territories, or customers) rather than in relation to the potential volume or profit from these units.

missionary sales person A type of manufacturer's sales job that involves nonselling activities such as performing promotional work and providing services for customers. The sales rep ordinarily is not expected or permitted to solicit orders.

MkIS See *marketing information system.*

modified rebuy An industrial purchasing situation between a new task and a straight rebuy in terms of time required, information needed, and alternatives considered.

money income The amount of income a person receives in cash or checks from salaries, wages, interest, rents, dividends, or other sources.

monopolistic competition A market situation in which there are many sellers. Each seller tries to differentiate its product or its marketing program in some way to suggest that its market offering is distinctive. Also known as *imperfect competition.*

monopoly A market situation in which one seller controls the supply of a product.

motivation The force that activates goal-oriented behavior.

motive A stimulated need that an individual seeks to satisfy with goal-oriented behavior.

multiple influence on purchases The situation where the purchasing decision is influenced by more than one person in the buyer's organization.

multiple packaging The strategy of packaging several units of a product in one container in the hope of increasing the product's sales volume.

national advertising Advertising sponsored by a manufacturer or some other producer. Also called *general advertising.*

national brand A brand that is owned by a manufacturer or other producer.

neighborhood shopping center A small group of stores centered around a supermarket and including other convenience-goods stores and specialty stores. Draws from a market located perhaps within 10 minutes by car.

net profit Gross profit minus all operating expenses. Or, sales revenue less both the cost of the goods sold and all operating expenses.

net sales Gross sales less sales returns and sales allowances.

new product A vague term that may refer

to (1) really innovative, truly unique products; (2) replacements for existing products that are significantly different from existing ones; or (3) imitative products that are new to the given firm.

new-product development process Developmental stages that a new product goes through. Starts with idea generation and continues through idea screening, business analysis, limited production, test-marketing, and eventually commercialization (full-scale production and marketing).

new task In the industrial buying process, the situation in which a company for the first time considers the purchase of a given item.

nonbusiness organizations A category that covers a wide spectrum of organizations that do not perceive themselves to be in business (even though they really are). Includes such groupings as educational, religious, charitable, social cause, cultural, health-care, and political organizations.

noncumulative quantity discount A discount based on the size of an individual order of products.

nonprice competition Competition based on some factor other than price—for example, promotion, product differentiation, or variety of services.

nonprofit, or not-for-profit, organization An organization in which profit making is not a goal. The organization neither intends nor tries to make a profit.

nonstore retailing A type of retail selling in which the customer does not go to the store.

observational method The method of gathering primary information in a survey by personal or mechanical observation of respondents. No interviewing is involved.

odd pricing Pricing at odd amounts ($4.99 rather than $5, for example) in the belief that these seemingly lower prices will result in larger sales volume. A form of psychological pricing that is also called "penny pricing."

off-price retailer Retailer whose standard pricing policy is to sell branded products

below the manufacturer's suggested retail price.

oligopoly A market situation in which only a few sellers control all (or most) of the supply of a product.

one-price policy The pricing strategy by which the seller charges the same price to all customers of the same type who buy the same quantity of goods.

operating ratio A ratio between any two items on an operating statement. Most commonly used are the ratios between some item and net sales.

operating statement The financial statement that shows an organization's revenues and expenses over a period of time. Also called an *income statement* or *profit and loss statement.*

operating supplies The "convenience goods" of the industrial market—short-lived, low-priced items purchased with a minimum of time and effort.

opinion leader The member of a reference group who is the information source and who influences the decision making of others in the group.

organizational portfolio analysis Same as *business portfolio analysis.*

packaging The activities in product planning that involve designing and producing the container or wrapper for a product.

party-plan selling A form of in-home retailing in which a personal sales rep makes a presentation to a group of potential customers gathered in a party setting in a person's home. The rep writes orders at this party, and the host or hostess receives a commission based on these sales.

patronage buying motives The reasons why a person or an organization patronizes (shops at) a certain store or some other supplier.

patterned interview A standardized list of questions used by all interviewers when interviewing a group of applicants for a given job.

penetration pricing Setting a low initial price on a product in an attempt to reach a mass market immediately.

percentage-of-sales promotional appro-

priation A method of determining the promotional appropriation. The amount is set as a certain percentage of past or forecasted future sales.

perception The meaning we attribute to stimuli received through our five senses, or the way we interpret a stimulus. Our perceptions shape our behavior.

personal interview A face-to-face method of gathering data in a survey.

personal selling The activity of informing and persuading a market on a person-to-person basis (face to face or on the telephone).

personal selling process Activities involved in making a personal sale, starting with presale preparation and including prospecting, the preapproach, the sales presentation, and postsale activities.

personality An individual's pattern of traits that are determinants of behavioral responses.

physical distribution Activities involved in the flow of products as they move physically from producer to consumer or industrial user.

physical distribution system The concept of treating all physical distribution activities as a total, interacting system, rather than as a series of fragmented, unrelated elements.

piggyback freight service Transporting truck trailers on railroad flatcars.

pioneer advertising Same as primary-demand advertising—stimulates demand for a product category.

place utility The utility created by having a product available at the location where a customer wants it.

planned obsolescence As used in this book, the same as *fashion* or *style* obsolescence, in contrast to technological or functional obsolescence. The altering of the superficial characteristics of a product so that the new model is easily differentiated from the old one. The marketer's intention is to make people dissatisfied with the old model.

planned shopping center A group of retail stores whose activities are coordinated and promoted as a unit to consumers in the surrounding trade area. The center is planned, developed, and controlled by one organization, typically called a shopping-center developer.

planning The process of deciding in the present what to do in the future.

possession utility The utility created by the transfer of a product's title from the seller to the buyer.

preapproach The stage in the personal selling process when a sales rep learns as much as possible about prospective customers and plans the best way to approach a given prospect.

presentation In personal selling, the activities that involve approaching the customer, giving a sales talk, meeting objections, and closing the sale. This is the AIDA stage in personal selling. See AIDA.

pretesting Field-testing a questionnaire, a product, an advertisement (or whatever item is being studied) by trying out the item on a limited number of people, prior to a full-scale market introduction of the item.

price What you pay for what you get. Value expressed in dollars and cents.

price lining A retail pricing strategy whereby a store selects a limited number of prices and sells each item only at one of these prices.

pricing objectives The goals that management tries to reach with its pricing structure and strategies.

primary data Original data (information) gathered specifically for the project at hand.

primary demand The market demand for a general category of products (in contrast to the selective demand for a particular brand of the product).

primary-demand advertising Intended to stimulate the demand for a generic product category, rather than a specific brand.

private brand A brand that is owned by a middleman.

processing in transit A railroad in-transit shipping privilege. The shipper can unload its product en route, have it processed, and then reload it to the final destination. The carload rate is charged from the original shipping point to the final destination.

product A set of tangible and intangible attributes which provide want-satisfying benefits to a buyer in an exchange. Such attributes include color, price, packaging, and the reputation and services of the manufacturer and the middleman. A ''product'' may be a physical good, a service, an idea, a place, an organization, or even a person.

product assortment Full list of products sold by a firm. Same as *product mix*.

product buying motives The reasons for buying a certain product.

product deletion The discontinuance of the marketing of a product; withdrawal of the product from the company's product mix.

product development The technical activities of product research, engineering, and design.

product differentiation A product strategy wherein a company promotes the differences between its products and those of its competitors.

product life cycle The stages a product goes through from its introduction, through its growth and maturity, to its eventual decline and death (withdrawal from the market or deletion from the company's offerings).

product line A group of similar products intended for essentially similar uses.

product manager An executive responsible for planning the entire marketing program for a given product or group of products.

product mix The full list of products offered for sale by a company.

product planning All the activities that enable an organization to determine what products it will market.

product positioning The decisions and activities involved in developing the intended image (in the customer's mind) for a product in relation to competitive products.

product warranty—express A statement in written or spoken words regarding compensation by the seller if its product does not perform up to reasonable expectations.

product warranty—implied The concept of what a warranty was intended to cover, even though it was not actually stated or written in words.

production orientation The first stage in the evolution of marketing management. The basic assumption is that making a good product will ensure business success.

promotion The element in an organization's marketing mix that is used to inform and persuade the market regarding the organization's products and services.

promotional allowance A price reduction granted by the seller as payment for promotional services rendered by the buyer.

promotional mix The combination of elements that constitute the promotion ingredients in an organization's marketing mix.

prospecting The stage in the personal selling process that involves developing a list of potential customers.

psychic income The intangible income factor related to climate, neighborhood, job satisfaction, etc.

psychoanalytic theory of personality Sigmund Freud's theory that behavior is influenced by the action and interaction of three parts of the human mind—the id, the ego, and the superego.

psychogenic needs Needs which arise from psychological states of tension.

psychographics A concept in consumer behavior which explains a market in terms of demographics, as well as consumers' attitudes and life-styles.

public relations A planned effort by an organization to influence some group's attitude toward that organization.

public service advertising Advertising (possibly by a manufacturer or a retailer) that urges people to support some public cause, such as a Red Cross drive or a campaign to drive carefully.

public warehouse An independent firm that provides storage and handling facilities.

publicity Nonpersonal promotion that is not paid for by the organization benefiting from it.

"pull" promotional strategy Aiming product promotion at end users so they will ask middlemen for the product.

"push" promotional strategy The producer directs its promotion at middlemen that are the next link forward in distribution channels.

quantity discount A reduction from list price when large quantities are purchased; offered to encourage buyers to purchase in large quantities.

questionnaire A data-gathering form used to collect the information in a personal, telephone, or mail survey.

quota sample A nonrandom sample that is "forced" in some way to be proportional to something.

rack jobber A merchant wholesaler that primarily supplies food stores with nonfood items. This middleman provides the display case or rack, stocks it, and prices the merchandise.

random sample A sample chosen in such a way that every unit in the whole has an equal chance of being selected for the sample.

raw materials Industrial products that have not been processed in any way and that will become part of another product.

readership test An indirect measure of the effectiveness of an ad and that measures how many people saw or read the ad.

real income Purchasing power; that is, what money income will buy in goods or services.

recall test An indirect measure of the effectiveness of an ad. Determines how many people remember seeing a given ad.

recognition test An indirect measure of the effectiveness of an ad. Determines how many people can identify a given ad.

reference group A group of people who influence a person's attitudes, values, and behavior.

regional shopping center The largest type of planned suburban shopping center (sometimes large enough to be a minidowntown). Usually includes two or more

department stores and many limited-line stores, along with service institutions such as banks, theaters, restaurants, hotels, and office buildings.

reinforcement In learning theory, the positive result of a rewarding (satisfying) behavioral reaction to a drive.

resale price maintenance A pricing policy whereby the manufacturer sets the retail price for a product.

response In learning theory, the behavioral reaction to cues.

retail sale The sale by any organization (producer, wholesaler, retailer, or nonbusiness organization) to an ultimate consumer for nonbusiness use.

retailer A business organization that sells primarily to ultimate consumers.

retailer cooperative chain A retailer-sponsored association of independent stores carrying essentially the same product lines.

retailing Activities related to the sale of products to ultimate consumers for their nonbusiness use.

return on investment (ROI) A measure of managerial performance and operating success in a company. The ratio of net profit to total assets or net worth. It is determined by multiplying the percentage of profit on sales by the rate of asset (or capital) turnover.

Robinson-Patman Act (1936) A federal law that amends the Clayton Antitrust Act by strengthening the prohibition of price discrimination that may injure competition.

salary plan (or straight salary) A sales-force compensation plan that pays a representative a fixed amount per period of time. Provides security and stability of income but generally does not provide much incentive.

sales branch A manufacturer's regional office that carries inventory stocks and performs the services of a wholesaling middleman.

sales-force composite A sales forecasting method based on estimates compiled by the field sales force.

sales forecast The estimate of what a company expects to sell in a given market during a specified future time period.

sales management The managerial efforts involved in planning, implementing, and evaluating the activities of a sales force.

sales office A manufacturer's regional location that does not carry merchandise stocks, but otherwise performs the services of a wholesaling middleman.

sales orientation The second stage in the evolution of marketing management, wherein the emphasis is on selling whatever the organization produces.

sales potential A company's expected sales of a given product in a given market over some time period.

sales promotion Activities that supplement and coordinate personal selling and advertising. Includes such elements as store displays, trade shows, and product samples.

sales-results test A method of measuring the effectiveness of advertising. Measure the sales volume stemming directly from an ad or a series of ads.

sales-volume analysis A detailed study of a company's sales volume over a given period of time.

sample A limited portion of the whole of a thing.

sampling principle The concept that, if a small number of parts (a sample) is chosen at random from the whole (the universe or population), the sample will tend to have the same characteristics, and in the same proportion, as the universe.

SBU See *strategic business unit.*

scrambled merchandising The practice of adding new product lines, quite unrelated to the products usually sold in a given type of store.

seasonal discount Discount for placing an order during the seller's slow season.

secondary data Information already gathered by somebody else for some other purpose.

selective demand The market demand for an individual *brand* of a product, in contrast to the primary demand for the broad product category.

selective-demand advertising Intended to stimulate the demand for a specific brand, in contrast to a generic product category.

selective distribution The strategy wherein a manufacturer uses a limited number of wholesalers and/or retailers in a given geographic market.

selectivity in perceptions The process that limits our perceptions. We perceive only part of what we are exposed to, and we retain only part of what we selectively perceive.

self-concept (self-image) The way you see yourself, and also the way you think others see you. The concept includes your actual self-image and your ideal self-image.

seller's market The situation in which the demand for a given item greatly exceeds the supply of that item.

selling Informing and persuading a market about a product or service; synonymous with *promotion.*

selling agent An independent agent wholesaling middleman that serves as an entire marketing department for a manufacturer. The agent markets the entire output of the manufacturer, and often influences the pricing and design of the products.

services Separately identifiable, intangible activities that provide want-satisfaction and are not tied to the sale of a product or another service.

Sherman Antitrust Act (1890) A federal law prohibiting monopolies and other combinations in restraint of trade.

shopping center A cluster of retail stores in a limited geographic area. Planned suburban shopping centers typically are planned, developed, and controlled by one organization. Their geographic market may be neighborhood, community, or regional.

shopping goods Consumer products that are purchased after the buyer has spent some time and effort comparing the price, quality, color, etc., of alternative products.

short-term planning Planning that typically covers a period of 1 year or less.

situation analysis The stage in a market-

ing research study that involves getting acquainted with the organization and its problems by means of library research and interviewing the organization's officials.

skimming pricing Setting a high initial price on a product, hoping to quickly recover new-product development costs.

small-order problem Individual sales orders that are so small as to be unprofitable relative to the cost of filling the orders.

social class A major division of society based on people's status in their communities.

social (societal) marketing A broadening and extension of managerial marketing. An organization must consider the social and environmental consequences of the production, marketing, and use of its products.

social responsibilities of marketing management Management's broad responsibilities for the effects that executive actions produce on our society.

specialty goods Consumer products with perceived unique characteristics, such that consumers are willing to expend special effort to buy them.

specialty store A retailer that carries only part of a given line of products. Or, in an alternative interpretation, a store that stresses its reputation, quality of merchandise, and abundant and excellent services.

stabilizing prices A pricing goal designed to stabilize prices in an industry. Often found in industries where one firm is a price leader. Other firms price so as to follow the leader and thus not "rock the boat."

stimulus-response theory of learning Learning occurs as correct responses to a given stimulus are reinforced with want-satisfaction and as incorrect responses are penalized.

stockturn rate The number of times the average inventory is sold (turned over) during a given period of time. It is calculated by dividing net sales by average inventory at retail, or by dividing cost of goods sold by average inventory at cost.

storage The marketing activity that creates

time utility. Involves holding and preserving products from the time they are produced until they are sold.

straight rebuy In the industrial market, a routine purchase with minimal informational needs.

strategic business unit (SBU) A separate major product and/or market division in a company. A separate strategic plan is prepared for each SBU.

strategic marketing planning The process of setting marketing goals, selecting target markets, and designing a marketing mix to satisfy these markets and achieve these goals.

strategic planning The managerial process of matching an organization's resources and abilities with its marketing opportunities over the long run.

strategy A broad, basic plan of action by which an organization intends to reach one or more goals.

style A distinctive presentation or construction in any art, product, or activity.

style obsolescence Same as *planned obsolescence.*

subculture A part of a total culture that is reasonably homogeneous with regard to race, religion, nationality, geographic location, or some other factor.

superego In Freudian psychology, the part of the mind that houses the conscience and directs instinctive drives into socially acceptable channels.

supermarket A large, departmentalized, self-service retailing institution offering a wide variety of food products, as well as an assortment of nonfood items. Emphasizes low prices and ample parking space. Also called *hypermarket* or *super-supermarket.*

superstore A large store carrying all that a supermarket typically carries plus a much wider assortment of the nonfood products that are usually purchased on a routine basis and at a low price.

survey of buyer intentions A method of sales forecasting in which a sample of potential customers is asked about their future plans for buying a given product.

survey method A method of gathering data by interviewing a limited number of people (a sample) in person or by telephone or mail.

tactic A detailed course of action by which a strategy (or a strategic plan) is to be implemented and activated.

target market A group of customers at whom an organization specifically aims its marketing effort.

target return A pricing goal that involves setting prices so as to achieve a certain percentage return on investment or on net sales.

task or objective method A method of determining the promotional appropriation. First, the organization decides what is to be accomplished, and then it calculates how much it will cost to reach this goal.

telemarketing A marketing communication system involving use of telephone, television, and computer to aid in a company's selling effort.

telephone selling/shopping Selling via telephone. The seller contacts a customer and makes a sales presentation over the phone. Or the customer contacts the seller and places an order over the phone. It is used in both retailing and wholesaling.

telephone survey or interview A method of gathering data in a survey by interviewing people over the telephone.

teleshopping In-home retailing where the consumer shops with the aid of a television set and possibly a home computer.

test marketing Commercial experiments in limited geographic areas, to determine the feasibility of a full-scale marketing program. The seller may test a new product, a new feature of an existing product, or some other element in the marketing mix.

theme In promotion, the central idea or focal point in a promotional campaign. The promotional appeals are dressed up in some distinctive attention-getting form.

time utility The utility created when a product is available when a customer wants it.

total cost The sum of total fixed costs and total variable costs, or the full cost of a specific quantity produced or sold.

total-cost approach In physical distribution, the optimization of the overall cost-customer service relationship of the entire physical distribution system.

trade channel Same as a *channel of distribution.*

trade (functional) discount A reduction from the list price, offered by a seller to buyers in payment for marketing activities that they will perform.

trademark A brand that is legally protected—essentially a legal term.

trading down A product-line strategy wherein a company adds a lower-priced item to its line of prestige goods, to reach the market that cannot afford the higher-priced items. The seller expects that the prestige of the higher-priced items will help sell the new, lower-priced products.

trading stamps Stamps that are given to the purchaser of a product or service and that can later be exchanged for merchandise. This is a form of nonprice competition.

trading up A product-line strategy wherein a company adds a higher-priced, prestige product to its line in the hope of increasing the sales of the existing products in that line.

trend analysis A sales forecasting method that projects future sales on the basis of past trends.

trickle-across concept In fashion adoption, a fashion cycle moves horizontally within several social classes at the same time.

trickle-down concept In fashion adoption, a given fashion cycle flows downward through several socioeconomic classes.

trickle-up concept In fashion adoption, a style becomes popular (fashionable) first with lower socioeconomic classes and then, later, with higher socioeconomic groups.

truck jobber or truck distributor A limited-function wholesaler, usually carrying a limited line of perishable products that are delivered in the jobber's own truck to retail stores. Also called *wagon jobber* or *truck wholesaler.*

tying contract A contract under which a

manufacturer agrees to sell a product to a middleman only if this middleman also buys another (possibly unwanted) product from the manufacturer.

ultimate consumers People who buy products or services for their personal, nonbusiness use.

uniform delivered price A geographic price strategy whereby the same delivered price is quoted to all buyers regardless of their location. Sometimes referred to as *postage-stamp pricing*.

unit pricing A form of price reporting where the price is stated per pound, per quart, or per some other standard measure—a consumer aid in comparison shopping.

upper-lower class A social class that includes blue-collar workers and the politicians and union leaders whose power base is with these workers.

upper-middle class A social class that includes successful executives in large firms and professionals.

upper-upper class A social class that includes the ''old wealth'' in a community.

utility The characteristic in an item that makes it capable of satisfying wants.

variable cost A cost that varies or changes directly in relation to the number of units produced or sold.

variable-price policy A pricing strategy in which a company sells similar quantities of merchandise to similar buyers at dif-

ferent prices. The price is usually set as a result of bargaining.

vending See *automatic vending*.

venture team An organizational structure for new-product planning and development. A small group that manages the new product from the idea stage to full-scale marketing.

vertical industrial market A situation where a given product is usable by virtually all the firms in only one or two industries.

vertical marketing system A distribution arrangement whereby a given channel of distribution is treated as a coordinated, integrated unit. Three common types of vertical systems are corporate, administered, and contractual.

voluntary chain A wholesaler-sponsored association of independently owned retail stores carrying essentially the same product lines.

wagon jobber Same as a *truck jobber*.

warehouse store Same as a *box store*.

warehouse/wholesale club A low-price, no-frills wholesaler/retailer that charges a membership fee and sells to small retailers (wholesaling transactions) and to ultimate consumers (retailing transactions).

warehousing A broad range of physical distribution activities including storage, assembling, bulk breaking, and preparing products for shipping.

wheel-of-retailing theory A theory which holds that (1) a new type of retailing institution gains a foothold in the retailing structure by competing on a low-status,

low-price, low-service basis; (2) then, to expand its market, this retail institution increases its services and product offerings, thus increasing its costs and prices; (3) this leaves room at the bottom for the next low-price, low-service type of retailer to enter the retailing structure; and (4) the ''wheel of retailing'' continues to turn as new institutions enter the retail market.

Wheeler-Lea Act (1938) A federal law amending the Federal Trade Commission Act by strengthening the prohibition against unfair competition, especially false or misleading advertising.

wholesaler A merchant middleman (takes title to the products) whose primary purpose is to engage in wholesaling activities. Also may be called a *jobber*, *industrial distributor*, or *mill-supply house*.

wholesaling All activities involving sales to organizations that buy to resell or to use the products in their businesses.

wholesaling middleman The broad category that includes all middlemen engaged primarily in wholesaling activities.

world enterprise The most advanced form of international marketing structure. Both foreign and domestic operations are fully integrated and are no longer separately identified.

zone delivered pricing A geographic price strategy whereby the same delivered price is charged at any location within each geographic zone. Sometimes called *parcel-post pricing*.

CHAPTER 15

p.333 Courtesy 7-11.
p.334 Tim Bieber, The Image Bank.
p.337 Courtesy, Mary Kay Products.
p.338 Courtesy, Chadwick's of Boston, Ltd.
p.339 Randy Matusow.
p.344 Courtesy, Supervalu.
p.344 Courtesy, Kroger.
p.349 Bullaty Lomea, The Image Bank.
p.353 The Image Bank.
p.357 Rivelli, The Image Bank.
p.358 Brett Frooman, The Image Bank.

CHAPTER 16

p.362 Courtesy, L'ESPRIT, photographers Alvio and Moulie Rosa Ballo.
p.362 Courtesy, L'ESPRIT, photographer, Olivero Toscani.
p.362 Courtesy, L'ESPRIT, photographer, Olivero Toscani.
p.365 Courtesy, Kroger.
p.366 Randy Matusow.
p.370 Randy Matusow.
p.371 (top) Wally McNamee, Woodfin Camp & Associates.
p.373 Courtesy, Mary Kay Cosmetics.
p.375 Courtesy, Supervalu.
p.376 Courtesy, L'ESPRIT, photographer, Alvio & Moulie Rosa Ballo.
p.378 Mark Godfrey, Archive Pictures.
p.379 Courtesy, Cerutti (1881).
p.382 Van Bucher, Photo Researchers, Inc.

CHAPTER 17

p.386 Courtesy, CSX Corporation.
p.386 Courtesy of Federal Express Corporation. All rights reserved.
p.390 Courtesy of General Dynamics.
p.390 Ran ty Matusow.
p.392 Courtesy, Kroger.
p.394 Courtesy, The Southland Corporation.
p.395 Courtesy, Kroger.
p.396 Courtesy, The Southland Corporation.
p.397 Photo courtesy of Genstar Corporation.

CHAPTER 18

Corporation. Photography by Paul Fusco, Magnum Photos.
p.399 Courtesy, Computerland Corporation.
p.400 (top) Courtesy, CSX Corporation.
p.400 (bottom) Roger Tully, NYNEX.
p.402 Courtesy, Union Pacific Railroad Company; photographed by Ovak Arslanian.
p.402 (bottom) Courtesy of Federal Express Corporation. All rights reserved.
p.403 Courtesy, NASA.

p.416 Randy Matusow.
p.416 Randy Matusow.
p.416 Randy Matusow.
p.419 Courtesy, Borden, Inc.
p.424 Courtesy, IBM and Lord, Geller, Federico Einstein Inc.
p.425 Leif Skoogfors, Woodfin Camp & Associates.
p.427 Randy Matusow.
p.427 Randy Matusow.
p.429 Randy Matusow.
p.432 Courtesy, General Mills, Inc.
p.433 Courtesy, American Cancer Society.

CHAPTER 19

p.438 (top) Joyce Ravid.
p.438 Rececca Collette, Archive Pictures, Inc.
p.438 Joyce Ravid.
p.438 Joyce Ravid.
p.440 Courtesy, Quaker Oats Co.
p.443 (top) Michael Heron, Woodfin Camp & Associates.
p.443 (bottom) Courtesy Joyce Ravid.
p.446 Rebecca Chao, Archive Pictures, Inc.
p.446 Rebecca Chao, Archive Pictures, Inc.
p.451 Courtesy, Avon Products, Inc.
p.452 Courtesy, Santo Laquatra, Beecham Products, Inc.
p.456 Courtesy, Beecham Products.

CHAPTER 20

p.460 Courtesy, Home Box Office, Inc.
p.460 Courtesy, Black & Decker, Black & Decker Spacemaker™.

p.462 Courtesy, Anheuser-Busch Companies, Inc.
p.463 (right) Courtesy, National Federation of Coffee Growers of Columbia.
p.463 (left) Randy Matusow.
p.464 Courtesy, Rolls-Royce Motors, Inc.
p.464 Courtesy, Rolls-Royce Motors, Inc.
p.464 Courtesy, Rolls-Royce Motors, Inc.
p.467 (left) As printed in *Coal Age*, A McGraw-Hill Publication. All rights reserved.
p.469 Courtesy, Mary Kay Cosmetics, Inc.
p.471 Courtesy, The Radio Advertising Bureau.
p.472 Courtesy, Zoological Society of San Diego.
p.475 Courtesy, Safeway.
p.478 Courtesy, Safeway.
p.480 Revlon, Inc., © 1985.

CHAPTER 21

p.494 Courtesy, American Express.
p.497 Randy Matusow.
p.497 Randy Matusow.
p.498 (top) Randy Matusow.
p.498 (bottom) Randy Matusow, Metropolitan Insurance Companies.
p.499 Tim Davis, Photo Researchers, Inc.
p.500 Fay Torresyap, Stock Boston.
p.501 Courtesy, Federal Express Corporation. All rights reserved.
p.502 Courtesy, Walt Disney Productions, Inc.
p.505 Courtesy, AT&T, 1986.
p.507 Vail Photo by David Lokey.
p.508 Randy Matusow.

CHAPTER 22

p.512 (top) Courtesy, Zoological Society of San Diego.
p.512 (bottom) Heine-Stillmark, The Image Bank.
p.512 Peter Miller, The Image Bank.
p.516 Courtesy, The American Cancer Society.
p.517 Courtesy, The Advertising Council, Inc.
p.519 Chgookee, Stock Boston.
p.521 Courtesy, The Episcopal Ad Project, a Ministry of St. Luke's Episcopal Church.
p.521 (bottom) Courtesy, The American Cancer Society.
p.525 Rentmeester, The Image Bank.
p.526 Courtesy, Dr. Lynn Tenney and Dr. Philip Kozlow.
p.527 Steve Hanson, Stock Boston.

CHAPTER 23

p.532 Randy Matusow.
p.535 Courtesy, Yamaha.
p.536 Courtesy of The United Nations.
p.539 Peter Paz, Image Bank.
p.540 Ethan Hoffman, Archive Pictures, Inc.
p.543 Marc Romanelli, The Image Bank.
p.545 Charles Harbutt, Archive Pictures, Inc.
p.545 Bruce Davidson, Magnum Photos, Inc.
p.549 Safeway.
p.550 Courtesy, Club Med Sales, Inc.
p.555 (top) Randy Matusow.
p.555 Bruce Davidson, Magnum Photos, Inc.

CHAPTER 24

p.568 Rod Hannah.
p.568 Rod Hannah.
p.577 H. Wendler, The Image Bank.
p.578 Tom Tracy, The Image Bank.
p.585 Arthur D'Arazien, The Image Bank.

CHAPTER 25

p.590 Joan Liftin, Archive Pictures, Inc.
p.590 Lisa Limer.
p.592 Randy Matusow.
p.593 Michael Pasdzior, The Image Bank.
p.594 Courtesy, Secret Solid, Procter & Gamble Co.
p.596 Randy Matusow.
p.598 (bottom) Randy Matusow.
p.600 Courtesy, American Cancer Society.
p.604 Mark Godfrey, Archive Pictures, Inc.
p.609 Randy Matusow.
p.610 Mark Godfrey, Archive Pictures, Inc.

Aaker, David A., 78, 218, 219, 294
Ackerman, Kenneth B., 395
Alsop, Ronald, 97, 246, 526
Andreasen, Alan R., 518
Ansari, Abdolhossein, 399
Anshoff, H. Igor, 52
Austin, Nancy, 3

Backman, Jules, 594
Bailey, Earl L., 200
Barach, Jeffrey A., 513
Barry, Thomas E., 420
Bates, Albert D., 331
Bean, Ed, 508
Belizzi, Joseph A., 148
Bello, Daniel C., 555
Bennett, Roger C., 208
Berlew, F. Kingston, 539
Berry, Leonard L., 499, 502, 508
Bertsch, Thomas M., 85, 558
Biglin, Ronald J., 501
Bird, Monroe M., 143, 152
Bishop, William S., 143
Blackwell, Roger D., 117, 166
Bloom, Paul N., 501, 513, 599
Bloom, Robert H., 191
Boddewyn, J. J., 601
Bonoma, Thomas V., 150, 168, 481, 576
Borden, Neil H., 419
Bowers, Michael R., 502
Bragg, Arthur, 336
Bragg, Daniel J., 399
Brasch, John J., 537
Brown, James R., 93
Brown, Stephen W., 504, 518, 523
Browning, E. S., 556
Browsh, Gani, 412
Buchanan, Bruce, 464
Buell, Barbara, 219
Buell, Victor P., 209

Bush, Alan J., 71
Buskirk, Richard H., 448, 633

Cady, John F., 381
Cannon-Bonventre, Kristina, 476
Carpenter, Lee Kimberly, 336
Cateora, Philip, 534
Cavusgil, S. Tamer, 537, 540, 548
Chadraba, Petr, 545
Chonko, Lawrence B., 607
Churchill, Gilbert A., Jr., 450
Coleman, Richard P., 118, 119
Colvin, Geoffrey, 96
Contractor, Farok J., 538
Cook, Victor J., Jr., 168
Cooke, Ernest F., 475, 614
Cooper, Philip D., 525
Cooper, Robert G., 201, 208
Coppett, John I., 444
Cossé, Thomas J., 209
Crow, Lowell E., 251
Cunningham, Isabella C. M., 239
Currim, Imran S., 514

Dahl, Jonathan, 285
Daniells, Lorna M., 69
Davis, Keith, 605, 607
Davis, Linden A., Jr., 79
Dawson, Leslie M., 15
Day, George S., 78
Densmore, Max L., 166
Dimsdale, Parks B., 514
Dirks, Laura M., 69
Dooley, Jim, 306
Dreyfuss, Joel, 337
Drumwright, Minette E., 525
Dubinsky, Alan J., 420, 578
Dwight, Maria B., 98

Eells, Kenneth, 117
Eitler, James, 85
Engel, James F., 117
Etzel, Michael J., 287

Farin, Laurence, 85
Faris, Charles W., 148, 149
Farrard, Alice, 541
Fern, Edward F., 93
Fisher, Anne B., 551
Folkes, Valerie S., 209
Foltz, Kim, 166, 495
Ford, Gary T., 294
Ford, Neil M., 450
Fornell, Claes, 603
Fox, Richard, 166
Fram, Eugene H., 560
Frederick, William C., 607
French, Warren A., 166
Funkhouser, G. Ray, 56
Futrell, Charles M., 445, 502

Garvin, David A., 246
Gaski, John G., 364, 604
Gelb, Betsy D., 499
George, William R., 508, 514
Gilman, Hank, 104, 163, 237
Goeldner, C. R., 69
Goldstucker, Jac L., 338
Graham, John L., 143
Greenberg, Herbert M., 450
Greyser, Stephen A., 599
Gubar, George, 106
Gumbert, David E., 140
Gutschick, Sharon, 558

Hafer, John C., 527
Hahn, Chan K., 399
Hair, Joseph F., Jr., 71

Haley, Russell J., 167
Hall, John F., 123
Hall, Trish, 233
Hansen, Richard W., 578
Hardy, Andrew P., 239
Harris, Brian F., 239
Hartley, Steven W., 450
Haspeslagh, Philippe, 50
Hawes, Jon M., 239, 339
Hess, John, 411
Hicks, Sue, 558
Hilger, Mary Tharpe, 102
Hill, John S., 544
Hill, Phil, 551
Hill, Richard M., 143
Hlavacek, James D., 373
Hollie, Pamela G., 238
Hoover, Robert J., 102
Hopkins, David S., 209
Hout, Thomas, 539
Hulse, Carolyn, 544
Hunt, Shelby D., 607

Imperia, Giovanna, 239

Jackson, Donald M., 373
Jackson, Donald W., Jr., 364
Jacobs, Laurence, 546
James, Don L., 287
Jeffries, Richard J., 614
Jones, J. Richard, 525
Jones, Michael H., 143

Kaikati, Jack G., 335
Katz, Elihu, 121
Kaufman, Sylvia, 166
Keegan, Warren J., 544
Keown, Charles, 546
Kerin, Roger A., 420, 429
Kiechel, Walter, III, 51, 52, 570
Kluckholn, Clyde, 116
Kluckholn, Richard, 116
Koffka, K., 125
Kohler, Wolfgang, 125
Konopa, Leonard J., 373
Kopp, Robert J., 479
Kosaka, Hiroshi, 556
Koten, John, 247
Kotler, Philip, 527, 528
Kotsos, Barbara, 209
Krampf, Robert F., 373
Kron, Joan, 363
Krum, James R., 78

La Barbera, Priscilla A., 602
Labich, Kenneth, 285
LaGarce, Raymond, 388
LaLonde, Bernard J., 388, 395, 412
Langer, Judith, 164
Langley, Monica, 14
Laver, James, 227
Lazarsfeld, Paul, 121
Lazer, William, 104, 116, 223, 556
Legum, Lynn T., 514
Lener, Jeffrey, 338
Levitt, Theodore, 448, 499, 508, 543
Levy, Michael, 429
Levy, Robert, 336
Lewin, Kurt, 125
Linden, Fabian, 98
Lloyd, David, 519
Lovelock, Christopher H., 497, 524, 527
Luck, David J., 78
Lumpkin, James R., 339
Lunt, Paul, 117
Luqmani, Mushtaq, 223

McCuistion, Tommy J., 373
McEnally, Martha R., 239
Machalara, Daniel, 387
McMahan, Harry W., 210
McNair, M. P., 340
McNeill, Dennis L., 433
McVey, Phillip, 148
Magnet, Myron, 216
Marcus, Stanley, 225
Martin, Lucy Z., 518
Martineau, Pierre, 117
Maslow, A. H., 112
Mason, Todd, 313
May, Eleanor G., 339
Mayer, David, 450
Mazis, Michael B., 433
Meeker, Marchia, 117
Mentzer, John T., 261
Miaoulis, George, 519
Michaels, Edward G., 14
Michman, Ronald D., 116
Milmo, Sean, 551
Mindak, William A., 168
Miniard, Paul W., 117
Mitchell, Arnold, 165
Mitchell, Lionell A., 81
Moore, Thomas, 91
Moore, William L., 202
Morgan, Fred W., 247
Moschis, George P., 338
Mufson, Steve, 591
Murata, Shoji, 556

Murphy, Liz, 335, 514
Murphy, Patrick E., 105

Nall, Janice R., 514
Neal, William D., 219
Nelson, James E., 83, 185
Novelli, William D., 513

O'Keefe, Robert O., 545
O'Reilly, Brian, 313
Oxenfeldt, Alfred R., 576

Parasuraman, A., 499, 502
Pearson, Michael M., 374
Peters, Thomas J., 3
Petre, Peter, 135
Pinto, Peter A., 399
Plank, Richard E., 169
Plummer, Joseph T., 165
Porter, Michael E., 51, 539
Posch, Robert J., Jr., 381
Pressley, Milton M., 72, 495

Quelch, John A., 476, 481
Quraeshi, Zahir, 223

Razzouk, Nabil Y., 523
Rees, C. William, 339
Reid, Brad, 247
Ricci, Claudia, 335
Robbins, John E., 519
Robbins, Stephanie S., 519
Roberts, Johnnie, L., 591
Robertson, Thomas S., 280, 395
Robey, Bryant, 91
Robinson, Patrick J., 148, 149
Rogers, Everett M., 205, 207
Rohrs, Walter F., 254
Ronkainen, Ilkka A., 202
Rudden, Eileen, 539
Rye, Daniel, 180

Saegert, Joel, 102
Salmon, Walter J., 339
Sanchez, Peter M., 518
Sands, Saul, 381
Saporito, Bill, 345
Sasaki, Laralyn, 520
Scammon, Derba L., 296
Schewe, Charles D., 98
Schleier, Curt, 476
Schneider, Kenneth C., 337
Schneider, Lewis M., 395

Schonberger, Richard J., 399
Schuchman, Abe, 576
Schumer, Fern, 73
Schwadel, Francine, 189, 231
Schwartz, David A., 202
Schwartz, David J., 261
Scott, James D., 425
Segal, Madhav, 102
Shansby, J. Gary, 218, 219
Shapiro, Benson P., 168
Shapiro, Roy D., 393
Sheffet, Mary Jane, 296
Sheth, Jagdish N., 339
Shostack, G. Lynn, 503
Sirgy, M. Joseph, 128
Skrzycki, Cindy, 23
Sloan, Pat, 296, 335
Smith, A. B., 340
Smith, Louise W., 501
Smith, Wendell R., 158
Solomon, Jolie, 157, 313
Sosa, Lionel, 102
Spragins, Ellyn E., 524
Stanley, Thomas J., 338
Stanton, William J., 180, 183, 448, 560, 633
Staples, William A., 105
Steinberg, Margery, 519
Stern, Aimée L., 96, 176, 238, 339

Still, Richard R., 544
Strang, Roger A., 239
Suss, Warren H., 140
Swan, John E., 209
Swartz, Steve, 220, 514

Talarzyk, W. Wayne, 166, 338
Tauber, Edward M., 238
Timmerman, Ed, 247
Timmons, Jeffry A., 140
Tracy, Eleanor J., 74, 233
Trager, Cara S., 319
Twedt, Dik Warren, 65

Upah, Gregory D., 143
Urbany, Joel E., 338
Urman, Harold N., 98

Valencia, Humberto, 239
Vamos, Mark N., 223
Van Doren, Doris C., 501
Vernon, Ivan R., 525
Vorhees, Roy Dale, 444

Wagner, William B., 388
Walker, Bruce J., 287, 364
Walker, Orville C., Jr., 450

Ward, Scott, 280, 395
Warner, W. Lloyd, 117
Waterman, Robert H., Jr., 3
Webster, Frederick E., 150
Webster, John, 429
Weigand, Robert E., 547
Weinberg, Charles B., 514, 524, 527
Weis, William L., 306
Wells, William D., 106, 123
Wengert, Lisa A., 183
Wentz, Laurel, 551
Westbrook, Robert A., 603
Whalen, Bernie, 461
White, Phillip D., 331
Wilkes, Robert E., 239, 604
Wilkie, William L., 433
Williamson, Nicholas C., 555
Wilson, John W., 520
Wind, Yoram, 148, 149, 150
Wittink, Dick R., 514
Wittreich, Warren J., 369
Worthley, Reginald, 546

Yanzito, Richard A., 537
Yovovich, B. G., 476

Zeithaml, Carl P., 22
Zeithaml, Valarie A., 22, 100, 499, 502
Zinszer, Paul H., 388

Accessory equipment, 197–198
Action programs, 607–609
Adoption process, new product, 205–207
Advertisement, 462
Advertising, 418
  careers in, 633–634
  costs of, 465–466
  criticisms of, 593–595
  evaluation (testing) of, 472–474
  in international marketing, 550–552
  media used in, 468–472
  in nonbusiness marketing, 525–527
  objectives of, 467–468
  organizational structures for, 474–475
  in promotional mix, 422–429
  target of, 462–465
  types of, 462–465
Advertising agency, 474–475
Advertising campaign, 468–472
Age groups, 96–98, 163
Agent middlemen, 314, 350, 355–358
  auction companies, 358
  brokers, 350, 357
  commission merchants, 357–358
  in international marketing, 538
  in major distribution channels, 380
  manufacturers' agents, 356–357
  selling agents, 358
Agribusiness, 137–138
Agricultural activity, 147–148
Air carriers, 400–401
Airline Deregulation Act (1978), 29
Allowances, 286–288
Analytical ratios, 624–627
Annual marketing plan, 46, 56–57
Area sample, 76
Attitudes in buyer behavior, 126–127
Auction companies, 358
Automatic vending, 339
Automobile Information Disclosure Act
  (1958), 29

Average costs, 269–271
Average revenue, 277–278

Balance sheet, 617
Base price, 264
Battle of the brands, 238–239
Bidding system, 139
Boston Consulting Group planning
  matrix, 52
Box store, 332–333
Brand label, 243
Brand mark, 232
Brand name, 232
Brand strategies and policies:
  branding of fabricating parts and
    materials, 235–236
  by manufacturer, 235–238
  by middlemen, 236–238
Brands, 232–240
  battle of, 238–239
  generic uses of, 235
  national, 232
  private, 232
  trademarks and, 232
  (See also Brand strategies and policies)
Break-even analysis, 274–277
Bribery in international marketing, 548–550
Brokers, 350, 357
Business cycle, 23–24
Buy class, 149
Buy grid, 149
Buy phase, 149
Buyer behavior:
  cultural influences on, 115–117
  decision-making process in, 129–131
  family influences on, 121–123
  psychological determinants of: attitudes
    and beliefs, 126–127
  learning experiences, 123–125
  motivation, 112–114

Buyer behavior, psychological
  determinants of (Cont.):
  perception, 114
  personality, 125–126
  self-concept, 127–128
  reference-group influence on, 120–121
  social-group influences on, 117–123
  (See also Buying habits; Buying
    motives; Consumerism)
Buying center, 149–150
Buying habits:
  consumer, 121–123
  industrial, 149–153
Buying intentions, survey of, 175–176
Buying motives:
  consumer, 112–114
  industrial, 148
Buying power of industrial market,
  147–148
Buying process, industrial, 148–149

Campaign:
  advertising, 468–472
  promotional, 431–432
Careers in marketing, 630–641
Carload freight rates, 401
Cash discounts, 287–288
Catalog showroom, 336
Celler-Kefauver Antimerger Act (1950),
  29
Chain stores, 326–328
Channels of distribution, 32, 268,
  314–316
  conflicts among members of, 364–371
  for consumer goods, 371–373
  control of, 365–366
  criticisms of, 593
  exclusive, 378–379
  factors affecting choice of, 373–376
  for industrial products, 373

Channels of distribution (*Cont.*):
  intensive, 377
  in international marketing, 547–550
  legal considerations in management of, 381–383
  multiple, 376–377
  in nonbusiness marketing, 523–525
  selection of, 371–377
  selective, 377–378
  in service marketing, 505–506
  and vertical marketing systems, 370–371
C.i.f. (cost, insurance, and freight), 543, 546
Cigarette Labeling and Advertising Act (1966, 1969), 29
Clayton Antitrust Act (1914), 29, 288
Client market, 515–516, 519
Cognitive dissonance, 130–131
Cognitive theories of learning, 124
Commission merchants, 357–358
Communication process, 421–422
Comparative advertising, 464
Compensating sales people, 453–454
Competition, 24–26
Conflicts in distribution channels, 364–371
Consolidated Metropolitan Statistical Area (CMSA), 95
Construction activity, 148
Consumer, ultimate, 92
Consumer behavior (*see* Buyer behavior)
Consumer Credit Protection Act (1968), 29
Consumer fraud, 603–604
Consumer goods, 192–193
  channels of distribution for, 371–373
  convenience goods, 28, 193–194
  shopping goods, 193–194
  specialty goods, 193, 195
  unsought, 195
Consumer Goods Pricing Act (1975), 29
Consumer income:
  distribution of, 103–105
  expenditure patterns of, 105–107
  types of, 102–103
Consumer Product Safety Act (1972), 29, 247, 600
Consumer Product Safety Commission (CPSC), 29, 247, 601
Consumer Product Warranty Act (1975), 29
Consumerism:
  business response to, 601–604
  careers in, 636

Consumerism (*Cont.*):
  conditions leading to, 598–599
  consumer response to, 599–600
  future of, 599
  government response to, 600–601
  meaning and scope of, 597–598
Containerization, 396
Contract farming, 138
Contract manufacturing in international marketing, 538
Contribution-margin (contribution-to-overhead) approach in cost analysis, 586
Contributor (donor) market, 515–516, 518–519
Control, 43
Convenience goods, 28, 193–194
Convenience stores, 28, 333
Cooperative advertising, 464
Copy, advertising, 472
Correlation analysis, 175
Cost, insurance, freight (c.i.f.) pricing, 543, 546
Cost of goods sold, 619–620
Cost allocation, 585
Cost analysis, 581–588
  of functional expenses, 581–585
  of ledger expenses, 581
  problems in, 585–586
Cost concepts in price determination, 269–272
Cost-plus pricing, 268–274
  based on marginal costs, 272
  cost concepts in, 269–272
  evaluation of, 274
  by middlemen, 272–273
Cost trade-offs, 391
Council for Mutual Economic Assistance (COMECON), 535–536
Cream-skimming pricing, 292–293
Criticisms of marketing, 592–597
Cultural forces in marketing, 26–28
Culture:
  changing patterns in, 116
  influence on buyer behavior, 115–117
  subcultures, 116–117
Cumulative discounts, 286–287
Custodian warehousing, 397
Customer service, 388, 392

Data gathering, 69–77
  experimental method in, 73–74
  observational method in, 72–73
  questionnaires for, 74–75
  through surveys, 71

Dealer selection, 381
Dealers (*see* Retailers)
Decision-making process in buying, 129–131
  cognitive dissonance in, 130–131
  patronage buying motives in, 130
Demand:
  derived, 141–142
  elasticity of, 265
  estimating, in pricing, 264
  fluctuating, 143
  in industrial market, 141–153
  inelastic, 142
  inverse, 266
  kinked, 279–280
Demography, 23
Department stores, 325–326
Depository Institutions Act (1981), 29
Deregulation, 394–395
Derived demand, 141–142
Descriptive label, 243
Design, product, 244–245
Desk jobber, 355
Devaluation, 547
Diffusion process, new product, 205–207
Direct-derivation analysis, 175
Direct mail, 470
Direct purchase, 151
Discount retailing, 332–336
Discounts, 286–288
Discretionary purchasing power, 102
Disposable personal income, 102
Distribution (*see* Channels of distribution; Physical distribution)
Distribution center, 395–396
Distributor (*see* Wholesalers; Wholesaling middlemen)
Diversification strategy, 53
Diversion-in-transit, 401–402
Donor market (*see* Contributor market)
Door-to-door selling, 336–337
Drop shipper, 355
Dual distribution, 376–377
"Dumping," 546

Economic conditions, 23–24
Economic order quantity, 398–399
Economy of abundance, 7–8
"80-20" principle, 577
Entrepreneurship franchising, 330
Environmental pollution, 608–609
Environmental Protection Agency, 601
European Community (EC), 535–536

European Free Trade Association (EFTA), 535–536
Evaluation of marketing performance (see Performance evaluation)
Exchange, 4–5
Exclusive dealing, 381–382
Exclusive distribution, 378–379
Exclusive (closed) territory, 382–383
Executive judgment (sales forecasting method), 177
"Expected" price, 266
Expenses, 620–621
 functional, 581–585
 ledger, 581
 of wholesaling middlemen, 352–353
Experimental method in marketing research, 73–74
Export-import agent middlemen, 538
Export Packaging and Labeling Act (1966), 29, 600–601
Export Trading Company Act (1982), 555
Exporting (see International marketing)
Express warranty, 246

Fabricating materials and parts, 196, 198
Fad, 225
Fair Credit Reporting Act (1970), 29
Fair Packaging and Labeling Act (1966), 29, 600–601
Fair Trade and Labeling Act (1966), 243
"Fair-trade" laws, 296
Family brand, 237–238
Family buying behavior, 121–123
Family life cycle, 98–101
 expenditure patterns and, 105–106
Farm market, 137–138
Farming, contract, 138
F.a.s. (free alongside ship), 546
Fashion, 224–228
 adoption process, 225–227
 fad, 225
 marketing considerations in, 227–228
 nature and origin of, 225
 and planned obsolescence, 224–225
Federal Trade Commission (FTC), 29, 595, 601
 labeling regulations by, 243
 and promotional activities, 432–434
Federal Trade Commission Improvement Act (1980), 29
Feedback in communication process, 421
Field theory of learning, 124–125
Field warehousing, 397
Fishyback service, 402
Fixed costs, 269–271

Flammable Fabrics Act (1953), 29
Flexible-price pricing, 293–295
F.o.b. (free on board) pricing, 290–291, 293–295
Focus-group interview, 71
Food, Drug, and Cosmetic Act (1938), 244
Food and Drug Act (1906), 244
Food and Drug Administration (FDA), 244, 601
Forecasting market demand, 172–177
 basic terms in, 172–174
 methods of, 174–177
Foreign Corrupt Practices Act, 548–549, 555
Foreign marketing (see International marketing)
Form utility, 8, 316
Forward dating, 288
Franchise systems, 328–331
Free alongside ship (f.a.s.) pricing, 546
Free on board (f.o.b.) pricing, 290–291, 546
Freight absorption pricing, 291–292
Freight forwarders, 402–403
Full-cost approach in cost analysis, 586
Full-service wholesalers, 353–354
Functional discounts, 287
Functional expenses, 581–585
Fur Products Labeling Act (1951), 29, 244

General merchandise store, 325–326
Generic brand name, 235
Geographic pricing strategy:
 f.o.b. point-of-production pricing, 290–291
 freight absorption, 291–292
 uniform delivered, 291
 zone delivered, 291
Gestalt theory of learning, 291
Goods (see Consumer goods; Industrial products)
Government, 28
 consumerism and, 600–601
 international marketing policies of, 554–555
 marketing to, 139–140
 regulation of promotional activities by, 432–434
 (See also Legislation)
Grade label, 243
"Green River" ordinance, 434
Gross margin, 620, 624

Image utility, 8–9
Implied warranty, 246
Impulse buying, 246
Industrial distributor (see Wholesalers)
Industrial goods (see Industrial products)
Industrial market:
 buying habits in, 149–153
 buying motives in, 148
 buying power of, 147–148
 buying process in, 148–149
 characteristics of demand in, 141–143
 determination of demand in, 143–153
 importance and scope of, 136–140
 regional concentration of, 146–147
 segmentation of, 168–169
 size of, 144–146
 vertical and horizontal, 147
Industrial products, 192–193
 channels of distribution for, 195–198
 classification of, 373
Industrial users, 92, 144–148
 (See also Industrial market)
Inelastic demand, 142
Inflation, 24
Informal investigation in marketing research, 68–69
Innovation, adoption and diffusion of, 205–207
Installations, 197–198
Institutional advertising, 462
Intensive distribution, 377
Interest rates, 24
International marketing, 533–556
 advertising in, 550–552
 bribery in, 548–550
 careers in, 638
 changes in, 536–537
 channels of distribution in, 547–550
 importance of, 534–535
 market analysis in, 539–543
 marketing research in, 539–543
 organizational structures for, 537–539
 physical distribution in, 548
 pricing in, 545–547
 product planning in, 543–545
International trade balances, 552–556
International trade policies in, 543–545
Inventory management:
 control systems in, 398–399
 distribution-center concept in, 395–396
 location and warehousing, 395–396
Inverse demand, 266

Jobber:
 desk, 355
 wagon, 355

Jobs in marketing, 630–641
Joint venture in international marketing, 538–539

Kefauver-Harris Drug Amendments (1962), 29
Kinked demand, 279–280

Labeling, 242–244
Lanham Trademark Act (1946), 29
Latin American Economic System (SERA), 535–536
"Leader" pricing, 296–297
Learning theories and buyer behavior, 123–125
Leasing, 152–153
Ledger expenses, 581
Legal forces in marketing, 28–30
Legislation, 28, 29, 244, 288–290, 432–434
consumerism and, 600–601
Liability, product, 246–247
Licensing in international marketing, 538
Life cycle:
family, 98–101, 105–106
product, 199, 220–224, 425–426
Life-style, 165–166
Limited-function wholesaler, 355
Limited-line store, 326
Long-range planning, 45

Magazines, 470
Mail-order selling, 338–339
Mail survey, 72
Management (see Marketing management)
Manufacturer:
and competitive conflicts in distribution, 366–369
competitive conflicts involving, 369–370
promotion by, 427–428
Manufacturers' agents, 356–357
Manufacturers' criteria for new product, 203–204
Manufacturers' sales branches and offices, 349–350
Manufacturing, careers in, 636
Manufacturing activity, 147
Marginal costs, 270–272
Marginal revenue, 277–278
Markdown, 625

Market:
definition of, 31–32
(See also Market segmentation; Target market)
Market aggregation, 92, 159, 169–170
Market development strategy, 53
Market factor, 172
Market-factor analysis, 174–175
Market index, 172
Market opportunity analysis, 92
Market penetration strategy, 52–53
Market potential, 172–173
Market segmentation, 92
by age groups, 96–98, 163
benefits of, 159–160
conditions for effective, 161
definition of, 158–159
demographic bases for, 93–101, 163
family life cycle basis for, 98–101
geographic bases for, 163
by income, 164
limitations of, 160
by population distribution, 93–96
product-related, 166–168
psychographic, 164–166
by sex, 98, 164
strategies for, 169–72
Market-share analysis, 580–581
Marketing:
careers in, 630–641
criticisms of, 592–597
definition of, 6
international (see International marketing)
nature and scope of, 4–6
in nonbusiness organizations (see Nonbusiness marketing)
present-day importance of, 6–10
selling and, 11–12
of services (see Service Marketing)
societal orientation to, 604–609
Marketing arithmetic, 617–629
analytical ratios, 624–627
markdown, 625
markup, 621–624
operating (profit and loss) statement, 617–621
return on investment, 625–627
Marketing audit, 576
Marketing concept, 10–12
broadening the, 15–16, 609–611
in service marketing, 500–501
Marketing cost analysis, 581–588
Marketing department, organization within, 571–574

Marketing environment:
external macroenvironment, 22–31
external microenvironment, 31–33
organization's internal, 33–35
Marketing evaluation, 576–588, 591–592
Marketing implementation, 570–576
managing the marketing operations, 575–576
organizing for, 570–574
staffing for, 574–575
Marketing information system, 61–64
benefits and uses of, 64
need for, 62–64
(See also Marketing research)
Marketing management:
evolution of, 12–15
process in, 40–41
social responsibility of, 605–607
Marketing mix, 54–56
Marketing performance, evaluation of, 576–588
Marketing planning, 44–46, 173–174, 570–576
Marketing research, 64–65
careers in, 634
experimental method in, 73–74
follow-up, 77
formal investigation in, 69–77
informal investigation in, 68–69
in international marketing, 539–543
in nonbusiness marketing, 527–528
observational method in, 72–73
organizations involved in, 77
procedure in, 65–77
questionnaires for, 74–75
scope of, 65
situation analysis for, 68
status of, 78–79
survey method in, 71
written report of, 77
Marketing system:
vertical, 370–371
(See also Marketing management)
Markup, 621–624
Meat Inspection Act (1906), 29
Merchandising:
scrambled, 326, 365
(See also Product planning)
Merchant middlemen, 314
(See also Retailers; Wholesaling middlemen)
Metropolitan Statistical Area (MSA), 94–95
Middlemen, 32, 314–316
agent (see Agent middlemen)
cost-plus pricing by, 272–273

Middlemen (*Cont.*):
  in international marketing, 547–549
  wholesaling (*see* Wholesaling middlemen)
Middlemen's criteria for new product, 204–205
Mingles, 100–101
Mining activity, 147
Missionary sales force, 443
Money income, 102–103
Monopolistic competition, 25–26
Motivation in buyer behavior, 112–114
Motor Carrier Act (1980), 29
Multinational economic organizations, 536
Multiple segmentation, 171–172

National income, 102
National Traffic and Motor Vehicle Safety Act (1966), 29
Natural Gas Policy Act (1978), 29
Net profit, 621
Net sales, 619
New products, 190–192, 200–205
  adoption and diffusion of, 205–207
  channels of distribution in, 523–525
  exchange concept in, 514–515
  importance of, 515–516
  managing of, 528–529
  market research in, 527–528
  marketing mix for, 56
  markets in, 515
  measuring performance in, 528
  physical distribution in, 524–525
  pricing in, 522–523
  product planning in, 520–522
  promotion in, 525–527
  target-market analysis in, 518–519
Nonprice competition, 299–300
Nonstore retailing, 336–339
Not-for-profit marketing (*see* Nonbusiness marketing)

Observational method in marketing research, 72–73
Occupational Safety and Health Administration (OSHA), 601
Odd pricing, 297
Off-price retailer, 334–335
Oligopoly, 26
One-price pricing, 293–295
OPEC (Organization for Petroleum Exporting Countries), 535–536
Operating expenses, 624
Operating statement, 617–621
Operating supplies, 197–198
Opinion leader, 121
Optimization concept in physical distribution, 391
Order processing, 399
Organization for Petroleum Exporting Countries (OPEC), 535–536
OSHA (Occupational Safety and Health Administration), 601
Outdoor advertising, 471–472

Packaging, 240–242
Party-plan selling, 336–337
Patronage advertising, 462
Patronage buying motives, 130
Penetration pricing, 292–293
Perception, 114
Performance evaluation:
  cost analysis in, 581–588
  market-share analysis for, 580–581
  marketing audit for, 576
  sales-volume analysis for, 579–80
Personal income, 102
Personal interview in marketing research, 71
Personal selling, 336–337, 418
  careers in, 633
  evaluating sales force performance in, 454–457
  importance of, 440–444
  jobs in, 441–444
  in nonbusiness marketing, 527
  process in, 445–448
  in promotional mix, 425
Personality and buyer behavior, 125–126
Physical distribution:
  careers in, 635
  and customer service, 388, 392
  future in, 403
  government deregulation and, 394–395
  importance of, 388
  in international marketing, 548
  inventory control in, 398–399
  inventory location in, 395–396
  materials handling in, 396
  in nonbusiness marketing, 524–525
  optimization and cost trade-offs in, 391
  order processing in, 399
Physical distribution (*Cont.*):
  total-cost approach to, 390
  total-system concept of, 389–391
  transportation in, 399–403
  warehousing in, 395–396
Piggyback service, 402
Pioneering advertising, 463
Place utility, 8, 316, 392–393
Planned obsolescence, 224–228
Planning (*see* Marketing planning; Strategic planning)
Point-of-purchase display, 480
Policy, 42–43
Political forces in marketing, 28–30
Pollution, environmental, 608–609
Population composition, 93–102
Population distribution, 93–102
Porter's generic-strategies model, 51
Portfolio analysis, 49–50
Positioning the product, 217–219
Possession utility, 8, 316
Postpurchase behavior, 130–131
Postsale activities, 447–448
Presentation, sales, 446–447
Price:
  importance of, 261–262
  meaning of, 259–261
Price competition, 298–299
Price determination:
  break-even analysis for, 274–277
  competitive market price in, 279–281
  cost-plus basis for, 268–274
  demand estimates in, 264
  "expected" price in, 266
  factors influencing, 264–268
  supply and demand balance as basis for, 277–279
  (*See also* Pricing)
Price lining, 294–295
Pricing:
  criticisms of, 593
  in international marketing, 545–547
  in nonbusiness marketing, 522–523
  objectives in, 262–264
  penetration pricing, 292–293
  in service marketing, 504–505
  skim-the-cream pricing, 292–293
  (*See also* Price determination)
Pricing strategies and policies:
  discounts and allowances, 286–288
  flexible price, 293–295
  geographic, 290–292
  "leader" pricing, 296–297
  nonprice competition, 299–300
  odd pricing, 297
  one-price, 293–295
  price competition, 298–299

Pricing strategies and policies (Cont.):
  price lining, 294–295
  psychological pricing, 297
  resale price maintenance, 295–296
  unit pricing, 294
Primary data, 69
Primary-demand advertising, 462–463
Primary Metropolitan Statistical Area (PMSA), 95
Printers' Ink statutes, 434
Private warehouse, 396
Processing in transit, 402
Product:
  criticisms of, 593
  life cycle of, 199, 220–224, 425–426
  meaning of, 189–190
  new (*see* New products)
Product advertising, 462
Product attributes (*see* Product features)
Product classification, 192–198
Product development (*see* Product planning)
Product development strategy, 53
Product differentiation, 170, 300
Product features, 231–248
  brands, 232–240
  color, 245
  design, 244–245
  labeling, 242–244
  liability, 246–247
  in nonbusiness marketing, 521–522
  packaging, 240–242
  quality, 152, 246
  servicing, 247–248
  supply, 152
  warranty, 246–247
Product innovation (*see* Product planning)
Product life cycle, 199, 220–224, 425–426
Product line, 215, 325–326
  (See also Product mix)
Product manager, 208, 635
Product mix, 215–220
  alteration of existing products, 217
  contraction of, 216–217
  expansion of, 216
  in nonbusiness marketing, 520–521
  positioning product in, 217–219
  trading down, 219–220
  trading up, 219–220
Product planning:
  importance of, 198–200
  in international marketing, 543–545
  new-product development process in, 200–205
  in nonbusiness marketing, 520–522

Product planning (*Cont.*):
  organizational structure for, 207–209
  in service marketing, 503–504
Product servicing, 152
Profit:
  determinants of, 199–200
  maximization of, as pricing goal, 262–263
  of wholesaling middlemen, 352–353
Profit and loss statement, 617–621
Promotion, 268, 300
  appropriation (budget) for, 429–432
  campaign concept in, 431–432
  communication process in, 421–422
  criticisms of, 593–595
  government regulation of, 432–434
  and imperfect competition, 419
  need for, 419–420
  in nonbusiness marketing, 525–527
  promotional mix, 417, 422–429
  in service marketing, 506–508
  and strategic market planning, 420–421
Promotional allowance, 288, 464
Promotional campaign, 431–432
Promotional mix, 417, 422–429
Promotional strategy, 425–429
Psychic income, 103
Psychoanalytic theories of personality, 126
Psychographics, 123
Psychological pricing, 297
Public relations, 482–483
  careers in, 635–636
Public service advertising, 462
Public warehouse, 396–397
Publicity, 418–419, 481–483
Pull strategy in promotion, 429
Purchasing, careers in, 634–635
Pure competition, 25
Pure Food and Drug Act (1906), 29
Push strategy in promotion, 428–429

Quality, 246
Quantity discounts, 286–287, 289–290
Questionnaires, 75–76
Quota sample, 76

Rack jobber, 354–355
Radio, 470–471
Railroads, 399–402
Random sample, 76
Ratios, analytical, 624–627
Raw materials, 195–196, 198
Real income, 103
Rebuy, 149

Reciprocity in industrial buying, 151–152
Reference groups and buyer behavior, 120–121
Resale price maintenance, 295–296
Reseller market, 139
Retailer cooperative chain, 329
Retailers, 32
  classification of, 320
    by forms of ownership, 326–328
    by method of operation, 331–339
    by product line, 325–326
    by sales volume, 321–324
  competitive conflicts involving, 369–370
  promotion by, 427–428
Retailing:
  careers in, 636–637
  costs and profits in, 318
  discount, 332–336
  economic justification for, 317
  future in, 339–341
  in metropolitan areas, 318–320
  nonstore, 336–339
  size in, 317
  supermarket, 331–333
  "wheel of retailing" cycle in, 340–341
Return on investment, computation of, 625–627
Robinson-Patman Act (1936), 29, 288–290, 432, 434
Rural population, 94–95

Sales, estimates at various prices, 265–266
Sales force:
  management of, 448, 575–576
    compensating the, 453–454
    selection and training of, 448–452, 574–575
    supervising the, 454
    organization of, 571–574
Sales-force composite, 177
Sales forecasting, 173–174
Sales potential, 172–173
Sales presentation, 446–447
Sales promotion, 418
  careers in, 634
  costs of, 478
  directed at end use, 479–480
  directed at middlemen and their sales force, 480
  directed at producers' own sales force, 480
  evaluation of, 480
  importance of, 476–477
  management of, 477–478

Sales promotion (*Cont.*):
  nature of, 475–476
  in nonbusiness marketing, 527
Sales-volume analysis, 579–580
Sampling, 75–76
Scrambled merchandising, 326, 365
Seasonal discounts, 288
Secondary data, 69–71
Selective distribution, 377–378
Selective-demand advertising, 462–464
Self-concept in buyer behavior, 127–128
Selling (*see* Personal selling; Promotion)
Selling agents, 358
Service marketing, 500–509
  careers in, 637
Services:
  characteristics of, 498–500
  definition of, 496–497
  growth in, 509
  importance of, 497–498
Servicing of product, 152
Sex of consumer, 98
Sherman Antitrust Act (1890), 29
Shopping centers, 320
Shopping goods, 193–194
Shopping mall intercept, 71
Short-term planning, 45
Single person, 100
Single segmentation, 171
Situation analysis, 53, 68
Skim-the-cream pricing, 292–293
Social class, 117–123, 164
Social forces in marketing, 26–28
Social responsibility of marketing
  management, 14–15, 605–607
Societal marketing, 604–609
Specialty goods, 193, 195
Specialty stores, 326
Staggers Rail Act (1980), 29
Standard Industrial Classification
  (S.I.C.), 144–145
State Unfair Trade Practices Acts
  (1930s), 29
Stimulus-response theories of learning,
  124
Stockturn rate, 624–625
Storage, 395–396
Strategic business unit (SBU) planning,
  45, 49–50
Strategic company planning, 45–53

Strategic planning, 38–58, 570–576
  marketing, 45, 53–57
  (*See also* Marketing planning)
Strategy, 41
Style (*see* Fashion)
Subcultures, 116–117
Suburban population, 94–96
Supermarkets, 331–333
"Superstores," 333
Supplier, 32
Supply-demand pricing, 277–279
Survey method in marketing research, 71

Tactic, 42
Target market, 54, 91
  selection of, 158
Technology, marketing systems affected
  by, 30
Telemarketing, 337–338, 444
Telephone selling, 337–338
Telephone survey, 72
Television, 471
Test marketing, 176
Textile Fiber Products Identification Act
  (1958), 29, 244
Time utility, 8, 316, 392–393
Total-cost approach in physical
  distribution, 390
Total population, 93
Trade associations and consumerism, 603
Trade balances, international, 552–556
Trade channels (*see* Channels of
  distribution)
Trade discounts, 287, 290
Tradeshow, 480
Trademark, 232, 239–240
Trading down, 219–220
Trading stamps, 479
Trading up, 219–220
Traffic management, 393–394
Transportation, 399–403
  (*See also* Physical distribution)
Trend analysis, 176–177
Trickle-across process in fashion
  adoption, 226–227
Trickle-down process in fashion adoption,
  226–227
Trickle-up process in fashion adoption,
  226–227
Truck distributor, 355
Trucks, 399–401
Truth-in-Lending Act, 601
Tying contracts, 382

Ultimate consumer, 92
Unfair-practices acts, 296–297

Uniform delivered pricing, 291
Unit pricing, 294
Unsought goods, 195
Urban population, 94–95
Utility, 8, 259–260, 316

Value, 259–260
Variable costs, 269–271
Variable-price pricing, 294–295
Vending machines, 339
Vertical marketing systems, 370–371
Voluntary chain, 329

Wagon jobber, 355
Warehouse club, 333–336
Warehouse store, 332–333
Warehousing, 395–396
Warranties, 246–247
"Wheel of retailing," 340–341
Wheeler-Lea Amendment (1938), 29,
  432–434
Wholesale club, 335–336
Wholesalers, 32, 346
  and competitive conflicts in
  distribution, 366–369
  future of, 359
  merchant, 349
    full-service, 353–354
    limited-function, 355
    rack jobber, 354–355
  (*See also* Wholesaling middlemen)
Wholesaling:
  careers in, 637
  definition of, 346
  economic justification of, 346–347
Wholesaling middlemen, 346
  agent, 350, 355–358
  auction companies, 358
  broker, 350, 357
  classification of, 347–350
  commission merchants, 357–358
  customers of, 351–352
  expenses of, 352–353
  manufacturers' agents, 356–357
  manufacturers' sales branches and
    offices, 349–350
  profits of, 352–353
  selling agents, 358
Wholly-owned subsidiaries, 539
Women, changing role of, 26–27
Wool Products Labeling Act (1940), 29,
  244
Worldwide enterprise, 539

Zone delivered pricing, 291